THE COMEDY OF
REVELATION

THE COMEDY OF REVELATION

Paradise Lost and Regained
in Biblical Narrative

FRANCESCA ARAN MURPHY

T&T CLARK
EDINBURGH

T&T CLARK LTD
59 GEORGE STREET
EDINBURGH EH2 2LQ
SCOTLAND

www.tandtclark.co.uk

First published 2000

ISBN 0 567 08718 2

British Library Cataloguing-in-Publication Data
A catalogue record for this book is available from the British Library

Typesetting by Waverley Typesetters, Galashiels
Printed and bound in Great Britain by Bookcraft Ltd, Avon

To my Mother

Contents

Acknowledgements

I should like to thank Jonathan Magonet for inviting me to Bendorf and thus providing the original stimulus for this project; my students at the College of St Mark and St John, 1989–91 and at St Martin's College, 1991–5, with whom I first read the Bible and witnessed the possibilities of dramatising it, particularly Vicky Morrell, Dan Clark, whose copy of *God Knows* I still have, and those unnamed souls who suffered most from having to act, script and direct Job, 1 Samuel, Exodus and St John's Gospel; Brian Gates whose open-mindedness made this latter exercise possible; Professor William Johnstone for the irascible patience which got me off the ground in Hebrew; Helen Bond for pressing me; Professor David Fergusson for constant encouragement; David Braine for an endless supply of fertile suggestions and philosophical rigour; Jack Trotter for a daily cybernetic dialogue about biblical comedy; my lodgers, Theodore Gillick, Lynsey Cowan and Christine James for putting up with me while I wrote it; and Gail, Tony and John Schmitz for providing a safe haven and constant companionship. I would also particularly like to thank Peter Andrews, whose copy-editing and proof-reading saved me from numerous errors.

Publishers' Acknowledgements

The author and publishers gratefully acknowledge permission to reproduce excerpts from the following:

And Also Much Cattle by D. S. Savage, reproduced by permission of The Brynmill Press Ltd, Pockthorpe Cottage, Denton, nr Harleston, Norfolk IP20 0AS.

Birds and *Lysistrata* by Aristophanes, edited by Alan Sommerstein, reproduced by permission of Aris & Philips Ltd, Teddington House, Warminster, Wiltshire BA12 8PQ.

The Book of Job, translated and with an introduction by Stephen Mitchell. Copyright © 1979 by Stephen Mitchell. Revised edition copyright © 1987 by Stephen Mitchell. Reprinted by permission of HarperCollins Publishers, Inc., New York.

The Corpus Christi Play of the English Middle Ages edited by R. T. Davies, reproduced by permission of Faber & Faber, 3 Queen Square, London WC1N 3AU.

The Dead Sea Scrolls in English by Geza Vermes (Penguin Books 1962, fourth edition 1995) copyright © G. Vermes 1962, 1965, 1968, 1975, 1987, 1995. Excerpts on pp. 73, 74, 81, 87 and 106.

Genesis. Translation and Commentary by Robert Alter. Copyright © 1996 by Robert Alter. Used by permission of W. W. Norton & Company, Inc., New York.

Genesis and Exodus by Everett Fox, translator. Copyright © 1983, 1986, 1990 by Shocken Books. Reprinted by permission of Schocken Books, a division of Random House, Inc., New York.

Highway 61 Revisited. Copyright © 1965 by Warner Bros. Inc. Copyright renewed 1993 by Special Rider Music, New York. All rights reserved. International copyright secured. Reprinted by permission.

Jonah reproduced by permission of Alfred A. Kalmus Ltd, London, on behalf of Theodore Presser Company, Pennsylvania.

The Thirst of the Salt Mountain by Marin Sorescu, published by Forest Books, reproduced by kind permission of Brenda Walker.

Extracts from the Authorized Version of the Bible (The King James Bible), the rights in which are vested in the Crown, are reproduced by permission of the crown's patentee, Cambridge University Press.

From Story to Drama:
An Anecdotal Preface

1. The Proof of the Pudding

I have a culinary prejudice against works of biblical criticism which begin with forty pages of methodology. The pudding is stone cold before the dinner guests taste it. Let us start with two anecdotes. In the 1970s, a student of 'the Old Testament' learned to relate disparate pieces of its text to a hypothetical history of Israel. The study of a classical prophet consisted in figuring out which bits of the text should be assigned to the various historical situations which the scholars had detected behind it. New Testament Form Criticism instructed us in what each of the church communities were trying to prove in each segment of their gospels. The one task which one never undertook was to read the Bible. To do so would have been a retreat to the pre-critical orthodoxy against which scholars had fought, and won, their battles a hundred years before, or to advance into Fundamentalism.

I might not have discovered that the Bible could be theologically interesting if I had not had to give a course on 'Sacred Texts'. I signed up for a summer school to refresh my memory and attended a seminar led by Philip Davies, Gabriel Josipovici, Francis Landy, Atalya Brenner and Jonathan Magonet. I was shocked to discover that scholars could simply read Second-Isaiah. This experience was *enjoyable*. The impulse of narrative criticism of the Bible was to recover its stories, as whole stories, and the words of the psalmists and prophets as whole poems.

2. Strengths and Weaknesses of Narrative Criticism

Literary criticism enables readers to find unity of action in the Bible. Literary works exhibit imaginative worlds, and one has to take their geography as it comes. One has to discover unity of action cumulatively, as the world is unfolded to us by the text.[1] The strength of holistic criticism is not that it *gives* us the Bible as a whole story, but that it offers the possibility of working one's way toward it, undergoing the narrative

---

1 Dale Patrick, *The Rendering of God in the Old Testament* (Fortress Press, Philadelphia, 1981), pp. 7 and 106–107.

process by which form is constructed. One cannot fast-forward to the conclusion if one wants to experience the meaning. If one wants to find in the Bible a unified imaginative world, one has to obey the laws of its development.

By an imaginative world, I mean not an alternative invented universe but an imaginative perception of this earth. Such an imaginative world is not an escape through a magical trapdoor from the boredom and pains of this world, but a way of seeing the world in which we live. To experience such an imaginative world is to live through it, knocking it against this world, working out whether or not it relates to the real world. Even a light reader tests characters and events against their experience; a serious reader who finds it to ring true has their perceptions of the world changed by it.

Narrative criticism tends to rule out study of the genetics of biblical texts. Its oppositional origin dictates that it does not elaborate hypotheses about how a 'hypothetical pre-text' was composed and spliced together with other texts.[2] If one reads the story as one finds it one may see that a web of meanings stretches all the way across it. The story is no longer one link in the process of inference back to 'those stages in the history of the religion of Israel that are exemplified in the textual strata'.[3] Narrative criticism is finished product criticism. Many narrative critics balk at tracing the story back to the history which to the untutored eye it appears to describe. They wrenched the *story* back from the historians, who had not displayed a keen interest in its emplotment.

The temptation of narrative criticism is not to ask whether the biblical world is true to the real world. The great achievement of a work such as Walter Brueggemann's *Old Testament Theology* is that it catches the excitement of the good stories of Genesis, Exodus and the rest; one returns to the biblical episodes with greater understanding after reading it. Does this advance on source criticism necessarily entail a complete retreat from correlating text and history? Brueggemann states that

> the Old Testament in the modern world is endlessly vexed by and tempted to historicity; that is, to 'what happened' . . . Enlightenment modes of history have almost nothing to do with Israel's sense of Yahweh. What 'happened' (whatever that may mean) depends on testimony and tradition that will not submit to any other warrant.[4]

Brueggemann says often that the Bible contains a 'plurality' of different testimonies. Why, then, should we take it all to be equally unhistorical? This is to impose a monolithic a-historicism on a text which contains different types of history, from legends to reportage to historical theology.[5] I doubt whether the current revulsion against historical questions will be sustained. The question of what actually happened is too humanly

---

2 Robert Polzin, *Samuel and the Deuteronomist: A Literary Study of the Deuteronomic History*, Part II, *1 Samuel* (Harper & Row, San Francisco, 1989), pp. 6–11.

3 Ibid., p. 2. I quote here from Polzin, but could have cited the same sentiments from many of the best narrative critics.

4 Walter Brueggemann, *Theology of the Old Testament* (Fortress Press, Minneapolis, 1997), p. 714.

5 Erich Auerbach, *Mimesis: The Representation of Reality in Western Literature*, translated by Willard Trask (Princeton University Press, Princeton, 1946, 1974), p. 21.

interesting to be permanently tidied away. If history and biblical theology had nothing to say to one another, biblical theology could not be changed by any *empirical* discovery: the Qumran scrolls indicate otherwise. It is narrow minded to make an a priori proscription of the contribution of archaeology to the investigation of an ancient body of texts. This book will draw on historical scholarship, without making any contribution to it. What is important for us is the warrant of the theological imagination. Our method does not rule out other kinds of warrant: the 'warrant of faith' is pretty feeble without that of historicity. Our intention is to find out what sort of imaginative world the Bible projects, in order to elucidate the model of revelation which it implies. Imagining the world and seeing the world *as it is* are not mutually exclusive activities.

3. The Bible as Drama

One way of avoiding the pitfalls of narrative criticism is to replace the metaphor of the Bible as a story with that of the Bible as a drama. The metaphor of a *story* evokes a picture of a circle of people, listening to one member of the circle speaking: the meaning of the story stays within a closed circle. Picture, in contrast, a drama. One then sees an action taking place between actors on a stage, before an audience. One may even picture an Elizabethan or Graeco-Roman theatre, which is open to the skies. Drama is tri-partite: the meaning of the performance is brought about by three responsive participants. The first is the script, or what the actors say to one another. The second participant is the audience. A piece which is read aloud gains its atmosphere from the audience response: 'Excitement generates excitement, yawning is contagious.'[6] The uncovered theatre is a symbol of openness: the third participant transcends the play. The biblical stories have a theological context: 'God's activity provides the larger framework for the story.'[7]

The Bible has some of the features of epic. But I should not ask undergraduates to turn the *Iliad* into a play. I spent some years experimenting with narrative criticism by requiring students to stage biblical books. I tested the hypothesis that the action of the Bible is moved largely by dialogue by asking students to create plays out of Exodus, 1 Samuel, Job and the Gospel of John: it works easily and well.[8] Readers can try my argument for themselves, by staging the biblical books. The lesson of holistic criticism must be well learned: stage whole books, and not the threads of 'P' or 'D'. A supply of tea towels and umbrellas has ensured that the tradition of staging the Passion on Good Friday has returned to many British towns. A young priest much attached to the canonical approach to the Bible remarked to me with reference to the liturgical cycle of biblical readings: 'We're trudging through Exodus now' (ending on a dying fall). By contrast, performances of biblical stories, whether amateur passion

---

6 Max Harris, *Theatre and Incarnation* (Macmillan, London, 1990), p. 65.
7 David M. Rhoads and Donald Michie, *Mark as Story: An Introduction to the Narrative of a Gospel* (Fortress Press, Philadelphia, 1982), pp. 74 and 116.
8 Robert Alter, *The Art of Biblical Narrative* (George Allen & Unwin, London, 1981), e.g. pp. 65–73

plays, oratorios, or rock operas, make for lively and spontaneous interpretations, because they allow scriptwriters and performers to imagine themselves into the biblical scenes.

The biblical narrative gets its shape partly from the reaction which authors wanted to evoke from a specific set of people.[9] The fact that the biblical narratives want to achieve meaning with a religious audience rules out the conception that they are solely *literary* texts. In the setting in which it is intended to be performed, the Bible is a sacred text. Gabriel Josipovici has distinguished the Bible 'from all other books' in the fact that, when one hears it read aloud in synagogue or church, one hears as a greedily believing and enchanted child.[10] On a phenomenological or descriptive level, the Bible is a sacred book. It is intended to be heard with awe and fidelity. It makes an absolute moral and religious demand not felt in the most serious of entertainments.

4. A Note on Method, Terminology, Texts and Order of Proceeding

I was given King James for my confirmation, and I make use of this entrusted document for some of the translations which I give here. The 'wots' and 'peravadventures' of King James can become wearisome. What the reader needs in a translation is a harmonious recollection of the language in which we first heard the Bible and a little dissonance to surprise us into seeing the story. I have chosen some of the translations I use for their vividness, such as Alter's *Genesis*, Everett Fox's *Exodus* and Stephen Mitchell's *Job*. Sometimes I alternate; I retain King James for the *Akedah* story, and allow Abraham to hold a 'knife', because Alter's 'cleaver' makes me think of Jack Nicholson in *The Shining*. In families given to religious debate, argument is either settled or prolonged by the production of whichever Bibles happen to be lying around the house: in families with very little Hebrew but some Greek, final recourse is made to the Greek text. I have reproduced something of this haphazard method, in the hope that it will accord with a common experience of the Bible.

Some argue that when we read the Bible in Jewish or Christian *traditions*, we are reading different books. There is an element of truth in this, but we also read books in *cultures*. Historically, Jews and Christians have not lived in absolutely distinct cultures; their gardens overlapped when mediaeval Christians went for help in interpreting the Bible, to Jews;[11] we had the same debates about literal, historical, allegorical and analogical readings of the Bible; in the modern world, we share the same divisions between conservatives, liberals, ideologues and fruitcakes. This book, which is entirely reliant on some Jewish interpretations of the Bible, places what it has gleaned in the context of Christian *tradition*. The idea of revelation

---

9 Meir Sternberg, *The Poetics of Biblical Narrative: Ideological Literature and the Drama of Reading* (Indiana University Press, Bloomington, 1985), p. 9.

10 Gabriel Josipovici, *The Book of God: A Response to the Bible* (Yale University Press, New Haven, 1988, 1990), pp. 7–8.

11 Beryl Smalley, *The Study of the Bible in the Middle Ages* (Basil Blackwell, Oxford, 1952), pp. 102–103 (on Hugh of St Victor).

which I educe from the Bible is Christian. I shall not pretend that I am reading anything other than the Old Testament and, with apologies to my best teachers, this is what I shall call it. Perhaps one should not apologise, if Seitz is right to say that 'Abandoning the term "Old Testament" would be to abandon a statement of the relationship of Christians to the literature of Israel and to modern Judaism'.[12]

The aim of this book is to find out whether a literary approach to the Bible can help us to see the imaginative basis of our doctrines of revelation and inspiration. Gilbert Keith Chesterton asserted that it is a good thing to bang cymbals together. We shall bang literary criticism of the Bible against a Christian conception of revelation. The clash of the symbols will show that the inspired images present revelation as a comic drama between God and human beings. We begin by asking *what* dramatic comedy is, then we ask *how* the biblical authors *imagined* the events they describe and we conclude by asking *why* they imagined them like that, and what this particular way of imagining says to theology. I turn to biblical narrative criticism in order to locate a *theological* paradigm.

12 Christopher Seitz, *Word without End: The Old Testament as Abiding Theological Witness* (W. B. Eerdmans, Michigan and Cambridge, 1998), p. 72.

1

The Human and Divine Comedy

1. Genres as 'Worlds'

Genres should be experienced before they are explained, so I shall not begin by subjecting the reader to a large dose of literary theory. We just need half a teaspoon of words about genre. Hegel spoke of three genres: epic, lyric and drama, which he subdivided into comedy and tragedy. Other writers attack the question of genre taxonomically. One could take a good empirical look at Hellenistic literature, and come up with a *list* which includes bucolic poetry, elegy, odes, lyric, epistle, history and βιος, Graeco-Roman biography.[1] The cutting and pairing of genres then depends on what the literary works 'look like'. If the animals look different, they belong in different parts of the zoo. The animals emerge, propagate and cross-breed. Burridge puts the empiricist's case:

> Genres do not resemble some kind of eternally immutable Platonic Ideal Forms, but are in a constant state of flux . . . consider for example the develop-ment of epic from Homer to Vergil and on through Spenser and Milton: there is still a family resemblance, but many of the specific *features* have altered immensely . . . genres . . . shift from age to age and according to locality . . . if we follow the term 'epic' still further to the film industry . . . the point is clear.[2]

The point is not so much unclear as a complete *non sequitur*. Homer's two poems defined the genre of the epic; he was imitated by Vergil and Milton. In the eighteenth century, Fielding and Richardson dropped the poetry and stuffed their comic novels into the template of epic. Today we have epic movies. It is imprecise, but not meaningless, to speak of an 'epic bowl of cornflakes'. As the everyday use of language indicates, epic thinks big because it wants to present *everything*.

What the empirical taxonomists call 'genres' I shall term 'literary structures'. Literary structures are the building materials of genres. Their elements are *quantitative*, such as poetic metres, or numbers of acts, in relation to theatre. The *novel* is a *literary structure*, not a genre. Most people

---

1 Richard A. Burridge in his *What Are the Gospels? A Comparison with Graeco-Roman Biography* (Cambridge University Press, Cambridge, 1992).
2 Ibid., p. 45.

take novels on holiday. Some novels are dramatic, like the court room tales of John Grishan; some are lyrical, as with Virginia Woolf's *Mrs Dalloway*; the five-volume family saga is epical. We do not have to be Platonists to know what to carry in our hand luggage: when we eschew *Malone Dies* and take a blockbuster, we tacitly imply that we prefer epic to lyric, on the beach. Our expectations are not only directed at literary structure but also at the bigger carrier of genre. Movies range across the genres. Eisenstein directed epics, like *Ivan the Terrible*, and dramas, like *The Battle-Ship Potemkin*; Tarkovsky restricted himself to lyrical cinema. However complex it is to articulate our tacit knowledge, we have an implicit expectation of what sort of world books or performances will show us.

Life worlds arrange themselves around perceptions: the museum curator, the ticket seller and the tourists inhabit the same space, but they each imagine the museum world differently. The writer arranges a life-world around the particular image which she wishes to present to her readers. For its audience, the literary life-world is a way of imagining. For the characters who live and breathe in this particular world, it is a way of being. The kinds of actions they can engage in depends upon the generic world which they inhabit. The literary world has its own geography, physical laws and chemical tables of elements. One life-world may be built up out of a dense accumulation of social detail; another may be as light and transparent as a watercolour; in another, everything spins past quickly and moves to a surprising conclusion. A genre is a literary life-world, the world inhabited by the fictional characters, as it can be imagined by readers or audience.

Different genres are constrained by different tempos, possibilities of dynamism and laws of gravity. The generic worlds projected, for example, by tragedy and by comedy are each ways of imagining how situations can turn out.[3] The genre contains the laws which govern what can happen and how one interprets what does happen, in a literary life-world. A *single* world cannot be governed by more than one set of laws. One cannot slip a bit of tragic drama into a lyric, because the event is attuned to its world. The love interest in epic is different from romance in a lyric; suffering in comedy is not the same as tragic suffering. The quality of an event depends on the genre which generates it.

2. The Dramatic World

A situation may be dramatic if it is conflictual. A dramatic moment is a turning-point. It sums up the story of the characters involved. When we are challenged our strengths and weaknesses are most visible. A dramatic moment is a cliff-hanging point which expresses the reality of character. In a drama the characters with whom the audience identify come into conflict with powerful opponents and express their true selves by the way in which they struggle against them. The most dramatic event is one which is directly seen, rather than narrated from the outside. A drama presupposes an audience. In order for a public conflict to be a drama, it must contain a

3 Louise Cowan, 'The Comic Terrain', pp. 1–18, in Louise Cowan (ed.), *The Terrain of Comedy* (Dallas Institute, Dallas, 1984), p. 7.

moral element. The background of order in drama is moral. You have to grasp that murder is a bad thing in order to understand *Macbeth*. It will be difficult to play Lady Macbeth as a heroine, although some directors may encourage it. But the essence of drama is not the achievement of virtue or vice by its characters. The Macbeths have done more than break the moral law. These villains have infringed *taboos*: they have encroached upon holy ground and trespassed against it. Macbeth's act is not murder, but regicide. The world of drama is in touch with the sacred. In its ancient form, theatrical drama had some of the trappings of a religious ritual. Drama is the genre closest to ritual. But the performances at the Festival Dionysia and the liturgies of the temple at the Acropolis are not *just the same thing*. Drama has an ethical strand and a religious strand, the two not being quite identical, even where we have to do with a moral God. The dramatic life-world is governed by *two* gravitational forces: one is outside the characters' power and one within it. Drama takes place in the *tension* between something transcendent and someone who is dependent. On one end of the rope finite human beings, on the other Tragic Fate: *or*, finite human beings dangling on a rope made of *grace* – or Comic luck.

The dramatic world has six elements: it is built upon conflict, it catches the meaning of the whole in suspenseful and important events, its characters are answerable to moral laws and are therefore free agents, its plot is unfolded by the characters' action and speech, it expresses its meaning as though it were being enacted before an audience, and the world which its characters and audience inhabit is subject to the laws of the Holy. These features are interrelated: the suspense attaches to a free person engaged in a moral conflict. The suspense pervades every scene. The story is presented publicly. It is open to view both by an audience and by the gods. Both the human and the divine audience make demands upon the actors, the one giving human meaning and the other a dimension of mystery. The meaning is thus created 'tri-logically': since we all know about dialogical meaning, I may as well invent a new logism. Tri-logical meaning is communicated in three ways: between the actors, between the actors and the audience, and to and from the deity above.

Dale Patrick defines dramatic action as 'the representation of deeds and occurrences within a spatio-temporal framework, exhibited in such a way that the audience enters as a participant'.[4] There would be no suspense if the story could go on for ever, and the moral conflict would not be serious if the decisions and their outcomes could be undone in a further story. Dramatic characters experience the repercussions of their actions within a specific timeframe. Drama clarifies the finitude and contingency of human action. And so the 'concentrating effect', which dramatists once aimed to achieve literally, through the three 'unities' of a single space, an unbroken action and focused time, stands for something crucial to dramatic action. The dramatic character is trying to answer one *single* question: this single focus 'constellates' the dramatic action into an 'explicit worldview'.[5]

---

4 Patrick, *Rendering of God*, p. 2.
5 Emile Staiger, *Basic Concepts of Poetics*, translated by Janette C. Hudson and Luanne T. Frank (Pennsylvania State University Press, Pennsylvania, 1991), pp. 153 and 159.

Thus, 'tragedy centres on one action and follows this continuously from beginning to end': it is because we cannot take our eyes off the 'un-avoidable' development of this one action that tragic drama focuses our senses on the *time* it takes for the resolution to be accomplished.[6] For the Greek tragedians, 'Time is a witness, and . . . a sovereign power: where these two qualities combine, he becomes . . . the most terrible of judges.'[7] Emile Staiger compares the single-mindedness of the author who puts a dramatic character through his paces to the method of a *judge*: both are interested only in what is essential. Like the dramatist, the judge 'selects from the material only what will help him come to a just decision'. The audience makes a judgement about the dramatic characters. Drama does not depict people, it tests them. And so, 'drama tends toward the external form of the court'.

Secular court room trials deal with criminals. An act of religious imagination perceives the criminal as a *sinner*. In *Crime and Punishment*, Dostoievsky presents Raskolnikov's murder of the old woman as a crime against the *sacred*. When the dramatic potential of the court room trial is realised in fiction, we have a literary drama. Since the emergence of novels of detection and suspense, drama has been put across in texts which are not intended to be staged. A drama is not the same thing as a play. The best novels of P. D. James are as dramatic as most contemporary staged plays.

3. The World of Comedy: The Desire for Communion

The later Wittgenstein was critical of the idea of a private language. He may as well have noted that a private joke is a shared joke. What about private jokes, jokes between old friends and lovers? Long after it ceases to be funny ha-ha, the private joke recalls friends to their lasting companion-ship, and so one laughs at the pleasure in one's shared knowledge of one another. One laughs out of the happiness of reciprocal friendship. One could speak of the public laughter of a community. P. G. Wodehouse mocked the fascist paraphernalia in the character of Sir Roderick Spode, Führer of the Brown Shorts and purveyor of lady's underwear. The British still laugh at goose-steps and toothbrush mustachios. When our humour drops its underdoggery, we laugh at the condescension, as in the 'Germans' episode of *Fawlty Towers*. When we are not afraid to mention the war, we laugh at it, because it is linked to the community *which we did not wish to become* and to the imaginatively real community which we dream of becoming again. Comedy expresses the heart's desire of a people.

Northrop Frye argued that the comic plot always follows an upward moving U. In its downward graph – the first stroke of the U – the plot moves away from a good situation and toward conflict and suffering. In its upward-graph, the second stroke, the plot turns toward happiness and communal festivity. We want to picture the U building itself, diachronically and dynamically, a chain of lights coming on one after the other to spell

---

6 Jacqueline de Romilly, *Time in Greek Tragedy* (Cornell University Press, Ithaca, New York, 1968), pp. 6 and 10.

7 Ibid., p. 161.

8 Staiger, *Basic Concepts*, p. 55.

out the U, one dot at a time. In a dramatic action, each unfolding event drives the next, and is contained in it. In *tragic drama*, a coalition of fate and hubris are mobilising the events. In *comic drama*, each scene is propelled forward by *desire* and by *grace*. At the summit of Frye's U stands the recovery of community: the good city is what we desire most.

Many people dream of *another world*. They dream about fairies, or about the future, about waking up and finding themselves in another time, about landing on a distant planet, about a complete 'Middle Earth', or a wood in which animals give tea parties and get speeding tickets. In its juxtaposition of two different worlds, comedy presents us with our secret yearning for a world which is both like and unlike this one. Peter Berger claimed to find a 'Signal of Transcendence' in New York City, because it offers such an unlimited variety of cuisines and costumes that one can walk down the street leading an elephant and beating a drum without attracting attention:

> when people say that New York City is a surrealistic place, they are . . . making an ontological statement about the reality of human life. Behind the empirical city lurks *another city*, a city of wonder and dreams. They are also making a soteriological statement, for redemption always comes into the world as a bit surprise . . . as a cosmic joke. Anything at all can come through the holes in the fabric of ordinary reality – a man leading an elephant by the leash, or a man riding on a donkey to inaugurate the mystery of our salvation.[9]

What is funny about that city is that Hasidic Jews in the garment district, Puerto-Rican taxi-drivers and Mafia garbage collectors all correctly regard themselves as native *New Yorkers*. And thus, although humour often springs from incongruity, the comic world makes two oddities – or twenty thousand – *one*. The togetherness of the untoward is the comic. Anachronism is a frequent comic device, as when the playwright uses a mug marked '**A gifte from Stratford**', in *Shakespeare in Love*. Anachronism is funny because people who ought not to belong *do*. Once having yoked those strange bedfellows together, comedy *marries* them. The great joy in the comic moment is the recognition that these disparate things, which can't stand each other, are made for one another. When the disparate things are temperaments, such as cleanliness and piggery, the characters become friends, still maintaining their disparity, as Walter Matthau and Jack Lemmon do in *The Odd Couple*. Comedy can interweave several fantasy worlds. An audience watching *A Midsummer Night's Dream* sees five interlocked worlds, the play, within that, the courtiers' Athens and that of the mechanicals, the forest of the fairies, and, in the very centre of all the worlds, Pyrramus and Thisbe, the mirror in which all of the realms see themselves. The mechanicals' play is intensely *satisfying*, because it pulls together the five worlds of the *Dream*. I shall avoid a definition of comedy which is so sophisticated that the funniness has been refined out: but there is a sense of comedy in which laughter and exhilaration are carried over into sheer satisfaction, or happiness.

9 Peter Berger, 'New York City 1976: A Signal of Transcendence', in Berger, *Facing Up to Modernity* (Penguin, London, 1979), pp. 258–268 (266–267).

Aristotle noted that one of the 'pleasure[s]' of Comedy is that 'the bitterest enemies in the piece . . . walk off good friends at the end, with no slaying of any one by any one'.[10] In Flannery O'Connor's short story 'Revelation', the hard-working and upright Mrs Turpin has a vision of all of the worst people going ahead of the good folks into heaven. Comedy does not describe the exclusive club, purged and purified of the reprobate hordes: 'The tendency of comedy is to include as many people as possible in its final society.'[11] Few comic villains are so bad as to be unreclaimable, in the last scene: 'You want the devils out but you also want them to return. Else no party next year.'[12] The Comedian is no dual predestinarian, but a universalist. Frye believed that comedy represents liberation from law.[13] It is better to say that comedy overthrows abstract or inhuman laws in order to create an ethos in which *friendship* flourishes. In the code of the comedians, eating and drinking, parades, parties, dances, and the pleasures of sex, which for the lucky follow from the above, are smiled upon. Pagans like Aristophanes celebrate excessive or illicit sensuous pleasures. Christian comedians from Dante to Flannery O'Connor regard them as the most minor of sins. The isolating sins, such as pride and treachery, land a man in the Ice at the centre of Hell. The shared enjoyment of sensual pleasures opens the door to emotion, which is the bond of friendship. The comic hero has a good companion, or two or three. Basil Fawlty would be doomed to the privacy of lunacy without Sybil, Polly and Manuel. The comic hero is filled with aspiration: his friends provide a mainstay to reality.

The comic adventurer is not guided by an imprudent or unrealistic moral code. One has not entered into the comic spirit if one can ask: 'Does Elizabeth Bennett love D'Arcy or does she love Pembroke?' The community takes up space, and a mansion will suffice. The domain to which comedy aspires must be sufficiently spacious and well endowed to support the most improvident members of the family. The comic spirit honours prudence because it is the least elevated of the virtues and is therefore best suited to creating a real human community, from below.

The comic story takes its adventurers 'upwards'. In comedy,

> Man is lifted up into a realm beyond himself, one that he has not gained by his own effort. Aristophanes' *Birds* portrays this realm symbolically . . . Here love is supreme; one is not required by one's own efforts to save the day – the natural tendency of things is upward. The pretty girl has become the vessel of reality and grace: Basileia, Beatrice, Portia, Miranda . . . The mark of it is not simply romantic love, the attainment of the beautiful lady, but the movement beyond her to that of which she has borne witness: universal love.[14]

---

10 Aristotle, *Poetics*, in *The Basic Works of Aristotle*, edited by Richard McKeon (Random House, New York, 1941), 1453a 13, 35.

11 Nelvin Vos, *The Drama of Comedy: Victim and Victor* (John Knox Press, Richmond, Virginia, 1966), p. 100.

12 Howard Jacobson, *Seriously Funny: From the Ridiculous to the Sublime* (Viking, London, 1997), p. 121.

13 Northrop Frye, *The Anatomy of Criticism: Four Essays* (Princeton University Press, New Jersey, 1957), p. 181.

14 Cowan, 'Comic Terrain', in *Terrain of Comedy*, p. 14.

The comic hero ascends toward a community of love. He uses prudence and discernment to reach it. He suffers as much as a tragic hero; he struggles against evil forces. But the swing of the comic plot hauls him up. Sometimes this narrative gravity is personified: Athena gets Odysseus home.

4. Aristophanes: Cosmic Laughter[15]

a. The Historical and the Cultural Context: Athens during the Peloponnesian War

During the attempted Persian invasions of Greece, in 480–479 BC, the Greek states allied themselves in the Delian League. Within ten years of victory, the islands were not allies but subjects of Athens. In 431, Pericles led Athens into war against the Spartan Peloponnesian League. Pericles launched a naval attack on the Peloponnese whilst withdrawing the citizens within Athens, where they starved whilst the Spartans wasted their farms. Pericles' successor was Cleon, an orator who manipulated the Athenian Assembly to pursue the war. Cleon and the Spartan General Brasidas both died in battle in 422. In 421, the Athenian Nicias and Sparta's King Pleistoanax drew up a peace settlement. Pericles' nephew Alcibiades was the genius behind the genocide of the people of the island of Melos, for having resisted conquest. He instigated the disastrous expedition to Sicily to 'help' the town of Segestus. The night before the Athenian expedition set out, in June 415, someone defaced the statues of Hermes; Alcibiades was the prime suspect; he left for Sicily with pending charges for impiety. The Athenian naval force perished in Sicily. Between 410 and 411, Athens endured the anti-democratic junta of the Four Hundred. In 404, Sparta besieged Athens into submission. Aristophanes (448–388) was the poet of the Peloponnesian War. His dirtiest jokes have an ethical purpose: to remind his audience that they truly desire reconciliation, that noble, sensuous and partially clad woman (played by a man). Old Comedy died with the Athenian Empire.

b. The Architecture of the Athenian Theatre and of Old Comedy

Friedrich Nietzsche considered that every Greek tragedy is about the death and rebirth of Dionysus. Nineteenth-century scholars such as Frazer could detect the myth of a dying and rising god in many facets of Ancient Mediterranean culture. In the first half of this century, the Cambridge School of Anthropology appeared to argue that tragedy and comedy arose automatically from the worship of Dionysus. They overlooked particularities, such as the role played in the *invention* of drama by historical individuals, such as the original actor, Thespis, an Athenian of the sixth century BC. Although the Frazerian *metanarrative* is now rightly disregarded as such, one does not need it in order to find Dionysus in Greek comedies, which 'were part of his cult and an outgrowth of his ritual'.[16]

One origin of Attic drama is certainly the *chorus*: a troupe of masked men, who danced and sang for entertainment and as a tribute to Dionysus.

---

15 Allardyce Nicoll said that Aristophanes' laughter is 'almost cosmic in its uproariousness'. *The Theatre and Dramatic Theory* (George G. Harrap, London, 1962), p. 128.

16 Katherine Lever, *The Art of Greek Comedy* (Methuen, London, 1956), p. 92.

Religious dance becomes drama once the mimed gestures begin to tell a story.[17] The dramatist was called the *chordidaskalos*, the Chorus teacher. The playwright did not merely script the *Bacchae* or the *Birds*, but also choreographed the chorus's dance, and trained them to play it.[18] The comic chorus provides a running commentary on the play from the sidelines. It also steps forward to play its own part, the choral 'parabasis' (meaning 'turn around' or 'come forward') in which the dramatist states his moral. The parabasis of Aristophanes' *Frogs* begins: 'Well does it suit the holy chorus to exhort the polis and to teach it what is good.'[19] The chorus stands for Athens: it was a 'staged metaphor for the community involved in the dramatic performance',[20] representing both audience and players.[21]

The first raised stage, or 'orchestra', was built in the precinct of Dionysus in 500 BC. The first comedies were performed at the festival of Dionysus in 487 BC. 'Old Comedy' now begins. The Old Comedian trained his troupe for competitions, which took place at the Lenaia Festival and the Greater Dionysia Festival. The Lenaia was held in January, when the winter seas precluded tourism. These plays were put on for an Athenian audience. Aristophanes' 'Lenaia' plays address events and figures whose fame is to be a footnote to his plays. The Greater Dionysia was celebrated in April, when the deities of fertility rose from their winter slumbers in Hades and Athens' subject-allies of the Delian League arrived with their tribute money. This was the pan-Hellenic festival. Aristophanes' plays for the Lenaia include the *Archanians*, *Knights*, *Wasps* and *Frogs*; his comedies for the Greater Dionysia are *Clouds*, *Peace* and *Birds*, perhaps more accessible than the former.

c. Peace (421 BC)

The Peace of Nicias was not yet signed when Aristophanes' *Peace* was performed; his hero, Trygaeus, has to achieve it. But the deaths of Cleon and Brasidas in 422 and the beginning of the peace negotiations indicated that this goal was attainable. Meanwhile, Trygaeus intends to ascend to Heaven, and demand that Zeus restore peace between the Greek states. He has procured a dung-beetle as his flying vehicle. A wonderful thing will be attempted, by scabrous means. In ritual, one approaches the gods through the sweet smells of sacrifice; in tragedy, a winged horse carries one to heaven, as in Euripides' *Bellerophon*. Trygaeus describes himself as 'an Athmonian, skilled in vines'.[22] This comic hero has his own fertile plan.[23]

---

17 Gerardus van der Leeuw, *Sacred and Profane Beauty: The Holy in Art* (Holt, Rinehart & Winston, New York, 1963), pp. 77–78.
18 Lever, *Art of Greek Comedy*, p. 89.
19 Aristophanes, *Frogs*, ll. 686, cited in ibid., p. 90.
20 Oddone Longo, 'The Theater of the Polis', in John J. Winkler and Froma I. Zeitlin (eds), *Nothing to Do with Dionysos?* (Princeton University Press, New Jersey, 1990), pp. 12–19 (17).
21 Victor Ehrenberg, *The People of Aristophanes: A Sociology of Old Attic Comedy* (Basil Blackwell, Oxford, 1943), p. 23.
22 Aristophanes, *Peace*, l. 190. Translated by D. B. Rogers, Loeb Classical Library (Heinemann, London, 1924).
23 A. M. Bowie notes that Trygaeus' flight is a direct parody of Euripides' *Bellerophon*: *Aristophanes: Myth, Ritual and Comedy* (Cambridge University Press, Cambridge, 1993), pp. 135–136.

The Athenian theatre swept its heroes aloft, and lowered deities on stage, by means of a crane, to which the actor was harnessed. Trygaeus invites his audience to share his dream that the beetle is another Pegasus, and shouts out to a man down in Peiraeus not to 'commit a nuisance', as his steed ducks and swerves earthward toward alluring smells. The audience must both be induced to believe that Trygaeus is flying over Athens, *and* is reminded that he is an actor dangling precariously on the end of a beam. Trygaeus calls out

> Zounds! how you scared me: I'm not joking now.
>
> I say, scene-shifter, have a care of me.
> You gave me quite a turn, and if you don't
> Take care, I'm certain I shall feed my beetle.
> But now, methinks, we must be near the Gods;
> And sure enough there stand the halls of Zeus.
> Oh, open, open! who's in waiting for me here?[24]

The Olympian gods have departed for the further regions of Heaven, leaving the Greeks in the care of the god War. War has buried Peace in a pit. Trygaeus finds him grinding the Greek states into a salad, throwing in Sparta as his leeks, Megara as garlic, Sicily for cheese and Attica as honey. His mortar is the Spartan general Brasidas; his pestle was to have been Cleon. Cleon is missing (the audience know that he is dead), so War leaves the stage to find another cooking utensil.

Trygaeus grabs his opportunity. He calls on the Chorus to drag Peace out of captivity. Once Trygaeus has bribed Hermes to assist them and poured a libation to the gods, the Chorus draws Peace out of confinement. Her sweet smell reminds Trygaeus of the world which war has expelled:

Hermes:	Not quite the odour of knapsack, eh?
Trygaeus:	Faugh! that odious pouch of odious men, I hate it.
	It has a smell of rancid-onion whiffs;
	But SHE of harvests, banquets, festivals,
	Flutes, thrushes, plays, the odes of Sophocles . . .[25]

Peace is attended by two maids, Opora (late summer, that is Vintage) and Theoria, Festival. Vintage and Festival are marriageable women; Peace is the goddess who provides these good things.[26]

The audience are drawn into the apparition: Trygaeus can discern their trades by their reaction, claiming to see dismay on the faces of arms sellers and pleasure in the rest. By pointing to public figures who are sitting in the auditorium, Aristophanes' script makes the world of his comedy encompass the audience. His actor both plays his own part and acts the 'actor', addressing the audience. Kenneth McLeish says that Aristophanes creates

---

24　Aristophanes, *Peace*, ll. 173–179.
25　*Peace*, ll. 527–531.
26　These are the preferred translations of Douglas McDowell: for his explanation, see *Aristophanes and Athens: An Introduction to the Plays* (Oxford University Press, Oxford, 1995), pp. 193–194.

a precise relationship between performer and spectator – a relationship . . . which still persists . . . between the modern stand-up comedian and his audience. Like such a comedian, Aristophanes invests the people and events taken from real life with a kind of illusory, fantasy existence . . . Because both comedian and spectator know that the comic creation is distorted from the original . . . a state of conspiratorial irony is established between them, with the parodied person as its butt . . . instead of stepping out of character to make a topical allusion, [Aristophanes' characters] draw . . . real people and events *inside* the comic plot. This absorption of 'real life' into the fantasy world is . . . central to Aristophanes' comic method.[27]

The audience has to play-act its audience status. The invisible spectator watching a story taking place on a raised stage is suddenly seen, and given its role, from the stage; the audience of comedy laughs at the fact that it is an audience. The real world is drawn into the play, and the comic fantasy expands to include the audience.

Trygaeus vows that the Greek states will never allow Peace to leave them again. Festival is promised in marriage to the Council, the symbolic restoration of public harmony. Hermes rewards Trygaeus with Vintage, advising him to: 'Take her and propagate young vines.'[28] Trygaeus and his friends prepare to celebrate the wedding, to which the audience are invited. Through his magnificent exploit, Trygaeus has achieved his desire, not for a philosophical or abstract 'peace', but for the physical delights of sex, food and good companionship which it represents.

d. Birds (414 BC)

The *Birds* was written and produced during the Athenians' attempt to colonise the Sicilian islands. Classicists have interpreted the play as a comment on this hubristic exploit and as a caricature of Athenian imperialism.[29] Alexandre Niçev reads it as a veiled 'political critique' of the Sicilian expedition and the 'threat to democracy posed by adventurers like Alcibiades'.[30] A. M. Bowie proposed that the *Birds* is a dystopia. Peisetaerus and his friend Euelpides are caricatures of Alcibiades and his followers, fleeing Athens and their creditors, in search of a new country.[31] The first bird they meet is Tereus. In Greek myth, Tereus was a bad egg: he married Procne, but raped her sister Philomena during their honeymoon. He cut out her tongue so that she could not spill the beans, but she wove her story onto a tapestry. Alerted to her husband's sexual offence, Procne killed their

27 Kenneth McLeish, *The Theatre of Aristophanes* (Thames & Hudson, London, 1980), pp. 17 and 85.
28 Aristophanes, *Peace*, l. 704.
29 J. W. Süvern was the first to take the play as a political allegory, referring to the Sicilian expedition; H. J. Newinger poses the more general interpretation. As McDowell notes, both theories are difficult to sustain, since Aristophanes' comedy is not subtle: he normally specifies the people and events he is sending up, and Sicily or Syracuse are never mentioned. See his *Aristophanes and Athens*, where these theories are discussed: pp. 222–224.
30 Alexandre Niçev, 'L'enigma des *Oiseaux* d'Aristophane', *Euphrosyne: Revista de Filologia Classica*, Nova Serie, 17, 1986, 10–30 (18).
31 Ehrenberg writes: 'Aristophanes' old ideal has not changed, but there seems now no chance left of realising it on earth. The result . . . is the flight of the two old men, and therefore of the poet.' *People of Aristophanes*, p. 43.

son Ithys and served him up to Tereus. Intervening before Tereus could axe-murder his wife, Zeus turned them all into birds. Tereus became a hoopoe, Procne a nightingale and Philomena a swallow:

> Aristophanes may suppress the unpleasantness, but Tereus is connected essentially with this one story, whose events act as a troubling *'sous-texte'* to the more cheerful aspects of the play.[32]

Since Peisetaerus and Euelpides will imitate this metamorphosis, Tereus might symbolise the kind of person who undergoes such a transition. Tereus gathers the Bird-Chorus who are to be Peisetaerus' allies in building a city in the sky. Peisetaerus persuades the birds to league with him in creating this urban 'Cloudcuckooland'. The pleasures which he claims it will entail for them are 'striking by their triviality or dangerous in their implications'. Having starved the gods into submission – with a reference to 'Melitian hunger' – Peisetaerus sets himself up as ruler of the city. Euelpides, the hopeful companion, leaves the stage. Cloudcuckooland loses all pretence of democracy, as Peisetaerus uses 'violence' to expel unwanted visitors.[33] At the end, Peisetaerus is called *turannos*, which Sommerstein translates as 'tyrant'.[34] The main item on the menu of the concluding feast is – bird.[35] Bowie says, 'if *Birds* is Aristophanes' greatest exercise in fantasy, it is also his best deconstruction of it'.[36] He contends that the play contains an 'implicit justification of imperialism': tactics like Peisetaerus' are necessary to maintain Athenian control of its allies.[37] Read as a political allegory, the *Birds* is a cynical exercise in showing that the retention of power requires the abuse of democracy. On this analysis, the play is as much of a comedy as *Animal Farm* written by a Soviet sympathiser. Niçev calls it 'the most pessimistic' of Aristophanes' works.[38]

At the start of Aristophanes' play, Euelpides and Peisetaerus depart from Athens carrying sacrificial implements, and a bird apiece, to show them the way: bird guides are common in myth, but not usually crows and jackdaws. They are 'wandering in search of a trouble free place', and they hope to find Tereus, because he ought to have a bird-eye view of the world and a human conception of a good place to live.[39] The play explores the logic of being a Man-bird. The two men encounter Tereus' bird-servant. They are surprised to discover that a hoopoe needs a servant, but he explains,

| Servant: | He does – I suppose because he once used to be a man. At one moment he gets a longing to eat Phalerum whitebait: |

---

32 Bowie, *Aristophanes*, pp. 166–167.

33 Ibid., p. 169.

34 Niçev emphasises the political point of the word *turannos*: 'Aristophanes' paradox is clear: for the ancient Athenians, the notions of kingship and democracy are irreconcilable.' 'L'enigma des *Oiseaux* d'Aristophane', 28.

35 Bowie sees a connection between cannibalism and metamorphosis (*Aristophanes*, pp. 167–170).

36 Ibid., p. 177.

37 Ibid.

38 Niçev, 'L'enigma des *Oiseaux* d'Aristophane', 30.

39 McDowell, *Aristophanes and Athens*, p. 204.

> I take the bowl and run for the whitebait. Or he wants
> pea-soup – we need a stirring spoon and a pot; I run for the
> stirring spoon.

Aristophanes has to give his dramatic life-world its own laws. The first
step into the illusion is that the Man-bird has two sets of culinary appetites.
Peisetaerus and Euelpides offend Tereus by laughing at him: the three
acknowledge that they are actors. For it is Tereus' threadbare bird-costume
which amuses them, and the audience. Tereus' feathers have seen better
days since he wore that costume in a Sophoclean tragedy. The comic
illusion mocks itself. Stepping back into role, Tereus explains that he is
'moulting for the winter'.[40] Aristophanes' replay of the myth brings out
Tereus' dual status on the boundary between man and bird. Tereus tells
his story when he calls his wife from their nest-house:

> Come, my consort, leave your sleep
> and let forth the melodies of sacred song
> with which from your divine lips you lament
> your child and mine, the much-bewailed Itys,
> quivering with the liquid notes
> of your vibrant throat.
>
> Through the leaf-clad green-brier comes
> the pure sound, reaching the abode of Zeus,
> where golden haired Phoebus hears
> and in response to your elegies plucks
> his ivoried lyre and stirs the gods
> to make music together . . .[41]

If this amorous lyric is anything to go by, Tereus' conjugal relations have
not been ill-affected by the unfortunate incidents which preceded their
metamorphosis. Their bird form has brought them nearer to the gods, in
the power of song.

Tereus explains that they eat 'white sesame, myrtle-berries, poppies
and bergamot', at which Euelpides exclaims: 'Why, you live the life of
newly-weds!' This prompts Peisetaerus to his vision: 'Ah ah! I see in the
bird race what could be a grand design and mighty power, were you to be
persuaded by me.'[42] Peisetaerus is staring into the sky: he has imagined
what human beings could do if they imitate the bird crafts of flight, love
and music. To a bird, these endowments are tools for survival; for a human
being, they would be magical gifts of release and empowerment. Instead of
copying Tereus' hermetic domesticity, Peisetaerus wants to build and
fortify a sky-city.

Tereus has taught the birds a language, and can mediate between his
new companions and the flocks of birds which walk onto the stage as he
sings. The Bird-Chorus is initially hostile. Tereus allays their suspicions by
telling them that Peisetaerus has been brought to the forest by

---

40 Aristophanes, *Birds*, l. 105.
41 Ibid., ll. 209–219.
42 Ibid., l. 163.

> A passionate desire [eros]
> For your life and your lifestyle
> and to share your home, too,
> And your whole existence.[43]

Peisetaerus' passionate desire gives him the gift of tongues: he pulls out a store of legends to win the birds to his dream: they once ruled over gods and humanity and can do so again. It is not the explanation which matters, but the *vision* of what the birds must do:

> I instruct you first of all that there should be a single great City of the Birds; and then you should completely encircle the whole of the air, and all this space between heaven and earth, with a wall of great baked bricks, like Babylon.

Cloudcuckooland will straddle heaven and earth. By thus controlling the pathways of the sky, they will be able to stop the heavenward aromas of sacrifice from reaching the gods and also obstruct the gods' amorous earth-bound missions. Starved of food and sex, the gods will be beaten into submission. Once the birds have been inspired to join in this lark, the two adventurers give their names for the first time: Euelpides, 'hopeful son', and Peisetaerus, 'Persuader of companions'. They leave the stage, later to return costumed as birds.

Peisetaerus projects a two-sided imagination: on the one hand, he sees the birds as wondrous and potent creatures; on the other, he is intensely literal minded. But even he is amazed when he hears of the vast wall which the birds have built around Cloudcuckooland:

Peisetaerus:	Poseidon, what a height! Who built it to such a size?
Messenger:	Birds, no one else . . . they did it with their own hands, so that I was amazed. From Africa there came some thirty thousand cranes, who had swallowed stones for the foundations; those were shaped by corncrakes with their bills. Another ten thousand storks made bricks. Water was brought to the air from below by the thickknees and the other river-birds.
Peisetaerus:	And who brought the clay for them?
Messenger:	Herons, in hods.
Peisetaerus:	But how did they get the clay into their hods?
Messenger:	That, my good sir, was really the cleverest idea they'd devised. The geese used their feet like shovels to dig into the clay and pitch it into the hods for them.
Chorus Leader:	Are you amazed that the fortification's been completed so quickly?
Peisetaerus:	Yes, by the gods, I am; it merits amazement. It seems to me truly tantamount to – a pack of lies.[44]

The birds have done the impossible, in a bird-like way. The joke would be lost if the birds become all powerful gods, or human beings. Rather than,

43 Ibid., ll. 412–414.
44 Ibid., ll. 1164–1167.

'deconstruct[ing] its own fantasy by showing how it is put together',[45] the comedy is about being two entirely different things at once: for

> Old Comedy astonishes . . . by its mixture of extreme reality and extreme unreality, by 'the romantic dissonance between real life and the fantasy of fairy tale.' The two ingredients cannot be separated . . . the poet . . . has contrived to blend two such different and . . . conflicting atmospheres in one picture, which despite all its variety is homogeneous.[46]

Seeing 'how it is put together', that is, seeing that the dream is both made of ordinary 'ingredients', and irreducible to them, is the fabric of the comic imagination.

Unwanted elements begin to intrude on the city, a Priest, an Oracle Monger, an obviously mad mathematical city-planner, an Athenian Inspector and a Decree Seller: perhaps Euelpides leaves the stage in order to play them.[47] The Athenian Inspector asks for the 'proxenoi', the informers who might hand the city over to Athens. Peisetaerus runs across the stage to drive the Inspector and Decree Seller out, with a whip, and, as Bowie says, the Inspector drops his 'voting urns'. But, when an audience sees one actor hitting another, they laugh, as with Laurel and Hardy or Basil and Manuel. Because the audience identifies with the protagonist, comedy permits it to do in make-believe what it cannot do in ordinary life, but might wish to: punch bureaucrats and incompetents on the nose. Peisetaerus' violence is neither a rebuttal of democracy nor an exhortation to take up the Attic burden: he assails popular hate-figures. Zeus sends Iris to find out what is going on. She makes a flappable landing with the help of the crane. Peisetaerus threatens to murder the immortal. Telling a goddess to get lost is a repressed fantasy which is most common in religious cultures: it can be heard in the Mediterranean store of curses for the saints and Virgin Mary.

Peisetaerus' attitude to Inspectors does not discourage other immigrants. 'Musical wings' and 'prophetic wings' and 'sea wings' have to be found for the 'ten thousand people coming here from down there'.[48] The Chorus Leader says: 'My city is the prevailing passion.' The Bird-Chorus advises Peisetaerus to 'examine each individual when you wing him'.[49] Peisetaerus has little time for his last guest. The Informer asks

| *Informer:* | And how, pray, can you give a man wings just by words? |
| *Peisetaerus:* | . . . By words a man is uplifted and his mind is made to soar aloft. And in the same way I want to give wings to your mind by my good advice, and make you turn to a lawful occupation.[50] |

Like Peisetaerus, the Informer understands the potency of words; but unlike him, his words are not directed to a vision. He understands the mechanics of the enterprise, but not its magic.

45 Bowie, *Aristophanes*, p. 171.
46 Ehrenberg, *People of Aristophanes*, p. 26.
47 McDowell, *Aristophanes and Athens*, p. 209.
48 Aristophanes, *Birds*, l. 1305.
49 Ibid., l. 1334.
50 Ibid., ll. 1437–1439.

Another informer arrives to sell the pass to Peisetaerus. Hiding under a parasol, Prometheus conspires with Peisetaerus for what terms to negotiate with Zeus. His devices have thus far succeeded, whispers Prometheus, for the Olympic gods are 'fasting' and the 'barbarian gods are . . . shrieking like Illyrians and threatening to march from up-country against Zeus, unless he secures the opening of the ports so that sliced offals could be imported'.[51] Prometheus advises Peisetaerus to hold out until Zeus 'gives his sceptre back to the birds and gives you Basileia to be your wife'.[52] Basileia is one of Aristophanes' inventions:

> [the] custodian of the thunderbolt of Zeus and of absolutely everything else – wisdom, law and order, good sense, dockyards, mudslinging, paymasters and three obolses.

Peisetaerus: You mean she looks after *everything* for him?

Prometheus: That's right: if you receive *her* from his hands, you've got everything.[53]

The 'moral rightness' of Peisetaerus' gift to the human race 'is symbolised by a kind of surreal inviolability, invincibility'.[54] A delegation of gods arrives from Olympus – an inarticulate Triballian, a snobbish Poseidon and a very hungry Hercules. Hercules is made desperate by having to watch Peisetaerus cook a delicious bird-supper and votes for peace; the Triballian's incomprehensible grunts are taken to count as a casting vote in favour. There is no doubt that Aristophanes was aware of the oddities of democratic government.

Their meal is certainly emphasised:

Herakles: Here, what sort of meat is this?

Peisetaerus: Its a number of birds who have been found guilty of attempting to rebel against the bird democracy.

Alan Sommerstein wonders 'how much real evidence there was of the bird's guilt . . . [and] by whom they were "found guilty"; and . . . what sort of "democracy" Cloudcuckooville enjoys'.[55] Although the hermeneutical task in relation to an ancient text is complex, it does not help matters to make one's interpretation turn on scenes which are not in the play. Birds were a delicacy for the Athenians, and thus – on the comic assumption of complete symmetry between gods and men – the food most likely to 'tempt Herakles'.[56] By the rationality of this fantasy, if Peisetaerus plans to seduce Herakles with the pleasures of the flesh, he needs cooked birds, and he uses the fairest means of attaining them; treason was punishable by death in Athens. The fact that they are eating bird is not a light comic touch: the scene harps on it. An Athenian audience probably found that funny, and not sad. McDowell notes that ancient Greece had no RSPB, and no

51 Ibid., ll. 1515–1520.
52 Ibid., l. 1535.
53 Ibid., ll. 1541–1543.
54 McLeish, *Theatre of Aristophanes*, p. 74.
55 In the endnotes to his edition of *Birds*, p. 303.
56 McDowell, *Aristophanes and Athens*, p. 224.

'sympathy for birds', which were 'considered primarily as a source of food'.[57] Peisetaerus does have a sympathy for birds, as winged and warbling love-makers; and none at all for birds as consumptible pigeons. St Francis of Assisi's compatriots, who combine their admiration for this great saint with an equal love of shooting, might understand him better than a post-Protestant Anglo-Saxon.

The Bird-Chorus are not disillusioned but delighted as the play ends in the apotheosis of Peisetaerus. Their leader begins the concluding wedding and victory song

> *Chorus Leader:*   Great, great is the good fortune that surrounds
> the race of birds
> thanks to this man; so now welcome
> with hymeneal chants and bridal songs
> our Lord and his Princess

The Chorus compare this wedding to that of Zeus and Hera; Peisetaerus is hailed, not only as *turannos*, which in many Greek texts is interchangeable with *Basileus*, and merely means 'king', but, more boldly, as the holder of Zeus' thunderbolt, the 'most exalted of gods [daimonwn upertate]!'

> *Chorus:*   O mighty golden blaze of the lightning!
> O immortal fiery bolt of Zeus!
> O thunders that rumble beneath the earth
> and at the same time bring down the rain!
> With you this man now shakes the earth;
> he has gained power over all that Zeus possessed
> and Princess too, what sat by Zeus' throne, is his.
> Hymen O, Hymenaeus O![58]

The conclusion is not cynical but 'jubilant'.[59] The celebratory Exit or 'Exodus' of the Chorus, the hero, and his bride-to-be, is called its *Komos*. The Greek *Komos* or *Komoidia* means 'a musical and dancing festivity'; it yields the English word 'comedy'. We may say, in secular terms, that comedy concludes with good things happening to good people. But, in the *quasi*-sacral world of Dionysian comedy, Peisetaerus dances out, 'brandishing the very thunderbolt of Zeus himself; and it becomes clear . . . that he is . . . to be regarded as a new Zeus'.[60] Peisetaerus' ethics are not defencible unless we regard his ultimate imaginative metamorphosis in the light of the sacred: he 'is' a new or replenished God-King. This is not supposed to be funny-reductive, at the expense of the hero and the audience who identifies with him, but rather, funny-hilarious, the rejuvenation of the human spirit.

Aristophanes' plays are neither a-political nor a-moral. Like those of the classical tragedians, the action of his comedies turns on the symbol of the *trial*. As von Balthasar says,

---

57 Ibid., p. 206.
58 *Birds*, ll. 1749–1754.
59 McDowell, *Aristophanes and Athens*, p. 223.
60 Francis Macdonald Cornford, *The Origin of Attic Comedy* (1934, Peter Smith, Gloucester, Mass., 1968), p. 59.

this dramatist who is often so wanton and frivolous is always dealing with the theme of justice . . . a symbol of which is the . . . arbitration court. Thus in the *Knights* the court is to decide who is the more base, Kleon or the sausage-seller; in the *Wasps*, the Athenian legal practice is . . . brought to the bar of the poet (with the splendid parody of the dogs' trial); and in the *Frogs* Dionysus . . . becomes the judge who puts the verses of Aeschylus and Euripides on the scales: Which of the two poets does more to further the common good? In the *Clouds* . . . the sophist debate between the *logos dikaios* and the *logos adikos* is naturally a judgement scene.[61]

Aristophanes goes to the heart of the ethical question: what does it mean to be human? The *Birds* is a joke and a liberating vision of what Athenian populist humanism is about. Although the reach of their ambitions had its dark and self-destructive side, that did not deter the playwright from appealing to their truest desires. He sought to persuade them by showing them an image of themselves: creatures with strong sensual appetites and soaring minds.

e. **Lysistrata** *(411 BC)*

Lysistrata is Aristophanes' least quotable play, in a work of philosophical theology, and the one most likely to be known to its readers. The plot is simple: Lysistrata has a plan! The women of the city have lost their menfolk to war; many will now grow old without the chance to marry. They must force the men to come to the peace table. She persuades the women of the city to lock themselves up in the Acropolis, thereby denying the men the two things which they need most: access to the treasury, and sex. The collapse of the men is swift and complete. Representatives of Sparta and Athens are very soon mapping out their peace treaty on the body of the beautiful Reconciliation.

The women of Athens have better political sense than their husbands, in *Lysistrata*. They do not take part in public life, in the Assembly. Their reliability in political judgement is founded on private life and on their participation in religion. The household occupation of Greek women was weaving wool into cloth. If Lysistrata had taken a fleece, cleansed it, carded it, made it into a ball and manufactured a garment, then she had as much practice in *politike episteme* as the Magistrate who reprimands her for interfering in politics. She explains:

> [j]ust like washing out a raw fleece, you should wash the sheep-dung out of the body politic in a bath, then put it on a bed, beat out the villains with a stick and pick off the burrs; and as for those people who combine and mat themselves together to gain office, you should card them out and pluck off the heads. Then card the wool into the work-basket of union and concord, mixing in everyone; and the immigrants, and any foreigner who's friendly to you, and anyone who's in debt to the treasury, they should be mixed in as well. And yes, there are also all the states which are colonies of this land: you should recognise how you now have them lying around like little flocks of wool, each one by itself; so then you should take the human flock from all of them, bring them together here and join them into one, and then

---

61 Hans Urs von Balthasar, *Theo-Drama: Theological Dramatic Theory: I Prologomena*, translated by Graham Harrison (Ignatius Press, San Francisco, 1988), p. 455.

make a great ball of wool, and from that weave a warm cloak for the people to wear.[62]

If we were to put words into his mouth, the Magistrate might have responded as Ehrenberg does: 'The whole idea of peace is simply a matter of prudent opportunism and prosaic self-interest, and is quite empty of a higher ideal.'[63] In comedy, ideals come wrapped in the warm cloak of the body. Since *Lysistrata* was performed at the Greater Dionysia, when Athens was open to all of her friends and allies, the audience may have been alert to the broader implications of Lysistrata's words. The comic peace-makers, Lysistrata and Trygaeus, are experts in domestic economy and farming. The Dionysian pleasures grow in the soil of peace.[64]

The women of Athens give the second reason for their political *nous*. The women say that they have a right to have a say in the good of the City:

> Women: Here we begin, all you citizens, to deliver
>   advice that will benefit the city;
>   and rightly so, for she nurtured me in sumptuous
>   splendour.
>   As soon as I was seven years old, I was an Arrephoros;
>   then I was a Grinder; when I was ten, at the Brauronia,
>   I shed my saffron gown as one of the Foundress' Bears;
>   and I was also once a basket bearer, a beautiful girl, wearing
>   a string of dried figs.

From their childhood upwards, they have taken part in the religious festivals of the city.[65]

Aristophanes often introduced real people into his plays. Lysistrata may have been intended to be the priestess of Athena Polias. In the late fifth century, the office was held by a woman named Lysimakhe. Lysimakhe means 'dissolver of battles', Lysistrata, 'dissolving armies', which is close enough. Lysistrata shows the leadership qualities of a priestess, and is at home in Athena's temple. Lysistrata stands for Athena, and, therefore, the city of Athens:[66] she and her supporters 'represent, not just a feminine attitude to war and politics, but also Athenian religious tradition'.[67]

f. Aristophanes' Audience
The theatre audience is the co-creator, not of the play itself, but of the play's performance. Anyone who writes for public performance structures their speech according to what their audience knows and what will achieve an immediate response with it. The meaning stock of the words, images and acted gestures which a writer sets out in a play is localised and specified by the audience before whom it will be performed. James Redfield says that a genre is

62 Aristophanes, *Lysistrata*, edited with translation and notes by Alan H. Sommerstein (Aris & Philips, Wiltshire, 1990), ll. 638–646.
63 Ehrenberg, *People of Aristophanes*, p. 222.
64 Lever, *Art of Greek Comedy*, p. 96.
65 According to McDowell, *Aristophanes and Athens*, p. 240.
66 Ibid., pp. 240–243.
67 Ibid., p. 242.

a disambiguating context, which creates a channel of communication. What happens in a comedy . . . is supposed to be funny, and the audience will do its best to take it so. In return, the audience expects the poet to play fair, and not abruptly to change the rules so that we feel ashamed of ourselves for laughing at something meant to be pathetic.[68]

Sophocles 'created' the character of Oedipus the king by expanding on a picture already implanted in his audience's minds by Pericles.[69] Old Comedy was even more 'exuberantly topical' than tragedy.[70] The play-wright writes 'with': the play is a dialogue with an audience. Theatrical convention makes the audience know in advance that, if they are watching a comedy, the crane is going to make them laugh. The author also writes 'to' the audience, re-arranging and transforming their conception of what is. Aristophanes' audience knew they would laugh at comedy and be uplifted by it, but they didn't take their seats expecting to see a wily old man, Peisetaerus, take the place of Zeus. Within both play and performance, author, actors and audience use both convention and spontaneity.

Cleon sued Aristophanes for libel on at least one occasion. In the following year, in the *Archanians* (425) Aristophanes counter-attacked, but stressed that he was assailing, not the people as a whole, but an individual: 'I do not say the state'.[71] It was permissible to criticise individuals, but not the city as a whole: 'In no other place or age were men of all classes attacked and ridiculed in public and by name with such freedom as in Old Attic Comedy.' It permitted 'complete parrhesia, freedom of speech'.[72] Such freedom of speech was not a general and unlicensed Athenian ideal. Greek culture recognised the significance of the 'public face', easily dishonoured by public derision. Athens' first law-giver, Solon (seventh century BC), gave citizens redress against libel and public calumny. The festival was an enclosure within which such censorship did not apply. One of the conventions of the comic theatrical performance was the possibility for 'spontaneous' abuse. The performers and audience are *playing*: they are acting in an arena which is set apart from normal life.[73] The theatrical experience is not properly speaking a political experience. The *Lysistrata* does not set out policy objectives. *Peace* does not explain how 'peace' is to be maintained in Greece and the Peloponnese. The *Birds* is not a project for the colonisation of outer space. Deliberation over practical policy took place in the Assembly, the locus of political experience. The dramatic festivals were *civic* occasions, paid for by the public purse. To say its theatrical experience was not political does not mean that the Greek theatre was 'private', in any modern sense. The public experience of comic theatre is aesthetic and ethical: it enables the audience to *see* and to *know* beauty and goodness. It does not tell the audience how to act on this knowledge. It

---

68 James Redfield, 'Drama and Community: Aristophanes and Some of His Rivals', in Winkler and Zeitlin, *Nothing to Do with Dionysos?*, pp. 314–335 (314).
69 Ibid., pp. 325–326.
70 Ibid., p. 329.
71 Aristophanes, *Archanians*, l. 515, cited in Ehrenberg, *People of Aristophanes*, p. 18.
72 Ehrenberg, *People of Aristophanes*, p. 19.
73 F. S. Halliwell notes that the Greek *paizein*, 'to play', is connected to dancing. 'The Uses of Laughter in Greek Culture', *Classical Quarterly*, ns. 41, 1991, 279–296 (283).

creates an imagined world in which these qualities are perceptible and thus enables the audience to give assent to them. As Redfield puts it,

> Drama is . . . a kind of dreaming in public, and on behalf of a public which, as it is drawn into the play, shares the dream of the poet. Theatre . . . is a kind of public event opposite to political debate. In the political Assembly, the practical life is brought . . . to lucidity by a procedure which clarifies, schematizes and facilitates the reconstruction of existing social relations. In the theater, the city shares an experience; because all share it equally, social relations are deleted. Because the action of the play is unreal, all can share in it without danger. A unity not attainable in practice was achieved on the level of theory – in the Greek sense: *theoria*, looking on. Debate is analytic, theatre synthetic. Through deliberation, the city could come to *act* as a unity; the theatre by contrast was a sphere of collective *knowledge*.[74]

We may read that Athenian theatre is entirely 'symbolic', achieving its effects through theatrical devices such as masks and costumes. That may have meant meant that the play was representative rather than real.[75] It might seem to follow that Old Comedy creates a world in which words bite only 'imaginary' objects. *In fact*, Athenian theatre is partly conventional and partly realistic. The use of the crane is evidence that the imagination required a little empirical assistance. And thus, by analogy, although the Athenian audience was instructed to enter the world of the imagination when it came into the theatre, that world is related to the real one – or else Cleon would not have sued. There is certainly a difference between meeting Cleon in the barber shop and calling him a warmonger, in front of the other men getting a haircut, and making Cleon the 'Pestle' in *Peace*. Comic drama is public humour set apart from the consequences of everyday life. The theatre is set apart from ordinary economic and political consequences, because its space of imagination is contiguous with a *religious* festival, over which the unruly god of wine presides. The 'Dionysiac liberation'[76] experienced during the theatrical experience allowed for the expression of violent, abusive and sexual energies which were normally suppressed. The Dionysian realm creates an 'interplay between norm and transgression'.[77] In a comic play-performance, nobodies like Trygaeus and Peisetaerus can overrun the normal boundaries of civic and religious life: they can curse their political leaders and their gods. Comic 'violence' is not only one of the conventions of the *theatre*, but is also attached to the *religious agon*, or contest, out of which theatre is said to have grown. The 'masked Dionysian procession', in which it was customary for the paraders to insult the bystanders, and comedy itself are 'close to . . . the sphere of ritual abuse'.[78]

Aristophanes' characters invoke the gods, pour libations and make sacrifices. The plays end with a sacramental wedding feast: the religion

---

74 Redfield, 'Drama and Community', p. 324.
75 McLeish, *Theatre of Aristophanes*, pp. 79–80.
76 Bowie, *Aristophanes*, p. 16.
77 Simon Goldhill, 'The Great Dionysia and Civic Ideology', in Winkler and Zeitlin, *Nothing to Do With Dionysos?*, pp. 97–129 (127).
78 Halliwell, 'Uses of Laughter in Greek Comedy', 295.

which is celebrated creates the opportunity to eat, drink, marry and bed.[79] This is allied to a lyrical and lofty perception of the gods; *Birds* 'pays homage to Apollo and Pan'. Likewise, '*Lysistrata* is filled . . . with the awe and power of Athene . . . running through all the plays is a theme of serious invocation of the gods and spirits connected with poetry, from Apollo and the Muses to the Graces'.[80] This seems hard to reconcile with the figures which the gods cut in the plays, such as the bribable Hermes in *Peace* or the Olympians' feeble capitulation to Peisetaerus. It is *impossible* to reconcile, unless comedy draws opposites together into a single image. The two rivers of whimsical mockery of the gods and the lyrical invocation of divine beauty run together in comedy. The paradox of the simultaneous mockery and awe of the gods in Aristophanic comedy is possible because it supplied the 'script' for a religious festival:

> Both Aristophanes and his audience would know the religious obligations of a poet writing for an Athenian festival; Aristophanes fulfils those obligations . . . by his constant association of worship with the simplest, deepest urges in man, the times when by moving in harmony with the natural order, he discovers his true self.[81]

The gods are not mocked in the tragedies of Aeschylus or Sophocles, although their effects are clearly felt. Perhaps we may say that, whereas Greek tragedy presents the proximity in *difference* of the gods, Greek comedy reflects the differerence in *proximity* of the divine: and thus human beings are permitted a 'come back'.

5. The Genre of Comic Drama

Old Comedy follows *structural* rules. Each of Aristophanes' plays starts with a prologue, which leads to an *Agon*, or contest, followed by the choral parabasis, after which comes a feast or sacrifice, which is variously interrupted; finally there is a *Komos*, the processional exit. This is the *literary structure* of Old Comedy. What follows concerns not these structural rules, which have probably not been widely observed outside of Old Comedy, but the *generic* form of comedy.

a. The Elements of Comedy

Drama does not argue, it shows. Aristophanes left it to his friend Socrates to argue philosophically for the divine in human nature: he shows it, in the *Birds*; he left it to Aristotle to explain what the political good of the city entails. The dramatist conveys a moral or a truth through the conflict in which the hero engages. The truth which the dramatist conveys is the resolution of an *aporia*, shown and experienced as an acted story. It is because the existence of a comic genre is a fact of experience that I failed to begin by contesting the notion that comedy is different in every age and culture. Perceiving the comedy of Aristophanes' plays is the best rejoinder

---

79 Ehrenberg, *People of Aristophanes*, p. 188.
80 McLeish, *Theatre of Aristophanes*, p. 59.
81 Ibid.

to the claim that the comedies of every culture are incommensurable. Any reader who laughed has the makings of a genre essentialist. If Aristophanes had been transported in a time machine to the twentieth century, he would have recognised the mechanics of Woody Allen's *Sleeper* as comic.

It may be because drama poses a provisional answer to the human quest to know that it has the six features which we named earlier: the presence of an audience, conflict, ethics, freedom, dialogue, symbolism and the sacred. The seventh feature, which qualifies these as comic, can be defined philosophically, as the spirit of desire, or aesthetically, as the presentation of a cosmos ruled by the laws of harmony, or in terms of the 'tripartite plot', which flows from problem to solution, to celebration.[82] What do these dramatic elements look like when they are driven by the spirit of desire? First, the *audience* enjoys the way that the hero resolves the *conflict*. Comic conflict is about endurance, the persisting will to win. The audience enjoys its identification with a hero or heroine who will fight on to the end. One person joking is funny, but two people bouncing insults off each other is better. Howard Jacobson calls this:

> *The come-back.* Where would cursing be without it? Curse a silent person or one who walks away, and invention dies on your lips. Your mouth becomes a grave. That's it; the party's over, the world's an empty place. A comeback . . . even sounds resurrectionary. A return from the dead. A living riposte.[83]

By wit, craft, strength of will, and imaginative power, the comic hero turns an unliveable situation into a paradise. Comic *dialogue* makes the audience laugh. The comic hero, or heroine, talks in order to get something done. The characters *attack* one another, and the gods, and the audience, and their plan. Comedy is about someone *being themselves*, in public, unravelling more and more of that fantastic energy. The audience *loves* the comic hero, or heroine, because their escapades flow out of what they *are*, and this is exhibited with great and extroverted obviousness. There is a double sense of *freedom* in the comic drama. In the first place, the comic *hero* is free. The freedom of the comic hero is expressed in the comic drama as his unbeatableness, his refusal to lie down and die. The comic hero is a life-force, because comedy 'is an image of human vitality holding its own in the world amid the surprises of unplanned coincidences'.[84] Comic heroes conceive schemes which enable them to transcend and to change their ambient world. This freedom of character is the complement of inhabiting a liberating *space*. In the space of play and fantasy created by comedy, form, species, gender and status are all open to negotiation and transformation: a farmer can marry a goddess, men can become birds, and women can take over the government of the city. The liberation from boundaries created by the comic space is fertile with possibilities. Where tragedy reminds its audience of their servitude to *necessity*, comedy shows them a space of freedom.[85] The freedom of the hero celebrates a fertile *world*, a world which

---

82 Ibid., pp. 50–52.
83 Jacobson, *Seriously Funny*, p. 122.
84 Suzanne Langer, *Feeling and Form* (Routledge & Kegan Paul, London, 1953, 1979), p. 231.
85 Redfield, 'Drama and Community', pp. 328–329.

can be changed for the better. The *symbol* which governs comic drama is the union of lofty and low, heavenly fantasy and concrete reality. It is therefore

> of the essence of comedy to kaleidoscope extremes, to jam together opposites so that they are simultaneously true; in this it defeats the laws of an inexorable linear logic of cause and effect, beginning and end, action and consequence.[86]

The comic hero's head is filled with dreams. But he or she is never *unworldly*. Jacobson hurls some fine invective at Cecil Collins's pictures of 'The Fool', that modern 'clown' who is a stranger to the 'dirt and filth' of this world and has eyes only for a distant, faery-realm. But once 'All pleasure in food is gone', then gone too is the game of *unifying* the gluttons and the angels.[87] The more sensual the hero's aspirations, the funnier it is to achieve them in Heaven. Woody Allen was never so funny once he set himself to playing the Swedish introvert. Rather than escaping elsewhere, the comic hero reinvigorates nature and culture. Ironies and incongruities are funny, but the comic world as a whole brings different things into harmony. In tragedy, the spatial and material conditions of existence are in shadow. In comedy, they are brilliantly illuminated, pointing up the contrast between fantasy and reality. Trygaeus marries the goddess Peace, always remaining a farmer; Cloudcuckooland is built of bricks; Lysistrata takes over a city while her opponents and allies remain true to *petit bourgeois* form.[88] The comic plot takes a literal fact to its logical conclusion: if you want to talk to the gods, fly to Heaven, and remember that the gods have to eat. The comic *symbol* is large and obvious, and thus laughable. A symbol is an analogy: it makes one thing into another. Aristophanes shows the Peloponnesian War as the god War, cutting and chopping the Greek states into a salad; he sees the need to escape one's creditors as the desire to fly, the desire for flight as literal metamorphosis into a bird, and being a bird – with wings and a beak – as an apotheosis of the human spirit. Aristophanes' symbols, or analogies, proceed from literal fact to idea and back again.

The comic *ethos* enjoys and pursues plurality and heterogeneity. The twenty-four different kinds of birds in the Chorus of that play remind its audience that they enjoy the differences between things. The ethic of comic drama is governed by the ideal of that perfect erotic companionship, which, in Plato's *Symposium*, Aristophanes pretends to believe existed before Zeus with his thunderbolt cut asunder all of the naturally joined, four-legged, soul mates:

> [E]very year Dionysios 'married' the king archon's wife, a marriage symbolizing the close relationship between the god and the city . . . In the *Symposium* Aristophanes contributes as his share of the discussion a myth of the origins of love which explains human restlessness as the constant search for a mate, and human bliss as the discovery of the mate and union. Sexual desire and satisfaction symbolize all human craving and joy.[89]

86 Jacobson, *Seriously Funny*, p. 240.
87 Ibid., p. 184.
88 Ehrenberg, *People of Aristophanes*, p. 27.
89 Lever, *Art of Greek Comedy*, p. 124.

Since the ending is a verdict on the characters' actions, happiness is the guide to what is good, for comedy. The good which is seen and created by comic protagonists is natural and human.

b. *The Levels of Comedy*

Comedies are sufficiently divergent that, if one wants to make a claim for a genre of comedy, one has to account for the variety. Despite what Northrop Frye's disciples tell us, it is not true that 'comedy' ends with a celebration or wedding. *Kind Hearts and Coronets* does not, and what is that, if not comedy? The tragic world is predominantly temporal. The comic world projects an image of *space*. Comedies can be categorised by the level of imaginative space in which their action occurs. Dante articulated the three realms of the comic imagination in the three stages of his journey to God. Comedies can be infernal, purgatorial, or paradisial.[90] Infernal comedies take place in an underworld of the human spirit. The world of black comedy is one in which we laugh, however bad it gets, *in order to survive*: the comic energy is still crackling in the underworld. In infernal comedy, the setting is dark, helpers absent, and the laughter ironic. Such comedies include Beckett's *Endgame*, *Kind Hearts and Coronets*, and Flannery O'Connor's *Wise Blood* and *The Violent Bear It Away*. The heroes of such works experience disaster. Infernal comedy includes darkness and death.

In purgatorial comedies the characters achieve their ends through an uphill struggle, in which helpers are present to assist: such, for example, is the 1980s movie, *Tender Mercies*. In the *Purgatorio*, Dante meets Beatrice, whose summons has brought him on this journey, at the summit of the Mount: assistance in purgatorial comedy very often comes from feminine figures. In *Tom Jones*, Mrs Miller gives the hero respite from his travails; Mrs Waters does so too, and her final disclosure that she is not his mother enables him to win Sophia. The quest belongs to purgatorial comedy. One could call it questing comedy, or Quixotic comedy. Although the papistical overtones may be off-putting to some, the word 'purgatorial' reminds us that there is suffering and struggle in this type of comedy. In purgatorial comedies, the characters are *on their way* to happiness, always on the verge of achieving their desire as the action concludes.

In paradisial comedies, the characters effortlessly achieve their dreams. The dream projects the characters into a celestial city: thus, in the movie *The Navigators*, a dream takes a group of mediaeval Yorkshire men into a modern New Zealand, where they climb a church tower and retrieve a cross which will avert Black Death from their village. In paradisial comedies the mood is light, and the heroes make their way into a heavenly banquet. This is visionary comedy, even where the vision is a cow jumping over the moon. There are not many examples of the type: the *Birds* is 'one of the world's few examples of true paradisial comedy'. In this play, Aristophanes tries to bring to life

> the city hidden within the earthly community where the right order of being resides. The city Aristophanes 'saved' in this and his other plays makes up a

---

90 Louise Cowan, 'Introduction: The Comic Terrain', in Cowan, *Terrain of Comedy*, pp. 9–14.

permanent part of the *mundus imaginalis* available to all citizens everywhere through the comic imagination – an image of that one city we keep dreaming of building.[91]

Aristophanes sent his heroes skyward because he had been there, in imagination: his 'vision', Louise Cowan says, 'is apocalyptic'.[92]

6. The Comic and the Sacred

A strange animal called *the sacred* has slipped out of its cage and put its head in the door a few times already. It popped its exotic face into the explanation of drama, and its Dionysian avatar has been rampaging in and out of the comic world. One may picture this creature with wings, six long giraffe legs and spots. It seems to have a taste for wine. But what is this animal, the sacred? The most lucid definitions come from the *Bestiaries* of the classical phenomenologists of religion, Rudolf Otto and Gerardus van der Leeuw, because they aimed to name what is specific and unique to *religion*. Classical, realistic phenomenology was as Aristotelian as it was experiential: it planned a *morphology* of the different human experiences. It attempted to show how specific experiences are related to their precise objects. The sacred is a field: we know it when we experience it. Otto is remembered for having ascribed irrationality to the sacred: the memory is inaccurate. Otto defined the sacred as *pre*-rational or *extra*-rational. The sacred is outside or before the hard rationalities of science, and the soft rationalities of mundane experience. The sacred enters the realm of human affairs as a stranger. But this visitor is bewitching: we want it to stay and become domesticated. The Egyptians worshipped the Cat, and alongside Him a menagerie of animal-headed divinities. Van der Leeuw writes that:

> [T]he animal is on the one hand the non-human, the wholly different, the sinister or sublime; on the other it is attached and familiar; and this union of both aspects renders the worship of the animal as a numinous object comprehensible.[93]

Rudolf Otto defined 'the holy' as a *'mysterium tremendum et fascinans'*, a terrifying and fascinating mystery. The mystery is 'the numinous'. To this numinous object there corresponds the human religious experience of simultaneous terror and yearning. When human beings encounter the numinous, we desire it fervently; and, that which we yearn for but can barely name, sometimes attains the character of the numinous. This *mysterium* is also horrifying. Otto distinguishes ordinary fear from the religious dread which we experience in the face of the sacred. When an unwary aspirant opens the book, or steps into the magic circle, or touches the side of the Ark, it blasts them to bits, or expels them from Paradise. The Hindu Kali, the Greek Pan and the Hebrew Yahweh are none of them

---

91 Cowan, 'Aristophanes' Comic Drama', in ibid., pp. 77, 82 and 85.
92 Ibid., p. 66.
93 Gerardus van der Leeuw, *Religion in Essence and Manifestation: A Study in the Phenomenology of Religion*, translated by J. E. Turner (George Allen & Unwin, London, 1938), p. 75.

chums to human beings: they are all dangerous gods. In the Buddhist countries of South-East Asia, 'image painters' still paint in the Buddha's eyes using mirrors.[94] To look in the Buddha's eyes is death without assurance of Nirvana. The sacred object is *taboo*, not because it is 'bad' – which is a category belonging to ethics, not to religion – but because it is dynamite: 'Tabu is a kind of warning: Danger! High voltage! Power has been stored up and we must be on our guard.'[95] Like a nuclear power plant, the sacred has to be enclosed within carefully demarcated boundaries. The 'sacred' can thus be defined as 'what has been placed within boundaries, the exceptional (Latin *sanctus*); its powerfulness creates for it a place of its own'.[96] Stories are attached to the *mysterium*: it gains a mythology in which it acts and does. The best 'sacral' event is the *miracle*, the advent of the god who reverses empirical laws. The sacred is a dynamic and performative category: sacred space is 'that locality that becomes a position by the effect of power repeating itself there, or being repeated by man. It is the place of worship'.[97]

Otto and van der Leeuw base their phenomenologies of religion in *experience*: Otto advises his readers to abandon his book on the second page if they can claim no experience of the holy. But he concedes one analogy to the sphere of the holy: that is, the aesthetic. The *mysterium tremendum* eludes definition, but we can develop some sort of net to catch it in, if we ask the *aestheticians*, the professional analysts of works of art.[98] The work of art is analogous to the sacred in that it is *set apart* from everyday life and even normal perception. The painting does not exist in normal space: it creates a 'virtual space' for itself.[99] The 'time' of the performance is not the time which ticks on the audience's watches. Within the dramatic world, time accelerates and slows down, according to the rhythm of the action which is being performed. The boundaries of the work of art are the limits of its aesthetic form. Both the sacred and the aesthetic attempt to capture that nameless stranger, the transcendent, in a limited form or shape. Both give laws to the anomalous and a name to the anonymous, and thereby make the other *present*. Van der Leeuw says that the sacred is experienced as the coalescence of untramelled Power with shaping Form and individual Will.[100]

The first human apprehension of 'Powers' comes about in dance. Dance extracts 'the sense of power from' everyday 'experiences'. Such 'dance creates an image of nameless and even bodiless Powers filling a complete, autonomous realm, a "world". It is the first presentation of the world as a realm of mystic forces.'[101] When we see dancers, moving away from and toward each other, we do not just see backward and forward motions: each dancer is a magnet, and the dancers are attracting and repelling each

---

94 Richard Gombrich, *Precept and Practice: Traditional Buddhism in the Rural Highlands of Ceylon* (Clarendon Press, Oxford, 1971), pp. 113–114.
95 Van der Leeuw, *Religion in Essence and Manifestation*, p. 44.
96 Ibid., p. 47.
97 Ibid., p. 393.
98 Otto, *The Idea of the Holy*, translated by John W. Harvey (Penguin, Harmondsworth, Middlesex, 1923, 1959), p. 56.
99 Langer, *Feeling and Form*, pp. 50 and 72.
100 Van der Leeuw, *Religion in Essence and Manifestation*, p. 148.
101 Langer, *Feeling and Form*, p. 189.

other. This is the performance of power. What we see are 'dance forces, virtual powers'.[102] The dancers create a 'magic circle', the boundaries of the sacred space.

Dance is 'unidirectional': it directs the powers here and there, but does not yet tell a story. It is only with the 'movement and countermovement' of drama that a myth can be told and re-enacted.[103] Van der Leeuw calls drama 'holy play', *sacer ludus*. Children play at being mothers and fathers, or royal families. In 'Holy Play', adults pretend to be, that is, imitate, the powers whose energies they want to channel: the rain and the sun, the stag and its hunters, the return of spring, and the autumn harvest. Religious 'playing' ensures food and fertility. The players 'represent' the sacred powers by pretending to be them. The best means of such pretence is dressing-up: the costume and the *mask* transform the actor into his part. As Van der Leeuw says,

> The mask belongs to the *sacer ludus* as the great means of stylization. Through it, all events are reduced to a single event which is . . . divine. At the Athenian Choe festival, a mask of Dionysius hangs on a pole during the mixing of wine. To it the new wine is offered first . . . The god is a mask; the mask, a god.[104]

Dionysus, the curious beast we were looking for, has been dogging us all along the way. But Frazer's metanarrative of dying and rising gods has been expelled from the canons of the classical scholars. How can we regain it for comedy? Frazer had a disciple in Francis Cornford, who found in the literary structure of each of Aristophanes' plays a re-enactment of the Frazerian myth. But his '*Origin of Attic Comedy* is almost as out of favour as . . . *The Golden Bough*'. One way back to a perception of comedy as related to rituals of fertility is *experience*. Howard Jacobson adjures us to 'Go to Bernard Manning's Embassy Club in Manchester on a Friday or Saturday night . . . and deny . . . that some sort of communal purgation is at work'. Having been there on our behalf, purely for the purpose of phenomenological research, Jacobson describes a policeman's dirty night out at the Embassy Club:

> an assembly of men, all belonging to the same profession, gathered . . . for the purpose of eating and drinking and laughing at the same jokes is ritual, or it's nothing. Over that assembly the comedian presides like a priest . . . his jokes should be familiar . . . they should evoke predictable responses – Amen! Hallelujah! . . . Every member of the congregation understands the formalized nature of the occasion . . . it bears upon the everyday but is not itself everyday . . . there is artifice at work. Drama. Play . . . transfigures reality.[105]

As with ritual, a crucial element in comic acting is pretending to be someone else. Actors disguise themselves in make-up and costume themselves in unlikely guises, and thus allow their everyday characters to encompass

---

102 Ibid., pp. 175–176.
103 Van der Leeuw, *Religion in Essence and Manifestation*, p. 78.
104 Ibid., p. 84.
105 Jacobson, *Seriously Funny*, p. 31.

the strange. Peisetaerus and Euelpides dressed as birds in order to take on their quasi-sacral aura and power. The strangest experience, in some sense the most religious, experience a man can have is to become a woman. This is one of the staples of comedy, as in *Some Like it Hot*, in which Jack Lemmon and Tony Curtis become wiggly girl saxophone players:

> of all the ways of figuring ourselves extended . . . the most universal – and . . . the most effective is transvestism . . . the whole of dressing-up works a miraculous transformation in the personality of the dresser . . . the effects of dressing-across are still more dramatic . . . To be herself, even on radio, Dame Edna Everage has to be dressed and equippaged as Dame Edna Everage.[106]

I need hardly remind the readers of a work of philosophical theology that the world's most famous cross-dresser is not Edna Everage but his Holiness the Pope. He wears his costume all the time, perhaps better to channel its feminine powers. Although some do their best to set themselves up for it, we do not usually laugh at the sight of priests. The Pope cuts a serious figure; so do Abraham, Isaac and Jacob. The reductionist may say that the comedy has been sublimated; the inflationist may argue that it has been sublated. When we turn to the Bible, we will find much that is literally comic: but we must also be on our guard for sublimated or sublated comedy, concealed under the serious religious purpose. Cross-dressing is but one of the crucial *analogies* between comic drama and religious ritual. A work of comedy is not a sacred text, and nor, for that matter, is the revealed word of God '*a* sacred text'. But perhaps they can form some sort of ladder, which we can best put together, not by reason, but by the pre-rational paradoxes which inform all three items. It is sometimes thought that the way of analogy from humanity to God is only passed through reason: but there are also *experiential* analogies, perhaps more fundamental than their rational counterparts. The loss of self in the roar of laughter and the loss of self in religion are friends. Let us, then, bring the experience of comedy to the Bible.

106 Ibid., p. 235.

2

The Master Images:
The Pentateuch

1. The Bible as Dramatic Comedy

The Bible is filled with comical episodes, verbal wit, parody and satire, humour of character and of situation. Alfred North Whitehead had to be pretty humourless to find none in it.[1] In contrast, some intrepid authors have gone so far as to find the *literary structure* of Old Comedy in various biblical books. I wish them well, but what I am looking for is neither humorous episodes, nor literary structure, but the *generic* world of dramatic comedy.

If Frye is right to define genre by its plot, we should be looking for a single plot in the Bible. Does it have one plot, or many? Genesis is narratively monogenetic: its genealogies remind the reader that it is about the family of Adam and Eve, Noah, Abraham and Sarah, Isaac and Rebekah, Jacob and Rachel, Joseph and his brothers. The 'subject of the covenant promises' of Exodus is the 'one people, *keneset Yisrael*'.[2] The Bible has a unity of actors because its story is about one unfolding dialogue between God and his chosen people. The Old Testament stories conceive character typologically: Jacob, rather confusingly, *is* Israel; Esau *is* Edom. The prophets look to a New David. The author of Galatians grafts Christianity into Abraham's story. If the single story is about a single people, Paul must identify baptism into Christ with birthing out of Abraham. Matthew makes Christ the new Moses, giving a new law. Christian theology joins the acts of the God of the Old Covenant with those of the New by finding Christ-like events in the scenes of the Old Testament, from Abraham's sacrifice of Isaac to the sufferings of Job. Frye defended biblical typology like this:

> [T]he Pharaoh of the Exodus, Nebuchadnezzar, Antiochus Epiphanes, and Nero are spiritually the same person. And the deliverers of Israel – Abraham, Moses and Joshua, the judges, David, and Solomon – are all prototypes of the Messiah or final deliverer.[3]

---

1 A. N. Whitehead remarked that 'the total absence of humor from the Bible is one of the most singular things in all literature'. Cited in Yehuda T. Radday and Athalya Brenner (eds), *On Humour and the Comic in the Hebrew Bible* (Almond Press, Sheffield, 1990), pp. 21 and 99.
2 Jonathan Sacks, *One People? Tradition, Modernity and Jewish Unity* (Littman Library of Jewish Civilization, London, 1993), p. 31.
3 Northrop Frye, *The Great Code* (Routledge & Kegan Paul, London, 1981), p. 171.

There is something slightly annoying about this suggestion, although we need not reject it out of hand for that reason. It is irritating because it subsumes the individual human actors of the Old and New Testaments into two single Actors, a good guy and a bad guy. We need not exaggerate the uniqueness of the biblical characters. Any successful long narrative holds itself together by kinships among its characters. The Rostovs in *War and Peace* are all musical, generous and impractical. If the biblical characters had nothing in common, we would go bumping along from one episode to another, and even the project of putting together the Pentateuch would seem perverse. There are family resemblances among the biblical characters: the tyrannical kings, such as the two Pharaohs of Exodus and Daniel's Nebuchadnezzar, are not completely dissimilar. This creates a comedy of the typical situation: we know that a stock-villain-king will send for his magicians. Nor are the good guys *absolutely* heterogeneous. Samson shares marginality and a way with women with the outlaw David of 1 Samuel. But the biblical characters would be boring if they lacked idiosyncrasy. Jacob is not only Israel: he is also a deceiving rascal. God enters into dialogues with many individuals. Our interpretation of the unity of the Bible cannot start from a theological univocity of character.

Gerardus van der Leeuw reminds us that

> The theological nature of ... drama [lies] in movement and countermovement. God moved; he came down to earth ... The most ancient drama, the drama that rules the world, is the drama of the meeting of God with man.[4]

A drama takes place within the boundaries of a world. The plot flows in the way that it does because it is coursing through this world. What we are looking for is not just a *plot*, but the world which contains it, with its specific forces and powers, its theological gravity. Since we speak of a *dramatic world*, we ask what sort of *action* runs through the Bible. Where are the stories going? One source of movement is 'alienation', moving *away* from something. Yahweh perpetually spurs the people of Israel to move away from their neighbours' rootedness in the cosmos. City dwellers are the most prolific authors of cosmic mythology. Herbert Schneidau argued that the dynamic of the Bible flows from the predilection of its Deity for bombing sacred piles of brick.[5] Each time human beings build a great city, God disperses it. The first shepherd is Abel, and the first murderer is Cain, who goes on to found a city. If the villains are city dwellers, the heroes are nomadic shepherds, like Abraham. The dynamic of movement away from cities into open pastures makes its way into the New Testament: 'I am the good shepherd', says Christ. The drama concludes with the overthrow of a Romish Babylon.

The first moving principle of the biblical stories is God's insistence that the heroes pull up their tent pegs. But the covenant promises direct the human actors into a land where they can put their roots down. The land is pictured as a place where good things happen: milk and honey flow and the fruits of the vine are easily harvested. The 'energy' of the biblical

---

4 Van der Leeuw, *Sacred and Profane Beauty*, p. 111.
5 Herbert Schneidau, *Sacred Discontent: The Bible and Western Tradition* (University of California Press, Berkeley, 1977): one has reluctantly to say '*passim*'.

narrative drives it toward integration.[6] The biblical story begins, Frye says, with the 'fall' away from unity with nature. Adam and Eve's departure from the natural Paradise is the inception of the 'downward' line of the U-shaped curve. The biblical characters learn to be at odds with nature and one another. As the plot begins its ascent to the new Paradise, its characters are driven by a vision of the reunification of nature: 'the wolf shall lie down with the lamb'. By culminating in the new Jerusalem, the biblical journey carries out the completed U of comedy. Frye claimed that 'the Bible gives us a vision of upward metamorphosis, of the alienated relation of man to nature transformed into a spontaneous and effortless life' in which there is 'energy without alienation'.[7] Comedy satisfied the desire for integration within space. If we downplay the thread of *integration* in the Bible, we lose the *space* in which the drama unfolds.

But the type of narrative of which Frye appears to speak could be depicted by an omniscient epic narrator. We can view an integrated cosmos from the outside. The biblical authors do not always narrate: they also make us watch people acting. The literary form of the Bible is not an epic in which God is almost as important as the cosmos, but a drama between God and human persons. The Bible tells the story of an event between *persons*, divine and human. The mark of a person, divine or human, is to be free. This is the moral or dramatic fabric of the biblical drama. A third way of marking the dynamic of the biblical world is given by Robert Alter's uncovery of a mixture of 'design and disorder' in its plot. The design is God's plan, the disorder is the unruly way in which it is implemented by human beings. The biblical narrative is realistic: it depicts psychologically real human beings by never letting go of the 'tension' between 'God's will ... and human freedom, the refractory nature of man'.[8] The Bible is dramatic because the spiralling of its plot is perceptible only in the *process* of decision-making and action by the characters. This is what happens if we *imagine* God acting in history. The dramatic God transcends the design and the disorder of the story. But, 'God is only funny when he is acting as if he were human':[9] that is, *reacting*, creating the hope and fear of response. The precise location of the divine side of the comedy is the join between a God who transcends nature and a God who enters into the human game. Likewise on the human side: there would be no comedy if God directed the play by dangling 'human' marionettes on strings.

There is no comedy without the odd coupling of earth and heaven. Human love is not disembodied. Because desire is humanly embodied, the 'higher world' which comedy seeks is not a-sexual. All comedy is about sex, and the Bible is no exception.[10] A fourth way of defining the plot-dynamism of the Bible is to say that the motor is Eros or love. Both in the translations which I use, and in the original, God is a chap, the subject of masculine verbs in the Hebrew and in the Greek. I shall refer to him as

---

6 Frye, *Great Code* (Routledge & Kegan Paul, London, 1981), p. 75.
7 Ibid.
8 Alter, *Art of Biblical Narrative*, p. 33.
9 Francis Landy, 'Humour as a Tool for Biblical Exegesis', in Radday and Brenner, *On Humour and the Comic*, pp. 99–115 (105).
10 Nelvin Vos, *The Drama of Comedy: Victor and Victim*.

such because the precise erotic quality of the encounter between God and human beings would be different if he were neuter or female. The biblical characters embark on their adventures because they have been promised a place in which they can build a community of love. The story ends in a paradisial City because its engine is love, the desire for communion. Thus, there are four elements of dramatic comedy in the biblical world: alienation, integration, freedom and eros. In the historical dialogue between God and human beings, human desire will be satisfied because the promised land, the New Jerusalem, is God's purpose and gift.

2. Genesis

a. Historical Background and Composition

In the 1870s, Wellhausen proposed that the Pentateuch is woven out of three 'documents', 'J', the Jahwist, 'E', the Elohist, and 'P', the Priestly writer. The three sources indicate three ways of understanding God and human nature. The Jahwist is supposed to have lived in the mid-tenth century BC, the Elohist in the ninth century BC.[11] The Priestly writer accentuated the liturgy. He is supposed to have written after the Exile of 597. The Deuteronomist took a hand in the final redaction of the book, again, after the Exile. Faith in hypothetical source documents like 'J' and 'E' has languished,[12] and the upshot has been to throw the weight of composition onto the post-exilic editors. Fewer contemporary exegetes ascribe authorial intentions to circumstances supposed to have existed before the Exile. Scholars now rely more on the post-exilic theologies of the Priestly and Deuteronomic *tradents*.

b. The Text

'In the beginning God created the heaven and the earth' (Gen. 1.1). From the beginning, the weight of the moving story rests on God. God creates the spatial dimensions in which the action will take place. These spatial dimensions probably *are* pre-scientific physics; but they are also the scene-setting of a drama. The upper domain belongs to God; the horizontal plane to the creatures which are placed in it. The stage needs an up and a down because God and his angels tend to enter from above. The perspective which makes 'up' above and 'down' here is human.

In the second creation story ('J'), God's creation is more directly oriented to the human.

> [T]he LORD God fashioned the human, humus from the soil, and blew into his nostrils the breath of life, and the human became a living creature. And the LORD God planted a garden in Eden, to the east, and He placed there the human He had fashioned. And the LORD God caused to sprout from the soil every tree lovely to look at and good for food, and the tree of life was in the midst of the garden, and the tree of knowledge, good and evil. (2.5–9)

---

11 Gerhard von Rad, *Genesis: A Commentary*, translated by John Bowker from the 9th German edition (SCM, London, 1961, 1972), p. 25.

12 Norman Whybray, *The Making of the Pentateuch: A Methodological Study* (Sheffield Academic Press, Sheffield, 1987).

Only 'the human' is given *nephesh*, God's breath of life. The dust and the *nephesh* are not quite the Platonic body and soul. But that which represents the 'below' – dust – and that which comes from above – God's 'breath of life' – have been mustered together to make Adam.

In the Jahwistic Chapter 2 God engages 'the human' in the speech-act of creation (Gen. 2.18–19). God has created the world from above; by naming the animals, Adam turns it into a human life-world. Adam does not meet his 'other' in any of the creatures. So God acts again, making the woman, whom Adam names as Eve. The first biblical alienation is the separation of Eve from Adam.[13]

Adam promptly blames both the human and the divine 'thou' for his failure in the first test which God posed to him: 'The *woman* whom you gave by me, she gave me from the tree, and I ate' (Gen. 3.12). Words both clothe the world in a meaning which unites, *and* cloak hollow, fantasy worlds. The villain of the piece uses language to seduce: 'God's creative word turns into the guile of the serpent, which divides man from himself and from the woman, from God and from the Garden.'[14]

Some commentators say that Genesis 1 is the beginning of the biblical *history*.[15] But God cannot initiate a *history* by himself: it takes two to tango. Adam fails his first test without knowing what good and evil are. Until he eats of the tree of the knowledge of good and evil, he is not a moral being: he has to obey the *religious* or sacral injunction of God not to eat the apple. He crosses a limit which is closer to a ritual taboo than a moral command. History begins once the human characters are both answerable to God religiously *and* can act morally. Drama begins beyond the garden, where Adam and Eve have become, as God notes 'as one of us, knowing good and evil' (Gen. 3.22).

God has told Adam that 'you are dust and to dust you shall return'. The 'breath of life' was not cemented into the human forms of Adam and Eve. The punishment which God imposes is to live 'on an accursed soil' (Gen. 3.19a), in a *place* from which God has removed himself: according to the wisdom of traditional biblical criticism, 'The three actors in the drama are condemned, not to death' but to live outside the security of the Garden where 'their life will be spent far from God, and near to death'. The displacement is traditionally articulated in the word 'fall'; the story indicates a decisive stage shift, *away* from the presence of God. The word 'fall' is educed from the implicit image of a movement *down*, from a garden-world close to God to a 'hostile world'.[16]

---

13 Gerhard von Rad comments on Eve's being made from Adam's rib: 'Whence comes this love "strong as death" (S of Sol. 8.6) and stronger than the tie to one's parents, whence this inner clinging to each other which does not rest until it again becomes one flesh in the child? It comes from the fact that God took woman from man, and they . . . were originally *one* flesh . . . The recognition of this narrative as aetiological is theologically important. Its point of departure . . . is for the narrator something in existence, present, not something "paradisiacal" and thus lost!' *Genesis*, p. 85.

14 Josipovici, *Book of God*, p. 69.

15 Von Rad, *Genesis*, p. 64.

16 Robert Martin-Achard, *From Death to Life: A Study of the Development of the Doctrine of the Resurrection in the Old Testament*, translated by John Penney Smith (Oliver & Boyd, Edinburgh and London, 1960), p. 19.

Mary Douglas explained why the ritual laws of Leviticus forbid the consumption of lobsters, crabs and creeping things but allow four-footed animals by suggesting that culinary rituals reflect a social order. Animals which are 'odd' and asymmetrical are placed outside the culinary pale.[17] By his trespass of the ritual injunction, Adam has built an ellipse into the human relationship with God. The characters can no longer revolve around God in a perfect circle. Adam has ingested oddity into history. Adam's fall makes the disjunctive outcomes of history possible. The dialectic of design and disorder can now begin. The tree of the knowledge of good and evil was an outpost of heaven, planted temptingly on earth. Adam and his descendants now incorporate more of the heavenly domain than had been originally given to the denizens of the dust. The tree of life dropped out of the plot in 2.19. It quietly reappears at the end of Chapter 3:

> And the LORD God sent him from the garden of Eden to till the soil from which he had been taken. And he drove out the human and set up east of the garden of Eden the cherubim and the flame of the whirling sword to guard the way to the tree of life. (3.23–24)

Adam and Eve ate of the tree of knowledge but not of the tree of life. Hence an incommensurability in their drives and desires: their urge to know lurches heavenward, while their span of life is earthbound. Their relation to God will be disjunctive because they have *too much* knowledge; their relation to themselves will be illogical, because they want more life than they can have. The two trees play no role in the Old Testament narratives: the characters' desires are played out in the drama of the land. The desires of the characters of Genesis, Exodus and Samuel are directed into their progeny. It is not until late in the Old Testament that the question centred in the tree of life is raised again.

Cain commits a crime against both the sacred and the moral order: God says, 'Listen! Your brother's blood cries out to me from the soil.' The blood is sacred: it is the spirit of life, which belongs to God. As in a fairytale, the earth replies to the breaking of the taboo by repelling him from her. God continues: 'And so, cursed shall you be by the soil that gaped with its mouth to take your brother's blood from your hand. And if you till the soil, it will no longer give you its strength. A restless wanderer shall you be on the earth' (Gen. 4.10–12). God's first words, 'Where is Abel thy brother?' mark Cain's loneliness. The brotherless man departs to build the first city. Schneidau notes that Cain 'is associated with various arts and crafts bespeaking culture. Through a conflation of legends, Cain is made the first city founder.'[18] Genesis 4 is more ambivalent than this implies:

> And Cain went out from the Lord's presence and dwelled in the land of Nod east of Eden. And Cain knew his wife and she conceived and bore Enoch. Then he became the builder of a city and called the name of the city, like his son's name, Enoch. And Irad was born to Enoch, and Irad begot Mehujael and Mehujael begot Methusael and Methusael begot Lamech. And Lamech took him two wives, the name of the one was Adah and the name of the other

17 Mary Douglas, *Purity and Danger: An Analysis of the Concepts of Pollution and Taboo* (Routledge & Kegan Paul, London, 1966, 1989), ch. 3, 'The Abominations of Leviticus'.
18 Schneidau, *Sacred Discontent*, p. 128.

was Zillah. And Adah bore Jabal: he was the first of tent dwellers with livestock. And his brother's name was Jubal: he was the first of all who play on the lyre and pipe. As for Zillah, she bore Tubal-cain, who forged every tool of copper and iron. And the sister of Tubal-cain was Naamah. And Lamech said to his wives,

> 'Adah and Zillah, O hearken to my voice,
>> You wives of Lamech, give ear to my speech.
> For a man I have slain for my wound,
>> A boy for my bruising.
> For seven fold Cain is avenged,
>> And Lamech seventy and seven.' (4.16–24)

Lamech is a man of violence but his offspring are Jabal, Jubal and Tubal-cain, the first tent-maker, organist, and metalworker. In 4.23 Lamech re-appears with his vengeance song. The text envelops the devices of civilisation in the skills of murder and vengeance. This is a matter of fact statement of what civilisation is like. Civilisation will be a medley and an intermixing of culture and violence.

God's opening of the heavens is not the start of a bad rain storm but the return of the primeval chaos. Noah and his family do not survive by dint of heroic struggle. Noah obeys silently, allowing himself passively to be rescued. This floating-deliverance is a re-creation narrative. Noah bears the sign of the comic hero by being effortlessly upheld above the waters. History will make peripatetic spirals, as God and humanity play grand-mother's footsteps, toward and away from each other.

Noah's descendants do not leave off building cities: Genesis 10 sees the construction of the Babylonian and Canaanite cities of Ninevah, Rehoboth, Calah and Resen: 'the same is a great city' (10.12). With comic exaggeration, the *human race* takes the lead in the subsequent building scenario:

> And the whole earth was of one language, and of one speech.
> And it came to pass, as they journeyed from the east, that they found a plain in the land of Shinar; and they dwelt there.
> And they said to one another, 'Go to, let us make brick, and burn them thoroughly'. And they had brick for stone, and slime had they for mortar.
> And they said, 'Go to, let us build us a city and a tower, whose top may reach unto heaven; and let us make us a name, lest we be scattered abroad upon the face of the whole earth'. (Gen. 11.1–4)

Humanity now has one 'language': that means one way of thinking, imagining and acting. This is why these comrades are all in it together. They all speak together at once. The perfect committee chants in unison rather than arguing about the project. All that we learn about the architectural plan is that the tower is to be high: the city-tower is not much of an intricate artefact and the builders not very great craftsmen. Their stones are 'brick' and their mortar is 'slime'. But, with their single imagination, the builders imagine its top will 'reach into heaven'. Their purpose in making the city-tower is to 'make a name', to create a permanent identity for their unitary self. That the heaven-reaching tower is not quite as stupendously tall as they hope is suggested by the next statement: 'And the LORD came down to see the city and the tower, which the children of men builded' (11.5). God has to come a long way down to see the tower block; an exploitation of the comic possibilities of envisaging God as being *literally* above the earth. Perhaps the endeavour strikes terror into his heart. But his mimicry – 'Go to' – implies irony rather than fear:

> Behold, the people is one, and they have all one language; and this they begin to do: and now nothing will be restrained from them, which they have imagined to do.
> Go to, let us go down, and there confound their language, that they may not understand one another's speech.
> So the LORD scattered them abroad from thence upon the face of all the earth: and they left off to build the city.
> Therefore is the name of it called Babel; because the LORD did there confound the language of all the earth: and from thence did the LORD scatter them abroad upon the face of all the earth. (Gen. 11.6–9)

The tower is a ziggurat, a typical Babylonian construction, used to make astrological calculations.[19] The people want to eliminate the borders of earth and heaven. They have exercised their creativity to effect a magical unity between heaven and earth. They want to escape the pluriformity of existence on the horizontal, human plane, in which they are vulnerable to adventure and mistake, and achieve absolute oneness, not only with each other but also with God.[20] The alterity between God and humanity enables the two to communicate with each other. If the Babel builders achieve their aim of theological monoglotism, there would be no more need for this. When God 'confounds' the people's single language, he recreates the space necessary for communication. The people want a single, univocal language: they want mechanism, not dialogue. God makes it necessary for them to use the many-sided language of analogy, without which there can be no history.[21]

If the Babel story rejects the desire for the good city as 'hubris' then it depicts a tragic downfall.[22] So who identifies with the builders? For a rural narrator and audience, the story is the pantomime of the felling of the dislikeably overblown city. London is a place of comical absurdity for the inhabitants of the small towns and villages of England. The felling of the tower block is desirable because it stands not for human aspiration fulfilled but for constriction and alienation. The perfect accord of the Babel workers reminds a modern audience of the synchronised action of workers on a mechanised conveyor-belt; automated factories were sent up in silent comedies of the 1930s, such as Chaplin's *City Life*. Such a scenario calls for the introduction of human chaos. The single-minded absolutist is a villain in comedy: his mockery is a happy ending, for the audience. After God throws the spanner of linguistic pluralism into the work, we are left with the return to the normalcy and freedom of rural life: 'this sense of freedom can still be perceived in the story of fallen Babel'. Fokkelman feels that the story effects a 'release' from the 'pressure ... experienced at the sight of the

19 Robert Alter, *Genesis: Translation and Commentary* (W. W. Norton & Co., New York, 1996), p. 46.
20 Leon Kass, 'What's Wrong with Babel', *American Scholar*, 58, 1, Winter, 1989, 41–60 (49).
21 J. Fokkelman, *Narrative Art in Genesis* (Van Gorcum, Amsterdam, 1975), p. 17.
22 Ibid., p. 17.

variety of that urban polity'.[23] But the intention of the workers of Babel is not 'variety' but uniformity of mind and univocity of language. Analogy of language requires careful contrast and comparison. It requires putting words and things *in context*. The dispersal of the worker comrades of Babel is not an absolute 'Fall' because God's purpose in dispersing humanity is to keep the balanced relationship between himself and humanity moving.

The desire for a name to be remembered by generations of descendants will be fulfilled by God's *gift* to Abram. In Genesis 12.1–3, God opens the covenant promise to Abram:

> Get thee out of thy country, and from thy kindred, and from thy father's house, unto a land that I will shew thee:
> And I will make of thee a great nation, and I will bless thee, and make thy name great; and thou shalt be a blessing:
> And I will bless them that bless thee, and curse him that curseth thee: and in thee shall all the families of the earth be blessed. (Gen. 12.1–3; cf. 12.6–7, 13, 15 and 17).

As Abram and Sarai travel through Canaan, God reappears, and pinpoints the promise: 'Unto thy seed will I give this land' (Gen. 12.6). Jack Miles finds in these promises a 'subtle aggression': by the feint of the promise, God is gaining control of Abram's 'fertility'. He is not only telling Abram 'to be' naturally fertile, but that He will make him so: why is his own power of procreation not enough? God is getting more than he is giving, and thus, says Miles, 'The premise of the narrative . . . is that in human fertility, as in mortal combat, whatever gives life to you takes life from me, and vice versa.'[24] God does not deliver on the nail: he repeats the offer again in the next chapter:

> 'Raise up your eyes and look out from the place where you are to the north and to the south and the east and the west, for all the land you see, to you I will give it and to your seed forever. And I will make your seed like the dust of the earth – could a man count the dust of the earth, so, too, your seed might be counted. Rise, walk about the land through its length and its breadth, for to you I will give it.' And Abram took up his tent and came to dwell by the Terebinths of Mamre which are in Hebron, and he built there an altar to the LORD. (Gen. 13.14–19)

God yet again defers Abram's gratification: he makes a fourth promise to Abram; the vista by which he defines it signals his satirical awareness of the difference between Abram's vision and his own:

> And he brought him forth abroad, and said, 'Look now toward heaven, and tell the stars, if thou be able to number them',

(a hint of mid-promise sarcasm there)

> and he said unto him, 'so shall thy seed be'. (Gen. 15.5)

Abram is a pragmatist, with a sense of human limits. His response to the fourth promise is to ask God how he can have so many seed when he and

Sarai are childless (Gen. 15.1–6). Perhaps, as Miles says, the 'effect of the
Lord's four times-repeated promise of fertility is to inspire not trust but
doubt in the reader ... A promise that was superfluous in the first place is
repeated, repeated, repeated again to what becomes, as it is not kept, an
effect of mounting unease'.[25] Finally, in Genesis 17, when Abram is ninety-
nine years old, God sets out the terms and conditions of the covenant: first,
he changes Abram's name, a sign of his possession of the actor:

> no longer shall your name be called Abram but your name shall be Abraham,
> for I have made you father to a multitude of nations ... (Gen. 17.4–6)

The covenant binds, and delivers, not only to the new Abraham, but to all
his promised descendants:

> And I will give unto you and your seed after you the land in which you
> sojourn, the whole land of Canaan, as an everlasting holding, and I will be
> their God. (Gen. 17.8)

The condition is quite steep:

> This is My covenant which you shall keep, between Me and you and your
> seed after you: every male among you must be circumcised. You shall
> circumcise the flesh of your foreskin and it shall be a sign of the covenant
> between Me and you. Eight days old every male among you shall be circum-
> cised through your generations, even slaves ... My covenant in your flesh
> shall be an everlasting covenant. And a male with a foreskin, who has not
> circumcised the flesh of his foreskin, that person shall be cut off from my
> folk. My covenant he has broken. (Gen. 17.10–15)

The first Jewish Matriarch must also give up her identity to God:

> And God said to Abraham, 'Sarai your wife shall no longer call her name
> Sarai, for Sarah is her name. And I will bless her and I will also give you from
> her a son and I will bless him, and she shall become nations, kings of peoples
> shall issue from her.' (Gen. 17.15–16)

Abraham and his descendants get the land of Canaan; God gets 'Abram's
penis – and the penises, the sexual potency, of his descendants': that is
what the covenant is *for*.[26] If, as Kass says, 'The promise answers Abram's
longing for a land, seed, and a great name' and therefore answers 'Abram's
deepest longings',[27] then, according to Miles, God *uses* his omniscient
knowledge of this longing in order to command Abraham to 'concede,
symbolically, that his fertility is not his own to exercise': this ownership is
signified by 'A physical reduction in the literal superabundance of Abram's
penis'. If the promise of a land contains that of a 'divine–human
relationship',[28] that relationship is a top-down one. Good jokes are often
put-downs: Miles's proprietorial God is laughing *down* at humanity.

---

25 Ibid., p. 50.
26 Ibid., p. 53.
27 Kass, 'What's Wrong with Babel?', 59.
28 David J. A. Clines, *The Theme of the Pentateuch* (*Journal for the Study of the Old
    Testament*, Supplement Series, 10, Sheffield, 1978), p. 31.

New role notwithstanding, Abraham narrowly misses laughing with disbelief in God's face:

> And Abraham fell upon his face, and laughed, and said in his heart, 'Shall a child be born unto him that is an hundred years old? and shall Sarah, that is ninety years old, bear?' (Gen. 17.7)

Abraham thinks just of '*a* child'. The gap between impossible desire and such an excessive fulfilment as is promised by God is ridiculous. Sarah is as prudent and worldly as her husband. Listening from behind the tent-door, as many a Bedouin wife was probably inclined to do, Sarah hears the promise repeated by three 'men', and 'laughed inwardly, saying "After being shriveled, shall I have pleasure, and my husband is old?"' (Gen. 18.12). Sarah cannot conceive of having good sex with her aged husband, let alone a child.[29] God overhears her: he overrides her denial, insisting that 'thou didst laugh'; he not does not tell her not to repeat the performance.

It is in the joy of this connubial laughter that Abraham comes up with the *chutzpah* to challenge God's plan to annihilate the cities of Sodom and Gomorrah. God intimates his strategy to Abraham (Gen. 18.22) and is questioned about the scope of the bombing. Would God kill them all if there are 'fifty righteous' in the cities? God politely demurs. What about forty-five righteous? God retracts. Forty? Thirty? Twenty? Ten? 'And he said, "I will not destroy it for ten's sake."' (Gen. 18.32). There are 'comic possibilities' in this dialogue. Abraham's first challenge to God means: 'Far be it from you, that the Judge of all the earth should not work justice.' 'With these words', Landy says, 'Abraham arraigns God, and few words are braver. "Far be it from you" in Hebrew has implications of "You desecrate yourself". Why? To destroy the righteous with the wicked.'[30] Why does God allow himself to lose the debate? Did he want to lose?

> The latter possibility evokes the ... image of God as the ... omniscient Father who permits and encourages his children to fight him, to feel their strength ... the sequence is a game through which ... subversive impulses are liberated.[31]

That implies that there is friction, or even sublimated aggression in the relation between the God who repeatedly promises an ever-ageing couple offspring, and who is capricious enough to argue the toss with Abraham about whether or not to annihilate the cities. Abraham is made confident and liberated so far as to be able to play with God. God's promise has boggled his imagination. The episode reminds us that he is playing with a God who can drop death upon whole cities, from his 'heaven'. No just man is found: the narration drops to Abraham's point of view, and we stand with him, looking 'toward Sodom and Gomorrah, and toward all the land of the plain, and [Abraham] beheld, and lo, the smoke of the country went up as the smoke of a furnace' (Gen. 19.28).

---

29 Robert Alter, *The World of Biblical Literature* (SPCK, London, 1992), pp. 36–38.
30 Landy, 'Humour as a Tool for Biblical Exegesis', p. 109.
31 Ibid., p. 110.

Their son, Isaac, is named after the 'contagious laughter' which he effects:[32] 'Sarah said, "Laughter had God made me, Whoever hears will laugh at me."' (Gen. 21.6). Or is it really, as Miles considers, 'bitter laughter', at a devious but inescapable dialogue-partner?[33] God threatens to take back what *he* has given, with the command to Abraham to sacrifice this 'laughter'. The God who teased an ever-ageing couple with the promise of babies now 'tempts' Abraham with the order to make Isaac a 'burnt offering' to himself. Without a word, Abraham takes ass, servants and son, and proceeds to the designated spot. Søren Kierkegaard adjures us not to forget that agonisingly slow, three-day journey to Mount Moriah.[34] Without further ado:

> Abraham took the wood of the burnt offering, and laid it upon Isaac his son; and he took the fire in his hand, and a knife; and they went both of them together.
>
> And Isaac spake unto Abraham his father, and said, 'My father': and he said, 'Here am I, my son.' And he said, 'Behold the fire and the wood: but where is the lamb for the burnt offering?'
>
> And Abraham said, 'My son, God will provide himself a lamb for a burnt offering': so they went both of them together.
>
> And they came to the place which God had told him of; and Abraham built an altar there, and laid the wood in order, and bound Isaac his son, and laid him on the altar upon the wood.
>
> And Abraham stretched forth his hand, and took the knife to slay his son. (Gen. 22.6–10)

Abraham's 'Here I am' designates 'his moral position in respect to God, who has called him'.[35] Everything is focused on Abraham's decision. Can he bring down the knife? We think of Abraham's sacrifice as a trial of his moral selfhood: can he subordinate his own desire to God's command, upon which all ethics hinges? Kierkegaard interpreted the scene in that light, and he pushed it one step further: Abraham is so stringently obedient to the command of the Infinite that he was willing to sacrifice the relative human ethical standard of paternal love to it.[36] In his readiness to bring down the knife, and the act is *in* the readiness, Abraham is either a murderer or a believer:[37] ethics is suspended, teleologically, or passed on to a higher source which transcends human morality. Abraham's sacrifice is not rationally comprehensible, but a paradox, which is one sort of joke:

> what a tremendous paradox faith is, a paradox which is capable of transforming a murder into a holy act well-pleasing to God, a paradox which gives Isaac back to Abraham, which no thought can master, because faith begins precisely there where thought leaves off.[38]

---

32 Cheryl Exum and William Whedbee, 'Isaac, Samson and Saul: Reflections on the Comic and Tragic Visions', in Radday and Brenner, *On Humour and the Comic in the Hebrew Bible*, pp. 117–159 (126).
33 Miles, *God: A Biography*, p. 53.
34 Søren Kierkegaard, *Fear and Trembling and the Sickness unto Death*, translated by Walter Lowrie (Princeton University Press, Princeton, NJ, 1941, 1974), pp. 62–63.
35 Auerbach, *Mimesis*, p. 8.
36 Kierkegaard, *Fear and Trembling*, pp. 80–81.
37 Ibid., p. 67.
38 Ibid., p. 64.

In God's eyes, the murder of this child is a 'well-pleasing' sacrifice. Willingness to sacrifice an innocent child is paradoxically joined to obedient faith. Child murder is thus turned into a holy act, and its victim becomes sacred, a 'burnt-offering' to God.

In innumerable watered down forms, a semi-Kierkegaardian reading of the Akedah as Abraham's immolation of his best-beloved to God held up for several centuries: nineteenth- and twentieth-century church, and, I guess, synagogue, goers, were exhorted to emulate Abraham's ethics. It held up, that is, for as long as one had, in public, to interpret the Bible *piously*. It was with a certain iconoclastic pleasure that one heard the words, composed in 1964,

> Oh God said to Abraham, "Kill me a son"
> Abe says, "Man, you must be puttin' me on"
> God say, "No." Abe say, "What?"
> God say, "You can do what you want Abe, but
> The next time you see me comin' you better run"
> Well Abe says, "Where do you want this killin' done?"
> God says, "Out on Highway 61."[39]

With that, the anti-ethical interpretations began to flood in. Do the innocent become sacred when violence is done upon them? René Girard suggests that we might think of God as a 'trickster', applying either a 'theology of *divine caprice*' or one of 'divine anger': 'In this perspective the god is fundamentally good but is temporarily transformed into a wicked god',[40] because what looks paradoxical from heaven does not feel very hilarious on earth. Such a 'trickster' God is not bound by such human and bourgeois constraints as truthfulness: Landy says that

> the *Akedah* is a double deception: Abraham is deceived into thinking that he will murder his son and that the Promise was a cheat; on the other hand, his lie 'The LORD will provide a lamb my son,' comes true.[41]

For Kierkegaard, the Akedah story is a *silent* movie, because there is nothing rational or intelligible for Abraham to say about his gesture.[42] Nor is there anything which one could really *say* to such a God. Miles reads Abraham's shut mouth as a tacit refusal to open up with this *Dialogue Partner*:

> Abraham resists even as he goes through the motions of compliance. At the end of the test as at the beginning, his only statement to God is the ostensibly willing but ultimately opaque 'Here I am.' Thus, when God declares that Abraham has passed the test and, for the seventh and final time, promises him abundant offspring, it is as much God who concedes defeat as Abraham. God says ... 'Because you have done this and have not withheld your son, your favored one, I will bestow My blessing upon you and make your descendants as numerous as the stars of heaven and the sands on the seashore' (22.16–17). But Abraham's action is ... far more ambiguous than God chooses to believe. He has not, after all, slain his son, and perhaps he

---

39 'Highway 61 Revisited', by Bob Dylan.
40 René Girard, *The Scapegoat*, translated by Yvonne Freccero (Athlone Press, London, 1986), pp. 84–85.
41 Landy, 'Humour as a Tool', p. 104.
42 Kierkegaard, *Fear and Trembling*, p. 122.

would never have done so. Abraham goes as far as he possibly can without actually doing the deed, and God chooses to be satisfied with this much . . . By the time he concludes this test . . . God knows how much acknowledgement he can get and how much he cannot get from Abraham.[43]

Miles's Trickster Lord-God is a *reductio ad absurdum* of the Kierkegaardian Deity who wilfully transmutes murder into well-pleasing sacrifice, who suspends the ethical to his own caprice. Only the bland, or the agonised, can imagine God like that without a tinge of hatred or aggression.

Homer's heroes are great kings. The milieu of the biblical heroes is 'domestic and commonplace'. The finite and the infinite are not wholly disjunctive in the biblical world

> In the Old Testament stories . . . The sublime influence of God . . . reaches so deeply into the everyday that the two realms of the sublime and the everyday are not only actually unseparated but basically inseparable.[44]

The biblical picture of God's relation to humanity brings him down into the realm of comic drama. And thus, where Kierkegaard *de-humanised* his conception of God, exhorting us to imitate Abraham, who 'gives up the finite in order to grasp the infinite,'[45] closer readers have humanised the scene, making the characters apprehensible. There is some good biblical everydayness in the discussion of the Akedah by the eleventh-century Jewish exegete, Rashi. God appears to Abraham and says,

> Take now thy son, thine only son, whom thou lovest, even Isaac, and get thee up into the land of Moriah; and offer him there for a burnt offering upon one of the mountains which I will tell thee of. (Gen. 22.2)

Rashi's comment:

> 'Thy son.' Abraham said, 'But I have two sons.' So God said, 'Thine only son.' To this Abraham parried, 'Each one is an only son: Ishmael to his mother Hagar, and Isaac to his mother Sarah.' God then added, 'Whom you love.' But Abraham argued 'I love them both.' So finally God explicitly said, 'Even Isaac.' Now why did God give His command in such a long-drawn-out way? The answer is that God approached the matter gradually to avoid upsetting Abraham too suddenly. This would of course have happened had He abruptly ordered Abraham to sacrifice Isaac. Another reason was to give Abraham the opportunity to earn a spiritual reward for complying with each separate part of the Divine command.[46]

The story is thus a 'lesson on the value of tact and thoughtfulness',[47] as exemplified by God. Rashi humanises God by making him considerate. He gives Abraham some come-back dialogue, because that fits his character. Rashi humanises Abraham, by remembering that the man who raised the anti with God over the men of Sodom and Gomorrah is likely to play a mean game of poker for his own son. We can also bring out the

43 Miles, *God: A Biography*, pp. 59–60.
44 Auerbach, *Mimesis*, pp. 22–23.
45 Kierkegaard, *Fear and Trembling*, p. 71.
46 Quoted in Chaim Pearl, *Rashi* (Weidenfeld & Nicolson, London, 1988), p. 54.
47 Ibid., p. 55.

everydayness of the episode by remembering the other character, who does *not* remain silent, but points out that 'you've got the sacrificial implements, and forgot to bring the sacrifice'. We can build on that wide-eyed irony, and picture Isaac as Gene Wilder, 'No way!, hosay!', and Abraham as an ineffectual Mel Brooks: let them bicker as Mel Brooks ineffectually wrestles an unwilling Wilder to the altar. If we bring the Bible down to earth, with its proper anthropomorphism, we may suppress our inclinations to Oedipal iconoclasm. We need not sublime the story out of its context, in the covenant promise of not just one – tragically beloved – son but un-countable seeds. The story *is* about the ethical, and its strange conjunction with the sacred, but both ethics and sacred are dramatically imaginable. Each character, from God to Abraham to Isaac is pictured in his deeds and his dialogue, and is thus close enough for communication.

Abraham does not know *what* is going to come of the sacrifice: God and Abraham are testing their trust in one another. All Abraham *knows* is that God will carry his story on. He does not *see* the ram, which has been there all along, but he has confidence that God will not desecrate himself:

> And the angel of the LORD called unto him out of heaven, and said, 'Abraham, Abraham': and he said, 'Here am I.'
> And he said, 'Lay not thine hand upon the lad, neither do thou any thing unto him: for now I know that thou fearest God, seeing thou hast not withheld thy son, thine only son from me.'
> And Abraham lifted up his eyes, and looked, and behold behind him a ram caught in a thicket by its horns: and Abraham went and took the ram, and offered him up for a burnt offering *in the stead of his son*. (Gen. 22.11–13)

If these are comic *characters*, we must look at what they *do*, rather than at their psychologies. In comedy, deceptions and role reversals enable the hero to achieve his aim. God does not play the name-game to deceive, but to transform human character: the victim becomes the victor.

Isaac has to sink this low in order rise into good fortune. The comic hero does not float into the air, at will: he rises because he allows himself to be earth-bound. Isaac is at the mercy of events, so he collides with them. His life and purposes are usually in the hands of others. But he lasts out: he is safeguarded, not from suffering but from disaster, by the laws of gravity in the world to which he belongs. Isaac's role in the Akedah scene is typical of his passivity and luck. Isaac is always given

> a joyous upswing which puts his story back in a comic light, a comedy in the shadow of threatened death, but nonetheless a comedy with its celebration of life ... Isaac ... is preeminently the victim in his near-sacrifice at the hands of his father ... he is a compliant son in the idyllic, romantic tale of Abraham's match-making on his behalf ... he is the one to yield ground in order to avoid conflict with the Philistines ... (Gen. 26); he is duped by his shrewd strong-willed wife and ... wily younger son ... into giving his deathbed blessing to the 'wrong' son ... he ... survives for ... twenty more years after the 'death-bed' debacle and after his death is buried by his two sons (Gen. 35.28–29).[48]

Isaac is the only courting groom who does not get to play in his own type scene of meeting the betrothed at the well. Rebekah is brought to him

48 Exum and Whedbee, 'Isaac, Samson and Saul', pp. 129–130.

by his father's servant, and it was clear from the moment that she 'lighted off the camel' to get a look at him who will take the active role in the partnership. Isaac 'loved her and ... was comforted after his mother's death' (Gen. 24.63–67). Isaac remains a son, a child-like position which ensures that he survives. He is not so much passive as *flexible*, like a rubber-boned baby. A comic adventurer who was helplessly passive would soon be shipwrecked: he would be 'sad' in the vernacular sense, maudlin rather than a transmitter of life.

Isaac plays the sacrificial offering (to have to play a ram is an absurd position to be in). His near-death experiences would not be funny if he were too high-minded to want to hang onto his body. Having told Abimelech, King of the Philistines in Gerar, that the beautiful Rebekah is his sister Isaac is spotted 'sporting with Rebekah his wife' (Gen. 26.8). But he gives ground to the Philistines when they countermand his wells (Gen. 26). Isaac loves his son Esau, the hunter, 'because he did eat of his venison' (Gen. 25.28). When he inadvertently blesses Jacob, he smells him[49] and imagines that he has passed on a fragrance, saying, 'See, the smell of my son is as the smell of a field which the LORD hath blessed' (Gen. 27.27). His role is to *give* his blessing/nature to a son. Isaac's comedy is a celebration of unbeatable life, and he is is a sensualist, who is glad to beat death. The story and the family are transmitted through him because he has life enough to be able to give it away.

Isaac's twin sons are the 'strugglers' of Genesis:

> And Isaac pleaded with the Lord on behalf of his wife, for she was barren, and the Lord granted his plea, and Rebekah his wife conceived. And the children clashed within her, and she said, 'Then why me?' and she went to inquire of the Lord. And the Lord said to her:
>   'Two nations – in your womb,
>   two peoples from your loins shall issue.
>   People over people shall prevail,
>   the elder, the younger's slave.' (Gen. 25.21–24)

'The children struggled within her' encapsulates the story. The twin sons' names *are* their characters:

> And the first came out red, all over like an hairy garment, and they called his name Esau. And after that came his brother out, and his hand took hold on Esau's heel; and his name was called Jacob. (Gen. 25.25–26)

Esau 'wears' a hairy redness, *admoni*; Jacob, *heel* grabber, is *eqeb*. Even in the birth passage, Jacob is getting ahead of the front-runner by unsporting tactics. Esau is a *'cunning hunter'* and Jacob a *'plain man*, dwelling in tents' (Gen. 25.27). This report is reversed by the brothers' first engagement: Jacob lures Esau into exchanging his birthright for 'this red, red stuff' (25.30). Esau is passive, controlled by his appetites. He is fascinated by something 'red' like himself; 'he despised his birthright' (Gen. 25.34).

The comic hero makes use of his interdependence. Jacob is not the prime mover in the second outmanoeuvring, by which he obtains the blessing

---

49 Alter thinks that the 'smelling' is a final test that this *is* Jacob, and that that is why Rebekah has dressed Isaac in Esau's clothes: *Genesis*, p. 140.

intended by Isaac for the first-born. Rebekah, who 'loved Jacob' (Gen. 25.28), is her son's *animator* in the feminine wheeze.[50] Nearly blind with age, and being either hypochondriac or very forward thinking, Isaac asks Esau to hunt and to cook for him one last plateful of the 'game ... of the kind that I love ... so that I may solemnly bless you before I die' (Gen. 27.4). Rebekah, who took the place of Isaac's mother, knows how to get the better of her husband: whatever doubts he may have about the provider will be suffocated by his desire to eat right away. Perhaps we were seeing through the eyes of Rebekah when we saw that Esau was 'red, all over like a hairy *garment*' (Gen. 25.25). Such a garment can be simulated. With Esau off-stage, Rebekah cooks the dinner which Isaac had ordered and disguises Jacob as Esau, by making him a hairy goat. Isaac is suspicious: 'The voice is Jacob's voice, but the hands are the hands of Esau' (Gen. 27.22). But he gives credence to the costume rather than the vocals. Survival and victory through deceptive disguise are comic ploys. Jacob has become who he pretends to be. He has transformed himself into the first-born, the inheritor of the blessing. Does the 'exceeding bitter cry' of Esau add a downbeat note? Portrayed by a novelist who can see into his psyche, Esau's loss is sad; seen as a staged action, it is comical. Their mother, still in control, instructs Jacob to 'flee to my brother Laban in Haran, and you may stay with him ... until your brother's rage against you subsides and he forgets what you did to him' (Gen. 27.43–45).

We learn the characters of Jacob and Esau by their actions in the contest. In the first scene, Esau sold his birthright: he 'does not hold on' to what is his.[51] In a second telling gesture, Esau casually married a Hittite woman (Gen. 26.34–35), without realising that his parents do not expect him to marry out (Gen. 28.8). He is unsuited for the role of first-born, having 'no sense of the special task of his family' and thus no awareness of the 'history'[52] which it is to create. Jacob has twice gained priority, by devious means. He can already 'be viewed as a rogue or trickster who by dint of his guile and wit makes his way successfully in the world'.[53] It was the helper-mother who enabled him to imagine the trick. Jacob masks himself as Esau in order to achieve his desire for the role of the first-born. Although Rebekah and Jacob pre-empted the predestination of God's oracle, there is a sense of rightness about the outcome. Once God has given the sacred power of blessing and name-giving into human hands, the story must be partly propelled by human natures and their wiles. If the picture were not painted by human desire, there would be no drama but a divine monologue.

After Jacob sets out for Haran, he has gained the blessing, but lost his birthplace. He is not in possession, not the victor. Now the curtains open on the heavenly plane:

> And he came upon a certain place, and stopped there for the night, and he took of the stones of the place and put it at his head and he lay down in that

---

50 James G. Williams, 'The Comedy of Jacob: A Literary Study', *Journal of the American Academy of Religion*, 45, 2, Supplement B, June 1978, 241–265 (253).
51 Ibid., 244.
52 Fokkelman, *Narrative Art in Genesis*, p. 106.
53 Exum and Whedbee, 'Isaac, Samson and Saul', p. 123.

place, and he dreamed, and, look, a ramp was set against the ground with its top reaching the heavens, and, look, messengers of God were going up and down it. (Gen. 28.11–12)

Jacob does not climb the ramp: he does not enter the upper world, but he sees into it, in a way undreamed of by the tower builders of Genesis 11. The ramp stands on the earth. It does not float in the sky. It provides a bridge, a visual focusing, of the 'space' between Jacob and God. The ramp has to stand on the earth because Jacob looks up along it, and it delimits the space between earth and heaven. The ramp makes the space imaginatively perceptible. This is Jacob's *dream*: this is how it appears to his human imagination. Jacob looks: he sees first a ramp, 'set against the ground', and second that it stretches up to heaven; thirdly he witnesses movement on the ramp. The messengers between heaven and earth are travelling up and down the ramp, making the space both sacred and dynamic. God gives the dream, but Jacob himself, the man of passionate desire, dreams it. The ladder is there in order to guide Jacob's eye toward God. God reiterates to Jacob the promise and blessing which he had given to Abraham (Gen. 28.13–14).

Haran reflects the scene which Jacob thought he had left behind, like a mirror. Jacob meets his image in his cousin Rachel. For this girl twin, Jacob 'served seven years, and they seemed in his eyes but a few days in his love for her' (Gen. 29.20). The family likeness between Rebekah and her brother Laban is apparent. Laban welcomes Jacob as 'my bone and my flesh': within a few weeks, he is asking, 'Because you are my kin, should you serve me for nothing? Tell me what your wages should be.' With an ironic pretence of generosity, Laban turns his nephew into his employee. Jacob meets his near-match in his uncle. The trick which he had played works on him. Expecting to be given Rachel in marriage, he wakes to find that Laban has slipped Leah between the sheets. Uncle Laban says, with sententious irony, 'It is not done thus in our place, to give the younger girl before the first-born' (Gen. 29.26). Jacob's desire for mimesis is thwarted for seven years. But he soon achieves a plethora of children. Leah, and Rachel, and their maids Zilpah and Bilhah, compete to produce offspring, and give birth to an excessive number. Not only is the trickster tricked, but the seizer is seized, in Haran. Such swelling lists of names, with their explanations, are funny, and, coming out of the loins of the fertile Jacob and his women, they indicate the hero's gift for life. Laban wanted to get Jacob to work for him for twice as long as he intended: but the doubling of wives gives him eleven heirs. The narrative of Jacob's stay in Haran, in Genesis 29.1–31.55 is structured so as to place Jacob and his wives' mass production of progeny in its middle.[54]

Once he has his children, Jacob wants out. Laban asks him to 'Name me your wages' (Gen. 30.28). Jacob has learned to use polite words to twist his uncle into the passive, giving position:

And Jacob said, 'You need give me nothing if you will do this thing for me: Let me go back and herd your flocks and watch them. I shall pass through all

54 Walter Brueggemann, *Genesis*, Interpretation Series (John Knox Press, Richmond, Virginia, 1982), pp. 249–250.

your flocks today to remove from them every spotted and speckled animal and every dark-colored sheep and the speckled and spotted among the goats, and that will be my wages. Then my honesty will bear witness for me in the days to come when you go over my wages – whatever is not spotted and speckled among the goats and dark-colored among the sheep shall be accounted stolen by me.' And Laban said, 'Let it be just as you say.'

And he removed on that day the spotted and speckled he-goats and all the brindled and speckled she-goats, every one that had white on it, and every dark-colored one among the sheep, and he gave them over to his sons. And he put three days' journey between himself and Jacob while Jacob herded the remaining flocks of Laban. And Jacob took himself moist rods of poplar and almond and plane-tree, and peeled white strips in them, laying bare the white on the rods. And he stood the rods he had peeled in the troughs, in the water channels from which the flocks came to drink – opposite the flocks, which went into heat when they came to drink. And the flocks went into heat at the rods and the flocks bore brindled, spotted and speckled young. And the sheep Jacob kept apart: he placed them facing the spotted and all the dark-colored in Laban's flocks, and he set himself herds of his own and he did not set them with Laban's flocks. And so, whenever the vigorous of the flocks went into heat, Jacob put the rods in full sight of the flocks ... for them to go into heat by the rods. And for the weaklings of the flock he did not put them, and so the feeble ones went to Laban and the vigorous ones to Jacob. And the man swelled up mightily and he had many flocks and female and male slaves and camels and donkeys. (Gen. 30.31–43)

The deception works by 'mirroring': if a goat is looking at a parti-coloured thing when it conceives, the offspring will be the image in its mother's eye.[55] When he tells his wives about his exploit, he covers up his part in the deception, attributing his success to the hand of God. He is 'at times an unseemingly deceptive man'. One may attribute the deceptive Jacob to 'J' and the pious Jacob to 'E'. But that would disjoin what the 'faith of Israel', and its sense of humour, put together: 'It is this earthy man through whom the resilient purposes of God are being worked out.'[56]

Why are parrots funny? Why do we laugh when we see identical twins? Why does the comedienne's art require the perfect mimicry of voices and mannerisms? Jacobson suggests that it is because 'Doubling gives life a second chance'.[57] We all want to be Buber's unique 'I's and 'Thous', but we also want as many chances as we can get. Jacob has found his identity 'repeated' in Haran. He has survived and proved exceptionally fertile. But nothing *new* can happen in the mirror wonderland. In order to get on his way to his history, Jacob has to confront his real twin. The LORD tells him to return to his own country (Gen. 31.3). Jacob sends messengers to tell Esau he is coming: he wants no surprise encounter with his impetuous sword-happy brother (Gen. 27.40). Jacob is dismayed to learn that his brother is riding out to engage him, with a welcoming party of 'four hundred men' (Gen. 32.6). He divides his entourage in half, so that half can

---

55 Again, lest the narrative critic stray too far from the literal sense, Alter cites Yehuda Feliks, 'an authority on biblical flora and fauna', to the effect that Jacob's means of multiplying his animals at the expense of Laban's works according to sound Mendelian 'animal breeding' principles. *Genesis*, p. 165.

56 Brueggemann, *Genesis*, pp. 251–252.

57 Jacobson, *Seriously Funny*, p. 232.

escape the slaughter. He reminds the God of his 'father Abraham and his father Isaac' in detail of the promises which have been made him. He does not ride ahead to meet his brother, saving his wives and sons at the expense of death. Prudential thought for survival is a virtue in comedy. Jacob presents a gift rather than his own face to Esau:

> two hundred she-goats and twenty he-goats, two hundred ewes and twenty rams; thirty milch cows with their young, forty cows and ten bulls, twenty she-asses and ten he-asses. (Gen. 32.14–15)

That will pacify the man who loved pottage! The present is given to control events. Not one servant, but three relays of them, each take a portion of the present to Esau. Jacob, 'the man of "I first!" ', jumps back behind 'the work of other people'.[58] Now all he can do is to wait.

> And he rose on that night and took his two wives and his two slavegirls and his eleven boys and he crossed over the Jabbok ford. And he took them and brought them across the stream, and he brought across all that he had. And Jacob was left alone, and a man wrestled with him until the break of dawn. (Gen. 32.22–24)

Once more, Jacob meets his destiny under the camouflage of the night. Jacob is engaged in a wrestling match by a mysterious 'man'. This is a greater *agon* than Jacob had ever bargained for.

> And he saw that he had not won out against him and he touched his hip-socket and Jacob's hip-socket was wrenched as he wrestled with him. And he said, 'Let me go, for dawn is breaking.' And he said, 'I will not let you go unless you bless me.' And he said to him, 'What is your name?' And he said, 'Jacob.' And he said, 'Not Jacob shall your name hence be said, but Israel, for you have striven with God and men, and won out.' (Gen. 32.25–28)

Jacob is no stranger to wrestling: he was born 'tripping' his brother 'by the heel' (*'qb*). This pattern of acting has led him to 'a wrestling (*'bq*) with a "man" which ... is the most shocking experience of his life'.[59] Jacob's capacity for leg throws is put out of action by the mysterious contender. Even without the use of his leg, Jacob continues to fight and to grasp his opponent. In this extreme crisis, Jacob is still demanding a blessing! The 'man' asks his indomitable fighting partner his name. The audience recalls Jacob's first naming and his long-disclosed identity. The blessing which Jacob obtains is a new name and acting identity: *Yisra'el*, meaning 'God fights'. We don't yet know *who* the man is, so

> Jacob asked and said, 'Tell me your name, pray.' And he said, 'Why should you ask my name?' and there he blessed him. And Jacob called the name of the place Peniel, meaning, 'I have seen God face to face and I came out alive.' (Gen. 32.29–30)

Jacob tells us that he has 'seen God face to face'. Alter claims that the strange figure is

---

58 Fokkelman, *Narrative Art in Genesis*, p. 205.
59 Ibid., p. 210.

in some sense a doubling of Esau as adversary, but he is also a doubling of all with whom Jacob has had to contend, and he may equally well be an externalization of all that Jacob has to wrestle with within himself.[60]

Jacob has done no internal wrestling before. *He* imagines that this was an *agon* with the person of God: Jacob 'has experienced the *mysterium tremendum ac fascinans'*.[61]

How new is Jacob's nature as Israel? Some commentators see no great novelty: Jacob's strength of desire and purpose is rewarded. Williams says,

> As Jacob had come in guile to steal Esau's blessing, so now by night he is blessed by 'someone' ('is, 32.25) who he concludes is God ('elohim, 32.31). These three episodes (25.19–26, 27.1–45, 32.23–33) suggest that *Jacob is he who is blessed in secret or in disguise as revealed in his ability to hold on.* He is a grasper, he is persistent, he prevails.[62]

Fokkelman concurs: God 'adorns him with the name "Israel" on the ground of (*ki!*) his recognition of Jacob's unique nature ... The line of his life has been confirmed.' But he notes a greater discontinuity here than in the renaming of Abraham. Only after having been 'purified' in this fight can the hero 'throw away' the 'evil ... name of Jacob', and be given a 'beautiful, theophorous name'.[63] The name-change does not stick: once God names Abram Abraham, so he remains for the rest of his story; but Jacob is 'in most instances' still Jacob.[64] A fictional David comments, 'We still call him Jacob.'[65] It is too simple to say either that Jacob's passionate, desirous nature is confirmed, or that the name Israel is a complete redirection of his life. Jacob likes himself, and likes people like himself, which is why he prospers. Jacob achieved material success in the land of his doubles, but he did not see himself. The gripper had to undergo the grip of the sacred 'man': he does not know himself until he is named by someone other than himself. The God whom he has lately reminded of his promises has taken him at his word. The hero is right and ripe for his new role, and has even surreptitiously tried it on, with Isaac, but he did not create it himself. A dramatic action is both continuous and surprising. A story would not be *dramatic* if the author could replace the identity of his character with another identity: every stage in a drama impels the next stage to come about. It is the linked *sequence* of stages which holds us in suspense. If Israel is just a substitute for Jacob, he is a *humana ex machina*. But comic drama throws up wild reversals. The transformations the comic actor undergoes are fitting, but they take congruity to a point of absurdity: they exceed hope in its own direction. The hero's new nature as 'Israel' emerges out of a drama in which God's 'I' gives the push forward to the human 'thou'.

Jacob/Israel orders his entourage in degree of endearment to him, with Leah to the front and Rachel and Joseph safe at the back, and goes ahead. Jacob comes 'near to his brother'. The volatile Esau 'ran to meet him, and

60 Alter, *Genesis*, p. 181.
61 Fokkelman, *Narrative Art in Genesis*, p. 220.
62 James. G. Williams, 'The Comedy of Jacob' (254–255).
63 Fokkelman, *Narrative Art in Genesis*, pp. 215–217.
64 Alter, *Genesis*, p. 182.
65 Joseph Heller, *God Knows* (Jonathan Cape, London, 1984, BlackSwan, 1985), p. 72.

embraced him, and fell on his neck, and kissed him: and they wept' (Gen. 33.3–4). The comic story concludes in fraternal harmony: 'the two brothers become reconciled in the end, even though they become founder[s] ... of two separate societies'.[66] Having achieved that degree of friendship which is possible for them, they prudently decide not to be neighbours.

The competitive welter of childbearing of Genesis 29–30 has created the characters who will carry the narrative line on. Rachel's first son, Joseph, is Jacob's favourite. The story of Joseph has a different mood from the tales of Abraham, Isaac and Jacob. Source critics attribute the atmosphere of the Joseph stories to their composition in a humanistic environment, perhaps the court of King Solomon, in around 900 BC.[67] The 'world' of the Joseph cycle is like that of the early Wisdom literature. In Proverbs 1–8, also written at this time, virtue has its natural reward. Joseph is the figure of the 'Wise Man', skilled in prudent, this-worldly and political action. Wisdom is

> a sense of how things are put together and how things work in God's inscrutable deployment of creation. It is the delicate recognition that reality is an intricate network of limits and possibilities, of givens and choices that must be respected, well-managed, and carefully guarded, in order to enhance the well-being willed by ... by Yahweh for the whole earth ... Joseph ... is ... 'discerning and wise' (Gen. 41.33). As a consequence of this special gift from God, Joseph is able to mobilize the resources of ... the Egyptian empire for the sake of 'bread for the world'.[68]

Rather than imagining God as making himself known by miracles, the Wisdom tradition conceives him as the unseen basis of order in creation and in human life: likewise, the 'story of Joseph ... features a well-hidden God'.[69] The author was writing for an audience which would not be convinced by a visibly present God: he lets God work through 'hints' and implications.[70] God appears in the story, although more intermittently than hitherto: he is Joseph's protector. But all that he seems to do is to make Joseph 'prosper' (Gen. 39.2–5). God is behind the scenes, and the stage is the more naturalistic for that. Joseph's dreams are not like Jacob's numinous visions; they have a 'secular orientation'.[71] Jacob dreams at night: Joseph seems to dream in the day. Joseph's dreams, and those which he interprets, are literal and allegorical. They mean just one thing, and Joseph

---

66 Exum and Whedbee, 'Isaac, Samson and Saul', p. 133.
67 On 'Solomonic humanism', see Gerhard von Rad, *Old Testament Theology*, I, 'The New Spirit', pp. 48–56. Von Rad comments that 'The stories about Joseph ... call for a totally different judgment from that passed on the stories about Abraham, Isaac, or Jacob, which are to some extent composed of cultic or local units of tradition. The Joseph stories are didactic narrative, such as we find in the Wisdom literature ... they are much more compact and straightforward in their theme ... God has himself directed all for good: in deep hiddenness he has used all the dark things in human nature to further his plans ...' (p. 172). Brueggemann claims that there are no longer many takers for a 'Solomonic Enlightenment': *Theology of the Old Testament*, p. 340.
68 Ibid., p. 465.
69 Ibid., p. 355.
70 Brueggemann, *Genesis*, p. 293.
71 Alter, *Genesis*, p. 208.

tells us what it is. The dreams guarantee success and survival, or foresee doom and death. Contemporary readers ask: Where is the *spirituality* in this round of material successes?

Cognisant of the advantages a costume can endow, Jacob made for Joseph 'a coat of many colours': the 'ornamented tunic', apparently a 'product of ancient *haute couture*' decorated with 'appliqué ornamentation',[72] should enable Joseph to act the king. The transformation exacerbates 'his brothers' (37.4): 'And Joseph dreamed a dream and told it to his brothers and they hated him all the more' (37.5). We learn that they hated him for it before we learn what the dream is: they hate him for having the dream, even before he tells it and they interpret it.

> And he said to them, 'Listen, pray, to this dream that I dreamed. And, look, we were binding sheaves in the field, and, look, my sheaf arose and actually stood up, and look, your sheaves drew round and bowed to my sheaf.' And his brothers said to him, 'Do you mean to reign over us, do you mean to rule us?' And they hated him all the more, for his dreams and for his words. And he dreamed yet another dream and recounted it to his brothers, and he said, 'Look, I dreamed again, and look, the sun and the moon and eleven stars were bowing to me.' And he recounted it to his father and to his brothers, and his father rebuked him and said to him, 'What is this dream that you have dreamed? Shall we really come, I and your mother and your brothers, to bow before you to the ground?' And his brothers were jealous of him, while his father kept the thing in mind. (Gen. 37.6–11)

The brothers think about what the dream means *for us*. For Joseph, the dreams are objective. His family cannot achieve this perspective. They must be diminished if Joseph is to be enhanced. *They* do not dream about how far the world can grow, or how spacious it can become.

Joseph *has* pictured himself up above the cosmos. Now he falls for the first time. His brothers intend to quench his dreaming.

> And they said to each other, 'Here comes that dream-master! And so now, let us kill him and fling him into one of the pits and we can say, a vicious beast has devoured him, and we shall see what will come of his dreams.' And Reuben heard and came to his rescue and said, 'We must not take his life.' And Reuben said to them, 'Shed no blood! Fling him into this pit in the wilderness and do not raise a hand against him' – that he might rescue him from their hands and bring him back to his father. And it happened when Joseph came to his brothers that they stripped Joseph of his tunic, the ornamented tunic that he had on him. And they took him and flung him into the pit, and the pit was empty, there was no water in it. (Gen. 37.19–24)

His brothers' murder plot is foiled at some expense to Joseph's dignity. While Joseph languishes in his waterless pit, his brothers eat dinner. Noticing a caravan of Ishmaelites on its way to Egypt, 'with their camels bearing spicery and balm and myrr', Judah figures that they can make more money by selling Joseph than by letting him die of thirst. Out of their narrow line of vision, some Midianite merchants drag Joseph out of the hole and sell him to the Ishmaelites. Reuben is distressed: 'where can I

---

72 Ibid., p. 209.

turn?' (37.30). His brothers' silent answer to the real, if implied question is to dip Joseph's coat in goat's blood (37.31). Rather than inventing a story about how they discovered the coat, they force their father to identify it:

> 'Recognize, pray, is it your son's tunic or not?' And he recognized it, and he said, 'It is my son's tunic.
> A vicious beast has devoured him,
> Joseph's been torn to shreds!' (Gen. 37.32–33)

Joseph dies in his first attempt to play the lord: he is 'stripped' of coat and kingship. The lordly son which Jacob had tried to tailor for himself has died, in the bloody coat. It is the descent, the literal fall into the pit, which propels Joseph into a wider world than that of his family. He is rescued by a walk-on cast of mercantile deliverers. Joseph is carried to Egypt, safely on the way to enslavement.

Having been bought by Potiphar, 'an officer of Pharaoh', Joseph enters the ambience of kingship. When she fails to get him into bed with her, Potiphar's wife accuses the 'Hebrew' of date rape (39.14, 17). Joseph falls again, into a dungeon. 'But the LORD was with Joseph ... and gave him favour in the sight of the keeper of the prison' (39.21). He springs forward in a verse, the prisoners' prison officer (39.22). He correctly interprets the Chief Cup Bearer's and the Baker's dreams, but his surviving contact in the Pharaoh's house 'did not remember Joseph, no, he forgot him'.[73]

The audience knows who is going to have the insight into Pharaoh's own dreams: first, that seven 'fatfleshed' ones consume seven 'ill-favoured' cows, and second, that seven full ears of corn are eaten by seven thin ones (Gen. 41.1–7). The hapless magicians of the Pharaoh are stock characters before they get into Exodus. Now the Butler tells the Pharaoh to send for Joseph. Joseph warns that the interpretation will not be his, but God's. In Joseph Heller's midrash, Joseph helped

> God to make good on His promises to Abraham ... by translating a con-
> founding dream of the Pharaoh's about stalks of corn and fat cows and skinny
> cows into a familiar two-word precept that might have earned a stinting
> accolade from Sigmund Freud and ignited a flash of esteem in the eye of
> every trader in commodity futures. The interpretation?
> 'Buy corn,' said Joseph.
> 'Buy corn?' said the Pharaoh?
> 'The dream,' said Joseph. 'The dream wants you to buy corn.'[74]

Joseph rises again, on the back on his hermeneutic foresight; he sees how 'thin' can ingest 'fat', and sees the practical link in the metaphor: store food so the vats of the years of plenty can overflow into the vats of the years of

---

73 Alter comments that, 'The verb for remembering also meant "to mention", and Joseph employs both senses of the root in his words to the cupbearer in verse 14 ... remembering is central to the larger story of Joseph and his brothers. When he sees them again after more than twenty years of separation, this same crucial verb of memory, *zakhar*, will be invoked for him, and the complicated strategy he adopts for treating his brothers is a device for driving them into the painful process of moral memory.' *Genesis*, p. 233.

74 Joseph Heller, *God Knows*, p. 52.

famine. God has given him both prosperity and disaster. Joseph sees that God will send good harvests and then withdraw them. Pharaoh gives Joseph his ring:

> And he made him to ride in the second chariot which he had; and they cried before him, [*deep voice*] 'Bow the knee ...' (Gen. 41.43)

The 'famine was over all the face of the earth': it affects Jacob and his remaining sons in Canaan. All except Benjamin, the youngest, go to Egypt to buy corn.

> As for Joseph, he was the regent of the land, he was the provider to all the people of the land. And Joseph's brothers came and bowed down to him, their faces to the ground. And Joseph saw his brothers and recognized them, and he played the stranger to them and spake harshly to them, and said to them, 'Where have you come from?' And they said, 'From the land of Canaan, to buy food.' And Joseph recognized his brothers but they did not recognize him. And Joseph remembered the dreams he had dreamed about them, and he said, 'You are spies!' (42.6–9)

Joseph's brothers do not know what they are doing: the dream is fulfilled, without their being conscious of it; it was the self-conscious bowing down to the youngest which they dreaded. They had been wrong to interpret the dream psychologically, and not scenically. Attempting to extricate themselves, they entangle themselves further, by listing their brothers. Playing the part of angry *Egyptian* governor, Joseph orders them to bring Benjamin to him. Now we have a flashback to the 'murder' scene, which replays something which the narrator had not told us there:

> And they said each to his brother, 'Alas, we are guilty of our brother, whose mortal distress we saw when he pleaded with us and we did not listen. That is why this distress has overtaken us.' Then Reuben spoke out to them in these words: 'Didn't I say to you, "Do not sin against the boy", and you would not listen? And now, look, his blood is requited.' (Gen. 42.21–22)

Joseph's *brothers* evidently have a mechanistic view of moral causality. Because they have killed one brother, another must die. Joseph is watching the scene, from outside, pretending not to speak their language: 'And they did not know that Joseph understood, for there was an interpreter between them' (Gen. 42.23). His detachment is a disguise: 'And he turn away from them and wept and returned to them and spoke to them, and he took Simeon from them and placed him in fetters before their eyes' (Gen. 42.24). The other brothers are packed off to bring Benjamin to Joseph.

Jacob has now lost three sons by dint of his brood's incompetence. Why, he wants to know, did you blab the whole family history?

> Could we know he would say, 'Bring down your brother?' (Gen. 43.6–7)

The confession of ignorance parallels their feigned ignorance of the provenance of the bloody coat. The brothers do not know *who* Joseph is. They do not want to. They see him as 'the man': their imaginations are severely limited. This is why they failed to recognise the tenor of Joseph's searching inquiry, which should have given him away.

Judah returns to Egypt with Benjamin. Joseph invites them to eat with him: Joseph, his brothers, and the Egyptians sit at three separate tables, 'for the Egyptians would not eat bread with the Hebrews, as it was abhorrent to Egypt' (43.32). Although the Egyptians know why Joseph is seated at a separate table from themselves, Joseph's brothers have yet to see through him. Joseph plays a last trick on his brothers. He conceals his cup in Benjamin's sack, and sends his servant to expose the thief. The brothers are brought back under guard to Joseph. They still do not know who this man is. Joseph asks them: 'Did you not know that a man like me would surely divine?' (44.15). The loss of Benjamin is the brothers' worst case scenario. They remind him of their story, picturing to themselves the pathos which they inflicted upon their father. Judah makes his confession of guilt (Gen. 44.19–34). Desperate to persuade 'the man' to let Benjamin go, the brothers imagine for him, and thus for themselves, what it is for the old man to lose his son. Judah goes through 'a process that induces recognition of guilt and leads to psychological transformation'.[75] Now that his brothers have exposed themselves, Joseph reveals himself:

> Then Joseph could not refrain himself before all them that stood by him; and he cried, 'Cause every man to go out from me.' And there stood no man with him, while Joseph made himself known unto his brethren.
> And he wept aloud: and the Egyptians and the house of Pharaoh heard.
> And Joseph said unto his brethren, 'I am Joseph; doth my father yet live?' And his brethren could not answer him; for they were troubled at his presence.
> And Joseph said unto his brethren, 'Come near to me, I pray you.' And they came near. And he said, 'I am Joseph your brother, whom ye sold into Egypt. Now therefore be not grieved, nor angry with yourselves, that ye sold me hither: for God did send me before you to preserve life.
> For these two years hath the famine been in the land: and yet there are five years, in the which there shall neither be earing nor harvest.' (Gen. 45.1–6)

Joseph interprets the meaning of his two dreams to the brothers: the purpose of his 'ascent' was to place him in a position to rescue his family from the famine. The brothers' deeds were overwritten by God's intention for Israel. Joseph establishes his father and brothers 'in the best of the land' and 'nourished his father, and his brethren ... with bread' (Gen. 47.11–12). He rose so that they could come up with him, into Egypt, ensuring that they survive the famine.

We began with some questions about Joseph's character, and the atmosphere of his cycle. The query which I left in abeyance was this: do our criticisms reflect our own spiritual prudishness? Genesis concludes with the family of Israel in the land of plenty. The humanistic 'Wisdom' ethos allows Joseph to be Pharaoh's good servant and God's, with no conflict between the two.[76] By skilfully managing the Egyptian empire, he can provide a respite from famine for his family. The comic action leads to a place of communion, including very concrete goods, not only the good of survival, but also of pastures for the shepherd's flocks and ample food to

---

75 Alter, *Genesis*, p. 265.
76 Brueggemann, *Genesis*, p. 320.

set on the festal table. It is good to exist: this fact is expressed, in comedy, by the material pleasures of food and wine.

The rhythm of the Genesis story depends on its sequence of characters, each with his little drama, death and burial. As Adam, Noah, Abraham, Isaac, Jacob and Joseph leave the stage, they pass on the blessing and the promise to their offspring. Each is important, but none is out of proportion to the others. The lives, decisions and crises of even these great mythical figures are relativised, in relation to the next generation which carries the thread of desire forward toward the land of promise. This is a mark not only of *comedy*, but also of good drama. It can be seen in the succession of lives in Thornton Wilder's *Our Town*.[77] Life goes on, without us: drama reflects that fact.

How does Genesis project the narrative world of comedy? In terms of plot, and the graph along which it carries its characters, we can without much difficulty map out a series of U-shaped curves for Abraham, Isaac, Jacob and Joseph. Abraham has to set out for an unknown land, Isaac to feel the knife at his throat, Jacob is exiled to labour in Haran for his oily uncle, Joseph is dropped into a pit, rises and drops again to prison, before a final elevation which hoists his whole family with it. The number of deceptions is one of the most striking features of the narrative. Abram twice passes Sarah off as his sister, bringing a plague of impotence and infertility on her Egyptian and Philistine suitors (Gen. 12.10–20; 20.1–7); Abraham conceals his deadly purpose from Isaac; Jacob pretends to be Esau to get his blessing; Rachel conceals the theft of her father's images by hiding them under the camel cushions, sits on them and pretends she cannot get up because she is menstruating (Gen. 31.32–36); Joseph 'plays the stranger' before his brothers. It would not take a Martian to conclude that if this is a sacred text, the religion in question is a thoroughly amoral one. Why is it all right for a patriarch and his wife to deceive? Many comic heroes and heroines disguise themselves. The disguise is a way of putting on power. A comic protagonist in a weak position uses it as a means of camouflage and survival, as with the various sex-changes in *Twelfth Night*, *Some Like it Hot* and *Tootsy*. Stronger heroines or heroes use it positively, as a tactical device, as when Portia reenters the scene as a sharper lawyer than her fiancé, in *The Merchant of Venice*. The strongest heroes become what they want to be: by disguising himself, Peisetaerus transforms himself into a man who can fly. Energy takes shape in a form borrowed from another, and the total ensemble clothes the 'will' of an 'I' which is more than just 'me'. All drama, *Birds* no less than *Oedipus the King*, turns on the question of the self, the question 'who am I?' The tragic hero asks the question alone, whereas the comic hero achieves identity by founding or enlarging a community. When the comic hero achieves his desire, he shows us a concrete universal self.

The 'gravity' of the world in which its characters move makes the genre. One of the actions in silent movies from which I always have to avert my eyes is that in which the camera dallies on a man standing on a ledge of a skyscraper. Each of the characters in Genesis undergoes such an ordeal.

---

77 Von Balthasar, *Theo-Drama I*, p. 412.

Genesis does not just perch its characters precariously on the ledge, but throws them off. Their deceptiveness makes them sufficiently unsublime for the fall to be funny. They do not just tumble: they are made to choose to leap off the edge. The power of God's *promise* engineers the fall into a progression. From Genesis 18, the Patriarchs live within the gravity of God's promise.[78] God does not promise the Patriarchs a bare, moral relation to himself. Rather, as Brueggemann says,

> The substance of the utterance ... is a blessing, the bestowal of life-force, as energy, prosperity, abundance, well-being. Yahweh is a God unlike any other, who has the gift of good life in Yahweh's own power ... The Book of Genesis understands the urgency of transmitting the solemn oath of Yahweh to the next generation of Israel, for *it is this oath that gives Israel power to survive and prosper in demanding and debilitating circumstance.* This oath is not a general promise that floats in the air. It is concrete and specific.[79]

The God of Genesis 'blesses' the sexual reproduction of the Patriarchs; above all, he 'gives' to these originally 'landless' people a space of their own. The good in comedy is something which one can see and taste and touch, like the fertility of the Patriarchs, and the good soil of the promised land. But the Patriarchs have been promised far more than they are given by the end of Genesis: 'All the persons of the house of Jacob, that came into Egypt, were seventy' (Gen. 46.27). That is a good round number, but not as many as the dust of the earth God had shown Abraham (Gen. 13).[80] The promise, which 'keeps the story moving', has yet to be fulfilled.[81] At the end of Genesis, desire is not satiated; the good which has been given is not commensurable either with the divine oath or with the human wishes which it has stimulated. The 'good' is still 'between', visible on an elusive horizon. The Patriarchs' drop into the abyss, and their onward moving quest are not marked by lonely fear: these characters are marked by a sense of 'security'. Both the 'elemental trust'[82] and the not-quite-thereness of the good are the signs of the realm of biblical comedy.

3. Exodus

a. The Evolution of the Species (and a Word about Genre)

The development of textual criticism of the Bible may be illuminated by comparison with the Darwinian paradigm of the origin of species. First to crawl out of the Wellhausian sea were the semi-amphibious reptiles, the source critics. The most leathery reptile to write about Exodus in English was Samuel Driver. In his *Introduction to the Literature of the Old Testament* (1891) and his Exodus commentary (1911), Driver argued that Exodus is constructed out of two sources, one 'JE' and the other 'P'. The reptiles could not withstand the onslaught of the much larger dinosaurs. The fossil record indicates that these beasts originated in Germany: they constructed a baggy

---

78 Brueggemann, *Theology of the Old Testament*, pp. 166–167.
79 Ibid., p. 168.
80 Clines, *Theme of the Pentateuch*, p. 45.
81 Ibid., p. 50.
82 Brueggemann, *Theology of the Old Testament*, pp. 466–467.

synthesis called the History of Traditions. The Tyrannus Rex among the dinosaurs was Gerhard von Rad; but it was von Rad's colleague, Martin Noth, who, like a great flying pterodactyl, circled around Exodus. The History of Traditions recaptures the development by which quasi-historical events were recollected in 'saga' form, rehearsed in the liturgy, and became biblical texts. On Noth's account of the origin of Exodus, Israel preserved in saga and in liturgical form a memory of a historical event: God's over-throw of the Egyptians at the Red Sea. This saga, or liturgy, is encapsulated in the 'seed' of Exodus 15.21b, which grew to become the biblical narra-tive of Exodus.[83] After an ice age, in which doubt was cast upon the 'speculative and arbitrary'[84] character of the History of Traditions, the field was taken by ostrich-like birds. They had little use for the Jahwist or the Elohist: Thomas Dozeman prefers to speak only of a 'pre-exilic tradition', by which he means the 'cultic mythology that supported the various monarchies in ancient Israel'.[85] The ostriches, or redaction critics, flew over the primeval 'sources', concerning themselves instead with 'later levels of the text where editorial activity and intention can be more certainly discerned'.[86] Contemporary redaction critics have found in Exodus *two* 'final' editions. One is the work of the Deuteronomistic school, the authors of Joshua to 2 Kings. The Deuteronomists constructed their version of Exodus during the exile. The second, and final, edition of Exodus is the work of the Priestly writers. But if the ancient cultic *Sitz im Leben* of the sagas and 'sources' like 'J' and 'E' have disappeared in the onward march of evolution, why not rationalise the progress still further? A horse appeared, who argued that the Exodus was largely the work of a single author, a Judaean writing in exile in Babylonia in the sixth century BC. The Yahwist makes a comeback: he is, according to John van Seters, an 'ancient historian', who having begun a history of Israel in Genesis continued in Exodus and Numbers with a 'biography' of Moses.[87] His construction is touched up by the Priestly writer, to produce the finished 'Exodus'. Seters's hypothesis of single authorship entails that the post-exilic Jahwist invented much of his 'biography', using the paradigms of the Deuteronomistic narratives and the prophets. If, following van Seters, one goes back 'to the ancient hermeneutical principle of "comparing scripture with scripture" ... in a source-critical manner'[88] then the task of the modern biblical historian is not a *long-range* affair, spanning centuries in which oral and written sources slowly evolved, but a *short-range* affair, focusing upon one man's construction of the 'history' of Israel by means of *contemporary* and *literary* models. Seters's 'J' is not a repository of ancient traditions, but a creative author, who uses literary *models* rather than semi-*historical*

83 William Johnstone, *Exodus* (Journal for the Study of the Old Testament Press, Sheffield, 1990), p. 68.

84 Ibid., p. 73.

85 Thomas Dozeman, *God at War: Power in the Exodus Tradition* (Oxford University Press, Oxford, 1996), p. 172.

86 Ibid., p. 75.

87 John van Seters, *The Life of Moses: The Yahwist as Historian in Exodus–Numbers* (Kok Pharos Publishing House, Kampen, The Netherlands, 1994), pp. 1–3.

88 Ibid., p. 247.

sources. Appearing out of sequence with the above, although he has hunted with the dinosaurs for the tasty morsels of saga, one may mention the humanistic theology of Martin Buber.

Karl Barth eschewed the history of religions: he refounded German theology in the light of faith. This act of faith gave rise to the Yale School, with which Brevard Childs, the Christian creator of canonical criticism, is affiliated. Some Jewish scholars also withheld their full assent from dissective exegesis: before Childs, Umberto Cassuto had set his hand to reading Scripture within Jewish tradition. Canon criticism may be interpreted in the light of Genesis: it constructs a pantechnical ark, containing all of the aforesaid beasts, and more. The ark of canon criticism takes on board the work of source, tradition-historical and redaction criticism. Cassuto and Childs pay attention to the sources, their redactions, the textual canon and the wider framework of Jewish and Christian tradition. Such a freighted ark floats precariously low in the water.

Trying to think how Exodus was written is an act of *historical imagination*. Does Exodus refer us back to an experience so mysterious that the legend can only be told in poetry? Or may we conceive the author at work on a text-based task of aetiology, a task sufficiently rational to be acceptable to the clearest thinking Houyhnhmn or empirical historian? What is the *genre* of Exodus? For Buber, Cassuto and for Childs, the text is a religious one with a historical basis. Childs comments that the 'problem' of the plagues and Pharaoh 'is not ultimately form-critical ... but ... theological'.[89] For Dozeman, Exodus is liturgical, and a-historical.

b. The Text

I have marked out four thematic sections in Exodus. The first, Exodus 1–11, is the Plagues against Pharaoh story. Its theme is miracle. The second section describes the Passover event and its subsequent ritual, creating a play within a play, in which the hearers are enjoined to take part. The theme of Exodus 12–18 is liberation. The third scenic section depicts Yahweh's theophany on the Mountain: the theme of Exodus 19–24 is revelation. The final scene, in Exodus 24–50, is the construction of the tabernacle. Both in the Exodus story, and in the Egyptian political reality, the Pharaoh was a representative character: the king of Egypt *is* the Egyptian people as a whole, standing in for the macrocosm.[90] The Pharaoh is both the representative of god on earth *and* the Egyptian people considered politically. The king is the state, taken as an immanent divine order. The conflict is thus between the God of Israel and the god of Egypt,

---

89 Brevard S. Childs, *Exodus: A Commentary* (SCM, London, 1974), p. 149.
90 Henri Frankfort says that 'The Egyptian state ... was a god-given, established when the world was created; and it continued to form part of the universal order. In the person of the Pharaoh a superhuman being had taken charge of the affairs of man ... the creator himself had assumed kingly office on the day of creation. Pharaoh was his descendant and his successor. The word 'state' was absent from the language because all the significant aspects of the state were concentrated in the king ... *l'état c'est moi* ... could have been offered by Pharaoh as a statement of fact in which his subjects concurred.' *Ancient Egyptian Religion: An Interpretation* (Harper & Row, New York, 1948, 1961), pp. 30–31. See also van der Leeuw, *Religion in Essence and Manifestation*, pp. 115–123 and 214.

who holds Israel in his power. The 'signs and wonders' with which God plagues Egypt drive the plot downwards. God 'hardens Pharaoh's heart' (Ex. 4.21; 7.4, 13; 8.15, 19, 32; 9.12; 10.1, 20, 27; 11.10). As Egypt's sources of life and fertility are destroyed, plague by plague, so Pharaoh's response rigidifies. Pharaoh is progressively mummified. The death of Egypt is Israel's escape from bondage, the subject of the second scene. Israel crosses the Sea to freedom and rebirth. The ascent continues in the third scene, in which Moses climbs the Mountain and God descends to meet him. In the concluding scene, the story rises with the lifting of the human spirit. In co-operation with God's careful instructions, artisans construct a 'house' for God. If the liberation from Egypt is brought about by God's 'hand' the tabernacle is the achievement of God and human hands, playing in unison. Exodus forms a unified dramatic action, beginning with the descent into conflict, turning at the peripeteia of Passover, and then rising, first to superhuman levels of the mountain theophany, and then to the divine–human creation of the tabernacle, the movable dwelling of a wandering God.

A rapid recapitulation of the 'names' of Jacob's twelve sons reminds us that 'all Israel' is in Egypt. 'Now there arose up a new king over Egypt, which knew not Joseph' (Ex. 1.8). This practised demagogue warns his subjects that the proliferating population of the 'children of Israel' consti-tute a military threat. The Egyptians burden the emigrant people with a project of city-building. Weighed down with extra 'bondage in mortar and in brick', the Israelites flourish. A deadlier threat is devised: their midwives are instructed to kill the male children at birth. The tone of the comic world is given by the presence of female helpers. The Hebrew midwives, Shiprah and Puah, outwit the Pharaoh's injunction, enabling the babies to evade the death-warrant: 'They are just being born too fast for us to stop them'. So the Pharaoh tells his own people to drown the Israelite males (Ex. 1.22).

The hero's first exploit is to escape Pharaoh's child murder policy, thanks to three women. When he grows too big for concealment, his mother builds him a little river-worthy boat. Pharaoh's daughter takes compassion on a baby who weeps at the expedient moment. His sister, a bright participant in various aquatic adventures, intimates that her mother could make a nurse. The king's daughter takes the child for her son and names him Moses (2.10). Moses steps full grown out of the enclave of the Egyptian palace in the next line:

> Moses went out unto his brethren, and looked on their burdens: and he spied
> an Egyptian smiting an Hebrew, one of his brethren.
> And he looked this way and that way, and when he saw that there was no
> man, he slew the Egyptian, and hid him in the sand. (Ex. 2.11–12)

The author's pictorial imagination does not miss a beat. The Israelites are no less observant:

> He went out again on the next day, and here: two Hebrew
> men fighting!
> He said to the guilty one:
> 'For-what-reason do you strike your fellow?'
> He said:
> 'Who made you chief and judge over us?

Do you mean to kill me
as you killed the Egyptian?'
Moshe became afraid and said:
'Surely the matter is known!' (Ex. 2.13–14)

Moses acts on the instant, then takes prudential thought for the consequences. He has the temper of a defender and judge of Israel: but he is also
terrified of exposure. He is both a natural leader and unwilling to risk
giving himself away. The other Israelites will be more liable to answer
back and to complain about his orders than the Egyptians are to their
monarchical microcosm.

> Now when Pharaoh heard this thing, he sought to slay Moses. But Moses
> fled from the face of Pharaoh, and dwelt in the land of Midian: and he sat
> down by a well. (Ex. 2.15)

Moses displays his resourcefulness in his 'well scene'. He assists a gaggle
of sisters in a brief argy-bargy with a gang of shepherds, who want the
well to themselves, and is invited to take his pick of the Priest of Midian's
daughters. He marries Zipporah and names their first son for his estrange-
ment from home and kin: 'Gershom [Ger, a foreigner], for I have been a
stranger in a strange land.'
   One Pharaoh exits and God enters the scene:

> And it came to pass in process of time, that the king of Egypt died: and the
> children of Israel sighed by reason of the bondage, and they cried, and their
> cry came up unto God by reason of the bondage.
> And God heard their groaning, and God remembered his covenant with
> Abraham, with Isaac, and with Jacob.
> And God looked upon the children of Israel, and God had respect to them.
> (Ex. 2.23–25)

The Israelite's cries 'come up' to God. He is drawn back into the story; he
hears their sighs of bondage and remembers his covenant. God responds
to the cries of the whole people, but he addresses his plan of action to their
single representative-to-be. Moses, a shepherd and more of a naturalist
than a mystic, sees a 'great sight': a bush which flames incandescently,
without burning up. Curious about this unnatural phenomenon, Moses
turns around to look,

> And when the LORD saw that he turned aside to see, God called unto him
> out of the midst of the bush, and said, 'Moses, Moses.' And he said, 'Here am
> I.' (Ex. 3.4)

Moses presents himself to his interlocutor; he must have stepped forward
to investigate, for he is warned back:

> Draw not nigh hither: put off thy shoes from off thy feet, for the place
> whereupon thou standest is holy ground. (Ex. 3.5)

Moses is in the presence of sacred fire, and of a power which speaks and
calls his name. The Power names himself as the God of Moses' fathers
(3.6). God tells Moses that he plans to 'deliver' the Israelites 'out of the
hand of the Egyptians'. He will send Moses to stand in for him before

Pharaoh. Remembering the king who intended to kill him, the hero promptly forgets who he is: 'Who am I, that I should go unto Pharaoh, and that I should bring forth the children of Israel out of Egypt?' (3.11). Moses' 'I' is wobbling. God promises to bind his own 'I' to Moses' wobbly one: 'Indeed, I will be there with you'. Moses responds with a delaying question: 'when I tell the Israelites that the "God of their fathers sent me to you", what shall I say when they ask for his name?' Don't the Israelites know who the God of their fathers is? The query is probably a dodge.[91] God's 'I AM THAT I AM' elicits from Moses neither theological questioning nor leadership qualities. As God enlarges himself Moses shrinks. Maybe focusing on the particulars will help: Moses must gather the people and ask Pharaoh's permission 'to journey into the wilderness to sacrifice'. The deliverance will take place in a dazzling display of miracles (Ex. 3.19–20). God has offered to show his hand, and Moses again refuses to take it: 'they will not believe me' (4.1). Undaunted by human resistance, God offers him 'signs': a rod which turns into a snake, a hand which can become leprous and non-leprous, and water which will turn into blood. Visual magic tricks are very well, but, '"W-w-w-why me? ... I st-st-st-stammer"'[92] (Ex. 4.10). The Creator of language can feed Moses his lines ('I will be with thy mouth', 4.12). 'Please send someone else', says Moses.[93] Enough is enough: 'God's anger was kindled against Moses'. Aaron can do Moses' talking for him: God will tell them both what to say.

What is the point of Moses' resistance in the face of the divine presence? Imagine this scene otherwise. Picture a Moses of quasi-mythical strength and resolution, ready to confront Pharaoh and to save his people. The comedy is lost and, with it, the humanity of Moses and the deity of the 'I AM'. The more titanic one makes Moses, the less dramatic is the event of God's speaking with him. Two very different actors are engaged in this scene. Not that God is too transcendent to be affected: his messenger eventually succeeds in annoying him. Never was the distance between God's plan and human disorder more succinctly dramatised. Moses of Exodus 3–4 is free to be a coward. God does not override Moses' fears, but accommodates the plan to his humanity.

For several centuries, the Bible was the focal point of Protestant Christianity; since the Second Vatican Council, even some cradle Catholics have got the general gist of the more well-known biblical episodes. And yet most Christians find the Bible a boring trudge. Taking account of our reluctance, various ecclesial bodies rewrote it in modern English. We still hear it unwillingly, perhaps even more so. It is not King James who made the Bible unreadable, but a moralising attitude, which pours cold water all over the drama. When the sermonist comments on Exodus 3, he wants to make a didactic point, and our private reading echoes it: Moses is *disobedient*. The finger points at the reader too, and who wants to have to identify with the moral condemnation of one character after another, all the way through the Book? The perception of the comedy does not detach the thread of ethics from the biblical drama, but it lightens it. We are not

91 Childs, *Exodus*, p. 75.
92 Heller, *God Knows*, p. 30.
93 Childs, *Exodus*, p. 79.

supposed to judge Moses, or to feel guilty for his faults, but to identify with his humanity. In the terrain of comedy, it is all right to be human: comedy contains no 'oughts' which carry us beyond the realm of human desire.

Exodus 3–4 is a recognition and identification scene. The voice from the flaming bush is not an 'alien God "discovered" by Moses on Sinai':[94] it tells Moses that

> 'I am the God of thy fathers, the God of Abraham, the God of Isaac, and the God of Jacob.' And Moses hid his face; for he was afraid to look upon God. (3.6)

A power of which Moses implicitly *knew* specifies himself. He defines himself further, in relation to the people, by articulating the act of hearing and remembering of 2.23–25. God tells Moses of his intentions for 'my people' in Exodus 3.7 and 10:

> In this word ᶜ*ammi*, 'my people', recurring at the beginning and the end of God's words, which unites the 'with' of human community with the heavenly 'my', the mystery of the nature and charge of Israel has found its most elemental formulation.[95]

God chooses Israel and makes it *his*: everything that is in store for Israel flows from this divine possessive genitive, ᶜ*ammi*. Israel's story is about the way in which it belongs to God: it is being named into its future as 'my people'. In 3.14, in response to Moses' quick-fire interrogation, God identifies himself: *ehyeh asher ehyeh* ('I am so that I am') and again *ehyeh shalhni alechem* ('I am sends me to you'). Some have found the answer to be evasive; but the moment when God acts on his recollection of Israel is one of dialogue made into deed, not word-games about Transcendence. The qal verb *hyh* often means 'to come about' or 'come to pass'; it is 'often used of action', 'especially with the creative fiats of Genesis 1.3 (*eyeh aur veyeh aur*: "let lights appear and lights appeared")'; it can also mean 'arise, come on the stage or scene'; it is used of the word of God 'coming' (or 'being to') a person, as in Genesis 15.1 or 1 Samuel 15.10, and 'constantly in the prophets'; it can mean become and become like, as in Genesis 27.32 ('his hands had become like the hands of Esau his brother, hairy'); it can also mean to be or to exist, always in a concrete sense, and thus 'be with, accompany'.[96] Buber takes the 'twofold ehyeh' to be a promise: 'I am and remain present.'[97] Yahweh defines and reveals what his role is, in the promise of presence. The scene is a revelation of the character of Israel and its God, exhibited in the encounter between Yahweh and a very common man.

94 Martin Buber, *Moses* (Phaidon Press, Oxford, 1966), p. 44.
95 Ibid., p. 32.
96 Francis Brown, S. R. Driver and Charles A. Briggs, *A Hebrew and English Lexicon of the Old Testament* (Clarendon Press, Oxford, 1951), *hyh*, pp. 224–228.
97 Buber, *Moses*, p. 52. Everett Fox comments that: 'Moshe refuses the commission five times, and five times God counters. In four of these cases, the assurance is given that God will "be-there" with him (3.12, 14; 4.12, 15), and the use of that verb carries in its essence one of the most significant motifs of the Bush Narrative: the interpretation of God's name.' *Now These Are the Names: A New English Translation of the Book of Exodus.* Translated with Commentary and Notes (Schocken Books, New York, 1986).

Nothing better expresses what we commonly mean by 'the sacred' than personal self-revelation: what is 'ours' is given to another; the dangerous and closely guarded space of the self is not just defined but opened up and handed over. Moses' quintuple scruples demonstrate Moses' freedom with respect to a call to become a prophet.[98] Exodus 3–4 presents an encounter between human and divine freedom. Freedom is self-possession. When Yahweh takes possession of Moses, and gives his self-possessed presence to Israel, divine and human freedom grip one another. Moses did not want his kinsfolk to be beaten like slaves, but by fleeing alone from Egypt he has achieved lonely exile. He quails before the impossible dream which God puts to him at Mount Horeb. God's vision of rescue meets his desire, but extends his conception of what can happen. Moses' freedom is finite; God's freedom is infinite; bound to 'my people', it will achieve an unlimited desire.

Moses learns that God will put the power of miracles into his human 'hand', when he comes before Pharaoh, but, says God, 'I will harden his heart', so that 'he shall not let the people go' (4.21).

> And thou shalt say unto Pharaoh, 'Thus saith the LORD, Israel is my son, even my firstborn. And I say unto thee, Let my son go, that he may serve me: and if thou refuse to let him go, behold I will slay thy son, even thy first born.' (Ex. 4.22–23)

Israel is God's 'first-born': if God cannot have it back, from Egypt, to 'serve' him, the first-born son of Pharaoh will die in substitution: because he is the 'macrocosmic' king, whatever happens to Pharaoh happens to everyone else, too. The substitution makes sense if we see Israel's servitude in Egypt as a kind of death: it is death for death. Israel is lying dead, burdened and weighted down by the pyramids: Egypt has to be sacrificed so that Israel can return to life.

Immediately after issuing these promises

> it came to pass by the way in the inn, that the LORD met him, and sought to kill him. Then Zipporah took a sharp stone and cut off the foreskin of her son, and cast it at his feet, and said, 'surely a bloody husband art thou to me'. So he let him go: then she said, 'A bloody husband thou art, because of the circumcision.' (4.24–26)

Cassuto conjectures that we have to read these lines in conjunction with the preceding ones:

> Zipporah *made* the foreskin *touch* Moses' feet, as though to say: Let the one take the place of the other. Just as the firstborn son sometimes suffers on account of the father … so shall the shedding of a few drops of the blood of Moses' firstborn son, which consecrates the infant to the service of the LORD, serve as a … decisive consecration of his father to the LORD's mission.[99]

---

98 Gerhard von Rad, *Old Testament Theology II: The Theology of Israel's Prophetic Traditions*, translated by D. M. G. Stalker (SCM, London, 1965; first German edition, 1960), p. 71.

99 Umberto Cassuto, *A Commentary on the Book of Exodus*, translated by Israel Abrahams (The Magnes Press, Hebrew University, Jerusalem, 1967), p. 60; Johnstone explains the story with reference to the Deuteronomist's focus on the offering of the first-born (as opposed to the P edition's emphasis on Passover). He says: 'It is fitting that Moses,

Zipporah saves Moses from death by bringing him into contact with his son's blood. The firstborn 'dies' on his behalf. The scene at the 'inn' repeats the message of 4.22–23, and foreshadows the drama between Pharaoh and God.

Cassuto finds that the succession of the plagues interlocks numerically. The plagues come in three rounds of three, first the blood, frogs and gnats, then the flies, pestilence and boils, and third the hail, locusts and darkness. In the first two rounds, each plague is preceded by an admonition; in the third, the plagues hail down without warning. He takes this symmetry to be evidence of an 'organically homogeneous composition'.[100] Cassuto envisages, standing behind the biblical Exodus, not 'various fragments of different sources',[101] but an 'epic poem', 'intended primarily to be chanted before' a 'general public ... fond of jocular and ironic observations'.[102] Brevard Childs considers that the plague cycle leads source archaeology back to 'a primary non-derivable stage', which seems to be a scholar's way of saying he has driven into a dead-end (a mystery).[103] For Dozeman the plague cycle began life as the liturgy of a 'night vigil', in which the gathered Israelite worshippers hear the tale of the plagues, until day comes and God's conquest is announced: 'the liturgy ends with a proclamation of Yahweh's victory over chaotic powers'.[104] The penultimate plague is Darkness: this is succeeded by the Death of the Egyptian firstborn, and then, as morning breaks, the crossing of the Red Sea. The earliest form of the plague cycle is about the Death of the Egyptian firstborn and the overthrow of the 'Egyptian armies' at the Red Sea. John van Seters finds that 'The whole plague narrative is ... consistent in its pattern and ... uniform in its outlook'; he infers from this that 'it must be the literary artistry of a single author, the Yahwist'. He attributes seven of the plagues to his 'Jahwist'. The Babylonian biographer invented his plagues on the bases of Deuteronomy's reference to 'diseases of Egypt' (Deut. 7.15; 28.60) and of the curse series in Deuteronomy 28 and Leviticus 26, in which Israel is threatened with '*sevenfold* punishment' if it does not keep God's law.[105]

Aaron and Moses approach Pharaoh, and meet a brick wall:

> Pharaoh said, 'Who is the LORD, that I should obey his voice to let Israel go? I know not the LORD, neither will I let Israel go.' (Ex. 5.2)

He ascribes the request to laziness, and increases the Israelites' brick quota. The Pharaoh is a deadly weight: trying to move him is as humanly impossible as the attempt, once made, to levitate the United States' Pentagon.

---

the leader of Israel, redeemed at the cost of the Egyptian first-born and consecrated by the dedication of their own first-born, should himself be redeemed by the blood of the circumcision, the symbol of the dedication to Yahweh, of his own first-born son.' *Exodus*, p. 109.

100 Cassuto, *Exodus*, p. 93.
101 Ibid., p. 93.
102 Ibid., p. 92.
103 Childs continues: 'the sense of the mystery of Pharaoh's resistance lies at the root of the tradition ... the ... problem ... is not ultimately form-critical ... but ... theological'. *Exodus*, p. 149.
104 Dozeman, *God at War*, p. 26.
105 Van Seters, *Life of Moses*, pp. 78–85, 95 and 91.

God knows that nothing short of a miracle will lift the Egyptian king from the Israelites' shoulders: he promises that his own 'strong hand' will topple the Pharaoh and carry the Israelites back into Canaan.

The overflowing Nile is the basis of Egypt's agriculture, its most potent natural life-force. Perhaps the Egyptians regarded the Nile as divine.[106] By the power of God, Moses turns every drop of Nile water into blood:

> the LORD spake unto Moses, 'Say unto Aaron, "Take thy rod, and stretch out thine hand upon the waters of Egypt, upon their streams, upon their rivers, and upon their ponds, and upon their pools of water, that they may become blood; and that there may be blood throughout all the land of Egypt, both in vessels of wood, and in vessels of stone."' (Ex. 7.19)

The destruction is comical because of the precision and plenitude of its outworking. Not a cup or a vase of water from the Nile evades the trans-formation. The supernatural has the exact natural effect one would expect: the land fills with the smell of rotting fish. The perfectly aimed miracle gives the Egyptians an escape route: they 'dig around the river for water to drink' (7.24).

Since Pharaoh will not let the Israelites go to sacrifice, the Egyptians are deluged with frogs: proliferating, irrational, inflating themselves, jumping left and right, in the beds, open the oven door and more leap out in your face, uncatchable, hopping over the kneading-troughs, escape next door to live with the servants, and find the frogs have already filled the house. Frogs, says Cassuto, were sacred to the Egyptians, as a 'symbol of fertility'.[107] They are certainly uncontrollably prolific. The Pharaoh's magicians had proudly imitated Moses' conjuring: they can turn rods into crocodiles, too. But was it wise to demonstrate that they can as powerfully invoke a plague of frogs as the prophet of Yahweh? They are on automatic pilot. Locked into mimetic rivalry with Moses, the magicians lose their sense of survival. Pharaoh wants his emblems of the divine to be tightly under control. It is with some irony that Moses asks him: 'when shall I entreat for thee ... to destroy the frogs ... that they may remain *in the river only*?' (8.9). Once Moses has asked God to hold back the outburst of frogs:

> the LORD did according to the word of Moses; and the frogs died out of the houses, out of the villages, and out of the fields.
> And they gathered them together upon heaps: and the land stank. (Ex. 8.13–14)

Within the logic of the miracle, the frogs do not just disappear; their smelly corpses are heaped high. Too many weird creatures could be as night-marish as Alfred Hitchcock's *Birds*, but the narrator keeps the fear below the surface, making it a giggling rather than a flesh-crawling horror. We don't have, and perhaps the Egyptians did not have, deep atavistic feelings about frogs: this plague is a mockery.

The Egyptians are given a remission of their humiliation by the fact that their magicians throw in the rod with the third plague: try as they

106 Cassuto, *Exodus*, p. 97.
107 Ibid., p. 101.

may, they cannot turn dust into lice, as Moses does. They warn their king:
'This is the finger of God' but 'Pharaoh's heart was hardened, and he
hearkened not unto them; as the LORD had said' (8.19). Pharaoh is on his
own.

The plague of flies introduces a new element: Goshen, where the
Israelites live, is exempt from its effects. God's omnipotence is hilarious.
He can create a neat demarcation between the Egyptians, plagued by flies,
and the Israelites, upon whom, he says, 'no swarms of flies shall be' (8.22).
Likewise with the pestilence of beasts: the Egyptians are told 'the hand of
the LORD will fall upon your cattle'. Rather than just 'sending' a plague,
God's hand will 'fall' (literally, 'be', *haya*, as in God's 'I am' of 3.14) upon
the Egyptians' cattle, and upon them *alone*.[108] Not 'one of the cattle of the
Israelites died'. Cassuto manfully attempts to explain many of the plagues
as events which might naturally occur in the middle East. He concedes that
the survival of all of the Israelite animals is 'possibly ... an exaggeration'.[109]
The too muchness of God's perfect aim is reflected in the moves from direct
speech to narration: everything which God instructs Moses to tell Pharaoh
will happen is reported twice, first as God's word and then as identically
consequent event:

> YHWH said to Moshe and to Aharon:
> 'Take yourselves fistfuls of soot from a furnace
> and let Moshe toss it heavenward before Pharaoh's eyes,
> it will become fine-dust on all the land of Egypt,
> and on man and on beast, it will become boils sprouting into blisters,
> throughout all the land of Egypt!'
> They took the soot from a furnace and stood before Pharaoh, and Moshe
> tossed it heavenward,
> and it became boil-blisters, sprouting on man and on beast. (Ex. 9.8–10)

In the earlier plagues, the Egyptian life-forces had been exaggerated to the
point of destruction. Now the instruments of the Israelites' slavery are
turned against their Masters. The Israelites had baked bricks, in vast kilns:
the soot which Moses takes from the furnace works its way under the skin
of Pharaoh and his people. Being covered in boils was, according to
Cassuto, 'an endemic affliction of Egypt ... a disease that spreads over the
whole body'.[110] Life has become progressively worse for the Egyptian
priesthood: the magicians are so systematically covered in boils that they
cannot stand up.

The plague of hail begins the third 'mini-cycle' of miracles. Moses
'stretched forth his rod toward heaven and the LORD sent thunder' (9.23).
Again, God is present in the plague: 'sent thunder' translates 'gave voices'
(*nathan qol*). The Egyptians are no longer mocked, but threatened with
death. They are getting an appropriate theophany. The plague of locusts is
announced:

> YHWH said to Moshe:
> 'Come to Pharaoh!

108 Ibid., pp. 110–111.
109 Ibid., p. 112.
110 Ibid., p. 113.

For I have made his heart and the heart of his servants heavy-with-stubborn-ness,
in order that I may put these my signs amongst them
and in order that you may recount in the ears of your son and of your son's son
how I have toyed with Egypt,
and my signs, which I have placed upon them –
that you may know that I am YHWH.' (10.1–2)

God describes the purpose of the plague: the Israelites will tell their children how he 'toyed with' or 'made sport of the Pharaoh:'[111] if this originates in *liturgy*, it was an exhilarating one.

And Moses and Aaron were brought again unto Pharaoh: and he said unto them, 'Go, serve the LORD your God: but who are they that shall go.'
And Moses said, 'We will go with our young and with our old, with our sons and with our daughters, with our flocks and with our herds will we go; for we must hold a feast unto the LORD.' (Ex. 10.1–2, 4, 9–10)

In the course of his negotiations with Pharaoh, Moses becomes a leader of his people: he takes up this role as the plot thickens. Standing over against Pharaoh, and with God's hand behind him, Moses can be a prince. The Moses who thought of five ways of evading the 'I Am' bargains with Pharaoh for his people, ineluctably increasing his demands, as he moves in to checkmate the king.[112] They both know that Pharaoh will never see his unwilling workforce again if they all go. Pharaoh the god tells Moses that only the men can go to sacrifice; God tells Moses to 'stretch out thine hand', and unleashes the plague of locusts upon Egypt.

If this is a game, between Pharaoh and God/Moses, it is a serious one. Too many frogs were a nuisance: the hail flattened the trees; clouds of locusts, jawing their way through every green thing they crawl across, can consume a countryside. Pharaoh says,

'... forgive, I pray thee, my sin only this once, and intreat the LORD your God, that he may take away from me this death ...' (Ex. 10.17)

God sends a westwind, on whose current the locusts ride out of Egypt.

But the LORD hardened Pharaoh's heart, so that he would not let the children of Israel go. (Ex. 10.20)

Pharaoh breaks his word again. God is pushing him to an unnatural in-flexibility. David Gunn believes that by this point Pharaoh has no mind and will of his own: he is simply a tool of God's will:

while in the early stages of the story we are invited to see Pharaoh as his own master, hardening his own heart (perhaps the legacy of the J story), as the narrative develops it becomes crystal clear that God is ... the only agent of heart-hardening who matters (the P legacy). 'Pharaoh's heart was hardened' thus becomes a kind of shorthand for 'Yahweh caused Pharaoh's heart to

---

111 'Made sport of' is the translation suggested by Childs, *Exodus*, p. 159.
112 Cassuto, *Exodus*, p. 125.

harden'. If Pharaoh may have been directly responsible for his attitude at the commencement, by the end of the story he is depicted as acting against his own better judgement, a mere puppet of Yahweh.[113]

Calvin took the Exodus 'hardening' motif as an illustration of dual predestination, in this case, to damnation. The Bible's Calvinists are the Priestly writers; its Arminians or humanists are the Jahwists. P's Pharaoh is a pantomime 'tyrant', a thorough-going Black Hat. 'J' shows us a

> Pharaoh who slyly spars with Moses, who passionately confesses his wrong, but with equal speed relents once the pressure has been removed ... when all is lost, the portrayal is not one of tragic despair, but of a sly fox still trying to salvage what he can (12.32).[114]

The question of *human* free will is not important for 'P': Pharaoh stands for the power of the gods of Egypt. The 'hardening' motif expresses the idea that the god of Egypt is clay in the hands of the God of Israel. The authors of 'J' and those of Chronicles, who exchange 'God hardened Pharaoh's heart' for 'Satan hardened his heart', are more concerned for the *humanity* of the history. The synthesis of the perspectives portrays the Pharaoh both as clay to be baked in a kiln by God ('P') and as the maker of his own destiny, intent on retaining his slaves by shifting his ground ('J'). Both by his inability to change, which reflects the 'static'[115] quality of Egyptian royal ideology, *and* by twisting and turning, deviously withdrawing his concessions as soon as they have achieved their end, Pharaoh makes himself game for God's sport. By the eighth plague, the mechanism is in control. He has no integrity left. This is less a theological predeterminism than a good literary psychology. The comic villain gets to the point where he can't stop. In the Egyptian theology of kingship, the Pharaoh is not an individual. He is Egypt. Pharaoh's inability to yield, his personal *rigor mortis*, corresponds to the death which is being inflicted by God on Egypt. The hardening moves the plot: 'P's theology underwrites the theme of

---

113 David Gunn, '"The Hardening of Pharaoh's Heart": Plot, Character and Theology in Exodus 1–14', in David Clines, David Gunn and Alan Hauser (eds), *Art and Meaning: Rhetoric in Biblical Literature* (*Journal for the Study of the Old Testament*, Supplement Series, 19, Sheffield, 1982), pp. 72–96 (79–80).

114 Childs, *Exodus*, p. 136.

115 Frankfurt says: 'Kingship, in Egypt, was as old as the world. It dated from the day of creation ... References to the creation turn up with great frequency in Egyptian texts; a large number of creation stories were current ... the concept played a very much larger part in Egyptian thought than in that of most other peoples. This is due to the Egyptians' view of the world. In a static world, creation is the only event that really matters supremely, since it alone can be said to have made a change. It makes the difference between the nothingness of chaos and the fullness of the present which has emerged as a result of that unique act ... the story of the creation held the clue to the understanding of the present ... In Egypt the creation stories displayed ... the articulation of the existing order ... The social order was part of the cosmic order .... a text describe[s] how Ptah made the local gods, the cities, and ... the whole order of existence. This passage ends with the following line which simply assigns to Ptah the title of King of Egypt: "Thus all the gods are at one with him (Ptah), content and united with the Lord of the Two Lands."' *Egyptian Religion*, pp. 50–51.

miracle. Thanks to 'J', Pharaoh is not enough of a victim of fate to revoke a hostile response.

Pharaoh had warned Moses: 'Look, for there is evil [ra^ca] before you' (10.10). This might be an allusion to the power of the Egyptian sun god Re.[116] In the early days of Egyptian monarchy, the Pharaoh was Re; later, he is identified with Horus.[117] If it is a reference to Re, God neatly reverses it. He orders Moses to

> 'stretch out thine hand toward heaven, that there may be darkness over the land of Egypt, even darkness which may be felt.'
> Moses stretched forth his hand toward heaven; and there was a thick darkness in all the land of Egypt three days:
> They saw not one another, neither rose any from his place for three days: but the children of Israel had light in their dwellings. (Ex. 10.21–23)

Maybe the Egyptians cannot walk around for fear of bumping into one another, and perhaps, as Cassuto suggests, the darkness could be felt because it came in the form of a 'sandstorm'.[118] Here Cassuto's literal mindedness shows its worth, even if this ghostly, tangible darkness represents more than a practical obstacle. It is the darkness of the grave, poured like mortar over the Egyptians, sitting as still as shades. Pharaoh bargains with Moses, and again Moses raises his game: he wants not just the whole people, but all of their livestock. Pharaoh breaks off the match:

> 'Get thee from me, take heed to thyself, see my face no more; for in that day thou seest my face thou shalt die.'
> And Moses said, 'Thou hast spoken well, I will see thy face no more.' (Ex. 10.28–29)

Pharaoh thinks that his divine gaze still has the power of death, when he is in the grip of death. His hardening and refusal instigates the final plague, promised by God from the beginning. Moses knows what is to come, and issues the injunction without a command from God:

> Moses said, 'Thus saith the LORD, "About midnight will I go out in the midst of Egypt:
> And all the firstborn in the land of Egypt shall die, from the firstborn of Pharaoh that sitteth upon his throne, even unto the firstborn of the maidservant that is behind the mill; and all the firstborn of beasts".' (Ex. 11.4–5)

The slaying of the firstborn is immaculately logical, extending from human beings to their animals. If God sends Pharaoh up, he sends up *everything* in his domain:

> it came to pass, that at midnight the LORD smote all the firstborn in the land of Egypt, from the firstborn of Pharaoh that sat on his throne unto the firstborn of the captive that was in the dungeon; and all the firstborn of cattle. (Ex. 12.29)

The Passover story is both about the advent of power and its repeated event, in the form of the liturgical ritual of Passover. The instructions for

---

116 Cassuto, *Exodus*, p. 126.
117 Frankfurt, *Egyptian Religion*, pp. 51–52.
118 Cassuto, *Exodus*, p. 129.

what the Israelites are to do on the night on which God will slay the first-born of the Egyptians and release the Israelites from Egypt are inter-mingled with instructions as to how to celebrate the event in the future: by acting it out again, dressed ready for departure, eating the same things, and re-telling the story. In Chapter 12, God tells Moses that each family must kill a lamb:

> And thus shall ye eat it; with your loins girded, your shoes on your feet, and your staff in your hand; and ye shall eat it in haste: it is the LORD's passover. For I will pass through the land of Egypt this night, and will smite all the firstborn in the land of Egypt, both man and beast; and against all the gods of Egypt I will execute judgement: I am the LORD.
> And this day shall be unto you for a memorial; and ye shall keep it a feast to the LORD throughout your generations; ye shall keep it a feast by an ordinance for ever. (Ex. 12.11–12, 14)

Moses tells the Elders what to do tonight, and what to do in later com-memoration, simultaneously:

> Now it will be,
> when you come to the land which YHWH will give you, as
> he has spoken,
> you are to keep this service!
> And it will be,
> when your sons say to you: 'What does this service (mean) to you?'
> then say:
> 'It is the slaughtered-meal of Passover to YHWH,
> who passed over the houses of the Children of Israel in Egypt,
> when he dealt-the-death blow to Egypt and our houses he rescued.'
> The people did homage and bowed low. (Ex. 12.25–27)

After the slaughter and the departure, the narrator repeats the injunction:

> It is a night to be much observed unto the LORD for bringing them out from the land of Egypt: this is that night of the LORD to be observed of all the children of Israel in their generations. (Ex. 12.42)

God restates the command to remember and to tell it over again to each generation (Ex. 13.8–10).

Passover-night, the night of death for the Egyptians and of liberation for the Israelites, is the turning point of the story, the peripeteia. God brings it about: his power is channelled into the form of the ritual which takes place on this night and hereafter. The Israelites have been crushed under a heavy weight. Plague by plague, divine power has been directed against this pyramid of human power. Now the pyramid is about to be lifted off. 'I love the sound of breaking glass', said Chesterton: an explosion can be uplifting and enjoyable. Untrammelled energy is aimless violence. The energy must be sealed off and trammelled, not only to destruction but also to creation. Comic violence kills *and* gives life. The Israelites were exempt from the effects of the first nine plagues by divine fiat. Now they are told to *do* something, to enact a ritual, which protects them from the violent force of God's advent. When they kill the lamb, the Israelites are to smear the blood on the doorposts of their houses, so that God will know which to omit, in his slaying of the firstborn. God knows who the Israelites are: the anthropomorphism is necessary because the rite particularises the exercise of divine energy. The lamb killed by the Israelites replaces the firstborn.[119] This substitutionary sacrifice deflects the power of God onto the Egyptians, and therefore releases the Israelites. They purify themselves, and make an oblation to God which wards off the danger of the sacred. The sacrificial lamb, and the ritual attending its consumption, embodies the power of freedom: 'The "charge" of the exodus is inexhaustible.'[120] So long as the Israelites continue to renew the story, they are a liberated people. They are freed for something specific: to move into the promised land. Here we have the movement of comic drama. The power and the energy of God impels the people 'upward', out of slavery and into the land of fulfilled desire. The people are rescued because God 'remembers' them; they are carried upward by the promise of the land. Promise and desire are two things, requiring two actors, but they constitute a single thread, along which the action travels. It is by being actors in this event and its 'festival' that the Israelites become a people.[121] The audience of the Passover narrative are to be actors in it. In the future, all of those who perform this drama, participating in this ritual field of force, are part of one acting company, a single community who eat together the unleavened bread and the lamb.[122] Every Israelite who acts out the drama of the Passover was present in Egypt: he experiences and undergoes the same divine 'charge' of liberation, which gives him a new land.

The story stops, at the Passover: we get an omniscient glimpse of what it will *always* mean to be an Israelite. The whole history of Israel is encapsulated in this moment. But the Israelites still have to move into the future. History does not come to a halt. There is always a further drama. Pharaoh is not yet conquered. His six hundred charioteers must chase the Israelites into the sea. God holds back the waters until morning, and then releases the watery chaos over the Egyptians. While the 'Israelites walked on dry land in the midst of the sea', the Egyptians drown in it (14.27–29).

Moses sings a song of God's victory. The 'Song of the Sea' (Ex. 15) tells of God's making his power present: we could call it the 'Poem of the Haya'. What the *presence* does is enlarged by stages. The prose narrative of the action (Ex. 14) describes the Israelites' perilous crossing, and the Egyptians' drowning; the poem focuses the hearers' attention on the power of God, the energy behind the event. In the prose narrative, the waters move back when Moses holds out his hand, at God's command. In the poem, 'the blast' of God's 'nostrils' drives the water back. The poem pictures God moving against the enemy, in response to his three-fold boast: 'Thou didst blow with thy wind, the sea covered them: they sank as lead in the mighty waters.' God's power 'grows' throughout the narrative: the first 'strophe' concludes with his dashing the opposing army 'in pieces'; the second ends with God's glory and miraculous power exalted above the power of the other gods; the final strophe projects God's power into the future.[123] The

119 Ibid., p. 138.
120 W. D. Stacey, *Prophetic Drama in the Old Testament* (Epworth, London, 1990), p. 51.
121 Ibid., p. 53.
122 Ibid., pp. 54–55.
123 Robert Alter, *The Art of Biblical Poetry* (T&T Clark, Edinburgh, 1985, 1990), p. 52.

accumulation of imagery carries the singer into a prophecy: the third strophe envisages what God will achieve for Israel in the promised land (Ex. 15.1–20). By singing a hymn to the power of God's past and present acts, the poet has a glimpse of the promise which the event contains. In 'the Bible ... God is movement'.[124] After 'Moses and the children of Israel' sing, Miriam and her women perform a victory dance. God's action is not complete until it has been integrated into human understanding. This takes place by performing it, in a song which tells the story in words, and in a dance which describes the action in movements:

> In Ex. 15.20, Miriam and all the women danced with timbrels to celebrate the victory at the Red Sea. If this verse is read historically, the dance is a reaction to the deliverance, but if it is read cultically, it may be either a reaction to the past or a celebratory anticipation of deliverance in the future ... By dancing, the women ... participate in the total event and give it greater 'presence'.[125]

The song dramatises the 'movement and countermovement' of God and his enemies; the dance, which contains only a single, forward circling 'movement', closes the action of the 'peripeteia'.

The biblical God is both the holy, the *mysterium tremendum*, and the source of justice. He is both glorious, *kabod*, and righteous, *mishpat*. The third thematic section of Exodus describes his self-manifestation. On Mount Sinai, Moses receives the law and is shown the glory of God. The people's undirected meanderings up and down the mountain, their mixture of rash attraction and fearful repulsion, dramatises the appearing of God. The 'ascending' motif reflects the 'attraction' of the holy, the descending motif its 'terror'. In 19.16–20, God descends, but what we see are the phenomenal effects of the 'descent'. The people in the 'camp' below 'trembled' when they hear God approaching with the noise of 'thunders and lightnings' and 'the voice of the trumpet exceedingly loud' and see the 'thick cloud' in which God is wrapped. The mountain turns into an erupting volcano: 'mount Sinai was altogether on a smoke, because the LORD descended upon it in fire: and the smoke thereof ascended as the smoke of a furnace, and the whole mount quaked greatly'. Moses leads the people forward, but they prudently remain at the lower reaches of the shaking Vesuvius. At God's call, Moses alone goes to the 'top of the mount': now, the people want to see more, so God tells him to make sure they do not come up: 'Go down, charge the people, lest they break through unto the LORD to gaze, and many of them perish.' They want to see, but they cannot bear to do so. The people's reaction contrasts with that of Moses. Moses changes in the course of the story, from the stuttering bundle of nerves who evaded the 'I AM', through his initially hesitant and unsuccessful dealings with the Pharaoh, to the leader who issued the last warning to Pharaoh off his own bat. Moses has learned how to play the role of mediator. The commandments of Chapter 20, and the elaboration thereon, in Chapters 21–23, are given to Moses. These are the laws which will enable the people of Israel to live as a community. Having received these regulations, Moses tells them to the people:

---

124 Van der Leeuw, *Sacred and Profane Beauty*, p. 74.
125 Stacey, *Prophetic Drama*, pp. 31 and 33.

and all the people answered with one voice, and said, 'All the words which the LORD hath said will we do.' (Ex. 24.3)

The people become a single community, in the unanimous agreement between the 'words' spoken by God and their own intended performance.[126] The God who explained his name to Moses in terms of a performance promised for the future *acts here*:

Yahweh is henceforth the God who brought Israel out of Egypt. Likewise, the people who benefit from the event derive their identity from the story.[127]

Moses performs the sacrifice which binds God and people together, sprinkling half the blood on the altar and half on the people. Moses writes the law down, in the 'book of the covenant'. Again he asks for the assent of 'the audience of the people' to them, and again, he gets it. On the first asking, the people agreed to the laws as embodied in Moses' memory, and, on the second, to the laws as written in a book. Revealed laws and words, mediated by a person, take precedence over the objectification of words and laws in the written text. The words are sealed in blood:

And Moses took the blood and sprinkled it on the people, and said, 'Behold the blood of the covenant which the LORD hath made with you concerning all these words.' (24.8).

God calls Moses to receive the law written by God, on tables of stone, as it were, the final version of the 'sacred text'. It is a calm, restful and passive Moses who disappears into the cloud of God:

And Moses went up into the mount, and a cloud covered the mount.
And the glory of the LORD abode upon mount Sinai, and the cloud covered it six days: and the seventh day he called unto Moses, out of the midst of the cloud.
And the sight of the glory of the LORD was like devouring fire on the top of the mount in the eyes of the children of Israel.
And Moses went into the midst of the cloud, and gat him up into the mount: and Moses was in the mount forty days and nights.

The whole people witnesses the outskirts of the epiphany of the glory of God. Moses' vision and mediatorship are at the centre.

Mediaeval Christian exegetes noted a correspondence between the 'signs and wonders' of the first scene of Exodus and the revelation in its third scene. The sending of ten plagues is followed by the giving of ten commandments.[128] The dramatised combat between good and evil gives

---

126 Jonathan Sacks notes that, in Jewish exegesis from the second century onwards, the unity of Judaism rests in its single-hearted assent to God's laws at Sinai. He cites Rashi, commenting on Ex. 19.2: 'And Israel camped there – *as one person with one heart*. But all their other encampments were marked by dissension and argument.' From here on, says Sacks, 'A Jew is born into obligations. There is no formal moment of acceptance of the commands. The born Jew is, as the Talmud put it, "already forsworn as from [the revelation at] Mount Sinai".' *One People*, pp. 18 and 122.
127 Patrick, *Rendering of God*, p. 68.
128 Childs notes that this tradition begins with Philo and is elaborated by Origen: *Exodus*, p. 165.

rise to absolute moral obligations. First God *acts* against Israel's oppressors. Israel becomes a people by the enactment of the Passover. The drama takes on its moral level in the next scene: God makes Israel a free people by giving it laws. The people know what it is to experience evil, and to be released from it. Then they are shown what the good is. They know what the good is by knowing this God:

> God does not wish to speak as the Lord of the world that He is, but as the One who has led them forth from Egypt. He wishes to find recognition in the concrete reality of that historical hour.[129]

The laws of Exodus 22 look back to the Egyptian exile and forward to the promised land. The laws are further particularised in Exodus 23. The laws are made for the construction of a good society in the land which they will be given, the land in which Yahweh will be king. As von Balthasar says,

> the commandments of Sinai are to be kept as the condition for receiving the promised land, *and* they will acquire the force of law when the land is received ... they are precepts for an existence on the basis of hope ... Israel exists in a state of being taken outside itself. It lives in the realm of the covenant.[130]

The comedy of the revelation of Exodus is the vision of the sacred; the drama of the revelation of Exodus is its relation to the conflict which has preceded it and to the future which it anticipates.

Exodus 25–40 is about building God's tabernacle; the authors are said to be the Priestly writers.[131] God gives Moses detailed instructions for the 'pattern of the tabernacle', and of its 'instruments'. God describes his design, including how to put the shittim staves into gold rings, the gold mercy-seat and cherubim 'of cunning work', the dishes, the spoons, the bowls, the tongs, the gold snuff-dishes, the curtains of fine twined linen of blue, purple and scarlet, each twenty-eight cubits long, the loops and the taches, the eleven goat's hair curtains, the boards 'and the forty sockets of silver', the veil for the mercy-seat, and the altar, with its horns overlain in brass, the pans and the shovels, the basins and the fleshhooks, all to be made of brass, and the grate and the net, the hangings for the court, and the pins; not forgetting the costumes for Aaron the priest, 'the curious girdle of the ephod', and broidered coat, mitre and the onyx stones with the names of the tribes of Israel, to be worn in the shoulders of the ephod, the breastplate with its four rows of stones, a ruby, a topaz, a carbuncle, an emerald, a sapphire and a diamond, a jacinth, an agate and an amethyst, and the rings for the breast plate, made of blue lace, and the robe of the ephod, fringed at the hem with 'a golden bell and a pomegranate, a golden bell and a pomegranate', and the plate for Aaron's forehead, and the bonnets and girdles for Aaron's sons: the itemisation fills three long chapters, from Exodus 25 to 28, such excessive plenitude being the delight

---

129 Buber, *Moses*, p. 131.
130 Hans Urs von Balthasar, *The Glory of the Lord: A Theological Aesthetics: Volume VI: The Old Covenant*, translated by Brian McNeil and Erasmo Leiva-Merikakis (T&T Clark, Edinburgh, 1991), pp. 179–180.
131 Von Rad, *Old Testament Theology I*, Section 6, 'The Priestly Document'.

of liturgiologists. God's injunctions for diverse sacrifices take three more chapters. Comedians pile one thing on another: 'Inventory is particularly appropriate to the comic spirit.'[132] God is telling Moses how to play when he orders him to get the tabernacle worship right. When children have finished building their dens, their next step is to make rules for their club. That is the human origin of religion, and God's idea of worship in Exodus 25–31 is analogous. The inception of the stately occupation of tabernacle construction is interrupted by the ridiculous incident of the golden calf.

> And when the people saw that Moses delayed to come down out of the mount, the people gathered themselves together unto Aaron, and said unto him, 'Up, make us gods, which shall go before us; for as for this Moses, the man that brought us up out of the land of Egypt, we wot not what is become of him.' (Ex. 32.1)

After three chapters of slow liturgical explanations, the compressed speed with which the idol is made is drily ironic. Building the tabernacle would require delicate and patient workmanship; slapping a calf together takes less time and trouble.[133] It takes five verses for the plan to be conceived, Aaron to collectivise the golden earrings, and 'fashion' them 'with a graving tool'. There is the childlike imagination which flows into the tabernacle, and the violent, semi-human energy which wants a calf.

> and they said: 'These be thy gods, O Israel, which brought thee up out of the land of Egypt.'
> And they rose up early on the morrow, and offered burnt offerings, and brought peace offerings; and the people sat down to eat and drink, and rose up to play. (Ex. 32.5–6)

They want to worship a calf, the image of their animal impulses. God instantly knows what is happening, and sarcastically hands the people back to Moses: 'watch out, the people *you* liberated have sunk themselves' (32.7–8). As Moses and Joshua return to the camp, Joshua thinks he hears a battle; 'they are not fighting, but singing', Moses dryly explains (32.17–18).

Something has been desecrated by the shrieking at the camp. So we begin again: Exodus 35–40 repeats everything we had heard in 25–31. As before, God 'calls' two artisans 'by name': he creates in Bezallel and in Aholiab the vocation of the gold and silver smith. We read again of the spinning of the cloth, the devising of 'curious works', the cutting, carving, casting, embroidering, coupling, making the altar, overlaying, engraving, weaving, making clothes, putting, fastening, binding, and tying, rearing up the tabernacle, setting up the veil, covering the altar, lighting, burning, and washing their hands. The tabernacle which is described in such meticulous detail cannot be reconstructed by biblical archaeologists. It is not their shortcoming. We cannot see how the different parts of the tabernacle fit into each other to make a finished building. In the twelve chapters of Exodus human workmanship is expended upon an object, in obedience to a plethora of rules about where it all goes, and the result is a

---

132 Robert Dupree, 'The Copious Inventory of Comedy', in Cowan, *Terrain of Comedy*, p. 175.
133 Josipovici, *Book of God*, p. 96.

splendid artifact which cannot be pictured as a whole. Perhaps the unpicturable tabernacle is contrasted with the 'visible tangible' god which the people make for themselves,[134] and maybe the Hebrew authors were more concerned with movement and action than with contemplating the form of the tabernacle, wanting to describe the constructing as much as the finished artifact.[135] The Israelites have been builders throughout, lifting bricks slab on slab to construct the Egyptian cities: this contrasts with the delighted making of the light tabernacle in which the accent is on the drama of pleasurable making. Brueggemann reads the story differently, commenting that 'visual' worship 'was a thing of joy for Israel, not a burden'.[136] Gorgeous vestments, golden bells and pomegranates are not invisible. *Two* opposing facts are brought together in the tabernacle. Buber describes the image which the *fusion* of the contradictory facts creates:

> The foundation of this great Sacrum ... came about as the realization of a paradox: an invisible God is sensed by the fact that He comes and goes, descends and rises ... The effect of the Ark symbol was ... so great that the movement of the God was virtually sensed as a corporeal thing; so that the invisible God was Himself apprehended. This is more than a continuous abiding; it is an ever-renewed coming, appearing, being present and accompanying. For the promise once developed from the name of the God that he would 'be there' from time to time, and always at the moment when His presence was necessary, there is no more adequate material substratum to be thought of than this. What the old wandering God of the Mesopotamian steppe means when he says to David that He has gone about until this day 'in tent and dwelling chamber' ... is not merely a simple state of being carried about; it is this coming and accompanying and disappearing and returning.[137]

The fusion of visibility and invisibility gives rise to a comic compromise: a wandering God about whose whereabouts one cannot be *absolutely* certain. The tabernacle/house will not stand in one place: it is a tent, which can be taken apart and put up again, when the Israelites make camp. The tabernacle passages are framed by the Sabbath commands, the first concluding with the command to rest on the Sabbath (31.12 – 31.17) the second beginning with it (35.1 – 3).[138] The tabernacle passages dramatise the meaning of the worship of a wandering God. They also let making stop, briefly, before it begins again:

> So Moses finished the work.
> Then a cloud covered the tent of the congregation, and the glory of the LORD filled the tabernacle.
> And Moses was not able to enter into the tent of the congregation, because the cloud abode thereon, and the glory of the LORD filled the tabernacle.
> And when the cloud was taken up from over the tabernacle, the children of Israel went onward in all their journeys:

---

134 Ibid., pp. 104–105.
135 Thorlief Boman, *Hebrew Thought Compared with Greek*, translated by Jules L. Moreau (SCM, London, 1960), p. 75.
136 Brueggemann, *Theology of the Old Testament*, p. 669.
137 Buber, *Moses*, pp. 159–160.
138 Childs, *Exodus*, pp. 541–542.

But if the cloud were not taken up, they journeyed not till the day that it was taken up.
For the cloud of the LORD was upon the tabernacle by day, and fire was on it by night, in the sight of the house of Israel, throughout all their journeys. (Ex. 40.33–38).

Exodus ends with the people in movement, journeying onward, with the 'cloud of the LORD' moving before their tabernacle, which is 'the symbol of the *moving* presence of God', going ahead of the Israelites on their travels. By fading out on the tabernacle, 'the end of Exodus ... points forward ... to the journeying that lies ahead'.[139] Neither the people nor God are fixed objects; the people are travelling in time and in space, and their God is moving with them. In the Jewish and the Christian imagination, there is, for human beings, no perfect point of complete knowledge and finished action, no static position outside of the drama. We cannot escape playing and the play.

4. *Theatrum Gloriae Dei*

What is the genre of the Exodus? The first way into the question is to ask: out of what matter is its life-world constructed? Both van Seters and Buber believe that a single mind lies behind it; there the resemblance ends. Van Seters thinks it is made of texts; Buber thinks it refers to experiences.

For van Seters, the motifs, scenes, episode-structure and overall plot of Exodus are derived by the 'Jahwist' from the writings of the Deuteronomist and the prophets, in order to provide a rational explanation of contemporary cultic practices. For example, in the mountain theophany of Exodus 19 Yahweh speaks with the sound of a trumpet: 'the Yahwist's intention is to construct a rather sophisticated etiology for the cultic use of the shofar as symbolic of the divine presence'.[140] Sitting in his office in Babylonia, the Yahwist invented a history of the twelve tribes of Israel, and an explanation of their cultic practices which was found sufficiently convincing and religiously satisfying to be taken up and canonised as the Torah. I wonder what was the *Sitz im Leben* for the transmission of this work of 'ancient antiquarian historiography'[141] into a sacred text? Such a metamorphosis would have been a magnificent act of manipulation.

The *ehyeh asher ehyeh* which radiates out of the encounter at the Burning Bush is integral to the drama. God is effectively present to Pharaoh, in the plague cycles; his forceful presence is commemorated at the Red Sea; the tabernacle is the vehicle of a God who 'accompanies', goes with, and makes to be: 'His power is the potency of one who *can*, who has at his disposal a tremendous space of freedom with which to act.'[142] Buber's methodological assumption is that the theology of Exodus emerges out of the experience of a mystery, gives it a narrative form, and leaves it unexplained. He claims that the dialogue of Exodus 3–4 'compels us to forsake the pale of literature

139 Clines, *Theme of the Pentateuch*, p. 26.
140 Van Seters, *Life of Moses*, p. 277.
141 Ibid., p. 457.
142 Von Balthasar, *Glory VI*, pp. 55–56.

for that singular region where great personal experiences are propagated in ways that can no longer be identified'.[143] We must go back to the religious experience of a historical individual in order to account for the existence of Exodus. Buber's phenomenology of religion turns on the biblical conception of Moses as the eminent prophet, the one who *knows* God: 'Yahweh's assertion, in Numbers 12.8, "With (Moses) I speak mouth to mouth, clearly, and not in dark speech; and he beholds the form of the Lord", is an apt characterisation of the Mosaic tradition.'[144] Does the *ehyeh asher ehyeh* name God, and, if so, *how* is the name known? It is as an empirical answer to this question that the figure of Moses assumes its centrality: Israel said that Moses wrote the Pentateuch because *'he was the only means by which Israel knew anything about God to begin with'*.[145] Phenomenology is nothing if not empirical. Buber answers the how question by reference to the experience of an individual. However much it has been reshaped and stretched beyond the breaking point of anything but sacred comedy, the *matter* of Exodus is experiential. If we fear the word experience, for its private or subjective connotations, we may take heart at the thought that although some experiences, such as swallowing, take place *inside* us, most experiences happen *between* us and our world. We hang on to the thought of *experience* because the *inspiration*, the originating impulse of the Exodus, is an encounter which happened to *somebody*.

A second question concerns the *form* of Exodus. Is that form a drama? Biblical theology has instructed us that biblical thinking is linear and progressive; Jürgen Moltmann says that salvation history is not just 'linear': it is eschatological.[146] In contrast, for such thinkers, 'Greek thought' and its drama are *cyclical*. Rather than moving forward to the time beyond time when 'all things are made new', it revolves in merely repetitive cycles. In Aeschylus' plays, the plot does not spread out to the future, but waits for the past to catch up with the protagonist. The past contains the guilt which will be punished in the present. The *span* of time is thus 'abolished under the pressure of archaic terror'. The past suffuses the present moment: Darius comes back to haunt the Persians: 'Nothing ever dies in Aeschylus', because the past never loses its potent life.[147] We are riveted in the now, waiting for the future while the sacred presences of the past intrude into the present:

> The result is a perpetual oscillation . . . between past and future . . . Aeschylus keeps for the center of his play the most distant 'flashback' . . . and joints it there with an anticipation and prediction about future events. So that the whole sequence of events stands there in the middle, as one great unity, where time's continuous course is gathered into a legible pattern.[148]

One does not have to turn to Greek tragedy in order to know that *drama* works traces of the past into the present and hints at the future, so that one

143 Ibid., p. 41.
144 Dale Patrick, *Rendering of God*, p. 23.
145 Seitz, *Word without End*, p. 126.
146 Jürgen Moltmann, *The Coming of God: Christian Eschatology* (SCM, London, 1996), p. 12.
147 Romilly, *Time in Greek Tragedy*, pp. 26–27.
148 Ibid., pp. 72–73.

has the aural sensation of standing still while the escalator keeps moving. If one listens to a Mozart symphony, one will find that

> The present moment ... is so full to the brim with tension that the genuine listener has neither time nor inclination to think of the past, let alone anticipate the future. With the passing of each note we sense the presence of the whole, which simultaneously comes into being in time and – in some incomprehensible supratemporal realm – always *is*.[149]

Whether we watch Aeschylus or the comic opera of Mozart's *Magic Flute*, the *action* of the drama, and not just its *temporality*, is moving in something like a circle.

At the centre of the Exodus, the Passover narrative is told in such a way as to make past, present and future present. The retelling of the story brings the potency of the past into the present, and directs it toward the future. The author does not name the Pharaohs. With its two mid-wives dealing with the families of 600,000 men, its ten demarcated plagues and its three million people, plus animals, who are supposed to have 'crossed a narrow stretch of water in one night',[150] Exodus deals in 'overstatements and generalizations' which 'defied standards of accuracy'.[151] The comedian delights to improve the story by making it push beyond the ordinary experience into the fantastic; Mark Twain's novels provide examples of legendary exaggerators. Exodus is a narrative which has gained in the telling. Perhaps its story reformulates the mundane process of the 'centuries-long' emigration of 'Semitic semi-nomads' from Egypt into Palestine.[152] What facts there are to be recovered

> suggest that the Exodus describes ... largely commonplace movements within great historical processes, military invasion, colonization, imperialism, decline of empire, and, particularly important so far as herdsmen are concerned, transhumance, the annual interchange of pasture grounds from desert to Delta and back ... Of these ... processes the Exodus narrative ... provides a drastically oversimplified account.[153]

Even if we consider that it is 'reasonable to infer from the central place assigned to the Exodus in Jewish tradition that Israel did win liberation and a victory of some kind over Egypt'[154] one must say that the mess of history has been, as de Romilly put it, 'gathered into a legible pattern.'

The Exodus needs its drastic oversimplification in order to dramatise the history. The historical imagination of the author of Exodus transforms 'common-place' history into what Calvin called a *theatrum gloriae Dei*, a theatre of the glory of God.[155] The histrionic analogy holds good:

> The deliverance of God's people from captivity in Egypt ... is recorded both as a spectacular event of historical import ... 'staged' at least in part with a view to its effect on Egyptian and Israelite 'spectators', and as an enacted

149 Von Balthasar, *Theo-Drama I*, p. 350.
150 Johnstone, *Exodus*, pp. 32 and 27.
151 Abraham Heschel, *The Prophets* (Harper & Row, New York, 1962), p. 13.
152 Johnstone, *Exodus*, p. 34.
153 Ibid., p. 18.
154 Miles, *God: A Biography*, p. 108.
155 Harris, *Theatre and Incarnation*, p. 6.

image of future grace. The exodus was theatrical not only in its scale but in its details: the successive rounds of the 'miracle plague' competition between Moses and Pharaoh's magicians; the comedy of Pharaoh's magicians summoning yet more frogs to prove that they can make life miserable too; the astonishing visual juxtaposition of devastated army and unarmed slaves; the triumphant closing dance of the Israelite women. It was theatrical too in its concern for audience, whether it be Yahweh's advance declaration that the action is designed so that the Israelites will 'know that I am the LORD your God' (Ex. 6.7) and the Egyptians 'may know that the earth is the LORD's' (Ex. 7.5, 9.29), or whether it be the fact that Moses and Aaron perform their miracles 'before Pharaoh and his servants' (Ex. 7.10). And it was theatrical finally in that it pointed beyond itself, 'imitating' the future defeat of the Canaanites (Ex. 15.14–17) or, as the Christian Church has understood it, the yet greater liberation to be accomplished by Christ.[156]

The Bible puts the Exodus across like a series of staged scenes. If we want to speak of its *aesthetic* effect upon an audience, we may say that Exodus looks like a movie:

> Cecil B. De Mille's *The Ten Commandments*, with its mighty throng crossing the sea, may be truer to the intended literary effect of the Book of Exodus than scholarship's reconstruction of a band of minor tribes slipping through the marsh.[157]

But if we want to speak of the *moral experience* of the handful of individuals who took part in the events, we have to refer ourselves to the narrower field of history. Buber claims that,

> In order to gain a historically possible picture . . . we must very much reduce the numbers given about the departing of the tribes; which . . . does not affect the . . . importance of the event; for the inner history of Mankind can be grasped most easily in the actions and experiences of small groups.[158]

It is because the moral and historical experience of the drowning of a couple of 'frontier guards' and the escape of a few fugitives dramatised the relationship between human beings and God that it laid itself open to the full-blown theatricality of the textual version. The story of Exodus was probably gathered into coherence for liturgical recitation. We live with the outrageous comic exaggerations of the whole text, because this is the form in which it becomes the communal possession of a *revelation*.

Stage shifts are significant in the Pentateuch. The first, the expulsion from the Garden, is conceived as a movement down and thus away from God: that is, as a movement in space. With the promise to Abraham, the movement of the narrative becomes a guided search for a place whose rich abundance represents the fellowship of God and humanity. Although temporality is present, there is no story in the Pentateuch in which a *temporal* tension is uppermost. Time is relaxed and flows in the big loops of generations, not in tight knots. The audience of the ten-plagues cycle are not sitting on the edge of their seats waiting for the crucial moment *when* the movement of time will expose God's judgement upon the Pharaoh.

156 Ibid., p. 8.
157 Miles, *God: A Biography*, p. 104.
158 Buber, *Moses*, p. 74.

The issue is: 'let my people go', out of the prison of Egypt and into the promised land; that is, spatial liberation. The biblical heroes want long life: that is a sign of divine blessing. The length of their days focuses the tension in the movement toward that physical but never quite concretised promised land. In each of its scenes, the Pentateuchal narrative imagines the divine–human relationship in terms of place: the Garden stands for intimacy with God, the wanderings in the wilderness for evasion of God's instructions, and the promised land for the fellowship of God and humanity. The Passover circles round the fullness of the *thing*, not the *time*.

5. Leviticus, Numbers, Deuteronomy

Some redaction critics argue that Exodus contains a 'Deuteronomistic' theology, with a stress on forward, historical, movement and a God known only in his 'name' *and* a 'Priestly' theology, in which God is made thickly visible in the liturgical cycle.[159] The Deuteronomic and Priestly theologies are in 'unresolvable tension'.[160] This dramatic tension propels the story *both* around and forward. The story is not 'unilinear': we have both a forward historical movement, fulfilling the human desire for newness, and a cylical movement, in accordance with the human need for completed rhythm.

This forward somersault can be seen in the law codes of Leviticus, which are held at the ready for the people's entrance into the land. The sacrifices, of bulls, fowls, meal, the peace offerings, sin offerings, and uncleanliness offerings, detailed in the first six chapters, sound so tasty. The anti-gourmand's negative menus are loving in their precision: the fowls which it is an 'abomination' to consume, the eagle, ossifrage, osprey, vulture, kite, raven, owl, night hawk, cuckow, little owl, cormorant, great owl, swan, pelican, gier eagle, stork, heron, lapwing, and, not to forget, the bat, and likewise, the 'unclean' creeping things, the weasel, mouse, tortoise, ferret, chameleon, lizard, snail, and the mole. The people must keep 'the law of the beasts, and of the fowl, and of every living creature that moves in the waters, and of every creature that creepeth upon the earth' *because* 'ye shall be holy, for I am holy' (Lev. 11.44–45). They *will* also, once that forward movement has carried them into the land, be *good*, and generously so, leaving the 'gleanings' of their fields and vineyards 'for the poor and stranger' *because*, 'I am the Lord your God' (Lev. 19.9–10). The high-point of Leviticus is the conditional promise: 'If you walk in my statutes and observe my commandments and do them ... I will walk among you, and will be your God, and you shall be my people.' (Lev. 26.3, 12–46).[161]

Dozeman claims that the Deuteronomist imbues the theology of his final text with a 'relational' image of divine power: once the people Israel have an agency of their own, God has to 'persuade' them to come with him.[162] Let us investigate one example of this divine–human relationality, in the Book of Numbers. The method and momentum of the journey is described thus:

159 Brueggemann, *Theology of the Old Testament*, p. 425.
160 Ibid., p. 429.
161 Clines, *Theme of the Pentateuch*, p. 51.
162 Dozeman, *God at War*, p. 69.

So it was alway: the cloud covered it by day, and the appearance of fire by night.

And when the cloud was taken up from the tabernacle, then after that the children of Israel journeyed: and in the place where the cloud abode, there the children of Israel pitched their tents.

At the commandment of the Lord the children of Israel journeyed, and at the commandment of the Lord they pitched: as long as the cloud abode upon the tabernacle they rested in their tents.

And when the cloud tarried long upon the tabernacle many days, then the children of Israel kept the charge and journeyed not.

And so it was, when the cloud was a few days upon the tabernacle; according to the commandment of the Lord they abode in their tents, and according to the commandment of the Lord they journeyed.

And so it was, when the cloud abode from even until the morning, and that the cloud was taken up in the morning, then they journeyed: whether it was by day or night that the cloud was taken up, they journeyed.

Or when it was two days or a month, or a year, that the cloud tarried upon the tabernacle, remaining thereon, the children of Israel abode in their tents, and journeyed not: but when it was taken up, they journeyed.

At the commandment of the Lord they rested in the tents, and at the commandment of the Lord they journeyed: they kept the charge of the Lord, by the commandment of the Lord at the hand of Moses. (Num. 9.16–23)

Then, in Numbers 10.11, as Clines says, 'the movement actually begins': 'on the twentieth day of the second month, in the second year ... the cloud was taken up from off the tabernacle of the testimony', and off the Children of Israel went. They are not embarking on a 'voyage into the void, but expressly, as Moses says to Hobab, a "setting out for the place of which Yahweh said, 'I will give it to you'.""[163] The people are dependent for their map reading and speed on the movement of the Lord. They also passively receive their food from God, until:

the mixt multitude that was among them fell a lusting: and the children of Israel also wept again, and said, 'Who shall give us flesh to eat?

We remember the fish, which we did eat in Egypt, freely; the cucumbers, and the melons and the leeks, and the onions, and the garlick;

But now our soul is dried away: there is nothing at all, beside this manna, before our eyes.'

And the manna was as coriander seed, and the colour thereof as the colour of bdellium.

And the people went about, and gathered it, and ground it in mills, or beat it in a mortar, and baked it in pans, and made cakes of it: and the taste of it was as the taste of fresh oil.

And when the dew fell upon the camp in the night the manna fell upon it. (Num. 11.4–9)

We want a change from bread from heaven every single morning, day in and day out, they kibitz. *We want meat with onions and garlick!*:

Even miracles become boring, often enough repeated ... We smile, too, at their ... short memories, the suppression that is an essential part of humour. 'We remember the fish = We've forgotten the slavery' (note the beautifully ironic 'that we ate for nothing'!).[164]

163 Clines, *Theme of the Pentatuech*, pp. 54–55.
164 Landy, 'Humour as a Tool', p. 113.

The satirical narrator has a light touch: he does not remind us what the Israelites were eating until after their complaint. God interacts with the request by telling the people they are going to eat 'flesh', 'until it come out of your nostrils' (Num. 11.20):

> there went forth a wind from the LORD, and brought quails from the sea, and let them fall by the camp, as it were a day's journey on this side, and as it were a day's journey on the other side, round about the camp, and as it were two cubits high upon the earth. (Num. 11.31)

Then God boils over:

> And the people stood up all that day, and all that night, and all the next day, and they gathered the quails: he that gathered least gathered ten homers . . . And while the flesh was yet between, ere it was chewed, the wrath of the LORD was kindled against the people, and the LORD smote the people with a very great plague. (Num. 11.32–33)

A people surfeited with a fixed menu of manna are not suffering too horribly in their passivity. A motif of the middle half of the Pentateuch is food, sacrificial food, unclean food, magical manna from heaven, and food cravings with which God does not comply.

Miles hints that the God of this biblical book is a 'whiny' number, like his dialogue partners:

> He complains endlessly about their complaining . . . a certain symmetry may be seen, never more clearly than in the Book of Numbers, as Israel complains about Moses, Moses complains about Israel, God complains about Israel, Israel complains about God, God complains about Moses, and Moses complains about God.[165]

Numbers 14 exhibits such whining, as the people weep to have died in Egypt, and God threatens them with death in the wilderness for their ingratitude. It is not too difficult to conceive of the right sort of *people* for dramatic comedy: so long as one remembers that human beings have stomachs *and* dream of other worlds, one will stay on the right track. In Numbers, the stomachs often get the upper hand. The hard part is to imagine the right sort of God. A God too pleasantly relational to overrule disobedience with irascible counter-measures would lose the drama. A God who could not be relied upon would lose the security required for comedy. If a theologian dramatises the story of a moral God who, with irascible patience, delivers a resoundingly recalcitrant people, the result is a comedy.

With this God behind them, the people are invincibly blessed. Balak, King of the Moabites, sees the people advancing toward Jericho, and messages Balaam to 'curse me this people' (Num. 22.6); God countermands the order so Balaam returns a refusal (Num. 22.12–13). Balak sends weightier princes: 'don't let anything stop you from coming to curse this people' (22.16–17). Balaam awaits further instructions, from the Israelite God: stay the night, and we'll see, he says.

---

165 Miles, *God: A Biography*, pp. 132–133.

> God came unto Balaam at night and said unto him, If the men come to call
> thee, rise up, and go with them; but yet the word which I shall say to thee,
> that shalt thou do. (22.20)

Balaam sets off, on his ass; God's illogical irritation with his compliance
takes shape as an angel:

> And the ass saw the angel of the Lord standing in the way, and his sword
> drawn in his hand: and the ass turned aside out of the way, and went into the
> field, and Balaam smote the ass, to turn her into the way.
> But the angel of the Lord stood in a path of the vineyards, a wall being on
> this side, and a wall on that side.
> And when the ass saw the angel of the Lord, she thrust herself unto the wall,
> and crushed Balaam's foot against the wall: and he smote her again.
> And the angel of the Lord went further, and stood in a narrow place, where
> there was no way to turn either to the right hand or to the left.
> And when the ass saw the angel of the Lord, she fell down under Balaam,
> and Balaam's anger was kindled, and he smote the ass with a staff. (Num.
> 22.23–27)

When the ass speaks God's word to Balaam, she comes out with the most
asinine, wet, pleading and 'whiny' complaint in Numbers,

> the Lord opened the mouth of the ass, and she said unto Balaam, 'What have
> I done unto thee, that thou hast smitten me these three times?'
> Balaam said unto the ass, 'Because thou hast mocked me: I would there were
> a sword in mine hand, for now would I kill thee.' (Num. 22.28–29)

The passive-aggressive ass talks exactly as an ass would, if it could: *What
did I ever do to you?*

> 'Am not I thine ass, upon which thou hast ridden ever since I was thine unto
> this day. Was I ever wont to do so unto thee?' And he said, 'Nay.'
> Then the Lord opened the eyes of Balaam, and he saw the angel of the Lord
> standing in the way, and his sword drawn in his hand: and he fell flat on his
> face.
> And the angel of the Lord said unto him, 'Wherefore hast thou smitten thine
> ass these three times? behold, I went out to withstand thee, because thy way
> is perverse before me:
> And the ass saw me, and turned from me these three times: unless she had
> turned from me, surely I now also I had slain thee, and saved her alive.'
> And Balaam said unto the angel of the Lord, 'I have sinned; for I knew not
> that thou stoodest in the way against me: now therefore, if it displease thee, I
> will get me back again.' (Num. 22.30–34)

God's death threat, obstructed and imparted by the ass, was, as it seems,
just a reminder:

> But the angel of the Lord said unto Balaam, 'Go with the men: but only the
> word that I shall speak unto thee, that thou shalt speak.' So Balaam went
> with the princes of Balak. (Num. 22.35)

Rendered dumb by the beast, Balaam tells his king, 'I've come, but so
what?': 'have I now any power at all to say anything? the word that God
putteth into my mouth, that shall I speak' (22.38). An altar is prepared for
the cursing, and as they stand, king, princes and prophet of Moab, by the
'burnt sacrifice', Balaam asks:

How shall I curse, whom God hath not cursed? or how shall I defy, whom
the Lord hath not defied?
For from the tops of the rocks I see him, and from the hills I behold him; lo,
the people shall dwell alone, and shall not be reckoned among the nations.
Who can count the dust of Jacob, and the number of the fourth part of Israel.
Let me die the death of the righteous, and let my last end be like his! (Num.
23.8–10)

Balak complains, I told you to curse and you blessed! Balaam goes on:
Jacob is unenchantable; there is no divinising against Israel (Num. 23.23).
Balak says, 'don't bless or curse': just shut up if this is your magic; but, says
Balaam, 'All that the Lord speaketh, that I must do'. They try it again, on
another mountain, and on another, and Balaam again describes the
beauteous plenty forthcoming to Israel. Balak whines: 'I told you to curse,
and three times you have blessed' (Num. 24.10).

By the end of Numbers, the people are in sight of their good. The
fulfilled good is existence: for Deuteronomy, 'to live is to subsist on the soil
that the Living God has chosen for Himself'.[166] The good life in relation to
God is not an abstraction:

> *Holiness is ... linked to the concreteness of material existence in the world.* Israel
> understands that full, whole life, life intended by Yahweh, requires land: a
> safe, fruitful, secure, productive place of one's own ... Israel testifies ... that
> Yahweh ... is a giver of land. Never again in the testimony of Israel will the
> sovereignty of Yahweh be separated from the legitimacy of land. The two are
> joined by the concreteness and specificity of utterance that has the force of
> oath.[167]

And yet, the Israelites do not gain their gift, and closure is not made upon
the promise. The full presence of this 'material existence' is postponed: the
Pentateuch shows 'a movement toward goals yet to be realized'.[168] Its
authors make the good concrete enough for the audience to put their hands
on it: but it remains incommensurable with the facts. The Pentateuch shows
God and humanity in the ethical relation of dialogue. Martin Buber defines
the Sinai covenant as 'a holy action performed which *institutes sacramentally
a reciprocity between the One above and the one below*'.[169] Reciprocity between
God and human beings is constituted by responsiveness, the creation of
mutuality, or likeness, or analogy in being. There is no comedy without the
trust that help is forthcoming. The biblical story shows not 'an' analogy of
being between God and humanity but an 'analogy brought into being', in
the dialogue between God and human beings. The conversation is inside
space and place: the Good which is God is incarnated in edible imagery:

> For the Lord thy God bringeth thee into a good land, a land of brooks of
> water, of fountains and depths that spring out of valleys and hills;
> A land of wheat, and barley, and vines, and fig trees, and pomegranates; a
> land of olive oil, and honey;

166 Robert Martin-Achard, *From Death To Life*, p. 7.
167 Brueggemann, *Theology of the Old Testament*, pp. 168–169.
168 Clines, *Theme of the Pentateuch*, p. 27.
169 Martin Buber, *The Kingship of God*, translated from the third German edition by
    Richard Schiemann (George Allen & Unwin, London, 1967), p. 123.

> A land wherein thou shalt eat bread without scarceness, thou shalt not lack any thing in it; a land whose stones are iron, and out of whose hills thou mayest dig brass.
> When thou hast eaten and art full, then thou shalt bless the Lord thy God for the good land which he hath given thee. (Deut. 8.7–10)

Walking in 'life', or living in the land, is being related to God:

> See I have set before thee this day life and good, and death and evil;
> In that I command thee this day to love the Lord thy God, to walk in his ways, and to keep his commandments and his statutes and his judgements, that thou mayest live and multiply: and the Lord thy God shall bless thee in the land whither thou goest to posssess it. (Deut. 30.15–16)

The people are enjoined to inhabit the Good; 'doing the good' is the basic analogy for the activity of being God. The analogy brought into being *is* drama, an acted analogy between God and his creatures, which God is in the course of constructing, in the biblical history. In the Garden, the analogy was junctive, although the possibilities for division were there. Afterwards, the analogy is created from a greater distance. With God's promises to Abraham, which are taken up again in the Wilderness journey, the symbol of divine–human relationship becomes the land; this is the *place* in which the relationship *will* take effect. That place and relationship are not fully grasped, in the Pentateuch.

I proposed that comedy has three levels: infernal, purgatorial and paradisial. The notion of the biblical as generically comic cannot work without a differentiation of levels; otherwise we will flatten the drama, or make a single sweeping curve out of it. The biblical narrative begins with God's opening 'fiats'. Eden is a locality close to heaven. From Genesis 3, the drama spirals around and away from heaven. In the Pentateuch, we travel through various *purgatorial* regions.

3

The Theatre of Old Testament History:
Political Comedy from Judges to Samuel

1. Judges

a. Historical Background, Composition and Theological Theme

What made Israel *a single sociological entity*? One answer has been located in the political unrest in Canaan in the era of transition between the Bronze and the Iron Ages. Two groups had entered the scene. One was the Philistine 'sea peoples', who poured into Transjordan and Palestine during the thirteenth century BC.[1] The other was the *'Apiru*. The *'Apiru*, or 'dusty ones', were 'donkey caravaneers' of the late Iron Age.[2] We learn of them from the correspondence between numerous Canaanite vassal kings and their Egyptian Pharaoh. The Canaanite side of the Amarna Letters contain querulous references to the *'Apiru* and the 'SA.GAZ'; and stern memoranda from the Managing God to the god-kinglets to hold the fort. To King Rib-Addi, in Byblos, 'Why have you sat [back] and done nothing so that the GAZ, the dog, takes your cities?'[3] Eighteen Canaanite kinglets, in cities from Byblos to Quatna, complain of or are rebuked for unrest caused by the *'Apiru*. *'Apiru*, usually transliterated as *habiru*, is cognate with Hebrew: perhaps the political disturbances to which the Amarna Letters attest are the historical parallel to the narratives of Judges and Samuel.

According to George Mendenhall, Israel underwent an extraordinary ethical experience after its escape from Egypt: the 'withering away of the state', in its liberation from peoples whose human kings were gods. Israel had no human king; its only king was Yahweh. It called the experience of *extra-political* and *personal* solidarity among equals under Yahweh the 'Sinai Covenant'. If the king is a god, the state is a power structure. If God is king, the society is 'egalitarian':[4]

> When the 'new' God of freedom and justice is accepted as covenant partner, the totalitarian, hierarchical social order is no longer necessary . . . the Israelite

---

1 George Mendenhall, *The Tenth Generation: The Origins of the Biblical Tradition* (Johns Hopkins University Press, Baltimore, 1973), p. 150.
2 Robert G. Boling, *Judges: Introduction, Translation, Commentary*, Anchor Bible Series 6a (Doubleday & Company, New York, 1969), p. 14.
3 Mendenhall, *Tenth Generation*, p. 124.
4 Ibid., p. 23.

order from Moses until the time of David, 1250–1000 B.C., represents a sociological experiment to determine if a society is possible when not sanctioned
and protected by the imperial gods.[5]

On this analysis, the ʿApiru became a single sociological entity by virtue of
a 'religioethical transcending of all tribal–political contrasts',[6] which flowed
from the experience and the practice of the Kingship of Yahweh. Israel was
one because the Sinai covenant had made it 'the earthly half of the kingdom
of Yahweh'.[7] Judges transposes into narrative the historical experience of a
'peasant revolt':[8] for Yahwism had not done with regicide *qua* Baal-bashing
when it emerged in Palestine.

The biblical books can be arranged according to their degree of 'disorder' or 'design': they are 'disorderly' when the authors have to synthesise
'the recalcitrant facts of known history' with 'the divine promise'; design
takes over when the facts are rather less palpable, as in Daniel.[9] The *habiru*
emerged in Palestine between the thirteenth and the eleventh centuries BC;
their progress was probably quite disorderly. For the authors of Judges,
the 'recalcitrant fact' is Israel's struggle to possess the land of Palestine.
The Philistine 'sea peoples' had two advantages over both the aboriginal
inhabitants and the *habiru*: they had camels, which are swifter and less
timid than donkeys, and they had entered the Iron Age ahead of their
Bronze-Age competitors. Joseph Heller's David explains that:

> we still had to learn from bitter experience with the Philistines that iron was
> harder than bronze and that a double-edged straight sword with a point
> was superior to our short hook-shaped ones sharpened just on the outside.
> That's the main reason you find us doing so much smiting all through the
> Pentateuch, and so little thrusting, hurling and shooting. Smiting is just about
> all you can do with an axe or a club or a curved sword molded like a sickle.[10]

Traditional critics believe that the history made its way into a body of
legends, by way of an 'oral narrative tradition'; the legends were written
down during Josiah's Reform, in the seventh century.[11] Recent critics focus
on the Deuteronomic 'tradents' who made a final edition during the Exile
or soon after the return. One can read Judges backwards, for the original
act of historical imagination which turned experience into narrative, or
forwards, for the act of aesthetic imagination which related the narrative to
an intended audience consisting of Israelites in exile.

If the theme of the Pentateuch is God's shepherding the people toward a
promised land which remains beyond their grasp, that of the Deuteronomistic History is what the people of Israel do with their freedom, once they
have gained the land. The post-exilic editors had good reason to think
about whether Israel had made the best use of its political freedom. The

---

5 Walter Brueggemann, 'Trajectories in Old Testament Literature and the Sociology of
  Ancient Israel', *Journal of Biblical Literature*, 98/2, 1979, 161–185 (167).
6 Mendenhall, *Tenth Generation*, p. 157.
7 Boling, *Judges*, p. 24.
8 Ibid., p. 12.
9 Alter, *Art of Biblical Narrative*, pp. 33–34.
10 Heller, *God Knows*, p. 84; cf. Mendenhall, *Tenth Generation*, p. 188.
11 Boling, *Judges*, p. 11.

Deuteronomist lays out a history in order to set out a political theology. The twelve tribes do not yet have secure tenure in the land. There is no hereditary monarchy: the Judges are individual 'deliverers' chosen by God, who sometimes marks this choice by breathing his spirit into them. There are foreshadowings of the temptations of monarchy. The moral framework for monarchy is set out in Deuteronomy 17.14–17:

> When thou art come into the land which the Lord thy God giveth thee, and shalt possess it, and shalt dwell therein, and shalt say, 'I will set a king over me, like as all the nations that are about me';
> Thou shalt in any wise set him king over thee, whom the Lord thy God shall choose: one from among thy brethren shalt thou set king over thee: thou mayest not set a stranger over thee, which is not thy brother.
> But he shall not multiply horses to himself, nor cause the people to return to Egypt, to the end that he should multiply horses: forasmuch as the Lord hath said unto you, 'Ye shall henceforth return no more that way.'

One will become disoriented if one imagines that the Book of Judges is about judges and the books of Samuel are about 'kings'. There are kings in Judges and judges in Samuel.

b. *The Text*
Othniel, Ehud, Deborah, Gideon, Tola, Jair, Ibzan, Elon, Abdon, Jephthah and Samson are the Judges. A sign that the editor is drawing on a body of legends is that he records not only the leaders who have stories attached to their names but also complete aesthetic nonentities. Von Rad claims that each of the Judges' stories shows a 'falling gradient', the inverted ∩ of tragedy: moreover

> The call is followed immediately by the public proof of the *charisma* effected by means of a victory over the enemy; but then the line curves steeply downwards. The one who was a special instrument of Yahweh's will in history falls into sin, degradation, or some other disaster. Thus these little narrative complexes ... have as their background a ... pessimistic conception of the charismatic leader. But for a moment was he able, in virtue of his charisma, to rise above the limitations of his being, only then simply to get himself more deeply entangled in deadly chaos.[12]

Von Rad thinks that deficiency at the centre of the lives of the Judges is the Deuteronomist's way of showing that it is not a human being but God who is the military protagonist in these wars of conquest.

Josipovici uncovers in the characters of the Judges little of the free will which 'Moses or Isaiah' had: one is 'asked ... to think of' its 'figures as like mechanical puppets with the electricity running down'.[13] Judges begins on the lower slopes of purgatory, and slides into an infernal comedy. If some of the Judge-Deliverers come across like automated machines that is because we are half-way to infernal comedy. People who behave like mechanical toys can be amusing, to a cold eye. There is something funny about the strict obedience of mechanical toys to instructions, keeping to

---

12 Von Rad, *Old Testament Theology I*, p. 329.
13 Josipovici, *Book of God*, pp. 121 and 123.

their logic when the mechanism goes wrong, particularly when that happens to someone else. One of the theories of comedy which has recommended itself to biblical critics is that set out by Henri Bergson in *Le Rire*. Bergson considered that people become laughable when they behave like machines: when we are expecting the 'flexibility' of a human being, we get a windup toy which cannot stop repeating itself.[14] Bergson says that 'the vice which makes us comical is one which we carry on the outside, like a frame into which we are inserted':[15] a figure of fun is stuck inside a self-moving contraption which keeps to its logic whatever the consequences. There are children's books in which knowledge of a secret verbal formula is all-important. Access to the source of power, which can be liberating *or* disastrous, is through the 'Open Sesame'. The characters of Judges possess, or are pursued by, an ineluctable Word.

Readers since Sir Flinders Petrie have depreciated the 'savage retaliations' portrayed in the book.[16] Josipovici finds the horrible tales of the deaths of the enemy leaders in Judges 'sinister'.[17] Each of the Judges has a simple task and the straight-forward adventure of helping their people to hold their ground against the Canaanite tribes. The narrator gives as much of an external view of the enemy as the old-fashioned Cowboy and Indian movies did. The battles and the murders are gruesome; the reader is no more asked to identify with the fallen than the audiences of John Wayne movies were with the 'Injuns'. But a tale of the struggles of purely good against absolutely evil can be either an amoral glorification of conquest, or morally banal, as when the Injuns become the purely good, in *Dances with Wolves*. The Deuteronomist history recognises the incommensurability of the goods which the Israelites eventually achieved. Some of the stories in Judges work on the level of 'how the West was won': but failure creeps in, and, with it, authorial satire. The weapon of authorial satire is the same as that employed by the heroes: the magical word.

On a first reading, the overarching pattern of the history of Judges is repetitive. Much of the story is told *in nuce* in the first two chapters of the book. God intended to give the Israelites the land of Palestine in its entirety. When the Israelite tribes entered Palestine, they neglected God's injunction to expel all of the native tribes, the Philistines, Canaanites, Perizzites, Jebusites and Midianites. Because the Israelites have intermingled and intermarried with these peoples, and have not, as he ordered, thrown down the altars of Baal (Judg. 2.2), these tribes will be, says God, 'a thorn in your sides' (2.3). Hereafter, the 'five lords of the Philistines, and all the Canaanites, and the Sidonians, and the Hivites' will be used by God to test and to teach those who had not learned the arts of 'war', and as a trial in keeping the Mosaic commandments (3.1–3). When the Israelites prove weak, God hands them over to one of their enemies. In Judges 3.4–11, the

---

14 Henri Bergson, *Le Rire: Essai sur la signification du comique* (Presses Universitaires de France, Paris, 1947), p. 8.
15 Ibid., p. 11.
16 Petrie described 'The invasion of the nomad horde of Israelites on the high civilization of the Amorite kings' as a 'crushing blow to all culture and advance in the arts; like the terrible breaking up of the Roman Empire by the northern races.' Quoted in Boling, *Judges*, p. 9.
17 Josipovici, *Book of God*, p. 125.

Israelites worship alien gods, are conquered by the Mesopotamian king, Chushanrishathaim, serve him eight years; they cry to God for help; he raises Othniel; when he goes to do battle, 'the Spirit of the Lord came upon' him; God 'delivers' Chushanrishathaim into Othniel's 'hand'; 'And the land had rest forty years'. The story of Othniel is a brief version of the bulk of the subsequent tales in Judges. Von Rad wondered whether the Deuteronomist had not given way to the 'ancient East's cyclical way of thinking',[18] so stereotyped is the rhythm of episodes which he finds in the book. There are detours from this simple rhythm. There are not only external but also internal threats to the peace of the land, for example. The Othniel story 'establishes a norm which can then be undermined'.[19] Many of the deviations make matters worse; the deliverance is less and less complete. Perhaps what we have is a circle which, like a line, is going somewhere: that is, a downward spiral. It may be better to revise the theory that biblical thought is linear than to regard the spirals as misplaced. If the plot movement in Judges is a downward spiral, that might indicate that charismatic theocracy could not create political cohesion.

Most of the deliverers are unlikely characters. Israel is weak, *vis-à-vis* its overlords, and so are its leaders, when they enter the scene. The narrator makes the enemy tribes and their armies vastly to outnumber the Israelites, in force of arms, and maybe they did. Charismatic deliverers often conquer by a trick. If the audience is fascinated by the clever device by which the alien overlords are outmanoeuvred, then the Spirit-led Judges may have more personal agency than some readers have assigned to them. The task of each of the heroes and heroines is to test their ingenuity against an enemy. In the Deuteronomist's rendition of the original legends, the Israelites are the underdogs and the surrounding tribes their masters. The tales of the Judges have been called 'resistance stories',[20] written to be read either by luckless Babylonian exiles or by the not much more happier returnees of 520. D. M. Gunn comments that 'beyond the end' of the Othniel story

> and the book and the larger story of which it is a part stands its contemporary audience, most likely Judean, in Mesopotamia ... For them the model story of Judah and its Mesopotamian oppressor must have conveyed an especially poignant irony.[21]

The ethos is that of comedy, sharpened by the situation of 'resistance': the underdog victors require the virtues of bravery, quick thinking and discretion; the vices are cowardice and treachery.

The rhythm of the book tells its audience what to expect: after Othniel dies, the people 'do evil' and therefore God 'strengthened Eglon King of Moab'. The Israelite tribes 'serve' Eglon eighteen years, cry to God for a deliverer, and God 'raises' Ehud. Ehud is a left-handed Benjamite. But 'by him the children of Israel sent a present unto Eglon the king of Moab' (3.15).

---

18 Von Rad, *Old Testament Theology I*, p. 330.
19 David M. Gunn, 'Joshua and Judges', in *The Literary Guide to the Bible*, edited by Robert Alter and Frank Kermode (Fontana Press, London, 1987), pp. 102–121 (105).
20 James A. Wharton, 'The Secret of Yahweh: Story and Affirmation in Judges 13–16', *Interpretation*, 27, 1973, 48–65 (54).
21 Gunn, 'Joshua and Judges', p. 113.

The Israelites only intend to use Ehud to deliver the tribute of a subject people to Moab. But the 'present' is literally double-edged: the word is a grim joke. On his own initiative,

> Ehud made him a dagger which had two edges, of a cubit length; and he did gird it under his raiment upon his right thigh.
>
> And he brought the present unto Eglon king of Moab: and Eglon was a very fat man.
>
> And when he had made an end to offer the present, he sent away the people that bare the present.
>
> But he himself turned again from the quarries that were by Gilgal, and said, 'I have a secret errand unto thee, O king': who said, 'Keep silence'. And all that stood by him went out from him.
>
> And Ehud came unto him; and he was sitting in a summer parlour, which he had for himself alone. And Ehud said, 'I have a message from God unto thee.' And he arose out of his seat.
>
> And Ehud put forth his left hand, and took the dagger from his right thigh, and thrust it into his belly.
>
> And the haft also went in after the blade; and the fat closed upon the blade, so that he could not draw the dagger out of his belly; and the dirt came out. (Judg. 3.16–22)

The elephantine Eglon is passive throughout the scene, engineered into defencelessness by Ehud. Ehud gets him alone in his private 'summer parlour' by means of his 'secret errand', about which Eglon makes a fatally false assumption. Both words and people have more than one side. Having discerned that Eglon's soft spot is his belly, the left-handed Ehud strikes unexpectedly from the 'wrong' side. Ehud saw that all kings are mortal: 'you can die' is the 'message from God' which he has for Eglon. Words have an uncanny valence in Judges; *Dabar* can mean either 'word' or 'thing'. Gunn discusses the interchange between the two:

> Ehud, truly YHWH's person . . . turns back (*shub*, 'return', 'repent'!) from The Images (or Idols, Pesilim, KJV: 'quarries') near Gilgal. 'I have a secret *davar* for you, king', he says (3.19); and Eglon, expecting perhaps an oracle (*davar*, 'word') from the gods near Gilgal, commands 'Silence!' Ehud's restatement confirms expectation: 'I have a divine word [*devar-'elohim*] for you' (v. 20). But the reader reads differently: the 'divine word' (or 'word of the gods') is rather the 'word of God [YHWH]', or then again, as Ehud draws his sword, it becomes a 'thing' (*davar*) of God. Like the sword which Ehud made for himself, his words are two-edged ('and [the sword] had two mouths,' v. 16). Thus against expectation is Ehud secured by a 'word' that does indeed, for him, spell silence. And so Ehud 'passes beyond the Idols' (v. 26) and YHWH delivers Israel.[22]

Having gained time by locking the doors behind him when he slips away, Ehud rouses the people to the slaughter of leaderless Moab: 'And the land had rest fourscore years' (Judg. 3.29–30).

On cue, at Ehud's death, the Israelites do evil: God sells them 'into the hand of Jabin king of Canaan'. Jabin is not the main adversary in this story: it is his captain, Sisera, with his nine hundred *iron* chariots, who is the figure of awe and the oppressor in the Israelites' eyes. Deborah, 'a pro-

---

22 Ibid., pp. 115–116.

phetess', is the Judge in Israel. Her name means 'honey bee';[23] though she may sting like one, Barak will lead her armies. She tells him that his masculine pride will not be augmented by their victory, for 'the Lord will sell Sisera into the hand of a woman' (Judg. 4.9). The prophetess and her captain take ten thousand men to Mount Tabor. On 'the edge' of Barak's 'sword', God forces Sisera to run away on foot, a comedown for a man with nine hundred chariots. In his thirsty flight, he reaches Heber the Kenite's tent. Sisera is enticed inside by the soothing words of Heber's wife, Jael: 'turn in, my lord, turn in to me, fear not'. She wants him in her tent. Maternally, 'she covered him with a mantle', and gave him a drink of milk (4.18–19). Sisera is unwary: he is used to giving orders:

> Again he said unto her, 'Stand in the door of the tent, and it shall be, when any man doth come and enquire of thee, and say, "Is there any man here?" that thou shalt say, "No."'
> Then Jael Heber's wife took a nail of the tent, and took a hammer in her hand, and went softly unto him, and smote the nail into his temples, and fastened it into the ground: for he was fast asleep and weary. So he died.
> (Judg. 4.20–21)

As in Judges 3, the narrative describes the scene of the tyrant's death with a cold and naturalistic eye. Having nursed Sisera into sleep, Jael uses a bit of imagination to see the weapon that is available to a lone woman in a tent. She hammers it right into the ground, through his skull: an unusual but precise use of a tent peg. The author's laconic comment about the heroine's prudent gesture is not negative: 'So God subdued on that day Jabin the king of Canaan before the children of Israel' (Judg. 4.23).

Ehud and Jael are pragmatists in desperate situations; they are heroes and heroines on the lower reaches of a purgatorial comedy. In the assassinations of Eglon and Sisera, the narrator does not romanticise violence but spells out how the deed of death is done. This is underdog comedy: the humour must be cold, rather than hot-blooded; laughter at death is grim. The *battles* of the book of Judges, the slayings of tens of thousands, have no particular human hero. Particular deaths are not described in the battle scenes, as they are in Homer's *Iliad*. Military strength is not glamorised. Israel's God achieves the victory in the battles. The Israelite heroes and heroines do not do *nothing*: it is for them to find the chink in their enemy's vast armoury.

A modern archaeological dig at Megiddo indicates that the city of Taanach was razed in 1125: it might be that the Song of Deborah records the destruction of this Canaanite city.[24] Together with Barak, Deborah sings the most extended, and the most bloodthirsty, monologue given to a woman in the Bible. In the prose story, the characters made use of whatever small thing came to hand; in Deborah's poem, the forces of nature quail as God marches into battle. In the first section, God swoops into the scene, from on 'high':

> Lord, when thou wentest out of Seir, when thou marchest out on the field of Edom, the earth trembled, and the heavens dropped, the clouds also dropped water.

23 Boling, *Judges*, p. 94.
24 Ibid., p. 116.

> The mountains melted from before the Lord, even that Sinai from before the
> Lord God of Israel. (Judg. 5.4–5)

The all-powerful God enlists the earth, clouds and mountains as his
weapons; the people of Israel, sneak along the smallest paths. In the second
section, we see how 'low' the people are:

> In the days of Shamgar the son of Anath, in the days of Jael, the highways
> were unoccupied, and the travellers walked through byways.
> The inhabitants of the villages ceased, they ceased in Israel, until that I
> Deborah arose, a mother in Israel. (Judg. 5.6–7)

The courage of Zebulun and Naphtali is praised, but not their skill in warfare. The stars and the 'ancient river' of Kishon are the heroes of this battle.
The only human being to be praised is the 'woman in the tent'. Jael's exploit
is pictured once again:

> He asked water, and she gave him milk; she brought forth butter in a lordly
> dish.
> She put forth her hand to the nail, and her right hand to the workmen's
> hammer; and with the hammer she smote Sisera, she smote off his head,
> when she had pierced and stricken through his temples.
> At her feet he bowed, he fell, he lay down: at her feet he bowed, he fell: where
> he bowed, there he fell down dead. (Judg. 5.25–27)

Jael does not just nail the head to the ground, but swings it in the air. Now
the low rise high above their masters. In the prose narrative, Sisera died
recumbent; here he bows before Jael, three times. The hymn has more of
the subjective exaltation of victory than mere reportage:

> The mother of Sisera looked out at a window, and cried through the lattice:
> 'Why is his chariot so long in coming? why tarry the wheels of his chariot?'
> Her wise ladies answered her, yea, she returned answer to herself,
> 'Have they not sped? have they not divided the prey; to every man a damsel
> or two; to Sisera a prey of divers colours, a prey of divers colours of needle-
> work, of divers colours of needlework on both sides, meet for the necks of
> them that take the spoil?'
> So let all thine enemies perish, O Lord, but let them that love thee be as the
> sun when he goeth forth in his might. And the land had rest forty years.
> (Judg. 5.28–31)

Sisera's mother *must* be an ambitious dreamer – imagining her son delayed
by dividing up the Israelite spoils, seizing the women and their handiwork
– when we know he has been killed by a woman. Where the punishment
fits the crime we have a dark comedy. The subjected Israelites and the conquering Canaanites exchange places: the fantasies of the strong will be
rudely replaced with humiliation; the low will swing up into the heavens
like the sun.

But, like a Jack-in-the-box working in reverse,

> the children of Israel did evil in the sight of the Lord: and the Lord delivered
> them into the hand of Midian seven years.
> And the hand of Midian prevailed against Israel: and because of the
> Midianites the children of Israel made them the dens which are in the moun-
> tains, and caves, and strongholds. (Judg. 6.1–2)

Von Rad believed that

> The story of Gideon's war against the Midianites pushes this idea of the all-sufficiency of Jahweh's action to the furthest ... extreme – Jahweh had given orders to reduce the number of the fighting men, and then he only stationed those left around about the enemy's camp ... The miracle came down from above, as it were into a vacuum – so rigorously does the narrator exclude the idea of any human co-operation.[25]

The Midianites try to force the Israelites out, driving them into the wildernesses and destroying their livelihood. The narrator depicts with heroic exaggeration the consuming Midianite hordes:

> And they came up with their cattle and their tents, and they came as grasshoppers for multitude; for both they and their camels were without number: and they entered into the land to destroy it. (Judg. 5.5)

The Israelites 'cried unto the Lord' (5.6). God sends an angel to call Gideon to be their leader. So many Israelites enlist that they may congratulate themselves, rather than thanking God, if they win. God tells Gideon to send the cowards home. That disperses twenty-two thousand. God wants a further troop cull: as the Israelites ford the river on the way to meet the Amalekites and the Midianites, 'whose camels are without number, as the sand by the sea-side' (7.12), some of the Israelites cup the water with their hands, others lap the water like dogs. God orders ten thousand more to depart, retaining for the holy war the dog lappers. Boling thinks he has kept back those who lie down without thinking to guard their rear, enlarging the scope for his own action, by employing 'those less suitable for a military enterprise'.[26] But maybe God selected the men who instinctively did not put their swords down, even when they were drinking: the doglappers. Gideon is not sure whether his three hundred *mannerless fighting men* will terrify the enemy as much as they do him. A Gideon with no stomach for this battle could not have achieved the victory: just in the way that Athena suggests a ruse to Odysseus, so Yahweh orders Gideon to make a nocturnal recce into the enemy camp. He hears a man telling his dream: a Midianite tent is overturned when a 'moldly barley bread'[27] hits it. Gideon's shakes are dispelled by this description of his troop. His 'hand' 'strengthened', Gideon divides his men into three companies, telling each man to carry a trumpet, and a torch inside an empty pottery urn. They may be few, but, Gideon reckons, they can make quite a spectacle and a tremendous din.

> And the three companies blew the trumpets, and brake the pitchers, and held the lamps in their left hands, and the trumpets in their right hands to blow withal: and they cried, 'The sword of the Lord, and of Gideon.'

> And the three hundred blew the trumpets, and the Lord set every man's sword against his fellow, even throughout all the host: and the host fled to Beth-shittah in Zererath, and to the border of Abelmeholah, unto Tabbath. (Judg. 7.20 and 22)

25 Von Rad, *Old Testament Theology I*, pp. 328–329.
26 Boling, *Judges*, pp. 145–146.
27 Boling's translation, ibid., p. 146.

As the Midianites run for their lives, the tribes of Naphtali, Asher and Manasseh pursue them: Gideon sends for the Ephraimites, who capture the Midianite princes. Rather than risk all of the Israelite tribes in one battle, God has held them in reserve, showing himself to be a fine military strategist. Gideon, his lieutenant, conceived for himself the piece of theatre through which the encamped Midianites are induced to flee for their lives. The author of Judges has constructed a subtle theological synthesis between the all-powerful God and the devious military intelligence of his chosen: rather than finding in Gideon a 'vacuum' through whom God's miracle has been worked, I would call it God 50 per cent and Gideon 50 per cent. Both of them exercised imagination about facts.

Now Gideon should die, the people do evil, and God give them into foreign domination. Instead, looking ahead to Saul's opening chapter to the Monarchy, we see the regression to the temptation not to be a people, but to be a *family*, that is, the temptation to a hereditary and tribal monarchy. The words by which the plot descends from the highpoint of victory over the Midianites are Gideon's own. Gideon asks the cornered Midianite princes,

> 'What manner of men were they whom ye slew at Tabor?' And they answered, 'As thou art, so were they; each one resembled the *children of a king*.'
> And he said, 'They were my brethren, even the sons of my mother: as the Lord liveth, if ye had saved them alive, I would not slay you.'
> And he said unto Jether, his first-born, 'Up, and slay them.' But the youth drew not his sword: for he feared because was yet a youth.
> Then Zebah and Zalmunna said, 'Rise thou, and fall upon us: for as the man is, so is his strength.' And Gideon arose, and slew Zebah and Zalmunna, and took away the ornaments that were on their camels' necks. (Judg. 8.18–21)

Gideon acts here more like a warrior chieftain than a judge; and he wants his son to display his valour. Recognising his potential, 'the men of Israel' ask Gideon to be their king: 'Rule thou over us, both thou, and thy son's sons also' (8.22) , they say. They are asking someone who looks as if he is built for it to replace the 'discontinuous',[28] one deliverer at a time, system. Gideon turns down the role, but immediately starts acting, not just like a king, but like a combination of Aaron at the foot of the mountain and a classically 'bad king'.[29] Contravening Deuteronomy on 'multiplying gold',

> Gideon said unto them, 'I would desire a request of you, that ye would give me every man the earrings of his prey' ... And they spread out a garment and did cast therein every man the earrings of his prey. And the weight of the golden earrings was a thousand and seven hundred shekels of gold ... Gideon made an ephod thereof, and put it in his city, even in Ophrah: and all Israel went thither a whoring after it: which thing became a snare unto Gideon, and to his house. (8.24–27)

Gideon 'multiplied wives', to the power of ten; his harem gave him seventy sons. Once he was dead, the Israelites 'went a whoring after Baalim, and

28 David Jobling, 'Deuteronomic Political Theology in Judges and I Samuel 1–12', in *The Sense of Biblical Narrative: Structural Analyses in the Hebrew Bible* (JSOT Press, Sheffield, 1986), p. 56.
29 Ibid., p. 67.

made Baalberith their god' (8.33). The author adds to the prescribed formula of their crimes that they did not 'shew kindness' to Gideon's house (8.35). The narrator had not hitherto noted that Israel owed a debt to the offspring of their deliverers.[30]

Gideon had a seventy-first, a bastard, whom he names Abimelech (8.31), which means 'My father is a king' (*Abi*, 'father', *mlk*, 'king'). The modern conception of race is paralleled by the ancient mythological notion of the common ancestor.[31] Buber elaborates in reference to our anti-hero:

> The theophoric name Abimelech was taken over from the Canaanites with whom it probably had the characteristic function of connecting with one another two different orders of divine denotation, the father-order and the king-order, thus the biological (the god as primeval father of the tribe) and the political conception (the god as overlord of the tribe) ... In the Bible this is the first Israelitish name formed with the divine designation *melekh*, and ... this is no coincidence.[32]

Abimelech prefers sacral kingship to the Sinai covenant; the first internal 'enemy of the theocratic' society of Israel tries to turn history 'into an arena of *merely* political interests'.[33]

Abimelech cuts his way through sixty-nine of his half-brothers to over-lordship. Abimelech's logic is one of which readers will hear more, in the books of Samuel and Kings: would you rather have one brother 'reigning over you' or seventy (9.2)? His brother Jotham has escaped to tell the Bible's first parable about kingship (9.8–15). The trees want an anointed king. The olive tree, then the fig and the vine each demur. Finally, the trees turn to the bramble:

> And the bramble said unto the trees, 'If in truth ye anoint me king over you, then come and put your trust in my shadow: and if not, let fire come out of the bramble, and devour the cedars of Lebanon.' (9.15)

The clearest candidate for the bramble is Abimelech: but he is unlikely to have noted with some 'irony' his own 'inadequacy' for the role; brambles do not cast protective shades.[34] Perhaps the bramble is Abimelech, in one sense, and Jotham, in another.[35] The object of Jotham's criticism is not Abimelech, but the people. He does not accuse them of choosing a king, but of permitting a usurper to overthrow Gideon's dynasty:

> And ye are risen up against my father's house this day, and have slain his sons, threescore and ten persons, upon one stone, and have made Abimelech, the son of his maid-servant, king over the men of Schechem, because he is your brother. (9.18)

Both the narrator and Jotham have censured Israel: 'the unspecified debt to Gideon's house (8.35) was to accept its ongoing rule, but ... the people

---

30 Ibid., p. 68.
31 Mendenhall, *Tenth Generation*, p. 179.
32 Buber, *Kingship of God*, pp. 73–74.
33 Ibid., p. 73.
34 Jobling, 'Deuteronomic Political Theology', p. 72.
35 Ibid., p. 75.

failed to monitor the hereditary system properly!'[36] By likening himself to a bramble, and by not seizing power after Abimelech's downfall, Jotham, the sole surviving legitimate son, stands aside from the kingship.[37]

Abimelech 'reigned three years over Israel'. The *ruah*/spirit which enters the Judges shows its darker side: 'God sent an evil spirit between Abimelech and the men of Schechem' (9.23). Gaal leads the men of Schechem against Abimelech. Abimelech 'fought against the city all that day; and he took the city, and slew the people that was therein' (9.45). The people incarcerate themselves in 'the house of the god Bereth', a tower or ziggurat; Abimelech and his troops incinerate them. Abimelech tries it again; the people of Thebez rush for safety into 'the top of the tower' of their city:

> Abimelech . . . went hard unto the door of the tower to burn it with fire.
> And a certain woman cast a piece of millstone upon Abimelech's head, and all to brake his skull.
> Then he called hastily unto the young man his armour bearer, and said unto him, Draw thy sword, and slay me, that men say not of me, A woman slew him.' And his young man thrust him through, and he died. (9.52–54)

The nameless woman is as much of a heroine in Israel as Jael.

In Judges 6–9 the people are bad, as per usual, but the outcomes are Gideon, a flawed judge, punishment not by Canaanite enemy but by means of tyranny and civil war, a self-chosen leader (Abimelech), and a possible king who steps aside, so that Judges can follow (Jotham). Although this 'cycle' looks epicentric, the chronology has been altered to place it at the centre of the book (Deborah's twelfth-century conquest of Taanach should come after this), and Gideon and Abimelech occupy more space than they merit,[38] perhaps because Judges 6–9 'meets the need for a proleptic treatment of kingship'.[39]

The Judge who follows Gideon is Tola. Tola is succeeded by Jair, a Gileadite, who judges Israel for twenty-two years and dies. Is he one of the lesser entities among the Judges? Jair

> had thirty sons that rode on thirty ass colts, and they had thirty cities, which are called Havothjair unto this day, which are in the land of Gilead. (Judg. 10.4)

'Judges', raised by God to meet an immediate emergency, are an inherently 'discontinuous' form of political government; kings, with their offspring to follow them, have an inbuilt continuity. The sense for political continuity takes some root, even in the 'Judges' system: these minor Judges are 'successful administrators',[40] says Boling. Are 'charismatic leaders' or their sons supposed to 'have' thirty cities? The long peace is created at the expense of the family principle finding a 'niche' for itself amongst the Judges.[41]

36 Ibid., p. 81.
37 Ibid., p. 84.
38 Boling, *Judges*, p. 184.
39 Jobling, 'Deuteronomic Political Theology', p. 86.
40 Boling, *Judges*, p. 189.
41 Jobling, 'Deuteronomic Political Theology', p. 56.

The 'cycle' begins again: the people do evil, God gives them into the hand of the Ammonites, they cry, they even put away their gods, and God tiredly repents of his anger: 'his soul was grieved for the misery of Israel' (10.16). We do not read that God raises a Judge: rather

> Then the children of Ammon were gathered together, and encamped in Gilead. And the children of Israel assembled ... and encamped in Mizpeh. And the people and princes of Gilead said one to another, 'What man is he that will begin to fight against the children of Ammon? he shall be head over all the inhabitants of Gilead.' (10.17–18)

The next verses backtrack to tell the biography of the hero who will deliver them:

> Now Jephthah the Gileadite was a mighty man of valour, and he was the son of a harlot: and Gilead begat Jephthah.
> And Gilead's wife bare him sons, and his wife's sons grew up, and they thrust out Jephthah, and said unto him, 'Thou shalt not inherit in our father's house; for thou art the son of a strange woman.'
> Then Jephthah fled from his brethren, and dwelt in the land of Tob: and there were gathered vain men to Jephthah, and went out with him. (Judg. 11.1–3)

Jephthah is a great soldier and whore's son, not unlike Abimelech. The irony is at the expense of Jephthah's family, who want him back to lead them in battle against the Ammonites. Jephthah realises that the name of the game is tribal leadership. He asks to be the Gileadites 'head' as payment for victory, and the Gileadites accept the bargain (11.9–10). Jephthah has been chosen, *by the people*. Wordplay before swordplay: Jephthah asks the Ammonite king, 'Why ... hast thou come to fight against me in my land?'; the king comes back, 'Because Israel took away my land when they came up out of Egypt'. Jephthah counters: we did not take this land from you, but from the king of Sihon. Why don't you keep to the land which your god Chemosh gives you? He pictures each land, with its god, as a tribal possession; maybe smart diplomacy on the part of a 'practical Yahwist'.[42] The 'Spirit of the Lord' did not take it amiss but 'came upon Jephthah'. 'Jephthah' means 'he opened'; as he goes to the Amorite encampment, Jephthah opens his mouth once too often and too wide.[43]

> Jephthah vowed a vow unto the Lord, and said, 'If thou shalt without fail deliver the children of Ammon into mine hands,
> Then it shall be, that whatsoever cometh forth out of the doors of my house to meet me, when I return in peace from the children of Ammon, shall surely be the Lord's, and I will offer it for a burnt offering.' (Judg. 11.30–31)

If that was verbal magic, it 'works': Yahweh delivers the submission of the Ammonites (11.32–33). The magic words spin out of control and Jephthah cannot step outside of the cycle of automotion:

> And Jephthah came to Mizpeh unto his house, and, behold, his daughter came out to meet him with timbrels and with dances; and she was his only child; beside her he had neither son nor daughter. (11.34)

42 Boling, *Judges*, p. 205.
43 Cheryl Exum, *Tragedy and Biblical Narrative: Arrows of the Almighty* (Cambridge University Press, Cambridge, 1992), p. 48.

The victory has unwittingly been pledged upon her life. Jephthah is entangled, not by forgetting the powerful word, but by refusing to let go of it: he becomes 'a prisoner of his words ... as he is a prisoner of his understanding of the immutability of both the vow ... and YHWH'.[44] The girl is Jephthah's 'only child'. Although the story echoes the sacrifice of Isaac, there is no 'comic resolution': no friendly ram emerges as the substitute for Jephthah's daughter.[45] We do not see Jephthah's hand raised to the slaughter: the horrific sacrifice is not described. The innocent girl asks her father for a respite:

> 'let me alone two months, that I may go up and down upon the mountains, and bewail my virginity, I and my fellows.'
> And he said, 'Go.' And he sent her away for two months: and she went with her companions, and bewailed her virginity upon the mountains.
> And it came to pass at the end of two months, that she returned unto her father, who did with her according to his vow which he had vowed: and she knew no man. And it was a custom in Israel, That the daughters of Israel went yearly to lament the daughter of Jephthah the Gileadite four days in a year. (Judg. 11.37–40)

God does not react. Cheryl Exum finds 'The source of the tragic in the story of Jephthah' to be precisely this 'divine silence'.[46] God neither asks for this sacrifice nor repeals the automatism of Jephthah's words. Jephthah reverts to the tribal mores of human sacrifice. Through the annual act of remembrance of 'the daughters of Israel', Jephthah's daughter rises above the bargaining of gift-blood for victory. What she asks to 'bewail' is not her life but her fertility. We end with the scene of the women annually commemorating the innocent girl, with songs of mourning. Cheryl Exum argues forcibly that the episode of Jephthah ends on a note of healing:

> To recount the story of Jephthah's daughter is to make her live again through words. This communal commemoration by women is an act of identification and integration, mitigating the wrong done by the word of the father. It cannot undo the word ... but it prevents that word from extinguishing memory along with life ... Because it contains ... both the tragedy and the human courage to face and rise above it, the story itself provides a palliative for the wound this terrible deed inflicts on our sensibilities. Jephthah's daughter finds life through communal recollection ... The recounting of the daughter's courage and the women's refusal to forget is not just a balance to, but a transcendence of the tragedy of the daughter's death. The word heals.'[47]

The dancing girl and her sacrifice is the 'one green leaf' in her soldier-father's 'history'.

Her sacrifice does not break the cycle of tribalism. Jephthah's story began with the search for a champion against the Ammonites: 'he shall be head over all the inhabitants of Gilead' (10.18). It ends with Gilead at war with Ephraim, and with an introversion into the dialect of the tribe:

---

44 Gunn, 'Joshua and Judges', p. 117.
45 Exum, *Tragedy and Biblical Narrative*, p. 51.
46 Ibid., p. 59.
47 Ibid., p. 61.

the Gileadites took the passages of Jordan before the Ephraimites: and ...
when those Ephraimites which were escaped said, 'Let me go over' ... the
men of Gilead said unto him, 'Art thou an Ephraimite?' If he said 'Nay';
Then said they unto him, 'Say now Shibboleth': and he said 'Sibboleth': for
he could not frame to pronounce it right. Then they took him, and slew him
... there fell at the time of the Ephraimites forty and two thousand.
And Jephthah judged Israel six years. (Judg. 12.5–7)

During the course of Jephthah's judgeship, the warring tribes take to killing
each other over words. Where the Judges of the earlier 'cycles' had succeeded in discharging the danger to Israel, Jephthah drives out one enemy,
the Ammonites, but leaves the Philistines in possession of part of the land.

The last Judge whose legend is told is Samson, with his magical hair
and weakness for women. As is biblically statutory, the hero's mother is
barren. Manoah's wife receives a visit from an 'angel of the Lord'. The
angel tells her to dedicate herself to God, forswearing wine and unclean
food. She will have a son: 'no razor shall come on his head; for the child
shall be a Nazirite unto God from the womb; and he shall begin to deliver
Israel from the hand of the Philistines' (13.5). When the angel returns,
Manoah asks him to whom they should pay homage. The angel replies:

Why asketh thou thus after my name, seeing it is secret? (13.18)

God is off-stage in the Samson stories: his name and actions are 'secret', the
clue to the riddle.

Samson makes no public pledge of his Nazirite vow: it was taken for
him when he was concealed in the womb. A Nazirite was 'dedicated to
God' (*nazir Aloihim*). His uncut hair was a sign of this sanctification. To
demonstrate his distance from the bibulous Canaanite fertility cults, the
Nazirite had to 'abstain ... from the drinking of wine, and to guard against
all ritual impurity'.[48] The annunciation story makes it clear that Samson is
called to be meticulously pure in ritual and in morals. Even before his tale
got into writing, the one thing which everyone knew about Samson is that
he sat loosely to the Nazirite rule. An era more austere in its code of sexual
conduct than our own took a dim view of Samson's helpless attraction for
the opposite sex. Gerhard von Rad considered that

anyone who comes from the pious story of the call ... must be astounded by
the whirlwind of very unspiritual adventures in which Samson gets lost. In
particular, Samson showed great interest in women ... the reader will not
forget ... the great mission with which God charged him, and will have to
think about the continuous alternation between humiliating weakness and
God-given power in which the life of Samson oscillates. But even the power
given him by God is increasingly squandered in ineffectual practical jokes,
and Samson finally founders in the great conflict between *eros* and *charisma*.
Thus, the stories about Samson ... show the failure of a charismatic leader,
and divine powers wasted.[49]

Samson is not even an averagely well-conducted Nazirite, rather, he has
the stock characteristics of the heroes of slapstick, vast physical strength

48 Von Rad, *Old Testament Theology I*, p. 62.
49 Ibid., pp. 333–334.

and a sex drive to match it. Joseph Heller makes David say that 'the Samson we remember was too coarse and obtuse to define himself as "eyeless in Gaza"'.[50] Some scholars cannot forgive Samson for being quite so unMiltonic. Von Balthasar called him a *less noble* brother of Hercules.[51] Von Rad took Samson to be 'the oddest figure among the judges'.[52] Apart from his way with women, Samson's idiosyncrasy lies in the fact that he is neither an army commander nor, according to Boling, a good administrator: his exploits are all solitary. Others say that Samson is *supposed* to live on the fringes of Israelite and Philistine cultures: his marginality is the point. But Samson is more than an outlaw: he would lose his precise incongruity if he were not both a big man who seems to male critics to be an 'oversexed buffoon',[53] whom women find irresistible, *and* a Nazirite. Samson is not unlike David, whose exploits are likewise condoned. David is misbehaved and he is God's favourite. Saul tries to pull things off with vows; David sits lightly to the code, because he has faith. The Deuteronomist is doing something similar, with Samson's Nazirite vow and his sexual entrapments, in a populist style. He never censures Samson's conduct.

God's secret use of Samson, uncurbed eroticism et al., is unfolded in his first adventure:

> the child grew, and the Lord blessed him.
> And the Spirit of the Lord began to move him at times in the camp of Dan between Zorah and Eshtaol.
> And Samson went down to Timnath, and saw a woman in Timnath of the daughters of the Philistines.
> And he came up, and told his father and his mother, and said, 'I have seen a woman in Timnath of the daughters of the Philistines: now therefore get her for me to wife.'
> Then his father and his mother said unto him, 'Is there never a woman among the daughters of thy brother, or among all my people, that thou goest to take a wife of the uncircumcised Philistines?' And Samson said unto his father, 'Get her for me; for she pleaseth me well.'
> But his father and mother knew not that it was of the Lord, that he sought an occasion against the Philistines ... (13.24–14.4)

Samson's desire is blunt and to the point: 'Get her', he says twice, his only apparent rationale for choosing a Philistine wench being that 'she pleases me'. When the three Israelites set off, a reluctant betrothal party, Samson slips away and 'the Spirit of the Lord' comes on him, to kill a lion. Samson returns to the scene of his kill to find that a swarm of bees have made their hive in the lion's carcass. Is it something of Deborah's *ruah redivivus*, in somewhat comical form?

At his wedding party, Samson bets the Philistines they cannot answer his riddle: 'Out of the eater came forth meat, and out of the strong came forth sweetness' (14.14). They can find him out through his wife: 'Thou dost but hate me and *lovest me not*' (14.16), his faithless bride coaxes him. The answer is seven days in coming, but Samson is no Sphinx in the face of

50 Heller, *God Knows*, p. 42.
51 Von Balthasar, *Glory VI*, p. 108 (my italics).
52 Von Rad, *Old Testament Theology I*, p. 333.
53 Wharton, 'Secret of Yahweh', p. 58.

a woman's reproachful tears. The Philistines triumph: 'What is sweeter than honey? and what is stronger than a lion?' You have 'ploughed with my heifer', he complains: unbowed, he kills and spoils thirty Philistines, to make good his lost bet. When Samson lays about him, we need not imagine him as a 'great big simpleton'[54] but as Crocodile Dundee. He is sexually and physically unconstrained. The audiences of comedies laugh at violence; especially when the blow lands on the national enemy. Samson

> constantly gets the better of the [Philistines], and the narrative shows a hearty, lusty approval of his unconventional conduct. Comedy can serve as a release from antisocial instincts and as a form of aggression. Samson is a comic hero not only in his ability to bounce back but also in his capacity to inflict pain on his enemies.[55]

Samson returns to find that his Philistine father-in-law has married his wife elsewhere. This is the springboard for an extravagant vengeance: Samson turns three hundred flaming foxes loose to fire the Philistine cornfields. The Philistines respond to the fox-arson in kind. Samson's setbacks are integral, not to his psychology, but to the action: he has to be pinned down by the Philistines so that his audience can watch him bounce back. When Samson smites his adversaries 'hip and thigh', even the Judahites turn against him: 'Don't you realise the Philistines are our rulers?' (15.11): 'subjection is no longer "oppression" but a *modus vivendi*.'[56] Samson's lonely outlaw status is a comment on his colluding compatriots. His fellow Judahites tie Samson up and hand him over to their masters. The Spirit of the Lord, who achieves some merely worldly ends in these stories, comes upon Samson: 'the cords that were upon his arms became as flax that was burnt with fire' (15.14). The unarmed Samson slays a thousand Philistines, while he chants,

> With the donkey jawbone
> One heap! Two heaps!
>
> With the donkey jawbone,
> I laid low a contingent! (15.16)

Perhaps that is the one-to-one vengeance of the donkey caravaneers against the camel riders.

Lest anyone think that Samson's miraculous strength is his own, Samson's deed leaves him thirsty: God makes water flow from the same donkey jawbone. If the Deuteronomist aimed to show that the 'divine power' is being 'wasted' or that Samson's lack of 'administrative charisma' makes him a 'tragic figure'[57] it is curious that the adventure concludes: 'And he judged Israel in the days of the Philistines twenty years' (15.20).

Samson's provocative proclivity for fulfilling his predilections on dangerous enemy territory has become the thematic joke of every scene:

---

54 Josipovici, *Book of God*, p. 123.
55 Exum, *Tragedy and Biblical Narrative*, p. 37.
56 Gunn, 'Joshua and Judges', p. 118.
57 Boling, *Judges*, p. 233.

> Then went Samson to Gaza, and saw there an harlot, and went in unto her.
> And it was told the Gazites, saying, 'Samson is come hither.' And they
> compassed him in, and laid wait for him all night in the gate of the city, and
> were quiet all the night, saying, 'In the morning, when it is day, we shall kill
> him.'

They think to seize him 'in the morning', when Samson is tired out from
lovemaking.

> And Samson lay til midnight, and arose at midnight, and took the doors of
> the gate of the city, and the two posts, and went away with them, bar and all,
> and put them upon his shoulders, and carried them up to the top of a hill that
> is before Hebron. (Judg. 16.1–3)

The enemy did not reckon with Samson's 'post-coital vigor' and 'rustic
craftiness', let alone his cartoon mastery of city gates.[58] To quieten the
moralists, the Spirit of the Lord is politely absent from this episode.

Samson attaches himself to that Philistine Mata Hari, Delilah; her name
means 'flirtatious'. This time it is 'love' (16.4), on the Israelite side. Her
Philistine lords bribe Delilah to 'entice him' to divulge the secret of his
strength (16.5). Samson and Delilah circle around each other in the game of
his secret. Samson relishes hairy situations: he is playing with the taboo
which guards his power. He tells her that if 'they bind' him with 'seven
green withs that were never dried', he will be theirs for the taking. Delilah
binds him. As the Philistine men leap out of their hiding place in the
bedroom, she cries: 'The Philistines be upon thee, Samson!' He breaks the
withs: 'the secret of his strength was not known' (16.9). Samson is the
injured party, but Delilah maintains her superiority: 'Behold, thou hast
mocked me, and told me lies.' Why not try new ropes? The Philistines leap
to Delilah's too-knowing warning. Is Samson too blinded with love to
know whose side she is on; or is he enjoying the tease? He is allowing her
to get warmer when, at the third feminine entreaty, he suggests that she
weaves 'the seven locks of my head with the web' of her loom (16.13). She
'fastens' him, and calls out, as the awaiting men jump (*pause*): 'The
Philistines be upon thee, Samson!' He walks away, carrying the loom with
him. Delilah's demand for love undoes Samson:

> And she said unto him, 'How can thou say, I love thee, when thine heart is
> not with me? thou hast mocked me these three times, and hast not told me
> wherein thy great strength lieth.'
> And it came to pass, when she pressed him daily with her words, and urged
> him, so that his soul was vexed unto death;
> That he told her all his heart, and said unto her, 'There hath not come a razor
> upon my head; for I have been a Nazirite unto God from my mother's womb:
> if I be shaven, then my strength will go from me, and I shall become weak,
> and be like any other man.' (Judg. 16.15–17)

The story does ask whether the power is *really* in the Nazirite's uncut hair
or a gift of God's spirit: it makes the two a single symbol. Samson's
sanctification to God *is* his hair. This story is not finicky about the fine line

---

58 Wharton, 'Secret of Yahweh', p. 52.

between magic and the sacred. Samson has emptied out his heart, and his secret strength goes with it:

> And when Delilah saw that he had told her all his heart, she sent and called for the lords of the Philistines, saying, 'Come up this once, for he hath shewed me all his heart.' Then the lords of the Philistines came up unto her, and brought money in their hand. (16.18)

Delilah, and the Philistines with their bribe money at the ready, know that they have got their man. Samson does not know: perhaps *he has* forgotten that the secret is God's.

> And she made him sleep upon her knees; and she called for a man, and caused him to shave off the seven locks of his head; and she began to afflict him, and his strength went from him.
> And she said, 'The Philistines be upon thee, Samson.' And he awoke out of his sleep, and said, 'I will go out as at other times before, and shake myself.' And he wist not that the Lord was departed from him. (Judg. 16.19–20)

Samson thinks *he* can do as before; his successful escapades have gone to his head.

Samson is blinded and imprisoned: his captors do not note that 'the hair of his head began to grow again' (16.21–22): since the camera pans in on it, we need not separate it from Samson's recovery of his heroism. The regrowth of his hair turns him back into a Nazirite. This is the logic of comedy, and not every act of religion is an advertant choice: not for a man whose witness to God is his natural force. Before Samson can grow strong again, the narrator presses home the theological irony: the Philistines 'praise their god' for delivering Samson to them, and 'when their hearts were merry' Samson is brought out for the 'sport' of three thousand Philistines, at a festival of Dagon. Samson has one last trick to pull; he asks his gaoler to let him feel the pillars of the house. To pull it off, he must *ask for help* and win by sacrificing himself, bowing between the pillars of the house:

> Samson called unto the Lord, and said, 'O Lord, God, remember me, I pray thee, and strengthen me, I pray thee, only this once, O God, that I may be at once avenged of the Philistines for my two eyes.'
> And Samson took hold of the middle pillars upon which the house stood, and on which it was borne up, of the one with his right hand, and of the other with his left.
> And Samson said, 'Let me die with the Philistines.' And he bowed himself with all his might; and the house fell upon the lords, and upon all the people that were therein. So the dead that he slew at his death were more than they which he slew in his life.
> Then his brethren and all the house of his father came down, and took him, and brought him up, and buried him between Zorah and Eshtaol in the burying place of Manoah his father. And he judged Israel twenty years. (Judg. 16.28–31)

Although I place the onset of Samson's renewal earlier, and do not see why we should shrink from God making himself present in hair, Cheryl Exum's interpretation of the scene is broadly accurate:

His prayer restablishes his relationship to Yhwh and thus gives the plot its upward surge. This restoration of the relationship is decisive for the classic vision in Judges 13–16 . . . His burial by his brothers in the tomb of Manoah, his father, symbolizes his ultimate integration into the society he represents.[59]

A comic hero may live alone, but his mark is trust and reliance on others. This acknowledged dependency is rewarded: when the hero lets himself fall, he is rescued. The people of Israel is a collective comic character in Judges: every time it cries to God to help, he delivers them. The Judges are like the people out of whom they are called. Cheryl Exum imagines the divine intervention in Samson's last scene as the *deus ex machina* who typically 'operates in comedy'.[60] Rather than make Israel's God a mechanical Deity, I should say that the Bible's comic heroes experience the operation of grace. The heroes and heroines of Judges have been found to lack character development, and thus free will. It is true that 'even if there were more Samson stories, they would be essentially the same'.[61] I should hesitate to concur with the judgement that, like all comic heroes, Samson is fundamentally 'amoral', simply a 'trickster'.[62] The seventh commandment is downplayed, in the Samson stories as in most comedies: but Samson is an innocent, not a worldly, figure. Samson is repetitive because he is 'too much': he has a superabundance of life. This makes him able and willing to sacrifice himself. Jephthah played with the sacred, with his vow: we find the jest bitter because it led to the sacrifice of someone else. But there is a kinship between the virginal daughter and Samson, the two childlike figures who are sacrificed for their people.

There are no more judges until Eli takes up the thread in 1 Samuel. There is no 'sheriff', and no law. Judges 17–21 expose the breakdown of the rhythmic pattern. These chapters relate three episodes with a freezing narrative irony: the landscape is like a ghost town after dark. The narrator's absolute detachment, with its note of satire verging upon cynicism, is more terrifying than any amount of moralising. Micah's name translates 'Yahweh is incomparable'.[63] The reader waits for the shoe to drop as Micah candidly remarks to his mother that he has stolen gold and silver from her: he uses it to make 'an house of gods'. A Levite moves in with him to become his priest.

> In those days there was no king in Israel: and in those days the tribe of the Danites sought them an inheritance to dwell in; for unto that day all their inheritance had not fallen unto them among the tribes of Israel. (18.1)

The invading Danites ride through Mount Ephraim, where Micah, his mother, his Levite, and his valuable 'house of gods' are living, and make off with his golden ephod. When the priest asks them where they are going, they tell him to shut his mouth and come along:

> 'is it better for thee to be a priest unto the house of one man, or that thou be a priest unto a tribe and a family in Israel?'

---

59 Exum, *Tragedy and Biblical Narrative*, p. 20.
60 Ibid., p. 31.
61 Ibid., p. 37; Exum and Whedbee, 'Isaac, Samson and Saul', p. 144.
62 Exum, *Tragedy and Biblical Narrative*, p. 30, citing Suzanne Langer.
63 Boling, *Judges*, p. 255.

And the priest's heart was glad, and he took the ephod, and the teraphim, and the graven image, and went in the midst of the people. (18.19b-20)

Micah sees that they are too strong for him and goes home. The Danites, hauling their ill-gotten 'porta-shrine'[64] (18.31), find a town named Laish, burn it to the ground, and build there a new city and 'called it Dan'. The story concludes as it began, without any intrusive moralising about idols:

And they set them Micah's graven image, which he made, all the time that the house of God was in Shiloh. (18.31)

In case we have not got the fact that 'At that time they simply didn't have a king in Israel'[65]

it came to pass in those days, when there was no king in Israel, that there was a certain Levite sojourning on the side of mount Ephraim, who took to him a concubine out of Bethlehem-judah.
And his concubine played the whore against him, and went away from him unto her father's house to Bethlehem-judah, and was there four whole months. (19.1–2)

He goes to get her back, and stays drinking with her father for three days. On the third day, the Levite says he really has to go: his 'father-in-law' detains him, and so they drink for another day, and then for a fifth. The sense of futility is deadening. In the afternoon, 'the man', his 'two asses' and 'his concubine' depart, but it is evening when they reach Jebus. Fearing to stay in 'the city of the stranger' (that is, the Jebusites), they travel on; as 'the sun went down' they reach Gibeah, a Benjamite city (19.11–15). They camp on the street until an old man invites them into his home:

Now as they were making their hearts merry, the men of the city, certain sons of Belial, beset the house round about, and beat at the door, and spake to the master of the house, the old man, saying, 'Bring forth the man that came into thine house, that we may know him.' (19.22)

When they refuse to disperse, the Levite flings them his concubine; they gang-rape her:

they knew her, and abused her all the night until the morning: and when the day began to spring, they let her go.
Then came the woman in the dawning of the day, and fell down at the door of the man's house, where her lord was, till it was light.
And her lord rose up in the morning, and opened the doors of the house, and went out to go his way: and, behold, the woman his concubine was fallen down at the door of the house, and her hands were upon the threshold. (19.25–27)

With a blood-chilling amnesia about the night's events,

he said unto her, 'Up, and let us be going.' But none answered. Then the man took her up upon an ass, and the man rose up, and gat him unto his place.
And when he was come into his house, he took a knife, and laid hold on his concubine, and divided her, together with her bones, into twelve pieces, and sent her into all the coasts of Israel. (19.28–29)

64 Gunn, 'Joshua and Judges', p. 119.
65 Buber, *Kingship of God*, p. 82.

In the Masoretic text, the narrator 'dryly records that "no one answered" the Levite'; it does not state that the concubine was dead before 'the man' chopped her into twelve pieces.[66] The scene is comparable to the one in 'comedy–horror films', where someone unwittingly talks to a dead body, which makes the audience giggle, 'O No, wait-for-him-to-find out', until the body flops forward; but here, since there is no 'horrified reaction' from our Levite, the audience is left boggling, its comic expectations blown.[67] Just as the inhabitants of Sheol, the dead-land, had no affective relations, so the sleepwalkers in this subliminal landscape have no personal contact beyond pride of possession. The spiral goes limp, dropping the reader into the region of black comedy. Lasine comments that

> the Levite's behaviour is comic because he is not acting like a social human being ... his actions are so bizarre that they burst the category of tragic villainy, just as they prevent the concubine from being viewed with tragic pity. What remains is the reader's awareness that this is a world in which unpredictability, incongruity, and chaos are the defining features.[68]

The Levite lies about the episode to his compatriots; leaving his own action out of it, he presents himself as the hapless victim of the mob.[69] The dismemberment rouses all the people to retaliation (19.30). The discrete tribes 'gathered together as one man' at Mizpeh (20.1), to repay the tribe of Benjamin. The spectacle of the consequences of their regression into individual tribes has reunited them. The remaining eleven tribes are reunited in a punitive war.

> And the Lord smote Benjamin before Israel: and the children of Israel destroyed of the Benjamites that day twenty and five thousand men: all these drew the sword. (20.3–5)

Ehud carried a word of power; Jephthah's refusal to relinquish his vow carried his daughter to death; Samson played deadly games with the secret of his Nazirite vow, locked into his easily snipped tresses. In the last chapter of the book, we meet a final vow, and it seems as if a spell is broken when the Israelites find a way to manoeuvre themselves out of it. 'Now the men of Israel had sworn in Mizpeh, saying, There shall not any of us give his daughter unto Benjamin his wife' (21.1). The Israelites do not like the consequences: both the male and also the female Benjamites have died in the war. We 'have sworn' but one of the twelve tribes will die out, if they have no-one to marry.

> Then they said, 'Behold, there is a feast of the Lord in Shiloh yearly in a place which is on the north side of Bethel ...'
> Therefore they commanded the children of Benjamin, saying, 'Go and lie in wait in the vineyards;

66 Stuart Lasine, 'Guest and Host in Judges 19: Lot's Hospitality in an Inverted World', *Journal for the Study of the Old Testament*, 29, 1984, 37–59 (45).
67 Ibid.
68 Ibid., 47.
69 'The basic lie is his failure to mention the fact that he himself threw his concubine out to the mob to save himself.' Ibid., 49.

And see, and, behold, if the daughters of Shiloh come out to dance in dances, then come ye out of the vineyards, and catch you every man his wife out of the daughters of Shiloh, and go to the land of Benjamin . . .'
And the children of Benjamin did so, and took them wives, according to their number, of them that danced, whom they caught: and they went and returned unto their inheritance, and repaired the cities, and dwelt in them.
And the children of Israel departed thence at that time, every man to his tribe and to his family, and they went out from thence every man to his inheritance.
In those days there was no king in Israel: every man did that which was right in his own eyes. (21.19–21, 23–35)

If there is a little irony at the lawlessness of the expedient, the daughters register no objection.

Judges 17–21 contains plenty of authorial comment, in the refrain, 'In those days there was no king in Israel: every man did that which was right in his own eyes'. The description of the concluding state of play in Palestine seems to be deliberately designed to make monarchy look appealing: Judges 17–21 states that 'that which you pass off as theocracy has become anarchy'.[70] Rule by judges is not working as a political system. This could give grounds for some negativity in our assessment of charismatic theocracy as it is portrayed in Judges as a whole. The Judges do not 'unify Israel' or 'deal adequately with foreign oppression' and 'anarchy' mounts in the 'gaps' between them.[71]

If we want to find analogies by which to understand what is going on in the Deuteronomic books, we may look particularly to *political* comedy. The thefts, murders, self-seeking and rapes of Judges 17–21 are about as funny as those in Joseph Heller's great anti-war novel, *Catch 22*. What kind of political comedy can we make of the book as a whole? According to Boling: 'the historian's task is enormously complicated in the Book of Judges by the sense of humour in the very narratives which witness to religious organisation in the period'.[72] The literary form of the original legends was, he thinks, 'historical romance', which tends either to idealisation or to comedy.[73] The fact that some of the protagonists are 'comic-ideal', some are satirised, and some belong to black comedy indicates that the editors had to hand a body of material which they could not cut without losing some of the history. Comic-ideal heroes and heroines, and comic villains and flirtatious villainesses are laid alongside one another in order to blend an anti-monarchial theology with a more pragmatic instinct. If the book is governed by what Buber calls a 'remarkable spirit of balancing' of the idealistic and the pragmatic, that makes it difficult to follow Mendenhall in calling this a *theocratic* political comedy. By demonstrating the 'thesis and counterthesis'[74] of judges-rule and rule by monarchs, the book shows us the virtues of the judges-theocracy and then throws us into its pitfalls.

It has been axiomatic in biblical theology that the earliest Israelite anthropology is collectivist: we ought to find in the evolution of the thought

---

70 Buber, *Kingship of God*, p. 78.
71 Jobling, 'Deuteronomic Political Theology', p. 60.
72 Boling, *Judges*, p. 19.
73 Ibid., p. 32.
74 Buber, *Kingship of God*, p. 78.

of Israel a gradual emergence of the concept of the individual. It is not all that difficult, even for the most primitive mentality, to imagine a great hero. The Yahwistic portions of Genesis gave us three: Abraham, Isaac and Jacob. It takes the historical experience of being a nation with its own territory to reflect upon the collective or societal problem of politics. On Buber's analysis, Homer's *Odyssey* is to Aristotle's *Politics*, or Thucydides' *Peloponnesian War*, as the Pentateuch is to the Deuteronomistic History: Judges 'deserves' to be called 'the biblical *Politeia*' as much as does Samuel.[75] Boling comments that 'In the Book of Judges the matter of justice is explored in cosmic perspective.'[76] And yet, its only *political* idea is really an *ethical* principle: the absolute, inflexibly applied obligation to serve Yahweh. Circumstances may allow one to serve a moral God by judge or they may require a king. Both ethical and historical-political themes run through the theme of the 'truly sacred'. That is why the common, as opposed to the Miltonic, reader knows that the Samson stories are the comic heart of the drama.

By the time that the Deuteronomist had edited them, the stories in Judges had become trilogic: they are acted out by human characters, watched by an audience, and encompassed by God. The first audience of the Samson legends may have been hard-pressed settlers in Palestine; the Deuteronomist retells the tale to an Israel which has known conquest by Persia, exile, and sorry return. Wharton suggests that 'As resistance stories, the earliest Samson anecdotes already betray a strong, this-worldly, political element'. But the purpose of this sacred comedy is not to exhort the Israelites to throw off the Philistine or Babylonian burden. The stories

> were not first told to stimulate a fiery peasantry to similar deeds. The bizarre character of Samson's exploits removes the Philistine problem from the realm of direct action to the realm of the imagination. The ribald humor provides a low-risk outlet for anger, fear, and hope among people who had little means to press their cause against the Philistines ... Nevertheless, the 'memory' crystallized in the early Samson stories embraces not only the ribald and the bizarre, but also the politically charged human realities of the community that preserved them.[77]

Through the hilarious recollection of the Samson stories, through memory and wild, hyperbolic imagination, the Israelites are encouraged to have faith that their story is a comedy: in the darkest times and places, a helper will be sent, take what form he may. We have to live in the comic realm in which God knows and fulfils our desires. Boling says wisely that,

> the exilic editor is profoundly concerned with [the] question ... how to sing the Lord's song in a pagan country ... [His] answer is a positive one. The final editor counters the disillusionment of exile, for 'comedy is an escape, not from truth but from despair: a narrow escape into faith'.[78]

Biblical faith is a way of thinking about 'the sum' of ethical experience. The assimilation of the disorder and the desires of history in the biblical

75 Buber, *Kingship of God*, p. 84.
76 Boling, *Judges*, p. 6.
77 Wharton, 'Secret of Yahweh', 53–54.
78 Boling, *Judges*, p. 38.

narrative is its most important theological statement: 'The appropriate retelling of the story *is* the theological affirmation.'[79] The very act of the Deuteronomist's telling the tale, and the Israelites' listening, is a statement that the comic narrative must continue. Now, because the legends and the editors have mined it out of history, the audience can contemplate an aesthetic image. Two elements in the Samson stories indicate that they are *moral* stories: the role which Samson plays for the Israelite community and the subtle interplay between Samson's comic exploits and God, who, although he is not the only agent, is the 'chief actor' in his story.[80] An actor and his audience make an act of the ethical imagination; God pins them to it.

2. Ruth

Judges begins with tales of conquest and resistance and concludes in a grim and deathly landscape. By placing Ruth after Judges, the Septuagint and the Christian Bible make the narrative flow toward integration. Ruth tells how a woman of the enemy tribe becomes an odd bedfellow to an Israelite, and a matriarch in Israel.[81] Their husbands-to-be had to go afield to find the matriarchs of Genesis. The Book of Ruth almost returns to this state of innocence. If we are congenitally averse to war stories, this fairytale of betrothal binds up the wounds of the Judges.

In 'the days when the judges ruled ... there was a famine in the land' (Ruth 1.1). The famine pushes Elimelech, his wife Naomi and their two sons into Moab. The sons are married to two Moabite women, Orpah and Ruth. The three women are widowed. Naomi tells her daughters-in-law to go back to their mothers. Orpah leaves, but Ruth will not. She clings to Naomi and in this gesture makes the promise which gives her a people: 'where you go, I will go; where you live, I will live; your people shall be my people, and your God, my God; where you die, I will die and be buried' (1.16–17). Naomi and 'Ruth the Moabitess, her daughter-in-law' go home to Bethlehem.

Ruth suggests to Naomi an initial advance to her father-in-law's 'kinsman'. Whilst Boaz is at work in his fields, Ruth will follow him, and 'glean ears of corn' behind him, collecting his leavings. Ruth's gleaning is a dramatic gesture which displays their poverty to the 'mighty man of wealth' (2.1). She wishes to show herself to Boaz, 'in whose sight I will find grace' (2.2). If the Patriarchs took the initiative in finding their foreign brides, the Book of Ruth 'rotate[s] the betrothal type-scene 180 degrees on the axes of gender and geography'.[82] Ruth comes to Boaz; he assumes the role of protector which she has cast upon him. He tells the young woman that his fields are her's for the gleaning; she may follow the young male harvesters, but they are to keep their distance from her. Ruth continues to act the part of the humble supplicant:

---

79 Wharton, 'Secret of Yahweh', 59.
80 Ibid., 59.
81 Robert Alter calls Ruth a matriarch in Israel, in *Art of Biblical Narrative*, p. 59.
82 Ibid., p. 58.

> Then she fell on her face, and bowed herself to the ground, and said unto
> him, 'Why have I found grace in thine eyes, that thou shouldest take
> knowledge of me, seeing I am a stranger?' (2.10)

Ruth's first task has been achieved: she has made herself 'seen' by Boaz,
and has been granted the blessing of his glance. Ruth departs, not only
with Boaz's *darshan*, but with an 'ephah of barley'.

The ephah hints that Boaz's kindly plans should not be followed *au pied
de la lettre*.

> Ruth the Moabitess said, 'He said unto me also, "Thou shalt keep fast by my
> young men, until they have ended all my harvest".'
> And Naomi said unto Ruth her daughter-in-law, 'It is good my daughter,
> that thou go out with his maidens, that they meet thee not in any other field.'
> And she kept fast by the maidens of Boaz . . . (2.21–23)

By this feminine reversal of Boaz's intentions, Ruth preserves the look of a
woman with no close male admirer. Her mother-in-law conceives the plot
to ensnare her kinsman in a mutually advantageous union. Boaz works on
the threshing floor by night: Ruth must beautify herself, and lie down
beside the tired man. Ruth gains her end by keeping up an appearance
of passivity. Boaz works, eats, drinks and, 'when his heart was merry',
kips down on a 'heap of corn' (3.7). He wakes to find the perhaps nubile
foreigner under his blanket and 'at his feet'.

> he said, 'Who art thou?' And she answered, 'I am Ruth thine handmaid:
> spread therefore thy skirt over thine handmaid; for thou art a near kinsman.'
> (Ruth 3.9)

Without ceasing to look submissive, the handmaid points out to her lord
his familial obligations. Boaz is not ready to submit to the stratagem: first
she must be offered to her nearest kinsman. But Naomi knows, on Ruth's
return home, that the game is nearly won. The nameless kinsman does not
want to rescue Ehimelech's family from dying out; by the removal of a
shoe, Boaz promises himself in marriage to Ruth. She will be the mother of
Obed, who begats Jesse, who begats David, God's favourite king. The baby
is on Naomi's bosom: she, too, has gained her end.

3. 1–2 Samuel

a. Historical Background and Composition

Israelite monarchy begins with Saul, in about 1050 BC. It spreads under
David to encompass both Israel and Judah. The dual kingdom achieved
its political high point with Solomon. Mendenhall considers that King
David, the 'Old Testament Constantine', 'represents a thorough-going
reassimilation to Late Bronze Age religious ideas and structures'.[83] Recent
scholars are not altogether impressed by the Monarchy's cultural achieve-
ments:

---

83 Mendenhall, *Tenth Generation*, p. 16.

The innovations and inventiveness of David and Solomon (expressed, e.g., in temple, bureaucracy, harem, standing army, taxation system, utilization of wisdom) embody an imitation of urban imperial consciousness ... and a radical rejection of the liberation consciousness of the Mosaic tradition.[84]

The practical Wisdom proverbs are said to have been written in the time of King David. According to a well-worn hypothesis, a school of scribes at Solomon's court compiled and edited the many oral sagas of Israel, assembling the ancient and diverse legends into great written texts: their work is said to include the Yahwist's history ('J'), the Joseph novella, the story of David's rise to power (1 Sam. 16–2 Sam. 5.12), the Succession Narrative (2 Sam. 6.12–1 Kings 2).[85] These editors were urban intellectuals, writing for a worldly and somewhat secularised audience. They were influenced by non-Israelite sources, such as Egyptian wisdom. Perhaps the Israelite scribes learned their trade from Egyptian intellectuals, like Solomon's Phoenician temple builders, specially imported for the task.[86]

The source critics have cut 1 Samuel 1–1 Kings 2 into three texts: the story of Saul, in 1 Samuel 1–15, the story of David's rise to power, in 1 Samuel 16–2 Samuel 5.12, and the Succession Narrative (2 Sam. 6.12–1 Kings 2). The story of Saul (1 Sam. 1–15) is said to conflate at least two sources. One is supposed to have been written within a generation or so of King Saul. It is 'reverent'[87] toward the monarchy (1 Sam. 9.1–10.16; 11.1–15; 31). The second was written after the debacle of 587: it indicts the monarchy in the figure of Saul (1 Sam. 7; 8.1–22; 10.17–27; 12.1–25). Thus, the editors of 1 Samuel are found to have bound together a 'favourable' and an 'unfavourable source'[88] with regard to the monarchy. But how could a 'credible' book be wrought out of two sources which are saying opposite things about monarchical government? The incommensurability of goods, and their attendant virtues, comes to light when we survey practical historical facts. If the Deuteronomist set out a theological *Politeia* in the books from Joshua to 2 Kings, he did so by means of a reconstruction of the history of Israel. Where better to lay out the virtues of judges, and the shortcomings which are tied to them, *and* the virtues and inveterate vices of monarchy? Buber said that 1 Samuel sets out to *balance* two 'antitheses'. By the end of Judges, we have seen *both* the ethical drawbacks of monarchy, in the self-sacralising Abimelech, *and* that monarchy is politically necessary.

The story of David's rise to power (1 Sam. 16–2 Sam. 5.12) is more of a 'clean block' than 1 Samuel 1–15. Scholars have found the marks of Solomonic naturalism in this text.[89] The Succession Narrative is thought to rely on various sources, such as a 'Military Source', through which the

84 Walter Brueggemann, 'Trajectories in Old Testament Literature', p. 169.
85 Von Rad, *Old Testament Theology I*, p. 49; Norman Whybray, *The Succession Narrative: A Study of II Samuel 9–20 and I Kings 1 and 2* (SCM, London, 1968), p. 4.
86 On the temple builders, von Rad, *Old Testament Theology I*, p. 48; on the Egyptians, Whybray, *Succession Narrative*, p. 3.
87 Georg Fohrer, *History of Israelite Religion*, translated by David Green (SPCK, London, 1972), p. 124.
88 John William Wevers, 'The First Book of Samuel', in Charles Laymon (ed.), *The Interpreter's One Volume Commentary on the Bible* (Collins, London, 1971).
89 Von Rad, *Old Testament Theology I*, p. 54.

narrator acquired his knowledge of the Ammonite war described in 2 Samuel 10.1–19 and 12.26–32,[90] and a 'very ancient' and disapprobative account of David's census (2 Sam. 24).[91]

The books of Samuel contain conservative warnings about the departure of monarchy from theocracy, an optimistic text composed during the heights of the monarchy's achievement, and a retrospectively pessimistic text. The end result is a book which is ironic about the political necessities of a monarchy, and of a human being who has to play the role of monarch. There is another contextual cause of the irony directed against those who play the role of monarch. Israel did not only import temple builders and scribes: it also acquired a theology built to harbour the fact of kingship. It is said to have shipped its political theology in from Egypt. Von Rad tells us that 'David's throne' gained

> sacral legitimation in the prophecy of Nathan (II Sam. VII) . . . form-critical comparison has . . . established . . . similarities to the Egyptian royal record. From the incidental remark 'sitting in his palace' at the beginning, and continuing with the king's expressed intention to build a temple . . . down to the divine declaration of the filial relationship granted to the king . . . all these . . . can be shown to be stylised in the court of Egypt. In the ancient Egyptian theology of kingship a special part is played by the so-called royal protocol, a document listing the king's throne name, attesting his divine sonship, his commission as ruler, the promise that his dominion would endure for ever . . . this document, allegedly written by the deity . . . was handed to the king at his accession.[92]

The author of the Succession Narrative transposed the Egyptian 'royal protocol' into an everlasting covenant, between Yahweh and the House of David.[93] The Israelite king will have three faces. In one light, the ancient image of the king as the representative of the people to God, and of God to the people gives him the stature of greatness. In a second light, the one who bears the role of king has to balance the absolute ethics of Yahwism against the pragmatic demands of politics. But, thirdly, Israel's historicising imagination, and the aptitude of the 'Solomonic humanists' for realistic portraiture shows the real man within the king. There is, then, an ironic contrast between what the religious imagination feels a king should be like and a close-up look at Israel's first kings. Von Rad notes that

> The Davidic dynasty came into being in the clear light of history: unlike the Babylonian dynasty . . . it did not 'come down at the beginning from heaven' . . . no mythic dignity . . . attaches to it . . . David's rise to power . . . sets before us with . . . matter of fact realism the tortuous path trodden by this erstwhile warrior in the service first of Saul and then of the Philistines . . . the Deuteronomic history works with a picture already idealised . . .[94]

David is undignified when he plays the king and dignified when he plays the man. He could not thus tergiversate if God were on stage to help him

90 Wevers, 'First Book of Samuel', p. 156.
91 Von Rad, *Old Testament Theology I*, p. 59.
92 Ibid., p. 40.
93 Ibid., p. 41.
94 Ibid., p. 308.

speak and act: but here we find a 'concept of God as working in a hidden way through the hearts and minds of men'.[95] This hidden God creates the space for the third round of ironies, as between Yahweh as king and the human kings, Saul and David. In its description of Israel under the monarchy, the biblical narrative spirals down to the lower realm of infernal comedy. Now good and bad intermingle in the leading characters. The realm of infernal comedy is *somewhat* analogous to the generic realm which Northrop Frye created for satire.

b. The Texts

The Hebrew Bible calls the books from 1 Samuel to 2 Kings the 'Former Prophets'. The richest field for the employment of satire in the Bible is prophecy. The character in the 'story of Saul' who represents the prophetic imperative is Samuel. The figure of Samuel seems to be partly cast in the mould of the *prophets* who decried the political alliances and religious compromises of Israel's later kings. Samuel as prophet gives voice to the satirical intent of the author. The story begins with Samuel's birth narrative. Hannah is distressed by her infertility: she prays in the temple at Shiloh that, if the Lord will grant her a son, she will 'give him unto the Lord all the days of his life, and there shall no razor come upon his head' (1 Sam. 1.11). The Shiloh priest who thought she was drunk has been deprecated by exegetes; maybe it was one importunate woman too far. God is open to the suggestion. When Samuel is weaned, she hands him over to Eli, the temple priest. She visits Samuel every year, bringing him a new 'little coat' (2.19). A prophet is known by his *call*[96] and God 'calls' 'the child Samuel' (3.1): 'whatever office the historic Samuel actually held, what the narrator wished to relate was the way in which a young man was raised up as a prophet (vs. 20).'[97]

The Deuteronomist interprets the figure of Samuel in the light of the later prophets:

> And Samuel grew, and the Lord was with him, and did let none of his words fall to the ground.
> And all Israel from Dan even to Beer-sheba knew that Samuel was established to be a prophet of the Lord.
> And the Lord appeared again in Shiloh: for the Lord revealed himself to Samuel in Shiloh by the word of the Lord. (3.19–21)

An earlier paradigm is also present: we are still in the realm of the Judges. The stories of Eli and Samuel show us the last of the Judges, the former flawed, and the latter less so.

We do not begin in the dark, but slide slowly down to it. The Ark of the Covenant gives a glimpse of a lighter comedy. It is carried into the fray against the fearstruck Philistines (1 Sam. 4.8). When a messenger reports the deaths of Eli's sons, Hophni and Phineas, Phineas' wife goes into labour

95 Whybray, *Succession Narrative*, p. 6.
96 Cf. the call narratives in 1 Kings 19.19–21 (Elisha); Amos 7–9; Isaiah 6; Ezekiel 1–3; Isaiah 40.3–8; Zechariah 1.7–6.8.
97 Von Rad, *Old Testament Theology II*, p. 55.

> And she named the child I-ch-bod, saying, 'The glory is departed from Israel': because the ark of God was taken, and because of her father in law and her husband. (1 Sam. 4.21–22)

The Philistines who had cried 'Alas!' at the sight of the Ark make off with the glory of Israel. Like the holidaymakers who towed King Kong from his island sanctuary to New York, they discover that the unchained animal is bigger than they had bargained for:

> [T]he Philistines took the ark of God, and brought it from Ebenezer unto Ashdod.
> When the Philistines took the ark of God, they brought it into the house of Dagon, and set it by Dagon.
> And when they of Ashdod arose early on the morrow, behold, Dagon was fallen upon his face to the earth before the ark of the Lord. And they took Dagon, and set him in his place again.
> And when they arose early on the morrow morning, Dagon was fallen on his face to the ground before the ark of the Lord; and the head of Dagon and both the palms of his hands were cut off upon the threshold; only the stump of Dagon was left to him.
> Therefore neither the priests of Dagon, nor any that come into Dagon's house, tread on the threshold of Dagon in Ashdod unto this day.
> But the hand of the Lord was heavy upon them of Ashdod, and he destroyed them, and smote them with emerods, even Ashdod and the coasts thereof. (5.1–6)

King James's *emerods* are 'haemorrhoids'.[98] The men of Ashdod get rid of the beast with due haste:

> 'Let the ark of the God of Israel be carried about unto Gath.' And they carried the ark of the God of Israel about thither.
> And it was so, that, after they had carried it about, the hand of the Lord was against the city with a very great destruction: and he smote the men of the city, both small and great, and they had emerods in their secret parts.
> Therefore they sent the ark of God to Ekron. And it came to pass, as the ark of God came to Ekron, that the Ekronites cried out, saying, 'They have brought about the ark of the God of Israel to us, to slay us and our people.'
> And they sent and gathered together all the lords of the Philistines, and said, 'Send away the ark of the God of Israel, and let it go again to his own place, that it slay us not, and our people': for there was a deadly destruction throughout all the city; the hand of God was very heavy there.
> And the men that died not were smitten with the emerods: and the cry of the city went up to heaven. (5.8–12)

The Ark is sent with its explosive contagion from Ashdod to Gath to Ekron. It is clear that 'there is something of the "carnivalesque" in 1 Samuel 5–6'.[99] If God's effects are hidden, it is in a very uncomfortable place. The Ark represents 'both the presence of the LORD and Israel itself; Israel is defined by the LORD present within the community'.[100] The Philistines ask their 'priests and diviners' how to get rid of this pain in the backside. The priests tell them to make a 'trespass offering' of 'five gold emerods and five gold

98 Private communication from Professor William Johnstone.
99 Polzin, *Samuel and the Deuteronomist*, p. 65.
100 Ibid., p. 66.

mice'. The five Lords of the Philistines will be represented by mice and by haemorrhoids. Each Lord offers an image of himself to the Ark, and it is carted away to Kirjath-je-a-rim. The books of Samuel juxtapose panels of light and panels of darkness, happy laughter, and satire. The descent from this laughing, divine king to the human kings will be steep.

Polzin says that the Ark stories look forward to the Exile of the people Israel. They also look backward to the last of the Judges. Samuel is the Judge who wearily tells the people that God will rescue them from the Philistines after they have once more put away their strange gods.

The conclusion of the Ark stories is of a piece with those of the Judges cycle:

> and the hand of the Lord was against the Philistines all the days of Samuel.
> And the cities which the Philistines had taken from Israel were restored to Israel, from Ekron even unto Gath ... and there was peace between Israel and the Amorites.
> And Samuel judged Israel all the days of his life. (7.13–15)

In the last, sunny scene of the Judges, the Israelites were protected by Yahweh, who smites the enemy with haemorrhoids, and governed in peace by Samuel. The implication of 1 Samuel 1–7 is that Israel needed no other king than Yahweh. Samuel seems like the pure model of a good judge, energetically and appropriately repelling the Philistines. But both Eli and Samuel deviate from the paradigm of the good judge: each has a pair of bad sons, *whom they institute as their successors*, as if judgeship could be hereditary, rather than open to the choice of Yahweh.[101] The unsuitability of Samuel's sons reopens the question of kingship.

The empowerment of the charismatic leader is described as 'The Spirit of the Lord clothing itself in Gideon' (Judg. 6.34).[102] How will the human kings act the part of God? Saul goes with a servant in search of his father's asses: inquiring for a 'seer' who may help them find the beasts, they are directed to Samuel. Samuel takes Saul into his house and anoints him in secret (1 Sam. 10.1). Saul cannot become king just as 'Saul': he has to be given the new role by God. Samuel sends Saul away with a prophecy: he is going to meet a troop of musical prophets, playing on the 'psaltery, and a tabret, and a pipe, and a harp':

> And the Spirit of the Lord will come upon thee, and thou shalt prophesy with them, and shalt be turned into another man. (10.6–7)

Samuel's words are carried out, to the letter:

> And it was so, that when he had turned his back to go from Samuel, God gave him another heart: and all those signs came to pass that day.

---

101 The people give the fact that Samuel's sons 'do not follow in your way' (1 Sam. 8.5) as one of their reasons for wanting a king. Jobling comments that 'the initiative which leads to monarch is Samuel's own; it is his own attempt to establish his sons as judges which provokes the people's request for a king ... it is *just* when Samuel has gloriously reestablished the integrity of judgeship (ch. 7) that he tries to subvert its very nature, into a continuous hereditary system; and thereby precipitates the replacement of judgeship by a continuous, hereditary, monarchy'. 'Deuteronomic Political Theology', p. 54.
102 Peter Ackroyd, *The People of the Old Testament* (Christophers, London, 1959), p. 66.

> And when they came thither to the hill, behold, a company of prophets met
> him; and the Spirit of God came upon him, and he prophesied among them.
> ... when all that knew him beforetime saw that, behold, he prophesied among
> the prophets, then the people said one to another, 'What is this that is come
> unto the son of Kish? Is Saul also among the prophets?' (10.9–12)

The people's question is ironic: already the narrative notes a gap between
the role which Saul is supposed to take on and what he is. Can God 'clothe
himself' in Saul? The question is reinforced when Saul conceals his transformation: he tells his uncle that the asses are found, 'But of the matter of
the kingdom, whereof Samuel spake, he told him not' (10.16). When
Samuel gathers the tribes for the 'election' of the king, God's chosen has to
be dragged out from his hiding place inside the Benjamites' luggage. Saul
does not want to act the part of God's chosen king.[103]

Modern 'commentators say' that the story of Saul is a tragedy, and 'all
but unanimously'.[104] E. M. Good thinks that seeing it dramatised will help
us to recognise its tragic potential:

> We have in the Saul story a masterpiece of structure, dramatic order and
> suspense, and tragic irony. Someday, someone will turn the story into a great
> tragedy for the stage. He will have to fill in characters and dialogue. But he
> will not have to alter a single episode. Then perhaps Saul will be recognized
> as a tragic figure of the same stature as Oedipus or Othello.[105]

Von Rad spoke of the story's 'close affinity with the spirit of Greek
tragedy'.[106] Saul has also been likened to *Shakespeare*'s tragic heroes, such
as Macbeth. Yahweh's reluctant acquiescence in the people's demand for a
king is soon retracted: unwilling and unwittingly, Saul bears the brunt of
the divine punishment for this demand. His coronation speech, given by
Samuel, is no eulogy: Saul and the people are told that they have taken
Saul as king instead of Yahweh (1 Sam. 12.1–12). Samuel makes no secret
of the order of events which have led to Saul's selection:

> Now therefore behold the king whom ye have chosen, and whom ye have
> desired! and, behold, the Lord hath set a king over you. (1 Sam. 12.13)

Samuel makes the man who hates publicity into an object of attention,
pointing to Saul, and saying, God has done *this* to you. The prophet calls
for a sign to show what Yahweh thinks of the coronation:

> 'Is it not wheat harvest today? I will call unto the Lord, and he shall send
> thunder and rain; that ye may perceive and see that your wickedness is great,
> which ye have done in the sight of the Lord, in asking you a king.'
> So Samuel called unto the Lord; and the Lord sent thunder and rain that day:
> and all the people greatly feared the Lord and Samuel.
> And all the people said unto Samuel, 'Pray for thy servants unto the Lord thy
> God that we die not: for we have added unto all our sins this evil, to ask us a
> king.' (1 Sam. 12.17–19)

---

103 Robert Polzin thinks that the way in which Saul is taken by lot emphasises that the
royal office is in itself a crime: *Samuel and the Deuteronomist*, p. 104; cf. 124–125.
104 E. M. Good, *Irony in the Old Testament* (SPCK, London, 1965), p. 56.
105 Ibid., p. 80.
106 Von Rad, *Old Testament Theology I*, p. 325.

Like Jeremiah, Samuel sets two ways before the assembled people: if they obey God, the king will prosper: if not, 'the hand of the LORD will be against you' (12.14) and 'you will be consumed, you and *your king*' (12.25). But it is clear which way he thinks it will go. It is easy to concur with the assessment that 'Saul, who never wanted to be king, is scarcely being given a fair chance'.[107]

Saul gathers an army. Jonathan makes an advance foray against the Philistine garrison at Geba. In the expectation of successful retaliation, the Philistines camp at Michmash. The Israelites make the same prognosis; some hide in caves and others speed off to Gad and Gilead (13.6–7).

> As for Saul, he was yet in Gilgal, and all the people followed him trembling. And he tarried seven days, according to the set time that Samuel had appointed: but Samuel came not to Gilgal; and the people were scattered from him.
> And Saul said, 'Bring hither a burnt offering to me, and peace offerings.' And he offered the burnt offering.
> And it came to pass, that as soon as he had made an end of offering the burnt offering, behold, Samuel came; and Saul went out to meet him, that he might salute him.
> And Samuel said, 'What hast thou done?' And Saul said, 'Because I saw that the people were scattered from me, and that thou camest not within the days appointed, and that the Philistines gathered themselves together at Michmash;
> Therefore, said I, The Philistines will come down upon me to Gilgal, and I have not made supplication unto the Lord: I forced myself therefore, and offered a burnt offering.' (13.7–12)

Recent discussion has focused upon the apparent ambiguity of Samuel's instruction.[108] Should Saul have waited seven full days, or until after seven days had elapsed, or any length of time, until Samuel arrived? Given the opacity of the order, is it just to blame Saul for misconstruing it? Robinson notes Saul's political and military dilemma: a good general does not wait for the arrival of the religious interest, particularly when his army is evaporating (13.8). Saul's urgent desire to sacrifice ('I felt compelled', 13.12, in Robinson's translation) can be seen as a mark of his piety.[109] Deaf to Saul's explanation, Samuel revokes the promised 'kingdom' (13.13–14). That may appear to be an overreaction to one misunderstood instruction. Perhaps the real agenda is not the sacrifice, but Yahweh's 'attitude' to what 'he represents', human kingship in Israel.[110]

Samuel tells Saul to

> go and smite Amalek, and utterly destroy all that they have, and spare them not; but slay both man and woman, infant and suckling, ox and sheep, camel and ass. (15.3)

107 Bernard P. Robinson, *Israel's Mysterious God: An Analysis of Some Old Testament Narratives* (Grevatt & Grevatt, Newcastle upon Tyne, 1986), p. 42.
108 Ibid., p. 43; D. M. Gunn, *Fate of King Saul: An Interpretation of a Biblical Story* (Journal for the Study of Biblical Literature, Sheffield, 1980), pp. 33–40.
109 Robinson, *Israel's Mysterious God*, p. 43; Gunn, *Fate of King Saul*, p. 38.
110 Gunn, *Fate of King Saul*, p. 40.

Having routed the Amelikites, 'Saul and the people spared Agag, and the best of the sheep' (15.9). Tipped off from on high that something is amiss, Samuel travels to Gilgal where he finds Saul, the best specimens and Agag. Saul claims that he brought them here to be sacrificed. Why assume without evidence that Saul is just a 'humbug'?[111] Gunn put Saul's lack of 'embarrassment' to his credit: maybe he saved the best of the animals to Gilgal to sacrifice them at Yahweh's shrine.[112] Now Samuel, instead of Saul, 'hewed Agag in pieces before Yahweh in Gilgal' (15.33).

Saul seems to fail as a king because of arbitrary interpretations placed after the event upon Yahweh's commands. A deity whose Will we cannot understand is like Fate. Gunn comments that

> From the moment of his anointing ... it is as though fate has become his active antagonist, thwarting and twisting his every move. In this respect he is remarkably like King Oedipus.[113]

Cheryl Exum pushes this line of interpretation further. After the confrontations at Michmash and at Gilgal, Saul is haunted and infested by an 'evil spirit': but this spirit is Yahweh himself. Samuel is like an inverted Judge: just as the breath of the divine Spirit propelled the Judges to victory, so Saul is pushed on to his own humiliating demise by the same divine spirit, the 'dark side' of God.[114] Exum claims that 'Saul is an pharmakos, the scapegoat for the people's sin of requesting a king'.[115] In tragedies of fate, the hero is wholly innocent. In constrast, there is the 'tragedy of the flawed hero', of which Shakespeare made use. Macbeth willingly accedes to the fate pronounced by the witches, because it tickles his ambition. Robinson notes that Saul ceases to be an appealing character once he begins to persecute David.[116] Some writers find in Saul at least one moral blemish: that is, jealousy. According to Gunn, Saul's story is a tragedy of flaw in that Saul's jealousy accelerates the doom of his dynasty, and a tragedy of fate in that his punishment exceeds his two crimes. What most interests Cheryl Exum is God's 'ambivalent' role in bringing about the tragedy:

> all the essential tragic ingredients meet us in the story of Saul, chief among them, and indispensable to the tragic vision, the Aeschylean paradox of human guilt and the wicked God.[117]

---

111 Robinson, *Israel's Mysterious God*, p. 44. Robinson thinks the narrator intended us to identify with Saul rather than Samuel: ibid., p. 45.
112 Gunn, *Fate of King Saul*, p. 47.
113 Ibid., p. 115.
114 Cheryl Exum remarks that: 'Saul ... knows the demonic side of God not only through divine absence, but also, paradoxically, through Yhwh's persecuting presence in the form of an evil spirit ... Saul's possession in these instances resembles Samson's when the spirit rushes on him (Judg. 14.6, 19; 15.14), and may also be compared to the cases of Othniel, Gideon, and Jephthah in the book of Judges. Divine possession leads to bizarre deeds. But we do not recognize it as especially problematic until after Saul's rejection, when we are told pointedly, "the spirit of Yhwh departed from Saul and an evil spirit from Yhwh tormented him" (1 Sam 16.14).' *Tragedy and Biblical Narrative*, p. 40.
115 Ibid., p. 38.
116 Robinson states that 'The Saul of 1 Sam 16 onwards ... is not a figure with whom the author wishes us to sympathize.' *Israel's Mysterious God*, p. 48.
117 Exum, *Tragedy and Biblical Narrative*, p. 17.

One of the questions which the Deuteronomist asks, in the figure of Saul, is whether Yahwistic obedience is compatible with human kingship. Perhaps we are looking at a work of political theology. The Deuteronomist was well aware that it is near to impossible for the king of a small country at war with its neighbours stringently to adhere to the demands of his prophet. He can see that Saul's actions serve political interests; he would probably see the point if David had asked him, 'For this you fire a king? Not by me you don't, even though I was the beneficiary.'[118] But he is equally certain that Saul, both as man and as king, must do exactly what Yahweh requires of him, through his prophet Samuel. It is this wielding together of the judgement on the man and on the king which makes for an ironic treatment of kingship.

Irony can be used gently and more forcefully: irony with intent to harm is satire. Aristotle interpreted comedy in the light of satire. He says that comedy begins with the iambic 'poetry of invective' set forth by Homer in his *Margites*.[119] *Invective* is verbal attack: once forceful irony turns to *satire* we have the use of comedy 'as a weapon'.[120] The poet trains the arsenal of satirical verse upon someone in order to make him look stupid. Aristotle defines comedy as

> an imitation of men worse than the average; worse . . . not as regards any and every sort of fault, but only as regards one particular kind, the Ridiculous, which is a species of the Ugly.[121]

Mel Brooks was a good Aristotelian when he said that 'tragedy is when *I* cut my finger; comedy is when *you* fall into an open sewer and *die*'. One does not *identify* with a ridiculous man. Elder Olson thinks that comedy is produced by our *detachment* from the hero's predicament: we must not 'sympathise' with the hero, or his problems would cease to be funny.[122] In Olson's Aristotelian conception of comedy, the protagonist is not a hero, but the butt of our laughter, a 'ridiculous man'.[123]

Robert Elliott has traced the origins of Greek satire to the figure of Archilochus, said to have lived in the sixth century BC. When Lycambes would not permit him to marry his daughter, Archilochus ridiculed his would-have-been father-in-law to suicide.[124] Archilochus' legendary satirical powers are due to the 'widespread popular belief in the destructive, supernatural power of ill-omened invective or imprecation'.[125] Elliott sketches the history of satire-as-magical-curse amongst the pre-Islamic Arabs, for whom 'The poet's chief function was to compose satire (*hija*)

118 Heller, *God Knows*, p. 152.
119 Aristotle, *Poetics*, 1448a 3 25–30.
120 Peter Berger, *Redeeming Laughter: The Comic Dimension of Human Experience* (Walter de Gruyter, Berlin/London, 1997), p. 157.
121 Aristotle, *Poetics*, 1449a 5 30–35.
122 Elder Olson, *The Theory of Comedy* (Indiana University Press, Bloomington, 1968), p. 17; compare the *Poetics* 1448a 2 10–15 and 1454b 5.
123 Olson, *Theory of Comedy*, p. 20.
124 Robert Elliott, *The Power of Satire: Magic, Ritual, Art* (Princeton University Press, New Jersey, 1960), p. 7.
125 Ibid., p. 8.

against the enemy'.[126] The pre-Islamic Arabs are not such distant cousins of the biblical authors.

The Irish also have a certain satirical prowess. Elliott relates an Irish myth which points us to the fact that comedy has more than one dimension:

> The major function of the filid was the familiar one of *laus et vituperatio*, praise and blame. It may be that the duality of the office is indicated symbolically in a story from *Cormac's Glossary* (a compilation of the ninth or tenth century) about the bard Senchán Torpeist, chief poet of all Ireland . . . Senchán and his retinue of fifty poets . . . were setting out on a pleasure cruise to Mann . . . A 'foul-faced gillie' insisted that he be taken along. His aspect was . . . hideous: '. . . when any one would put his finger on his forehead, a gush of putrid matter would come through his ears on his poll . . . Rounder than a blackbird's eggs were his two eyes; blacker than death his face; swifter than a fox his glance; yellower than gold the points of his teeth; greener than holly their base; two shins bare, slender; two heels spiky, black speckled under him. He shouted . . . to Senchán . . . "I should be more profitable to thee than the proud and wanton crew that is round thee".'
>
> After the foul gillie outdoes Senchán in completing the mysterious quantrains of a female poet, he is suddenly metamorphosed into a 'young hero with golden-yellow hair curlier than cross-trees of small harps: royal raiment he wore, and his form was the noblest that hath been seen on a human being . . . It is not . . . doubtful that he was the Spirit of Poetry'.[127]

Those who define the comic as the satirical may have wondered why the audiences of comedy laugh at actions in which they would not engage: why do bank managers laugh at bank robberies and muggings, bungled or otherwise, when these exploits are presented in comedies; why are persons of impeccable sexual morals amused by dirty jokes? Anti-clerical humour is a special instance of the same question: the elderly and three-quarters mad Father Jack, who jumps out of a plane with a parachute and the drinks trolley, could hardly have been conceived outside of Ireland. Do we laugh at *Father Ted*'s alcoholic priest because he is ridiculous, and therefore entirely unlike ourselves?[128] When he made the Athenian demagogue Cleon the pestle with which the god War is grinding the states of Greece into a salad, in *Peace*, Aristophanes perfected the art of satire as political cartoon.[129] But not all of Aristophanes' characters are Cleons: we sympathise with Trygaeus, Peisetaerus and Lysistrata; their exploits are set out for our delight. Nor is it only the comic *hero* who is empathetic. Even though the leading figure in Monty Python's Dead Parrot Sketch is ridiculous, anyone who has met an obstructive wall of lies from a salesman identifies with Cleese's character. We can identify with bad comic *heroes*. When we laugh at Woody Allen in *Take the Money and Run*, it is because we have been there, if not as failed bank robbers, as failures in other lines of business. AA members laugh at alcoholics because it hurts. Audience detachment is not the clue to the good citizen's delight in the apparent

---

126 Ibid., p. 15.
127 Elliott, *Power of Satire*, p. 22.
128 Olson, *Theory of Comedy*, p. 37.
129 Ibid., pp. 69–71.

amoralism of some sorts of comedy. The comic hero inhabits a space of freedom; the audience experiences this freedom as unexpectedly fulfilled desire. If not all comedies are satires, that is because some comedies project an *area of grace* upon their leading figure. Samson lives in an area of grace. The area of grace is not genuinely anti-moral. The law-breaking miracle of grace requires a moral context. But there is more to being moral than being law-abiding. The comic figure, representing this arena in which we can take pleasure in law-breaking, stands for this common intuition. He is often opposed by the stickler for the laws. The satirist's *butt* is sometimes a real, but more often a fake, Puritan; the comedian's *hero*, with whom we identify, and who opens up an imaginative space of freedom for us, breaks abstract laws in the name of life, a tricky business for the moral theologians to explain without recourse to the notion of the sacred.

The comedy which makes fun of people with whom we do not identify is *satire;* here the actors are objects of derision, who are viewed by the audience as an *enemy.* Modern examples of the art are *Spitting Image* and *Private Eye.* The aggression is not haphazard: satire is 'the comic used in attacks that are part of an *agenda* on the part of the satirist … Most often the attack is directed against institutions and their representatives, notably political or religious ones'.[130] Contemporary satirists feed off politics: they hang around newspapers and television studios in capital cities. The satirists of Israel *c.* 1000–550 BC also hung out at the court of the king's capital city: they were the prophets.

God treats Saul and David very differently. Brueggemann lists the disparities: Saul is deprived of his kingship for failing to spoil the Amalekites; David will later attack the 'same Amalekites', seize their booty, and receive only congratulation for his cunning (cf. 1 Sam. 30.19–20, 23–25); Saul is not granted forgiveness, but David is, after sending Uriah to death on the front line:[131] 'For David, Yahweh is "Providence"; for Saul, Yahweh is "Fate".'[132] This is because David's freedom enables him to present an area of grace. This is not given to everyone: it may, as Brueggemann says of Yahweh's treatment of David, be 'arbitrary'. It is not equitable that Saul appears to be a hard-trier who gets nowhere, whilst David springs buoyantly from one misdemeanour to the next; he can even charm God. If we insist on rule-abidingness for all, we would have consistent fairness but no areas of grace. The story of Saul is interleaved with that of David. In the first part of the story, David is played off against Saul: here Saul is the area of bondage and David the area of grace. In so far as Saul represents bondage, he is treated satirically.

Samuel's sons practise bribery and extortion: they cannot succeed him as judges (1 Sam. 8.1–5). That might give some people the idea that the hereditary principle does not work very efficiently, but it makes the 'elders of Israel' demand a king. Yahweh instructs his prophet to tell them what a king will be like, and he does so, extravagantly blackening the character of kingship:

---

130 Berger, *Redeeming Laughter*, p. 157.
131 Brueggemann, *Theology of the Old Testament*, pp. 367–371.
132 Gunn, *Fate of King Saul*, p. 116.

> He will take your sons, and appoint them for himself, for his chariots, and to
> be his horsemen; and some shall run before his chariots.
> And he will appoint him captains over thousands, and captains over fifties;
> and he will set them to ear his ground, and to reap his harvest, and to make
> his instruments of war, and instruments of his chariots.
> And he will take your daughters to be confectionaries, and to be cooks, and
> to be bakers. (1 Sam. 8.11–13)

The caricature is blown larger and larger: the obvious answer to Samuel's
warning is a change of mind: the people blithely persist in wanting 'a king
over us', who will 'fight our battles' for us (1 Sam. 8.19, 20). The scene
shifts to the family of Kish, who 'had a son, whose name was Saul, a choice
young man, and a goodly: and there was not among the children of Israel a
goodlier person than he' (1 Sam. 9.2). Samuel anoints him, in private. The
charism seems to 'take': we find Saul 'among the prophets' (10.11). He
neglects to mention these exploits to his family: they will be as surprised as
anyone when the tribes gather at Mizpeh to chose a king, and the lot
indicates *him*. Dragged from under 'the stuff', Saul stands up, and is
'higher than any of the people from his shoulders and upward' (10.23).
Saul is empowered by the 'Spirit of the Lord' to call the Israelites to arms to
rescue the people of Jabesh-Gilead from the Ammonites (1 Sam. 11). This
single unalloyed victory is followed by Saul's public anointing, with the
warning signs from heaven (1 Sam. 12). Downfall follows swiftly: Saul
makes his first false step by seizing the day, and sacrificing before Samuel
arrives at Michmash Pass. Some take Saul's excuses at face value, but it
may be asked: did the victor of Jabesh-Gilead sacrifice in order to get it
over with and on with the real business, the war against the Philistines? Do
we say 'I forced myself' when we did?

Saul goes forth to battle against the Amalekites, having been instructed
by Samuel to 'utterly destroy all that they have, and spare them not;
but slay both man and woman, infant and suckling, ox and sheep, camel
and ass' (15.3). These are the rules of holy war, as the Deuteronomist
conceives them. Samuel goes to find out whether his instruction has been
obeyed:

> Samuel came to Saul: and Saul said unto him, 'Blessed be thou of the Lord: I
> have performed the commandment of the Lord.'
> And Samuel said, 'What meaneth then this bleating of the sheep in mine
> ears, and the lowing of the oxen which I hear?'
> And Saul said, 'They have brought them from the Amalekites: for the people
> spared the best of the sheep and the oxen, to sacrifice unto the Lord thy God;
> and the rest we have utterly destroyed.' (15.13–15)

If the scene were staged, this could hardly fail to be funny. On the page, we
may wonder about Saul's intentions, but if we saw the unconcealably noisy
animals, in person, crowded around Saul the ayes would have it (guilty).
The animals make him look ridiculous. Saul unheroically blames someone
else: 'the people took of the spoil, sheep and oxen, the chief of the things
which should have been utterly destroyed, to sacrifice unto the Lord thy
God in Gilgal' (15.22). He knows he was supposed to destroy. How would
the Deuteronomist take the suggestion that Saul did mean to sacrifice? He
might unkindly, and anachronistically, point Saul to Isaiah's satirical
commentary on a later king:

'What to Me is the multitude of your sacrifices?'
Says the Lord;
'I have had enough of burnt offerings of rams
and the fat of fatted beasts;
I do not delight in the blood of bulls,
Or of lambs, or of he-goats.' (Is. 1.11)

Samuel replies to Saul in analogous terms to the prophet:

hath the Lord as great delight in burnt offerings and sacrifices, as in obeying the voice of the Lord? Behold, to obey is better than sacrifice, and to hearken than the fat of rams. (1 Sam. 15.22)

Samuel pronounces the hard words of rejection: Saul continues to blame the people:

I have sinned: for I have transgressed the commandment of the Lord, and thy words: because I feared the people, and obeyed their voice. (15.24)

If we think that Saul's punishment exceeds his crime, we should point the finger at kingship: can anyone please the people and obey God in equal measure? Saul the king is the object of satire, and is viewed with detachment. Elliott develops a theory of satire as ritual curse, as a subsection of the Cambridge school's conception of comedy as fertility rite. Aristotle had noted, rather vaguely, that Comedy 'originat[es] with the authors of ... phallic songs'.[133] Elliott claims that

The entire rite is magical. Its purpose was to stimulate fertility, the sacred energy of life ... The ceremonial had two aspects, as it were: the invocation of good influences through the magic potency of the phallus, the expulsion of evil influences through the magical potency of abuse. Cornford says: '... the simplest of all methods of expelling ... malign influences of any kind is to abuse them with the most violent language'.[134]

Like the verses of the primitive satirists, the poetic words and the strange gestures of the biblical prophets are agents of a power which, von Rad says, we need not scruple to regard as magical.[135] The prophetic word unleashes the negative power of God: 'Isaiah speaks of the word of Jahweh as if it were a material thing, achieving its effect by its physical weight: The Lord has sent a word against Jacob, and it has lit upon Israel (Is. 9.7).'[136] The satirist '"kills", at least symbolically':[137] when Ezekiel had done abusing him, Pelatiah dropped dead (Ezek. 11.13).[138] The Deuteronomist used the prophetic idea of the powerful word of God.[139]

Northrop Frye claims that satire requires a shared *moral* point of view between satirist and audience. Berger notes in response that satire can *create* such a perspective:

---

133 Aristotle, *Poetics*, 1449a 5–10.
134 Elliott, *Power of Satire*, p. 5.
135 Von Rad, *Old Testament Theology II*, pp. 82–86.
136 Ibid., p. 90.
137 Elliott, *Power of Satire*, p. 4.
138 Von Rad, *Old Testament Theology II*, p. 91.
139 Ibid., pp. 93–94.

Satire can also be educational: it may be as a *result* of the satirist's labors that the audience comes to understand the undesirability of what is attacked.[140]

One of the purposes of the prophets' 'campaign' against compromising kings was an exercise in moral education;[141] we tend to notice the didacticism more than the artistic means by which it is put across. The prophets' dramatic gestures not only signal but also bring about the destruction which they express. Prophetic satire is a form of 'ritual cursing'. Samuel has put a curse on Saul.[142]

He turns his back on the distressed man and tears his own robe, a prophetic gesture which signals that God has torn the kingship from Saul.[143] Threatened with public humiliation, Saul stops shifting the blame, and begs Samuel not to shame him publicly: 'honour me now, I pray thee, before the elders of my people, and before Israel, and turn again with me, that I may worship the Lord thy God' (1 Sam. 15.30). Saul is too much interested in his stage appearance to be a good actor. Samuel

> turned again after Saul; and Saul worshipped the Lord.
> Then said Samuel, 'Bring ye hither to me Agag the king of the Amalekites.' And Agag came unto him delicately. And Agag said, 'Surely the bitterness of death is past.'
> And Samuel said, 'As thy sword hath made women childless, so shall thy mother be childless among women.' And Samuel hewed Agag in pieces before the Lord in Gilgal. (15.31–33)

Saul's story is over: he has been pushed back onto himself. Samuel mourns Saul, with the sorrow of the first prophet to Israel's king for her first king, whose disobedience typifies all of Israel's historical kings. God is used to beginning again. He tells his prophet to stop mourning, get his anointing equipment, and go to see Jesse. Samuel is afraid: 'Saul will kill me if he sees me.' So God tells him to 'lie a little': take a heifer too and pretend it is for a sacrifice. Brueggemann comments that 'This Yahweh is not committed to the moral civility of an entrenched order.'[144] Jesse's seven sons are paraded before the prophet: each looks good enough to him, but God tells him that only one who can see the outside and the inside of the candidates can decide; leave it up to him. The youngest is brought in, not tall, but 'beautiful' (1 Sam. 16.12); the last one in is the best.

140 Berger, *Redeeming Laughter*, p. 158.
141 Ibid., p. 157.
142 As Elisha 'was going up by the way, there came forth little children out of the city, and mocked him, and said unto him, Go up thou bald head, go up thou bald head. And he turned back and looked on them, and cursed them in the name of the Lord. And there came forth two she bears out of the wood, and tare forty and two children of them.' (2 Kings 2.23–24). Is W. C. Fields also among the prophets?
143 W. D. Stacey comments that 'Tearing garments was a serious matter, as mourning rites show. There are many references to the tearing of a kingdom from a king in which the same Hebrew verb is used (I Sam. 28.17; I Kings 11.11f., 31; 14.8) ... defeated monarchs were humiliated by the spoliation of their robes.' *Prophetic Drama*, p. 77. He also notes that these lines are ambiguous: it may be that the 'he' is *Saul*, grabbing Samuel's mantle and inadvertently ripping it.
144 Walter Brueggemann, *David's Truth in Israel's Imagination and Memory* (Fortress Press, Philadelphia, 1985), p. 26.

Samuel took the horn of oil, and anointed him in the midst of his brethren: and the Spirit of the Lord came upon David from that day forward. So Samuel rose up, and went to Ramah.
But the Spirit of the Lord departed from Saul, and an evil spirit from the Lord troubled him. (16.13–14)

The two anointings are thus directly contrasted. David, resilient actor, harpist, and dispeller of evil spirits is first presented as a 'refreshing' (16.23) agent of liberation to Saul.

The narrator sends Saul's armour bearer back to obscurity, so that he can emerge as an unknown, short champion against another tall man.

And there went out a champion out of the camp of the Philistines, named Goliath, of Gath, whose height was six cubits and a span.
And he had a helmet of brass upon his head, and he was armed with a coat of mail; and the weight of the coat was five thousand shekels of brass.
And he had greaves of brass upon his legs, and a target of brass was between his shoulders.
And the staff of his spear was like a weaver's beam; and his spear's head weighed six hundred shekels of iron: and one bearing a shield went before him. (17.4–7)

His father sends David to go-fer bread and cheese for his brothers on service. David asks who the hell does this 'uncircumcised Philistine' think he is, 'that he should defy the armies of the living God' (17.26). News of this singular, unfrightened man is carried to King Saul. He offers the boy his armour. David tries on armour, helmet and sword, and removes them. The mighty armoured hero challenging his equal is not the stuff of comedy, or of great faith. But only the dullest sermonists depict the episode as an act of *empty-handed* and *blind* faith against a humanly invincible enemy: David enters with the skills of a shepherd. He *looked*, and saw the weak spot; he also took in that an over-freighted giant cannot move fast in his gear. Heller construes his heroism as an act of imagination: here were the Benjamites, the Ephraimites and the men of Manasseh, God's 'chosen people', but

in no other brain but mine did the obvious consideration arise that Goliath might be successfully met in single combat on conditions different from those implied in his own preparations for the fray ... Away from home with my flocks for weeks at a time, I would spend hours on end ... practising on my lyre, composing songs, and slinging stones at broken clay flasks placed atop a wooden fence as standing targets, or at rusty tin cans ... I would spend whole mornings and afternoons practising with my sling in order to help the time go faster. I knew I was good ... And with Goliath that day, I knew that if I could get within twenty-five paces of the big son of a bitch, I could sling a stone the size of a pig's knuckle down his throat with enough velocity to penetrate the back of his neck and kill him, and I also knew something else: I knew if I was wrong about that, I could turn and run ... and dodge my way back up the hill to safety without much risk from anyone chasing me in all that armour. I paused a moment on the peak of the low ridge to let everyone get a good look. I was far from uninterested in the effect I was creating ... If you want to believe what you've heard, I halted along the way to choose five smooth stones out of the brook. That was just for show. Any slinger worth his salt always carries his stones with him; and as I knelt with my knees in the water, I was unobtrusively removing two from the leather pouch at my waist, concealing them in the palm of my right hand.[145]

The warrior's boast is a diluted form of the satirical curse:[146] the champion and the go-fer match insult to insult. But it was 'that stick I carried that really touched him off':[147] the Philistine roared, 'am I a dog, that thou comest to me with staves?' and 'cursed David by his gods' (1 Sam. 17.43). Goliath is going to feed David to the birds: David has Power behind his imagination:

> Thou comest to me with a sword, and with a spear, and with a shield: but I come to thee in the name of the Lord of hosts, the God of the armies of Israel, whom thou hast defied. (17.45)

David insults in the Lord; and his prognosis of the possibilities of the contest prove accurate;

> David put his hand in his bag, and took thence a stone, and slang it, and smote the Philistine in his forehead, that the stone sunk into his forehead; and he fell upon his face to the earth. (17.49)

Saul shrank before the oversized Philistine. A chorus of women chant the truth: 'Saul has slain his thousands, and David his ten thousands' (18.7). Why do a few impressionable women make Saul fear for his kingdom? Elliott explains the story by reference to the satire practised by Arabic women:

> the odd poetic power wielded by these women explains 'why King Saul was so upset when the "dancing women" in their songs of triumph . . . "gave" to David the slaying of ten thousands and him only thousands . . .'[148]

Jonathan hands over his armour to David, denuding himself of the symbols of his inheritance. That raises the hypothetical question: *what if Saul* had taken Samuel's blunt hints and given up his kingdom, thus following in the footsteps of Jotham? A Saul party would have formed to resist the usurper, the hot-heads around the new king would have insisted that the old king, and his sons, were a dangerous liability and must be put to death. Saul is too much himself to play well on the political stage: and *so is his son Jonathan.* The narrative contrasts Jonathan's straight-forward honesty and David's ability to conceal his intentions. Saul is too bad to be a good king, Jonathan too good even to be a bad king. David is sufficiently devious to become a great king: but once he is tarred with the brush of kingship, the man begins to surface. And so we have an infernal comedy, in which the incommensurable demands of God, politics and humanity cannot all be met.

The encomiums for David spark Saul's jealous wrath. The next day,

> the evil spirit from God came upon Saul, and he prophesied in the midst of the house, and David played with his hand, as at other times: and there was a javelin in Saul's hand.

---

145 Heller, *God Knows*, pp. 88, 90, 96–97.
146 Elliott, *Power of Satire*, p. 16.
147 Heller, *God Knows*, p. 98.
148 Elliott, *Power of Satire*, p. 17, quoting S. D. Gotein.

And Saul cast the javelin: for he said, 'I will smite David even to the wall with it.' And David avoided out of this presence twice.

And Saul was afraid of David, because the Lord was with him, and was departed from Saul. (1 Sam. 18.10–12)

Saul cannot carry the role of the prophet. But he will be forced into parodying it. David flees to Samuel at Ramah. Saul pursues him. There follows a scene in which Saul plays the inverted prophet:

Saul sent messengers to take David: and when they saw the company of prophets prophesying, and Samuel standing as appointed over them, the Spirit of the Lord was upon the messengers of Saul, and they also prophesied. And when it was told Saul, he sent other messengers, and they prophesied likewise. And Saul sent messengers again the third time, and they prophesied also.

Then went he also to Ramah, and came to a great well that is in Sechu: and he asked, and said, 'Where are Samuel and David?' And one said, 'Behold, they be at Naioth in Ramah.'

And he went thither to Naioth in Ramah: and the Spirit of God was upon him also, and he went on, and prophesied, until he came to Naioth in Ramah.

And he stripped off his clothes also, and prophesied before Samuel in like manner, and lay down naked all that day and all that night. Wherefore they say, 'Is Saul also among the prophets?' (19.20–24)

Samuel repels the attack by the use of sympathetic magic. It is Saul's habit to 'prophesy', in the name of who knows what gods or spirits; the Spirit of the Lord, invoked by Samuel, reduces first his messengers and then Saul himself to gibbering wrecks. Under the influence of the Spirit, Saul involuntarily and unconsciously tears off the clothes which had given him the bearing of a man, if not a king. Saul is now a 'disintegrated personality'.[149] The question of 1 Sam. 10.12 is repeated, its irony now obvious: 'Is Saul also among the prophets?' Robert Polzin comments that

the murderous conduct of Saul in chapter 19 characterises as evil his and his servant's prophesying at the chapter's end. 'Is Saul also among the prophets?' (19.21) asks a question about one of Saul's most abominable practices.[150]

The Deuteronomists who edited the histories of Israel's monarchs had earlier taken a hand in cultic reform, directing the theological spring-cleaning of the Jerusalem Temple (2 Kings 22–23), which took place under King Josiah (seventh century BC). The Deuteronomist reformers centralised the cult in Jerusalem, expelling cult prostitutes and spirit-mediums from the Temple precincts. In the light of their moral imagination, Saul's madness takes the shape of prophesying in the name of evil spirits.

Saul offered his daughter to any taker against Goliath. David can have Merab, he says. David prudently demurs: he is not great enough to join such an illustrious family. Saul learns a helpful fact: 'Michal, Saul's daughter, loved David: and they told Saul, and the thing pleased him' (1 Sam. 18.20). Saul can use Michal as a decoy to trap David. The putative son-in-law protests his unworthiness until he learns that the prize will cost him only a hundred Philistine 'foreskins'. The hero bounces back, exchang-

149 Exum, *Tragedy and Biblical Narrative*, p. 40.
150 Polzin, *Samuel and the Deuteronomist*, p. 185.

ing the double-bounty of two hundred foreskins for the woman who loves him. She would be wrong to take it personally, and so would we; so long as monarchies mattered, few princesses made love-matches. The narrator neither admires nor mourns the facts of politics. Saul has given away his pawn only to make her David's ally.

David flees to Nob, where a frightened priest wonders why he is at large. David cannot divulge the deadly secret business from the king which has brought him here: but he is extremely hungry, and 'what is under thine hand? give me five loaves of bread' or whatever you have got there (1 Sam. 21.3). This, Ahimelech tells the young man, pompously, is *not* ordinary bread, but 'the consecrated shrewbread', and, eyeing David, is reserved for 'young men who have kept themselves at least from women' (21.4). David assures him that he and his friends have done just that, and in any case, playing with words, the bread is 'in a manner common, yea, though it were sanctified this day in the vessel' (21.5). So the apprehensive 'priest gave him the bread'. Lying to a priest and church robbery are now to David's credit: it would be a sterner reader than this who did not find the absoluteness of the amorality amusing. David is still on the run. He plants himself for safety on Achish, king of Gath. Achish learns his identity, which puts David in some danger. So

> he changed his behaviour before them, and feigned himself mad in their hands, and scrabbled on the doors of the gate, and let his spittle fall down upon his beard.
> Then said Achish unto his servants, 'Lo, ye see the man is mad: wherefore then have ye brought him to me?
> Have I need of mad men, that ye have brought this fellow to play the mad man in my presence? shall this fellow come into my house?' (1 Sam. 21.13–15)

Von Balthasar takes this as one of David's 'humiliations': 'at the low point of his flight he has to play the lunatic and so invite contempt (21.10ff)'.[151] The manoeuvre is actually the pragmatic equivalent of a pratfall. But von Balthasar is right to recognise that *humility*, the self-giving which every actor and actress requires,[152] is one of David's virtues, and stocks-in-trade. A band of debt-ridden outlaws join David (being in debt is never a sin in comedy). Brueggemann says that the text 'celebrates' the 'bandit' status because bandits are *habirem*, characters alienated from urban society, and fighting back.[153] The Canaanite King Rib-Addi repeatedly called the *'Apiru* stray dogs;[154] in the biblical narrative, the *habiru* emerge triumphant in David:

> He lost status in the Israelite community by flight caused by the enmity of the king. There gathered about him other refugees motivated by economic as well as other concerns. All were similarly without legal protection and had to maintain themselves by forming a band under the leadership of David, which

---

151 Von Balthasar, *Glory VI*, p. 112.
152 Von Balthasar, *Theo-Drama I*, p. 294.
153 Brueggemann, *David's Truth*, pp. 20–21.
154 Mendenhall, *Tenth Generation*, pp. 124 and 130: 'A stray dog is one who has become alienated and is beyond the control of his master.'

was then able to survive by cleverness combined with a considerable degree
of mobility ... the Philistines themselves label David and his gang 'Apiru-
Hebrew', and relieve David of the embarrassing moral choice of open breach
of either his political obligations to Achish or his religious obligations to
Israel.[155]

By dint of his outlaw status, David returns to the primeval ethico-religious
experience of the *'Apiru*: 'It began to look as though every deadbeat, misfit,
rascal and freebooter in the land was anxious to join me.'[156] David is attractive because he is outside the law. The attraction derives from the human
need to break taboos. That desire is not that there should be no taboos –
how much more rational! One intuition tells us that taboos are not just
sociologically necessary, but real channels of power; a counter-intuition
tells us that on the other side of the taboo there is an even larger area of
grace. It is not at all fair that the miracle works for some and not others. As
Saul hunts David through the hillcountry of Palestine, the narrative sets
out the pre-rational explanation for our identification with the man. Saul
enters the cave in which David and his men are hiding: the mischievous
taboo-breaker cannot resist cutting off a slice of the king's robe. Remorseful,
he steps up, bows to the 'Lord's anointed', tells him that he could have had
his life, and shows the evidence (1 Sam. 24.11). Although David's action is
not exactly motiveless, von Balthasar puts his finger on one reason for
David's 'arbitrary' appeal:

> After friendship, David's great gift is magnanimity, the thoroughly human,
> Aristotelian sort: the *grandezza* which, in its sovereignty, knows how to
> forgive. This is David's constant attitude towards Saul as he flees from the
> latter's disfavour.[157]

David the man is a generous giver. We like his escapades, because we
identify with them. Heroes such as David nourish other people; that is one
definition of grace. What will happen when that great *humanity* has to sit
on a throne, 'so that the bandit becomes the new authority' is a darker
story.[158] It is indicated by David's collection of a pair of new wives, Abigail
and Ahinoam of Jezreel, a large harem being the prerogative of a man on
the way to political power. The narrator comments laconically, in the next
verse, that 'Saul had given his daughter, David's wife, to Phaltiel' (1 Sam.
25.44).

The Philistines are still around to help to conclude one story, and to
bring the spirits of the underworld into the closing scenes of Israel's first
monarch. Re-enter Saul, and remember that the Deuteronomists had a hand
in clearing necromancers out of the Jerusalem Temple:

> Now Samuel was dead, and all Israel lamented him, and buried him in
> Ramah, even in his own city. And Saul had put away those that had familiar
> spirits, and the wizards, out of the land.
> And the Philistines ... pitched in Shunem: and Saul gathered all Israel
> together, and they pitched in Gilboa.

155 Ibid., pp. 135–136.
156 Heller, *God Knows*, p. 229.
157 Von Balthasar, *Glory VI*, p. 111.
158 Brueggemann, *David's Truth*, p. 22.

And when Saul saw the host of the Philistines, he was afraid, and his heart greatly trembled.
And when Saul enquired of the Lord, the Lord answered him not, neither by dreams, nor by Urim, nor by prophets.
Then said Saul unto his servants, 'Seek me a woman that hath a familiar spirit, that I may go to her, and enquire of her.' And his servants said to him, 'Behold, there is a woman that hath a familiar spirit at Endor.'
And Saul disguised himself, and put on another raiment, and he went, and two men with him, and they came to the woman by night: and he said, 'I pray thee, divine unto me by the familiar spirit, and bring me him up, whom I shall name unto thee.' (28.3–8)

Cheryl Exum comments perceptively on the dark-scene painting: the visit to the witch takes place by night, a clue that death is portended for the traveller. She asks

Why does Saul seek out the prophet Samuel, who has already rejected him? When Gunn answers that Saul can stand no more ambiguity, he identifies the root of the dilemma of the tragic hero. Not content to let his tragic destiny unfold, the tragic hero stalks it. Like Oedipus, who relentlessly pushes for the full truth to be disclosed while the answers steadily close in upon him, Saul *must* know.[159]

The irony of the biblical passage is blunt to the point of being bludgeoning: as the first line (1 Sam. 28.3) indicates, Saul goes to gather information from the profession which he has just criminalised. We are not intended to sympathise with the object of such plain satire. Oedipus urgently sought his own identity. Saul's motive is fear of the Philistines. He cannot face them without some oracle. Even a forced oracle will do. Compulsion is his stock-in-trade, used both against himself and others. Would the king who fought the Philistines, and won, be this apprehensive if his situation were genuinely ambiguous to him? He does not seek knowledge, but rather, desperately evades reality. Sophocles' hero put his eyes out because he saw the truth; Saul goes in the dark because he does not want to do so, if he cannot control the outcome.

And the woman said unto him, 'Behold, thou knowest what Saul hath done, how he hath cut off those that have familiar spirits, and the wizards, out of the land: wherefore then layest thou a snare for my life, to cause me to die?' And Saul sware to her by the Lord, saying, 'As the Lord liveth, there shall no punishment happen to thee for this thing.' (28.9–10)

The king will make sure of that.

Then said the woman, 'Whom shall I bring up to thee?' And he said, 'Bring me up Samuel.'
And when the woman saw Samuel, she cried with a loud voice: and the woman spake to Saul, saying, 'Why hast thou deceived me? for thou art Saul.'
And the king said unto her, 'Be not afraid: for what sawest thou?' And the woman said unto Saul, 'I saw gods ascending out of the earth.'
And he said unto her, 'What form is he of?' And she said, 'An old man cometh up; and he is covered with a mantle.' And Saul perceived that it was Samuel, and he stooped with his face to the ground, and bowed himself.

159 Exum, *Tragedy and Biblical Narrative*, p. 23.

And Samuel said to Saul, 'Why hast thou disquieted me, to bring me up?'
And Saul answered, 'I am sore distressed; for the Philistines make war against
me, and God is departed from me, and answereth me no more, neither by
prophets, nor by dreams: therefore I have called thee, that thou mayest make
known unto me what I shall do.'
Then said Samuel, 'Wherefore then dost thou ask of me, seeing the Lord is
departed from thee, and is become thine enemy?
And the Lord . . . hath rent the kingdom out of thine hand, and given it . . . to
David:
Because thou obeyedst not the voice of the Lord, nor executedst his fierce wrath
upon Amalek, therefore hath the Lord done this thing unto thee this day.
Moreover the Lord will also deliver Israel with thee into the hand of the
Philistines: and tomorrow shalt thou and thy sons be with me: the Lord also
shall deliver the host of Israel into the hand of the Philistines.' (28.11–19)

It is only when the witch 'sees Samuel' that she 'recognizes Saul'.[160] But
Samuel can only tell Saul what he 'knows already'. Saul the king has had
to stand for imprisonment. Now the narrator shows him collapsing back
into his humanity:

Then Saul fell straightaway all along on the earth, and was sore afraid . . . and
there was no strength in him; for he had eaten no bread all the day, nor all the
night. (28.20)

If there is one thing which a sublime Sophoclean hero is not supposed to
feel, it is his stomach rumbling in his climactic scene. The woman sees the
man's shivering human need:

'let me set a morsel of bread before thee; and eat, that thou mayest have
strength, when thou goest on thy way.'
But he refused, and said, 'I will not eat.' But his servants, together with the
woman, compelled him; and he hearkened unto their voice. So he arose from
the earth, and sat upon the bed. (28.22–23)

The witch turned helper kills a calf and bakes bread:

And she brought it before Saul and before his servants; and they did eat.
Then they rose up, and went away that night. (28.24)

If this scene has taken to the depths of a satirical hell, turning our attention
to the physical body changes the tone:

In a scene built around dialogue, Saul's words are dramatic in their brevity,
'I will not eat.' The meal which Saul finally allows to be prepared and which
he eats with his servants ameliorates the despair and pathos of the scene.
Saul would have it otherwise, but he gives in, as he has before, to human
urging. Pure tragedy would have left him without any recourse.[161]

Saul began as the most average of guys. An errand for, of all banalities,
missing donkeys, takes him to 'the seer'; on Yahweh's instructions, he
returns home an anointed king. Saul is so ordinary that he *is* the people,
who want a king. His only egregious feature is his height, 'from the neck
up'. Saul is still a human figure in his last scene. He can only speak his own

160 Ibid.
161 Ibid., p. 24.

lines, but his personality is less free than that of his actor-rival. The requirement that he be obedient to the prophet's commands was an invitation to assume a role, by drawing on resources within and beyond himself. When he tried to 'do the prophet', what comes out is not the word of God but a naked man yelping; his efforts to play the king crumple before the savage satire of Samuel, and, since he directs the drama, of God. This is a black comedy. Tragic heroes take their lives; the objects of satire are driven to suicide.[162] Saul stands for the worldly kings of Israel. If that were all that we saw in him, he would have no pathos. Saul's humanity is visible under the ridiculously misfitting robes of the king. His failure is pathetic, because we identify with the *humanity*. But how far? When we think back to his little, self-serving lies to Samuel, his efforts to murder David, and finally to the self-delusive hypocrisy of the visit to the witch, we do not really want to follow him, if we can avoid it. The narrative's treatment of Israel's first king is satirical, whilst preserving a respect for his humanity, the too-smallness of the tall man.

The Philistines send the body 'round about to publish it in the house of their idols' (1 Sam. 31.9). But Saul has made a few friends, and the narrative does not forget the disorderly fact. The Philistines

> put his armour in the house of Ashtaroth: and they fastened his body to the wall of Bethshan.
> And when the inhabitants of Jabeth-gilead heard that which the Philistines had done to Saul;
> All the valiant men arose, and went all night, and took the body of Saul and the bodies of his sons from the wall of Beth-shan, and there came to Jabesh, and burnt them there.
> And they took their bones, and buried them under a tree at Jabesh, and fasted seven days. (31.11–13)

W. Lee Humphreys comments that

> this ... dark ... moment has a constructive subtone as well ... the men of Jabesh-Gilead come, grateful still to their former deliverer, and take his and his sons' exposed bodies and give them an honourable burial. In death Saul attains a stature that escaped him in life.[163]

The author does not conclude the first book of Samuel with the desecration of the hero's body. The judgement on Israel's first king is eased by the intuition that his corporeal humanity deserves respect. The author of the books of Samuel is too much of a realist to imagine his protagonists in a monotone. He sees the good intermingled with the bad, the mark of the ironist. We do not *know* that there was a humanistic *renaissance* at the court of King Solomon: we *do* know that there was *one* humanist present, that is, the author of the Saul and the David cycles. Scholars have been led by the narrator's realistic perception of character to take Saul's story as a tragedy. The Deuteronomist's humanism is balanced against a moral absolutism which takes fire in prophetic satire: he sees matters both from a human and from a divine perspective.

---

162 Eliott, *Power of Satire*, p. 77.
163 W. Lee Humphreys, 'The Tragedy of King Saul: A Study of the Structure of 1 Samuel 9–31', *Journal for the Study of the Old Testament*, 1978, 18–27 (24).

One may cast a cynical eye on David's public displays of grief. The Amalekite messenger who brings the news of the deaths of Saul and Jonathan, and boasts that he put the spear into Saul, showing the trophies of Saul's royal insignia, is put to death for those crown and bracelets. David comments:

> Thy blood be upon thy head; for thy mouth hath testified against thee, saying, I have slain the Lord's anointed. (2 Sam. 1.16)

David laments 'Saul and Jonathan his son':

> The beauty of Israel is slain upon thy high places: how are the mighty fallen!
>
> . . .
>
> Ye mountains of Gilboa, let there be no dew, neither let there be rain, upon you . . . for there the shield of the mighty is vilely cast away, the shield of Saul, as though he had not been anointed with oil.
>
> . . .
>
> Ye daughters of Israel, weep over Saul, who clothed you in scarlet, with other delights, who put on ornaments of gold upon your apparel.
>
> . . .
>
> I am distressed for thee, my brother Jonathan: very pleasant hast thou been unto me: thy love to me was wonderful, passing the love of women.
> How are the mighty fallen, and the weapons of war perished. (2 Sam. 1.19, 21, 24, 26–27)

David describes Saul the king as the glory of Israel. The stories of 1–2 Samuel present three sides of kingship. Here, in the words which the narrator gives to him, David places the theocratically idealistic and the human together, in the face of King Saul. This is a great act of imagination. We need not assume that an undercurrent of irony is present here. David believes that the king does not emerge out of political expediency but is chosen by the Lord. David sends God's blessing to the men of Jabesh-Gilead, for 'showing this kindness' to Saul (2 Sam. 3.4–5). When Ishbosheth succumbs to the inevitable at the hands of his captains, David shows no mercy to the murderers. He takes Mephibosheth, Jonathan's crippled son, into his house (2 Sam. 9). He interprets family and blood allegiance differently than does Joab.

Michal is the only woman in the Bible of whom it is clearly stated that she loves her man;[164] David owes his life to this 'feminine helper'. When she was warned that Saul's men are coming to take David: 'Michal let David down through a window: and he went, and fled, and escaped' (1 Sam. 19.12); 'out the window I went, like some hairylegged clown in a dirty burlesque'.[165] Michal is not just adoring, but smart with it; she

> took an image, and laid it in the bed and put a pillow of goat's hair for his bolster, and covered it with a cloth.
> And when Saul sent messengers to take David, she said, 'He is sick.'
> And Saul sent the messengers again to see David, saying, 'Bring him up to me in the bed, that I may slay him.'
> And when the messengers were come in, behold, there was an image in the bed, with a pillow of goat's hair for his bolster. (1 Sam. 19.12–16)

164 Alter, *Art of Biblical Narrative*, p. 118.
165 Heller, *God Knows*, p. 205.

The scene is reminiscent of Rebekah and Rachel at their most tricksterish. If the house stands for her female body, 'Michal figuratively births David into freedom'.[166] David *the king* will inhabit the world of infernal comedy. There is little room here for unselfish love. One of the marks of infernal comedy is that the 'pretty girl ... is either absent or victimized'.[167] Michal's release of David into the cheerful masculine camaraderie of the *habiru* gave Saul the pretext to marry his daughter to Phaltiel.

Abner makes the last Saulide fighting man, Ishbosheth, king. David and Ishbosheth go to war for the kingdom of Israel. In the camp of David are three brothers, Joab, Abishai and Asahel. Abner kills the youngest, Asahel (2 Sam. 2.22–24). Abner and Ishbosheth fall out over Saul's concubine, Rizpah. Abner offers his suit to David, who tells him that the price of the alliance is Michal (2 Sam. 3.13). Michal becomes the token of Abner's new fealty: she is also David's human claim to political legitimacy. 'Michal stands for Saul's succession',[168] and she cannot be left to breed Saulide pretenders. So

> David sent messengers to Ishbosheth Saul's son, saying, 'Deliver me my wife Michal, which I espoused to me for an hundred foreskins of the Philistines.' And Ishbosheth sent, and took her from her husband, even from Phaltiel the son of Laish.
> And her husband went with her along weeping behind her to Bahurim. Then Abner said to him, 'Go, return.' And he returned. (2 Sam. 3.14–16)

Phaltiel follows his wife until he reaches Bahurim, the border set by Abner between domestic and political life. Like Michal, he is 'a mere pawn in the game being played out between "Saul and David" and their descendants'.[169] After his rise to power, David retains his freedom as a man, before God; as a king he will be bound by political expediency, as indicated to him by right-hand men such as Joab. Joab does not feel himself bound by the terms of David's alliance with Abner: he and Abishai take their blood vengeance on Abner. It is David 'the king' who mourns (2 Sam. 3.24–34): 'all the people took notice of it, and it pleased them ... for all the people understood ... that it was not of the king to slay Abner' (3.36–37). David must now act in the public face of the king: 'Does he protest too much?'[170]

David captures Jerusalem: the Ark of the Lord must be brought there. After coming out of retirement, the Ark is no less a channel of divine energy than before: as it is conveyed on a cart to the city of David, with a parade of celebrating musicians going before it, Uzzah, putting out his hand to steady the mysterious beast, gets a fatal electric shock from the Lord (2 Sam. 6.6–7). Carting an Ark is a dangerous business. David is quickly discovering the difference between the rules which govern shewbread and the laws which Arks impose. Suitably terrified, David calls a halt until he has the Lord's permission to continue. The second stage is judiciously decorous: with excruciating care, David sacrifices an ox every six feet of the Ark-

---

166 Exum, *Tragedy and Biblical Narrative*, p. 89.
167 Louise Cowan (ed.),*The Terrain of Comedy*, introduction 'The Comic Terrain', p. 11.
168 Josipovici, *Book of God*, p. 191.
169 Ibid.
170 David M. Gunn, *Story of King David: Genre and Interpretation* (JSOT Press, Sheffield, 1978), p. 90.

cart's journey. He lets himself go when the Ark reaches Jerusalem, 'exhibiting corybantic behaviour before'[171] the Ark:

> David danced before the ark of the Lord with all his might; and David was girded with a linen ephod. (6.14)

Like the Scotsman in his kilt, David's whirling leaves little to the imagination. David's dance releases not only his own sexual energy but also 'Yahweh's creative energy'. All of that channelled fertility should have concluded with a pregnant Michal.[172] The wife brought back by David's captain to witness this spectacle gives him a cold douse of sarcasm:

> as the ark of the Lord came into the city of David, Michal Saul's daughter looked through a window, and saw king David leaping and dancing before the Lord; and she despised him in her heart.
> Michal the daughter of Saul came out to meet David, and said, 'How glorious was the king of Israel today, who uncovered himself to day in the eyes of the handmaids of his servants, as one of the vain fellows shamelessly uncovereth himself!'
> And David said unto Michal, 'It was before the Lord, which chose me before thy father, and before his house, to appoint me ruler over the people of the Lord, over Israel: therefore will I play before the Lord.
> And I will be yet more vile than thus, and will be base in mine own sight: and of the maidservants which thou hast spoken of, of them shall be had in honour.'
> Therefore Michal the daughter of Saul had no child unto the day of her death. (6.16, 20–23)

The feminine helper, who has been shifted from man to man, is confined inside the house, as befits a king's wife: she could hardly fail to be unimpressed by his display of sexual potency. Now that the David she loved is king 'the politics of gender serve the politics of state'.[173] David's ritual dance is an expression of potency: but perhaps it does make him look stupid, or half-human, as out-of-control gestures tend to do. Peter Berger pictures David's semi-naked dancing before the Ark as the gesture of the prototypical 'holy fool'. He remarks that Michal's lifelong barrenness is 'a severe penalty ... for lacking a sense of humor'.[174] The king has here a political face, and a human face. But the third dimension, of Yahweh's anointed king, is also overlaid into the narrative. The Hebrew verb 'to dance' appears three times in the Old Testament: twice, here, in 2 Samuel 6.5 and 21. The third occasion is in Proverbs 8.27–31, where Wisdom dances before God at the creation of the world:

> When he established the heavens, I was there ...
> when he marked out the foundations of the earth,
> then I was beside him, like a little child;
> and I was daily his delight,
> rejoicing before him always,
> rejoicing in his inhabited world
> and delighting in the sons of men.

171 Von Rad, *Old Testament Theology I*, p. 237.
172 Stacey, *Prophetic Drama*, p. 32.
173 Exum, *Tragedy and Biblical Narrative*, p. 87.
174 Berger, *Redeeming Laughter*, p. 187.

The theologians have found that the narrator implicitly links David, God's chosen, with Wisdom.[175] Heller makes David enjoy his dancing so fantastically that it recalls the day of creation:

> You never heard so much music or saw so much rejoicing as there was on the day we brought the ark of the covenant into the city . . . There was never such music and such song and such shouting for joy since the spirit of God first moved upon the face of the waters and He said: 'Let there be light.' And there was light. And there was I right out in front, leading them all, dancing before the Lord.[176]

The story of the shepherd and *habiru*-bandit pictures David as a public actor, whilst that of the monarch is largely about David's private misfortunes. Once the path to kingship is cleared, David is played off against himself. When David stands alone, in the 'Succession Narrative', *David* and *the king* wrestle with each other. There are three ways of being David: as a man, as the Lord's anointed king, and as a worldly monarch. Which self should he play? In the terms of the comic drama, we no longer have Saul to play the buffoon and the *habiru* the area of grace: David will have to do both.

Nathan the prophet gives David the command to build a temple to Yahweh in Jerusalem. This is a crucial moment of integration in the biblical narrative: now the city becomes the representative image of God's promise. James Dougherty comments that

> In their nomadic years the Jews depicted Yahweh as a citybreaker . . . when David and Solomon amalgamated Israel, Judah, and Canaan into one kingdom with a throne city, Jerusalem, God became the protector of that city. This development is negotiated in scripture by a series of dreams, prophecies, rituals, and prayers in which the nomadic Yahweh accepts a permanent 'house' like the king's house and adjacent to it in the citadel on Zion.[177]

Now God makes this promise to David: 'thine house and thy kingdom shall be established for ever before thee: thy throne shall be established for ever' (2 Sam. 7.16). The urban monarchy inaugurated by David receives God's eternal blessing. If we read the text only for the strand of irony at the expense of kingship, we may say that, as 'state truth' begins, imagination is 'placed in the hands of ideology'.[178] 2 Samuel 7 will then be the 'pivot' between the two putative stories, the moment at which royal ideology takes over from the truths of 'trust' of the earlier narrative.

David stays in Jerusalem while Joab does the hard work at which he excels, of smiting the Ammonites; Uriah the Hittite is with him. There is a freedom which is played out between human beings and God, and there is the liberty exercised amongst human beings, of which kings may have the lion's share. David, 'walk[ing] on the roof of the king's house' (11.2) espies

---

175 Hugo Rahner, *Man at Play: Or Did You Ever Practice Eutrapelia?*, translated by Brian Battershaw and Edward Quinn (Burns & Oates, London, 1965), pp. 19–20.
176 Heller, *God Knows*, p. 335.
177 James Dougherty, *The Five-Square City: The City in the Religious Imagination* (University of Notre Dame Press, Notre Dame, 1980), pp. 5–6.
178 Brueggemann, *David's Truth*, pp. 71–72 and 84.

a sun 'bathing beauty'.[179] Once 'the woman' is pregnant, how to deal with the husband? Bring Uriah home from the Ammonite war; try to get him to sleep with his wife (11.6–8); when the soldier insists that he cannot 'lie with my wife' while his comrades and the Ark are in danger, invite the subject to the palace and make him 'drunk'; when he proves unseduceable, send him back to the army with orders to Joab to put him 'at the forefront of the hottest battle' (11.15). Once having satirised yourself and killed Uriah, add Bathsheba to the harem,

> And when the mourning was over, David sent and fetched her to his house, and she became his wife. But the thing that David had done displeased the Lord. (11.27)

Nathan pronounces God's judgement: the child will die. The child falls sick, David prays face down for seven days, sees that the child has died, worships God and goes home and eats. The servants ask him how he can 'rise up' so quickly. David replies

> While the child was yet alive, I fasted and wept: for I said, Who can tell whether God will be gracious to me, that the child may live?
> But now he is dead, wherefore should I fast? can I bring him again? I shall go to him, but he shall not return to me. (2 Sam. 12.22–23)

Death has touched him, and David sees that it will do so again. Seeing his own death in his child's, he recognises that his culpability makes him free and mortal. The two main themes of the Succession Narrative are the 'inter-relation' of 'political and personal' and of 'giving' and 'grasping' in David's life.[180] David's seizure of Bathsheba leads to disaster: but as the first of its consequences works itself out, he knows that he cannot grasp God. Like David, God is free, and David leaves him that way. It is David, the most energetic comic character in the Old Testament, who comes closest to being its best tragic actor, because his *trustingness* is related to an unblinkered perception of death.

David the king has a fine brood of heirs and a palace to house their mis-demeanours. Where bumbling and confusion leads to Saul's debacle, the consequences of David's freedom work themselves out with a hard irony, a finger's breath from tragic necessity. David is 'enmeshed':[181] his grasping of Bathsheba is paralleled by his son's rape of Tamar. Amon falls in love with his virgin sister, gets her into his room by pretending to need a nurse for his sickness, and 'being stronger than she ... forced her, and lay with her' (13.14). Now he hates her for her defilement and kicks her out:

> Then he called his servant ... and said, 'Put now this woman out from me, and bolt the door after her.'
> And she had a garment of divers colours upon her: for with such robes were the king's daughters that were virgins apparelled. Then his servant brought her out, and bolted the door after her.
> And Tamar put ashes on her head, and rent her garment of divers colours that was on her, and laid her hand on her head, and went on crying. (13.17–19)

179 Alter, *Art of Biblical Narrative*, p. 77.
180 Gunn, *Story of King David*, p. 14.
181 Brueggemann, *David's Truth*, p. 44.

The special robe which reappears throughout the biblical drama, the emblematic costume of Joseph, of Samuel, and of others, always beautiful and always torn, is here the dress of the king's daughter. The narrator focuses our pity in the robe. The rape is both desecration of kingship and its consequence: this is what the new human freedom of self-government does to women.

Another brother, Absalom, takes her into his house. He bides his time, gets Amnon drunk, and has him murdered. He flees the consequences:

> And the soul of king David longed to go forth unto Absalom: for he was comforted concerning Amnon, seeing he was dead. (13.39)

David's family drama is not only political by default. Here he is 'King David'. It is given to kings to have too many arrogant sons, and to have to uphold their position before them.

Absalom is soon back, 'praised' by everyone for his 'beauty' (14.25). He is without 'blemish', a Bronze Age André Agassi, his best feature his 'two shekel's' weight of hair. The vain man drives around town in his chariot, gathers followers, sends out spies with the code signal for uprising, and leads an army against the king his father. David is practised in the art of a fast get away:

> David said unto all his servants that were with him in Jerusalem, 'Arise, and let us flee; for we shall not else escape from Absalom: take speed to depart, lest he overtake us suddenly, and bring evil upon us, and smite the city with the edge of the sword.' (15.14)

What other hero of a warlike age has his supreme moment in running away? When he courts death, the comic hero knows how to run away in style; he does not want to go out in sublime smoke and ashes. But even the wily Odysseus fights his way out of the Cyclop's cave. Even Samson took a lot of Philistines away with him. David is the lowest of the lowly comic heroes. The comic hero is bound by love of his solid mortal frame: the episode takes us back down into David's physical mortality. It is a faithful, but no less an intelligent, move: 'my chances of emerging successful from any battle were greater in an open field than inside a city in which I could not deploy my troops to best advantage and in which I did not know who was loyal to me and who was not'.[182] David and his entourage make with their feet, Zadok the Levite burdened with the Ark. If this is no time for a leisurely procession, the Lord's anointed knows that the Ark is not a good-luck trophy:

> the king said unto Zadok, 'Carry back the ark of God into the city: if I shall find favour in the eyes of the Lord, he will bring me again, and shew me both it, and his habitation:
> But if he thus say, "I have no delight in thee"; behold, here am I, let him do to me as seemeth good unto him.' (15.25–26)

David willingly abandons the apparatus of kingship; he cheerfully trusts himself to God: 'David knows ... that he is being watched and that the

---

182 Heller, *God Knows*, pp. 401–402.

watcher will decide things.'[183] Thrown back upon being a man, in the hands of God, he lets others take control: 'we see again ... the magnanimous David who will allow the matter of the kingdom to rest in the hands of others (2 Sam. 15–18)'.[184] The fugitive David has to exercise generosity: he is met in Bahurim, the border of the political and the human, by one of Saul's fellow tribesmen:

> he came forth, and cursed still as he came.
> And he cast stones at David, and at all the servants of king David: and all the mighty men were on his right hand on his left.
> And thus said Shimei when he cursed, 'Come out, come out thou bloody man, and thou man of Belial:
> The Lord hath returned upon thee all the blood of the house of Saul, in whose stead thou hast reigned; and the Lord hath delivered the kingdom into the hand of Absalom thy son: and behold, thou art taken in thy mischief, because thou art a bloody man.'
> Then said Abishai the son of Zeruiah unto the king, 'Why should this dead dog curse my lord the king? let me go over, I pray thee, and take off his head.'
> And the king said, 'What have I to do with you, ye sons of Zeruiah? so let him curse, because the Lord hath said unto him, "Curse David." Who shall then say, "Wherefore hast thou done so?"'
> And David said to Abishai, and to all his servants, 'Behold my son, which came forth of my bowels, seeketh my life: how much more now may this Benjamite do it? let him alone, and let him curse; for the Lord hath bidden him.
> It may be that the Lord will look upon mine affliction, and that the Lord will requite me good for his cursing this day.' (2 Sam. 16.5–12)

Shimei, perhaps a third cousin of Saul, satirises the king from close up. David puts up decently with being made into a buffoon. He has touched the rock bottom into which comic heroes fall: his 'own son, which came forth from my bowels' is trying to kill him. Shimei's raillery is a joke by comparison. David knows that a human king is mortal, dependent upon the Lord. His expansive gesture to Shimei is of another order to Joab's narrow conception of justice. As Gunn aptly says,

> Joab's principle, 'you should love your friends and hate your enemies', is a human commonplace, but David's feeble resistance to this law is the resistance of true humanity, which feels itself trapped in this law.[185]

David is happiest when he is free to be an area of grace. Once more in his best role of outlaw, David again has to receive the kingdom from others.[186] The people will not let David, their cynosure, go into battle: send Joab and Abishai (2 Sam. 18.1–3). The actor who knows all about the social construction of meaning tells Joab in everyone's hearing (18.5) not to kill Absalom. That hair was bound to get him eventually; snagged by his locks in the branches of a tree 'he was taken up between the heaven and the

---

183 Brueggemann, *David's Truth*, p. 54.
184 Gunn, *Story of King David*, p. 95.
185 Ibid., p. 103.
186 Ibid., p. 101.

earth; and the mule that was under him went away' (18.9). He is left there to hang until Joab kills him (18.14). Two messengers, Ahimaaz, raring to go but who does not know the full story, and Cushi, who does, run to tell David. Ahimaaz outpaces the messenger who knows:

> And David sat between the two gates: and the watchman went up to the roof over the gate unto the wall, and lifted up his eyes, and looked, and behold a man running alone.
> And the watchman cried, and told the king. And the king said, 'If he be alone, there is tidings in his mouth.' And he came apace, and drew near.
> And the watchman saw another man running: and the watchman called unto the porter, and said, 'Behold another man running alone.' And the king said, 'He also bringeth tidings.' (18.24–26)

Perhaps the only time that king is willingly self-deceived:

> And the watchman said, 'Me thinketh the running of the foremost is like the running of Ahimaaz the son of Zadok.' And the king said, 'He is a good man, and cometh with good tidings.' (18.25)

The king has almost convinced himself:

> Ahimaaz called, and said unto the king, 'All is well.' And he fell down to the earth upon his face before the king, and said, 'Blessed be the Lord thy God, which hath delivered up the men that lifted up the hand against my lord the king.'
> And the king said, 'Is the young man Absalom safe?' And Ahimaaz answered, 'When Joab sent the king's servant, and me thy servant, I saw a great tumult, and I knew not what it was.'
> And the king said unto him, 'Turn aside, and stand here.' And he turned aside, and stood still.
> And, behold, Cushi came; and Cushi said, 'Tidings, my lord the king: for the Lord hath avenged thee this day of all them that rose up against thee.'
> And the king said unto Cushi, 'Is the young man Absalom safe?' And Cushi answered, 'The enemies of my lord the king, and all that rise against thee to do thee hurt, be as that young man is.'
> And the king was much moved, and went up to the chamber over the gate, and wept: and as he went, thus he said, 'O my son Absalom, my son, my son Absalom! would God I had died for thee, O Absalom, my son, my son!' (18.26–33)

David, even David the king, is so rich that he would have given his life for his son. The king who signed the death warrants of the Amalekite who claimed to have killed Saul, and of Ishbosheth's murderers, does not remonstrate with Joab for the execution of his son. David the man may mourn, but David the king is reliant on a general who knows that real politics requires that any man who leads an uprising against the king be executed. David wants to return to his simple humanness, but his entourage will not permit him. His people are embarrassed, shying off into the city, like cowards who escape from a battle (19.3) while 'the king covered his face' (19.4) and sits publicly mourning his son. Joab tells him that a king disgraces himself – loses his face – if he 'loves his enemies and hates his friends': the king will lose all of his supporters unless he pulls himself together (19.6–7):

Then the king arose, and sat in the gate. And they told unto all the people, saying, 'Behold, the king doth sit in the gate.' And all the people came before the king: for Israel had fled every man to his tent. (19.8)

He has to be a king for his people. He is now reliant on others, who give him his representative role.

David, the hero of the dark comedy of the monarchy, has kept three incommensurable goods in uneven balance throughout his career: he has tried to be human, a father of sons, and the public face of Israel's worldly monarchy, the father of ambitious princes, and the Lord's anointed king, an actor in a wider sense. For all of his effort, Cheryl Exum thinks that David 'seems to lack true tragic greatness, choosing to compromise, to adjust to circumstances, rather than struggle heroically against his lot'. Despite 'fall[ing] short of realizing its full tragic potential',[187] the Succession Narrative must, she says, be counted as a tragedy, because it tells of a 'fall from prosperity to misery'.[188] We might stand back and take a look at the whole David, prose and poetry included. David certainly is enfeebled: Goliath's slayer has to be rescued from a giant Philistine by Abishai (2 Sam. 21). Following this last victory over the Philistines, the penultimate chapter of 2 Samuel is a psalm, put into the mouth of David, in which he thanks God for his salvation:

The Lord is my rock, and my fortress, and my deliverer:
The God of my rock; in him will I trust: he is my shield, and the horn of my salvation, my high tower, and my refuge, my saviour; thou savest me from violence.
I will call on the Lord, who is worthy to be praised: so shall I be saved from mine enemies.
When the waves of death compassed me, the floods of ungodly men made me afraid;
The sorrows of hell compassed me about; the snares of death prevented me;
In my distress I called upon the Lord, and cried to my God: and he did hear my voice out of his temple, and my cry did enter into his ears.
Then the earth shook and trembled; the foundations of heaven moved and shook, because he was wroth.
There went up a smoke out of his nostrils, and fire out of his mouth devoured: coals were kindled by it.
He bowed the heavens also, and came down; and darkness was under his feet.
And he rode upon a cherub, and did fly: and he was seen upon the wings of the wind.
And he made darkness pavilions round about him, dark waters, and thick clouds of the skies.
Through the brightness before him were coals of fire kindled.
The Lord thundered from heaven, and the most High uttered his voice.
And he sent out arrows, and scattered them; lightning, and discomfited them.
And the channels of the sea appeared, the foundations of the world were discovered, at the rebuking of the Lord, at the blast of the breath of his nostrils.
He sent from above, he took me; he drew me out of many waters.
. . .

187 Exum, *Tragedy and Biblical Narrative*, pp. 120–121.
188 Ibid., p. 122.

> He brought me forth also into a large place: he delivered me, because he
> delighted in me.
> . . .
> Therefore I will give thanks unto thee, O Lord, among the heathen, and I will
> sing praises unto thy name.
> He is the tower of salvation for his king: and sheweth mercy to his anointed;
> unto David, and to his seed for evermore. (2 Sam. 22.1–17, 20, 50–51)

David the man imagines the great gift to himself of God's kind of kingship.
The Deuteronomists' image of sacred kingship towers over worldly
politics. Without the monumental backdrop of the image of divine–human
kingship, the gift of kingship to humanity from God, the story might be
tragic: we would have the story of a David torn apart between worldly and
human justice. As the Succession Narrative stands, from 2 Samuel 6 to 2
Kings 2, the drama narrowly balances the three incommensurables, and
we are presented with a black comedy. Von Balthasar accentuates the
vertical dimension of David's standing before God. He thinks that the
'tension' between human freedom and its call to obedience to the infinite
freedom of God is so taut that 'Scripture can portray it only in dialectical
and tragic fashion'.[189] The narrative becomes 'dialectical' if we make the
level of the divine–human relationship the only issue in the story. If we
attend to both horizontal and vertical levels, we may see the ironic
interrelation of three goods: humanity, worldly kingship and kingship as a
gift from God. David plays out his freedom in the role of a worldly king.
The public man of 1 Samuel, the show-off, persists into 2 Samuel and
enables David to be a human king. Isaac's sons quarrelled over his blessing:
David's sons want his throne. That is the robe he has to wear. God gives
the people the freedom to create a monarchy, since the ramshackle tower
of kingship is what they 'desire', the space in which their freedom will
design their own dispersal into exile, and the loss of the promised land.
The narrative satirises worldly kingship, and makes such kings its butts; it
gives to David the *man* a tremendous quality of bouncing and generous
faith, which enables him to be an area of grace; and it sets both off against
an image of God's promise of a perfect king. The 'vertical' image, the
prophetic conception of how *God* sees all three faces of kingship is behind
the story:

> This is indeed the theatre of the world; the action, however, is enveloped by a
> God who not only remains a spectator of the play . . . but a God who, in the
> actions of his 'images', remains the archetype that also participates in the
> action, both in hidden and manifest ways. He lets man explore the extremest
> possibilities of his freedom, and yet he conducts events as a play of his mani-
> fold elections and directions. He both ties and loosens the knots, and through
> it all he wants to further this kingdom and this dynamic promise. But he also
> wants to exhibit the tragic mask of the old king with the bleeding heart, who,
> if only he had been allowed to, would have so gladly died in the place of his
> lost son.[190]

David would be unique amongst *tragic* figures in singing that God has
'delighted in me' (2 Sam. 22.20). The Deuteronomist has a high image of

---

189 Von Balthasar, *Glory VI*, p. 106.
190 Ibid., pp. 113–114.

the king, a worldly image and a human image. Do we ever see David *acting* the high and dignified king? Not often. It would have given him a plinth from which to fall. But he would have lost the passivity and the pragmatism of the comic hero. How can a man who suffers so many blows be a comic hero? Because David never stops thinking that he is on the plinth. David lives under the shadow of a God-given myth in which he believes. When Helmut Thielicke was preaching in Stuttgart during World War II,

> there was an air raid, without warning, with the most frightening noises of ... airplanes, machine-gun fire and countering flak. Thielicke shouted from the pulpit: 'Everyone flat on the ground! We sing "Jesus, my Joy" ("*Jesu, meine Freude*, ...").' The organist and the congregation followed the instruction. Thielicke could no longer see them from the pulpit, as everyone was crouched under the pews ... the situation impressed Thielicke as acutely funny. He started to laugh wholeheartedly ... he thought that this was ... laughter that pleased God.[191]

Von Balthasar says, 'Israel is happy when it sings.'[192] The legend remembers David as a happy singer. Everyone sings in paradisial comedies; but to sing right through the divine and the human air-raids of 2 Samuel is miraculous. David pleases God because he has the guts to carry on playing the harp, imagining himself as that area of grace which is the Lord's anointed king.

The human king never becomes impeccable: the last story of 2 Samuel tells of David's census of Israel's 'fighting men': he needs to know exactly how many troops he has at his disposal. The Lord duly punishes him for this lack of trust. He gives his anointed three options. Either

1. seven years of famine?
2. flee three months before your enemies?
3. three days pestilence?

David says he will go with the pestilence: 'let us now fall into the hand of the Lord: for his mercies are great; and let men not fall into the hand of man' (2 Sam. 24.14), displaying the boundless optimism and the prudent knowledge of human nature of the great comedian that he is. God sends a pestilence, and 70,000 Israelites die: it is remarkable that no-one has put this down as a tragedy.

4. The Ironies of History

Many of those who contributed to the emergence of the literary study of the Bible want to keep it that way. According to D. M. Gunn, the genre of 1 and 2 Samuel is not history, but 'serious entertainment' like Icelandic 'family sagas'.[193] Gunn argues that the author of the David saga does not write like an ancient Assyrian Annalist: his purpose cannot be historical, for he describes many things which are superfluous to the requirements of historical knowledge. No historian would carefully describe the relay of

---

191 Berger, *Redeeming Laughter*, p. 202.
192 Von Balthasar, *Glory VI*, p. 211.
193 Gunn, *Fate of King Saul*, p. 16, and *Story of King David*, pp. 61–62.

messengers, bringing to David the news of Absalom's death.[194] Gunn does not contend that the Saul and David stories are devoid of historical content, but that their overarching aim is storytelling, not history telling. He thinks that as David ceases to be the public king and becomes simply a man, we find in him something 'essentially' and universally human. According to Aristotle, he says, that universal touch of humanity is the stuff of poetry rather than of history: this is why the stories of Saul and David still strike a chord with us today. Aristotle stated that:

> the poet's function is to describe, not the thing that has happened, but a kind of thing that might happen, i.e. what is possible as being probable or necessary. The distinction between historian and poet is not in the one writing prose and the other verse – you might put the work of Herodotus into verse, and it would still be a species of history; it consists really in this, that the one describes the thing that has been, and the other a kind of thing that might be. Hence poetry is something more philosophic and of graver import than history, since its statements are of the nature rather of universals, whereas those of history are singulars. By a universal statement I mean one as to what such or such a kind of man will probably or necessarily say or do – which is the aim of poetry, though it affixes proper names to the characters; by a singular statement, one as to what, say, Alcibiades did or had done to him.[195]

When Aristotle assigns to poetry the function of telling 'what such or such a kind of man will probably or necessarily do', he is thinking of fiction as the construction of an *imaginary* world. If imagination is an act which vanishes into the ethereal beyond without a glance at the facts, it creates a world which runs *counter* to the possibilities of this one. But if, conversely, imagination is an act which makes its way into facts, then the imaginary world is the seizure of *what could be*, on the literal ground of *what is*. Joseph Heller found such possibilities in the biblical David. By a devious act of comical anachronism, he makes David a New York Jew, that is, a universal man; a composer for the harp who wrote the 'Air for the G String', the 'B-Minor Mass, Mozart's Requiem, and Handel's Messiah'.[196] Heller's concrete and particular Palestinian David is even a universal *old man*:

> They grew tired of hearing me tell them I'd begun life as a shepherd.
> 'O no,' said Amnon.
> 'Not again,' said Absalom.[197]

Anachronism is funny because it exposes the relation between our conscious knowledge of incorrigible temporal particularity and our unconscious intuition of universal human nature. Because it works primarily in space, rather than in time, comedy can juxtapose and synthesise temporally distanced scenes, and the greater the scenic density, or historical exactitude, the more amusing is the explosion of the weight of historicism. Aristotle went on to say that the particular *can* contain the universal:

194 Gunn, *Story of King David*, pp. 43 and 57–58.
195 Aristotle, *Poetics*, 1451a 9 35–1451b.
196 Heller, *God Knows*, pp. 169 and 349.
197 Ibid., pp. 310–311.

the poet must be more the poet of his stories or Plots than of his verses, inasmuch as he is a poet by virtue of the imitative element in his work, and it is actions that he imitates. And if he should come to take a subject from actual history, he is none the less a poet for that; since some historic occurrences may very well be in the probable and possible order of things; and it is in that aspect of them that he is their poet.[198]

The poetic art lies in choosing the event which is 'probable and possible': the universal can get inside the particular when poetry creates, not a counter-world of fantasy but an imagined world.

Meir Sternberg considers that the Bible has three 'functions': historiography, aesthetics and ideology.[199] The first 'would like nothing better than to tack fact onto fact in an endless procession, marching across all artistic and ideological design'. For 'aesthetics', 'the plays the thing ... with no strings attached to what is, or was, or should be'.[200] Alter is one of the objects of Sternberg's artillery. Alter describes the Bible as running between 'historicized prose fiction', in some of its earlier parts, and 'fictionalized history' 'when we move into the period of the Judges and Kings'.[201] He finds that the David 'cycle'

> provides an instructive central instance of the intertwining of history and fiction. This narrative, though it may have ... folkloric embellishments (such as David's victory over Goliath), is based on firm historical facts, as modern research has tended to confirm: there really was a David who fought a civil war against the house of Saul, achieved ... sovereignty over the twelve tribes, conquered Jerusalem, founded a dynasty, created a small empire, and was succeeded by his son Solomon.[202]

Where Sternberg thinks that the biblical writers were trying to achieve three exclusive aims at once, Alter thinks that they put imagination and history in the service of one another. An agnostic historian need have few doubts about the broad outlines of the Deuteronomist's *history*. The facts have been related in drier and fuller forms than those found in the Bible. The act of assent which is required of *faith* is to the *meaning* imposed by the biblical writer upon his tale, a meaning which is inextricable from the act of imagination which gives the history its shape.

Alter's 'new critical' intuition is that the genius of the biblical writers is their 'imaginative grasp' of their 'protagonists as distinctive moral and psychological figures'. Sternberg says that,

> To the Bible, history is an affair between heaven and earth, with the heavenly side figuring as a maker and bent on advertising his makership by imposing his will and order on the normal logic of events ... Hence the alignment of divine ... artistic pattern-making against earthbound recording.[203]

If the storytelling urge and the ability to write reasonably reliable history sometimes combine in the same head, there is no reason to speak of divine

---

198 Aristotle, *Poetics*, 1451b 9 25–30.
199 Sternberg, *Poetics of Biblical Narrative*, p. 41.
200 Ibid., p. 44.
201 Alter, *Art of Biblical Narrative*, p. 29.
202 Ibid., p. 35.
203 Ibid., p. 46.

and artistic pattern making as *working against* earthbound recording. Neither Herodotus nor Thucydides are dull plodders. The impulse to design is not restricted to ideologists; it is a human desire. Alter makes a suggestive parallel between the Deuteronomic history and Shakespeare's history plays: in his 'imaginative reenactment of history',

> The author of the David stories stands in . . . the same relation to the Israelite history as Shakespeare stands to English history in his history plays. Shakespeare was . . . not free to have Henry V lose the battle of Agincourt or to allow someone else to lead the English forces there, but, working from the hints of historical tradition, he could invent a kind of *Bildungsroman* for the young Prince Hal; surround him with invented characters that would serve as foils . . . obstacles, aids in his development . . . That is . . . what the author of the David cycle does for David, Saul, Abner, Joab, Jonathan, Absalom, Michal, Abigail, and a host of other characters.[204]

The RSC lately put on the whole cycle of Shakespeare's histories, to run from Richard II through Henry VIII. Perhaps we should conceive the Deuteronomic History as an inspired version of the same performance. That would entail that we give a greater weight to the free hand of the human historian than has traditionally been done. The Deuteronomic narrative gives us history in which divine and human intentions are inextricably intermingled, both at the literary and the historical level.

The narrative's adherence to an ironic grasp of *history* is mirrored by its literary content. It would have been easier for the narrator to have all good judges, or all bad judges, or to make the judges start from perfection and serially to degenerate. A given body of legends made it impossible to impose a perfect pattern on the history. It would have been simpler to make David an ideal king, or a good man who goes to the bad as soon as he is surrounded by the apparatus of the state, or otherwise to separate the ideal king, the real king, and the individual man. But the narrative sticks to their ironic interplay. One can recreate a black and white picture by finding out behind the particular aesthetic form of the Bible a history in which the 'face to face personal relationships' of the Sinaitic *habiru* overcame 'the impersonal power structure'[205] of the pagan state(s), only to be repressed by the 'paganism' of 'David and Solomon'. On Mendenhall's analysis, such pagan politics results in a notion of the 'exercise of legitimate power', which is 'irrelevant' to the Mosaic ethical community in which 'power, like the absolutes, derives from God alone'.[206] In the biblical narrative, however, God delegates to his chosen people a space in which human beings can exercise power. The narrative records that they did so rather badly, but the freedom to leap into one's own space is not withdrawn. Human freedom is not condemned; in the figure of the king, the archetypal human being, it is set alongside another and higher good, that of the divine king. The Deuteronomist mixes without homogenising the goods of divine and human kingship. If he is not quite a liberal political pluralist, he has a wider view of the possibilities of human freedom than those who admire it only

204 Ibid., pp. 35–36.
205 Mendenhall, *Tenth Generation*, p. 208.
206 Ibid., p. 195.

in spontaneous gestures of theocratic disruption. The balancing act is possible because the human is a created image of God, even when the likeness is seen from below, in an infernal comedy. Sometimes the likeness is almost blacked out; God goes silent on Saul. David keeps the likeness spinning, by singing. By this act of freedom, he maintains the spoken analogy between God and humanity; and God continues to respond to him, with a trace of satire.

The historical imperative makes the narrator qualify the absoluteness and autonomy of each episode by interleaving it with successors. The intention to tell the story of the whole of Israelite monarchy relativises and qualifies the importance of each individual king. If we spoil their narrative by considering all of the sources separately, we also fail to read it holistically if we treat the Saul and the David stories independently. Harold Fisch comments that *Saul* could have been a tragic figure,

> but he can only fully realize this role if his story is isolated from its context, which ... emphasizes the history of the royal house to be founded by ... the young David. Saul's replacement by David rather than his tragic death in battle is what ultimately counts and it is on that that our attention ... focuses ... biblical stories of the 'fall' of a hero lack the closure that tragedy seems to require; instead of fable rounded in on itself, we have the undetermined movement of historical time, a witnessing to purposes still to be disclosed and by no means confined to the fate of the hero.[207]

This relative 'indetermination' of the narrative is exhibited by the fact that we are shown morally imperfect characters, such as Gideon, Saul and David, of whom it cannot be entirely certain what they will do next. A political history has to deal in the currency of human freedom. The Deuteronomic History shows what the possibilities are: what sort of government we may expect from judges, and what sort of government under kings. As Jobling says,

> The Deuteronomic History is neither pro-monarchic nor anti-monarchic ... nor ... 'balanced' between the two. It lets monarchy be seen for good and bad, and judgeship for good and bad ... Out of these elements, Israel is free to create its 'political theology'![208]

The Deuteronomic History is committed to human freedom. If we keep our eyes on how disgracefully they exercised their freedom, we may find it a tragedy; if we say how good that the history happened, we may call it a comedy. This is a much darker comedy than that of the Patriarchs, because the divine and the human good are at their most incommensurable in the realm of politics. The history will grow much darker. After Solomon's death, in 922, the kingdom breaks in half, into Judah and Israel; two hundred years later, 'The Assyrians take Samaria, capital of Israel ... in 722 BCE; the Babylonians take Jerusalem, capital of Judah (2 Kings 30) in 587 BCE; and a divine effort that, by the Bible's reckoning, has lasted for

---

207 Harold Fisch, *Poetry with a Purpose: Biblical Poetics and Interpretation* (Indiana University Press, Bloomington and Indianapolis, 1990), p. 42.
208 Jobling, 'Deuteronomic Political Theology', p. 87.

more than a millenium ends in wreckage, slaughter, and the ignominy of exile'.[209] The biblical narrative continues its search for the good, beyond Solomon's palace-temple complex and beyond the Second Temple of Ezra and Nehemiah.

209 Miles, *God: A Biography*, p. 186.

4

A New Look on Job

1. Setting the Scene

Composed sometime between the sixth and the fourth centuries BC, Job
belongs to the Wisdom tradition. The earliest form of biblical Wisdom
literature is practical wisdom: 'As the door turns on its hinge, so the
sluggard turns over in bed' (Prov. 26.14). The 'lower' wisdom uses
natural causes and effects as illustrations of the kinship between types
of human behaviour. The *Hokmah* or skill which is wisdom was inculcated
in young men for its practical benefits: obedience to moral law entails
prosperity. The problem of Job surfaces out of the lack of fit between
a utilitarian idea of goodness and the realities of providence. Proverbs
also contains 'higher' wisdom: speculation about the nature of 'Wisdom',
as an attribute of God. Wisdom dances before the Creator at the formation
of the world (Prov. 8.22–31). Job 28 is a hymn to a figure of semi-divine
Wisdom.

The Book of Job has been supposed to consist of at least three and
perhaps four separate texts. The prose prologue (1–2) and epilogue (42) are
taken originally to have formed a consecutive narrative. Much later, a
higher-wisdom sophisticate adapted this prose tale into a longer poem.
The Elihu speeches of chapters 32–37 are to textual critics an obvious
interpolation. Some have suggested that Job 28 is also a later addition.
Robert Gordis notes that we can do better than to treat this book as a
'conglomeration of separate documents, unrelated and at times even
opposed to one another' which were 'either haphazardly or deliberately
manipulated to produce a masterpiece'.[1] Horace Kallen argued that the
text is modelled on the tragedies of Euripides: he sets the whole book out
in five acts, to demonstrate the thesis.[2] It is at least true that the text of Job
looks like a drama: apart from the prose prologue and epilogue, it consists
of the speeches of Job, the friends, Elihu and God. Luis Alonso Schökel

1 Robert Gordis, *The Book of God and Man: A Study of Job* (University of Chicago Press,
Chicago, 1965), p. 15. Walter Brueggemann has claimed that 'Many scholars now
agree that the three parts of the book . . . are to be seen as a dramatic, artistic whole'.
Theology of the Old Testament, p. 489.
2 Horace M. Kallen *The Book of Job as a Greek Tragedy: with an Essay* (first published by
Moffatt, Yard & Co., 1918, reprinted by Hill & Wang, New York, 1959).

recommends that the way to find unity in the book of Job is to *imagine* its *action*. One of the speakers is God: if we are going to 'see' the book's action, we have to look 'up' and 'down'. If we imagine God and the Satan placing their bet, Job falling victim to his numerous woes, and his friends coming to prosecute him for blasphemy, we will see that the story sets out the intellectual 'drama' of a 'search' for justice.[3] Reading Job as a 'drama' means *visualising* the action and participating in it by letting it communicate with us tri-logically. We must picture actors before us on a stage, and God above them; and we must put ourselves in the audience, which identifies with the actors' predicament. The Prologue sets out these stage directions. In Job 1.1–5, the reader/audience sees 'earth', or the land of Uz, and Job with his family. The scene then shifts to heaven: the sons of God come to present themselves to him. God asks the Satan where he has been, and the Tempter replies, 'From going to and fro in the earth, and from walking up and down in it' (1.7, repeated in 2.2). This encourages the reader to picture an earth below and a heaven above. Schökel suggests that we

> imagine a stage with a second floor on the left side . . . which remains invisible to the actors on the floor below. In this upper realm the prologue in heaven unfolds, the speeches of God with Satan; here God is seated and continues to observe without being seen or heard by Job until the final act. This gives an advantageous position to the audience but a powerless one to Job. His ignorance is necessary because we are concerned here with a wager and a test . . . God is somewhat of a spectator of the reactions of Job and his friends, he overhears without being seen, he is addressed but does not respond, they seek him without finding him . . . The spectator must be aware of this presence of God . . . this triangular vision is a source of irony that very much enriches the drama. Only at the end of the fourth act will the barrier be removed so that Job can see and hear God: pleased to see him, but appalled to discover that God has been listening all the while.[4]

Act I, the beginning of the verse poem, starts with Job wishing that the day in which he was born could be nullified; or, could he not have died 'when I came out of the belly?' (3.11). The point about being dead is that one is *invisible*: 'O that thou wouldest hide me in the grave, that thou wouldest keep me secret, until thy wrath be past' (14.13). It is bad enough being covered from head to foot in boils: it is worse to be *watched*. Job demands to be hidden from prying and prurient eyes, but he also wants his case to be answered, which requires that he witness in his own defence. He swings between asking to be hidden and demanding that his case be heard. Job's friends appear as the witnesses in God's defence *and* the council for Job's prosecution. Eliphaz and Bildad repeat the truisms of wisdom: 'your predicament proves that you have sinned. No innocent man suffered thus'. As his case falls on the deaf ears of the human prosecution, Job begins to insist that the Judge present himself. The trial/drama is about visibility and invisibility.

---

3 Luis Alonso Schökel, 'Toward a Dramatic Reading of Job', *Semeia*, 7: *Studies in the Book of Job*, edited by Robert Polzin and David Robertson, 1977, Society of Biblical Literature, 45–59 (46).
4 Ibid., 46–47.

Act II is initiated by Eliphaz's response to Job: 'Thine own mouth condemneth thee; and not I: yea, thine own lips testify against thee' (15.6). Faced with such 'miserable comforters' (16.2) and wooden replies, Job turns to the audience. He 'wants us to see ourselves reflected and even embodied in himself'.[5] Now Job asks for pity, complaining about the lack of eyes to see him, the universal invisibility and inaudibility of the wretched to the happy (Job 19). In Act III, Job does something no-one expected: he questions God.[6] He still wants a trial (23.3–5); God remains invisible (23.8–10). In Act IV, a member of the audience jumps onto the stage, bursting to defend God. If 'the book was composed ... to transform the audience into the cast', Elihu exemplifies the drama's 'provocative power'. Elihu fails to defend God or to condemn Job. God's entrance in the final act is now a dramatic necessity: 'God must speak in order to transfer the lawsuit of the four friends to a higher court, for God is the subject of the lawsuit.'[7]

The biblical image of God develops, and so does its 'patterning of dramatic action'.[8] After the Exile, the imaginative distance between heaven and earth lengthens. The God of the Priestly writers, and the higher wisdom school is more transcendent than that of earlier writers.[9] Some authors have given an 'existential interpretation' of God's speeches in Job: the 'answer' is God's *presence* to Job.[10] Gordis contests this, because God 'does *not* assure Job of his protection and love for his suffering creature'. All that we see is 'the divine transcendence, the majesty and mystery of God, far removed from man'.[11] If the dramatic gesture of entering the stage is as significant as what God says, we may think otherwise. Job's demands create an expectancy that he will appear: but everyone knows he is making an impossible request. This is what makes God's entrance dramatic. It is the heightened sense of God's transcendence which makes *this* appearance startlingly theatrical. Job says that seeing God has touched him where words about God failed.

2. A Performance of *Job*!

If candidates were to be put forward for a modern Job, the list being restricted to European theologians, many people would offer Søren Kierkegaard. Against Hegel's all-knowing rationalism, Kierkegaard insisted that the religious life consists in the existential realisation of the difference between the finite human being and the infinite God. When a human being, submerged in relative concerns, applies herself to being *religious*, she experiences the gap between what she is and what she should be. Kierkegaard suffered in his heroic attempt to put this intuition across

---

5 Ibid., 49.
6 Ibid., 54.
7 Ibid., 48, 50.
8 Tom F. Driver, *The Sense of History in Greek and Shakespearean Drama* (Columbia University Press, New York, 1960), p. 69.
9 Fohrer, *History of Israelite Religion*, p. 356.
10 Von Rad comes near this in his *Wisdom in Israel*, translated by James D. Martin (SCM, London, 1972), p. 217.
11 Gordis, *Book of God and Man*, pp. 14–15; cf. 130–132.

to the self-satisfied denizens of Danish 'Christendom'. The insight led Kierkegaard to a number of 'Joban' conclusions. One is that *suffering* is the mark of the 'religious individual'. Suffering is *essential* because the 'religious individual' must learn 'that he is nothing before God', or, because 'self-annihilation is the essential form for the God-relationship'.[12] The 'religious individual' must suffer because it is a painful business to divest oneself of one's 'certainties' about God: this is the only way of faith. Kierkegaard tells us that 'uncertainty is the criterion'[13] of a religious, as opposed to an 'aesthetic', relationship to God. 'Aesthetic' stands for a way of life, and of theology, which has woven God, world and humanity into a single synthetic web so that it knows God as well as it knows itself.

If the religious insight is that suffering is integral to life, then, says Kierkegaard, the poet and the actor half know it.[14] The poet as 'humorist' knows it, because comedy consists in *contradiction*.[15] But the humorist-poet – with his attachment to *aesthetics* – shies away from suffering, turning it into a joke, or a 'jest': 'He touches upon the secret of existence in the pain, but then he goes home again.'[16] The religious individual experiences the *contradiction* between himself and God and is thus a brother to the 'humorist'. Both the religious man and the comedian apply themselves to incongruity. And so comedy may appear to be analogous to religion. But Kierkegaard was sick to death of Hegel's construction of similarities between the human enterprise and God. Instead of letting comedy provide an upward *analogy* for religion, we should *start* with religion and work our way back down to comedy.[17] The theologian of Paradox will not expand on the analogy from below to above – from the comic sense of the humanly human to that of the religiously human – for that would expel the contradiction, by making *comedy* a neat ladder to God. Kierkegaard develops it from the other direction: if you want *real*, non-escapist comedy, look at the life of the religious individual. The religious man is a comical contradiction in two ways. First, in that he 'looks like other men' but is absolutely different: therefore, 'humor is his incognito'.[18] Second, the religious individual has to grow out of the adolescent enthusiasm which is so passionate about God that it 'see[s] God directly in everything' and imagines that it has God in its 'pocket' – a temptation to magic or aesthetic certitudes.[19] Like Job, perhaps, the religious individual needs to develop a sense of irony about himself, if he is to gain 'maturity' of faith. His faith must not be located in anything outward: it must be disguised even from himself. This 'incognito' of faith is the life in contradiction:

> He does not conceal his inwardness in order to be able to apprehend others comically, but conversely: in order that the inwardness that is within him may be inwardness in truth, he conceals it, and in consequence of this concealment

12 Søren Kierkegaard, *Concluding Unscientific Postscript*, translated by David F. Swenson and Walter Lowrie (Oxford University Press, London, 1941), p. 412.
13 Ibid., p. 407.
14 Ibid., p. 397.
15 *Vide supra*, p. 40.
16 Kierkegaard, *Unscientific Postscript*, p. 400.
17 Ibid., p. 413.
18 Ibid., p. 447.
19 Ibid., pp. 451–452.

he discovers the comical, which, however, he does not give himself time to dwell upon. Nor does he feel himself to be better than others, for such a comparative religiosity is precisely externalism, and hence is not religiosity.[20]

Kierkegaard's theology appears to be peculiarly apposite to a consideration of the book of Job as a dramatic comedy. Von Balthasar is at his most Kierkegaardian when he says that the 'unashamed objective' of the Book of Proverbs,

> is to equip the government official with the know-how and the polish necessary for a successful career ... while all the while providing him with a religiously based ethic. From the Christian perspective, what is offered here is an anthropocentric philosophy with a religious backdrop, or an enlightened, liberal theology.[21]

The Wisdom tradition *naturalises* the idea of the good: as the tree which spreads its roots deep in the earth blossoms, so the moral person flourishes in worldly 'goods'. The friends, and Job himself, have taken the organic metaphors which flourish in the Wisdom literature literally. Once recompense for piety and retribution for criminality have become automatic, it is possible to believe in God without having *faith*. The comic possibilities become evident when we recall that Bergson defined the object of laughter as 'something mechanical encrusted on the living': for example, on living faith.[22] The Wisdom tradition stood in danger of turning suggestive similarities between God and creation into magical univocities, where the meaning of 'good' for human beings is *identical* to the meaning of 'good' in the eyes of God. Kierkegaard thought that Hegel *aestheticised* the relation between God and human spirit, by creating a harmonious *identity* between the two. The ancient Near Eastern equivalent of aesthetic theology was 'magic'. The drama and the test of Job could thus be his way of learning that we cannot be *certain* about God. Through God's majestic crushing of his anthropocentric universe, Job learns the way of *faith*. As E. M. Good puts it:

> magic is focused on man's self-fulfilment, faith on the will of God ... The issue of the Book of Job is *faith*, the true and proper relationship between man and God ... the book shows Job's movement from a position of magical dogmatism to his ultimate stance of faith.[23]

For Kierkegaard, the transition from the aesthetic to the life of faith passes through the ethical – and, as God's command to slay Isaac indicates, goes beyond it. According to Terrien, the author of Job uses 'the story of the man from Uz' as a 'celebration of a theology which transcends even an ethical conception of the divinity'.[24]

William Whedbee has argued that Job is a comedy of contradiction. He says that we can see the generic form of comedy in Job if we

---

20 Ibid., p. 454.
21 Von Balthasar, *Glory VI*, p. 124.
22 Bergson, *Le Rire*, p. 39.
23 Good, *Irony in the Old Testament*, pp. 197–198.
24 S. Terrien, 'The Yahweh Speeches and Job's Response', *Review and Expositor*, 68, 1971, 497–509 (509).

focus on that vision of comedy which has two central ingredients: first, its perception of incongruity that moves in the realm of the ironic, the ludicrous, and the ridiculous; and secondly, a basic plot line that leads ultimately to the happiness of the hero and his restoration to a serene and harmonious society.[25]

I shall attempt to imagine how a director would reconstruct the drama of Job as a comedy of incongruity. The comic performance of *Job!* should enable us to observe the degree of kinship between the ideas of faith and of comedy in Kierkegaard's *Concluding Unscientific Postscript* and those in the Book of Job. The director will follow Schökel's stage instructions. He figures thus: if I put the text into three dimensions, enabling an audience to see a man on stage building up a bigger and bigger picture of God's injustice to him, and to everyone else, but especially to him, the funny side of it will be apparent. The comedy of incongruity will be perfected when God appears to debunk Job's illusions: the audience will realise that the author was a 'comedian' who 'pricks the bubble' of human 'pretentiousness'.[26]

The book enables its audience to see two 'stage' levels: a ground level, on which Job, his family and 'friends' speak their parts, and an 'upper storey', upon which God and the celestial court are visible. Job is set amidst his plenty: 'the greatest of all the men of the east' (Job 1.3). The audience's attention shifts to heaven. The interplay between these Olympian regions and earth is underlined: God asks Satan 'where did *you* come from', and Satan replies, 'From going to and fro in the earth' (1.7). The Satan of the Book of Job is not the devil of later Judaeo-Christian imagining, but a 'Puck' figure: the game which is going on beyond the clouds between the Almighty God and his pet mischief-maker casts a shadow of fantasy over the beginnings of the drama. The Satan is given permission to throw a spanner between good deeds and prosperity.

Those who take comedy to be foreign to the spirit of the Book of Job make two suppositions:

1. Job is devastated by the loss of his children (and oxen, camels, slaves, etc.);
2. Job is a thoroughly *good* and innocent man.

We are supposed to take his loss of his family very seriously, and we are supposed to take what Job says about the total inappropriateness of his divine punishment at face value. The director puts the 'fairytale' Prologue into the slide projector:

> Once upon a time, in the land of Uz, there was a man named Job. He was a man of perfect integrity, who feared God and avoided evil. He had seven sons and three daughters, seven thousand sheep, three thousand camels, five hundred yoke of oxen, and five hundred donkeys; and also many slaves. He was the richest man in the East.

25 William Whedbee, 'The Comedy of Job', *Semeia*, 7, 1–39 (4–5).
26 Graeme Garrett, '"My Brother Esau is an Hairy Man": An Encounter between the Comedian and the Preacher', *Scottish Journal of Theology*, 33, 3, June 1980, 239–256 (251).

> Every year, his sons would hold a great banquet, in the house of each of
> them in turn, and they would invite their sisters to come feast with them.
> When the week of celebration was over, Job would have them come to be
> purified; for he thought, 'Perhaps my children have sinned and cursed God
> in their hearts'. Job did this every year.

The director of *Job!* observes that the final author was not lumped with his
folktale: if he had wanted to give richer characters to the seven sons and
three daughters, it was not beyond his literary competence. The number of
Job's children, seven and three, are 'stylized':[27] they are not real enough for
audience identification. The director would be false to the text if he deepened their characterisation by giving them lines to speak. He is true to
what he finds if he presents them as glossy cartoon figures, raising their
glasses to their lips for one more toast, sinking their knives into the
celebratory ox with relish, unaware of the typhoon which is about to blow
them away. The loss of offspring so casually drawn cannot pierce the
audience's heart. His audience will *not* be overly set back by Job's loss
when all they have seen is a breakfast cereal advertisement family.

Job asks his director, 'What's my motivation? How *pious* am I really
supposed to be?' The director is suspicious of Job's perfection and has been
encouraged to learn from one Hebrew scholar that this man is not merely
innocent, but 'hyper-pious', an 'impossible example' for any audience to
follow.[28] There is something odd about Job's practice of 'pre-emptive
sacrifice': to perform sacrifices to God *just in case* anyone has 'sinned and
cursed God in their hearts' is 'uncalled for even by the Priestly Code'; the
author of Job cannot have intended it as 'unqualified praise'.[29] The Job of
the first two chapters is too good to be true: the Prologue is setting him up
for a fall. The director tells the actor playing Job to go watch some French
movie comedies like *Le Cop*, and to play these first scenes like the novice
policeman who tries to run his section by the book, is shaken out of his
compulsive rule consultations by the disastrous consequences, and falls
into his humanity when he falls in love with a prostitute. The director says:
the audience is not supposed to *like* the way you carry on. Smirk a bit as
you sacrifice, and look over-washed, barbered, slicked back and mani-
cured. 'Few things', says Jacobson, 'are more irreducibly comic than faeces
coming out of the sky',[30] and God is going to dump a ton of horse manure
on you. Wear a white suit.

Our knowledgeable director has read the books of Samuel, too, and he
cannot forget the story of the two messengers running to tell David of the
death of Absalom, as good as anything in Aeschylus. He asks himself how
the author of Job puts across his messenger scene:

> That same day, as Job's sons and daughters were feasting in the house of the
> eldest brother, a messenger came to Job and said, 'The oxen were plowing

27 Whedbee, 'Comedy of Job' 217–249, in Redday and Brenner (eds), *On Humour and the
   Comic*, p. 222.
28 Athalya Brenner, 'Job the Pious? The Characterization of Job in the Narrative
   Framework of the Book', in David J. A. Clines (ed.), *The Poetical Books* (Sheffield
   Academic Press, Sheffield, 1997), pp. 298–313 (302).
29 Ibid., p. 306.
30 Jacobson, *Seriously Funny*, p. 1.

and the donkeys grazing and the Sabeans attacked and took them and killed the boys and only I escaped to tell you'. Before he had finished speaking, another came up and said, 'Lightning fell from the sky and burned up the sheep and boys and only I escaped to tell you'. Before he had finished speaking, another one came and said, 'Chaldeans attacked the camels and took them and killed the boys and only I escaped to tell you'. Before he had finished speaking, another one came and said, 'Your sons and daughters were feasting and a great wind came out of the desert and knocked down the walls of the house and it fell on them and they're dead and only I escaped to tell you'.

The one-thing-on-top-of-the-otherness of the staged scene can be funny. Three breathless messengers on each other's heels, each interrupting his forerunner and ending on the same formula ('only I escaped to tell you'), can easily smack of comical exaggeration: he instructs each messenger to talk fast. Job reacts *exactly* how an all-too-perfect man is supposed to do:

> He said, 'Naked I came from my mother's womb, and naked I will return there. The Lord gave, and the Lord has taken; may the name of the Lord be blessed'.

The audience can hardly blame the Satan for demanding permission to repeat the test on this paragon, or God for giving it. It is not easy to convince Equity that we need just one actor for Bildad and for the Satan, but when Equity agree the costume people put him in Calvin Klein jeans and airtex shirt, with alligator. When Job is covered from head to foot in boils, with that omnipotent divine ability to make things perfectly awful, the audience know it is witnessing the cursing power of God. To play *Job!* as a comedy of incongruity is to perform the play as a satire, an infernal comedy.

The first thing which the God-fearing, mishap-fearing man does, when the event which he performed all of those sacrifices to avert comes about, is to proclaim himself a complete solipsist. He turns to the audience and says:

> God damn the day I was born
> > and the night that forced me from the womb.
> On that day – let there be darkness;
> > let it never have been created;
> > let it sink back into the void.
> Let chaos overpower it;
> > let black clouds overwhelm it;
> > let the sun be plucked from its sky.
> Let oblivion overshadow it;
> > let the other days disown it;
> > let the aeons swallow it up.
> On that night – let no child be born,
> > no mother cry out with joy.
> Let sorcerers wake the Serpent
> > to blast it with external blight.
> Let its last stars be extinguished;
> > let it wait in terror for daylight;
> > let its dawn never arrive.
> For it did not shut the womb's doors
> > to shelter me from this sorrow.

The director instructs the Job-actor to say it like you are getting into a coffin and shutting the lid. Make the audience see the speed of your transition from perfect piety to cosmic negation. You are talking about light and darkness, the first things which God created at the beginning of the world, and you are saying you prefer dark to light: 'every flicker of light is wished into darkness, swallowed up by darkness, or cancelled into non-being by the chain of "nots" or "nones" that run down the poem'.[31] Every time you spit out a 'not' and 'none', we turn out a light. We keep you in a partially illuminated circle of darkness until the end of the play. Directly above you, the platform where God is is dark too, so you can't see him; but horizontally, the platform is still lighted, so God is visible, to the audience. You let slip your real motivation for your piety at the end of your speech:

> My worst fears have happened;
> My nightmares have come to life.

Then, you turn from the audience, look up to the raised platform where God is, and start insulting your Creator. Hit back the ironies at God:

> What is man, that you notice him,
>   turn your glare upon him,
>   examine him every morning,
>   test him at every instant?
> Won't you even give me
>   time to swallow my spit?

The guy who was so obedient and God-fearing turns out to be a closet satirist. You, says the director, for he is not sure how well his actor knows his Bible, are making a 'parody' of Psalm 8.4–5:

> What is man that thou rememberest him,
> Or the son of man that thou visitest him?
> Thou hast set him little below God,
> And with glory and honor thou dost crown him.[32]

Most of the actors are in therapy and it is clear to them that Job must have built up a lot of destructive anger in his pre-emptive sacrificing days, if this is how he vents his spleen upon the Almighty. Where the Psalmist pictured God visiting man as a 'ceremony of reward', Job imagines God's every visit to human beings as a 'court at law', in which the divine Judge tries human beings for their slightest crimes.[33] The mask of obedient constraint has come off.

On come Zophar in an academic's corduroys, Bildad as before, and Eliphaz in Armani. The director reminds them that their group title of Friends is ironic. If they want to drink whiskey, smoke cigars, and read the *New Yorker* while the other Friends and Job are talking, that is fine. Talk very smoothly, advises the director: the proverbs roll off Bildad's tongue:

---

31 Robert Alter, *Art of Biblical Poetry* (T&T Clark, Edinburgh, 1985, 1990), p. 78.
32 Good, *Irony in the Old Testament*, pp. 225–227.
33 Ibid.

Can papyrus grow without water?
    Can a reed flourish in sand?
As crisp and fresh as it looked,
    it wilts like a blade of grass.
Such is the fate of the impious,
    the empty hope of the sinner.
His peace of mind is gossamer;
    his faith is a spider's web.
Though he props up his house, it collapses;
    though he builds it again, it falls.

But the righteous blossom in sunlight,
    and the garden is filled with their seeds.

You know the Wisdom tradition, says the director, like merchant bankers know the stockmarket: you are too good at it: you are giving advice to a bankrupt as if you were talking to someone on £100,000 a year. Now Job is going into denial. He picks up half of what you are saying, and takes it to its logical conclusion. God is, he says, completely unknowable:

I know this is true:
    no man can argue with God
or answer even one
    of a thousand accusations.
    . . .
he talks to the sun – it darkens;
    he clamps a seal on the stars.
He alone stretched out the heavens
    and trampled the heights of the sea;
he made the Bear and the Hunter,
    the Scorpion, the Twins.
His workings are vast and fathomless,
    his wonders beyond my grasp'. [*Here he begins to look up to make sure God is listening*]
If he passed me, I would not see him;
    if he went by, I would not know.
If he seized me, who would stop him
    or cry out, 'What are you doing?'
He will never hold back his fury;
    the Dragon lies at his feet.

Job says: yes, you are right, *I should just submit to my fate.* Make it sarcastic: the Sky-Walker is not to be trifled with. What am I saying about God?, asks the Job-actor. You read *Beyond Good and Evil*? You are saying God is sheer power – outside ethics. You are being ironic about the friends' idea of God: if God is as far from us as they say, he cannot be as good as they want to believe – not good on human terms. The Guy who killed the Dragon of chaos would have you for breakfast, so you have no rights.

    Your language takes control. You are more irascible in every scene. You have become an arch-satirist, and your enemy is God. Cut him down to size; accuse him of being an ignorant slob:

Are your eyes mere eyes of flesh?
    Is your vision no keener than a man's?

Job jeers,

> For you keep pursuing a sin,
> > trying to dig up a crime,
> though you *know* that I am innocent
> > and cannot escape from your grip.

Go back to your first view. Yes, God is all-powerful, and we know it by the chaotic way in which he behaves. In the Old Testament, dames like Hannah and guys like David lyricise about God kicking down the high and mighty from the thrones, and raising little people like them. Say it as a parody of these self-serving magnificats: God is supposed to be keen on order, but when it suits his whim, he creates chaos. Say it rudely and pointedly:

> Power belongs to him only;
> > deceived and deceiver are his.
> He turns great lords into morons,
> > priests into drivelling fools.
> He pushes kings off their thrones
> > and knocks the crown from their heads.
> He strips the wise of their reason
> > and makes the eloquent mute.
> ...
> He drives great rulers insane
> > and drops them alone in the wilderness.
> They grope about in the dark,
> > staggering as if they were drunk.

Now the Job-actor is perturbed: am I supposed to sound like a raving lunatic? Yup, says the director. You want to look like John Cleese by the end of *Clockwork*. Cleese plays a very anal headmaster who is always on time, and intolerant of his subordinates' unpunctuality. He drives off to a headmaster's conference to give a lecture on time management. Events start making him run behind time; he gets together with an attractive chick, they get lost, their car breaks down. Posing as hitch-hikers, they persuade a driver to go into the forest and undress with them, steal his clothes and make off with his car. The headmaster reaches his conference and tries to walk dignifiedly to the podium in a wide lapelled suit two sizes too small for him, and the police hot on his trail. Play Job like the clock-keeping headmaster who has gone too fast from rigid hyperperfection to criminality: your hair should be flying every which way by Act III, and your tie round your ear.

Remember that the purpose of these tirades is to demand justice. God *must* appear, and speak to you, because

> I have prepared my defence,
> > and I know that I am right.

In the logic of the Wisdom tradition, God has no moral right to make Job suffer as he does. You have a clearer and more 'direct perception' of the world and of God than the Friends do, but your 'moral imagination' is 'only somewhat less conventional' than theirs.[34] Like them, you are trapped

---

34 Alter, *Art of Biblical Poetry*, pp. 90 and 106.

in magic, or what Kierkegaard called the aesthetic. The Job-actor is not too clear on what Kierkegaard meant by the 'aesthetic', so the director borrows another tack, from Samuel Terrien. You know, he says, what the Pharisees and mediaeval Catholics were like? Well, Job was being good because he 'assumed that he could buy his own salvation'.[35] But make the audience respect you a little bit: you are a puny man shaking your fist at God and saying:

> Grant me one thing only,
>   and I will not hide from your face:
> do not numb me with fear
>   or flood my heart with your terror.
> Accuse me – I will respond;
>   or let me speak, and answer me.
> What crime have I committed?
>   How have I sinned against you?
> Why do you hide your face
>   as if I were your enemy?

The audience should giggle uneasily when you gun God down. Because of the lighting, they can see a lot more of God than you can. They can see God, up on the 'higher stage', watching this increasingly bizarre performance.

The producer suggests that the Friends should be fed their replies by lap-top computer. They push a button and the answers roll out – the audience sees them pushing the 'suffering' button again and again, and reading off the printout. Bildad the Shuhite should be the most gruesome of the trio:

> Should the earth be changed for *your* sake
> and mountains move at your bidding?
>
> It is true: the sinner is snuffed out;
>   his candle flickers and dies.
> His arrogant steps are hobbled;
>   he is tripped by his own deceit.
> A net catches his legs;
>   he stumbles into a pit.
> His heels stick in a trap;
>   a noose snaps his neck.
> The terrors of death surround him
>   and make him piss in his pants.

You are telling Job: Why *should* God care about you? That cosmic Engineer has created a built-in sinner-self-destruct mechanism within this world.

---

35 Terrien, 'Yahweh Speeches', 503. Terrien says that 'the poet uses the scandal of innocent suffering in order to study the ambiguities of faith ... the theological dimension of moral man's sinfulness, and the folly of human efforts toward self-justification ... the poet proves himself to be the theologian of pure grace, over against the fallacies of proto-Pelagianism' (497–498). He adds that Job, 'Like his friends ... had accepted the folkloric belief in individual retribution based on a commercial accounting between deeds and rewards ... The poet anticipates the theological discussions of a later age on salvation by faith and the vanity of good works'.

You say you are innocent, but you can't be innocent, in the eyes of God (*and never, never look away from the computer and upto heaven*):

> How can a man be pure
>> or a son of woman be sinless?
> If God despises the moon
>> and thinks that the stars are tainted,
> what about man, that worm
>> that vile, stinking maggot?

Am I supposed to be believable, asks the Job-actor? Nope, says the director. The audience starts wondering whether it can be as bad as you say. They have not seen any of *these things*:

> I am jeered at by streetboys,
>> whose fathers I would have considered
>> unfit to take care of my dogs.
> What were *they* but mongrels?
>> No one would have called them men.
> . . .
> And now I am their fool;
>> they snigger behind my back.
> They stand beside me and sneer;
>> they walk up and spit in my face.
> When they see me, frenzy takes them;
>> they turn into savage beasts.
> They rush at me like a mob;
>> they raise seige-ramps against me.
> They tear down my defences;
>> they swarm over my wall.
> They burst in at the breach
>> and come pouring through like a flood.

Has Job caught the contagion of the Friends' compulsive exaggeration? Job has got to sound like the most hyperbolic of hypochondriacs: 'The comedian practises an art of exaggeration, or overstatement'.[36] You are doing it unintentionally.

Now Job the word-spinner makes his tremendous boast, throwing down the gauntlet to the Almighty. Looking up at the sky, you say: If I have seduced a woman

> let any man take my wife
>> and grind in between her thighs!'

If I have neglected the poor, let my arms fall off! If I took anything without paying for it, may my crops be overgrown with thistles! If I kissed my hand to the moon . . . ! Job presents his case:

> Oh if only God would hear me,
>> state his case against me,
>> let me read his indictment.

36 Wylie Sypher, 'The Meanings of Comedy', in Henri Bergson, *Comedy, an Essay on Comedy by George Meredith and Laughter* (Doubleday Anchor, New York, 1956; Johns Hopkins University Press, Baltimore, 1980, 1984), p. 239.

I would carry it on my shoulder
    or wear it on my head like a crown.
I would justify the least of my actions;
    I would stand before him like a prince.

The audience know God is up there, listening to this. Now he *must* appear.
'We expect God – and we get Elihu!'[37] The director characterises his actors
in line with Whedbee's observation that

> Incongruity and parody pervade the representation of Job's friends includ-
> ing young Elihu, Job's God, and *Job himself*... are not the friends correct
> to a point in their estimate of Job's pride? ... is it not the case that Yahweh's
> magnificent parody of Job's heroic posture has elements of truth?[38]

The Friends are right to be offended by the way that Job speaks of God: 'it
is Job's titanism that so exercises the friends. No man has any right to talk
of God as Job does'.[39]

    The director has foiled the rules of the American Equity by shipping in
an aristocratic Englishman of recusant stock to play God. He wears his
tiara with complacency, and made play with his pince-nez during the Satan
scenes. For his concluding monologues, he doesn't need the director to tell
him to play it like he is giving a blessing from the balcony. If the director
has to nudge him a little bit in the direction of the story, telling him that he
is puncturing Job's fantasies, the cradle-catholic needs no reminding of the
first line of his catechism: *You* created the world. Ask him if *he* could! You're
amused by his determination to judge the world *you* made by how well it
treats *him*. God puts a stream of ironically bemused and 'satirical
question[s]'[40] to Job:

Where were you when I planned the earth?
    Tell me, if you are so wise ...
    Who laid down its cornerstone
While the morning stars burst out singing
    and the angels shouted for joy!

Where were you when I stopped the waters,
    and they issued gushing from the womb?
when I wrapped the ocean in clouds
    and swaddled the sea in shadows?
when I closed it in with barriers
    and set its boundaries, saying,
'Here you may come, but no farther;
    here shall your proud waves break.'

Now the director suggests some surreal stage directions: take out a
giant teaspoon and start tapping on the head of your little solipsist.
Make Job look *out* at the world which you pronounced good. The little
creep is a narcissist. Make him to look around himself a bit. He made a
death wish on your creation in his first speech. As you speak, the director
tells the God-actor, we bring all of the lights on – in every colour in

37 Whedbee, 'Comedy of Job', 19.
38 Ibid., 23.
39 Good, *Irony in the Old Testament*, p. 206.
40 Whedbee, 'Comedy of Job', 23.

the spectrum. We want to 'reverse' everything Job said about your creation.[41]

The God-actor says, Look, I am supposed to come on, and stand in the dock Job has built for me, and defend my idea of justice. Why the hell do I just start talking about antelopes and ostriches! He stays in role in and out of rehearsals and doesn't like the idea that the lighting crew are going to project some sort of *David Attenborough* film onto the stage walls, distracting the audience from his speech. But he knows his Ming from his Sung, and it helps to learn that it will be like a *Chinese landscape*. The God-actor is able to explain to the Americans that the Chinese were painting naturalistic portraits of animals two millennia before the English learned to paint a horse that looks like a horse. He says that is because the Chinese have a *'Different conception of Man's Importance*. In a small child's conception of the universe animals play quite as important a part as men'.[42] Once the landscapes are projected onto the stage walls, thinks the God-actor, even an American audience can see that they are looking at the 'face of the earth' from an 'aircraft'.[43] Once the director says the magic words 'Feng Shui', even the producer twigs. Its like a conflation of the Jewish God and the Taoist Chi, says the director. You made this landscape and you like all of it equally: just remind Job of his place in it by teasing him a little bit. You boasted to Satan about Job; now boast to Job about your animals. 'God' takes his turn in the dock in the spirit of his favourite poet, Lewis Carroll:

Do you tell the antelope to calve
    or ease her when she is in labour?
Do you count the months of her fullness
    and know when her time has come?
She kneels; she tightens her womb;
    she pants, she presses, gives birth.
Her little ones grow up;
    they leave and never return.

Who unties the wild ass
    and lets him wander at will?
. . .
Do you deck the ostrich with wings,
    with elegant plumes and feathers?
She lays her eggs in the dirt
    and lets them hatch on the ground,
forgetting that a foot may crush them
    or sharp teeth crack them open.
She treats her children cruelly,
    as if they were not her own.
For God deprived her of wisdom
    and left her with little sense.
When she spreads her wings to run,
    she laughs at the horse and rider.

41 Alter, *Art of Biblical Poetry*, pp. 96–97.
42 Arthur Waley, *An Introduction to the Study of Chinese Painting* (Ernest Benn, London, 1958), p. 153.
43 René Grousset, *Chinese Art and Culture*, translated by Haakon Chevalier (Andre Deutsch, London, 1959), p. 251.

Do you give the horse his strength?
    Do you clothe his neck with terror?
Do you make him leap like a locust,
    snort like a blast of thunder?

Job is thus decentred: God turns the issue from justice in the universe (a human ideal) to order in the universe (a divine prerogative). Perhaps he has not learned *blind* faith:

With ear's hearing I had heard of you.
But now my eyes see you. (42.5)

But he speaks those lines self-deprecatingly: he has dropped his belief in magic and learned to be ironic about himself.[44] Job has learned the double 'incognito' of faith. His original picture of himself has been underwhelmed by a God who is far greater than he had imagined, and this 'is the quietus on magic … The irony of reconciliation is that man is reconciled to God on God's terms, not on man's'.[45] If Job was tearing his hair out before God appeared, he *dies* during the God speeches. God now teaches him the absolute contradiction between the most religious individual and the Absolute: he learns the 'overwhelmingness of God'. For the God 'over whom Job and his friends have debated is … one of the images prohibited by the terrible God of Sinai'.[46] *Job!* is a comedy of inverted ideas: Job inverts the Wisdom tradition, and turns the Friends' wisdom upside down; but when Job takes it too far, God appears to invert Job's pretensions. If *Job!* is set out as a comedy of incongruity, Job is the final object of this satire – the satirist satirised.

If we wish to put on *Job!* as a comedy, we cannot leave the protagonist stranded, repenting in dust and ashes, after God has dressed him down. If we take note of the prose epilogue, Whedbee argues, it will be obvious that plot carries out the U-shaped curve typically attributed to comedy. *Job!* ends with an enormous party – whilst the second round of beautiful daughters (named Dove, Cinnamon and Eye-Shadow)[47] and a dozen of their friends do a cancan routine at the back of the stage.

Not all of the critics give rave reviews to this performance. Two of them say it began well, but began to go wrong with the God-speeches; Job's repentance is insufferable. James Williams writes that God's 'parad[e] of his cosmic power apparatus' left him cold; he was rather hoping that Job would never succumb to a God who 'never really deal[s] with the questions'.[48] Williams thinks the director is right to make God sound ironic. But then, he says, the director and his cast had two choices. One: we could have played God as an *alazon* – the biggest Imposter in the book. Two: If we thought our audience was not up to date enough for that we have to make God show real contempt for human beings. The actor playing God should

---

44 Good, *Irony in the Old Testament*, p. 198.
45 Ibid., pp. 239–240.
46 Brueggeman, *Theology of the Old Testament*, p. 391.
47 Mitchell's translation, not the director's invention.
48 James G. Williams, '"You Have Not Spoken Truth of Me": Mystery and Irony in Job', *Zeitschrift für die Alttestamentliche Wissenschaft*, 83, 1971, 231–255 (247).

have stated more clearly that his response to Job's suffering is to tell him about 'Man's nothingness'.[49] The director feels like Cleese's headmaster when he reads that 'Man is not valued in the Book of Job – except when we re-enter the folk-tale world, where God in effect condemns himself!'[50] In an exceptionally biting review, David Robertson says that a God who is so infinitely different from Job that he cannot be bothered to answer his complaint, a God who responds to the cries of unjust suffering by telling the victims that their pains suffer tremendous diminution when seen from above, is a 'charlatan'.[51] Robertson says that Job should have winked at the audience when he made his phoney submission to this Faker: the director leaves his newspaper on the side of the table, goes back to his Bible, and finds consolingly little textual evidence for that one. It *is* true that he gave himself little room for manoeuvre on the dynamics of the U-shaped curve: *why* does Job's trial end in triumph? And why does God say that Job alone has 'spoken well of me' (Job 40.7)? These are matters for the incognito of faith. He comforts himself with the thought that his audience were insufficiently Kierkegaardian to enjoy his black comedy. Not even Catholics know how to be Jansenists any more, gripes the God-actor, who lost his faith during the first sitting of the Second Vatican Council (1962–1965).

3. Humanising Job

Job! as a comedy of the infinite contradiction between humanity and God either goes too far or not far enough. Williams and Robertson are right to find this way of putting on the drama of Job unbelievable. That indicates a *lacunae* in the comic Bible à la Bergson. Henri Bergson's book is called *Le Rire*, that is, *Laughter*. Bergson's essay answers the question, not what is comedy but 'what do we laugh *at?*': he is asking not about comedy but about *the comical*.[52] If we are going to laugh at a man falling down, we cannot pity him. Bergson's first condition of laughter is the suppression of emotion, an 'anesthése momentanée du coeur'. The object of laugher, *le comique* is 'addressed to the pure intelligence'.[53] The object at which such a pure intelligence laughs is someone who is locked into a mechanical compulsion: 'The attitudes, gestures and movements of the human body are laughable in exact proportion as that body reminds us of a mere machine'.[54] Sypher lodges a well-considered protest against the casting of *all* comedy as satire:

> the range of comic action is far wider than Bergson supposed when he remarked that . . . the comic hero . . . makes only . . . automatic motions, which look ridiculous when they are 'interrupted'. Bergson [saw] . . . the comic figure . . . from only one angle, treating him as if he were a toy manikan which, wound up, is geared to execute the same motion wherever he is put.

---

49 Ibid., 249.
50 Ibid., 250.
51 Cited in Whedbee, 'Comedy of Job', *Semeia*, 7, 21; Robertson defends his position in 'The Comedy of Job: A Response', *Semeia*, 7, 41–44.
52 The philosopher David Braine alerted me to the significance of this distinction.
53 Bergson, *Le Rire*, p. 4.
54 Ibid., p. 29.

Bergson's comic hero is only a caricature of man. Yet Don Quixote ... enters
the realm of human action as a figure like Tartuffe cannot. In Dickens and
Dostoievsky, too, the characters are ... not merely comic machines like
Tartuffe and Harpagon.[55]

Bergson defines comedy as the means by which society 'restrains
eccentricity' and 'corrects' 'rigidity': he compares comic audience and
victim to a cat and its mouse.[56] The French philosopher reduces laughter to
a means of *punishment*, and the objects of such laughter to *victims*. He says
that 'Being intended to humiliate', laughter 'must make a painful impression on the person against whom it is directed'.[57] This accounts for the
element of aggression in comedy, but not for the existence of comic *heroes*,
such as Lysistrata, the Wife of Bath, Falstaff, Tom Jones and Job.

Job is too human to stand for mechanical overdrive. We shall attempt to
describe the drama of Job as a *purgatorial* comedy. What rings true and
false in our first experiment? An audience could learn something about
God's mystery by laughing *at* Job and his Friends, and by laughing *with*
the ironic God who appears to despatch them all to their various rewards
and punishments. It would be wrong entirely to dispose of this satirical
element, in the direction of an earnest consideration of the problem of evil.
If there is funny ha-ha in the messenger scene, in which the feasting
offspring are despatched with the swift piling up of disasters beloved by
satirical cartoonists, and if Job *sometimes* seems to enlarge his woes sky-
high, thus gaining an audience reaction of a wry, disbelieving smile,
perhaps we are to learn that suffering is not, after all, *unendurable*. If it
were, there could be no comedy which includes it, except that directed at
an enemy from whose misfortunes we are detached. If the audience is to
learn this from Job's performance, then we must identify with him.
Kierkegaard distinguished the art of the ironist and that of the humorist
thus: 'But because humor is always a concealed pain, it is also an instance
of sympathy. In irony there is no sympathy.'[58] The audience neither pities
Job nor views him with ironic detachment: rather, they see *themselves*, and
their own all too frequent descents from perfection to chaos, in him. If Job
is to have this effect on his audience, they must be sufficiently detached
from him to think about him and sufficiently empathetic to feel like him.
Why do we find it so easy to imagine that Job is an object of divine satire?
Is it because we project backwards the diminishment which appears to fall
upon Job during the God-speeches? Terrien tells us that the God-speeches
exhort Job to 'liberate himself from the microcosm of his own egocentricity,
to borrow the perspective of God ... and to discover the broad horizons of
the macrocosm of life on the grand scale'.[59] Don't we know that God comes
on to redirect Job's sight away from its limited human focus? Doesn't God
overwhelm Job's anthropomorphic conception of justice by lifting him up
and letting him see the *whole* cosmos from above? How else could Job learn
the incongruity between his idea of the good and God's? We smile when

55 Sypher, 'Meanings of Comedy', p. 226.
56 Bergson, *Le Rire*, pp. 20–21, 71.
57 Ibid., pp. 200–201.
58 Kierkegaard, *Unscientific Postscript*, p. 491.
59 Terrien, 'Yahweh Speeches', 502.

we see tiny cars making their way along a tiny motorway, from air-plane windows, because from that height, things

> do not just appear distant and small, they look *too* small, due to the fact that the interval between viewer and ground is almost unstructured. This perspective not only shrinks people and objects, it dominates them.[60]

The actor who advises the hero to look at the world with such 'despising sight' is not God but Bildad. Bildad tells his friend that human beings are 'unclean worms and maggots'.[61] God depicts the animals, not from far away, but 'close up', with warmth and intimacy. We have forgotten to dramatise the book if we omit to show that God's words bring him down to earth. His omniscient sight gives him an 'aerial view'[62] of creation. Does Job learn to see the world from God's point of view, so that he may put away his close-up focus on human injustice, and emulate the aerial perspective? What would he learn from it? He knows already the *distance* between God and cosmos:

> His workings are vast and fathomless,
> his wonders beyond my grasp.
> *If he passed me, I would not see him;*
> *if he went by, I would not know.*

If, by the end of the play, Job has seen God with his own eyes, and in that seeing, perceived the world, perhaps he has learned that one *can* see like God and like a human being at the same time; one can even see God and the cosmos in one integrated vision. As Lasine puts it:

> God denounces Job's initial attempt to make the correct perspective for earthly vision of social injustice into a total perspective of cosmic validity. This is not a zero-sum game, where one mode of vision is validating by calling the other blind or upside down. God himself indicates as much when he uses many of Job's expressions in describing the bird's-eye view of the world. This implies that the speeches are designed not to replace Job's world-picture, but to coincide with it, in the way that two slides create depth which are made to coincide in a stereoscope. Because Job – like all other humans – has a place in the cosmos seen through God's eyes, the bird's-eye and worm's-eye views *both* reveal essential dimensions of human reality.[63]

We mistake the purpose of the drama of Job if we read it as a tract against being human.

In order to recreate the theatrical experience which could be made of it, we need, first, to attend to the audience's reaction to Job. He is to be the object neither of their enmity nor of their tearful pity: rather, he has to remind them of themselves. Brueggemann has well described Job as the most complete 'dramatic ... reflection on humanness in the Old

---

60 Stuart Lasine, 'Bird's Eye and Worm's Eye Views of Justice in the Book of Job', in Clines, *Poetical Books*, pp. 274–297 (278).
61 Ibid., pp. 279 and 280.
62 Ibid., p. 276.
63 Ibid., p. 294.
64 Brueggemann, *Theology of the Old Testament*, p. 489.

Testament',[64] and we do not regard our own selves with contempt, even or especially when we turn the face of our humanness toward God. And if we are not merely to stage Job but to reflect upon its inherently dramatic qualities, we need to meditate on what the characters are doing by speaking. We have to look more closely at the dramatic situation which the book sets up. The memory of the characters in Job reaches back to Genesis 2.7, where 'Adam' is made out of red earth, or soil (*'adam*). Job reminds his Creator:

> Hast thou not poured me out like milk, and curdled me like cheese?
> Thou hast clothed me with skin and flesh,
> and hast fenced me with bones and sinews. (Job 10.10–11)

Job continues, a few lines on, 'Why then hast thou brought me forth out of the womb?' (Job 10.18). Such a Creator-God is *answerable* to Job's come-back. Fisch comments that

> The force of the question resided not in any implied answer but in the question itself. The very power to ask the question becomes . . . a testimony to God's purposefulness . . . Job is saying 'You made me, and here I am, capable of asking you questions about it'. Job's questioning of God – and the book is conducted largely in the form of such questions – implies its own answer.[65]

Genesis' way of imagining creation has lowered God and man into each others' sights. The biblical God can be 'summon[ed]' by Job 'to interview – and the interview is granted!'[66] If there is a beautifully visualised intimacy in God's external description of the animals, there is a more internal intimacy in the unbroken dialogue between God and Job.

Kierkegaard wrote little about God as the Creator, or humanity as God's creation. It is not an omission which one would readily attribute to any Hebrew author. By talking back to God, Job insists upon his createdness. The purpose of the God-speeches is not to alienate Job, but to help him to find his own home within this creation. If we imagine the book within the context of creation, the tension between human and divine does not collapse, but it is relativised. 'Creation' is the language of metaphysical theology: let us restrict ourselves to the biblical *hayyim* ('life', related to the verb *haya*, to be). In the drama of Job, *hayyim* is an *ethical* question. Job is God-fearing, but fearful of life. He passes through a test, in which he is 'driven to ask himself the question "To be or not to be?"' Job begins by withdrawing into himself and rejecting an all too strange creation. But, because Job hangs onto his demand for justice, never ceasing to believe that the Creator God ought to care for created humanity, by the end of the play, the 'answer forced out of him is that life, however unwelcome, has to be endured'.[67]

Frye's diagrammatic conception of the tragic and the comic plot gives us a helpful short-hand for talking about these things. But we are inclined to follow Fisch in departing from any theory which 'requires us to be

65 Fisch, *Poetry with a Purpose*, p. 32.
66 Ibid., pp. 30–31.
67 Ibid., p. 37.

hunting for Us or inverted Us'. Fisch argues that Job breaks the mould of
the literary genres, both tragic and comic. He is rightly antipathetic toward
an overstructured, plot-based conception of genre. Comedy is the untidy
genre, lacking the remorselessly logical passage of tragedy toward disaster.
Sypher comments that it is the messiness and illogicality of comedy which
allow it to break through the surface of life, and dig down to water:

> the comic experience can reach as deeply down [as tragedy], perhaps because
> the comic artist begins by accepting the absurd, 'the improbable', in human
> existence. Therefore he has less resistance than the tragic artist to representing
> what seems incoherent and inexplicable, and thus lowers the threshold of
> artistic perception. After all, comedy, not tragedy, admits the disorderly into
> the realm of art; the grotesque depends upon an irrational focus.[68]

Comedy is created by the kind of world which it builds, the 'terrain'
which its characters inhabit. Job's experience of the prerational immerses
him in a world he did not make, a mysterious, multiplicitous and funny
world, created by God. Fisch says that God's concluding speeches

> celebrate the *vitality* of the universe: abundant life and creation are their
> theme ... Crude, barbaric, even chaotic the creation may seem, but it is
> bursting with energy and purpose.

When God questions Job,

> The point is not that Job doesn't know, but that God does. The world is ...
> ruled over not by a god of death, by Hades, but by a living god, the God of
> the spirits of all flesh, *'elohê harûhot lekol basar*. Job in his life is linked with the
> sportive leviathan ... and with the sons of God shouting with joy ...
> Wherever he looks there is an abundance of life, of creativity, and of beauty.
> He is bound up in the bond of that creativity.[69]

The terrain of comedy is a land of fertility and splashing life. This is the Uz
in which Job dwells, a real and solid world in which one can take some
very hard knocks, but from which it is possible to recover. We have resisted
a definition of comedy which hands it over to what Jacobson called the
'stomachless clowns' of the spiritualisers, the other-worldly fools. The
comic hero learns to be at home in this world. This is why he needs to have
bones that bounce, pragmatism and imaginative flexibility. Disasters
happen to the comic hero, but none that is absolute and final. Comedy
resists closure at the catastrophic moment; it shows the next scene.

After God has praised Job for speaking well of him, he leaves the stage.
In Job's last scene his friends and relatives come 'to his house to celebrate';
and

> So the Lord blessed the end of Job's life more than the beginning. Job now
> had fourteen thousand sheep, six thousand camels, a thousand yoke of oxen,
> and a thousand donkeys. He also had seven sons and three daughters: the
> eldest he named Dove, the second Cinnamon, and the third Eye-shadow.
> And in all the world there were no women as beautiful as Job's daughters.
> He gave them a share of his possessions along with their brothers.

68 Sypher, 'Meanings of Comedy', p. 201.
69 Fisch, *Poetry with a Purpose*, pp. 39–40.

> After this, Job lived for a hundred and forty years. He lived to see his grandchildren and great-grandchildren. And he died at a very great age. (Job 42.12–17)

How is that possible, after all that he has been through? Fisch remarks that people can survive the most hideous things. He does not take this as a 'fairytale' ending, but in a realistic sense:

> The survivors of Auschwitz have been known to establish new families and set themselves up in business. This may not have the aesthetic tidiness of art, but human beings are resilient – and that . . . is what the book of Job is saying.[70]

I have known two such people, Igor and Sonia, who met in Auschwitz, married, and ran a coffee-shop on Sixth Avenue. For the lucky survivor, infinite contradictions are *integrated* and lived with, grant us faith in *hayyim* ('being'). The Job who did not scruple to remind God that the poor require justice has learned to see humanity afresh: 'If Job continues to view the world through God's eye, he will do so in a very human way ... like a biblical prophet.'[71]

4. Death

Staging *Job!* as an infernal comedy seemed to make Job into a Ridiculous Man who is put through his paces by an utterly incomprehensible God. And so, it breaks apart the dramatic nexus which the biblical drama creates, between Job and the audience, on the one side, and between Job and God, on the other. A God who first parodies the sufferer, and then arbitrarily rehabilitates him might be respected by the pious as a 'truly hidden' *Deus Absconditus*, but it does not require an excess of Voltairean scepticism to find such a deity demonic. It makes better sense of the relatedness of the human Job and the Creator God if we present the story as a purgatorial comedy. If we read the book as a 'trial' of the hero our concern is focused upon Job's *humanity*. What does Job's comic bravado consist in? To what extent does the earth-centred presentation encompass the complete drama of a book which vividly depicts *Sheol*, earth *and* heaven? Wylie Sypher claims that, 'At the radiant peak of "high comedy" ... laughter is qualified by tolerance, and criticism is modulated by a sympathy that comes from wisdom'.[72] Perhaps the drama of Job leans toward paradisial comedy. This is a designation which we have intended to retain for apocalyptic literature, because it is there that the hero travels through the cosmos. We will see how far we can press the case for paradisial comedy in the Book of Job. This will enable us to show how the four corners of Job's world are connected; it will permit us to draw in the whole canonical text of Job, including Job's speech about wisdom, and Elihu's speech. What does the inclusion of these 'cosmic' poems do to the text?

Job is not the first person to decide that he might as well be dead. His wife shrewdly advises him to 'curse God and die' (Job 2.9), and his Friends perform a ritual of mourning for the dead in the sight of the sick man: 'they

---

70 Ibid., p. 41.
71 Stuart Lasine, 'Bird's Eye and Worm's Eye Views of Justice', p. 297.
72 Sypher, 'Meanings of Comedy', p. 211.

lifted up their voice and wept; and they rent every one his mantle, and sprinkled dust upon their heads toward heaven' (Job 2.12).[73] Following upon these gestures, Job formally 'unbirths' himself (Job 3). The identification of 'life' with 'happiness' did not come to Job from a 'Pelagianism' so 'Proto' as to be prophetic:[74] it is one of the foundational images of the Pentateuch. As the Hebrew imagination envisaged it, life *is* vigorous and forceful existence: a second of its images is *light*. In the Old Testament light means both the reality of existence in this world, and seeing and being seen by God.[75] In asking 'darkness' to unmake the day upon which he was conceived, Job is setting his face toward unbeing. He conceives himself in Sheol, the 'subterranean region'[76] in which the Old Testament writers had placed the dead. Not-being is a place, the land where 'kings and counsellors', the 'wicked', the 'weary' and the 'princes' of the earth are 'prisoners ... together' (3.14–18), not as 'souls', but as 'shadowy' replicas of their former selves.[77]

Life, *hayyam*, is 'an operative force' or an 'active power'.[78] The dead are designated as the *rephaim*, 'the weak'.[79] The dead 'exist': they do not 'live'.[80] Life is not a given, but a gift from God: it is a conditional blessing. Death is the absence of blessing: it takes from the human person everything which mediates the presence of God to them. Life is also 'water', 'rains', 'wells', 'springs' and 'dews': in Psalm 1.3, the believer is 'like a tree planted by streams of water, that yields its fruit in its season, and its leaf does not wither'.[81] In dusty Sheol the dead croak with thirst; drought is death. God exercises his life-giving power upon the world of the living, upon his chosen people, and upon history.[82] The dead are removed from these spheres. They are impotent because life *is* forceful being. Life is communion with other people: this is denied to the dead. The authors of the Patriarchal narratives believe that the shades in Sheol have gone beyond an impassable 'gulf':[83] 'the dead man is the absent, *par excellence*, the vanished man'.[84]

Sheol is under the world: it is as far away as one gets from God's heaven. This 'place' is a social 'state'.[85] The inhabitants are cut off from God: Job imagines himself as being like them. The round of life on earth is joyless if

---

73 On mourning rituals and their significance, see Robert Martin-Achard, *From Death to Life*, p. 27, and Walther Eichrodt, *Theology of the Old Testament*, Vol. II, translated by J. A. Baker (SCM, London, 1967), p. 215.

74 Samuel Terrien's terminology.

75 Martin-Achard cites Psalm 36.9: 'For with thee is the fountain of life; in thy light do we see light'. He comments: 'The believer prays his God "to lift up the light of his countenance upon him", that is to say, to save him (Ps. 4.6; Ps. 31.16) or "to grant him light" which means to restore his strength (Ps. 13.3).' *From Death to Life*, p. 9.

76 Ibid., p. 36.

77 Eichrodt, *Theology of the Old Testament*, Vol. II, p. 214.

78 Martin-Achard, *From Death to Life*, p. 5.

79 Eichrodt, *Theology of the Old Testament*, Vol. II, p. 214.

80 Martin-Achard, *From Death to Life*, p. 32.

81 Ibid., p. 10.

82 Eichrodt, *Theology of the Old Testament*, Vol. II, p. 222.

83 Ibid., p. 222.

84 Martin-Achard, *From Death to Life*, p. 42.

85 Ibid., p. 43.

Sheol beckons at the end. After Chapter 3, Job appears to choose death over life at least three times (7.1–3, 9–10, 15). Life is not filled with immanent meaning if it empties itself out into Sheol. Transcience merely slides into forgetfulness:

> Are not my days few? cease then, and let me alone, that I may take comfort a little,
> Before I go whence I shall not return, even to the land of darkness and the shadow of death;
> A land of darkness, as darkness itself; and of the shadow of death, without any order, and where the light is as darkness. (10.18–22)

In the earlier Hebrew conception, life on God's given land is a complete container of meaning. The goods of this world keep the invading forces of chaos and incoherence at bay. For later Hebrew authors, the familial ties between the dead and the living were insufficient comfort:

> 'The dead know nothing,' Ecclesiastes complains, '... the memory of them is lost ... they have no more for ever any share in all that is done under the sun' (Ecclesiastes IX.5–6; cp. Job XIV.21). Here then is expressed a conception of the beyond much more pessimistic than the ... older one, according to which the departed, through his offspring and through funerary rites remains in contact with the land of the living. It is partly ... a consequence of the evolution of ideas in Israel, and particularly of the growing sense of the importance of the individual that developed among the Chosen People. Thus the bridges between the perished and the living are broken down. Between Yahweh and the dead, relationships are as if they were non-existent.[86]

Job's 'evolution' into an 'individual' is achieved by the loss of his sons and daughters.

The biblical conception of death is the product of imagination, not philosophy. It contains elements which are experientially true, even if they are not logically coherent. It is God who gives the life-giving *ruah* to human beings, and it is God who takes it away. Thus, death is 'no cruel enemy' but 'the end of life, determined by God, and to be as readily accepted as his decision as the gift of life itself'.[87] Death is part of the ordered world constructed by Yahweh. But, because it is the opposite of God-given life, death is the welling up of the 'monster' of chaos, over the sea-barriers which had been set up to protect human beings against such disorder.[88] And yet, that portion of chaos which is death is given to human beings from the hand of God. To fight against this nothingness is to defend oneself against God:

> Alongside this peaceful conformity with God's order ... there is ... another attitude to death ... which as times go on becomes ... the dominating melody. This is *lamentation over death* as the ... most painful disturbance of the condition of life established by God.[89]

And so, Job can assert that, by turning his life to dust, God has murdered him (Job 16.11–18). For Job, everything, both good and evil, order and

86 Ibid., p. 41.
87 Eichrodt, *Old Testament Theology*, Vol. II, p. 500.
88 Martin-Achard, *From Death to Life*, p. 42 (Is. 5.14; Prov. 1.12; 27.20; 30.15 ff.).
89 Eichrodt, *Theology of the Old Testament*, Vol. II, pp. 501–502.

chaos, come from the hand of God: it is God who is inflicting the death-force upon him. Job's certainty that it is God who is his attacker is also his conviction that God's power stretches into every blackhole in the universe; it is his enraged and partially unwitting witness to the omnipresence of God. Like Jacob, Job engages in a hand-to-hand combat with God. And what an unremitting verbal fight-back he puts up. It is said that Job's story is not a 'theodicy' but an 'anthropodicy': Job wants God to appear, so that he can justified.[90] God may be invisible, but Job has been a visible representative of the 'way of life' set forth by Deuteronomy and the prophets (23.8–12). God, present in the 'words of his mouth' has always been life to Job. He fights back on behalf of this presence of God to and in himself.

God makes himself present in cosmic and moral order: when Job loses his perception of God's justice, he is plunged into a 'Sheol' in which God is invisible to him, and yet the cause of his condition. Job is fighting an unseen Opponent. Job says he is 'dead' because he has been removed from God's presence. Job does not merely wish that he were dead: he insists that he *is* dead

the grave [Sheol] is mine house; I have made my bed in the darkness.
I have said to corruption; thou art my father: to the worm, Thou art my mother, and my sister. (17.13–14)

Just as the dead are cut off from communion with the living, so Job is shunned by his wife, his Friends and his servants (19.1–23). He is a living inhabitant of Sheol: his complaint is an assertion that he *ought not to be*. The commentators have taken Job's demands that God *ought to be* just as 'Promethean', or rationalist: but Job's 'oughts' are the oughts of faith in a moral God, a God who is true to his life-giving word. Like Abraham, Job cannot believe that God will 'desecrate himself' by harming a righteous man, and, with no less chutzpah than the Patriarch, he challenges God to be himself. If we make the idea that death is ordained by God confront the idea that death is an invasion of nothingness, it becomes apparent that the second limits the sphere of God's mastery. Job is an inveterate believer in the ordering power of the Creator. He carries that belief into his own 'Sheol', where, he says, the God of the living will appear to him:

For I know that my redeemer liveth, and that he shall stand at the latter day upon the earth;
And though after my skin worms destroy this body, yet in my flesh shall I see God. (19.25–26)[91]

The Job who speaks has not yet 'really' entered the grave: 'Job wants vindication here in this world, and before he dies ... Before he dies – for the whole drama originates and is enacted in this world – Job will hear his Lord's voice, and behold His majesty.'[92] Nonetheless, by dint of his faith in the 'reach' of God's own goodness, Job has momentarily taken a crucial

---

90 Good, *Irony in the Old Testament*, p. 214.
91 Martin-Achard gives the literal translation: 'And after (or "behind") my skin, they have torn this to shred and from (or "without") my flesh, I shall see God.' *From Death to Life*, p. 169.
92 Ibid., pp. 172 and 180.

step which will after many centuries become belief in the vindication of the 'pious', after death.

Job goes on a journey in search of God. His imagery is consistently cosmic (cf. 9.5–10). He is looking for the secret, hidden place where Wisdom is hidden like a buried treasure:

> There is a path which no fowl knoweth, and which the vultures eye hath not seen:
> The lion's whelps have not trodden it, nor the fierce lion passed it by.
> He putteth forth his hand upon the rock; he overturneth the mountains by the roots.
> He cutteth out rivers among the rocks; and his eye seeth every precious thing.
> He bindeth the floods from overflowing; and the thing that is hid bringeth he forth to light.
> But where shall wisdom be found? and where is the place of understanding?
> Man knoweth not the price thereof; neither is it found in the land of the living.
> The depth saith, It is not in me: and the sea saith, It is not with me. (28.7–14)

It is not in the 'land of the living', and cannot be mined even in 'Ethiopia' (27.19). The living cannot see it, and the dead know of it only by reputation: knowledge of it echoes around the globe, but only the scope of God's sight can find it out:

> Whence then cometh wisdom? and where is the place of understanding?
> Seeing it is hid from the eyes of all living, and kept close from the fowls of the air.
> Destruction and death say, We have heard the fame thereof with our ears.
> God understandeth the way thereof, and he knoweth the place thereof.
> For he looketh to the ends of the earth, and seeth under the whole heaven;
> To make the weight for the winds; and he weigheth the waters by measure.
> When he made a decree for the rain, and a way for the lightning of the thunder:
> Then did he see it, and declare it: he prepared it, yea, and searched it out.
> And unto man he said, Behold, the fear of the Lord, that is wisdom, and to depart from evil is understanding. (28.20–28)

In his search for Wisdom, Job begins to wander up and down amidst the strange treasures of the universe: first the 'earth', out of which 'bread' comes, but under which is a fire (28.5), then in the sky, amidst the high-flying vultures (28.7), then amongst the mountain lions, or in the veins of the earth, (28.16–17), plunging down to the bottom of the sea, amongst the 'coral' and 'pearl' (28.18), and up again to the winds and the rain. Whoever added Chapter 28 to the poem

> chose the new material with a firm sense of how it could help tune up the proper attentiveness for God's concluding speech. That tuning up is a matter ... of poetically defining a *place* where we can begin to imagine the un-fathomable workings of the Creator. A whole world of sprawling expanses and inaccessible depths and heights is evoked ... 'A path unknown to the hawk,/ungrazed by the falcon's eye' (28.7), unguessed realms of hidden recesses that only God can see or bring to light if He chooses.[93]

---

93 Alter, *Art of Biblical Poetry*, p. 93.

Job has begun to paint for himself the scenery which God will show to him. He has to look upward when God appears to him. Job does existentially what the later apocalyptic writers will do more literally: he depicts the scenery of the cosmos, as it looks from above.

His ability to do this depends upon his own *well-grounded* self-belief. For Job has not ceased to be occupied with determining his innocence. Job's self-justification leads him to the recollection that he *himself* was a channel of life to those who lacked it: he was life-giving water. Job makes a further voyage, into memory. He brings himself back to life, as one who *gave* life:

> When the ear heard me, then it blessed me; and when the eye saw me, it gave witness to me:
> Because I delivered the poor that cried, and the fatherless, and him that had none to help him.
> The blessing of him that was ready to perish came upon me: and I caused the widow's heart to sing for joy.
> I put on righteousness, and it clothed me: my judgement was as a robe and a diadem.
> I was eyes to the blind, and feet was I to the lame.
> I was a father to the poor: and the cause which I knew not I searched out.
> And I brake the jaws of the wicked, and plucked the spoil out of his teeth.
> . . .
> My root was spread out by the waters, and the dew lay all night upon my branch.
> . . .
> After my words they spake not again; and my speech dropped upon them.
> And they waited for me as for the rain; and they opened their mouth wide as for the latter rain.
> . . .
> I chose out their way, and sat chief, and dwelt as a king in the army, as one that comforteth the mourners. (29.11–17, 19, 22–23, 25)

Job remembers himself as a damp and dewy tree of life: a king. *Because* his daring is over the top, the Job who dies and returns to life in this poem is not a Ridiculous Man, but an 'area of grace'. The comic hero is a *giver* precisely in his suffering humanity. When do we see Job giving? Gustavo Guttierez claimed that the figure of Job begins to change when he notices the 'injustice that mark[s] the life of the poor'.[94] When Job makes his final 'protestation of his integrity' he is not at his 'Promethean best':[95] in order to understand Job's speeches, we have to divest ourselves of the prejudice that it is impossible for a human being to be humanly good. This prejudice is expressed by the Friends. Eliphaz says that God

> putteth no trust in his saints; yea, the heavens are not clean in his sight.
> How much more abominable and filthy is man, which drinketh iniquity like water? (15.15–16)[96]

---

94 Gustavo Gutiérrez, *On Job: God-Talk and the Suffering of the Innocent*, translated by Matthew O'Connell (Orbis Books, New York, 1987), p. 16.
95 Whedbee, 'Comedy of Job', 18.
96 See also (4.17–19 (Ehud); (11.26) (Zophar the Naamathite); and (25.4–6) (Bildad).

The Friends believe that God, rightly, has nothing but contempt for the creation which he pronounced 'good' (*tob*) in Genesis 1. Unless we believe that it was impossible to abide by the Torah, an opinion which has taken some knocking in recent decades, and unless we place an invisible standard above Job, which he cannot know he has failed to reach, we need not imagine that he overstates his case when he concludes his 'protestation of innocence' and throws it down like a red carpet, as he goes to meet his Judge: 'as a prince would I go near unto him' (31.37). Job has preserved the bridge between himself and the living God, his experiential knowledge of his own goodness. He has searched the cosmos and his memory, and he knows that wisdom and life have been found in himself.

Unlike the Friends, Elihu admires his Creator: he speaks of God as one who 'delivers man' 'from going down into the pit', who saves from death (33.18, 24, 28). Elihu heightens the debate. Job's 'Sheol' speeches have taken us as low as we can go. His 'Wisdom' speeches begin a shift upward; Elihu's speeches lift up the minds of actors and audience to the life-giving elements which drop from God's heaven. Elihu prepares the scene for God's entrance by 'weav[ing] into his abuse of Job images of God as the mighty sovereign of a vast creation beyond the ken of man'.[97] Elihu speaks of God as the rain-maker and snow-maker. His words drench Job's drought: you parched your throat whinging about the dust of Sheol – here comes a downpour of rain, hail, frost, sleet and snow:

> Behold, God is great, and we know him not, neither can the number of his years be searched out.
> For he maketh small the drops of water: they pour down rain according to the vapour thereof:
> Which the clouds do drop and distil upon man abundantly.
> Also can any understand the spreadings of the clouds, or the noise of his tabernacle?
> Behold, he spreadeth out his light upon it, and covereth the bottom of the sea.
> . . .
> God thundereth marvellously with his voice; great things doeth he, which we cannot comprehend.
> For he saith to the snow, Be thou on the earth; likewise to the small rain, and to the great rain of his strength . . .
> Then the beasts go into dens, and remain in their places.
> Out of the south cometh the whirlwind: and cold out of the north.
> By the breath of God frost is given: and the breadth of the waters is straitened.
> . . . he scattereth his bright cloud;
> And it is turned round about by his counsels . . .
> . . .
> Dost thou know when God disposed them, and caused the light of his cloud to shine?
> Dost thou know the balancings of the clouds?
> How thy garments are warm, when he quieteth the earth by the south wind?
> Hast thou with him spread out the sky, which is strong, and as a molten looking glass? (36.26–30, 37.5–6, 8–10, 11b–12a, 15–18)

Elihu speaks of the reciprocity between the heavens and the earth: the seasonal downpours fertilise the earth. The round of the seasons, envisaged

97 Alter, *Art of Biblical Poetry*, p. 91.

from a cloud's perspective, are directed by the personal behest of God. The sky is 'like a molten looking glass': it mirrors the needs of the earth. Like a tardy stage hand, Elihu hurries on to paint the movement of clouds, winds and light below the 'upper level' where God sits and orders them here and there. If Elihu cannot quite haul Job up to heaven, he has the beginnings of a paradisial imagination, with its combination of the fantastic and the literal. Job 28 and the Elihu speeches begin to close the 'incongruous' gap between God and human beings.

God orders Job to get ready for an ordeal: 'Bind thy loins like a strong man! (38.3a). The Hebrew word used here for 'strong man' is *Gebher*: 'The *gebher* is akin to the *gibbor*, the "hero" of legend. The incongruity of the contrast between Job, sitting, exhausted ... alienated, on his pile of manure, and still in revolt, with such a grandiose specimen of virility only deepens the irony.'[98] God inquires: 'Where wast thou when I laid the foundation of the earth, declare, if thou hast understanding' (38.4). He continues: Who laid the measures? Who stretched out the line? Where were the foundations fastened? Who laid the corner stone? The only possible answers are not me, not me, not me, no. Job encounters the otherness of the Creator. If our hero had gone forth to meet ... a warm and nurturing God, *that* would have been a genuine anticlimax, and the surest proof that the text deals neither in *drama* nor in *comedy*. With his string of questioning 'Who's' the *personal* God which Elihu had evoked contrasts his 'I' to that of the human 'thou' who had demanded his presence. Behind the negatives, which distinguish God's 'I' from Job's, is the positive answer. *Who* was there

> When the morning stars sang together, and all the sons of God shouted for joy?
> Or who shut up the sea with doors, when it brake forth, as if it had issued out of the womb?
> When I made the cloud the garment thereof, and thick darkness a swaddling band for it. (38.7–9)

The Job who had unbirthed himself into Sheol is confronted with the power of life:

> Job ... prayed for cloud and darkness to envelop the day he was born. Cloud and mist reappear here ... as the matitutinal blanket over the primordial seas, as the swaddling bands of creation (verse 9) ... Against those doors of the belly (3.10) that Job wanted shut on him forever, the Voice from the Whirlwind invokes a cosmic womb and cosmic doors to a very different purpose ... The doors are closed ... so that the flood will not engulf the earth, but ... the waves surge, the womb of all things pulsates, something is born.[99]

The Job who had believed himself dead is forced to imagine the birth of all creation. If we are inclined both to feel that Job is *overwhelmed* by the God-speeches and that they are inexplicably *satisfying*, that may be because this is what a Job who had been present in Sheol *needs*. If he is to undergo a rebirth, Job needs to see the beginning of creation.

That comes about because he is questioned by the Rain-Maker himself:

98 Terrien, 'Yahweh Speeches', 501.
99 Alter, *Art of Biblical Poetry*, pp. 98–99.

Who hath divided a watercourse for the overflowing of waters, or a way for
the lightning of thunder;
To cause it to rain on the earth, where no man is; on the wilderness, wherein
there is no man;
To satisfy the desolate and waste ground; and to cause the bud of the tender
earth to spring forth.
Hath the rain a father? or who hath begotten the drops of dew?
Out of whose womb came the ice? and the hoary frost of heaven, who hath
gendered it?
. . .
Canst thou lift up thy voice to the clouds, that abundance of waters may
cover thee?
Canst thou send lightnings, that they may go, and say unto thee, Here we
are? (38.25–29, 34–35)

Terrien pictures Job as a 'royal figure' who is 'symbolically put to death',
expiating the crimes of his nation, and brought back to life by the 'autumnal
rains': those rains, predicted by Elihu, now begin to fall.[100] Job had been
into the depths, and now God is making him experience the heavens. God
is making Job feel the Creator's 'Who'. Terrien makes a second, biblical,
comparison:

If the date of the poem may be ascribed to the first generation of the exile . . .
The servant of Yahweh becomes the symbol of the people of Jahweh.
Innocent, he is brought to utmost destitution and misery. He has lost all, and
. . . he has died, but he will live again, by faith.

We may not say that Job *is* a 'suffering servant', but we may suggest that
people respond to him as a figure who is given life, and who is life-giving.
If comedy is 'a Carrying Away of Death, a triumph over mortality by some
absurd faith in rebirth, restoration and salvation', Job has shown such
faith.[101]

Job envisaged his whole world as submerged in the power of death. He
stringently objected to being relinquished to the monster of Chaos. His
refusal to lie down and die was a demand that God prove himself the
master of Chaos. Now God invokes the monsters: Behemoth, and the
mighty Leviathan, who stands for Chaos. The corollary to his 'can yous?' is
'I can':

Canst thou draw out leviathan with an hook? or his tongue with a cord which
thou lettest down?
Canst thou put an hook into his nose? or bore his jaw through with a thorn?
Will he make many supplications unto thee? will he speak soft words unto
thee?
Will he make a covenant with thee? wilt thou take him for a servant for ever?
Wilt thou play with him as with a bird? or wilt thou bind him for thy
maidens?
Shall the companions make a banquet of him? shall they part him among the
merchants?
Canst thou fill his skin with barbed irons? or his head with fish spears?
Lay thine hand upon him, remember the battle, do no more. (41.1–10)

---

100 Terrien, 'Yahweh Speeches', 508–509.
101 Sypher, 'Meanings of Comedy', p. 220.

God answers that Leviathan is his 'toy', a thoroughly domesticated monster. In his fantastical, and whimsical, portrait of the sea monster, God both exaggerates, or 'mythologises' the power of the beast, and affirms that Leviathan is merely 'part of nature': he is not only under God's command, but a toy who is 'available for his enjoyment'.[102] God concludes his speech by rebuking the Friends, and commending Job, who alone has 'spoken well of me' (42.6). He has taken Job on a journey, over mountain, sky and sea. Now he plants his hero back on earth and restores his prosperity.

There are thus three ways of reading Job as a comedy. We may set it in the *theological* framework of an absolute incongruity between God and humanity, or in the imaginative framework of an infernal comedy, in which, as Bergson claims, the 'opposite' of the object of our laughter is 'grace'.[103] We will find that the text tells of a

> 'God beyond God,' who denies to Job (and to Israel) the comfort of moral symmetry. Job (and Israel) now are required to live in a world where *nothing is settled or reliable except the overwhelmingness of God*.[104]

Or we may identify with Job's humanness: then we will find that, like the Patriarchal narratives, the book makes Job pass through a desperate trial but ultimately affirms faith in this world. We may argue, thirdly, that God's presentation of the cosmos, which carries Job from the moment of creation, through the 'carnival of animals', up into the skies, and into the watery depths where the Leviathan lurks, creates what a modern student of apocalyptic literature calls an 'open heaven'. We are shown God 'seeing' the whole creation and this conveys a tremendous sense of liberation. Guttierrez locates the new element in Job in the discovery of divine and human freedom:

> The final chapters ... tell us of the meeting of these two freedoms. Job's freedom finds expression in his complaints and rebellion; God's freedom finds expression in the gratuitousness of the divine love that refuses to be confined within a system of predictable rewards and punishments. Job's freedom reaches its full maturity when he encounters without intermediaries the God in whom he hopes; God's freedom comes to light in the revelation that divine gratuitous love has been made the foundation of the world and that only in the light of this fact can the meaning of divine justice be grasped.[105]

I should plump for the second: Job is a purgatorial drama. But it has glimpses both of Sheol and of paradise. The author has an inkling that the realm of comedy can be widened. He is beginning to lay out a new map of the analogy of being, of the multiform integrations of God and his world.

---

102 Jon D. Levenson, *Creation and the Persistence of Evil: The Jewish Drama of Omnipotence* (Harper & Row, San Francisco, 1988), p. 16.
103 Bergson, *Le Rire*, p. 22.
104 Brueggemann, *Theology of the Old Testament*, p. 391.
105 Gutiérrez, *On Job*, p. 80.

5

Paradisial Comedy

1. Pause for Breath

If we wander with a friend into the lingerie section of a department store, the detection of a *really* enormous pair of underpants may amuse us. Henri Bergson explains that *'Any incident is comic that calls our attention to the physical in a person'*. We find comedy wherever we see *'the manner seeking to outdo the matter, the letter aiming at ousting the spirit'*. Comedy is an *agon* between the soul and its ungainly baggaging. The 'moral personality with its intelligently varied energy' descends into risibility when it is loaded with 'the stupidly monotonous body, perpetually obstructing everything with its machine-like obstinacy'.[1] Peter Berger puts this intuition in a religious framework. He takes the elephant as a symbol of the comically sacred; as with the Hindu Ganesha. The out-sized elephant 'represents the vastness of the universe in which man finds himself'.[2] Comedy is related to our sense of transcendence by way of the feeling of 'discrepancy', between man and elephant, or finite and infinite.[3] Berger claims that the comic proceeds out of the *anthropological* split within human beings, who are both body and spirit, and out of the *ontological* discrepancy between human beings and the cosmos, 'suspended in this ridiculous position between microbes and the stars'.[4] Someone looking *from the outside* finds us ridiculous in that posture.

A wider imaginative terrain than this is held open to view by the lifeworld of comedy. Jokes make for a great *moments,* but not for much of a story, and still less for a play like *Peace.* Comedy exaggerates discrepancies and cuts pretensions, and salads, down to size. Having done so, it marries Peace's maidservant Vintage to a farmer. Comedy prunes, and then fertilises with large dollops of manure. Because it can generate a great number of unique but interlocking worlds, New York City is a great comic 'signal of transcendence'. Looking back to his youth in that great city, Peter Berger

---

1 Bergson, *Le Rire*, pp. 52–54.
2 Peter Berger, 'A Lutheran Looks at an Elephant', in Berger, *A Rumour of Angels: Modern Society and the Rediscovery of the Supernatural* (Doubleday, New York, 1969, revised edition, 1990), pp. 109–122 (116).
3 Ibid., p. 118.
4 Berger, *Redeeming Laughter*, p. 209.

still recall[s] with pleasure my lunch hours: I would buy a bialy with lox in the old Essex Street Market, munch it while strolling through the teeming street life at the foot of the Williamsburg Bridge, and then have a quiet coffee with baklava in one of several Turkish cafes on Allen Street, surrounded by old men smoking waterpipes and playing checkers ... [These] mundane facts contain a mighty promise ... that God loves the human race in *all* its incredible variety, that His redemptive grace embraces *all* of humanity without any exception, and that His Kingdom will mean not the end but the glorious transfiguration of every truly human expression.[5]

The comic imagination enjoys variety, and especially the mixed marriages which follow in its train. If the last place in which one should expound Body–Soul dualism is in a theory of comedy, clean-minded wit is as out of place in the lyrics of Victoria Wood as in those of Aristophanes, and, if comedy relishes sex, perhaps there is a grain of wheat in the notion that comedy emerges out of the worship of fertility. All but one of Aristophanes' comedies concludes with a marriage. If we make the god of procreation

appear incarnate in a human form ... we shall have the first actor, the hero of our supposed ritual drama, which ends – how else should a fertility drama end? – in the sacred marriage of the divine protagonist, that mystical and magical union by which the whole creation is moved to bring forth the fruits of the year in due season.[6]

Comedy has to do with procreation, symbolised in the sacred wedding of Peisetaerus and Basileia, Tom Jones and Sophia; Mariel Hemingway and the neurotic hero are half-way there in *Manhatten*.

The comic characters have been divided into the *bomolochus* (buffoon), Eiron (the Ironic man) and Alazon (Impostor). The *Impostors* are the comic hero's antagonists in the comic debates, scuffles, contests, and Agon. The 'ironical jester' may have a buffoon as a side-kick. But often, the comic hero 'combines both types, and we have, over against the Impostor, one character only – the Ironical Buffoon'.[7] Why should ancient comedy be beset by Impostors? Their expulsion allows for some Bergsonian violence. If there is any truth in the notion of a ritual killing of an Old God-King which enables a New God-King to emerge, then the participants must do violence to the sacred: they must commit regicide. This is made tolerable if we make the Old King the Impostor, who is the loser in the contest: 'The reviling and expulsion of the Antagonist-Impostor is the darker side of the Komos which brings in the new God, victorious over him in the Agon.'[8]

Comedy is a way of putting our experience into shape which brings us into touch with *reality*. In the comic world, the characters are pushed into a recognition of the human reality of being embodied and limited, and we imaginatively follow them in. William Lynch calls this recollection of what it means to be human the 'comic anamnesis'.[9] Comedy would not be *satisfying* if it did not make us suffer *reality*. Finding the place

---

5 'New York City 1976', p. 262.
6 Cornford, *Origin Of Attic Comedy*, pp. 113–114.
7 Ibid., p. 120.
8 Ibid., pp. 131–132.
9 William Lynch, *Christ and Apollo: The Dimensions of the Literary Imagination* (Sheed & Ward, London, 1960; University of Notre Dame Press, Notre Dame, 1975), p. 95.

where the comic and the sacred meet is not an easy way out, but the hard way in:

> especially for those of us who have lost the taste of being, the way of comedy taxes the imagination and the whole soul more than does tragedy, and requires even more courage as a way into God. It is a more terrible way ... requiring more faith in the finite.[10]

The peripeteias through which the comic actors pass make them drop down into their finite bodies. Once having suffered that reality, they spring back with greater fertility in their step. The comic anamnesis requires an imaginative certainty that, if one pushes down to the bottom of what it means to be human one will find transcendence. The comic anamnesis looks up from below; it shows the picture from the *inside*. It does not only negate, or satirise, but engages in the richer field of what *is*. The real comedy is the 'congruity' between finite man and infinite God, 'the tie between earth and Christ, with all the logic omitted'.[11] Comedy shows similitude in dissimilitude: the fact that heaven and embodied human beings are *like* each other is even more surprising than that they are unlike. The poets and the ritualists spoke of a cosmic *fertility* engendered by the sacred wedding of earth and sky; the philosophers and the theologians speak about God's creativity: the divine goodness freely overflowing into a creation which flows back to him, because it wants to be more like the Likeness. The outflowing and the inflowing is the analogy in being of God and his world. Woody Allen pointed out the funny side of the *analogia entis* when he noted that there are two questions about heaven: '*How long does it stay open? And can you get there by cab from midtown Manhattan?*' A third question is whether he could keep his eyes off the metre.

Genre is more encompassing than literary form: like Jonah's whale, it can swallow the lot of them. Genres should be defined by the type of world which they imaginatively project. Different literary worlds present their action in their own ways, for example, extensively in the comic epic and intensively in the comic drama. Epic allows for an all-round inspection of its characters. Dramatic characters are put across sidewise; the adventure of entering the land of milk and honey is, as it were, condensed. The world of comedy takes up *space*. For the tragic hero, finitude spells *mortality*; for the comic, being finite means being a *body*. The tragic hero's world is governed by time; the tension in comedy is spatial. The leaven in comedy is liberation; the comic hero has a great spatial freedom.

The biblical history looks especially like a search for the *good*. As von Balthasar says,

> For the Hebrew, the transcendentals are disposed in a total mutual compene-tration, such that the statements about the good stand together in the centre, and the truth and beauty of this good scarcely appear in any other way than as its modalities. Thus the truth (*emeth, emuna*) of God is ... the truthfulness, freedom from deceit and reliability of his person, which is made known to Israel in the grace of his promise, of his covenant, and of his conduct in keeping with the covenant.[12]

10 Ibid., pp. 93–94.
11 Ibid., p. 109.
12 Von Balthasar, *Glory VI*, p. 144.

Likewise, John's Gospel assimilates 'truth' to the good: 'For every one that *doeth* evil hateth the light ... But he that *doeth* truth cometh to the light' (John 3.20, 21). When it is represented by a *comic hero*, the good is fertile: Abraham, blessed with his 'fertility covenant'[13] is the mother of all the life-giving comedians. This world sets its blessing on the *human*, and thus on the *imperfect*: a comic hero can set out as a coward with a speech defect. The good is down to earth: this realism can be represented either by the pragmatism of Joseph or by the passivity of Isaac; both the doers and the sufferers are open to what life brings; they are nourishing *survivors*. Even nervy Job felt sufficiently at home in *creation* to demand justice from God. The comic hero's realism requires a trust in life, in *hayyim*, and through that, in *Haya*, the 'I am' whose hand can be trusted to help. The heroines, like Rebekkah, are often the closest to the source of help; they are intimate enough with the providential clues to act pre-emptively. All of the biblical heroes and heroines act in the faith that the absolute good which is God will respond to them. The words for the *dramatic* good are the four laws which rule what the characters in the biblical life-world can achieve. The human actors are at a distance from their destination: this is the law of alienation. God intends to create a form out of the movement of the 'pieces' but there is an interplay between 'design and disorder' because all of the characters are free. The characters are pushed on into a perfect space: this is the law of integration. They want to get there: the motor of the action is love, the desire for perfect friendship. Paul satirises his former co-religionists in his letter to the Galatians, and his current ones in 1 Corinthians; he balances such alienations with the integrations of Romans 9–11. The complete movement of comic drama requires a free person being lifted into integration, with a backward, debunking wave of alienation, and finally achieving the fullness of desire in communion: 'all *Israel* will be saved' (Rom. 11.26) and 'God hath concluded them all in unbelief, that he might have mercy on *all*' (Rom. 11.32). The comic good is always *somewhere*; the good in drama is always *doing* something: an exceptionally fertile hero can promise to 'draw all' to himself (John 12.32).

The main type of comedy which Berger claims to find in the Bible is *satire*:

> Anyone surfing through the Bible (Old and New Testament alike) or the history of Christian theology in search of the comic is bound to be disappointed. The God of the Hebrew Bible is ... mentioned as laughing a number of times, but it is virtually always a laughter of derision over the vain ambitions of human beings (as in Psalms 2 and 59).[14]

It depends on where the eye of the narrator is placed, and whether or not we are supposed to identify with the victim or hero. Comedie Française à la Bergson is sometimes on the mark. God takes a satirical view of the Babel builders whom he has to descend so far down to see. God looks from the outside at the Pharaohs of Exodus. In Judges, a concealed God enables his heroes to contest the ownership of the land through a series of deadly practical jokes. Israel constructs its own rickety Babel in the monarchy.

---

13 Miles, *God: A Biography*, p. 224.
14 Berger, *Redeeming Laughter*, p. 197.

Israel's human kings are satirised by their prophets. Meanwhile, the viewpoint of the comedy is being immanentised. As a human king, David can be treated satirically; but the audience also *identifies* with the exploits of the man who is the Lord's anointed. Israel's monarchy 'was not finally effective in sustaining Israel'.[15] The prophets fire irony at the *'shepherd-kings'*:

> 'Woe to the shepherds who destroy and scatter the sheep of my pasture', says the Lord. Therefore thus says the Lord, the God of Israel, concerning the shepherds who shepherd my people: 'It is you who have scattered my flock, and have driven them away, and you have not attended to them.' (Jer. 23.1–2)[16]

As God becomes so invisible as to be questionable, by Job, so the eye of the comedy further identifies with the victim-hero. By the eighth century BC, 'the dramatic rendering of God has largely passed from the narrative prophet to the prophetic word, and ... with Amos, to the prophetic books'.[17] Jack Miles notes that 'From Genesis through II Kings, no-one doubts, ever, that God is knowable. Then, in the Book of Isaiah, God's unknowability begins to be asserted'. Moreover, Isaiah's God speaks of love and of pity for Israel. The terminology of the *passions* had seldom hitherto been applied to him: 'The combination of ... divine access to the human heart and divine omnipotence and mystery – has remained the defining incongruity at the core of the word *God*.'[18] This ever-more mysterious God sympathises with human beings. As God becomes more transcendent, so the narrator's position becomes more internal to the drama. God's Word becomes increasingly immanent in the drama of the prophet's lives: von Rad asks 'whether this entry of the word into a prophet's bodily life is not meant to approximate to what the writer of the Fourth Gospel says about the Word becoming flesh'.[19] Now *God* is looking up, from below; a perspective which has tremendous comic power.

From Genesis to First Isaiah, the space of liberation was the promised land of Palestine. The Edict of the Persian Emperor Cyrus, in 538 BC, enabled the Jews to return from Babylonian exile. Palestine was governed from Persia, until 332 BC, when it was conquered by Alexander the Great. It was ruled by the Hellenistic Seleucid dynasty, until 64 BC, when it was overrun by Roman armies. After the repeated conquests, the land lost its hold on the biblical imagination. The good is further off: the search for it will require up and down stage directions. With the development of apocalyptic this space can be made to show the interplay between God's eternity and the realm of history.

The first, proleptic microcosm of the land, as a symbol of the divine–human relationship, was the Ark. In 1 Kings 6–8, Solomon builds a temple; God first sends a commendation and a warning (1 Kings 6.11–12); when the Ark is brought inside, he consents to the act: 'the glory of the LORD had filled the house of the LORD' (8.11). But his concluding

---

15 Brueggemann, *Theology of the Old Testament*, p. 614.
16 Brueggemann's translation: cited by him in ibid., p. 615, as an illustration of this point.
17 Patrick, *Rendering of God*, pp. 23–24.
18 Miles, *God: A Biography*, pp. 234 and 236.
19 Von Rad, *Old Testament Theology II*, p. 92.

remarks about his new dwelling are one-third blessing and two-thirds threat:

> And the LORD said unto him, 'I have heard thy prayer ... I have hallowed this house, which thou hast built, to put my name there for ever; and mine eyes and mine heart shall be there perpetually.
>
> And *if* thou wilt walk before me, as David thy father walked, in integrity of heart and uprightness, to do according to all that I have commanded thee, and wilt keep my statutes and my judgements:
>
> Then I will establish the throne of thy kingdom upon Israel for ever, as I promised to David ...
>
> But if ye shall at all turn from following me, ye or your children, and will not keep my commandments and my statutes ... but go and serve other gods, and worship them:
>
> Then will I cut off Israel out of the land which I have given them; and this house, which I have hallowed for my name, will I cast out of my sight ...'
> (1 Kings 9.3–7a)

The editor had half an eye on Nebuchadnezzar's armies, which razed the First Temple in 587. The exilic prophet Ezekiel describes being lifted by his hair into a *heavenly* temple. Through a concealed 'door' he sees 'creeping things, and abominable beasts, and all the idols of the house of Israel, portrayed upon the wall' (Ezekiel 8.10): this is the earthly temple. Ezekiel sees cherubim around the throne of God:

> Then the glory of the LORD went up from the cherub, and stood over the threshold of the house; and the house was filled with the cloud, and the court was full of the brightness of the LORD's glory.
>
> . . .
>
> And when I looked, behold the four wheels by the cherubs, one wheel by one cherub, and another wheel by another cherub ...
>
> And as for their appearance, they four had one likeness, as if a wheel had been in the midst of a wheel.
>
> . . .
>
> As for the wheels, it was cried unto them in my hearing, O Wheel!
>
> . . .
>
> And the cherubims were lifted up. This is the living creature that I saw by the river of Chebar.
>
> And when the cherubims went, the wheels went by them: and when the cherubims lifted up their wings to mount from the earth, the same wheels also turned not from beside them.
>
> . . .
>
> Then the glory of the Lord departed from off the threshold of the house, and stood over the cherubims.
>
> And the cherubims lifted up their wings, and mounted up from the earth in my sight: when they went out, the wheels also were beside them, and every one stood at the door of the east gate of the LORD's house; and the glory of the God of Israel was over them above. (Ezek. 10.4, 9–10, 13, 15, 16, 18–19)

Ezekiel sees the glory of the LORD taking lift-off from the Temple, leaving it to the Babylonians: 'One result of the traumatic break with the traditions of the past caused by the destruction of the temple and the exile ... is a new feeling of distance between God and humanity ... Ezekiel's vision of God on a chariot-throne is a response to the fact that the temple, once the centre of religious experience, is no longer available.'[20] Although 'Ezekiel's charges are' no doubt 'grossly exaggerated', they attest to an intuition that the earthly temple is 'defiled'. After the Persians became the political masters of Palestine, a group of Judaeans, led by Ezra, returned and built a Second Temple. A belief that the Temple and its ritual have lost their perfection results in the relocation of the glory. Because 'The Second Temple is never able to emerge from the shadow of the disengagement of the glory of God', the Jerusalem Temple loses some of its religious potency: 'this desacralization of the earthly temple' will eventually 'open the way' for the apocalyptic narratives of ascent to heaven.[21]

It is as if the earthly stage-level had dropped several feet. Does the gap allow a space in which God has no power? *Where* can the relationship between God and man be completed? It is hard to enter the realm of death if one pictures it as being eaten alive by an outsized shark. Can the monster invade and break off the human relationship to God? Between the mid-sixth and the third century, a prophet composed the 'Isaianic Apocalypse' (Is. 24–27). The author *alludes* to a defeat of death, announcing that 'He destroys death forever' (Is. 24.8), that 'Death shall be no more' (25.8), exulting 'May the dead revive!' (Is. 26.19). The striking chords pronounce that the monster is done for:

> In that day the Lord will punish
> With His great, cruel, mighty sword
> Leviathan the Elusive Serpent –
> Leviathan the twisting Serpent;
> He will slay the Dragon [*tannin*] in the sea. (Is. 27.1)[22]

The 'primal myth' of the conquest of chaos will be re-enacted at the end of time. The Isaianic Apocalypse imagines the slaughter of the Serpent being celebrated in a 'victory banquet of YHWH on his mountain' (Is. 25.6–8): 'the feast is a ratification of the claim to sovereignty of the deity'.[23] The issue of death is primarily about the omnipresence of God, and secondarily about the lifespan of human beings. God's sovereignty must be established *somewhere*. In this Apocalypse, 'God no longer permits death to mar the rejoicing of his guests. Here hope of immortality is bound up with expectation of the coming of the Kingdom of God.'[24]

The Jews put up a good fight for the promised land, in the Maccabean War. If individuals are to be martyred for the land, which represents 'God's sovereignty on earth', then that sovereignty must be established by 'the abolition of death'.[25] Daniel is the first biblical book which affirms a

20 Martha Himmelfarb, *Ascent to Heaven in Jewish and Christian Apocalypses* (Oxford University Press, Oxford, 1993), p. 69.
21 Ibid., pp. 11 and 13.
22 As translated in Levenson, *Creation and the Persistence of Evil*, p. 27.
23 Ibid., p. 28.
24 Martin-Achard, *From Death To Life*, pp. 129–130.
25 Eichrodt, *Theology of the Old Testament*, Vol. II, p. 510.

bodily resurrection of the dead.[26] The prophecies of Isaiah 24–27 and of Daniel 12.1–2 are set in the future: the beast's lair has yet to be invaded. Human beings are still vulnerable to attack,

> a clear, impassable boundary-line is drawn before the appearing of God's glory: the fact that death has not been overcome ... this means that *man's radical problem has not been overcome*, even in the presence of God ... In the old covenant God's power and the abyss of chaos stood mythologically over against one another.[27]

One final combat must take place: the bridge between the old and the new covenant can only be built by 'an invisible collision of the absolute weight of God with what is other'.[28]

2. Apocalyptic Imagination and Paradisial Comedy

The Fall Story of Genesis 3 was composed by the Priestly writers in the sixth century BC. Apocalypticism began to develop a century later. Like the branch of Wisdom which flowed into Job, it is preoccupied with the source of evil. If we put Job's trial into history, let the question of evil gather momentum, picking up traces of Zoroastrian dualism on its way, apocalyptic will emerge. It will imagine history as a 'battleground' between the power of God and the powers of darkness.[29] This calls for a specification of the shadowy spear-carrying parts which earlier Hebraic writers had allotted to the heavenly characters. There are new roles for good angels, such as Gabriel, Michael and Raphael. The heavenly villain changes: 'the Satan', God's interrogator, becomes 'Satan' by the time Chronicles is composed, and the laird of a counter-kingdom of bad angels by the second century BC.[30]

Both the Wisdom tradition and apocalyptic literature are driven by the quest for knowledge. The mark of an *apocalypse* is 'a belief in the direct revelation of the things of God which was mediated through dream, vision or divine intermediary'.[31] As the etymology indicates, an 'apocalypse' is a lifting of the veil. Collins defines the *apocalypse* as: '*a genre of revelatory literature with a narrative framework, in which a revelation is mediated by an other-worldly being to a human recipient, disclosing a transcendent reality which is both temporal, insofar as it envisages eschatological salvation, and spatial insofar as it involves another, supernatural world*'.[32] Both the Book of Revelation and Daniel may be defined as apocalypses, because both contain

26 Fohrer, *History of Israelite Religion*, p. 389; von Balthasar, *Glory VI*, p. 334.
27 Hans Urs von Balthasar, *The Glory of the Lord: A Theological Aesthetics. Volume VII: Theology. The New Covenant*, translated by Brian McNeil (T&T Clark, Edinburgh, 1989), p. 82.
28 Ibid., p. 83.
29 Fohrer, *History of Israelite Religion*, p. 377.
30 Paolo Sacchi, *Jewish Apocalyptic and Its History*, translated by William J. Short, *Journal for the Study of the Pseudepigrapha* Supplement Series, 20 (Sheffield Academic Press, Sheffield, 1998), p. 224.
31 Christopher Rowland, *The Open Heaven: A Study of Apocalyptic in Judaism and Early Christianity* (SPCK, London, 1982), p. 21.
32 John Collins, *The Apocalyptic Imagination: An Introduction to Jewish Apocalyptic Literature* (William B. Eerdmans, Michigan, 1984, 1998), p. 5.

'the conviction ... that man is able to know about the divine mysteries by means of revelation, so that God's eternal purposes may be disclosed, and man, as a result, may see history in a totally new light'.[33] In apocalyptic literature, a seer is carried to heaven to learn the secrets of the cosmos as in 1 Enoch, or to see an angelic preview of historical battles to come, as in Daniel.

Jacques Le Goff finds that 'most of the "apocalypses" tell of a journey to Heaven rather than a descent into Hell, typical of the hopeful, expectant climate of the period during which Christianity emerged'.[34] If that is true, apocalyptic is the product of a lively and fertile imagination, which ranges freely from earth to the infernal and celestial realms, but prefers the latter. Likewise, for Martha Himmelfarb, the apocalyptic journeys attest to a hopeful faith in the human: 'The examples of the heroes of the ascent apocalypses teach their readers to live the life of this world with the awareness of the possibility of transcendence.'[35]

I have claimed that the literary cosmos of dramatic comedy has three 'levels': infernal, purgatorial and paradisial, and that we can find these three levels in the Bible. This appeared to require that we apply a schema, exhibited in the fourteenth century by Dante in *The Divine Comedy*, to biblical texts which antedated it by a millennium and a half. My apologia for doing so is that it is the apocalypticists – some biblical, some extra-canonical – who gave Dante the notion of travelling between the three realms. The apocalyptic imagination is like that which belongs to the authors and producers of science fiction. In the 1950s, when motorists first became a menace to the countryside, it was suggested by optimistic engineers that the car could one day be supplanted by the personal propulsion unit, which would act like a vacuum cleaner in reverse, enabling the man who strapped it on to fly, rather than to motor, to his destination. The personal propulsion unit failed to take off. Those optimistic engineers had been anticipated by the apocalypticists. What energy is it that propels the visionary into heaven? Is it a desire which will stop at no less? Dan O. Via asked: 'May it be that for apocalyptic in general the catalytic moving power is the comic sense of life?'[36] It is a hypothesis worth testing. *At its best*, the apocalyptic imagination enters the realm of paradisial comedy, and presents the most dramatic images of the Bible. The time machine is a typical invention of paradisial comedy, as in *The Navigators*. Some apocalyptists seem to be fixated with *dating* the end time: perhaps what they really want is to see time fly. Purgatorial comedy is about a hard-won quest. In Paradisial comedy, *once the hero or heroine hit upon their great plan*, they float, rather than climb, toward their goal. Its heroes, like Peisetaerus on his way to Cloudcuckooland, or Dante in Paradise, are given a certain weightlessness: they must keep their bodies, for the journey to be funny, but their burdens are lightened. If comedy

33 Rowland, *Open Heaven*, p. 13.
34 Jacques Le Goff, *The Birth of Purgatory*, translated by Arthur Goldhammer (Scholar Press, London, 1984), p. 30.
35 Himmelfarb, *Ascent to Heaven*, p. 71.
36 Dan O. Via, *Kerygma and Comedy in the New Testament* (Fortress Press, Philadelphia, 1975), p. 89.

moves upwards, paradisial comedy does so *almost* effortlessly. Paradisial comedy exhibits the perfect achievement of the object of human desire. It propels the human imagination to its outer limits: this type of comedy concludes with a party in the perfect city.

a. *Extra-canonical Apocalyptic: 1 Enoch*

1 Enoch is a compilation of five books, the Book of the Watchers (1–36), the Similitudes (37–71), the Astronomical Book (72–82), the Book of Dreams (83–90) and the Epistle of Enoch (91–108). Aramaic fragments of 1 Enoch have been unearthed in Qumran Cave 4, indicating that much of the text is pre-Christian. The earliest treatise in the Enoch literature, the Book of Watchers, has been variously dated from the fifth century BC to the mid-second-century BC.[37]

The Book of the Watchers is about 'the problem of evil'.[38] The biblical Genesis 6.1–4 contains an enigmatic story of the mating between the 'sons of God' and the 'daughters of men'. The offspring were 'giants' who nonetheless did not survive the flood of Genesis 7. The Book of the Watchers describes the marriage between the 'angels, the sons of heaven' and the beautiful daughters of men. The wicked angels teach the human race the lore of magic and astrology (1 Enoch 6–9). Evil is transmitted to the human world through ritual pollution, the mixture of angelic and human blood. This sacral transgression is articulated in the passing on of magical lore.

The question about how the divine and the human good are connected bends in the middle in the Book of Job: on the one hand the Friends offer a naturalistic ethics, founded in organic metaphors, which aligns God's reward to human good deeds; on the other hand, the same trio imply that the human is not *worth* divine justice. There may be a hint that the human is inherently sinful, that there is an 'ontic impurity' which throws the cosmo-ethical order off balance.[39] In 1 Enoch, evil is presented as a quasi-natural reality: thus the myth of angelic pollution. 1 Enoch considers evil and good *naturally*, the one as black magic and the other as an ethereal but substantial perfection.

The Enochic 'fall narrative' is followed by a 'cry of pain' from 'the souls of those who have died' (9.3, 10): immortal *souls*, as opposed to Sheolite *shades*, have entered the Jewish imagination. Genesis 5.24, states, 'Enoch walked with God: and he was not; for God took him.' What happened to him? He was taken up into heaven, to record God's punishment of the wicked angels (1 Enoch 12): 'the book continues with Enoch's journey in the "in-between world", where he sees, since they already exist, the places destined to await the souls of the just and the unjust in view of the Great Judgement'.[40] Enoch is taken to a house where he sees one at whom

---

37 Sacchi, *Jewish Apocalyptic*, p. 61, argues for the earlier dating. According to Sparks, Book I, chs 1–36, dates from the mid-second century BC; Book II, chs 37–71, may be as ancient; Book III, chs 72–82, dates from the third century BC; Book IV, chs 83–90, is familiar with the Maccabean Revolt and thus dates to somewhere after 164 BC; Book V, chs 91–108, was perhaps written in around 50 BC. H. D. F. Sparks (ed.), *The Apocryphal Old Testament* (Clarendon Press, Oxford, 1984), Introduction to 1 Enoch.
38 Sacchi, *Jewish Apocalyptic*, p. 53.
39 Ibid, p. 217. Citing Job 14.1–4.
40 Ibid., p. 52.

no creature of flesh could look. A sea of fire burnt around him, and a great fire stood before him, and none of those around him came near to him ... And the Lord called me ... Come hither, Enoch, to my holy word. And he lifted me up and brought me near to the door. And I looked, with my face down.[41]

You send your narrator into heaven, so that, like a metaphysical astronaut, he can see the whole cosmos, and return with the picture. We see, in 1 Enoch, as in Job, the Wisdom writers' delight in creation, with the earth standing firm on its pillars.[42] The Angel Uriel takes Enoch to the place in which the wicked angels will be made to stand. The purpose of the trip is to exhibit the secret treasures of heaven and earth to Enoch. Sometimes the writer over-elaborates:

> And I came to the Garden of Righteousness, and I saw ... the tree of wisdom from which they eat and know great wisdom. And it is like the carob-tree and the fruit is like the bunches of grapes on a vine, very beautiful, and the smell of this tree spreads and penetrates afar. And I said, This tree is beautiful! How beautiful and pleasing is its appearance! And the holy angel Raphael ... said to me, This is the tree of wisdom from which your old father and your aged mother, who were before you, ate, and learnt wisdom; and their eyes were opened, and they knew that they were naked, and they were driven from the garden.[43]

It spoils things to learn exactly what the tree of knowledge looks like. The impulse for 'design' and to knowledge turns into an obsessive quest for empirical information. The author of 1 Enoch can be tone-deaf and tactless, the effect of an imagination which cannot hit on the simple gesture which tells what matters, and descends from drama into soap opera.

We seem to have sauntered past some suspicious activity without inquiring. If the 'fall', the origin of evil, has been transferred from Adam and Eve's transgression to a cosmic misdemeanour, what are the 'tree' and the human culprits doing in Enoch's 'itinerary'? According to Himmelfarb,

> First, the Garden is never called Eden, but rather the Garden of Righteousness. Next ... the tree of life has been transplanted from the Garden to the mountain west of Jerusalem. Thus the importance of the Garden ... has been ... diminished ... Raphael responds to Enoch's exclamation about the beauty of the tree of knowledge ... with a brief version of the expulsion from Eden that is notable for what it leaves out. 'This is the tree of knowledge of which your father of old and your mother of old before you ate; and they learned knowledge, and their eyes were opened, and they knew that they were naked, and they were driven out of the garden' (32.6). The author has avoided any mention of the serpent, the fruit, and the fact that Adam and Eve had sinned.[44]

The authors of 1 Enoch ask where good and evil can be found, and they answer all too literally. Evil is a 'disorder of nature', so one goes outside of nature, and its temporal and contingent conditions, in order to see where

41 1 Enoch 14, in Sparks, *Apocryphal Old Testament*, pp. 202–203.
42 1 Enoch 18, in Sparks, *Apocryphal Old Testament*, pp. 206–207.
43 1 Enoch 32, in Sparks, *Apocryphal Old Testament*, p. 219.
44 Himmelfarb, *Ascent to Heaven*, p. 74.

the disorder has been reversed: 'there exists already a world not polluted by evil; it already is', as a mythological archetypal reality, 'but in another sphere. The eschaton is not at the end of times', not in the future, but a 'reality within the reach' of the righteous.[45] Enoch travels to the far west of the in-between world (17 and 22) in order to see the souls of the good: they are placed beside 'a spring of the water of light': 'the expression 'water of light' attests to our author's immaterial and absolutely spiritual conception of the life of the soul'.[46] We are in the region of the stomachless. Since their souls have already been separated out from those of the wicked, they need not *act* in order to achieve their identities. This world will finally be taken into the higher world, but without its 'historical dimensions: it will be the *souls* of individuals that will ... enter into the dimension most properly theirs'.[47] If we consider the good cosmologically, it is not an action, not something dynamic which is caught sight of in the transpiring. It is a literal fact to be photographed, with no elliptical hovering outside the freeze-frame. The biblical narrative of journeying towards the good symbolises *movement*. In 1 Enoch the good is congealed. 1 Enoch is not all that exuberant: the bubbles are weighed down by over-description. The author has an idea of paradise, but little means with which to dramatise it. Like the other apocalyptic 'lives' of the Old Testament heroes, 1 Enoch reads between the lines and after the close of the biblical stories to feed the reader's curiosity about what happened next. Like the contemporary sequels to the novels of Jane Austen, they fall below the standard of the original. Once the urge to know and tell all predominates, the desire for a complete and fixed conception of the cosmos obscures the drama.

b. Daniel

The Seleucid king Antiochus IV Epiphanes attempted to force the Jews in Palestine to assimilate to the social and religious practices of his Hellenised kingdom, such as monarch-worship. To this end, he set up a statue of himself in the Jerusalem Temple. A military revolt, led by Judas Maccabeus and his sons, induced him to desist. The Book of Daniel was probably written between 167 and 164 BC: most scholars consider that its aim is to encourage Jews to resist apostasy.[48] Here 'historical apocalyptic is born'.[49] The stories of Daniel 1–6 make an *aesthetic* play of the conflict of good and evil, whereas the visions of Daniel 7–12 take the same topic *ethically*.

Daniel 1–6 tells six stories of conflict between a group of Jews and three Babylonian kings: Nebuchadnezzar, his son Belshazzar and Darius the Mede. In each story, a trio or quartet of Jews are put to the test by their ruler. The villains are political incompetents; the heroes effortlessly play-act their tests. In the first, Daniel, Hananiah, Mishael and Azariah, Jews resident in Babylon, are brought to the king's court to learn the language and wisdom of the Chaldeans. The four are renamed Belteshazzar, Shadrach, Meschach and Abednego, in that order: they are thus costumed

---

45 Sacchi, *Jewish Apocalyptic*, p. 54.
46 Ibid., p. 100.
47 Ibid., p. 84.
48 Norman Porteous, *Daniel: A Commentary* (SCM, London, 1965, 1979), p. 16.
49 Sacchi, *Jewish Apocalyptic*, pp. 66 and 67.

as Babylonian subjects. Nebuchadnezzar decrees that they eat unclean meats. The four heroes ask to subsist on water and pulses for ten days, and then to be compared for fitness with those who eat from the king's table. The dieters emerge fatter than the eaters; all four are found by Nebuchnezzar to be 'ten times' wiser than his own magicians (1.20).

Nebuchadnezzar requires that his Chaldeans, astrologers and sorcerers tell him what he dreamed, and then interpret it. When the sorcerers fail, the King commands that every wise man in his kingdom be put to death. Daniel prays for help: 'then was the secret revealed to Daniel in a night vision' (2.19). Despite the echo of Exodus, in *apocalyptic* God 'reveals the deep and secret things: He knows what is in the darkness, and the light dwelleth in him' (2.22). Daniel tells Nebuchadnezzar that he saw a vast man, with a head of gold, arms and chest of silver, thighs of brass, legs of iron, and feet part iron and part clay. A stone appears, grows into a mountain, and bashes the image. Nebuchadnezzar is the head of gold: after him, there will arise kingdoms of silver, of brass and of iron–clay, 'partly strong and partly broken' (2.42). This is not the last kingdom, for

> in the days of these kings shall the God of heaven set up a kingdom, which shall never be destroyed. (2.44)

Nebuchadnezzar makes Daniel the governor of the largest province in Persia and offers minor satrapies to the three friends.

In the third story, he sets up a golden image of himself and calls his princes, governors, captains, judges and sheriffs to its dedication:

> Then an herald cried aloud, 'To you it is commanded, O people, nations, and languages,
> That at what time ye hear the sound of the cornet, flute, harp, sackbut, psaltery, dulcimer, and all kinds of musick, ye fall down and worship the golden image that Nebuchadnezzar the king hath set up:
> And whoso falleth not down and worshippeth shall the same hour be cast in the midst of a burning fiery furnace.'
> Therefore at that time, when the people heard the sound of the cornet, flute, harp, sackbut, psaltery, and all kinds of musick, all the people, the nations and languages, fell down and worshipped at the golden image that Nebuchadnezzar the king had set up. (3.4–7)

Some people are worried that the decree is not being carried out properly. They remind their lord:

> Thou, O king, hast made a decree, that every man that shall hear the sound of the cornet, flute, harp, sackbut, psaltery and dulcimer, and all kinds of musick, shall fall down and worship the golden image:
> And whoso falleth not down and worshippeth, that he shall be cast into the midst of a fiery furnace. (3.10–11)

Shadrach, Meschach and Abednego are summoned by Nebuchadnezzar: when they hear the cornet, flute, sackbut and so forth, they had better fall down and worship the image. The three are flung into a furnace seven times hotter than the norm:

> Then Nebuchadnezzar the king was astonied, and rose up in haste, and spake, and said unto his counsellors, 'Did not we cast three men bound into the midst of the fire?' They answered and said unto the king, 'True, O king.'

> He answered and said, 'Lo, I see four men loose, walking in the midst of the fire, and they have no hurt; and the form of the fourth is like the Son of God.' (3.24–25)

The trio are not merely unsinged but do not even smell of fumes. The kings of the stories are bad *politicians*; they are not usually *bad* politicians.

In the fourth story, Nebuchadnezzar dreams of a vast tree, which is cut down by an angel (4.13). Daniel tells the king that he is the tree. The king is incorrigibly boastful:

> At the end of twelve months he walked in the palace of the kingdom of Babylon.
> The king spake, and said, 'Is not this great Babylon, that I have built for the house of the kingdom by the might of my power, and for the honour of my majesty?'
> While the word was in the king's mouth, there fell a voice from heaven, saying, 'O king Nebuchadnezzar, to thee it is spoken; The kingdom is departed from thee.' (4.29–31)

When he blesses God for stumping him, the king is restored: 'Yahweh is not, in principle, opposed to superpowers, but only to those that ... arrogate to themselves ultimate power.'[50]

Belshazzar is a buffoon, like his papa. He gives a party, and sends for the Temple cups so that he, 'and his princes, his wives and his concubines might drink' from them (5.2):

> They drank wine, and praised the gods of gold, and of silver, of brass, of iron, of wood and of stone.
> In the same hour came forth fingers of a man's hand, and wrote over against the candlestick upon the plaster of the wall of the king's palace: and the king saw the part of the hand that wrote.
> Then the king's countenance was changed, and his thoughts troubled him, so that the joins of his loins were loosed, and his knees smote one against another.
> The king cried aloud to bring in the astrologers, the Chaldeans and the soothsayers. And the king spake, and said to the wise men of Babylon, 'Whosoever shall read this writing, and shew me the interpretation thereof, shall be clothed with scarlet, and have a chain of gold about his neck, and shall be the third ruler in the kingdom.' (5.4–7)

The hand is creepy because it is a *thing* making words. The Chaldeans will not pass this test. Daniel suggests this interpretation:

> And this is the writing that was written. MENE, MENE, TEKEL, UPHARSIN.
> This is the interpretation of the thing: MENE; God hath numbered thy kingdom, and finished it.
> TEKEL; Thou art weighed in the balances, and found wanting.
> PERES; Thy kingdom is divided and given to the Medes and Persians.
> Then commanded Belshazzar and they clothed Daniel with scarlet, and put a chain of gold about his neck, and made a proclamation concerning him, that he should be the third ruler in the kingdom.

Last orders indeed; the king who made that proclamation was too stupid to be *evil*:

50 Brueggemann, *Theology of the Old Testament*, p. 513.

In that night was Belshazzar the king of the Chaldeans slain.
And Darius the Median took the kingdom . . . (5.25–31)

In the sixth story, Darius the Mede makes Daniel his chief governor; his people persuade Darius to decree that anyone who prays in the next thirty days will be eaten by lions. Darius has a worse night than the unbeatable Daniel. When he wakes to examine the remains of his governor, Daniel calls out that his 'God has sent his angel, and hath shut the lion's mouths'. Darius cheerfully consigns the accusers, their wives and their families to the lions for a late dinner.

With their repetitions designed to be stomached by nine-year olds, these stories are pantomime comedies. The narrative section of Daniel is a 'subversive' comedy, in which a harsh law is overcome, so that a 'new age' can bloom.[51] The stories are 'comedies in little': in each, the hero surmounts a 'situation of danger' brought on by a wicked decree, and is rewarded for success.[52] If this is so, the notion that they were composed to put backbone into the fight against Antiochus IV becomes less obvious. The Maccabean war is perhaps not the right context for Daniel's stories:

> Tales of Jewish success in pagan bureaucracies will hardly stiffen resistance when Jews who would take positions in the Seleucid state were turn-coats . . . This is the fiction of a world so different from the one in the streets outside that its impact is purely on the imagination . . . Perhaps the comic improbability of success makes these stories so appealing, the success in the face of every threat of a God who is acknowledged even by Nebuchadnezzar and Darius to be in charge.[53]

Whenever he wrote his pantomimes, Daniel's 'Babylon' is not a real country: it is a realm in which God always vanquishes evil and rescues the faithful. It is because the good and the bad are so neatly rewarded and punished that we have a comedy which can best be appreciated by someone who can read it to a child in a way that would make the child laugh.

Good considers that the visions of Daniel 7–12 are uncomic. This is in keeping with the consensus of scholarship, which maintains that Daniel 1–6 and 7–12 began life as separate books. The pagan tyrants of the tales, in the first half, are 'reformable', and the mood 'optimistic'; in the visions, the pagan kingdoms are 'rebellious monsters that could only be destroyed'.[54] The alteration in atmospheres is due to the fact that the tales deal with moral questions aesthetically, whereas the visions deal in the sources of moral order which are working behind the scenes of history and achieving celebratory ends for its heroes.

There are elements which transcend pantomime in the stories: such as the eternal kingdom of saints which Daniel perceives in Nebuchadnezzar's first dream. On Alter's spectrum of 'disorder and design' apocalyptic is on the far side of 'design'. The four Jews endure a human predicament with

---

51 E. M. Good, 'Apocalyptic as Comedy: The Book of Daniel', *Semeia 32: Tragedy and Comedy in the Bible*, edited by Cheryl Exum, 1985, 40–65 (42).
52 Ibid., 48.
53 Ibid., 56.
54 Collins, *Apocalyptic Imagination*, pp. 88–89 and 97.

the inflexibility of angels. Daniel has the 'surreal invincibility' of Peisetaerus and the ethics of the Torah and the prophets. This is what the conflict between good and evil looks like, from above:

> The opening up ('apocalypse') of the space between Heaven and earth in the central vision of the Book of Daniel (ch. 7) allows us to see both the drama of the forces of history in the presence of God – in the form of the four 'monstrous' apocalyptic beasts – and the scene of judgement in Heaven: the judge's throne set up, the fiery seat of God's glory, the myriads of angels, and 'with the cloud one like a son of man, and he came to the Ancient of Days'.[55]

The comedy of Daniel makes use of the dramatic resources of apocalyptic. The stage space between heaven and earth becomes the visible object of the drama. A divine being travelling down from a visible heaven to earth or an earthly scene watched by a human being from heaven is better theatre than an event which takes place on the single plane of earth.

In his first night vision, Daniel sees four beasts rising out of the sea: a lion with eagle's wings, a bear, a winged leopard and a ten-horned stamping monster with iron teeth, 'whose look was more stout than his fellows' (Dan. 7.20). The beasts are four successive empires: when 'the books are opened', Daniel learns that each will some day lose its power. Before the throne of the Ancient of Days, the God who is outside the stream of history, Daniel sees, in the eye of eternity, that 'one like the son of man' will be given 'dominion, and glory, and a kingdom ... his dominion is everlasting, which shall not pass away, and his kingdom that which shall not be destroyed' (7.14). The kingdoms above and below 'shall be given to the people of the holy ones of the Most High' (7.27). The second vision says that the world empires will be destroyed. The Friends' answer to Job's question is rejected: '*at the present time*, Israel's suffering cannot be understood exclusively as God's punishment'. A 'dualistic' philosophy of history, and ethics, enables the author to demonise the world powers: these 'forces of evil ... will eventually be destroyed'[56] by God. In the third vision, Daniel sees the Angel Michael going forth to do battle against the king of Persia (9–11). What had happened at a human level, in the stories of 1–6, and in the Maccabean wars, reflects a perpetual conflict: 'This homology is quite explicit in Daniel 10, where the struggle between the Jews and the Greeks is viewed as a battle between their angelic patrons.'[57] Human history is determined by heavenly movements and countermovements. In the final vision, the narrator sees Michael on the other side of a river; the angel tells him that at a given time, 'thy people shall be delivered, every one that shall be found written in the book' (12.1). At the fixed hour, their names shall leap off the page, to eternal life:

> And many of them that sleep in the dust of the earth shall awake, some to everlasting life and some to shame, and everlasting contempt.
> And they that be wise shall shine as the brightness of the firmament; and they that turn many to righteousness as the stars for ever and ever. (12.2-3)

55 Von Balthasar, *Glory VI*, p. 321.
56 John Riches, *Jesus and the Transformation of Judaism* (Darton, Longman & Todd, London, 1980), p. 74.
57 Collins, *Apocalyptic Imagination*, pp. 105–106.

Angels are associated with stars, in the apocalyptic literature: perhaps the resurrected will 'mingle with the angels' after death.[58] Although this is bodily resurrection, and not mere 'immortality', the promised land has left behind most of its earth. Daniel is to 'shut up the words, and seal the book, even to the end of time' (12.4), when *some* shall be judged sufficiently righteous to keep company with angels or bad enough for eternal social exclusion.

The apocalyptic mind tries to grasp the mystery of power: are the armies of the emperors the axis of history, or are moral forces at work beyond it? Daniel answers the question from the point of view of eternity: he presents a spectacle of the combat between heaven and the worldly empires. Daniel assures his readers that there is a 'good city' beyond the movements of worldly empires. Is he avoiding the vicissitudes of real politics or is his apocalyptic vision of the 'triumph of the saints' a tremendous leap of imaginative faith toward paradise? His historical dualism transcends the cosmological ethics of 1 Enoch. Without the childish tales, his visions might have put the good beyond taste, touch or sight.

c. *Extra-canonical Apocalyptic: Qumran*

The high priesthood in Jerusalem belonged to the Zadokite family. During the conflict between Antiochus IV Epiphanes and the pious Jews, the succession to the high priesthood became muddled. A Hellenising high priest, Onias III, was murdered and his brother Jason deposed. These were the last Zadokite high priests. One of the brothers who had instigated the war against Antiochus IV, Jonathan Maccabeus, accepted the high priesthood from the Seleucid Alexander Balas. He died by the sword, and was succeeded by his brother, Simon Maccabeus. Some liturgically legitimist Jews took these proceedings to have invalidated the Jerusalem priesthood. Refusing to participate in this debased cult, they formed a community which took itself to be the faithful remnant of Israel. The Qumran sect retreated from this politically polluted temple to the desert. There they conceived of themselves as re-enacting the past history of Israel and rehearsing its apocalyptic future. The Qumran scrolls are dated to between the late second century BC, when the Covenanters withdrew from normal Jewish life, and AD 70, when Roman armies invaded Palestine and the caves were sealed.

The Qumran community was founded by the 'Teacher of Righteousness'. The Teacher was believed to have established a new covenant, on divine mandate. He was able to interpret the Law and the Prophets as denoting his community, because God showed him the eschatological meaning of the Scriptures.[59] He passed on to the community's 'Guardians' the means by which to interpret Scripture as a series of allegories which achieve fulfilment in themselves.

The Teacher of Righteousness preferred a logical to a mythological explanation of the origin of evil: he gave the 'first explanation of evil in rationally acceptable terms'. The Teacher thought it 'Better' to have 'a God

---

58 Ibid., pp. 112–113.
59 Geza Vermes, *The Dead Sea Scrolls in English* (Penguin, London, 1962, 4th edn, 1995), p. 45.

who creates bad angels' than one 'whose work of salvation remains inexplicably half-done', as it does in 1 Enoch.[60] God has created a spirit of evil and a spirit of good. Those angels and human beings in whom the 'spirit of truth' is uppermost are the sons of light. Others are the sons of darkness, the followers of the 'spirit of falsehood'. The dualism of good and evil is not at the rockbottom of reality: God has designed this disorder. The conflict between the 'two spirits' is set out in the oldest extant Qumran scroll, the *Community Rule* (c. 100 BC):

> From the God of Knowledge comes all that is and shall be. Before ever they existed He established their whole design, and when, as ordained for them, they come into being, it is in accord with His glorious design that they accomplish their task without change. The laws of all things are in His hand and He provides them with all their needs.
> He has created man to govern the world, and has appointed for him two spirits in which to walk until the time of His visitation: the spirits of truth and injustice. Those born of truth spring from a fountain of light, but those born of injustice spring from a source of darkness. All the children of righteousness are ruled by the Prince of Light and walk in the ways of light, but all the children of injustice are ruled by the Angel of Darkness and walk in the ways of darkness.[61]

The sons of the spirit of falsehood have 'a blaspheming tongue, blindness of eye and dullness of ear, stiffness of neck and heaviness of heart, so that man walks in all the ways of darkness and guile'. Their fate has already been decided: they will be visited with 'a multitude of plagues by the hand of all the destroying angels'.[62] The *Rule* adjures its readers to

> separate from the habitation of unjust men and . . . go into the wilderness to prepare there the way of Him; as it is written, *Prepare in the wilderness the way of . . . make straight in the desert a path for our God* (Is. xl, 3).[63]

Such social dualism fits a picture of apocalypticism as gloomy and judgemental. Such an assessment might be altered by the beautiful *Hayyodot* (psalm of praise) with which the *Rule* concludes:

> I will sing with knowledge and all my music
> shall be for the glory of God.
> (My) lyre (and) my harp shall sound
> for His holy order
> and I will tune the pipe of my lips
> to His right measure.
> With the coming of day and night
> I will enter the Covenant of God,
> and when evening and morning depart
> I will recite His decrees.
> I will place in them my bounds without return.
>
> For the source of His righteousness
> is my justification,

---

60 Sacchi, *Jewish Apocalyptic*, p. 55.
61 *Community Rule*, III, in Vermes, *Dead Sea Scrolls*, p. 73.
62 Ibid., IV, p. 74.
63 Ibid., VIII, p. 81.

and from His marvellous mysteries
is the light of my heart.
My eyes have gazed
on that which is eternal,
on wisdom concealed from men,
on knowledge and wise design
(hidden) from the sons of men;
on a fountain of righteousness
and on a storehouse of power,
on a spring of glory
(hidden) from the assembly of all flesh.[64]

This poem is a metaphorical ascent. The Teacher of Righteousness does not literally travel to heaven, but the revelation is implicit in everything the Qumran sect did. The Teacher composed most of the *Hayyodot*. The Seer convinced the Qumran community that paradise was realised on earth, amongst themselves. By throwing in one's lot with him, and with frequent showers, one can be absolved 'of the fault of being human and can then obtain the pardon of successive sins'.[65] The Teacher describes the catharsis from sin which is effected by the gift of eternal life:

For your glory, you have purified man from sin so that he can make himself holy for you from every impure abomination and blameworthy iniquity, to become united with the sons of your truth and in a lot with your holy ones, to raise from the dust the worm of the dead to an [everlasting] community, and from a depraved spirit, to your knowledge, so that he can take his place in your presence with the perpetual host and the [everlasting] spirits, to renew him with everything that will exist, and with those who know in a community of jubilation.[66]

Such hymns reflect 'The belief that the community enjoyed present fellowship with angels'.[67] Resurrection is not so important here, because the Sectarians are *already* living as angels do:

the profound meaning in the thought of the Teacher of Righteousness ... must be sought in a certain Gnostic attitude. Unlike Daniel, who did not feel saved in the world in which he lived, the Teacher of Righteousness feels himself already saved (and here he is close to the Book of Watchers), inasmuch as he enjoys a knowledge which, finally, is the very knowledge of God. His salvation coincides with the knowledge of his position in the economy of the divine plan. He is not eternal, but his knowledge is.[68]

One does not have to go *up* to heaven, because it is *here, for sectarians, anyhow*. Leviticus lists those who are ineligible for the priesthood: 'he that hath a blemish ... a blind man, or a lame, or he that hath a flat nose or anything superfluous, or a man that is brokenfooted, or brokenhanded, Or crookbackt, or a dwarf, or that hath a blemish in his eye, or be scurvy or scabbed, or hath his stones broken' (Lev. 21.18–20). Qumran has similar

---

64 Ibid., X and XI, pp. 86–87. I do not cite the whole psalm.
65 Sacchi, *Jewish Apocalyptic*, p. 70.
66 Collins, *Apocalyptic Imagination*, pp. 173–174, citing 1QH 19.10–14; formerly 1QH 11.
67 Ibid.
68 Sacchi, *Jewish Apocalyptic*, p. 70.

'priestly' membership restrictions, excluding deformed people and eccentrics, a perennial liability of sectarian communities: 'No madman, or lunatic, simpleton, or fool, no blind man, or maimed, or lame, or deaf man, and no minor, shall enter into the Community.'[69] The Teacher manages to be both an ethical naturalist and hostile to nature: he

> carries to extreme conclusions the apocalyptic idea that nature . . . was contaminated by evil . . . The human person is bad by nature, as an impure being, of an impurity that cannot be purified even by all the water of the sea (1QS 3.4–5). There is no water deep enough nor fresh enough to be able to purify the human of the fault of being human: humans are guilty right from the womb (1QH 4.29–30).[70]

Apocalyptic Qumran-style is dominated by the image of the battle to be fought between the Angels of God and the powers of Satan.[71] Since it pictures its soldiers in battledress like that worn by the Romans, the *War Scroll* is said to have been written in the last decade before Christ.[72] If it is modelled on contemporary warfare, it has a dreamy conception of military engagement. It gives the exact order of battle for the army of light, as it lines up against and eliminates the army of the darkness. With its precise wordings for the labels to be inscribed on the trumpets and standards, its careful descriptions of the soldiers' shields, spears and swords, and other martial paraphernalia, it reads like a parodic conflation of the Tabernacle of Exodus and the battle orders of Numbers. Here is a slice:

> And after them, three divisions of footsoldiers shall advance and shall station themselves between the formations, and the first division shall hurl seven javelins of war toward the enemy formation. On the point of the javelins they shall write, *Shining Javelin of the Power of God*; and on the darts of the second division they shall write, *Bloody spikes to Bring Down the Slain by the Wrath of God*; and on the javelins of the third division they shall write, *Flaming Blade to Devour the Wicked struck down by the power of God*. All these shall hurl their javelins seven times and shall afterwards return to their positions.[73]

The current of the Hebrew Bible achieves some odd remixings when it runs through the strangely wired fantasies of the Qumran scrolls. The detail with which Exodus' tabernacle is described reflects the joy of the *maker*, and a pleasure in pluriformity: the writers who enumerated the unreal battle equipments of the *War Scroll* are not making anything. Seeing and knowing have replaced drama. There is none of the coarse vulgarity of the struggles of the Book of Judges; the Qumran priests who lead the soldiers into battle must be careful not to permit their white robes to be smattered with blood.[74] The paradisial imagination lends weightlessness to its leading characters; but nothing as systematically disembodied as the Qumran community's 'last battle' can really be called comedy. Qumran

---

69 *The Damascus Document*, XV, in Vermes, *Dead Sea Scrolls*, p. 106. See also the *War Scroll*, VII, in Vermes, *Dead Sea Scrolls*, p. 132.
70 Sacchi, *Jewish Apocalyptic*, p. 69.
71 Vermes, *Dead Sea Scrolls*, p. 59.
72 Vermes sets out the arguments in ibid., p. 124.
73 *War Scroll*, VI, in ibid., p. 131.
74 Ibid., IX, p. 134.

apocalypticism is too anti-worldly in its conception of the good community to carry the flesh and blood human being with it into heaven.

We have not found the rare fruit of paradisial comedy in extra-canonical apocalyptic literature. Neither 1 Enoch nor the Qumran literature can place a dramatically telling gesture at its centre. Le Goff and Dan O. Via rightly perceived the mood of apocalyptic as comic. In 'the perspective of salvation history we must say ... that the atmosphere of Jewish apocalyptic is providential':[75] but this optimistic surge upwards wants an object upon which to focus its image. With the advent of Christianity, heaven itself is personalised, without losing its spaciousness. The liberating space is found in the body-person of Christ: paradise takes the form of a person.

d. Paul's Letters

First-century 'Normative Judaism' has been defined by the belief that right behaviour takes place within a God-given covenant.[76] The Qumran community regard the Mosaic Covenant as being in abeyance. A *new* covenant has been issued to them. The entrance requirements set out in the *Community Rule* and the *Damascus Document* describe postulants to the community as *deciding* to join the community.[77] One is born into the Covenant of normative Judaism: one had to '*transfer*' into the Qumran covenant. Failure to do so will lead to extirpation by the divinely powered swords, spears and javelins at the Last Battle.[78] Paul shares with Qumran the eschatological belief that salvation is no longer a matter of belonging to the Covenant but of joining a new one. For Paul, the body of Christ takes the place of the Covenant. His soteriology is a 'participatory eschatology': an historically final act of God has created a new realm of grace.[79] One enters the new world constituted by the apocalyptic moment of Christ's death and resurrection by union with the body of Christ. For Paul, and for primitive Christianity, the body of Christ is both the historical humanity of Christ and the corporate 'body' of the eschatological Israel, the redeemed community.[80]

---

75 Hans Urs von Balthasar, *Theo-Drama: Theological Dramatic Theory: V The Last Act*, translated by Graham Harrison (Ignatius Press, San Francisco, 1998), p. 20.

76 The picture of intertestamental Judaism given in this chapter, and of Paul's relation to it, evidently depends upon Krister Stendahl's *Paul among Jews and Gentiles and other Essays* (SCM, London, 1977) and upon E. P. Sanders's works. Sanders's theses have been much debated: a good resumé of the issues is given by S. J. Hafeman, 'Paul and His Interpreters', in Gerald F. Hawthorne, Daniel Reid and Ralph P. Martin (eds), *Dictionary of Paul and His Letters* (Intervarsity Press, Downer's Grove, Illinois, 1993).

77 'Community Rule', in Vermes, *Dead Sea Scrolls in English*, pp. 70 and 75.

78 Sanders, *Paul and Palestinian Judaism* (SCM, London, 1977, 1989), pp. 257, 268–270, 283.

79 Sanders, *Paul and Palestinian Judaism*, p. 552.

80 Von Balthasar says that for Paul, 'all the characters in the play are explicitly included in him, the Head of the Body that consists of living, personal members'. The Pauline statements in which Christ is said to include all humanity are restatements of pre-Pauline Christological hymns, that is, very primitive Christian theology. Von Balthasar, *Theo-Drama: Theological Dramatic Theory: III Dramatis Personae: Persons in Christ*, translated by Graham Harrison (Ignatius Press, San Francisco, 1992), p. 26. E. P. Sanders also notes that, 'Paul deepened the idea of the possession of the

The Christian image of atonement as victory over the satanic power of Death has its seeds in the image of battle between the forces of good and evil which is first found in the apocalyptic writings. The complex angelology and demonology of apocalyptic literature are narrowed down to Christ and the Evil One. Paul distinguishes two spirits (Gal. 5.16–23) in a manner similar to the Covenanters.[81] Paul combines a moral conception of right and wrong doing with a sacral or cultic notion of good and evil. Good and evil are not just discrete acts, but powers to be channelled through specific fields of force. The crucified and resurrected Christ is a field of force opposed to the field of evil:

> When Paul speaks of the conflict between 'spirit' and 'flesh' (Gal. 5.16–25) it would be better to capitalize the two words ... The Spirit which is here engaged in struggle is the same Spirit which Christians have, which dwells in them; it is not the human spirit at war against corporality ... The war ... is not within one's self, but has to do with which power one – body and soul – belongs to ... Paul's view seems to owe as much to the apocalyptic theory of two aeons as to the Hellenistic theory of the struggle between soul and body ... One finds ... the Hellenistic tone of slavery and the apocalyptic scheme of opposing world powers.[82]

One enters the 'Christ field' and participates in its power through the ritual repetition of his death and resurrection in baptism and in the Eucharist.[83] The apocalyptic image of Christ as Combatant, who through crucifixion and resurrection conquers the *powers* of death runs through Paul's letters. The Pauline image of Christ as 'Victor–Victim' is paradisial because Christ's conquest of death makes present, in the course of time, the triumphal dénouement of the drama of human history. Christ's death and resurrection are seen together in Paul's conception of the Eucharist. Nelvin Vos claims that

> In dramatic action, the Last Supper is also at one with the New Testament's many other intertwinings of Christ's roles as Victim and Victor. Paul perceives the essential truth when he says: 'For Christ, our paschal lamb, has been sacrificed. Let us, therefore, celebrate the festival' (1 Cor. 5.7–8). Christ's sacrifice as the Lamb of God for the sins of the world is the inauguration of the whole eschatological drama of Christ's reign.[84]

In the conflict between Christ and the forces of evil, suffering and conquest make a single image. Christ is both wounded and winner, both dead and conquering death: 'The first characteristic of the comic victim–victor is his

---

Spirit ... so that it became participation in one Spirit, or the idea of Christ's death as cleansing former trespasses so that it became the means by which one *participated* in Christ's death to the power of sin ... herein lies the heart of his soteriology and Christology ... when he expresses [such ideas] Paul does not consider himself as an innovator, but only to be remininding his readers of the implications of their Christian experience'. Sanders, *Paul and Palestinian Judaism*, p. 453.

81 Raymond E. Brown, 'The Dead Sea Scrolls and the New Testament', in Charlesworth, *John and Qumran* (Geoffrey Chapman, London, 1972), pp. 2–6.
82 Sanders, *Paul and Palestinian Judaism*, pp. 553–554.
83 Ibid., pp. 453–467; D. E. H. Whitely, *The Theology of Saint Paul* (Blackwell, Oxford, 1964, 1974), pp. 126–167.
84 Vos, *Drama of Comedy*, p. 19.

awareness of paradox and mystery ... Nature is not in blissful harmony ... nor is nature in jarring discord ... but ... is a tension of continuity and discontinuity.'[85] The comic imagination pushes its heroes 'down' into reality, 'in such a way that the plunge down causally generates the plunge up'.[86] The 'Victor–Victim' of comedy brings opposites together and unites them. The kenotic hymn in Philippians brings the high and the low together; in this drama, the descent *brings about* the elevation: 'And being found in human form he humbled himself and became obedient unto death, even death on a cross. Therefore God has highly exalted him' (Philippians 2.8–10).

e. The Synoptic Gospels (Especially Mark)

Richard Burridge argues that all of the Gospels belong to the Graeco-Roman genre of βιος. Drawing on examples such as Tacitus' *Agricola* and Philostratus' *Life of Apollonius of Tyana*, he builds a composite picture of the Graeco-Roman βιος:

> βιοι are works in prose narrative ... and of medium length, 5,000 to 25,000 words; into a bare chronological framework of birth/arrival and death is inserted more chronological narrative (especially for statesmen – e.g. Plutarch) and topical material (especially for philosophers or literary men ...); the scale is narrowly focused on the subject; a similar range of literary units is used, notably anecdotes, stories, speeches and sayings, taken from a wide range of oral and written sources to display the subject's character indirectly through words and deeds.[87]

Burridge says the Gospels exhibit these empirical features: they certainly contain the materials of the 'literary structure' of 'biography'.

Alexander the Great's conquests made theatre-goers of the ancient Mediterranean world. Herod the Great [74–4 BC] built theatres throughout Palestine, in Jerusalem, Caesarea Maritima, Damascus, Sepphoris and Sidon; actors' guilds existed from Nimes to Cyprus.[88] Much of Graeco-Roman education consisted in the study of the dramatic classics.[89] It is not implausible that the New Testament writers were affected by Hellenistic theatre. The generic theory of drama derives from Aristotle's *Poetics*. One

---

85 Ibid., p. 89. Berger says that 'this humiliated Jesus is the same as the triumphant victor of the Resurrection. The central paradox of the Christian message, as preached by Paul, is the immense tension between the kenotic Christ of the Passion and the *Christus Victor* of Easter morning ... To proclaim this paradox is to engage in an act of folly ... In speaking as a fool, the apostle does at least two things: He is faithful to the extraordinary character of the message that has been trusted to him. And, in his own weakness, he also imitates the weakness assumed by the kenotic savior, who was crowned and crucified as a royal fool (or, more precisely, as a fool who thought himself a king). From that time on, every fool for Christ's sake both participates in and symbolizes the *kenosis* of God that brings about the redemption of the world'. *Redeeming Laughter*, p. 190.

86 Lynch, *Christ and Apollo*, p. 12.

87 Burridge, *What are the Gospels?*, p. 177.

88 Gilbert Bilizekian, *The Liberated Gospel: A Comparison of the Gospel of Mark and Greek Tragedy* (Baker Book House, Grand Rapids, 1977), p. 37.

89 Mary Ann Beavis, *Mark's Audience: The Literary and Social Setting of Mark 4.11–12*, *Journal for the Study of the New Testament*, Supplement Series, 33 (JSOT Press, Sheffield, 1989), pp. 21–23.

may also define dramatic plot quantitatively, in terms of numbered acts: this is to define drama in terms of literary structure. In his *Ars Poetica*, Horace (65–8 BC) argued that a tragedy must have five acts, divided by choruses. These quantities were utilised by playwrights such as Seneca.[90] Mary Anne Beavis finds five acts divided by choruses in Mark's Gospel.[91] But she tends to rely on what the textbooks said drama ought to be like. The Greek playwright's 'task ended not with the script, but with the performance'.[92] Anyone influenced by Hellenistic theatre would owe more to the image of the performance than to Horace's dicta. Aristotle sets out a qualitative conception of drama:

> Every tragedy has two parts, complication (desis) and unravelling or dénoue-ment (lusis). Complication I shall call all that extends from the beginning up to the time where there is the turning point. The unravelling is that which extends from the beginning of that change to the end. Accordingly, in an ideal tragedy we look for a true beginning (which is only to be found conditionally in every tragedy we know), a true central point, and a true consummation or end. Towards the central point the whole action must ascend in orderly sequence, and from it descend in an equally ordered sequence to the end.[93]

An audience is gripped by an unresolved dilemma. The 'complication' builds up the suspense: the tension is based on an unanswered question: what is the hero going to do? (Antigone); who will he be shown to be? (Oedipus); will he be blessed or cursed? (Orestes, in the *Eumenides*). The climax or peripeteia marks the answer to the mystery. Now the audience knows who, or what, or whither: the dénouement tells us what springs from it. Aristotle's theory is *qualitative* because he is describing the shape of an *action*. The qualitative conception of drama defines its 'rhythm of action'.[94] The action of Greek tragedy is a progression from doing, *poiema*, in the complication, to suffering, *pathos*, at the peripeteia, to knowledge, *mathema*. One plunges into action, one suffers, and one learns.

Gilbert Bilezikian says that Mark's Gospel is *qualitatively analogous* to Hellenistic tragedy.[95] He finds the complication in Mark 1.1–8.26: Jesus is 'transcendent' but none of the other human characters can perceive this or understand what it means.[96] Jesus does not destroy the plot-development by proving his transcendence with 'signs'. He largely keeps his miracles a 'secret': he does not want to be taken for a political Messiah. He cannot force the plot: he becomes who he is through the progressive stages of the announcement of the kingdom. Dramatic and theological necessity are at one: 'Jesus accepts the consequences of the complication in order to fulfil the peculiar demands of his redemptive mission, which ... requires

---

90 Ibid., pp. 126–127.
91 Ibid., pp. 128–129.
92 Oliver Taplin, *Greek Tragedy in Action* (Methuen, London, 1978), p. 2.
93 Aristotle, *Poetics*, 1455b 18 25.
94 Francis Fergusson, *The Idea of a Theatre* (Princeton University Press, New Jersey, 1949), p. 18.
95 Bilezikian does not think that Mark's Gospel follows Horace's quantitative rules for drama: *Liberated Gospel*, p. 137.
96 Ibid., p. 58.

vicarious suffering as a means to victory.'[97] Bilezekian finds the climax at Peter's Confession (8.27–30). Having been recognised in this role, Jesus must play it openly to the end. Once the mystery of his transcendence is discovered, the messianic task, proclaiming and presenting the Kingdom, becomes the central theme.[98] Mark's second 'part' is 8.31–16.8. The dénouement begins as Jesus goes to Jerusalem, there to meet rejection and death.[99]

Dan O. Via finds the literary structure of Aristophanic comedy in some of Paul's letters and in Mark's Gospel.[100] Via shows how the 'plot' of 1 Corinthians 1.17–2.5 and the course of Mark move from repeated conflict to celebration. In 1 Corinthians, the 'Wisdom of the Cross' is set against 'Worldly Wisdom': the *komos* or victory of the hero is the achievement of true wisdom through the Word. The 'elemental logic' of Mark's Gospel is the drama of the encounter of opposing forces, as Jesus moves from verbal conflicts with the Pharisees to combat with the hostile power of death. Via calls Peter's Confession the *parabasis*, the moment in comedy where the chorus turns to the audience; the *komos*, or victory-celebration is the Resurrection.[101]

Sanders and Davies claim that the generic purpose of the Synoptic Gospels is 'theodicy'. They locate the Gospels against the imaginative world of the Old Testament. Matthew 'may have written that Jesus went up a mountain because he actually did so; yet once he was on the mountain he became, in Matthew, a kind of second Moses'.[102] The formative images, in Matthew and in Mark, are the Old Testament figures of the prophets: Mark's Jesus is like Elijah.[103] For the Gospel writers, the proximate exemplars of the Hebraic imagination are the apocalypticists. Job demanded the appearance of his Judge; from Enoch to Revelation, the apocalyptic narrator travels to find out the sentence to be passed on humanity. Compare the Jesus of Matthew:

> The Matthaean Jesus is not taken on a heavenly journey … but he is inspired by the Spirit of God (Matt. 3.16; 4.1 … 1 Enoch 91–104) and reveals God in his earthly life and teaching. Not only are visions of the future and of a transcendent world related to people on earth in chapters 24–25 and 28, but Jesus' earthly life … provide[s] knowledge of God … The revelation is focused in Jesus and the story of his life, death and resurrection is not just a biography of an individual but a microcosm of God's heavenly judgement. Hence the story of the Messiah and prophetic martyr has become a theodicy, a vindication of God's justice and mercy.[104]

Likewise in Mark, the way of seeing and of being is primarily eschatological, and the 'story is not a tragedy of innocent martyrdom, but a

97 Ibid., p. 59.
98 Ibid., p. 79.
99 Ibid., p. 55.
100 Via, *Kergyma and Comedy*, Figure 17, p. 141.
101 Ibid., pp. 124–127.
102 E. P. Sanders and Margaret Davies, *Studying the Synoptic Gospels* (SCM, London, 1989), p. 258.
103 Ibid., p. 272.
104 Ibid., p. 264.

theodicy of creation, fall and recreation through suffering and death'.[105] Although Burridge protests that '"Theodicy" is not a genre',[106] Sanders and Davies indicate that the key question in the Gospels is God's judgement on humanity and a human judgement upon the justice of God. Jesus *is* both: he is the drama of the Gospels, appearing to judge and be judged even more plainly than the Voice out of the Whirlwind; but also dramatically effecting anthropodicy. Drama creates a conflict, a test and a judgement between God and humanity.

The first 'half' of Mark – its 'complication' – is not dramatic in the sense of having an integrated plot. The consecutive episodes get their drama, not from the plot, to which Horace would award low marks, but from the impact of *personal* encounters with Jesus. Jesus is the first person who has *seen* the 'woman with an issue of blood' (Mark 5.25–34). In such healings a clearly visualisable picture emerges: the crush around Jesus, the woman who, in good Old Testament style, does not merely think, but *says*, 'If I may touch but his clothes, I shall be made whole', Jesus feeling the intention in the gesture, the woman telling him 'all the truth', Jesus sending the 'daughter' away healed: action turns into gesture, which turns into a spoken and understood truth. Down to the turn-around of Peter's confession, it is not the plot which is dramatic, but the character of Jesus. His character generates the drama, creating the world in which the action takes place. Mark makes Jesus' exorcisms into crowd-pullers, as in the tale of the healing of the boy with the dumb spirit (8.17–29), where Jesus stages an action, and the crowd is an audience whose comments reflect the action. The disciples are part actors, part audience.

Mark's Christ is carrying forth the apocalyptic battle against the powers of darkness in his exorcisms and in his healing miracles. He diminishes Satan to finite proportions:

> And the scribes which came down from Jerusalem said, 'He hath Beelzebub, and by the prince of the devils casteth out he devils.'
> And he called them unto him, and said unto them in parables, 'How can Satan cast out Satan?
> And if a kingdom be divided against itself, that kingdom cannot stand.
> And if a house be divided against itself, that house cannot stand, but hath an end.
> And if Satan rise up against himself, and be divided, he cannot stand, but hath an end.
> No man can enter a strong man's house, and spoil his goods, except he will first bind the strong man; and then he will spoil his house.' (Mark 3.22–27)

Mark's Jesus is 'binding the strong man'; Satan is the man of power. The 'strong man' makes us think of circus-wrestlers, perhaps Mark's Roman audience connected it with gladiators from the arena. Satan is a *finite* field of force. If Mark's Jesus is picturing the devil as a muscle-bound gladiator, he is envisaging himself as a shrewd burglar, who ties the big man up before making off with his property – not the occupation of law-abiding citizens.

---

105 Ibid., p. 275.
106 Burridge, *What are the Gospels?*, p. 104.

The comic hero is attractive because he embodies the human need for some thing which is outside the law; we called such a person a field of grace. We need moral laws; and we need a space where the law does not count. The heroes of comedy sometimes personify such gracious lawlessness. Jesus compares himself to one of them:

> And it came to pass that he went through the corn fields on the Sabbath day; and his disciples began, as they went, to pluck the ears of corn.
> And the Pharisees said unto him, 'Behold, why do they on the Sabbath day that which is not lawful?'
> And he said unto them, 'Have ye never read what David did, when he had need, and was an hungered, he, and they that were with him?
> How he went into the house of God in the days of Abiathar the high priest, and did eat the shewbread, which is not lawful to eat but for the priests, and gave also to them that were with him?'
> And he said unto them, 'The Sabbath was made for man, and not man for the Sabbath:
> therefore the Son of man is Lord also of the Sabbath.' (2.23–28)

David never wavered in believing that God was *for* him, and he took such liberties as he could get away with on those grounds. The power of the sacred is channelled through forms like the Sabbath in order to be accessible to man. The sacred is to be taken seriously, but as we take play seriously: it liberates. The passage follows the comment about putting old wine in new bottles: Jesus is making something which is eschatologically new – a new Sabbath – but also comparable. His mission to preach the Kingdom of God leads him and his disciples to do things which are outside the scheme of things; but he is also doing something which is humanly imaginable and desirable.

Matthew's nativity scene repeats the phrase 'that it may be fulfilled' five times. Matthew's Jesus goes consistently to demand 'too much':

> The appeal is to a fuller law, now becoming evident but implicit in the original creation; it will now be restored in the excess of a new order of creation (19.28) ... When seen in its fullness it holds guilty of murder or adultery if one simply hates or lusts (5.28).[107]

It was not easy to rationalise David's *habiruisms*, his church-robberies and so forth: no matter how charming he is, the narrator lays himself, and God, open to the charge of arbitrariness, in failing to censure David's freedom with respect to the rules. The Gospel authors have an analogous task, for '*Épater les Pharisiens*, to dumbfound the Pharisees, seems to have been Jesus' motive on a number of occasions', and he often sets up situations which are wantonly destructive of the religious conventions, using 'Dada tactics of provocation'.[108]

The most widespread *explanation* of Jesus' outrageous buffoonery has been that Judaism merited his antics: he came to replace external legalism with a new teaching of love. It seems reasonable to say that Jesus and his opponents had different ethical frameworks: the former eschewed the

---

107 Frank Kermode, 'Matthew', in *The Literary Guide to the Bible*, pp. 387–401 (390).
108 Harris, *Theatre and Incarnation*, pp. 62 and 64.

'Pharisaical purity regulations which regulate the Jews' conduct to one another and those outside by means of ritually enforced barriers'.[109] Judaism had been reinterpreted in a ritualistic direction by the Sadducees. With the final redaction of the Law and the Prophets, the dead letter of the law was substituted for the living word of life.[110] When such priestly piety was translated into a lay phenomenon by the Pharisees, it excluded ordinary people by its perfectionistic standards. One of Sanders's contentions against this paradigm is that Jews in a state of ritual impurity were not regarded as *sinners*. If a person contracted impurity, they went to a priest and had it removed.[111] Jesus' attack upon the Jewish establishment must then be taken, not as the intelligent rejection of hypocritical piety, but as an extra-rational, that is, religious gesture: He did not merely open the Kingdom to the *impure*, but to 'those who *by the normal standards of Judaism were wicked*'.[112] The debate between Jesus and his fellow Jews is not about Pharisaic 'hypocrisy', but about 'who spoke for God?'.[113] Does Jesus have the right to perform that most irrational of actions, the announcement of the eschaton?

Matthew describes Jesus' *exousia* (power and authority) not as an *incongruous, purely antithetical* break with the past, but as an 'excess over something old, namely the law, the ancient source of authority'.[114] There is a break with the old law, because Jesus' preaching of the Kingdom is not a new *thing* – apocalyptic*ism* – but a new *person*. A Jesus who simply breaks with the law would present an absolute alienation between Torah and the Kingdom. Kermode calls Jesus' claim to go beyond the law 'pleromatic'; it carries the integrations of paradisial comedy into fulfilment.[115]

Before he goes to his death, Jesus praises another amoral action:

> And being in Bethany in the house of Simon the leper, as he sat at meat, there came a woman having an alabaster box of ointment of spikenard very precious; and she brake the box, and poured it on his head.
> And there were some that had indignation within themselves, and said, 'Why was this waste of the ointment made?
> For it might have been sold for three hundred pence, and have been given to the poor.' And they murmured against her.

---

109 Riches, *Jesus and the Transformation of Judaism*, p. 138.
110 Ibid., p. 67.
111 E. P. Sanders, *Jesus and Judaism* (SCM, London, 1985): 'The common people ... kept most of the law most of the time, observed the festivals and paid heed to some of the more serious purity regulations. It was only the special purity laws of the haberim which they did not observe' (p. 182). Failure to be a *habirem* did not make one wicked, ibid., p. 186; reentry to the Jewish community was an easy legal passage, ibid., p. 202; Jesus' mission to the wicked was unconnected with willingness to break purity codes, ibid., p. 209.
112 Ibid., p. 187.
113 Ibid., p. 281.
114 Kermode, 'Matthew', p. 392.
115 Kermode comments that 'Revelation is not the only part of the New Testament that deals with the last things. There are the Synoptic "little apocalypses" (Mark 13; Matt. 24; Luke 21) and the famous eschatological passage in 1 Thessalonians 4.16–17 ... And there is a sense in which the entire New Testament exhibits the eschatological attitudes that are an important element in apocalypses ... the idea of fullness, pleroma, is essential to the New Testament'. Ibid., pp. 385–386.

And Jesus said, 'Let her alone; why trouble ye her? she hath wrought a good
work on me.
For ye have the poor with you always ...
She hath done what she could: she is come aforehand to anoint my body to
the burying.' (Mark 14.3–8)

The woman's generosity, which should have been expended on dis-
advantaged people, goes to make a gift to Jesus. Jesus has compared
himself with David, the gift-giver. Now, like David, Jesus becomes passive.
His body, the field of grace, becomes the *recipient* of generosity. He cannot
just fight his way through to the finish. Jesus has to be a victim *in order to be*
a victor, in Mark.

In answer to the question, which is the higher genre, epic or tragedy, a
key consideration for Aristotle is the quality of the audience. Epic, Aristotle
says, 'is said to address a cultivated audience, which not need the accompaniment of gesture', whereas tragedies are stacked with histrionic
gestures because they are put on for 'an uncultivated one' and are thus a
'vulgar art'.[116] Auerbach tells us that the classical tragedy of Greece, and
the rhetorical history of Rome, never 'mixed the styles': it did not bring the
proletarian or the peasant together with the aristocrat. High and low must
not mingle. When Roman authors brought 'low' characters on stage, they
showed no interest in their background, or in their reality as people. It is
otherwise with the description of Peter's betrayal, in Mark's Gospel:

> Peter is no mere accessory figure ... He is the image of man in the highest
> and deepest and most tragic sense ... this mingling of styles ... was rooted
> ... in the character of Jewish-Christian literature; it was graphically and
> harshly dramatized through God's incarnation in a human being of the
> humblest social station, through his existence on earth amid humble
> everyday people and conditions, and through his Passion which, judged by
> earthly standards, was ignominious ... Peter, whose personal account may
> be assumed to have been the basis of the story, was a fisherman from Galilee
> ... The other participants in the night scene in the court of the High Priest's
> palace are servant girls and soldiers.[117]

Mark is *able* to show us the conflict, torment and failure of a fisherman
because Peter is part of the 'world' which Jesus' story creates; Mark has
begun by showing us Jesus, the carpenter's son from Judaea, and so he can
tell us about servant girls and soldiers.

There is a kinship between Mark's Gospel and Grimm's fairy stories.[118]
Like a children's story, Mark's Gospel was written to be read aloud by one
person. Maybe Mark did it first;[119] the evangelist lays down guidelines for
future readers (Mark 13.14). The text was probably circulated to be read by
other 'interpreters' from an early date. No scholar has claimed that Mark's
Gospel was intended to be presented on stage by actors.[120] Burridge is right

---

116 Aristotle, *Poetics*, 1462a.
117 Auerbach, *Mimesis*, pp. 41–42.
118 John Drury, 'Mark', in Alter and Kermode, *Literary Guide to the Bible*, pp. 402–417
   (403).
119 Ibid.
120 Bilezikian states: 'Mark did not intend to write a Greek tragedy. His was the task of
   putting together a new form of literary composition that would promote the unique
   impact of a dynamic and effervescent religious experience.' *Liberated Gospel*, p. 109.

about its *literary structure*. It is set out as the historical Life of a Hero. Beavis claims that 'A reader/audience familiar with Aristotle might have regarded Mark as a *Bios* or *Plasma* modelled on the tragedy of suffering (*Poetics* 1452, 145b32)'.[121] If the tradition that Mark was Peter's interpreter is correct, Mark was telling the life story of a man who was known to some of his first hearers. Mark has taken the biographical materials and framed them within the world of comic drama: he imagines Jesus as a dramatic world.

3. The Book of Revelation as Paradisial Comedy

Three structures have been proposed for the Book of Revelation: it could belong to Jewish Apocalyptic, it could be a letter, and it could be a drama. John Wick Bowman and James Blevins argue for a syncretistic genre, in which drama predominates. The book begins and ends in the style of a letter but, 'All that lies between is drama'.[122] Like a Greek tragedy, Revelation has a prologue (1.1–8) and an epilogue (22.6–21). This leaves us with seven 'Visions' or Acts. Act I is called 'Visions of the Faith: The Son of Man in its Midst' (1.9–3.22). Act II is the 'Vision of God in Heaven' (4.1–8.1). Bowman comments that

> The throne of God is henceforth the principal prop on the stage ... John's drama is akin to all the apocalypses. God is sovereign over all creation – such is its import. In tabernacle and temple, God's throne was the portion of the lid of the Ark of the Covenant between the worshipping cherubim. As the Ark stood in the inner part of the sanctuary ... it is clear that John visualizes the open sanctuary as always present on this heavenly stage.[123]

Act III Bowman terms 'Visions of the Seven Angels of the Presence: The Church in Tribulation' (8.2–11.18). Act IV is a 'Vision of the Church Triumphant' (11.19–14.20 and 15.2–4). Act V is a 'Vision of the Seven Angels of God's Wrath: The World in Agony' (15.1–16.21). Act VI is a 'Vision of Babylon's Overthrow: The Drama of Judgement' (17.1–20.3, 7–10). Bowman finds in Act VII a 'Vision of the Church in the Millennium: Consummation of God's Purpose' (20.4–6, 11–20.5).

Although drama proliferated in the first century before Christ, 'The numerous tragedies composed in Latin by thinkers, poets, and literary dilettanti were generally not intended for stage presentation. On learning that his *Medea* was being produced on the stage, Ovid objected that he had not written for the theater.'[124] Once Horace had prescribed its formula, tragic drama lost its stuffing. Anyone who has seen *Quo Vadis* needs no reminding that Nero was a playwright. Nero is said to have mounted his private stage and played the harp during the great fire of Rome (AD 66), for which the Emperor inculpated the Christians of Rome. One of the victims of Nero's fire was the first permanent Roman amphitheatre, which

---

121 Beavis, *Mark's Audience*, p. 129.
122 John Wick Bowman, *The First Christian Drama: The Book of Revelation* (Westminster Press, Philadelphia, 1955), p. 11.
123 Bowman, *First Christian Drama*, p. 43.
124 Bilezikian, *Liberated Gospel*, p. 44.

had been constructed at the behest of the first divine Emperor, Augustus. At the end of the first century, Vespasian ordered the construction of a Coliseum in Rome. Finished under Domitian, the 'monument was of grandiose proportions'.[125] It was not alone of its kind. The

> Flavian Amphitheatre (Colosseum) at Rome seated some 50,000 spectators. The very largest amphitheatres include in addition those at Capua, Verona and Milan in Italy, Pola in Yugoslavia, Augustodunum (Auton) in Gaul, Carthage and Thysdrus (El Djem) in Africa. None of these can have held less than 30,000 people. Amphitheatres holding 20,000–25,000, like the well-preserved ones of Nimes and Arles ... were numerous.[126]

The amphitheatres were arenas in which convicted criminals fought one another and wild animals at the games. By the time that they were staged in the great amphitheatres of the first century of the Pax Romana, the games expressed the political religion of the Roman people: they were 'dedicated ... to the emperor, about whose person all the religious feeling aroused by the spectacles would crystallise'.[127] Roman aristocrats and intellectuals attended, along with the lower classes, although some such as Tacitus claimed that they disapproved of the effect upon the spectators. The historian Dio Chrysostom 'records how he himself chewed on a laurel leaf from the wreath on his head to stop himself giggling, presumably from sheer terror'.[128] The amphitheatre was as well known to the Christian writers of the New Testament as the literary theatre.

The Book of Revelation is a dramatic unity: the course of its 'action' is the progressive development of a small number of central images, which gather around a single meaning. John delivers seven 'promises' to the seven churches of Asia. The first, to the church in Ephesus, is

> To him that overcometh will I give to eat of the tree of life, which is in the midst of the paradise of God. (Revelation 2.7)

The second, to the church in Smyrna:

> He that overcometh shall not be hurt of the second death. (2.11)

The third, to the church in Pergamos:

> To him that overcometh will I give to eat of the hidden manna, and will give him a white stone, and in the stone a new name written, which no man knoweth saving he that receiveth it. (2.17)

The fourth, to the church in Thyatira:

> But he that overcometh, and keepeth my works unto the end, to him will I give power over the nations:
> And he shall rule them with a rod of iron; as the vessels of a potter shall they be broken to shivers: even as I have received of my Father.
> And I will give him the morning star. (2.26–28)

---

125 Roland Auguet, *Cruelty and Civilization: The Roman Games* (George Allen & Unwin, London, 1972), p. 33.
126 Colin Wells, *The Roman Empire* (Fontana, London, 1984, 1988), p. 272.
127 Auguet, *Cruelty and Civilization*, p. 29.
128 Wells, *Roman Empire*, p. 277.

The fifth promise, to the church in Sardis:

> He that overcometh, the same shall be clothed in white raiment; and I will
> not blot his name out of the book of life, but I will confess his name before my
> Father, and before his angels. (3.5)

The sixth promise, to the church in Philadelphia:

> Him that overcometh will I make a pillar in the temple of my God, and he
> shall go no more out: and I will write upon him the name of my God, and the
> name of the city of my God, which is new Jerusalem, which cometh down
> out of heaven from my God; and I will write upon him my new name. (3.12)

The 'letter' to the lukewarm Laodiceans concludes with the best-promised
gift:

> Behold, I stand at the door, and knock: if any man hear my voice, and open
> the door, I will come into him, and sup with him, and he with me.
> To him that overcometh will I grant to sit with me in my throne, even as I
> also overcame, and am set down with my Father in his throne. (3.20–21)

He does not promise seven different rewards. Through his messenger, Christ
is promising eternal life to each of the members of the seven churches.
Since the 'seven' churches stand for completion, he is making the gift of an
eternal, individual and corporate resurrection to the whole church, to all
Christians who continue to combat their temptations. These images will
return in the triumphal presentation of the New Jerusalem, in the last
chapters of the book. The plot, or image-sequence of Revelation travels in a
spiral, from the promises given to the church on earth by one who names
himself as the 'Alpha and Omega' (1.8; 21.6) to their achievement. The two
ends meet in Christ, who encompasses the whole of humanity.

Drama has to do with the showing of the true self. Revelation sets out
a drama in which the opposing forces achieve their moral identity in
relation to the Truth or Lie to which they witness. In the seven letters,
the 'name' is mentioned twice, as a reward for conquest. Each man and
woman will gain their own unique identity, by holding onto the Truth. If
divine judgement is a form of social construction, then the 'name' is that
which one is publicly recognised as having achieved. The 'name' is *both* a
unique sign of individuality, and a mark of selfhood grasped by joining
a community. The two communities are the forces of light and dark:
those who carry the name of the Lamb on their foreheads are matched by
those whose faces or hands are marked by the sign of the beast (14.1
versus 13.6). Personality is achieved by seeing and loving another
person: 'And they shall see his face; and his name shall be in their
foreheads' (22.4).

Revelation makes use of the stage levels of 'earth', 'heaven', 'sea' and
below the earth. John is propelled 'up' into heaven by the voice. Even in
this heaven, the mechanics of human movement are not left behind. A
physical thing – John's body – has to get into heaven through the means by
which it would enter any house. The narrator does not beam up but goes
into heaven through an 'open door'. Christ had advised the Laodiceans to
'open the door' (3.20): on the other side of it, they can eat together. The
paradise which John enters is the body of Christ.

John's vision of God has a light touch. He keeps the description of the ineffable simple:

> And immediately I was in the Spirit, and behold, a throne was set in heaven, and one sat on the throne.
> And he that sat was to look upon like a jasper and a sardine stone: and there was a rainbow round about the throne, in sight like unto an emerald. (4.2–3)

John is carried into heaven *en pneumati*.[129] John's soul is not taken to heaven while his body remains on earth: his soul would not have to use the door. John is transported 'into Christ', or into Christ's paradise, 'in the Spirit', that is, by the Holy Spirit. He sees the throne of God. Four beasts represent its supernatural aura. A lion, the calf, a beast with a man's face and an eagle are not that fabulous, but then we read that each has six wings full of eyes. The wings represent the *mysterium*: the book is about flight between heaven and earth, and about visionary seeing.

The dream-like character of Revelation is constructed by focusing: first an object is noticed, comes to the foreground; then action begins to swell out from around it. In the first phase, we see a picture: we notice an object and start wondering what it is for. The longer that this goes on, the stranger and more compelling the object becomes. The second phase is cinematic: the object's powers are set in motion by one of the characters. It is like a dream; but it is also like witnessing a religious ceremony in a strange temple, and not knowing what any of the cultic *things* is going to *do*.

> And I saw in the right hand of him that sat on the throne a book written within and on the backside, sealed with seven seals.
> And I saw a strong angel proclaiming with a loud voice, Who is worthy to open the book, and to loose the seals thereof?
> And no man in heaven, nor in earth, neither under the earth, was able to open the book, neither to look thereupon. (5.1–3)

Someone *must* open the book but who? John cries with the uncertainty of it: no-one has clean enough hands to touch the book. The author does not *say* 'the book is *extremely* sacred', but, rather, he shows it by the reluctance of any of the worshippers in this heavenly temple to go anywhere near it. If it is *this* untouchable, the book is theophanic. One of the elders tells John that the 'lion of Judah' will do it. Suddenly, a seven-horned, seven-eyed Lamb, marked with sacrificial incisions, appears and takes the book. Revelation 3.5 mentions a 'book of life', whose contents are currently fluid, but which will contain the names of the true witnesses. In Revelation 5.6 the Lamb opened a book. A philosopher might say that the words written in this book are 'performative': when they are spoken something happens. A student of religions would call the book magical: its words take effect by being exposed. The book is the archetypal sacred text; its contents incarnate the divine intentions. The gradual loosening of its seven seals puts the script of the first seven plagues into action.

The narrator resorts to synaesthesia, using images which call on more than one sense at a time. At the opening of the book, John hears the

---

129 Richard Bauckham discusses the meaning of the expression in *The Climax of Prophecy: Studies on the Book of Revelation* (T&T Clark, Edinburgh, 1993), pp. 151–159.

heavenly chorus singing *and* he *smells* the 'golden vials of odours, which *are* the prayers of the saints' (5.8). In 5.8 the chorus take up their harps and John smells perfume: the song is the incense. The figure who John saw in Patmos had a 'voice as the sound of many waters' (1.15). In Chapter 14, John sees the Lamb again, and hears a voice like waves crashing,

> And I heard a voice from heaven, as the voice of many waters, and as the voice of a great thunder: and I heard the voice of harpers harping with their harps:
> And they sung as it were a new song before the throne, and before the four beasts, and the elders: and no man could learn that song but the hundred and forty and four thousand, which were redeemed from the earth. (14.2–3)

The voices like waves crashing recur in Chapter 19:

> And I heard as it were the voice of a great multitude, and as the voice of many waters, and as the voice of mighty thunderings, saying, Alleluia: for the Lord God omnipotent reigneth. (19.6)

Being near the Lamb is compared with being drowned in voices like the sea. The voyager is at the source of divine power: this is what it is like being inside the fount of living water. In the Old Testament, water is both destructive and the means by which God creates and liberates. The spirit of God broods over the waters in Genesis; the hand of God drives back the Red Sea, to swallow the Egyptians and release the Israelites; in Mark's miracles of new creation, Jesus walks on the Sea of Galilee, calming the storm (Mark 4.39). Water is also the medium of baptism: the Spirit descends on Jesus as he emerges from the Jordan (Mark 1.10). In the Gospel of John, Jesus' offer of 'living water' is connected with his possession of the Spirit. Both as a biblical and as a natural symbol, water stands for birth. We float in the waters of the womb before we are born. A man or woman whose bodily weight is held up by water is easily carried toward someone else; they do not have the autonomy of someone 'standing on their own two feet'. In this fluid medium, it is easy to float towards another person. When we are in water, we are 'in between': we are immersed in the water of the womb before we become independent personalities, at birth, and immersed in the waters of chaos again, at baptism and rebirth to a newer self. We become a self or transform a given self in water. Water and Spirit come together in the actions of creation and baptism: this is the aspect of God which brings about *relation*.[130] Water is a sign of a communication which is not just a transfer of information from one ego to another, but a flowing exchange of self. Coming out of the water is the moment of liberation, the birth of the person. When John's attention is drawn to the Lamb who holds the book and feels all around him voices like the booming of the sea, he is immersed in something wild and primeval, but also in a medium of communication, which transforms his understanding.

As the Lamb unwinds the scroll/book, opening the first four seals, conquest appears as a white horse, the lust for murder as a red horse, starvation as a black horse, and death as a white horse. The fifth seal pre-

---

130 John V. Taylor, *The Go-Between God: The Holy Spirit and the Christian Mission* (SCM, London, 1972), pp. 44–45.

sents the effects of the domination of the evil powers: the narrator sees the souls of the 'them that were slain for the word of God, and for the testimony which they held' (6.9). The performative or magical consequences of the manifestation of the divine words are not solely an earthbound *divine* action: we also see the *God-bound* actions of human beings. The Lamb holds the book, and lets its powers forth, but the human actors also make their part. When the Lamb opens the book down to the sixth seal, the sun goes black, the moon becomes as red as blood, and

> the stars of heaven fell unto the earth, even as a fig tree casteth her untimely figs, when she is shaken of a mighty wind.
> And the heaven departed as a scroll when it is rolled together; and every mountain and island were moved out of their places. (6.13–14)

The stable heavenly sky which has presided over the biblical story is being put away, like a stage prop when the play is over, and like a completed book.

With no heavenly roof above, there can be no breath of wind. Four angels wait to pull away the winds like blankets. The event is forestalled: the four winds cannot be dispersed until the martyrs have been marked with the name of God. So the reader's attention is directed away from that picture, to the martyr/army of the twelve tribes of Israel, who appear before the Lamb:

> These are they which came out of great tribulation, and have washed their robes, and made them white in the blood of the Lamb.
> Therefore are they before the throne of God, and serve him day and night in his temple: and he that sitteth on the throne shall dwell among them.
> . . .
> For the Lamb which is in the midst of the throne shall feed them, and shall lead them unto living fountains of waters: and God shall wipe all tears from their eyes. (7.14–15, 17)

Blood can wash white in the realm of the Victor–Victims. John's martyr army have won their holy war by losing it. Unless we want to envisage Revelation's martyrs as stomach-less clowns, we need not exaggerate the contrast which the book makes, between an 'earthly' and a 'heavenly' way of seeing. All of the Bible's heroes have suffered, and have made it a springboard into a deeper grip on life. Isaac, Jacob and David endured and survived because they let life roll over them. The new element in John is that survival and its celebration are to take place in the 'fountain of living waters', which rebaptises the heroes into eternal life.

The most dramatic sound completely changes the pace, like blowing a trumpet in a silent auditorium. The most dramatic gesture crosses the widest space, like throwing an incense censor all the way down from heaven to earth:

> And when he had opened the seventh seal, there was silence in heaven about the space of half an hour.
> And I saw the seven angels which stood before God; and to them were given seven trumpets.
> And another angel came and stood at the altar, having a golden censer; and there was given unto him much incense, that he should offer it with the prayers of all saints upon the golden altar which was before the throne.

And the smoke of the incense, which came with the prayers of the saints, ascended up before God out of the angel's hand.

And the angel took the censer, and filled it with fire of the altar, and cast it into the earth: and there were voices, and thunderings, and lightnings, and an earthquake.

And the seven angels which had the seven trumpets prepared themselves to sound.

The first angel sounded, and there followed hail and fire mingled with blood, and they were cast upon the earth: and the third part of trees was burnt up, and all green grass was burnt up.

And the second angel sounded, and as it were a great mountain burning with fire was cast into the sea: and the third part of the sea became blood;

And the third part of the creatures which were in the sea . . . died . . . and the third part of the ships were destroyed.

And the third angel sounded, and there fell a great star from heaven, burning as it were a lamp, and it fell upon the third part of the rivers, and upon the fountains of waters. (8.1–10)

Just as God created the world in seven days, in Genesis, so in the Book of Revelation, he folds it back up into the box in seven days.[131] Josipovici saw in the first chapters of Genesis a pattern of breaking and joining, uniting and dividing. Perhaps these patterns are repeated in the unmaking and re-creation of the world in Revelation. There is a break followed by a join in Revelation 8 and 10 respectively. Richard Bauckham explains the incense censers thus:

In the morning service in the temple . . . the offering of incense was . . . *the high point of the ritual*, preceded by the sound of an instrument that could be heard throughout Jerusalem . . . the ascending smoke of the incense was seen as symbolizing and assisting the ascent of prayers to God in heaven . . . the incense offering . . . is mentioned as requiring the silence of the angels, so that the prayers of Israel might be heard . . . Revelation portrays the heavenly reality which the earthly ceremony had symbolized. The incense in heaven accompanies the prayers of God's people and ensures that they reach the throne of God. The early Jewish belief that the angels bring human beings' prayers to God (Tob. 12.12, 15; 1 Enoch 47.1–2; 99.3 . . . 3 Bar. 11–16 . . .) is here dramatized in terms of the liturgy of the heavenly temple.[132]

In Exodus 24.5–8, Moses sprinkles some of the blood of the sacrifice upon the altar, giving it to God, and some of the blood on the people, binding God and people together. Revelation 8.2–3 is an uncovenanting: an angel sprinkles some of the incense on the altar and then throws some of the fire of the altar onto the earth – causing thunder, lightning and an earthquake.

John hears an angel with a voice like a lion. The sound of the beast reflects what it looks like: it is luminously bright – the cloud and the rainbow indicate diaphanous light; the fiery feet something solider. John hears thunders whose language he understands but is forbidden to explain:

131 Austin Farrer, *A Rebirth of Images: The Making of John's Apocalypse* (Dacre Press, Westminster, 1949), ch. 3, pp. 59–91.
132 Bauckham, *Climax of Prophecy*, pp. 80–81.

I saw another mighty angel come down from heaven, clothed with a cloud: and a rainbow was upon his head, and his face was as it were the sun, and his feet as pillars of fire:

And he had in his hand a little book open: and he set his right foot upon the sea, and his left foot on the earth,

And cried with a loud voice, as when a lion roareth: and when he had cried, seven thunders uttered their voices.

And when the seven thunders had uttered their voices, I was about to write: and I heard a voice from heaven saying unto me, 'Seal up those things which the seven thunders uttered, and write them not.'

And the angel which I saw stand upon the sea and upon the earth lifted up his hand to heaven,

And sware by him that liveth for ever and ever, who created heaven, the earth, and the things that therein are, and the sea, and the things which are therein, that there should be time no longer:

But in the days of the voice of the seventh angel, when he shall begin to sound, the mystery of God should be finished, as he hath declared to his servants the prophets.

And the voice which I heard from heaven spake unto me again, and said, 'Go and take the little book.' And he said unto me, 'Take it, and eat it up; and it shall make thy belly bitter, but it shall be in thy mouth sweet as honey.'

And I took the little book out of the angel's hand, and ate it up; and it was in my mouth sweet as honey: and as soon as I had eaten it, my belly was bitter. And he said unto me, 'Thou must prophesy again, before many peoples, and nations, and tongues, and kings.' (10.1–10)

Comedy moves toward the unification of the incongruous – as in Laurel and Hardy, and in seaside postcard couples. Here we see an angel standing with one foot on the earth, one foot on the sea, and one hand reaching up into heaven. His face is like the sun and his feet are like pillars of fire, to round up his giganticism. He symbolises the three realms – earth, sea and heaven. He announces the end of time, swearing by the Creator of heaven and earth and sea. John, the human narrator, is standing right alongside him. We are supposed literally to picture this enormous angel and little John and to draw from it a meaning – of heaven and earth conjoined, in the figure of the angel, and communicating with human beings, like John.

We heard first of a 'book of life'; then we saw the great Book with seven seals, which the Lamb holds. Now a third book appears. The enormous angel passes on to John a minimised book which he must assimilate, or become, before he can speak the words of Revelation to his Christian audience. We see first the Word of God, and its effectiveness, and then its passing over into the humanised word of prophecy. Once John has consumed the book, he *is* the book: he has the creative speech of a prophet.

The seventh angel, with his seven thunders, extends from heaven to the earth to the sea. Time is measured experientially by the rotation of the sun around the earth, and by the tides. The seventh angel represents the structuring passage of time. He can therefore dismantle time. When he sounds, the play is over ('the mystery of God shall be finished'). John sees the angel, but cannot repeat when and how the plot will conclude. The heavenly voyager is not given perfect knowledge to repeat to initiates. He cannot return to earth bringing the secret of when the end of time will be. He has to tell less than he has seen, in the eye of eternity, so that the story can remain open. If he told all, he would effect complete closure, rather than prophesying; he would turn the mystery into a finished puzzle. The revelatory word is a person and their actions, not a text to be pored over.

The centre of the book is the 'war in heaven'. A 'woman clothed with the sun, and the moon under her feet, and upon her head a crown of twelve stars' fills the sky: she goes into labour and, as the child is born, is attacked by a dragon. As John sees it, the birth of the saviour is not a singular historical event, but an archetypal action. When 'Michael and his angels' defeat the dragon 'that old serpent, called Devil and Satan' (12.9), a voice in heaven tells that the Saints have overcome him 'by the blood of the Lamb and by the word of their testimony' (12.11). The dragon is not yet down and out: he spits a flood of water at the woman (12.15). Then he goes off to continue his attack upon the witnesses. Revelation 12 interweaves different times: the birth of Christ, which is past, for John, the persecution of the martyrs, which is present reality for the author, the victory of the martyrs, which is future, and the dragon's battle against the powers of good, which continues through history. The Book of Revelation does not 'foretell' the future: it presents a simultaneous vision of the whole of human time. Aeschylus' *Agamemnon* transforms the 'history' of the House of Atreus 'into a vision' because

> Cassandra sees not only the past and future, she also sees the present action, which she reveals to us almost as if she were a messenger. Her vision compresses past, present and future so closely together that we see all as parts of one picture, and the present becomes . . . one phase of a cycle . . . The formative principle in the *Oresteia* is the desire for vision, not action, a fact which accounts for its ending in ritual celebration. The play's greatness lies in the fact that the principle of 'historic' action pushes against, but does not break the 'visionary' form.[133]

The drama of Revelation has the same form: here, time moves, not in a straight line, but in a circle. John, standing at the 'still centre' can see *three* concentric and revolving wheels, the past, the present and the future. As they spin, past can suddenly catch up with present, or spin ahead of it; the future can appear alongside of the present, or even affect present and future, making their wheels run faster to catch up. Greek drama expresses a circular, or completed, sense of time: so does the liturgy. The Priestly tradition in the Old Testament assimilated the sense and reality of salvation history into the recurrent round of Israelite festivals. In the Priestly Genesis 1, creation is both originary event and a week of days culminating in the Sabbath. In Exodus 12–13, the last night in Egypt is both 'then' – history – and 'now' – Passover ritual. John's Revelation likewise integrates history into liturgy, not only in its setting, but also in its sense of time.

Like the beasts of the Book of Daniel, Revelation's beasts from the earth and sea (Revelation 13) stand for worldly political powers which demand worship. In contrast, the dragon of Revelation 12 represents something greater than any particular world-empire: he is evil itself.[134] The tape of

---

133 Driver, *Sense of History*, p. 125.
134 Commenting on the relation of this creature to the serpent of Genesis 3, Richard Bauckham says that 'As 12.9 shows, this image of the devil as the Dragon has been made possible by the identification of Leviathan, the dragon who is destined to eschatological defeat by God, with the serpent of Genesis 3. The latter is recalled . . .

history is being unwound and rewound: because he 'sees' them both at the same time, John can identify the primeval serpent of Genesis with the 'eschatological' dragon.

The dragon gives 'authority' – power – to the 'political' beast from the sea. The Qumran Covenanters pictured the combat of the spirit of the truth and the spirit of falsehood. The Johannine writings draw the antithesis into a theology in which the Book is the divine presence and intention and the book of life contains the 'names' – of the persons – who will witness to the Word. The sea-beast makes an image of itself: all must worship the 'spirit of the lie':

> And he made everyone have a mark on their forehead or their right hand and no-one could buy or sell unless they had the name of the beast or his number. (13.16–17)

This way of gaining identity is immediately contrasted with that of the 'spirit of truth'

> And I looked, and lo, a Lamb stood on mount Sion, and with him an hundred forty and four thousand, having his Father's name written in their foreheads. (14.1)

With the voice of a satirising prophet, John pronounces doom on Babylon. He says that those who have been intoxicated on the 'wine of the wrath' of the 'fornication' of Babylon will be forced to drink the 'wine of the wrath' of God:

> And there followed another angel, saying, 'Babylon is fallen, is fallen, that great city, because she made all nations drink of the wine of the wrath of her fornication.'
> And the third angel followed them, saying with a loud voice, 'If any man worship the beast and his image, and receive his mark in his forehead or in his hand,
> The same shall drink of the wine of the wrath of God, which is poured out without mixture into the cup of his indignation; and he shall be tormented with fire and brimstone in the presence of the holy angels, and in the presence of the Lamb.' (14.8–10)

---

in 12.9, but also by the enmity between the Dragon and the Woman (12.1–4, 13–16) and the enimity between the Dragon and her children (12.4, 17), alluding to the curse on the serpent in Genesis 3.15. The serpent of Genesis 3 was ... already associated with ... the devil in Jewish interpretation (Wisd. 2.23–24; 1 Enoch 69.6; ...), but for any hint, outside Revelation, of an identification of this serpent with Leviathan we have only two Christian texts. Romans 16.20 assures Paul's readers that "the God of peace will shortly crush Satan under your feet" ... In a later text, Odes of Solomon 22.5, Christ is represented as saying: "He who overthrew by my hands the dragon with seven heads, and placed me at his roots that I might destroy his seed." The first line refers to Leviathan, the second to the serpent's seed in Genesis 3.15. Thus it may be that Revelation 12 stands in some kind of exegetical tradition, buts its exegetical basis for identifying Leviathan and the serpent of Genesis 3 is probably Isaiah 27.1, where Leviathan is described both as "בהש (LXX: ophis) and as תבי‎ן (LXX drakwn)". That Isaiah 27.1 lies behind Revelation 12 is confirmed by the promity of the image of Israel as a woman in the throes of childbirth (Isa. 26.17–18). But ... John ... does what no-one had done before: he brings the Old Testament text to imaginative life in the visionary figure of a great red dragon.' Bauckham, *Climax of Prophecy*, pp. 193–194.

Wine has to be planted, harvested and fermented before it can be drunk. Having started at the top of the scale, John doubles back. The image of wine makes us think of harvesting. And so the angels go forth with their sickles, and then gather the grapes, and trample them in the winepress:

> And another angel came out of the temple, crying with a loud voice to him that sat on the cloud, 'Thrust in thy sickle and reap: for the time is come for thee to reap; for the harvest of the earth is ripe.'
> And he that sat on the cloud thrust in his sickle on the earth; and the earth was reaped.
> And another angel came out of the temple which is in heaven, he also having a sharp sickle.
> And another angel came out from the altar, which had power over fire; and cried with a loud cry to him that had the sharp sickle, saying, 'Thrust in thy sharp sickle, and gather the clusters of the vine of the earth; for her grapes are fully ripe.'
> And the angel thrust in his sickle into the earth, and gathered the vine of the earth, and cast it into the great winepress of the wrath of God.
> And the winepress was trodden without the city, and blood came out of the winepress, even unto the horse bridles, by the space of a thousand and six hundred furlongs. (14.15–20)

Through a logical and prophetic progression of imagery, the people of 'Babylon' *are* the grapes; their blood is the wine. If you drink the wine of Babylon, you will *be* the wine of the wrath of God.

The next step in the temple liturgy is the presentation of the seven 'golden vials full of the wrath of God' (15.7):

> And the temple was filled with smoke from the glory of God, and from his power; and no man was able to enter into the temple, till the seven plagues of the seven angels were fulfilled. (15.8)

As each of the seven bowls is poured out, it unlooses a plague. The seven plagues of Revelation are parallel to the ten plagues of Exodus. The first plague gives 'sores' to those marked with the sign of the beast; the second and third turn the sea and the river to the 'blood of a dead man'; the fourth causes scorching heat. The fifth fills the kingdom of the beast with darkness: 'and they gnawed their tongues for pain'. The sixth dries up the river Euphrates, making 'unclean spirits like frogs' to emerge from the mouths of the dragon, the beast and the false prophet. The seventh plague finishes it: 'it is done', says a voice,

> and the cities of the nations fell: and great Babylon came in remembrance before God, to give unto her the cup of the wine of the fierceness of his wrath.
> And every island fled away, and the mountains were not found.
> And there fell upon men a great hail out of heaven, every stone about the weight of a talent . . . (16.19–21)

A few chapters before the culmination of all things, the biblical imagination retains its concreteness: the hail stones weigh 'about' a 'talent'.

The seventh angel takes John into the wilderness, where he sees the woman sitting on a 'scarlet beast': she is dressed in red and purple, and holds 'a golden cup', from which she drinks the 'blood of the saints' (17.3–6). The woman 'is that great city' (17.18). Given that the city of Babylon stands for supernatural evil, its fall is not without its lighter moments. For the merchants, the shopkeepers and seatraders, the fall of Babylon represents above all a commercial disaster:

> And the merchants of the earth shall weep and mourn over her; for no man buyeth their merchandise any more.
> The merchandise of gold, and silver, and precious stones, and of pearls, and fine linen, and purple, and silk, and scarlet, and all thyine wood, and all manner vessels of ivory, and all manner vessels of most precious wood, and of brass, and iron, and marble,
> And cinnamon, and odours, and ointments, and frankincense, and wine, and oil, and fine flour, and wheat, and beasts, and sheep, and horses, and chariots, and slaves, and souls of men. (18.11–13)

Like the ineffectual kings of Daniel, these merchants are, after all, rather silly: the universe is being systematically taken to pieces and its inhabitants judged: their main concern is for the effect on the splendid things which they have bought and sold. They do a final stock-taking, and far down the list, after gold, linen, ivory, marble vessels, beasts, sheep, horses, come ... the souls of men. Merchants and shipmasters are shrewd enough to keep well out of the disaster which they mourn:

> And the merchants of these things will stand afar off for the fear of her torment, weeping and wailing,
> And saying, Alas, alas that great city, that was clothed in fine linen, and purple, and scarlet, and decked with gold, and precious stones, and pearls! (18.15–16)

And at the same time, 'every shipmaster' and every seatrader will keep a prudent distance, and pour dust on their heads and bewail the city which made us rich!

> And a mighty angel took up a stone like a great millstone, and cast it into the sea, saying, 'Thus with violence shall that great city Babylon be thrown down, and shall be found no more at all.
> And the voice of harpers, and musicians, and of pipers, and trumpeters, shall be heard no more at all in thee; and no craftsmen, of whatsoever craft be he, shall be found any more in thee; and the sound of a millstone shall be heard no more at all in thee;
> And the light of a candle shall shine no more at all in thee; and the voice of the bridegroom and of the bride shall be heard no more at all in thee: for thy merchants were the great men of the earth; and by thy sorceries were all nations deceived.
> And in her was found the blood of prophets, and of saints, and of all that were slain upon the earth.' (18.21–24)

It seems that human endeavour (musicians and craftsmen) is being annihilated. God destroys in order to create: the voice of 'many waters' and 'great thunderings' is heard again, and announces that

> 'the marriage of the Lamb is come, and his wife hath made herself ready.'
> ...
> And he saith unto me, 'Write, Blessed are they which are called unto the marriage supper of the Lamb.' And he saith unto me, 'These are the true sayings of God.' (19.7, 9)

The Lamb which had held the divine book is transformed into a warrior, riding a white horse:

> His eyes were as a flame of fire, and on his head were many crowns; and he had a name written, that no man knew, but he himself.
> And he was clothed with a vesture dipped in blood: and his name is called the Word of God. (19.12–13)

Now the armies of the beast go into battle against the Word/Warrior; they are thrown into a lake of fire; the 'old serpent, the Devil and Satan' are tied up and imprisoned in a bottomless pit. The 'book of life' is opened, and 'death and hell delivered up the dead which were in them', and 'whosoever was not found in the book of life was cast into the lake of fire' (20.12–13, 15).

The Book of Revelation has spiralled around past, present and future. Now the circle begins to close. As we return to the promises of the first chapter, the human city is reborn:

> And I saw a new heaven and a new earth: for the first heaven and the first earth were passed away; and there was no more sea.
> And I John saw the holy city, new Jerusalem, coming down from God out of heaven, prepared as a bride adorned for her husband.
> And I heard a great voice out of heaven, saying, 'Behold, the tabernacle of God is with men, and he will dwell with them, and they shall be his people, and God himself shall be with them, and be their God.
> And God shall wipe away all tears from their eyes; and there shall be no more death, neither sorrow, nor crying, neither shall there be any more pain: for the former things are passed away.'
> And he that sat upon the throne said, 'Behold, I make all things new.' And he said unto me, 'Write: for these words are true and faithful.'
> And he said unto me, 'It is done. I am Alpha and Omega, the beginning and the end. I will give unto him that is athirst of the fountain of the water of life freely.
> He that overcometh shall inherit all things; and I will be his God, and he shall be my son.' (21.1–7)

The dramatic alienation of the destruction of the worldly city leads to a comic and paradisial integration. The three dismantlings, opened by the seals of the divine Book, trumpeted by the angels, and consummated by the pouring of the plagues of wrathful judgement, were necessary only to bring about this fulfilment. Eros now creates a community of love. The Lamb's wife is the new Jerusalem, humanity transfigured: this is the wedding *Komos* of earth and heaven which the comic imagination anticipates. The demolition of Babylon clears the stage for a new creation. Comedy plain juxtaposes two worlds to give a glimpse of miraculous transcendence; comedy paradisial takes its heroes into heaven. The drama of Revelation takes us step by step through the abolition of the empirical cosmos, in order to present a new heaven and earth, the spacious realm that was promised to the Patriarchs. Even this 'fivequare city', which 'descends out of heaven from God' is constructed to fulfil human desire. Human beings and even kings, bring *something* into the city of God:

> And the city had no need of the sun, neither of the moon, to shine in it: for the glory of God did lighten it, and the Lamb is the light thereof.

And the nations of them which are saved shall walk in the light of it: and the kings of the earth do bring their glory and honour into it. (21.23–24)

The river of life flows through the city; and here is planted 'the tree of life ... and the leaves of the tree were for the healing of nations' (22.2). Revelation ends with a vision of a restored humanity, gazing on the 'face of God', and knowing themselves in him: 'his name shall be in their foreheads' (22.4). Revelation presents a vision which is deeply satisfying to the human imagination. The promises of eternal life made by the 'Alpha and Omega' at the beginning of the book are followed by three acts of destruction; when they are needed, when there is no worldly space left to sit on, the promises wheel around again. Comedy is about the 'indestructibility of the finite': the 'comic anamnesis' makes us laugh because it strikes us with the reminder that 'in my end is my beginning'.[135]

The speaker returns to earth. The penultimate sentences of the book are a bloodthirsty curse:

> For I testify unto every man that heareth the words of the prophecy of this book, If any man shall add unto these things, God shall add unto him the plagues that are written in this book:
> And if any man shall take away from the words of the book of this prophecy, God shall take away his part out of the book of life, and out of the holy city, and from the things which are written in this book. (22.18–19)

The Book of Revelation describes three times and three books. There is the great Book, with its seven seals: this is the mind of God. There is the book of life, containing the names of those to whom eternal life is given. This is the human world as it will be, in heaven. There is also the book of prophecy which John is to compose, the worldly text. The conflict at the heart of the book is moral: it is about truth and falsehood. But it is also religious. The conflict is about who should be worshipped, the visible powers of this world or the invisible power above the world. The Book of Revelation was designed to be read to a gathering of Christians for the Lord's Supper – the setting is the 'Lord's Day'. The Book of Revelation is not only *about* Worship, but was intended to be read out in the course of Eucharistic worship. The theme of Eucharistic worship runs through Revelation:

> eating and drinking, wine and blood, the tree of life and the water of life, manna and images from the feast of Tabernacles, grain harvest and grape harvest, being sealed and encountering Jesus ... Each scroll contains explicit Eucharistic scenes: the first scroll closed with the invitation to the common table; the second promises to satisfy hunger and thirst (7.16) and closes with 'We give you thanks, O Lord', a form of Eucharistic prayer; the third includes the explicit invitation: 'Blessed are those bidden to the marriage supper of the Lamb' (19.9), and closes with a scene nearly every element of which parallels Eucharistic celebrations.[136]

---

135 Lynch, *Christ and Apollo*, p. 109.
136 David Barr, 'The Apocalypse of John as Oral Enactment', *Interpretation*, 40, 1986, 243–256 (254).

Barr finds a number of parallels between the Book of Revelation and the primitive Eucharistic services described in the Didache. The messianic banquet is a common symbol in apocalyptic prophesy. The audience of Revelation are being invited to imagine their own worship as such a banquet, through the performance of the text. Sacred liturgy and drama both take place in a space which is distinguished from the ordinary world. In both, people behave oddly. Actors and liturgical celebrants dress in ways which mark their characters off from a man on the street. They become 'another', just as children do when they play spacemen or cowboys and Indians. With their costumes, their expressive actions, and their words, they create a different world. The imagined world of the play or children's game is set aside from the ordinary world. In the case of the liturgy, the world which is thus imagined becomes real. The participants in the 'celebration' at which Revelation was first read took the world created by this drama to be the real world, and themselves to be participants in it: by 'putting on' the Apocalypse they were led to 'experience of the Kingdom of God'.[137] The celebration made the Kingdom of God present in the room in which it was performed for those who heard and believed. In this way, the audience entered the world of the book. A genre is a mode of experience, and it communicates a means of knowing the world beyond itself. The audience of Revelation learn to understand their own world in terms of the ethos and the images of that book.

4. John's Gospel as Comic Drama (Paradisial)

In John's Gospel, the ethical theme of light and darkness operates as a kind of stage-setting, indicating which character is illuminated and which is in shadow. When the narrator steps on stage to speak the Prologue, he indicates a point of light which moves down from heaven to earth.

> In the beginning was the Word, and the Word was with God, and the Word was God.
> The same was in the beginning with God.
> All things were made by him ...
> In him was life; and the life was the light of men.
> And the light shineth in darkness; and the darkness comprehended it not (John 1.1–3, 4–5).

The third word from the end is *katalaben*: the darkness did not seize, take hold, put an end to, stop, overtake, or catch the light: perhaps a little collision on the way into the cosmos. A plain fact intrudes on the philosophical poem:

> There was a man, sent by God, name him John
> The same came to bear witness (*marturian*), so that he could witness (*marturese*) about the light, so that all might believe. (John 1.6–7, my literal translation)

Form critics interpret the interruption of the bystander as a put-down of John the Baptist and his disciples by the Johannine community:

---

137 Ibid., 255.

He was not the light, but in order to bear witness (*marturese*) about the light. (John 1.8)

The shift to the witness sets up a trilogical or three-way perspective upon the descent of the Word into the world: it does not just happen, objectively and cosmologically, but an ordinary human being testifies that it happens. We see the Baptist standing on the earthly stage-level, pointing to the Word.

Some features of the style of the biblical narratives can be explained by the fact that it was written to be read out loud. The repetitions in Exodus may derive from the need to ensure that an audience easily distracted by disobedient camels got the main elements of the story, if not the first, then the third, time.[138] John Robinson said in reference to John's Gospel that

> J. B. Lightfoot noted ... 'the conversational character of the Gospel ... Adolf Deissmann made the observation that 'St. Luke's is written Greek; but St. John's is spoken Greek' ... H. E. Edwards ... suggests that the characteristic Johannine links like *oun*, 'so when', or *meta tauta*, 'another time', or unnecessary repetitions which would be slovenly in literary composition, reflect resumptions in spoken and ... episodic teaching material ... An interesting phenomenon ... is the curious ... use of *outos*, which could represent ... a gesture of hands in the telling (cf. John 4.6 and 13.25).[139]

Apart from indicating an Italianite origin for the Gospel, the implication of the proximity of John's language to direct speech and gesture is that it began life by being read aloud.

However gripping the tale, a *narrative* is about *what* happened, leaving its hearers with a space to shift away. The *actress* seeks to make an audience experience what is happening to her. Her 'pathos' is 'impressed upon or hammered' into 'the listener'. Actors attack their audience. We cannot bear the brunt of their attack without a space between us: anyone who behaves like that 'cannot remain among the listeners as a mere story-teller. He must be separated or otherwise differentiated from them ... must stand on an elevated ... platform, must wear a cothurn and mask'.[140] The 'New Testament audience' are not only 'invited to participate in the drama',[141] but also *under attack*. The speaker insists that this is a drama with which he has some personal contact. He requires the distance of a stage. What stage? Probably not the dinner parties at which the Roman upperclasses were regaled with Tacitus' *Agricola*. The question of setting hinders assent to the conception of the Gospels as βιοι. It seems as if something is being omitted. The theological lacunae is foregrounded when Burridge comments on the 'topics' shared by Gospels and βιοι

> Ancestry: βιοι often begin by tracing the ancestry of the subject back to an impressive forebear in the realm of the legendary or semi-divine; thus Matthew and Luke follow Jesus' origins back to Abraham and Adam or God

138 Alter, *Art of Biblical Narrative*, p. 90.
139 John Robinson, *The Priority of John*, edited by J. F. Coakley (SCM, London, 1985), p. 160.
140 Staiger, *Basic Concepts of Poetics*, pp. 141 and 145.
141 Harris, *Theatre and Incarnation*, p. 50.

respectively. John, however, 'leaves the other three far behind in a single super leap by starting its account in the time before creation, in eternity'.[142]

It is an idiosyncratic biography which traces a chap's ancestry back to God the Father.

The Gospel of John lacks 'many formal features of the genre of drama, such as poetic metres, choruses and so on'.[143] Those who look for the literary structure of drama in this Gospel limit themselves to the Horatian prologue, five acts and epilogue. John 1.1–18 is the 'Prologue'. The 'Complication' runs from John 2 to 10. That can be broken into Act I (John 2–4) and Act II (John 5–10).[144] The raising of Lazarus in John 11 is the Gospel's peripeteia: 'the mathematical centre of the work which is its moral centre also'.[145] The dénouement is John 13–20. Act IV (John 13–19) contains Jesus' farewell speeches, his trial before Pilate and the Crucifixion. The fifth act is the recognition of the Risen Christ by Mary Magdalene (20.28). In the Epilogue, Jesus appears to the other disciples. If we are looking for *qualitative* drama, John's Gospel falls into three clear sequences. The 'beginning' is Jesus setting out his claims on the world, through dialogues and untoward actions, such as the two Sabbath healings at chapters 5 and 9. The peripeteia/parabasis is the resurrection in advance, the raising of Lazarus. As the plot unravels to the end, all of the scenes lead to Jesus' death. The surprising reversal at the end is the *anagnoresis* or recognition in the garden.

The dialogue between Philostratus and Theseus which inaugurates the Mechanicals' Play of Pyramus and Thisbe in *A Midsummer Night's Dream* reminds us of some principles of genre theory:

> *Philostrate*   There is a brief of how many sports are ripe.
> (*giving a paper*):   Make choice of which your highness will see first.
>
> *Theseus:*   . . .
>   *A tedius brief scene of young Pyramus*
>   *And his love Thisbe; 'very tragical mirth'*
>   Merry and tragical? Tedious and brief?
>   That is, hot ice and wondrous strange snow.
>   How shall we find the concord of this discord?
>
> *Philostrate:*   A play there is, my lord, some ten words long
>   Which is as 'brief' as I have known a play.
>   But by ten words, my lord, it is too long
>   Which makes it 'tedious'. For in all the play
>   There is not one word apt, one player fitted.
>   And 'tragical', my noble lord, it is,
>   For Pyramus therein doth kill himself
>   Which when I saw rehearsed, I must confess
>   Made mine eyes water: but more 'merry' tears
>   The passion of loud laughter never shed. (Act V, Scene 1)

---

142 Burridge, *What are the Gospels?*, p. 231.
143 Ibid., p. 225.
144 Mark Stibbe, *John's Gospel* (Routledge & Kegan Paul, London, 1994), p. 35.
145 R. M. Hitchcock, 'Is the Fourth Gospel a Drama?', in Mark Stibbe (ed.), *The Gospel of John as Literature: An Anthology* (E. J. Brill, Leiden, 1993), pp. 15–25 (16). Hitchcock's article was first published in *Theology*, 7 (1923), 307–317.

Mark Stibbe claimed that the plot of John's Gospel ultimately obeys the U-shaped curve of comedy.[146] But he does not rest content with this suggestion: he has found all four of Frye's genres in successive stages of the Gospel. Stibbe thinks that we may discover in John the plots of Romance, Tragedy and Satire; it concludes with the 'mythos of comedy', in the Resurrection.[147] It beggars credulity to believe that John's Gospel contains four generic plots, each projecting its own world, and yet converging to create a dramatic and harmonious whole. Shakespeare suggested the possibility, but he was joking. Stibbe has also noted a 'hide-and-seek' theme in this Gospel. People 'seek' Jesus (*zetein* occurs thirty-four times); they seldom find him, for John's Jesus is signally 'elusive'. He is constantly moving away, escaping from scenes of danger (e.g. 11.53–54; 10.39); his movements are like those of a secret agent (e.g. 7.10): 'For the first-time readers of John's story, the elusiveness of Jesus is the key factor in the creation of suspense, movement and tension. John's Gospel, for such a reader, is . . . a combination of an adventure story ("where is he?") and a mystery story ("who is he?").'[148] The crucial question in John's Gospel is, Where are you from? Those who ask him do not know: '*But he knows* (7.29; 8.14; 13.3). This . . . is a presupposition of the whole Gospel.'[149] If we press Stibbe's fine idea of a combined adventure and mystery story further, and bear in mind that the Prologue tells us that the hero is *monogenetes theos*, we may find that we are dealing with the *summative* biblical deception: God has placed himself in disguise.

Small wonder then, that

> He was in the world (*kosmo*), and the world came to be by him, and the world did not know him.
> He came to his own, and his own did not receive him.
> To those who received him, he gave them the power to become children of God, those who believe in his name:
> Not from blood nor from the will of flesh nor the will of man, but from God they are born.
> And the word became flesh and *eskenosen en hemin* [dwelt among us] and we beheld his glory, glory of the only begotten of the Father, full of grace and truth. (John 1.10–14)

Skenoo means 'to live or dwell in a tent'. God's *shekinah*, his presence, was said to dwell in the Ark, and in the Temple. On the matter of that *eskenosen en hemin*, Gerald Vann comments that

> the Word 'pitched his tent within our midst': in thus evoking the distant nomadic past of his people, John evokes both the transience and the intimacy of nomadic life, and the sense of intimacy is strengthened by the prepositional phrase, which almost means 'within us' . . . the idea of living in a tent (or being 'tabernacled') leads us straight back to the Old Testament, to the tabernacle which housed the ark of the covenant, the place where God's glory dwelt . . .[150]

146 Stibbe, *John's Gospel*, p. 66.
147 Ibid., p. 72.
148 Mark Stibbe, 'The Elusive Christ: A New Reading of the Fourth Gospel', in Stibbe, *Gospel of John as Literature*, pp. 232–247 (246).
149 Robinson, *Priority of John*, p. 357.
150 Gerald Vann, *The Eagle's Word: A Presentation of the Gospel according to St John with an Introductory Essay* (Collins, London, 1971), p. 14.

The Word of God takes on the biblical mode of alienation, *in order to* integrate believers into himself. Although the Prologue ends at verse 14, we may allow the Baptist to continue his interruption:

> out of his *pleromatos* we have all received, and grace for grace.
> For the law was given through Moses, grace and truth is through Jesus Christ.
> God (Θεον) no-one has ever seen, the only begotten God (θεος) who is out of the bosom of the father, has *egegesato* (expounded, interpreted, described) him. (1.16–18)

The parallelism of Moses and Christ is not as antithetical as it looks at first sight: if first-century Judaism lived spiritually in the interpretation of the law, the Johannine Christ is the exegesis of the Father, the *pleromatos* of the biblical *Dabar* as word and as person.

Verbal communication between this Word-man and others is often blocked by literalism. The disciples tell him that he ought to eat something, and he says he has plenty of meat: they ask whether anyone has got him some food without their knowing (John 4.31–34). Such verbal misunderstandings are plentiful in John, and rather funny, unless we feel it our duty as readers of the Bible to make mournful moral judgements on the actors. John's ironies flow from a lack of fit between Jesus and his world. These incongruities are placed alongside an overarching sense of *pleromatos*. In contrast to the Synoptics, and to Qumran, 'the eschatology of the Fourth Evangelist is *predominantly* "realised" or "realising"'.[151] In apocalyptic literature and in paradisial comedies, the hero is taken *up* into heaven. John's Gospel is an upside down apocalypse: it is about the divine *Dabar*-Person who descended to earth. Instead of conveying a human hero into the skies, it brings paradise down to earth. The author knows the form of apocalyptic well enough to turn it on its head. What would it be like if the Word became flesh and dwelt among us? It would be a terrifying judgement, for those who prefer the darkness. It would also be comedy. Instead of a man witnessing opaque signs in heaven, we have the divine Word-Man performing perplexing signs on earth. John calls the miracles *semeia*, 'signs'. In apocalyptic literature, signs are objects of knowledge; in John's Gospel, they are transforming actions. If Job imaginatively ascended through all three realms of comedy, John makes his hero descend through the regions of paradise, earth and hell.

An imaginative or real world generates the possibilities for its own peculiar stories. Odysseus is not on a voyage, he *is* a voyager. Within the framework of John's Gospel, the central religious axis is that between Jesus and 'the Father'. The gravitational movement of the plot of John, which the hero embodies, describes a circle, moving from above, the realm of the Father, to below, the realm of human beings. John's Christ *is* this spiral from heaven to earth and back. His plot is framed by a 'cosmic journey from the Father'.[152] Christ *is* an *apocalyptic* journey. The author of Enoch

151 James Charlesworth, 'A Critical Comparison of the Dualism in 1QS 3.13–4.26 and the "Dualism" contained in John's Gospel', in *John and Qumran*, p. 94.
152 Fernando F. Segovia, 'The Journey(s) of the Word of God: A Reading of the Plot of the Fourth Gospel', in *Semeia, 53: The Fourth Gospel From a Literary Perspective*, edited by R. A. Culpeper and Fernando F. Segovia, p. 33.

had an idea of Paradise but scarce means of dramatising it. In John, the person of the descending-ascending Christ *is* the apocalypse, and gathers the world around himself in a visualisable drama.

Neither Christ's friends nor his opponents know where he is coming from. He reminds them that 'the Father' gave them 'true bread from heaven' in the wilderness.

> Then the Jews murmured at him, because he said, 'I am the bread which came down from heaven.'
> And they said, 'Is not this Jesus, the son of Joseph, whose father and mother we know? how is it then that he saith, "I came down from heaven?"' (6.41–42)

When he says that his journey will take him back to heaven, they guess he is planning to commit suicide (8.22). The misconceptions arise from literalism, as if the interlocutors were looking at a three-dimensional object from underneath, and seeing only the one, flat dimension.

> He said unto them, 'Ye are from beneath; I am from above; ye are of this world; I am not of this world.' (8.23)

Stibbe is puzzled by the fact that John's story begins with the wedding at Cana: shouldn't the wedding come at the end?[153] This is a paradisial comedy which inverts the expectations of the apocalyptic imagination. Once the wine has run out, Jesus turns the contents of the stone waterpots into the best wine which the partygoers have ever drunk: this 'manifestation of glory' (2.11) is what comedy is for. John the Baptist puts this pleromatic interpretation on the scene:

> He that has the bride is the bridegroom. The friend of the bridegroom who stands and hears rejoices with joy at the voice of the bridegroom. This my joy is fulfilled (*peplerotai*).
> . . .
> He from above (*Ho anothen*) is above all. He who is from the earth is earthly and speaks of the earth. He who comes from heaven is above all. (3.29, 31)

The bridegroom has come down from heaven: the story begins with the celebration: the actor and his action now proceed backwards.

The wedding at Cana seems to provide us with an escape for one of the trickier *cruces* of the attempt to present the Gospels as comedy, the fact discovered by John Chrysostom[154] and underlined by Presbyterians, that Jesus *never* smiles. Perhaps if we stage the scene, the actors' 'tone of voice' and 'facial expression' will throw a different complexion onto the Biblical text. Harris urges us to 'imagine' the Wedding at Cana like 'a first century counterpart of Bruegel's *Peasant Wedding*'.[155] Jesus' Mother urges him to redress the shortfall in wine, and he replies, 'what's me and you, woman? my hour has not yet come' (2.4). Harris comments

---

153 Stibbe, *John's Gospel*, p. 67.
154 'John Chrysostom (d. 407) taught (PG, LVII, 69) that Christ had never laughed.' Ernst Robert Curtius, *European Literature and the Latin Middle Ages*, translated by Willard Trask (Routledge & Kegan Paul, London, 1953), p. 420.
155 Harris, *Theatre and Incarnation*, p. 99.

we tend to read the words ... as if they were spoken in irritation. But this requires us to explain Jesus' legitimate short temper and his subsequent bounteous compliance. Commentators have shown great ingenuity in doing so. One can ... imagine a very different kind of theatrical commentary in Jesus' delivery of the text. Envisage Jesus turning to his mother with a grin on his face, a twinkle in his eye, and a full cup of wine in his hand, and saying with good humour 'My good lady, what's that to us? I'm not on call right now!' ... If Mary were then to laugh, looking at her son with love and full confidence in his ebullient generosity, the exchange would have an entirely different flavour and would lead more naturally into the jovial miracle that follows.[156]

I think the Presbyterians are right about Jesus' habitual facial expression. Nothing could kill the joy in the hearts of an audience more than to see the actors in front of them dissolving into humour. You can't even tell a good joke if you find it so funny that you cannot keep a straight face. No comic hero smiles, nor the cast of an Ealing comedy: they are too intent upon implementing their purpose to laugh. But Homer's Aphrodite is always laughing; the buxom Barbara Windsor of the *Carry On* films giggles; Elizabeth Bennett smiles at Darcy, superlative comic *heroine* that she is. In Genesis, Rebekah enabled Jacob to get the first son's blessing before God had a chance to rename him Israel; Zipporah moved zippily to circumcise Moses; Hannah importuned the Lord for a son so noisily that she annoyed a priest, and got her way with God. The biblical women ardently *want* the promise. Jesus' Mother is the last of a long line of women who jump the gun. Wheezing their way through the two Testaments, the heroines are importunate. Their stratagems flow out of a sure feeling for divine providence. Jesus' comment to his Mother is: Woman! You almost blew my cover!

Jesus turns on his heel from that near-pleromatic party for a scene of condensed violence: he assaults the Temple.

> And he found in the temple sellers of oxen and sheep and doves and the usual changers of money. And he made a rope out of cord and he threw them out of the temple and the sheep and the oxen, and the little coins flew out, and he overthrew the tables. And he said to the dove sellers; get out of here, don't make my father's house into an emporium. (John 2.14–17)

John places the foray against the Temple at the beginning of the ministry; in the Synoptics, Jesus concludes his ministry with this gesture. The attack on the Temple is mentioned by Jesus' accusers in Matthew and in Mark, and is repeated at their crucifixion scenes (Matt. 26.61; 27.40; Mark 14.57; 15.29). With such multiple attestation, the Temple-assault is very likely historical. What did Jesus mean by it? Sanders is convinced that it was not a 'cleansing', because there was nothing to *cleanse*. He thinks that scholars have considered that Jesus naturally attacks Temple worship, because of its externality. But, he says, no Jew contrasted inward and outward faith in this way. Rather, for a first-century Jew:

> sacrifices require the supply of suitable animals. This had always been true of the temple in Jerusalem ... no one remembered a time when pilgrims,

156 Ibid., p. 24.

carrying various coinages had not come ... what would be left of the service
if the supposedly corrupting externalism of sacrifices, and the trade necessary
to them, were purged?[157]

Thus, from the fact that a private religiosity is not to be preferred to an
external one, he infers that there can have been nothing amiss in the
activities of the dove, ox and sheep sellers in the Jerusalem Temple. I should
advise anyone who buys that not to purchase an ice cream in the Vatican
city. Not all *factual* instances of public religion are alike. Sanders's *Jesus and
Judaism* is based, or as he says, 'presuppose[s]' his earlier *tour de force, Paul
and Palestinian Judaism*.[158] The oral and the written law functioned through
the deliberations of the rabbis; the Temple was run by the Sadducees. The
question of *Torah* piety is not identical to that of *Temple* piety. The Pharisees
had social influence; the Sadducees had the appearance of political power.
The activities of the *rabbis* were *relatively* a-political; not so those of the
priests. One reads of the political manoeuvrings of the high priests; one
does not do so about Hillel. Perhaps 'the Rabbis ... never embraced the
nationalism which had been embraced by many Jews from the time of the
Maccabees'.[159] The Second Temple was a public religious monument which
happened, historically, also to be a political monument. Since the time of
Herod the Great, the high priests had 'held from' the Roman governors of
Palestine: 'the high priest's authority was clearly dependent on the Roman
authorities. He was appointed by the Roman governor, and a Roman
garrison kept a watchful eye over the Temple courts'.[160] First-century
Palestine 'was a country where control of power was uneasily balanced
between the traditional families', such as the aristocratic Sadducees, 'and
the Roman governor'.[161] The Temple was implicated in this political
alliance. The Qumran sectarians withheld their approbation from the
consequences. In Daniel, Revelation and *The War Scroll*, the worldly powers
demand worship, and persecute those who refuse it. Sanders interprets the
scene described in John 2 as a 'symbolic action' of 'destruction'.[162] But it is
also a political judgement upon the willingness of the priesthood to make a
supine working compromise with the agents of the Roman Empire.
Perhaps the assault is less of a reasoned statement about Saduccean-Roman
political alliances than a pronouncement of doom by an eschatological
prophet, although, in the light of the historical dualism of Qumran and
Daniel there seems little reason rigidly to demarcate the two. Sanders
concludes that 'A blow against the temple, even a physically minor one,
was a blow against the ... *religio-political* entity: Israel'.[163] We may combine
the judgement of Sanders that Jesus engages in an apocalyptical gesture of
destruction with the belief that it is launched against what Jesus sees as 'the

157 Sanders, *Jesus and Judaism*, p. 63.
158 Ibid., p. 17.
159 David Braine, 'The Inner Jewishness of St. John's Gospel as the Clue to the Inner
     Jewishness of Jesus', *Studien zum Neuen Testament und Seiner Umwelt* (SNTU), Serie
     A, Band 13, 1988, 101–157 (108).
160 John Riches, *The World of Jesus: First Century Judaism in Crisis* (Cambridge University
     Press, Cambridge, 1990), p. 23.
161 Ibid., p. 29.
162 Sanders, *Jesus and Judaism*, pp. 69–70.
163 Ibid., p. 296; my italics.

very seat of corruption that paralyses the nation'.[164] Sanders connects Jesus' prophetic gesture to the image of the destruction of the old Temple and the instauration of a new, eschatological temple which is found in the apocalyptic literature (Is. 60.3–7; Micah 4; 1 Enoch 90.28 ff.; and the Qumran Temple Scroll).[165] John's Jesus says that he is the destroyed and the to-be-recreated Temple:

> Jesus answered and said to them, 'Destroy this temple and in three days I will raise it.'
> The Jews said, 'It took forty six years to build this temple and you will raise it in three days.'
> He spoke of the temple of his body.
> And when he was raised from the dead the disciples remembered ... (2.19–22)

He identifies himself no less with the old than with the new Temple: he is not a new and perfect Temple, but the old turning into the new, through life, death and rebirth. John's Christ does not embark upon a satirical destruction of the Temple from outside: the Gospel identifies him completely with what is to be destroyed. If his opponents are 'the Jews', he is 'the Jew'. Comedy deals *both* with the violent expulsion and murder of a victim, *and* with the exploits of a *hero*: 'the Pharmakos', the scapegoat of tragedy and the Eironic Buffoon of Comedy, 'is a representative both of the power of fertility and of the opposite powers of famine, disease, impurity, death'.[166]

Bultmann believed that the Gospel of John is about the man from elsewhere, who is a stranger in this world.[167] It does not tell the life of a disembodied spirit. Such a Gnostic βιος would have no ironies, for the initiated among the hero's companions would recognise that they are dealing with someone whose language works differently from their own. Not so Nicodemus, the Pharisee with whom Jesus has his first 'discontinuous dialogue'.[168] Nicodemus professes to know where Jesus is from: 'we know that you are a teacher come from God' (3.2). Jesus responds to this profession of faith,

> 'Amen, amen, I say to you, if he is not born *anothen* (from heaven) he will not be able to see the kingdom of God.'
> Nicodemus said to him, 'How is a man able to be born when he is old; no one can come out of his mother's belly twice and be born.' (3.3–4)

That is not the last time that someone will envisage carrying out Jesus' instructions too literally:

164 Riches, *World of Jesus*, p. 106.
165 This is Sanders's list. 1 Enoch 90.28 ff. states 'And I stood up to look until he folded up that old house, and they removed all the pillars; and all the beams and ornaments of that house were folded up with it; and they removed it and put it in a place in the south of the land', in Sparks, *Apocryphal Old Testament*, p. 290. That might conceivably be about a new temple!
166 Cornford, *Origin of Attic Comedy*, p. 11.
167 Rudolf Bultmann, *Theology of the New Testament: Volume II* (SCM, London, 1955, 1979), p. 33.
168 Mark Stibbe, 'The Elusive Christ', p. 237: the phrase is Stibbe's, although he does not directly apply it to Nicodemus.

Jesus answered, 'Amen, amen, I say to you, unless he is born of water and spirit, he will not enter the kingdom of God.
That which is born of the flesh is fleshly, and what is born of the spirit is spiritual.
. . .
The wind (*pneuma*) blows where it will and you hear the sound but you do not know whence it comes and where it goes; thus are all who are born of the Spirit.' (3.3–6, 8)

Jesus attempts to lift his hearer to his own level by means of word play. The wind (*pneuma*) which does as it wills is like the spirit (*pneumatos*): although you can hear them (*akoueis tēn phōnēn*), you cannot see (*all' ouk oidas*) where they are coming from: 'Divine puns such as these emanate from an integrative consciousness which rejoices in metaphorical unions.'[169] Nicodemus decided to come 'by night': he is in the dark, thinking literally, but he does want to hear 'the teacher come from God' (3.2). Jesus cannot resist the ironic question: 'You are a *master in Israel*, you do not know this?' (3.10). Of all the Gospel writers, John is the 'most concerned with the Word becoming *flesh*'.[170] Coming down from above entails a peculiar way of knowing. Jesus' conversations and actions exhibit a comic divergence between the levels of earthly and heavenly meaning, and then, in an action designed to bring about *anagnoresis*, or recognition, a fuller concretisation of the transcendent. John's Jesus sets up the confusions; he makes a game of working patiently from misunderstanding to understanding. He did not have to initiate a dialogue about 'living water' standing next to a well.

John uses the Old Testament type-scenes: the Samaritan woman is the last of a long line to be met at a well, although she is the first to be no spring-chick; there is a play on audience expectation. On his journey from Judaea to Galilee, Jesus travels through Samaria. The Word is 'wearied with his journey' comes to the πηγη (*pēgē*) or 'Well' of Jacob and sits down (*oun . . . ekathezeto outos*; one of H. E. Edwards's gestures making their way into writing: he sat down 'like this') at the *pēgē*/well (4.6). A woman of Samaria comes to draw water, and Jesus demands 'Give me to drink'. She points out that it is an odd request for a Jew to make of a Samaritan 'for the Jews do not have dealings with the Samaritans' (4.9): because he is, in all matters except the Sabbath, a law-abiding first-century Jew, 'social intercourse between Jesus and non-Jews is notable and exceptional'.[171] He tells her

> 'If you knew the gift of God and who it is saying to you give me to drink, you would have asked and he would have given you living water.'
> She said to him, 'You have no *antlema* (water-drawer/bucket), and the φρεαρ/*phrear* (water-tank) is deep. From where can you get the water of life?'

The language reflects the perspective of the characters: where Jesus and his narrator see a *pēgē*, a spring or well, the woman sees the prosaic and closed water-tank. She has not forgotten her ancestry: our father Jacob gave us the *phrear*, and his twelve sons and their cattle used it! (4.12). There remains the difficulty of how to get living water without a water-dipper:

169 Ibid.
170 Robinson, *Priority of John*, p. 344.
171 Braine, 'Inner Jewishness', 110.

Jesus answered her,
'All who drink this water thirst again
But those who drink the water I will myself give (*hou egō dōsō autō*)
will not thirst ever.
But the water I will give will become in him a spring (*pēgē*) of water to
everlasting life.'
The woman saith unto him,
'Lord give me that water
So that I will never thirst nor come hither to draw it up.'

Jesus has raised the woman's hopes that she will no longer have to haul
buckets of water up from the well and carry them back into the city. Jesus
addressed this woman because she is no Laodicean, but a woman of strong
desires. He understands her simple desires – not to have to labour so hard
for her boyfriends – perfectly well:

'Retire and call your man to come here.'
The woman answered and said, 'I do not have a man.' Jesus said to her,
'Too true! You say that you do not have a man
For you have had five men, and the one you have now is not your husband.'
(4.16–18)

You got at least that bit right! That insight indicates to the woman that this
is no ordinary conversation:

'Lord, I see that you are a prophet.
Our fathers worshipped in this mountain
You say that in Jerusalem is the place where it is necessary to worship.
Our fathers worshipped in this mountain; and ye say that in Jerusalem is the
place where men ought to worship.'
Jesus saith unto her, 'Woman, believe me, the hour cometh, when ye shall
neither in this mountain, nor yet at Jerusalem, worship the Father.
Ye worship ye know not what: we know what we worship: for salvation is of
the Jews.
. . .
God is a Spirit: and they that worship him must worship him in spirit and in
truth.'
The woman saith unto him, 'I know that Messiah cometh, which is called
Christ: when he is come, he will tell us all things.'
Jesus saith unto her, 'I that speak unto thee am he.' (4.19–22, 24–26)

Jesus is not transcending the concrete facts which the woman understands,
but pushing into them and exploring their depths. The dialogue began with
the question: how can a Jewish man take a drink from a Samaritan woman?
The Word-man who is from above *and* from Nazareth[172] explains: 'salvation
is from the Jews' and is therefore universal. He is not amused by the *distance*
between himself and his friends. His symbolic word-plays are his means of
tunnelling down to earth, getting into role. The human apocalyptic voyager
goes to heaven in order to see strange signs, beasts with eyes in their wings.
The Word comes to earth and plays with ordinary words like water: 'the
water I will give will become in him a spring (*pēgē*) of water to everlast-

---

172 'He is from or out of Nazareth *and* he is from or out of the Father, and not one at the
   expense of the other': Robinson, *Priority of John*, p. 367.

ing life'. He causes confusion: what sort of magical water generates – more and more water? One can see why the woman is thirsty for it. In the Book of the Watchers, Enoch is led by angelic guides to 'the water of life'.[173] When Enoch sees the bunkers in which the damned and the saved await judgement, those for the latter are aquatic:

> Then I asked about . . . the judgement on all and I said, 'Why is one separated from another?' And he {Raphael} said . . . 'These three places were made in order that they might separate the spirits of the dead. And thus the souls of the righteous have been separated; *this is the spring of water and on it is the light*. Likewise a place has been created for sinners when they die and are buried in the earth and judgement has not come upon them during their life.'[174]

Objects which are allegorical, in Enoch's *heaven*, do not stay heavenly when they are brought down to earth. When the Word 'plunges down' in order to generate paradise, the objects he uses have to become more concrete, not less so.

John's Gospel has the driving theme of apocalyptic: the desired good to be achieved is eternal life. This is what Jesus promises (4.14; 5.24–29; 5.39; 6.26–27; 6.31–33; 6.40–44; 6.46–59; 6.66–68; 7.37–39; 10.27–28; 12.24–33; 17.1–3). His imagery is concrete: water, bread, flesh and blood, corn and sheep are tangible and often consummable symbols of the body being born again. The promise of resurrection, the realised good, flows from the hero's sacred-comic fertility. The dramatic energy of the Gospels radiates from the nuclear, apocalyptic figure of Christ. So too, he *is* the comedy. In Mark, he is the victim of hateful laughter *in order to* become a fertile comic victor. John's Jesus talks about his own life-giving powers; rather startlingly so in his 'bread discourses':

> I am (εγω ειμι) the bread of life
> Your fathers ate manna in the wilderness and they are dead.
> The bread which came down from heaven, this you eat and do not die.
> I am the living bread that is come down from heaven – If you eat of this bread you will live forever, and the bread which I will give is my flesh for the life of the kosmos. (6.48–51)

How can he give us his flesh to eat? Rather than taking the symbol 'up', Jesus makes it more literal:

> if you do not eat the flesh of the son of man and drink his blood, you will not have life in you.
> Whoever τρωγων (gnashes, chews, gnaws) my flesh and drinks my blood has everlasting life and I will raise him up at the last day.
> For my flesh is the true meat and my blood is the true drink.
> Whoever bites on (τρωγων) my flesh and drinks my blood stays in me and I in him.
> Thus as the living Father sent me and I have life by the father, and who bites on me lives in me. (6.53–57)

The nexus is narratively broader in John's Gospel because it redeploys the episodes of the ministry. John puts the destructive cleansing of the

---

173 1 Enoch XVII, in Sparks, *Apocryphal Old Testament*, p. 206.
174 1 Enoch XXII, in ibid., pp. 211–212.

Temple at the beginning (and the words about the Temple of his body); his bread discourses replace the Institution/Passover narratives of the Synoptics. In Mark, the words about the bread and wine lead straight into the Crucifixion. If, the 'emphasis' in tragedy 'has come to fall on the death, the resurrection surviving only in rudiments', whereas, 'in Comedy the emphasis still falls on the ... fertility marriage',[175] Mark's narrative focus is closer to the former. In John, where the scene is presented earlier, the wine is taken out and allowed to breathe over the Gospel. The penultimate scene in Aristophanic comedy is a Feast: Cornford finds in such 'scenes of cooking and feasting' a *'cauldron of apotheosis* through which the God passes to his resurrection'.[176] Jesus' interlocutors in John 6 bring out the point: how can you eat, not just a man, but a *living* man? John's Christ speaks here as the dead-*and*-living, the resurrected Christ. A proleptically resurrecting Christ defines himself as the dramatic and comic dynamism of John's Gospel.

The crowd in the Roman amphitheatre had a sense of the histrionic: so did Caesar when he turned his thumb up. A staged effect can have dramatic force without the actor's saying anything. An actor's silence can be dramatic: speechlessness can convey that something awful is going on. At the beginning of Aeschylus' *Agamemnon* the prophetess Cassandra has been conveyed on her captor's chariot to the palace of the house of Atreus. She stands beside Agamemnon and Clytemnestra: and does not speak for the first thousand lines of the play. When the dumb Cassandra 'breaks her long silence' the effect of her prophecy of doom on the house of Atreus is enormously heightened. The silence is an irony: she knows more than any of the other characters.[177] Such a silence exemplifies one of drama's most important instruments: 'gesture also belongs to the expression of pathos'.[178] The representative gesture is 'the unique action which is brought about by, and which often epitomises, the dramatic impact of a particular moment'.[179] Where the dramatic gesture is maintained through one or many scenes, it can be termed a 'tableaux'. The dramatist arranges his actors on stage to 'sum up a sequence of the play so as to create a pictorial impression which will remain as a kind of after-image'.[180] In the brief gesture or in the tableaux, the actors 'mime' the meaning of the play.

John Robinson spoke of John's technique of 'focusing' on one small detail within a larger, lightly described image. One is given the larger scene, and then, as it were, the camera rapidly pans in the one small area within it. John's Gospel is the most 'talkative' of the Gospels. Intimate dialogues and harsh debates take the place of the Synoptics' miracles and parables. And yet, a great deal of what happens in John could be conveyed without words. John's Gospel would work as a silent film. John uses silence at the beginning of Chapter 8:

> the scribes and Pharisees brought unto him a woman taken in adultery; and when they had set her in the midst,

175 Cornford, *Origin of Attic Comedy*, pp. 22–23.
176 Ibid., p. 53; my italics.
177 Taplin, *Greek Tragedy in Action*, pp. 102–105.
178 Staiger, *Basic Concepts of Poetics*, p. 145.
179 Taplin, *Greek Tragedy in Action*, p. 58.
180 Ibid., p. 101.

They say unto him, 'Master, this woman was taken in adultery, in the very act.

Now Moses in the law commanded us, that such should be stoned: but what sayest thou?'

This they said, tempting him. But Jesus stooped down, and with his finger wrote on the ground, as though he heard them not.

So when they continued asking him, he lifted up himself, and said unto them, 'He that is without sin among you, let him first cast a stone at her.'

And again he stooped down and wrote on the ground.

And they which heard it, being convicted by their own conscience, went out one by one, beginning at the eldest, even unto the last: and Jesus was left alone, and the woman standing in the midst.

When Jesus had lifted up himself, and saw none but the woman, he said unto her, 'Woman, where are those thine accusers? hath no man condemned thee?'

She said, 'No man, Lord.' And Jesus said unto her, 'Neither do I condemn thee: go, and sin no more.' (8.3–11)

The reader takes away from John's Gospel a series of simple pictures: the Samaritan woman drawing water from the well, Jesus and the woman taken in adultery sitting on the sand, the spit-ball being smeared on the blind man's eyes, and Lazarus hopping in his shroud. The actions form a sequence of mimed gestures, the divine Judge saying nothing. One is shown an expressive gesture before the meaning is articulated; action precedes knowledge.

The 'conflict' in John's Gospel is represented in a series of lesser trial scenes, whose recurrence leads to the trial before Pilate.[181] Jesus' debates with 'the Jews' are at: 5.16–17, after the healing of the impotent man; 7.14–32 and 8.13–59, after the episode with the woman taken in adultery; 9 narrates a trial of the blind man whom Jesus has healed, a trial of a disciple (9.28: Pharisees: 'You are his disciple; but we are Moses' disciples'); 10.24–33, where 'the Jews' want to stone Jesus for the claim to be God; and, finally, in 11.45–53, a council of Pharisees, chief priests and Caiaphas, the High Priest, decide in Jesus' absence that 'it is expedient, *for us*, that one man should die for the people' (11.50). The cycle of pre-trials' have a *literary* purpose. In John's Gospel 'each ... episode contains in itself, implicitly, the whole of the Gospel'.[182] In the Gospels, 'God – the Father – is hidden ... present behind the scenes, seldom rendered as actor. This change of dramatic centre ... embodies the claim that God has identified with Jesus'.[183] God the Father has identified with Jesus in his function as Judge. The trial scenes express a central symbol of the Gospel: as in Job, the judge judges by being judged. It is not just that, 'ironically', the Prosecutor is being judged, but that there is a heightening of the give and take between the human characters' judgement upon God, and his upon them.

The *leitwort* of the Gospel is 'to bear witness' (*marturei*). Related keywords are 'testify', 'bare record', 'give evidence' and 'judge', and the noun 'witness'. The theme of trial and witness also refers to John's

181 A. E. Harvey, *Jesus on Trial: A Study in the Fourth Gospel* (SPCK, London, 1976), pp. 50–55, 58, 62–63 and 76.
182 C. H. Dodd, *The Interpretation of the Fourth Gospel* (Cambridge University Press, Cambridge, 1965), p. 384.
183 Patrick, *Rendering of God*, p. 137.

audience. Where the audience of Mark's Gospel are intended to identify
with the bumbling **disciples**, that of John's Gospel are asked to be
witnesses. The drama expresses a moral conflict, in which the audience is
asked to take sides. The audience is being asked to make a response which
will implicate them on one side or another of a moral conflict.

Some sort of dualism belongs to the narrative structure of John's Gospel.
Many of the terms which John has in common with Qumran are linked to a
dualistic perspective. Charlesworth lists eleven Johannine terms which
have close parallels in *The Community Rule* (1QS): 'the spirit of truth' (John
14.17; 15.26; 16.13; cf. 4.24); 'the holy Spirit' (14.26; 20.22); 'sons of light'
(12.36); 'eternal life' (3.15, 16, 36; 4.14, 36; 5.24, 39; 6.27, 40, 47, 54, 68; 10.28;
12.25, 50; 17.2, 3); 'the light of life' (8.12); 'and he walks in darkness' (12.35)
or 'he will not walk in darkness' (8.12); 'the wrath of God' (3.36) (linked to
'by the furious wrath of the God of vengeance' 1QS 4.12); 'the eyes of the
blind' (10.12); 'full of grace' (1.14); 'the works of God' (6.28, 9.3); and 'the
men ... because their works were evil' (3.19). Of these common terms, four
relate to a dualism of light and dark.[184] John's Gospel presents at least three
dualistic images: that of the world above and the world below, that of light
and dark, and that of truth and its enemies. These dualisms do not exactly
run parallel. The world below is not, *per se*, the world of darkness: Jesus is
bringing light into this world, 'so that light and darkness are opposed to
one another *in this world*'.[185] The purpose of the 'cosmic voyage' is to put
light and darkness on trial in this world, and thus to realise the eschaton.
An 'ethical' and 'soteriological' dualism, symbolised by the conflict of light
and dark, is more important to this Gospel than a dualism of two worlds.[186]
John's dualisms are not intended to portray the world as evil. The
Qumran scrolls lacked intentional humour, because of their ethereal
quality. John's Gospel presents a comedy of embodied heaven. In the
Community Rule, one of the *attributes* of the 'ways of the spirit of falsehood' is 'blindness of eye': it results in the fact that 'man walks in all the
ways of darkness'. Although John has no 'spirit of falsehood', he has
plenty of wilfully blind evil doers. The progressive stages of the episode of
the restoration of sight to the man born blind put light and darkness on
trial:

> And as Jesus passed by, he saw a man which was blind from his birth.
> And his disciples asked him, saying, 'Master, who did sin, this man, or his
> parents, that he was born blind?' (9.1–2)

The episode begins with a reminder of Job's question, and one of the
Friends' answers. Jesus replies by changing the metaphor of what the good

184 Charlesworth, 'Critical Comparison of the Dualism in 1QS 3.13–4.26', pp. 98–103.
     As to the historical question of when and where John was written, Charlesworth
     comments that 'If the Rule is behind Johannine "dualism" then ... it becomes more
     probable that the *sitz im Leben* of John's traditions is Palestinian ... there is no
     evidence that 1QS was read outside Palestine'. This may not demonstrate that the
     Gospel was '*written* in Palestine', since the author could have got his terminology
     from John the Baptist. 'However', Charlesworth says, 'it is more probable ... that
     John was written, perhaps only in a first draft, in Palestine.' Ibid., pp. 104–115.
185 James L. Price, 'Light from Qumran on Some Aspects of Johannine Theology', in
     Charlesworth, *John and Qumran*, p. 20.
186 Ibid., p. 19.

is about: not something natural, but something dramatic, which God does in history:

> Neither hath this man sinned, nor his parents: but that the works of God should be made manifest in him. (9.3)

The man born blind is the cosmos sunk in darkness; one man's healing out of blindness/sin to sight/life expresses what the 'light of the world' (9.5) does to the cosmos. The way out of the ethical dilemma, the existential sense of 'ontic impurity' which weighs down inter-testamental apocalyptic, is not by knowledge, but by action. This is the only Johannine sign in which Jesus works with physical implements, as if to emphasise that he has made the comic gesture of deepened embodiment, touching the earth in order to heal the world: 'he spat on the ground, and made clay of the spittle, and he anointed the eyes of the blind man with the clay' and told him to go and wash it off in 'the pool of Siloam' (9.6–7). The hands are the hands of the man from Nazareth; the voice is the power of the God of Israel. We learn, mid-miracle, that this is the Sabbath. 'The Jews' try to get an explanation out of the man's parents, who are evasive

> We know that this is our son, and that he was born blind:
> But by what means he now seeth, we know not; or who hath opened his eyes, we know not: he is of age; ask him: he shall speak for himself. (9.20–21)

John's Pharisees reject the miracle for what it stands for:

> Then said they to him again, 'What did he to thee? how opened he thine eyes?'
> He answered them, 'I have told you already, and ye did not hear: wherefore would ye hear it again? will ye also be his disciples?'
> Then they reviled him, and said, 'Thou art his disciple; but we are Moses' disciples.
> We know that God spake unto Moses: as for this fellow, we know not from whence he is.' (9.26–29)

The unblinded man replies with a blunt sarcasm liable to get a man booted out of any community,

> Why herein is a marvellous thing, that ye know not from whence he is, and yet he hath opened mine eyes. (9.30)

John's Jesus is overturning the rational order of the world of darkness: anyone who knew enough to know they were blind would be on their way to the light.

> And Jesus said, 'For judgment I am come into this world, that they which see not might see; and that they which see might be made blind.' (9.39)

John's Pharisees object: are you calling *us* blind? (9.40). Jesus replies

> If ye were blind, ye would have no sin: but now ye say, We see; therefore your sin remaineth. (9.41)

One is not at fault by living in the condition of the world, which the blind man represented. The apocalyptic seer, *looking* down from above, *sees* the ethical divisions between human beings in black and white. The divine apocalyptic voyager brings about a situation which *creates* ethical divisions:

> the ironic movements of the narrative ... are the same simultaneous upward and downward movements we have ... observed in the Gospel as a whole. The man born blind ... sees with increasing clarity; the ones who claim sight plunge into ... thickening night ... With artful restraint the author withholds the word judgement (krima) until the last scene ... Now we recall the grimmer aspect of what Jesus has said about the light. The light is not only ... life ... it is 'the judgement' (3.19) – the dreaded brilliance which exposes the deeds of those who fear it (3.20), and so drives them into the deepest darkness of all, the willing refusal to see.[187]

Jesus' presence thrusts the Pharisees into an infernal world of darkness. They are no more spiritually derailed than anyone else, before or since: they look dark in *his* eye, and his actions. Jesus' perspective is represented by language which 'bends upwards': beginning from the literal, one travels into the symbolical. The perspective of 'the Jews' in John's Gospel is represented by a linguistic 'down-turn': they take the metaphor downwards. The nastiest example is perhaps this:

> 'I speak of that which I have seen with my Father: and you do what you have seen with your father.'
> They answered and said, 'Our Father is Abraham.' Jesus said to them, 'If you are the children of Abraham, then do the deeds of Abraham.
> Now you seek to kill me, a man who has told you the truth that he has heard from God. Abraham did not do that.
> You do the deeds of your father.' (8.38–41)

He is not just calling them sons of camels:

> They said to him, 'We are not offspring of fornication, we have a father in God.'
> Then Jesus said to them, 'If God were your father, you would love me, for I come from God, nor did I come of myself, but he sent me.
> You do not understand my speech because you cannot hear my word.
> You have the devil for your father, and you want to do the lusts of your fathers. He was a man-slaughterer from the beginning because he did not live in the truth. When he speaks a lie, he speaks of his own, because he is the father of lies.
> Because I speak the truth, you don't believe me.' (8.41–45)

The prophets flamed their contemporaries with satire. John's Jesus likewise curses 'the Jews'. John aligns universal infernalisation to universal salvation. His Jesus speaks of his saving 'all' ($\pi\alpha\nu$), as in

> Except a grain of wheat fall into the ground and die, it abideth alone: but if it die, it bringeth forth much fruit.
> ...
> And I, if I be lifted up from the earth, will draw all men unto me. (12.24, 32)

He identified with all, 'the Jews', in order to redeem all.

187 Paul Duke, *Irony in the Fourth Gospel* (John Knox Press, Atlanta, 1985), pp. 118 and 126.

A performance is dramatic to the extent that it is going somewhere. Drama catches its audience up into a *directed* movement. We ought to receive the impression that it *had* to come out that way. The skilled dramatist builds this feeling of purposeful movement into the play by making each scene a clue and a link, which anticipates the conclusion. John has told how the apocalyptic voyager has come from the realm of eternal life to that mortality, promising eternal life in a series of symbols, such as 'living water' and 'bread from heaven'. The scene of the raising of Lazarus is the peripeteia or parabasis of the Gospel because it expresses the drama *in nuce*. The raising of Lazarus from the dead presents Jesus at his most human. Martha has sensibly gone to fetch Jesus.

> When Jesus therefore saw her weeping, and the Jews also weeping . . . he groaned in the spirit and was troubled,
> And said, 'Where have ye laid him?' They said unto him, 'Lord, come and see.'
> Jesus wept.
> Then said the Jews, 'Behold how he loved him!'
> . . .
> Jesus therefore again groaning in himself cometh to the grave. It was a cave, and a stone lay upon it. (11.33–36, 38)

Jesus has travelled further and further down into humanity, and the human world. Now he comes face to face with death: this is the lowest point in the almost circle of Jesus' journey. Now he begins to reascend the circle, bringing about the most comic comment in the Gospel:

> Jesus said, 'Take ye away the stone.' Martha, the sister of him that was dead, saith unto him, 'Lord, by this time he stinketh: for he hath been dead four days.' (11.39)

Undeterred by such epistemological disjunctions, Jesus

> cried with a loud voice, 'Lazarus, come forth.'
> And he that was dead came forth, bound hand and foot with graveclothes: and his face was bound about with a napkin. Jesus saith unto them, 'Loose him, and let him go.' (11.43–44)

Within the logic of comedy, a resurrection scene involves hopping around in one's winding sheet until someone – presumably Martha – unwinds it. The Johannine ascent into eternal life will not be disembodied. The promise of eternal life will be realised existentially. The reascent is going to take more struggle than the descent. As the narrative puts in position its gestures towards the death of Jesus, it retains its feeling of calm. John's anointment scene is more deliberative than Mark's:

> Then took Mary a pound of ointment of spikenard, very costly, and anointed the feet of Jesus, and wiped his feet with her hair: and the house was filled with the odour of the ointment. (12.3)

In the preliminary acts, the Word, *as it were*, half into the role, had spoken 'high' and been understood to say something low; now, fully transformed into the guise, he will be low in order to be high. Gerald Vann describes the mission of the Johannine Christ as a 'dark journey', a paradoxical journey which by being one thing becomes another; the voyage into darkness turns the dark into light:

> The fourth gospel emphasizes the idea of looking for life in death and light in darkness by its use of the word *hypsoun*, to be lifted up, to signify simultaneously the crucifixion and the ascension of the Son of Man.[188]

David played three roles: the shepherd/*habiru*, the worldly king, and God's anointed king. As *habiru*/shepherd, he created an area of freedom. As worldly king, he was forced back into passivity. It is as the man who gives, and who receives from others, he is the Lord's anointed. The 'Good shepherd' discourse, in John 10, is an eschatological midrash on biblical kingship:

> I am the good shepherd, and know my sheep, and am known of mine.
> Even as the Father knoweth me, even so know I the Father: and I lay down my life for the sheep.
> . . .
> Therefore doth my Father love me, because I lay down my life that I may take it again.
> No man taketh it from me, but I lay it down of myself. I have power to lay it down, and I have power to take it again. This commandment have I received of my Father. (10.14–15, 17–18)

As John's Jesus goes to the Cross, he is already imagining himself as victor. In and alongside the incongruities, John presents the historical life of Jesus in an extended image of *completeness*. He has been described as the 'king of Israel' (1.49; 6.14–15; 12.13), and has not rejected the designation. The 'Old' King, the representative Jew, becomes the means by which Israel's desire for a king is mocked. When John pictures 'the Jews' outside Pilate's Praetorium as crying 'We have no king but Caesar', he is making a *political* judgement on first-century Judaism. John's judgement scene before Pilate presents the apocalyptic conception of the absolute demarcation between worldly and heavenly power. The world chooses the world as its emperor. In the apocalyptic writings the visionary seer watches from on high as the beasts representing the world-empires are destroyed by the sons of light. Pilate's trial of Jesus presents God's judgement on political power and on 'the world', from below. Pilate is 'a symbol of "worldly" kingship ... of power-politics and political expediency'.[189] John's Gospel does not satirise Pilate. It satirises the *desire for a king*. It is not the hero who is mocked, in the trial scene. If Jesus is the Eironic-Buffoon of the Gospel, the collective 'Jews' are its 'Impostors'.

The scenes of the trial before Pilate move between the inner Praetorium, or judgement hall, and the courtyard outside, where 'the Jews' await the judgement. The picture is thus that of 'two stages ... a front stage and a back'.[190] 'The Jews' are depicted as not wanting to go inside a gentile's house during the Passover: they take Jesus to the door and skip out again.

---

188 Vann, *Eagle's Word*, p. 26.
189 Ibid., p. 17.
190 Duke, *Irony in the Fourth Gospel*, p. 127.

Pilate has to go outside to them (*these unbending people*) to find out what the charge is. Is he out of control of the situation already? Not entirely, for his action forces the admission of political dependency: 'It is not lawful for us to put any man to death' (18.31; *we can't get anywhere without asking **you** for permission*). Pilate goes back inside and asks Jesus a question which we know so well that we may not recognise its oddity: 'Art thou the king of the Jews?' Jesus asks where he got his information (18.34). Pilate prevaricates: you must have done something if your high priests have delivered you to me for judgement. Jesus tells him he is not a worldly-king; but 'a king?' asks Pilate again (8.37); he is digging for that answer. Convinced that Jesus is not a political threat, Pilate goes back outside, and tells the crowd their man is innocent. He does so in a way which is designed to inflame them, imposing the man as their king, like it or not: 'But ye have a custom, that I should release unto you one at the Passover; will ye therefore that I release unto you the King of the Jews' (18.39). Such 'ironic' digs at a subservient nation without a monarch 'seem calculated more to embitter "the Jews" against Jesus than to win his release'. He plans to use Jesus to 'humiliate "the Jews" and to ridicule their national hopes',[191] deploying a *faux-naive* pretence of belief in Jesus' kingship in order to force the Jews to testify to the Roman Caesar. Returning inside, Pilate has his victim scourged and costumed in the dress of a monarch. This enables him to return to 'the Jews' with a 'mock-king'.[192] Jesus is not the direct object of Pilate's mockery: he is the means by which the crowd are satirised. Jesus permits Pilate ritually to abuse him in the trial, because he must be sacrificed as 'king of the Jews':

> At a deeper level ... John's irony stands the mockery of Pilate on its head: this is in truth the king, and this is royal epiphany. 'The Jews' ... see only the bitter burlesque of Jewish royalty, and neither Pilate nor the reader could ... expect them to respond otherwise than as they do. 'Behold the man!' he says and *now*, beholding him, the chief priests cry out, 'Crucify!' (19.5–6).[193]

Pilate ironically tells his subjects to go 'crucify him yourselves': it has already been pointed out that they have no power to do so. The penultimate repetition of the innocent insult brings the answer which Pilate has been requiring all along: 'Shall I crucify your king? The chief priests answered, We have no king but Caesar' (19.15). The last word from Pilate is the sign fixed to the cross. John's Gospel overthrows the static ethical dualisms: evil is overcome, not by separating off from it, but by engaging in it and transforming it.

By dint of Pilate's malice, the Christ of *all* the Gospels dies as the 'Mock King' of the Jews:

> the soldiers led him away into the hall, called the Praetorium; and they call together the whole band.
> And they clothed him with purple, and platted a crown of thorns, and put it about his head.

191 David Rensberger, *Overcoming the World: Politics and Community in the Gospel of John* (SPCK, London, 1989), p. 92.
192 Ibid., p. 93.
193 Ibid., p. 94.

And began to salute him, 'Hail, King of the Jews!'
And they smote him on the head with a reed, and did spit upon him, and
bowing their knees worshipped him.
And when they had mocked him, they took off the purple from him, and put
his own clothes on him, and led him out to crucify him. (Mark 15.16–20)

The 'Impostor' or Old King is, and is not, 'split off' from the New King.
The soldiers, the crowd and Pilate make a fool, or Impostor, of Christ: he is
mocked in the robes and dies under the sign of 'the King of the Jews'. He
becomes the object of *violent* laughter. In the soldiers' parody of a
coronation:

Jesus is mocked by being treated as if he were a bogus royalty of the
Bacchanalia ... just before his crucifixion, Jesus was crowned as a king of
folly.[194]

The crucified Christ of the Gospels enters the infernal realm. He does not
hit back: and in this passive endurance, not only of the consequences of
worldly messianism, but of *human sin*, our propensity for dark laughter,
he becomes *comical*. The victim-hero is both as a character who seems
wilfully to invoke a violent response, and a life-giver. The comical/comic
has a duality like that of the *sacred*. The sacred is a *mysterium tremendum et
fascinans*, a terrifying and attractive mystery. The comic hero curses *and*
blesses; he is the object of violence *and* the sign of fertility. The God of the
Old Testament has cursed and blessed from 'heaven', from a stage above
the earth. Bring him down to earth, and he will curse, consigning 'the Jews'
to the devil, and bless, drawing 'all' to his power of resurrecting life. In
order to do so, he must be the object of invective and violence; the 'Judge'
at whom a fictional Job hurled abuse appears on the stage of history. John's
Jesus dies in explicit awareness that he has achieved the thing towards
which the story of the Bible has been making its way:

Jesus knowing that all things were now accomplished, that the scriptures
might be fulfilled, saith, 'I thirst'. (19.28).

The comic *hero* rebounds from that inferno, carrying with him the Judaism
with which he has completely identified, and thus all humanity. Christ has
experientially realised the three realms:

Jesus becomes the true possessor, through his own experience, of what 'Hell'
... it is from this point that we see the emergence of concepts of Hell,
purgatory and Heaven, which for the first time are theologically meaningful.[195]

Death and Paradise are encompassed by his person.
Nicodemus enters the scene with a ton of burial stuffs: 'And there came
also Nicodemus, which at the first came to Jesus by night, and brought a
mixture of myrrh and aloes, about an hundred pound weight' (John 19.39):
'John's Gospel makes it clear that Jesus' body did not suffer *niwwul*, i.e.
disgrace debarring from Jewish burial.'[196] Nicodemus' effort does not

194 Berger, *Redeeming Laughter*, p. 189.
195 Von Balthasar, *Glory VII*, p. 233.
196 Braine, 'Inner Jewishness', 110.

inspire the exegetes' approbation: he 'shows himself capable only of bury-ing Jesus ponderously, and with a kind of absurd finality'.[197] The heavier the better, so far as comedy, which never looks down on carnality, is concerned: let's see him explode out of that dead weight.

The rules of the comedy are not broken by the Resurrection. Mary Magdalene goes to the garden, finds the sepulchre empty: the disciples come and look; the 'disciple Jesus loved' seeing the graveclothes on the floor 'believed', and leaves. But Mary knows there is something more to be had than this bodiless believing. *He* is where his body is. Where have they taken the beloved body?

> she turned herself back, and saw Jesus standing, and knew not that it was Jesus.
> Jesus saith unto her, 'Woman, why weepest thou? whom seekest thou?' She, supposing him to be the gardener, saith unto him, 'Sir, if thou have borne him hence, tell me where thou hast laid him, and I will take him away.' (20.14–15)

The gardener disguise is transparent; perhaps it has seen better days since he last wore it in Genesis:

> Jesus saith unto her, 'Mary'. She turned herself, and saith unto him, 'Rabboni'; which is to say, 'Master'.
> Jesus saith unto her, 'Touch me not; for I am not yet ascended to my Father: but go to my brethren, and say unto them, I ascend unto my Father, and your Father; and to my God, and your God.' (21.16–17)

The sacred space of paradise is now a human presence.

Should a paradisial comedy end with a perfect feast in heaven? Many of the images of incarnation in John's Gospel are about descent and re-ascent, which would give us the narrative circle of Greek drama (1.51; 3.13–15). The idea is that the human desire for perfected communal life requires a cumulative and inclusive circular movement. Segovia comments that 'Jesus has survived death and can now return to the world of God, thus bringing the cosmic journey to a proper closure'. But the return is not 'directly portrayed'. One gathers it from the 'future reference' of the 'narrator or Jesus himself'. There is no 'formal closure' on the 'cosmic journey of the Word'.[198] In the last scene, Jesus comes to meet the disciples where they are fishing, by the sea of Tiberias. He asks them about a matter which has worried them throughout: 'Children, have you no meat? They answered him, No' (21.5). Once having followed his instruction to fish on the other side, and netted their breakfast, the disciples 'come to land' and find that Jesus has made a fire and is toasting some bread:

> Jesus saith unto them, 'Come and dine'. And none of the disciples durst ask him, 'Who art thou?' knowing that it was the Lord.
> Jesus then cometh, and taketh bread, and giveth them, and fish likewise. (21.12–13)

The upside down apocalypse ends with a meal by the seaside, on earth, in the domestic proximity of the Lord. We do not arrive in the City of heaven,

197 Rensberger, *Overcoming the World*, p. 40.
198 Fernando Segovia, 'Journey(s) of the Word of God', pp. 45–46.

but in the most human image of communion. As the great drama concludes, the circle is still spiralling. Paradise on earth is a fish breakfast,
with God.

Robinson helps to sum up what I have said about the Gospels of Mark
and John:

> In the Synoptists the teaching is contained in separate poetic oracles, parables
> and apophthegms, in John in connected argument and dialogue. The
> difference is partly due to the ... techniques of the evangelists, Mark's being
> more that of the cinema with its rapid flashing scenes, John's that of the
> theatre with its slowly building drama in carefully staged acts ... both the
> isolated pericope and the set piece are ... the work of the church, the former
> being no less than the latter shaped ... by the evangelistic ... and liturgical
> uses of the Christian community.[199]

If John used the dialogue with the Samaritan woman for its comic and
dramatic potential, it scarcely follows that he invented the conversation.
Some of his materials may be as biographical or factual as the Synoptics.
Like them, he makes apocalyptic history take on the imaginative form of a
drama. But where they make Jesus reveal and conceal a divine intent
behind *words*, John makes the Word conceal himself within flesh. The
narrator of this Gospel has the perspective of a producer who has thought
about how to stage the journey from heaven to earth of a hero who cloaks
his divine nature.

The notion of Incarnation as divine deception may worry us. For those
of us of an older generation, the idea came up in the context of patristic
images of atonement as a '*deceit* of the devil', and was quickly dismissed,
on that ground. Origen is said to be the first to pose the amoral suggestion,

> The Evil one had been deceived and led to suppose that he was capable of
> masting the soul and did not see that to hold Him involved a trial of strength
> greater than he could successfully undertake. Therefore Death, though he
> thought that he had prevailed against Him, no longer prevails against Him.
> Christ, then, having become free among the dead ... and so much stronger
> than Death, so that all who will among those who are mastered by death may
> follow Him.[200]

Grensted comments, 'That such an action is unworthy of God does not
seem to occur to Origen',[201] who did not have the advantage of an English
public school education. Gregory of Nyssa embroiders the same image:
'The Deity was hidden under the veil of our nature, that, as is done by
greedy fish, the hook of the Deity might be gulped down along with the
bait of the flesh, and thus life being introduced into the house of death and
light shining in the darkness, that which is contradictory to light and life
might vanish away': but at least Gregory was 'aware of the moral problems
involved'.[202] Later writers recalled that Jahweh had played a similar trick

199 Robinson, *Priority of John*, p. 304.
200 Origen, *Commentary on Matthew*, xvi.8, quoted in H. E. W. Turner, *The Patristic
    Doctrine of Redemption* (A. R. Mowbray, London, 1952), p. 55.
201 L. W. Grensted, *A Short History of the Doctrine of the Atonement* (Manchester
    University Press, Manchester, 1920, 1962), p. 37.
202 Turner, *Patristic Doctrine*, p. 57, citing Pope Gregory the Great's, *Great Catechetical
    Oration*.

on a mighty fish: 'Canst thou draw out Leviathan with a hook?' (Job 41.1).[203] The idea of divinity so well disguised that it can be swallowed by a fish may strike less stringent moralists as funny. Origen's notion, which so infiltrated the patristic mind, is said to have been drawn from Gnostic mythology:[204] its source may equally well have been meditation upon John's Gospel, which makes some play with the drama of Job. Another word for our divine disguise is Barth's 'veiling and unveiling'. John's resurrected Christ invites Thomas to *experience* his divinity: 'Reach hither thy finger, and behold my hands; and reach hither thy hand, and thrust it into my side and be not faithless but believing' (John 20.27). Barth emphasises that the experience is defined by its object: 'the biblical witnesses', such as John, 'point beyond themselves ... what makes a man a witness is ... that other, the thing attested'.[205] There is, nonetheless, a human acknowledgement: 'this actual occurrence, this being ascertained and acknowledged, is the historicity of revelation ... in the Bible revelation is a matter of impartation, of God's being revealed, by which the existence of specific men in specific situations has been singled out in the sense that their experiences and concepts, even though they cannot grasp God ... in the dialectic of veiling and unveiling, can at least follow Him and respond to Him'.[206] If, and only if, we see the *difference* between God and earthly 'Adam', then the tension of their congruity in Christ is an action, a drama. If it is 'of the essence of comedy to kaleidoscope extremes, to jam together opposites so that they are simultaneously true',[207] then God's wriggling into the human form, in order to perform the *analogia entis*, is divine comedy.

5. Typology and Tradition

Cornford notes that tragedies subordinate character to mythic action, whereas in comedies,

> The characters can take the primary place and shape the incidents as they please. Human nature is so complex ... that, wherever writers are not bound by the demands of a given plot, they always tend either to group people in certain classes of stock types, or to copy individual characters from the life and let them bring about the action as they will. Aristophanes inherited ... a small group of stock characters or masks, and there were no exigencies of plot to force him to abandon them.[208]

The characters wear 'stock masks': the best comedians can pour into those moulds a 'personality' which 'remains what Aristotle calls universal'.[209] Henri Bergson argues that, whereas no *tragedy* is named after a universal vice or virtue, many comedies are:[210] moreover, 'Every comic character is a

203 Grensted, *Short History of the Doctrine of the Atonement*, p. 43.
204 Ibid., pp. 34–35.
205 Karl Barth, *Church Dogmatics I/1 The Doctrine of the Word of God*, translated by G. W. Bromiley (T&T Clark, Edinburgh, 1st edn, 1936, 2nd edn, 1975), pp. 111–112.
206 Ibid., p. 330.
207 Jacobson, *Seriously Funny*, p. 240.
208 Cornford, *Origin of Attic Comedy*, p. 175.
209 Ibid., p. 177.
210 Bergson, *Le Rire*, pp. 15–16, 162–168.

type'[211] because 'what is most comic of all is to become a category oneself into which others will fall, as into a ready-made frame; it is to crystallise into a stock-character'.[212] This is what the Gospel writers sensed, when they made *Christ* the dramatic comedy of their narratives. His figure will become the stock-character of the Christian liturgy: he is capacious enough to feed the characters of Abel, Isaac, David, the Suffering Servant and Jonah. Those critics who have sensed in the summative and thus typological character of the New Testament a *thinning down* of the concrete realism of the Old Testament have not taken account of the abundance of the stock-heroes of comedy, their ability to include similarity and difference, and thus to enclose without engulfing a near infinite number of individuals. I have hinted, by reference to the quite literary and non-theological category of the comic figure of grace, that a holistic reading of the Scriptures can gain a toe-hold in typology. Such literary categories suggest themselves most properly in the performance, and I have little doubt that fresh dramatisations of the Scriptures would yield many others, and more ingenious and interesting ones. When the RSC try their hand at the Bible, we will see for ourselves; anyone can have a go at it.

---

211 Ibid., p. 152.
212 Ibid.

6

The Unoriginality of the Thesis

If Jews and Christians had been poring over the Bible for two thousand years and had found no comedy there, common sense should incline us to this *consensus fidelis*. If I have *invented* the idea that the Bible is a dramatic comedy, the hypothesis is extraordinarily *improbable*. A modest sketch of the history of the dramatisation of the Bible will show the experiment has been successfully performed before. Theologians, exegetes and preachers transpose the Scripture into schemas which do not require the assent of faith. Stage directing the Scriptures is close to the art of preaching, and is likewise a *cultural* transposition of the Gospel. The Bible has been performed as tragedy and as comedy. I shall be hard and fast about the dramatic quality of Scripture, but will resist the temptation to contend that Bach's *St Matthew's Passion* or Milton's *Samson Agonistes* have missed the comic potential of their material. My aim is to show that the conception of the Bible as dramatic comedy is neither novel nor idiosyncratic, not to demonstrate that *tragic* interpretations distort the text.

St Paul interpreted Christian baptism through, with and over against the Hebrew Scriptures. He was creating the tradition by which Scripture was interpreted as a unitary whole. He held the threads of Old and New Covenant together typologically. The compilation of the Christian Bible was the work of the church over time, that is, of tradition. Patristic theologians channelled the biblical narratives into the liturgy by finding in them a few crucial landmarks, which their congregations would sacramentally encounter. One reason why we have to speak of a *tradition* is that the liturgical foregrounding of certain episodes marked out *one* story as 'the' narrative.

Do we wish to demonstrate that those who are repeatedly subjected to the Catholic liturgy and lectionary are prone to laugh not only at the clergy but also at the Scriptures? The contents of Christian *tradition* are revealed to the eye of faith. Revealed tradition has influenced the performances of Scripture. But the history of Christian *cultures*, of which the story of the dramatisation of the Scriptures is a sub-section, is not the unfolding of revealed tradition. We cannot always be *certain* whether our culture is obfuscating the Gospel or enlightening it. The brief history of the comic performances of the Scriptures does not demonstrate that the Bible *must* be thus interpreted; it yields only the *probability* that there is something in the idea. Von Balthasar comments that

The theme of the fool, which receives its first metaphysical treatment in the poetry of Wolfram, is not really a tragic theme … It is no accident that, in Christian literature, comedy on the whole outweighs tragedy. In Shakespeare, the two are finely balanced, but in the English novel, right up to Chesterton, it is humour which increasingly has the upper hand. Molière has more penetration than Racine. In Austria, with Mozart, Raimund, Nestroy, Hofmannsthal, Christian light triumphs over the bogus gravity of Germany.[1]

Does the history of its performances tell us more about the Bible or about the cultures which put them on? It would not be disagreeable to argue that there is one type of culture which has been most open to the expression of biblical comedy. The vista of Feasts of Fools, Carnivals, pre-Lenten Mardi Gras, and other bacchanal epiphenomena of Mediterranean cultures, capable of live export to South America, but not to these wet and Protestant Islands is hardly displeasing, and could grow into the thesis that belly laughs went the way of *communitas* at the Enlightenment. I shall bid *vade retro* to this vision. Since we are looking for a probable, and not a certain, judgement, the hypothesis that comedy is intrinsic to the Book holds more water if a variety of cultures has agreed on the point. Discovering comedy in the Bible is not a matter of being a merrie Englander, or a merry Mexican. What tradition put together in the Bible did not altogether lose its potency when Catholic, Orthodox and Protestant cultures went their ways.

The imagination of the Roman world was not baptised in comedy overnight. The less poetical Church Fathers lengthened the step, by repeatedly condemning drama. Von Balthasar notes that it 'may seem unfortunate that it is the rigorist Tertullian who begins the series of anti-theatrical Church documents with his *Concerning Plays* (*c.* 197)'. The theologian who asked, 'What has Athens to do with Jerusalem?' 'repeats the stoic objections' to drama, that it stimulates 'the passions'.[2] Even those such as Clement of Alexandria and Augustine, who use theological metaphors in their theology,[3] are rigorists with respect to the real stage. The condemnations were thumped out after Charlemagne had reclaimed some of the remnants of the Roman Empire as Christendom: 'The Church assemblies of Mainz, Tours, Rheims, Chalon-sur-Saone (813) forbade bishops and other clerics to attend all plays whatsoever, under pain of suspension; Charlemagne ratified the decree in the same year.'[4] If the green room and the footlights were off-limits to the clergy, the altar was out of bounds to

---

1 Von Balthasar, *Glory V*, pp. 152–153.
2 Von Balthasar, *Theo-Drama I*, pp. 93–94.
3 'Paul (I Cor 49.9) says of the Apostles that God appointed them to death as a spectacle (θεατρον) for the world, angels and men. Here the idea in mind is not the stage but the Roman circus. We find a related concept in Clement of Alexandria: "For from Zion will go forth the law and the word of the Lord of Jerusalem, the divine word, the true fighter for the prize, who gains the crown of victory on the theater of the whole world" … Here the cosmos is seen as a stage. In Augustine (Enarr. ad. ps., 127) we read: "Here on earth it is as if children should say to their parents: Come! think of departing hence; we too would play our comedy! For nought but a comedy of the race of man is all this life, which leads from temptation to temptation."' Curtius, *European Literature*, p. 138.
4 Von Balthasar, *Theo-Drama I*, p. 99.

actors: from the Synod of Elvira (305) until the twelfth century actors were forbidden to receive the sacraments.[5]

Anyone who has received the impression that mediaeval biblical exegesis is holistic should test this conviction against the page in Pope St Gregory the Great's *Morals on the Book of Job* at which they abandon hope of illumination. Gregory gave the imprimatur to the practice of finding three senses in Scripture: literal/historical, allegorical/Christological, and moral. He discovered these three senses in every *sentence* in his text. By detecting a disparate literal, allegorical and moral application for every single verse, and by not linking them into a continuous narrative, Gregory cuts the scenic wholeness of Job as thoroughly as the most dissective of modern biblical critics. Gregory analysed prefigurations in each individual *proposition* of the Old Testament. Little sense of the complete *gestalt* of salvation history emerges: the analogy of drama is far from Gregory's intention.

If we want to grasp the meaning of typology for the Patristic *homme moyen sensuel*, we had better turn from the hermitage to the liturgy. The liturgical practice of the early church reflects the recognition that 'we have to do with *one* divine discourse, here to the Fathers through the prophets, there to us through Christ'.[6] Christian typology is not a matter of the discovery of a foreordained design in God's eternity, which finds its lustreless reflection in an otherwise empty and secular history. It discerns the movement of meaning through history. The types are not primarily something we *know* but something that happens, an action, not a rationalisation. They display the fulfilment of horizontal time in historical scenes. Daniélou says that for the Patristic liturgiologists,

> the sacraments carry on in our midst the *mirabilia*, the great works of God in the Old Testament and the New: for example, the Flood, the Passion and Baptism show us the same divine action as carried out in three different eras of sacred history, and these three phases of God's action are all ordered to the Judgement at the end of time.[7]

The typologies draw the Christian into the drama. The theologians found, not only Old Testament prototype and Christic type, but also 'anti-types', the sacramental actions:[8] 'Cyril of Jerusalem shows us the descent into the baptismal pool is as it were a descent into the waters of death which are dwelling place of the dragon of the sea, as Christ went down into the Jordan to crush the power of the dragon who was hidden there.'[9] Thus articulated by the poetic imaginations of the Fathers, the vivid experience of liturgical typology became the means by which some parts of the biblical narrative were made to drive the whole. Mediaeval dramatists will make multiple-act plays of the biblical story. Scholars puzzle over the exact basis of selection. Episodes which are central in the liturgy are seldom absent from

---

5 Ibid., pp. 97–99.
6 Gerhard von Rad, 'Typological Interpretation of the Old Testament', in Claus Westermann (ed.), *Essays on Old Testament Hermeneutics* (John Knox Press, Richmond, Virginia, 2nd edition, 1964), pp. 17–39 (36).
7 Jean Daniélou, *The Bible and the Liturgy* (Servant Books, Michigan, 1979), p. 5.
8 Ibid., pp. 44–45.
9 Ibid., p. 41.

such plays. The sense of the contemporaneity of past history with the eternal Christ event, and with the existential or moral reference of the text to present behaviour, was communicated as much by the liturgy as by textual exegesis. By making the drama take place in the congregation's own time, the liturgical typologies gave the biblical story into the hands of Christian worshippers.

1. 'To Play in Paradise': The N–Town Cycle

André Malraux remarks that 'Christianity did not originate the dramatic scene; what it originated was the spectator's participation in it'.[10] Amalarius, Bishop of Metz (780–850), invented the 'allegorical' interpretation of the Mass which gave rise to the liturgical performance of 'playlets' by priest, deacons and people.[11] A moral, or contemporary, reference was also involved. In his *Liber Officialis*, Amalarius stage-directed the Mass, assigning roles to all of the participants in the Passion and Resurrection of Christ. He understands the Mass as a real repetition of the Passion, but *also* as an imaginative dramatisation of the Passion narrative. What happens on the altar is real; what the celebrants and the people are instructed to do around that reality is a play–pretend game. The congregation must 'be' the people of Jerusalem, welcoming Christ into their city. Children say that pieces of furniture 'are' boats and castles and moats. For Amalarius, an Episcopal bossy older sister, the altar above which the Host *is* raised 'is' the Cross; the priest and deacons gathered around it 'are' 'the disciples and holy women who remained with Christ during the Passion'.[12] Then the priest 'becomes' the Centurion, who plunges the spear into Christ's side: he says 'truly this was the Son of God' and raises the chalice. The priest wraps the chalice in a cloth which 'is' the grave-linen of Christ: the altar becomes the Tomb. Three sub-deacons approaching the altar 'are' the Three Marys. The priest, now an angel, pronounces: 'He is risen; He is not here.' Back to being a priest, he mixes the consecrated elements, the body and blood of Christ, and raises the ensemble for all to see: 'The commingling reunites body and blood' and thus 're-creates the miracle of the Resurrection'.[13]

The purpose of this Passion is atonement, conceived as descent into hell and victory over Satan.[14] The plot of the Mass centres on a conflict theme. This staged Mass reaches its high point, not at the Passion of Christ, but at the *Resurrection*, present in the elevation of the consecrated Host. The Eucharistic drama of death and Resurrection moves from disaster to happy conclusion. Hardison found a classical comedy in the Romanesque Easter liturgy. 'The Mass', he says,

---

10 André Malraux, *The Voices of Silence*, translated by Stuart Gilbert (Paladin, London, 1953, 1974), p. 224.
11 O. B. Hardison Jnr., *Christian Rite and Christian Drama in the Middle Ages* (Johns Hopkins Press, Baltimore, 1965), p. 37.
12 Hardison, *Christian Rite*, p. 66.
13 Ibid., p. 73.
14 F. W. Dillistone, *The Christian Understanding of Atonement* (SCM, London, 1968, 1984), pp. 98–100.

is comic in structure, having a descending action, a crisis, a reversal-recognition, and a joyful resolution. In terms of emotion this represents a movement from *tristia* to *gaudium*. In terms of allegory it is a presentation of the central events of Christian history: the Crucifixion, entombment and Resurrection. The Easter liturgy has the same structure, emotional pattern, and historical associations. Its descending action begins with Lent. The point of crisis is reached on Good Friday, and Holy Saturday and Easter Sunday are devoted to the entombment and Resurrection, respectively. The reversal-recognition occurs early on Easter morning and is followed by a week of ceremonial rejoicing known in the ninth century as *octavia in albis*, 'the octave of white robes' ... this *gaudium* is more than simple joy over a happy ending. Something fundamental has happened to the participants as well as to the protagonist. During the *octavia in albis* they share in the life of the Heavenly Jerusalem; their joy is that of saints dwelling with God. The transformation of the participants as a result of the peripeteia is essential to both Mass and the cyclical drama. It has implications for the ... subject of dramatic catharsis.[15]

A thespian *manqué*, like one or two other bishops, Amalarius appreciated the significance of timing. The bishop had the good fortune to set out his liturgical stage directions when the first Holy Roman Emperor had taken it upon himself to create liturgical uniformity within his territorial Christendom. The Mass was produced in accordance with the *Liber Officialis* both at Charlemagne's court and throughout the provinces. By focusing the congregation's attention upon a glorious hero, apparently defeated, but conquering at the conclusion, Amalarius had overlaid upon the Mass a child's pantomime, which the unlettered and Latinless laity could enter into and enjoy.

Following in Amalarius' path, various Benedictine monks decorated the margins of the Mass with this crucial episode, to be chanted by several deacons:

Quem quaeritis?	Who are you looking for?
Responderunt ei:	They reply
Jesus Nazarenum.	Jesus of Nazareth.
Quem quaeritis?	Who are you looking for?
Illi autem dixerunt:	They say to him:
Jesus Nazarenum.	Jesus of Nazareth

The tenth-century manuscript playlet of the women's visit to the Tomb ('Visitatio Sepulchro') comes from the Benedictine monastery of St Gall: the monastic libraries of Europe preserve more than four hundred such texts. The English 'Visitatio Sepulchro' is set out in the *Regularis Concordia*, including 'stage directions'. The *Regularis Concordia* was put together by Bishop Aethelwold of Winchester in 970: he intended that the play should be used to teach the laity the Easter story, and that it be put on in the same way in every Benedictine monastery.[16]

The little 'Visitatio Sepulchro' gave rise to more ambitious *Quem Quaeritis* plays. These became an autonomous, extra-liturgical addition to

15 Hardison, *Christian Rite*, p. 83.
16 A. M. Kinghorn, *Mediaeval Drama* (Evans Brothers, London, 1968), pp. 27–29.

the Easter ceremonies. On Maundy Thursday, the consecrated host is set aside in the 'place of repose'. The Benedictine church saw that it is dramatically out of place to consecrate the host on Good Friday, since Christ is dead and buried. But, 'if the Host is "buried" on Maundy Thursday, it must later be "revived". The idea of resurrection from the sepulchre is implicit in this revival'.[17] The *Quem Quaeritis* play makes a piece of theatre of the Easter Resurrection: three deacons, dressed as the Three Marys, search the altar space for the body of Christ; an angel/deacon tells them that he is risen: they 'recognise' the Resurrection of Christ by the absence of his body. This is the basic text:

> *Quem queritis in sepulchro, O Christicole?*
> [Whom seek you in the tomb, O followers of Christ?]
>
> *Ihesum Nazarenum crucifixum, o celicole.*
> [Jesus of Nazareth who was crucified, O heaven dwellers.]
>
> *Non est hic, surrexit sicut ipse dixit; ite nunciate quia surrexit.*
> [He is not here, he has arisen as he said; go announce that he has risen.]

Hardison comments that

> the Resurrection is both the *peripeteia* and the *anagnorisis* of the Christian mythos. It is the point at which the action of history 'veers around in the opposite direction', and it is the moment when humanity . . . first recognizes the full significance of the Incarnation. The *Quem quaeritis* dramatizes this moment.[18]

Once the margin is decorated at one point, one will be inclined to illuminate the whole. Plays of the ascension, prophets and nativity follow in the wake of the *Quem Quaeritis* drama. The stage business around the manger was invented by St Francis of Assisi, who 'made a live model of the *praesepe* at his altar in the forest with men and women impersonating the main figures and with a live ox and ass to complete the scene'.[19] The Franciscans looked to the *affective* import of the Bible. The mediaeval dramatisation of the Bible was originated by the Benedictines; later impulses came from the Franciscans and the laity. Dramatisation emerged from the monastic liturgy and lay piety of pre-Reformation Christianity, rather than from its theological front. Long after Anselm and the scholastics had set aside the conception of atonement as a duel with Satan, and with it the image of the Descent into Hell, the theology of the combat was kept alive in popular drama. It was for the purpose of this 'combat' that Christ had worn his 'disguise'. Von Balthasar says that the Easter plays,

> are uniquely illuminating; naively portraying Christ's descent into the underworld, they mediate the awareness of an all-transforming action. Thus they continue the work of a theology that was alive in patristic preaching and in the frescoes and icons of the Eastern church but which had been . . . stifled by the systematization of the scholastics . . . this play had been part of

---

17 Hardison, *Christian Rite*, p. 125.
18 Ibid., pp. 178–179.
19 Murray Roston, *Biblical Drama in England: From the Middle Ages to the Present Day* (Faber & Faber, London, 1968), p. 21.

the Church's liturgy ever since the tenth century; from the eleventh century on it gradually became independent and was ... the fruitful seed from which sprouted the other spiritual plays ... The consequence for theology of a genuinely dramatic grasp of the *descensus* are immeasurable.[20]

The first performance of a full-fledged liturgical 'opera' is the *Ludus Danielis*, the 'Play of Daniel', a musical drama, in Gregorian chant.[21] It was staged at the Benedictine monastery in Beauvais, in 1180.[22] The first complete 'play' of a biblical episode may have been *Le Mystère d'Adam*, written in 1150 in the French vernacular, and performed by trained actors outside the church doors.[23]

Did the lay vernacular performances evolve out of the Latin liturgical plays or are they two distinct species? Current opinion runs against von Balthasar's statement of the case. The narrative by which biblical drama begins inside the church, proceeds down the nave out to the 'porch', escapes the cloister, shedding the Latin along with the hood, and is triumphantly performed by the laity in the 'market-place' can 'no longer stand',[24] says Kolve. The liturgical plays had had their longest run on the Continent, but the extant secular plays produced on the European Continent add up to one or two.[25] Secular biblical drama flowered in England. Dozens of fragments and four complete cycles of English plays survive. On the one hand, then, as Miri Rubin argues, 'England had never developed a liturgical dramatic repertoire as vast as those of Northern Italy or Germany, and yet it had produced the elaborate Corpus Christi cycles'; and on the other, 'The Corpus Christ drama never "left" the church; it always retained a liturgical component, and more importantly, a strong didactic orientation'.[26]

Kolve notes the different terminology used for the sung, Latin, liturgical dramas and the vernacular Corpus Christi cycles. The former are described in terms which connote *theatrical* or *imitative* action. The *Concordia Regularis* uses words like *imitatione, similitudo, exemplum, miraculum* and *repraesentatio* in relation to the liturgical plays. The words for vernacular drama include: *processe, processyon, pageant, shewe* and *miracle: ludus* appears most often. The French called such a play a *jeu*, as in Jean Bodel's *Jeu de Saint Nicholas*; the Germans termed it a *spiel*, as in the *Fronleichnamspiele* of Southern Germany.[27] The secular plays are usually called *ludi*, games.

20 Von Balthasar, *Theo-Drama I*, pp. 113–114.
21 Kinghorn, *Mediaeval Drama*, p. 35.
22 It is available on CD: *Daniel: Opéra Sacré*, Ensemble Venance Fortunat, Harmonia Mundi (ED 13052), Eguilles, France.
23 Kinghorn, *Mediaeval Drama*, pp. 37–40; Claire Sponsler claims that *Le Jeu de Saint Nicholas*, composed in the last decade of the twelfth century, has priority: 'Festive Profit and Ideological Production: *Le Jeu de Saint Nicholas*', in Meg Twycross (ed.), *Festive Drama: Papers from the Sixth Colloquium of the International Society for the Study of Medieval Theatre* (D. S. Brewer, Cambridge, 1996), pp. 66–79 (67).
24 V. A. Kolve, *The Play Called Corpus Christi* (Edward Arnold, London, 1966), p. 50.
25 R. T. Davies (ed.), *The Corpus Christi Play of the English Middle Ages* (Faber & Faber, London, 1972), p. 26.
26 Miri Rubin, *Corpus Christi: The Eucharist in Late Medieval Culture* (Cambridge University Press, Cambridge, 1991), p. 274.
27 Kolve, *Play Called Corpus Christi*, pp. 11–12.

The only mediaeval theologian of weight to 'make allowances' for actors was St Thomas Aquinas.[28] He states that 'the acting profession ... is not unlawful in itself'. Nor are actors in a state of sin provided their 'art is temperate', and since actors have 'other serious and virtuous activities', such as prayer and almsgiving, 'those who support them in due season do not sin, but rather act justly by rewarding them for their service'; but one must not 'support ... indecent plays'.[29] St Thomas discusses *ludi* in relation to ethics, asking first, 'Whether there can be a moral value in outward bodily action'.[30] Having said 'yes' to that, he asks whether 'there can be a moral virtue engaged with play?' (*Utrum in ludis possit esse aliqua virtus*), whether 'superfluous play is wrong?' (*utrum in superfluitate ludi possit esse peccatum*), and 'is too little playing sinful?' (*utrum in defectu ludi consistat aliquod peccatum*). There can be such a moral virtue, Aquinas says, because the soul needs to rest in 'words and deeds in which nothing is sought beyond the soul's pleasure', and these can be 'playful or humorous' (*ludicra vel jocosa*) actions and speech. Because it is ruled by reason, 'there can be a moral virtue about playing'; Aristotle called it *Eutrapelia*.[31] Those who have no spirit of play (*illi autem qui in ludo deficiunt*), that is, 'those who never say anything to make you smile, or are grumpy with those who do' sin.[32] There are provisos: play must not be 'indecent', or unpoised, or unsuitable to the circumstances. Excessive play is sinful.[33] One can play morally, in a fertile spirit, and immorally, in a spirit of violence.

St Thomas scripted the celebration of Corpus Christi. The feast of devotion to the Eucharist which had begun in 1252, in Liège, was made obligatory for the whole church by Urban IV, in the Bull *Transiturus*, in 1264. The universality of the Feast was confirmed in England in 1311. Lay fraternities, with a stake in staging the Corpus Christi procession, emerged in England from the mid-fourteenth century. These fraternities engaged in the Easter 'playlets': 'The fraternity at Caistor (Lincolnshire), founded in 1376, provided illumination on the procession to the tomb' on Easter Friday, supplying the candles 'around the shrine into which the Eucharist, as Christ's crucified body, was being placed'.[34] The first sign that a *play* took place on Corpus Christi is in Robert Holcot's *Book of Wisdom* (c. 1335), in which, like Aquinas, 'Holcot distinguishes between three types of plays: vile plays, joyful devotional ones, and plays which comfort the soul. His example of the second type is "the devotional play" [*ludus devocionis*] and spiritual "gaudy" which Christians do on the day of Corpus Christi'.[35]

There are four extant English Corpus Christi 'cycles': Chester, dated to 1375, the 'Primitive' York plays of 1378, the 'Second' York, or Wakefield plays of the 1430s and the 'N-Town' Cycle, the *Ludus Coventriae*. What do we mean by calling these plays *cycles*? One view is that the liturgical cycle,

28 Von Balthasar, *Theo-Drama I*, pp. 99–100; Kinghorn, *Mediaeval Drama*, p. 37.
29 St Thomas Aquinas, *Summa Theologiae*, 2a2ae, Question 168, Article 3 Is Superfluous Play Wrong, Reply.
30 Ibid., 2a2ae, Question 168, Article 1.
31 Ibid., 2a2ae, Question 168, Article 2, Reply.
32 Ibid., 2a2ae, Question 168, Article 4, Reply.
33 Ibid., 2a2ae, Question 168, Article 3, Reply.
34 Rubin, *Corpus Christi*, p. 236.
35 Ibid., p. 273.

with its annual rehearsal of the biblical episodes, gave rise to the secular 'cycles' of the Corpus Christi plays.[36] That is, the Corpus Christi plays are 'cycles' because they tell the history of the world, from Creation to Doomsday: everything between Genesis and Apocalypse is 'filled partly by figuration, partly by imitation, of Christ'.[37] As a recent commentator concludes,

> all the surviving pageant-wagon cycles have a basic structure in common. The great story that composed the Corpus Christi play (the whole cycle was called a *play*, while the individual portions were *pageants* ...), a history of the universe from just before its Creation to its ending at the Day of Judgement, was parcelled up into episodes. Each episode was delegated to a separate group ... Each group had or shared a mobile stage also called a *pageant*, which when their turn came they pulled through the city along a traditional route, stopping at prearranged *stations* (the word means 'stopping places') to perform their episode.[38]

Kolve popularised the notion that the plays 'cycle' round the story of redemption: 'To English ears the "plaie called Corpus Christi" meant a play of the history of the world.'[39] Kolve relied on the typological principle: all of the episodes relate to the *single theme* of the 'three advents of God', in Creation, Incarnation and Judgement.[40] There is thus, he argued, an underlying 'protocycle', which necessarily informs the extant plays, including pageants of 'The Fall of Lucifer', 'The Creation and Fall of Man', 'Cain and Abel' (Abel prefigures Christ), 'Noah and the Flood' (the flood foreshadows Baptism), 'Abraham and Isaac' (the sacrifice of Isaac is a type of the Passion), 'Nativity', 'Raising of Lazarus', 'Passion' and 'Resurrection'. If one starts from the typological foregrounding of these scenes in the liturgy, this is a coherent group. Take away the liturgical link, and one may be hoist with one's own petard. Miri Rubin turns Kolve's logic against him:

> By historicising the play so brilliantly Kolve produces a model of Corpus Christi drama which fits three of the four elaborate cycles which we know from the English towns. But ... the dramatic enterprises which Corpus Christi inspired are increasingly being revealed as a far more heterogeneous and a less neatly classifiable lot. They were living events, bound by some aesthetic rules, but of a far less fixed meaning and form than has been appreciated.[41]

Some other offshoots of the Corpus Christi festival appear to place their audience within a cosmo-history which runs from Genesis to Revelation. Alexandra Johnstone has studied two productions of the York Corpus Christi Guild, the 'Creed Play' and the 'Pater Noster' play. Johnstone suggests that the 'Creed Play' was presented in twelve episodes, each

---

36 Kinghorn, *Mediaeval Drama*, p. 31.
37 Auerbach, *Mimesis*, p. 158.
38 Meg Twycross, 'The Theatricality of Medieval English Plays', in Richard Beadle (ed.), *The Cambridge Companion to Medieval English Theatre* (Cambridge University Press, Cambridge, 1994), pp. 37–84 (39).
39 Kolve, *Play Called Corpus Christi*, p. 48.
40 Ibid., p. 50.
41 Rubin, *Corpus Christi*, p. 272.

staged on its own pageant wagon. Each hypothetical 'pageant' represents one article in the creed. Thus staged, it looks like a Viewer's Digest of the Corpus Christi Cycle.[42] Most of the article/pageants can be aligned with one from the Corpus Christi cycle. The first pageant: 'I believe in God the Father Almighty maker of heaven and earth' is parallel to Creation I, and presents the same scene, of God enthroned. Likewise, in the Pater Noster play, which borrowed the pageant wagons used by the guilds for Corpus Christi, each petition of the Lord's Prayer could represent a scene from the 'protocycle' of the mediaeval dramatisation of salvation history.[43] It is possible that Rubin has overstated the case for the thematic heterogeneity of the English mediaeval dramatic impulse.

The pageant wagons enabled the players to move about on three tiers: God the Father, God the Son and the angels could ascend and descend from the top of the wagon to the 'first floor', and the Devil could make his entrances and exits in and out of the undercarriage. The players were assisted in these manoeuvres by various hauling devices:

> When the York Jesus is about to ascend into heaven he says, 'Sende doune a clowde, fadir', and a cloud comes down; He gets into it and is hoisted aloft out of sight. The action was not designed to resemble reality, but ... to translate it into a game mode, a play equivalent.[44]

Aristophanes' comedies employ similar devices, such as the beam which lifts Trygaeus into Olympus, in *Peace*, and drops Iris into Cloudcuckooland, in *Birds*. In Greek comedy, such devices did not disperse the illusion of theatre, but rather make the audience collude with the construction of the fantasy, by revealing its mechanics. An analogous aspect of the Corpus Christi plays is the speaker's direct address to the audience. A well-known example is the Marriage Guidance offered to the people of York in the Wakefield 'Noah and his Sons', apparently deriving not from the Bible but from folklore.[45] Noah's wife breaks off from abusing her husband to turn to the 'women in the audience':

Noah's Wife:	We women must harry	all ill husbands.
	If I have one – by Mary	that loosed me from my bands!
	. . .	
	But still, otherwise,	
	What with game and with guile,	
	I shall smite and smile,	
	And pay him back dear.[46]	

The quarrel continues after Mrs Noah has been persuaded to board the Ark:

42 Alexandra Johnston, 'The Plays of the Religious Guilds of York: The Creed Play and the Pater Noster Play', *Speculum*, 50, 1975, 55–90 (66–69). The Creed Play was performed in York in 1483, 1495, 1505 and 1535.

43 Ibid., 79.

44 Kolve, *Play Called Corpus Christi*, p. 26.

45 Howard H. Schless, 'The Comic Element in the Wakefield Noah', in MacEdward Leach (ed.), *Studies in Medieval Literature* (University of Pennsylvania Press, Pennsylvania, 1961), p. 233.

46 'Noah and His Sons', ll. 208–216, in John Russell Brown, *The Complete Plays of the Wakefield Master in a New Version for Reading and Performance* (Heinemann, London, 1983), pp. 26–46.

Noah (to the men in the audience):

	Ye men that have wives,	while they are young,
	If ye love your own lives,	chastise their tongue.

. . .

	But I,
	So may I have bliss,
	Shall chastise this.

Wife:	Yet may ye miss,
	Nichol Neddy!

Noah:	I shall make thee still as stone,	beginner of blunder!
	I shall beat thy back and bone,	and break all in sunder.
		They fight.[47]

Commenting on the 'heroic scale' of the Corpus Christi cycles, which took two or even three days to perform, Meg Twycross notes that 'We are looking here at an appetite for theatre that can stand comparison with the days of ancient Athens'.[48] I should say that the two had more in common than size, and I am not referring to the Cambridge School's idea of the origin of May-Pole Dancing. The use of direct address to the audience, burlesque and slapstick are first seen in Aristophanes' plays; they are all present in the mediaeval cycles. These routines turn the *illusion* of theatre into a game. The audience knows that Christ is not really ascending into heaven just as well as it knows that Noah and his wife are not really beating one another up. There are instructions for the use of stage props in the Chester 'Noah': '"Then Noy with all his familie shall make a signe as though they wrought ypon the shipe with diuers instrumentis." When the ark is ready to be filled, painted boards representing the birds and the beasts are brought on.'[49] More 'play-pretend' was required of mediaeval actors and audience than of their successors: Elizabethan dramatists restricted themselves to naturalistic actions which can be shown on stage, whereas the actors in the medieval *ludi* do 'miraculous' things, such as building an ark and sailing in it: 'In every cycle Noah builds the ark in front of the audience ... always he claims that it is taking him a hundred years, and the audience enjoys the speed with which the ark is actually readied.'[50] Athenian audiences witnessed a dozen birds constructing a Sky-City, and *of course* they did not believe that it was really happening; and, *of course*, they did, if they let themselves go and enjoyed the play. Neither in the comedy of Aristophanes nor in that of the English cycles does the audience's collusion in the pretence detract from the theatricality of the event. Both the *Birds* and the 'Noah' text incite disbelief in the possibility of the action: that makes watching it funnier and more 'miraculous'. The pleasure of the appearance of the supernatural in the midst of the natural world, which the Corpus Christi festival was instituted to commemorate, concerns the suspension of empirical laws, the inclusion of the impossible in the midst of the everyday. The 'ludic cycles' are game imitation miracles, *analogous* to the real miracle of the Eucharist.

47 Ibid., ll. 388–407.
48 Twycross, 'Theatricality of Medieval English Plays', p. 66.
49 Kolve, *Play Called Corpus Christi*, p. 24.
50 Ibid.

How could a reverent mediaeval player act the part of God, Father or Son? Kolve says, not *theatrically*: 'those who played God would not have sought ... to be God, nor to get inside His personality ... They presented not the character of God but certain of His actions'.[51] In the biblical narrative, the character of God *is*, and is defined by, his actions. The Gospel authors convey Christ's inner life by telling his outer life. Luke and Cleophas recognise the risen Christ by his *own* expressive gesture, breaking the bread (Luke 24.30). The English Cycles are *interpretations* of the Old and the New Testaments. If their attitude to the supernatural characters of the Bible is not psychological, that may indicate that they were careful readers, who had gained a great inwardness with their text. The 'pretence' of the mediaeval *ludi* differed from some modern conceptions of 'acting':

> In York, there were at least twenty-two actors playing Christ. This meant that there was less danger of identifying the role with any one star actor. In performance it creates an extremely strong sense of the role itself, detached from any one particular performer. This happens – not totally accidentally – to mesh very well with medieval views on the relationship between 'images' (pictures or statues) and the sacred persons and truths they represent. The actor, as image, does not become but represents the person he plays.[52]

Whereas Eastern Christianity developed a theology of the artefact as an Icon, or sacramental *container* of the holy, Western Christians attributed a moral or didactic value to religious art. Efficacious powers were assigned by Western Christians to relics, but not, in strict theology, to artefacts. The biblical text was taken to have three to four senses, the literal/historical, the allegorical, the analogical and the moral. The mediaeval dramatic interpretation of that text is an achievement of the moral, that is, the practical, imagination. The English mediaeval 'actor as image' is a didactic picture, not a sacramental icon. The authors' aptitude for imagining the biblical narrative as if it were happening in Mediaeval England is expressed by the Wakefield 'Second Shepherd's Play'. Do not, then, sacramentally *become* a shepherd, but imagine doing as the Shepherds did, and giving the 'little tiny Mop' of a Christ child a bob of cherries, a bird and a tennis ball.[53] Drama, like ethics, is connected with *doing*; the Greek is *dromenon*; the underlying thought is *praxis*. If the theme of the mediaeval *ludi* is moral, they still imagine analogically: the analogy which is sought is the moral-historical, which finds kinships between past and present actions. The *imitatio* of the actions of the 'good' role models of the biblical stories is the ethical message of the medieval cyclical *dramas*. The senses of Scripture were sometimes computed as three (literal, allegorical, moral), as by Gregory the Great; later a fourth, the analogical, is 'added'. The triplet of literal-allegorical-moral presupposes and requires the analogical sense: without it, one is left with discrete ideas rather than typological *Gestalten*. Biblical theatre is in search of an analogy of the good, as between God and human beings, and between the moral decisions and actions described in the ancient text and its presentday application.

51 Ibid.
52 Twycross, 'Theatricality of Medieval English Plays', pp. 42–43.
53 'The Second Shepherds' Play', ll. 710–736, in Brown, *Complete Plays of the Wakefield Master*, pp. 68–97.

In the first vernacular play, the 'Anglo-Norman' *Mystère d'Adam*,

> Adam talks and acts in a manner any member of the audience is accustomed
> to from his own ... house; things would go exactly the same way in any
> townsman's home or on any farm where an upright but not very brilliant
> husband has been tempted ... by his vain and ambitious wife who has been
> deceived by an unscrupulous swindler.[54]

There was no greater gift to the comedian in the author of the Wakefield
Cycle than his duty to show the contemporary moral relevance of a story
which even Mediaeval Man knew took place a thousand and more years
ago. *Anachronism* is a feature of comedy because it juxtaposes two
startlingly different worlds, and thereby exposes their kinship. To represent Abel's sacrifice of a lamb and Cain's sacrifice of corn as willing and
grudging attitudes to the laws of tithing, and to make Cain request to be
buried 'in Goodbower at the quarry's head'[55] is the mark of an author who
is a comedian because he is a moralist, directing his audience at the
contemporary implication of his story. When the Wakefield Master set
out as a prologue to the Nativity of the Son of God the boozy Shepherds'
loss of a sheep to Mak, the thief, his wife's swaddling of the long-snouted
animal, its concealment in a crib, and the Shepherds' drawn-out exposure
of the substitution, he made a little free with the Birth Narratives. But this
'carefully contrived visual pun' on their next move, which is to go to the
'real' stable and manger, to worship 'the new-born Lamb'[56] is an interpretative commentary on the story which is thoroughly *Johannine* in spirit.
Behold the stolen sheep, as it were.

No one knows where the 'N-Town' Cycle was first performed. The
banns proclaim:

> A Sunday next yf that we may
> At vi of the belle we gin oure play
> In N-town.

The N-Town Play was once assigned to Coventry and is still sometimes
called the *Ludus Coventriae*. 'N-Town' has three main themes: the deflation
of the proud, wisdom and play.

Pricking the bubble of the villain is a staple of comedy:

Lucifer:	A worthier lord, forsooth, am I,
	And worthier than he ever will be.
	In evidence that I am more worthy
	I will go sitten in Godes see.
	Above sun and moon and starres on sky
	I am now set as you may see.
	Now worship me for most mighty,
	And for your lord honour now me,
	Sitting in my seat.

God expels the seat-grabber. Exile does not puncture the adversary's pride:
the angel turned devil goes out saying: 'For fear of fire a fart I crack.'[57] The

---

54 Auerbach, *Mimesis*, p. 151.
55 'The Killing of Abel', l. 367, in Brown, *Complete Plays of the Wakefield Master*, pp. 8–25.
56 Harris, *Theatre and Incarnation*, p. 82.
57 'Creation and Fall', in Davies, *Corpus Christi Play*, pp. 73–86 (76).

pageant of 'Creation and Fall' expands on non-canonical inter-testamental apocalyptic, and on the canonical Isaiah 27.1 and Revelation 12 rather than on Genesis. The author makes the theme of the deserts of pride run through the cycle.

The theme of wisdom is focused on the 'tree of cunning' which God orders Adam and Eve not to 'touch': the serpent, likewise, tempts Eve to become 'Wise of cunning' by biting the apple.[58] God's plan for human history appears to have been overthrown:

> *Deus:*   Unwise woman, say me why
>   That thou hast done this foul folly?
>   And I made thee a great lady
>   In paradise for to play.

In the next pageant, Cain interprets his punishment for manslaughter thus:

>   In field and town, in street and stage,
>   I may never make mirthes mo.[59]

In the N-Town Ludus, Noah and his wife enjoy no marital battles; Noah's wife, and those of Shem, Ham and Japeth are models of simpering obedience. Once the octet have finished their 'God forbids' that we do any impiety, one may wonder whether the author of 'N' had less sense of humour than the Wakefield Master. Lamech walks on, boasting about what a fine archer he is. His boy directs him to fire into the bushes, where he bags a villain:

> *Lamech:*   Now have at that bush, yon beast for to spill!
>   A sharp shot I shot, thereof I shall not fail.
> *Cain:*   Out! out! and alas! My heart is asunder!
>   With a broad arrow I am dead and slain.
>   I die here on ground. My heart is all to tunder:
>   With this broad arrow it is cloven in twain.

In some earlier versions, Isaac protests vigorously all the way to the sacrifical altar: 'Kill me, father? Alas! what have I done?'; what if my mother saw you pulling a sword on an innocent child, he asks in the Brome and the Chester Plays.[60] The N-Town Ludus extracts no comedy from an unwilling Isaac. The boy is passive and obedient to a fault.

Just as the biblical writers pinched and pulled the mess of history into a theological schema, so the N-Town Cycle highlights the moral of the biblical ensemble, by commentaries in the form of dramatic scenes. The Cycle dramas do not tell the whole biblical history: they are encapsulative. 'Moses' telescopes the Exodus narrative into one episode: God's revelation of his name at the burning bush is summed up in his giving of the ten commandments, which Moses expounds to the audience.

---

58 Ibid., pp. 77–79.
59 'Cain and Abel', in Davies, *Corpus Christi Play*, pp. 86–92 (92). The older, Dominican translation of Aquinas' *Summa Theologica* translates *ludus* as 'mirth'.
60 'Brome', in Davies, *Corpus Christi Play*, pp. 377–391 (382); David Mills (ed.), *The Chester Mystery Cycle: A New Edition with Modernised Spelling* (Colleagues Press, East Lansing, 1992), p. 76.

In the 'Parliament and Annunciation' pageant the Virtues conduct an intellectual tournament. Mercy pleads the case for God's compassion while Justice and Truth contend that it is irrational to rescue an Adam who has been condemned to eternal death. The Son offers the Anselmian argument: to make good the claims of Mercy, a man must die; to satisfy Truth and Justice, he must be sinless; 'hell may hold him by no law'.[61] Since the Virtues are agreed that no man is sinless, the Persons of the Trinity hold a council to decide which will become Incarnate man. God the Father tells the Son that he must take the role, because man was created in the image of the Wisdom of God.

The late-mediaeval tract *Dives and Pauper* finds a scriptural basis for 'mirth' in David's dancing before the Ark, in 2 Samuel 6.[62] Had the author of 'N-Town' also considered the theological justification of *ludi*? Father, Son and Spirit, represented by three lights, descend upon Mary, and she immediately 'feel[s]' in her 'body' 'Perfect God and perfect man'. Gabriel takes his leave saying 'Farewell, Godes sister, and his playing-frere [playmate]'.[63] Mary, Virgin mother of an already formed Christ, is carrying Eden within her.

Roston argues that the Old Testament heroes are less saintly than those of the New, and thus that their pageant counterparts are more 'amenable to dramatic realism', and to humorous characterisation.[64] The greater the proximity to the 'circle of sanctity' around Christ and his Mother, the less *naturalistic* the presentation: the Hebraic scenes are replete with gargoyles whereas the New Testament pageants 'were presented like beautiful frescoes'.[65] Roston contrasts the exaggeration of Cain's rudeness with the diminution of the comic potential of Joseph's plight.[66] No funny business can happen near Christ.[67] Roston believes that comedy and bawdy are walled off into the Old Testament because the mediaeval authors set the New Testament figures on an other-worldly pedestal. It could be that the *text* of the Old Testament contains a larger measure of funny ha-ha than the text of the New, which is one reason for not being a Marcionite.

The 'Mother of Mercy: Joseph' pageant initiates a division in the *ludus* theme: there are good games and bad games. Joseph attributes the latter to his betrothed. Returning home from abroad, Joseph immediately notices her condition and comments pointedly upon it:

---

61 'Parliament and Annunciation', in Davies, *Corpus Christi Play*, pp. 123–134 (128).
62 *'Dives et Pauper'* (c. 1405–1410) gives this scriptural proof in defence of miracle plays and dancing: 'But michol saules doughter and Dauydes wyf scornyd dauyd for his daunsynge and for his skyppynge/& sand. that it was nat semely to a king to skippe & daunce as a kanaue. before the people and bifore her maydens. Dauyd saide to her/I shal pley and daunce bifore my lorde god þat hath chosen me to be a kinge. & put thy fader & al thy kyn from þe crowne I shall pley bifore my lorde god/... and for þat mychol sconyd so dauyd for his skippynge & his daunsynge and his lownesse/therefore god made her bareyne.' Cited in Kolve, *Play Called Corpus Christi*, pp. 131–132.
63 'Parliament and Annunciation', in Davies, *Corpus Christi Play*, pp. 132–133.
64 Roston, *Biblical Drama in England*, p. 30; see also Kolve, *Play Called Corpus Christi*, pp. 138–139.
65 Roston, *Biblical Drama*, p. 33.
66 Ibid., pp. 31–32.
67 Ibid., p. 26.

Joseph:	Thy womb too high does stand.
	I dread me sore I am betrayed,
	Some other man thee had in hand.
	. . .
	Say me, Mary, this childes father who is.
	I pray thee, tell me, and that anon.
Maria:	The Father of heaven and you it is –
	Other father has he none.
	. . .
Joseph:	Godes child! Thou liest in fay [upon my word]!
	God did never jape so with may
	[God never played such games with maidens]
	. . .
	But yet, I say, Mary, whose child is this?
Maria:	Godes, and you, I say, iwis [for sure].

Joseph's rejoinder, unmuffled by the requirement of good taste, is addressed to the audience:

Joseph:	Yea! yea! all old men to me take tent [pay heed].
	And weddeth no wife in no kindes wise [any manner whatsoever]
	That is a young wench, by my assent,
	For doubt, and dread, and such service, [fear, treatment]
	Alas! alas! my name is shent.
	All men may me now despise,
	And say, 'Old cuckold, thy bow is bent
	Newly now, after the French guise',

Mary tells him that she has conceived the child during the visit of an Angel:

Joseph:	An angel! Alas! alas! fie! for shame.
	. . .
	It was some boy began this game
	That clothed was clean and gay
	. . .
	Here may all men this proverb trow,
	That many a man does beat the bough –
	Another man has the bird.[68]

The couple take part in a crude test of their chastity: the probably unbiblical 'Trial of Joseph and Mary'. The Summoner calls the audience to an 'ecclesiastical court' hearing.[69] The Detractors introduce themselves as gossip-mongering termagants:

Secundus Detractor:	I am Back-Biter that spilleth all game,
	. . .
	Hark! Raise-Slander, canst thou ought tell
	Of any new thing that wrought was late?[70]

68 'Mother of Mercy: Joseph', in Davies, *Corpus Christi Play*, pp. 135–137.
69 'Trial of Joseph and Mary', in Davies, *Corpus Christi Play*, pp. 147–160.
70 Ibid., p. 149.

The pleasure-destroying detractors exchange their information about the unmarried couple:

> *Primus Detractor:*   Some fresh young gallant she loveth well more
> That his legges to her has laid,
> And that does grieve the old man sore![71]

Bishop Abiyachar proposes the test: Joseph must drink a magical potion from the 'bottle of God's vengeance', and circumambulate the altar seven times; guilt will be expressed in prompt facial disfigurement.[72] As the old man picks his way around the altar, the detractors tell him he walked fast enough when he danced with the damsel. His perambulations prove him chaste. Is he a cuckold? Mary circumambulates with the sex education advice of the Detractors in her ears:

> *Primus Detractor*   In faith, I suppose that this woman slept
> Withouten all covert while that it did snow,
> And a flake thereof into her mouth crept,
> And thereof the child in her womb does grow.[73]

At her clean-faced finish, the first Detractor insinuates that the Bishop, her cousin, must have spiked the drink. The Bishop instructs him to test its efficacy with a swig: '*Hic bibet et sentiens dolorem in capite cadit* – here he drinks & feeling ill falls on his head.'[74] The purpose of the Pageant is to make the saintly pair miraculous winners in a competitive game. It was a tradition of the mediaeval *Lives* to make a comedy of the saints' miraculous powers over their enemies; sometimes 'the comedy is on the other side – in refractory mockers, who are then drastically punished'.[75]

Joseph is not ungrouchy, for a canonised saint; his miraculously pregnant wife has the food whims of any woman in her condition. As they travel to Bethlehem for the birth, his Lady spies some tasty cherries at the top of a tree. Her hapless husband heaves himself up, grumbling, 'let him pluck you cherries begat you with child!'[76]

Hans Urs von Balthasar has issued a reproof to the creativity of some traditional biblical commentary: for example, that which claims that the Virgin gave birth without labour-pains.[77] The tradition derives from the apocryphal Protoevangelium of James. N-Town makes use of it. Its Mary is no less of a Gothic smiler than the stone angel at Reims. Joseph returns from a search for midwives to find his wife *Subridendo* – smiling:

> *Maria*:   The child that is born will prove his mother free [gracious]
> A very clean maid, and therefore I smile.
>
> *Joseph*:   Why do you laugh, wife, you are to blame!
> I pray you spouse, do no more so.

71 Ibid., p. 150.
72 Ibid., p. 155.
73 Ibid., p. 157.
74 Ibid., p. 159.
75 Curtius, *European Literature*, p. 428.
76 'Birth of the Son', in Davies, *Corpus Christi Play*, p. 160–170 (161–162).
77 Von Balthasar, *Theo–Drama. Theological Dramatic Theory II. The Dramatis Personae: Man in God*. Translated by Graham Harrison (Ignatius Press, San Francisco, 1990), p. 125.

Joseph begs his wife to act seriously lest the midwives he has summoned to an emergency birth depart in a huff. But she cannot restrain herself:

> *Maria:*　　　　Husband, I pray you, displease you not,
> 　　　　　　　Though that I laugh and great joy have.
> 　　　　　　　Here is the child this world has wrought, [who]
> 　　　　　　　Born now of me, that all thing shall save.

The concluding scene of the Birth Pageant is equally a *commentary* on the biblical narrative: the midwives, Zelomy and Salome, feel inside the woman, to prove that she is still a Virgin. The N-Town plays do permit buffoonery into the sacred circle of Mary and Joseph. The theme of 'Wisdom' is carried by the Son; that of playing in Paradise is represented by Mary. All the games are not good: like Aquinas, the N-Town author clearly distinguishes good and bad *ludi*.

The 'Herod' episodes obey the simple mechanics of the 'bad game' and braggart themes. The hyperbolic villain presents himself:

> *Herod:*　　　　As a lord in royalty, in no region so rich,
> 　　　　　　　And ruler of all realmes, I ride in royal array.
> 　　　　　　　. . .
> 　　　　　　　I ding with my doughtiness the devil down to hell,
> 　　　　　　　For both of heaven and of earth I am king certain.[78]

Herod splutters his alliterative order to slaughter the innocents.[79] The Roman soldiers speak in short rhyming half-lines, like a child's stomping and chanting game:

> *Secundus miles:*　　For swordes sharp
> 　　　　　　　As an harp
> 　　　　　　　Queenes shall carp.　[talk]
> 　　　　　　　And of sorrow sing.
> 　　　　　　　Bairnes young,
> 　　　　　　　They shall be stung:
> 　　　　　　　Through liver and lung
> 　　　　　　　We shall them sting.[80]

On the soldiers' return with assignment accomplished, Herod's boasting is loud enough to be heard by Death, who joins in the king-and-soldiers-game:

> *Mors:*　　　　Ow! I heard a page make praising of pride!
> 　　　　　　　[churl, servant]
> 　　　　　　　. . .
> 　　　　　　　I am Death, Godes messenger.
> 　　　　　　　. . .
> 　　　　　　　What man that I wrestle with he shall right soon have
> 　　　　　　　shame –
> 　　　　　　　I give him such a tripett he shall evermore lie soon.
> 　　　　　　　[I so trip him up]

---

78 'Herod and the Three Kings', in Davies, *Corpus Christi Play*, pp. 176–186 (176).
79 'Slaughter of the Innocents', in Davies, *Corpus Christi Play*, pp. 193–201 (193).
80 Ibid., p. 195.

For Death can no sport!   [knows]
. . .
Both him and his knightes all,
I shall them make to be but thrall,
With my spear slay them I shall,
And so cast down his pride.[81]

As the soldiers boast of the 'boys sprawled' on their 'speares end', Death enters to kill Herod and his two soldiers, and to hand them over to the Devil as suitable playmates. The Devil promises to 'teach' the trio 'plays fine',

Diabolus: And show you sportes of our glee.
                           [games with which we entertain ourselves]
                           Of our mirthes now shall you see,
                           And ever sing welaway.[82]

Christ's first scene interweaves the theme of Wisdom with that of the dispatch of overblown intellectuals:

Primus Doctor: *Scripturae sacrae esse dinoscimur doctos*
                           [In sacred Scripture we are recognised to be
                           distinguished experts]
                           We do bear the bell of all manner clergise.
                           [to be the best in all kinds of learning][83]

The Doctors rhyme the areas of their research excellence: of reading, writing, grammar, cadence and of prosody, they are the masters; of 'versifying' and of 'sweet music', 'look no further but to our presence'; in dialectic, sophistry, logic and philosophy, 'Against our argument is no resistance'; in calculation and necromancy, 'And for indicting with rhetoric, The highest degree is ours'.[84] They cannot match their wits to the Second Person in a contest to spell out the ratio of Trinitarian theology. The scene splits to Mary and Joseph, in search of their offspring. When she finds him, she all but boxes his witty ears:

Maria: Your Fatheres will must needes be wrought:
                           It is most worthy that it be so.
                           Yet on your mother had you some thought,
                           And be nevermore so long from me![85]

Nor is the Incarnate Christ protected from proximity to some dirtier humour. If 'The Woman Taken in Adultery' was taken 'in the act' (John 8.4) that entails a young man running off the wagon with his trousers down, protesting loudly about his discomfiture:

Juvenis: My breech be not yet well up-tied –
                           I had such haste to run away.[86]

81 Ibid., pp. 198–199.
82 Ibid., p. 200.
83 'Jesus and the Doctors', in Davies, *Corpus Christi Play*, pp. 202–211 (202).
84 Ibid., pp. 202–203.
85 Ibid., p. 210.
86 Ibid., p. 216. The stage instructions state: 'Here a certain young man runs out in his doublet with his shoes unlaced and holding his trousers in his hand.'

Caiaphas and Annas are made real for their audience by assuming the trappings of the Catholic hierarchy. The Jewish priests meet in a bishop's oratory to plot Jesus' death. Annas' doctor councils that Christ be hung, drawn and burnt. But how can the desecration of the Passion be shown on a pageant-wagon stage? The action is distanced by turning it into a game: the soldiers

> are shown killing Christ in outbursts of great energy, violence, laughter, and delight; they are shown turning the tasks assigned to their masters into a sequence of formal games, into a changing metamorphosis of play, and adding to them further games of their own devising.[87]

The N-Town Jews make a game of beating a blindfolded Jesus:

> *Quartus judeus:* Ah! and now will I a new game begin,
> That we may play at, all that are herein:
> 'Wheel and pill, wheel and pill, [turn and tear off the hair]
> Cometh to halle whoso will' – [haul?]
> Who was that?[88]

The Devil sees it, the whole 'salvation-history' as a game – which he is about to lose:

> *Satan:* My game is worse than I weened here. [thought]
> I may say my game is lorn. [lost][89]

The mockery of Jews and of soldiers continues through the Passion pageants. The bad game is connected with violence, and with an evil satirical appetite, the good game with the pastimes of Eden. As Christ sets out to harrow Hell he states:

> *Anima Christi:* Now all mankind in heart be glad,
> With all mirthes that may be had!
> For mannes soul, that was bestead [beset]
> In the lodge of hell,
> Now shall I rise to live again,
> From pain to plays of paradise plain.
>   [delights of perfect paradise]
> Therefore, man, in heart be fain,
> In mirth now shalt thou dwell.[90]

The soldiers do not perform their cruelties upon the Christ figure as such. By turning their work into a game, they objectify and distance their 'object' from their actions:

> First ... there is a frequent substitution of a game figure for Christ as a real person, as when the Towneley Caiaphas in the *Buffeting* names Christ as 'kyng copyn in oure game' ... the *tortores* actions then become governed by the game rather than by any direct awareness of Christ; He serves as a passive figure in a series of games largely played for their own sake. Second, there is a ... substitution of game action for ... parts of the *tortores'* task, as when

87 Kolve, *Play Called Corpus Christi*, p. 180.
88 'Passion II: Before Annas and Caiaphas', in Davies, *Corpus Christi Play*, pp. 282–286 (286).
89 'Passion II: Dream of Pilate's Wife', in Davies, *Corpus Christi Play*, pp. 296–299 (298).
90 'Passion II: Harrowing of Hell I', in Davies, *Corpus Christi Play*, pp. 315–316 (315).

they turn the raising of the cross into a contest of strength, thus separating themselves ... from the ... terrible purpose of the action.[91]

A Blind Roman Knight is induced inadvertently to execute the last stroke in the game:

Primus Miles:	Lo! Sir Longeus, here is a spear,
	Both long and broad and sharp enough.
	Heave it up, fast, that it were there.
	For here is game – shove! man, shove![92]

He is healed of his blindness when the blood splashes his sleeve.

Annas, Caiaphas and Pilate are determined to keep the jack-in-the-box sealed down:

Annas:	Lo! here is wax full ready dight! [prepared]
	Set on your seal, anon, full right,
	Then are you secure, I you plight,
	He shall not risen again!
Pilatus:	On this corner my seal shall sit,
	And with this wax I seal this pit.
	Now dare I lay he shall never flit
	Out of this grave, certain.[93]

The Roman soldiers take their stations, setting out in their rhyming half-lines a 'keep him hidden' game:

Affraunt:	Now in this ground
	He lieth bound,
	That tholed wound [suffered]
	For he was false.
	This left corner
	I will keep here,
	Armed clear
	Both head and hals. [neck]
Cosdram:	I will have this side
	Whatso betide.
	If any man ride
	To steal the corse
	I shall him chide
	With woundes wide,
	Among them glide
	With fine force.
Amoraunt:	The head I take
	Here by to wake.
	A steal stake
	I hold in hand
	Masteries to make: [to exercise my skill]
	Crownes I crack
	Shaftes to shake
	And shapen shond.[94]

91 Kolve, *Play Called Corpus Christi*, pp. 181–182.
92 'Longeus and Burial', in Davies, *Corpus Christi Play*, pp. 318–322 (320).
93 'The Setting of the Watch', in Davies, *Corpus Christi Play*, pp. 322–327 (325).
94 Ibid., pp. 326–327.

Although these clipped chants are not merry, but menacing, the game is enjoyable because we know that they are staking out a loss. As they sleep 'a wink', Christ continues his progress through Hell, releasing its prisoners to 'finded mirthes many one/in play of paradise'.[95]

Christ appears to Cleophas and Luke: when the 'signs' of Jonah and the other types fail to recall him, he makes himself known by linking his Gospel of the new Eden with his own sign:

> *Christus:*   Be merry and glad, with heart full free,
> For of Christ Jesu, that was your friend,
> You shall have tidings of game and glee
> Within a while, ere you hence wend.
>   With my hand this bread I bless,
> And break it here as you do see.
> I give you part also of this,
> This bread to eat and blithe to be.[96]

As Christ sends for his 'clowd' and re-ascends to the Father, his last injunction to the Disciples is to live in charity 'With mirth and melody and angel song',[97] a comic vision of Christian life.

The N-Town Corpus Christi play has most of the eight features which I have attributed to comic drama. The symbols are over-sized and obvious: the self-inflating villains, Lucifer, Cain and Herod, *talk* themselves into destruction. These are villains so Toadish that the toughest scholars would be taxed to rescue them for the side of the Angels. A conflict is set up: the contest in heaven which ranges Mercy against Truth and Justice; the trial of the chastity of Mary and Joseph, against the Detractors; and that of Mary's Virginity by the Midwives. The conflict episodes are played out against the larger theme of the bad and the good game: once Eden is lost, the purpose of the drama is to permit humanity once more to play in a eutrapelic paradise. The dialogue and stage-business are funny. Far from being kept at a safe distance from the Holy Family, this humour surfaces in a hard-done-by Joseph, and in the sexual comedy of the Woman taken in Adultery. The lofty and the low are not brought together in the same way as in the Wakefield Cycle, which pastoralises the sublime story. Here, low-liness is not a social condition, the gift of a shepherd, but a moral condition, a playful humility. Didacticism is balanced by a design to produce an enjoyable drama. The joke is the villains' descent from high to low. The bad games of the schemers are devised to pin down a larger-than-life hero: no other dramatist, in setting out to create a hero who will not lie down and die was so literal in taking God as his protagonist. The good game generates the victory of the eternal life-force, the resurrection to Paradise of Christ and of his good companions. Fulfilment of desire in companion-ship belongs to the intention of the N-Town Cycle. At least, that is, in part. Not everyone's desires are fulfilled. The 'Doomsday' finale packs those convicted of the seven deadly sins off to Hell:

---

95 John the Baptist, in 'Harrowing of Hell II', in Davies, *Corpus Christi Play*, pp. 328–330 (329).
96 'Appearance to Cleophas and Luke', in Davies, *Corpus Christi Play*, pp. 347–354 (353).
97 'Ascension', in Davies, *Corpus Christi Play*, pp. 359–360 (360).

Animae damnandum:	Ah! mercy! mercy! we rub, we rave,
	Ah! help us, good Lord, in this need.
Deus:	Why ask you mercy now in this need?
	What you wrought your soul to save?
	To whom have you done any merciful deed,
	Mercy for to win?[98]

If comedy is supposed to invite its villains to its concluding feast, all of the English Corpus Christi Cycles fail us here. The element of my definition of comedy which is missing is a delight in heterogeneity. Black and white comedy has its downside:

> the opponents and enemies become stylized, the devil on one side and the Jews on the other. If Christ is portrayed as the loser in the Passion play, it is followed by the *Vengeance de Notre Seigneur*, a light-hearted little history of the Jewish people in which the Victor visits just retribution and annihilates his enemies.[99]

The parts of the Eutrapelists and the bad sports are fixed for Paradise and for Hell. There is a bit of cardboard in the personae of mediaeval biblical drama. No matter how far the circuit which the pageant wagons traversed was from the Cathedral nave, they put on a *strict* repetition of the sacred history. It is only after the pageant wagons had been forcibly dismantled that human freedom, with its inclination to particolours, will be fully celebrated in Christian drama.

First Interlude

Divine Folly is the narrator of Desiderius Erasmus' most well-known book. The cackling and orange peel throwing audience seated in the 'gods' are the gods, and even God. Folly confides the secrets of the gods' leisure hours:

> when they are soused with nectar and no longer want to do anything serious, they take their seats at the place where heaven juts out farthest, and lean forward to watch what mankind is about ... Good lord, what a theatre! ... One man ... marries the dowry, not the wife ... One man who is in mourning – good grief! what foolish things he says and does! He even hires professional mourners, like actors, to put on a show of grief. Another weeps at his stepmother's grave ... For the gods watching the spectacle, both types provide the most extraordinary entertainment, when the tricksters themselves are outwitted by their victims.[100]

The divine laughter at the expense of human foibles is satirical. Erasmus took the lead in encouraging Humanist scholars to return to the original, unglossed, biblical texts: and he found the Christian God, both Father and Son, to be no less cutting in his humour than the Greek gods. If, as the Psalmist has it, 'He that sitteth in the heavens shall laugh: the Lord shall

---

98 'Doomsday', in Davies, *Corpus Christi Play*, pp. 368–373 (370).
99 Von Balthasar, *Theo-Drama I*, p. 107.
100 Desiderius Erasmus, *The Praise of Folly*, edited with an introduction and commentary by Clarence Miller (Yale University Press, New Haven, 1979), pp. 76–77.

have them in derision', that means that 'Those whom the Father laughs to scorn, Christ our Lord derides. Both are laughing in derision at sinners'.[101] The technical word for such 'harsh, railing satire' is *diasyrm*.[102] The Greek διασυρω (*diasurō*) means 'to tear in pieces, to worry, disparage': *diasyrm* is the laughter which cuts. It has a biblical legitimisation in the laughter by which Elijah cursed the children who mocked his bald head. In his *Praise of Folly*, Erasmus exploited a scything 'close to Elijah's diasyrm'[103] to cut a division between the human and the Christian life. If 'human life is *nothing but* a stage play of Folly'[104] acted within the shadows of Plato's cave,[105] then *Christian* life is sheer madness. How are the folly of humanity and the folly of Christianity related? One figure which presents itself is the 'hour-glass', which a well-known theologian used to describe the Karl Barth's *analogia fidei*, except for that Erasmus omits a meeting place at the centre.[106] We have to do with opposing kinds of madness. A second metaphor is a distorting mirror: the man standing on his feet is reflected in the image of a man floating upside down. Perhaps the simplest way of getting the idea of the thing is take a pair of scissors ✂, and swivel it 90 degrees so that it stands upright on its pins. The human world in the cutting triangle has an inverted value in the upper triangle of the handles. Speaking for the lower half of the scissors, Folly derides the emotionless Stoic: 'what state would choose such a man for civic office ... what woman would consent to marry him'?[107] The Christian piety of the upper V roots up and discards natural emotions, such as love of parents.[108] The illogicality of the mundane world 'recognises human limitations and does not strive to leap beyond them';[109] the Christian folly, of which 'Plato had a glimmer when he wrote that the madness of lovers is the height of happiness', yearns only for 'that future life in heaven' in which 'the spirit ... will absorb the body'.[110] There are two realms of folly, one in the lower half of the scissors, the other in the higher. The follies which flourish 'beneath the mind', including emotion, friendship and prudence, and the supernatural follies whose demesne is 'above the mind'[111] can no more become incarnate in one another than Plato's Ideas can become embodied in the world of delusory sense. Human and Christian folly cannot construct *one* world: Erasmus' theology presents two closed circles,

◯   Divine Folly
◯   Human folly

101 M. A. Screech, *Laughter at the Foot of the Cross* (Allen Lane, London, 1997), pp. 50–51.
102 Ibid., p. 40.
103 Ibid., p. 188.
104 Erasmus, *Praise of Folly*, p. 120; my italics.
105 Ibid., pp. 72–73.
106 Hans Urs von Balthasar, *The Theology of Karl Barth*, translated by John Drury (Holt, Rinehart & Winston, New York, 1971), p. 170: 'We might describe Barth's thought as an intellectual hourglass, where God and man meet in the centre through Jesus Christ.'
107 Erasmus, *Praise of Folly*, p. 46.
108 Ibid., p. 135.
109 Ibid., p. 44.
110 Ibid., p. 136.
111 Von Balthasar, *Glory V*, p. 165.

The two circles do not intersect in a sanctified terrain of comedy: 'Erasmus' natural and chosen territory was wit, not comedy.'[112] For, as von Balthasar claims,

> Erasmus would not be Erasmus if he did not end – inexplicably! – by committing the folly of fleeing from the folly of world and Church in Platonic flight into the realm of pure spirit. The ecstatic flight of spirit from body, of the mind from the world up into God – that is the illogical conclusion of his treatise, which in the end closes its eyes to the radiant glory of true folly.[113]

Erasmus presents a figure of Christ as *disincarnate* Folly. He abolishes comedy as an *analogy* for the heaven to which human beings aspire. For Erasmus, comedy is an equivocal, that is, referentially disjunctive term: the folly of *being human* is the opposite of the madness of *being spiritual*.

It was only by 'fleeing' the world that Erasmus could *see through* human fantasy: it is by rising above the world that he is able satirically to deflate the web of social gestures through which human beings make their world into a meaningful drama. Folly observes that if

> you could look down from the moon ... and see the innumerable broils of mortals, you would think you were looking at a great cloud of flies or gnats quarrelling among themselves ... It is ... incredible ... what tragedies can be stirred up by such a tiny creature, so frail and short-lived.[114]

Erasmus is funny-reductive at the expense of histrionic social actions, such as the ceremonies of the hunt and the rituals of funerals.[115] From the Platonic 'moon', most religious festivals are transparent mummeries. If, as Erasmus said, 'all buffoonery should be excluded from Christian life',[116] then the Feast of Fools was likely to win light applause from the author of the *Praise of Folly*. The Erasmian propensity to describe play-pretend as pretentiousness, and re-presentation as a doubling of the shadow-play of the cave, reaches its peroration in his onslaught upon the monastic orders. The stage directions of monastic life excite Erasmus to unsmiling satire:

> All levels of society rejoiced in the permitted licence of Twelfth Night and Shrovetide. Erasmus would have none of it. They were survivals of the ancient Bacchanalia. He was moved to write passionately against such excesses in his exposition of the psalm *Quam dilecta*. The Gentiles celebrated the harvest with wantonness, 'in honour of their ridiculous Bacchus' ... Erasmus was especially distressed by preachers who made concessions to the antics of the unlearned and the illiterate to be found in all ranks of society. There was a tradition of deliberately funny sermons on Easter Day. They formed part of what was known as 'Easter Laughter'. Erasmus judged such sermons to be shameless. Preachers tell 'manifestly made-up stories', so obscene that no decent man would repeat them even during a banquet ... The kind of laughter he most detested is the kind often associated with friars and monks.[117]

---

112 Screech, *Laughter at the Foot of the Cross*, p. 216.
113 Ibid., p. 168.
114 Erasmus, *Praise of Folly*, p. 78.
115 Ibid., pp. 60–61 and 67.
116 Quoted in Screech, *Laughter at the Foot of the Cross*, p. 219.
117 Ibid., pp. 214–216.

'But I am glad to be done with these play-actors': thus Folly concludes her tribute to the monastic orders.[118] Erasmus took the Greek root of to act, *hupocrites*, literally. The Renaissance humanist could not perceive any medium between telling the truth and lying. This medium is the area of dramatic representation, in which one person or thing stands for, and points to, another. It was ruled out of court by the Either/Or of fifteenth-century English Wycliffites. The Wycliffite preacher,

> is unable to see the dramatic artefact as something analogous, but in a root sense 'unrelated', to real life . . . He believes that drama teaches men that hell is only a locus on a pageant stage, and that the wrath of God is only a dramatic attitude, for it is obvious to any spectator that the damned souls are not really punished in any Judgement Day pageant: 'Not he that pleyith the wille of God worschipith hym, but onely he that doith his wille in deede worschipith hym.'[119]

A moral is not to be communicated by an analogy: images either are *what* they represent, or they trick, deceive and hold up an image for worship, *instead of* the reality. Truth should be seen *directly*, and not through the medium of body language, pictures, or symbols. If comic drama is not an *analogous* term, either the man on stage *is* Christ or he is not. If he is not, he should not be pretending to be. This line of thought extends from the Wycliffites to Erasmus, and to the Reformers:

> Behind the repudiation of ceremonial by the reformers lay a . . . conceptual world . . . in which text was everything, sign nothing. The sacramental universe of late medieval Catholicism was, from such a perspective, totally opaque, a bewildering and meaningless world of dumb objects and vapid gestures, hindering communication. That spirit of determined non-comprehension had been the life-blood of Lollardy, and [was] . . . encouraged by the spread of reformed teaching and practice.[120]

Erasmus completed the first edition of his *Praise of Folly* at Thomas More's house, in 1511. Henry VIII beheaded the 'Feast of Fools' in 1541. Erasmus' cutting satire achieved its political incarnation in the various Edwardine injunctions, which banned processions, and, in 1548, abolished Corpus Christi. But the Henrician Reformation did not put an end to Christian drama. In the 1540s,

> The Protestant play *The life and repentaunce of Marie Magdalene* sold itself as 'not only godly, learned and fruitful, but also well furnished with pleasant mirth and pastime, very delectable'. Another biblical play, the *Historie of Jacob and Esau*, was described as 'mery and wittie', an interlude on the story of King Darius as 'piithie and pleasaunt'.[121]

Some of the Reformers were too reformed for Henry: in 1538 he issued a proclamation which 'repudiated the "contentious and sinister opinions . . . by wrong teaching and naughty printed books" . . . a reference to the

---

118 Erasmus, *Praise of Folly*, p. 106.
119 Kolve, *Play Called Corpus Christi*, p. 21.
120 Eamon Duffy, *The Stripping of the Altars: Traditional Religion in England 1400–1580* (Yale University Press, New Haven and London, 1992), p. 532.
121 Patrick Collinson, *The Birthpangs of Protestant England: Religious and Cultural Change in the Sixteenth and Seventeenth Centuries* (Macmillan Press, Basingstoke, 1988), p. 98.

Protestant primers set out ... by protégés of Cromwell'.[122] One such protégé was John Bale (1495–1563), ex-Carmelite, and a convert to Lutheranism. Known for his vituperative wit as 'Bilius Bale', this playwright and pamphleteer was one of several men whom Abbot Feckenham termed 'the preachers and scaffold players of this new religion'.[123] Bale made his way to the Continent when Cromwell went to the block. In 1543–1544 laws were set out 'forbidding interludes' which the Henrician Church judged heretical. Bale's work was 'condemned by proclamation' in 1546.[124] He spat back by having several plays printed in Wesel in 1547–1548. Edward VI rewarded Bale with a bishopric in Ossory. On hearing of the accession of Queen Mary, 'Bilius' had his triolet of *God's Promises, Johan Baptystes Preachynge* and *The Temptation of our Lord* performed in the Irish market square. The first is labelled by Bale as a 'tragedy'; the last two are subtitled comedies. John the Baptist preaches to the multitude to 'Flee mennys tradycyons'; the Saduccees ask him 'By whose autoryte/doest thu teache thys newe lerynge? ... /Wyth a lytle helpe/of an heretyke he wyll smell'.[125] Bilius Bale is happier clothing Satan as a monk or Pharisee, than the Pharisees and Sadducees as bishops and monks. In 'The Temptation of our Lord', Satan tempts Christ in a monastic habit; Rowan Atkinson could smirk suitably in the role. With hands primly folded, he tells Christ

It is a grat joye,	by my holydome, to se
So vertuouse a lyfe	in a yonge man as yow be,
As here thus to wander	in godly contemplacyon,
And to lyve alone	in the desart solytarye.[126]

He responds to Christ's Scriptural ripostes with 'Scriptures I knowe non/ for I am but an hermyte, I'.[127] When the play was performed in Ireland, it caused, in Bale's words, a 'small contentacion of the prestes and other papistes there'.[128] If 'Early Protestantism ... created a new religious and moral drama of its own for ... propagandistic and didactic purposes',[129] then Bale's most biting work along those lines is his allegorical 'A newe comedy or enterlude concernyng thre laws' (printed 1562). Deus Pater creates the three laws, of Nature, Moses and Christ, 'of Nature/of Bondage, and of Grace'.[130] Infidelity destroys each of the laws. For the corruption of Nature, Infidelity's henchpersons are Sodomy, dressed as a monk, and Idolatry, costumed as a witch. Sodomy perverts 'the clergye at Rome' for 'want of wyves':[131] the best line is Infidelity's injunction to Sodomy to

---

122 Duffy, *Stripping of the Altars*, p. 410.
123 Cited in ibid., p. 103.
124 'Introduction', John Bale, *The Complete Plays of John Bale: Volume I*, edited by Peter Happé (D. S. Brewer, Cambridge, 1985), p. 8.
125 John Bale, 'Johan Baptystes Preachynge', in *The Complete Plays of John Bale: Volume II*, edited by Peter Happé (D. S. Brewer, Cambridge, 1986), pp. 39 and 41.
126 'The Temptation of our Lord', in Bale, *Complete Plays II*, p. 55.
127 Ibid., p. 56.
128 Cited in 'Introduction', in Bale, *Complete Plays I*, p. 7.
129 Collinson, *Birthpangs of Protestant England*, p. 102.
130 'Three Laws', in Bale, *Complete Plays II*, p. 66.
131 Ibid., p. 83.

> Stodye the Popes decretals,
>   And mixt them with buggerage.[132]

Idolatry's Hail Marys and the lures of Sodomy give Nature leprosy. The Law of Moses is assailed by Ambition, clothed as a bishop, and Avarice, dressed 'lyke a Pharyse'.[133] Moses' Law is blinded and lamed.[134] The reign of Christ is signified by 'Evangelium', the Gospel. Evangelium states that his is not the church, 'Of apysh shavelynges/or papystycall sodomytes'.[135] According to Collinson,

> On a Friday afternoon in May 1560 a Canterbury tailor found work to do in cutting out what he laughingly called 'an ape's coat'. This was the costume for the part of a popish friar in a play which Bale was to 'set forth' (and perhaps it was the *Thre lawes*) and which was to be given a public performance in one of the large houses of the town, with a charge made for admission.[136]

Bale's own stage instructions put Hypocrisy into the garb of a 'graye frye'; perhaps he wore the ape-suit on top. False Doctrine is garbed like a 'popysh doctour'. Evangelium rebukes them both

Evangelium: Wo, Pharysees, wo!   Ye make cleane outwardlye,
                But inwardes ye are full   of covetousnesse and baudrye.[137]

Under Elizabeth, such energetically vituperous satires co-existed for a time with the pre-Reformation cycles: the Corpus Christi plays survived the outlawing of the festival which they had been created to celebrate by thirty years. The York, Wakefield and Chester plays were banned in the 1570s; Coventry was 'laid down' in 1580, 'to be replaced four years later by a new and Protestant play "of the Destruction of Jerusalem"'.[138] In 1599, Elizabeth banned all plays 'wherein either matters of religion or of the governance of the estate of the common weale shall be handled or treated'.[139]

And yet, Elizabethan drama opened the way to the theatrical representation of the *person*. Elizabethan England was fed by the humanism, not only of Erasmus but also of John of Salisbury, whose *Policratus* was reprinted in 1476, 1513 and 1595.[140] That helped English 'Baroque literature' to Christianise the meaning which Erasmus gave to drama: 'Shakespeare will take advantage of this meaning: even when he gives Jacques his speech, "All the world's a stage" (*As You Like It*, II, 7), it is a world that has inbuilt categories giving order . . . to the various strata.' In 1599, the year in which Elizabeth issued the death-warrant to the Cycle-Dramas, the Globe Theatre was built, 'sport[ing] an inscription from John of Salisbury's *Policraticus*: *Totus mundus agit histrionem*'.[141]

132 Ibid., p. 85.
133 Ibid., p. 93.
134 Ibid., p. 101.
135 Ibid., p. 103.
136 Collinson, *Birthpangs of Protestant England*, p. 104.
137 Bale, 'Three Laws', p. 112.
138 Collinson, *Birthpangs of Protestant England*, p. 101.
139 Roston, *Biblical Drama in England*, p. 114.
140 Curtius, *European Literature*, p. 141.
141 Von Balthasar, *Theo-Drama I*, pp. 161–162.

Sensing the analogy of being is like feeling one's way through a forest, along a path which disappears and returns; that is, it is like making moral decisions. The openness of being is best shown opaquely or elliptically, as, for example, in symbolic gestures. In the fourteenth century, Dante discovers the openness of being between God and the world, not in metaphysics, but along the road of ethics. 'Dante's new way is the primacy of concrete personal existence over the essentialist world view of scholasticism.'[142] If there are analogies between actors and their parts, and thus between the roles which God gives us and the outwardly expressed path of our own moral decision-making, then, although our acting may lack in philosophical articulation, we do not have to be Thomists in order to *experience* these connections. If we can find our way back to 'concrete personal existence', that will show us a way to discern the analogies between the goodness of God and human virtue. Elizabethan England had the most reliable guide to 'concrete personal existence' in a narrative which incarnates the analogy of real communication; the text achieved its most euphonious and affectively accurate translation in the reign of James I. Even if we live in an era in which theologians are hard put to give a convincing explanation of analogy, we have an infallible, *pre-theoretical* guide to the analogy of being, if we inhabit the biblical narrative. The Bible can be misinterpreted, but it holds us to its description of the experience of divine–human dialogue, slipping in under our philosophical categories.

It would be difficult to disagree with Collinson that 'it would require a singular perversity to prefer *The life and repentaunce of Marie Magdalene* to *Hamlet* or *Measure for Measure*'.[143] Shakespeare was a finer playwright than the authors of Chester, York, Wakefield, or N-Town: 'If we compare Shakespeare's drama with the Mystery plays, we see that the dramatic power is heightened ... and the situations secularized and universalized.'[144] When the salvation history is 'secularized and universalized' the sacred figures are set free to become human characters: Christ can be Cordelia. In the era in which neither Erasmus nor the theologians whom he pictured 'rise[ing] up en masse and march[ing] in ranks against' him[145] could find a convincing medium between reductionist naturalism and the theology of equivocity, and which, therefore, gave birth to a savage *literalism* with respect to iconic symbolism, it was secular dramatists who showed what analogy is. Once drama is loosed from the obligation *literally* to convey the biblical story, it can convey it *analogously.* Every individual in human history, every commonplace and unique person, can re-present the salvation history in their own inimitable way: Falstaff can be Christ. If time can carry meaning, meaningful time does not belong only to the biblical history. The mediaeval dramatists educated their audience in prefiguration: Shakespeare creates 'postfigurations' of Christ.[146] A unique human

142 Von Balthasar, *The Glory of the Lord: A Theological Aesthetics III: Studies in Theological Style: Lay Styles*, translated by Andrew Louth, John Saward, Martin Simon and Rowan Williams (T&T Clark, Edinburgh, 1986), p. 34.
143 Collinson, *Birthpangs of Protestant England*, p. 114.
144 Driver, *Sense of History*, pp. 201–202.
145 Erasmus, *Praise of Folly*, p. 87.
146 Roston, *Biblical Drama in England*, p. 69.

being has that many more free choices to make. If Erasmus' anti-Stoical praise of emotion and his encomium of Christian asceticism cancel one another out, Shakespeare found the balance between the two: *Hamlet* must have its grave-digger scenes:

> The comic disapproval of the fact that a person of such high rank should be subject to weariness and the desire for small beer . . . is a satire upon the trend – no longer negligible in Shakespeare's day – toward a strict separation between the sublime and . . . everyday realities.[147]

The mediaeval drama cycles mixed the styles by bringing bumpkins into the nativity: the comic nature of the beast is summed up in the proximity of the profane to the sacred. The same fusion can be effected in the secular theatre's mixture of the 'rough' and the 'holy'. It takes great ingenuity because the sense of the dangerous contact of the sacred with the profane must be communicated to an audience which has paid for entertainment, not sanctification or edification.[148] The Elizabethan dramatist revisits the theme of the 'Doomsday' pageant. The 'Christian mystery play' of *Measure for Measure* 'marks the high point of the problem of justice versus mercy'.[149] Because the exercise of mercy is delegated from God to a passible woman, the actors can show the

> cost of forgiveness, which is a kind of miracle in our life; indeed, it must be a rarity if it is to have its full effect. This is expressed in *Measure for Measure*, which has the Old Testament concept of justice in its title . . . but its whole thrust lies in the fact that it goes beyond this level.[150]

Now the scenes of salvation history are translated into staged stories, just as that history is translated, in human life.

2. Handel's Oratorios

The *Ludus Danielis* of Beauvais has a good claim to be the first oratorio. The vernacular mystery plays dropped the music; the Baroque oratorios would recapture their comedy.[151] The Italian Franciscans expressed their affective spirituality in the *laudi*, 'rhapsodic' hymns.[152] St Philip Neri (1515–1595) founded the Congregation of the *Oratorio* (Oratory), in Rome, in 1564. If we find the exuberance of the Baroque imagination apt to the comic terrain, St Philip will be our patron saint:

> During the Counter-Reformation the question whether the pious Christian might laugh still played a part in the intellectual battles of the time. Jansenism and Rancé's 'Malheur à vous qui riez!' are characteristic of an ethical rigorism which in the present-day judgement of Catholic historians represents a blame-worthy extreme. In contrast, Henri Bremond has celebrated San

---

147 Auerbach, *Mimesis*, p. 312.
148 Harris, *Theatre and Incarnation*, pp. 95–97.
149 Von Balthasar, *Theo-Drama I*, p. 470.
150 Ibid., p. 466.
151 Winton Dean, *Handel's Dramatic Oratorios and Masques* (Oxford University Press, Oxford, 1959, 1972), p. 5.
152 Paul Henry Lang, *George Frederic Handel* (Faber & Faber, London, 1964), p. 69.

Filippo Neri, whose favorite reading was a book of *facetiae*, as 'le saint patron des humoristes'. The saint's maxim was: '*Lo spirito allegro acquist piu facilment la perfezione christiana che non lo spirito malinconico.*'[153]

Von Balthasar notes that 'it bespeaks a sense of humor when the Catholic Church ... responds to the Reformation with the putti of the Bavarian Baroque';[154] although no German Catholic theologian has yet felt himself equal to a 'book on the humor of the saints', Goethe 'has given us a short exerpt of it in his *Philipp Neri, der humoristische Heilige* (the humorous saint), particularly in the latter's far-from-reverential exchange of notes with Clement VIII'.[155] The musically buoyant among St Philip's oratorians dramatised the *laudi*: these performances, which served as a devotional epilogue to the Mass, were called *rappresentazioni*. These representations of biblical episodes had a spoken part, read by a priest-narrator (or *testo*), and a sung response, the responsibility of the congregation.[156] The word *oratorio* was first used in 1595, in reference to these performances. The first work now designated as an *oratorio* was Cavalieri's *La Rappresentazione di Anima et di Corpo* ('The Representation [play] of the Spirit and the Body'), put on in St Philip's church in 1600. St Ignatius Loyola and St Francis Xavier were canonised in 1622: the event was celebrated in Rome with an *oratorio* about their lives, composed by Kapsberger, and enhanced with 'elaborate scenery and action'.[157] Stefano Landi set *Il Sant Alessio* (1632) for which the 'future pope Clement IX' wrote the libretto, and which contained 'dance, stage machinery, a chorus of devils and two characters for comic relief';[158] Palermo did an oratorical *Sansone* (Samson), in 1638; Loreto set *Il Sagrifizio d'Abramo* to music (1648). Carissimi composed short (twenty-minute) Latin oratorio-dramas of Abraham and Isaac, Jephtha, Solomon and Belshazzar. The librettist for Carissimi's *Sacrifizio di Isacco* (1655) was a Jesuit, and von Balthasar comments that the idea of dramatic 'representation' 'underlies not only ... the entire Jesuit mission, but also the theatre' of the Baroque, bringing with it 'a new awareness of the manifestation of the divine glory in the world'.[159] 'Nonetheless', von Balthasar complains,

> deductions came to be made, in the style of the Counter-Reformation, that Ignatius had not made ... Bellarmine did this in ecclesiology, and Baroque art, with its tendency toward extravagant glorification, extended it to all the phenomenal aspects of the Catholic Church ... theology and art accomplish all this in a conscious act of faith and loyalty to mother church, in a conscious rejection of the Protestant rejection of the idea that divine revelation can have any real visibility in the times of the Church's history or in the charisms of sanctity ... and which the art of Tintoretto, El Greco, Zurbaren, Rubens ... tried to represent visibly as the splendour of grace. And yet ... the crisis of the late middle ages could not be undone ... Luther was a fact. And so ...

153 Curtius, *European Literature*, p. 422.
154 Hans Urs von Balthasar, *The Office of Peter and the Structure of the Church*, translated by Andrée Emery (Ignatius Press, San Francisco, 1987), p. 304.
155 Ibid., p. 306.
156 Lang, *George Frederic Handel*, p. 77.
157 Dean, *Handel's Dramatic Oratorios*, p. 7.
158 Ibid.
159 Von Balthasar, *Glory V*, pp. 106–107.

there was something contrived about triumphantly celebrating ecclesiastical forms as revelatory icons of the eschatological Jerusalem, as anticipatory glimpses of a gorgeous Pozzo and Tiepolo kind of heaven, full of saints and angels ... whatever the subjective sincerity of those who made this profession of faith, there was something objectively untrue about it ... the scandalous form of the cross and the humble form of the Church were treated as if they were, without qualification, forms of worldly beauty.[160]

It is possible, then, that he would not have approved of the marzipan *trionfo* (triumphs) with which the *cantate spirituali* which were performed at the Papal Palazzo Apostolico were enhanced. Such *cantate spirituali* were music-dramas: this one was performed annually between 1695 and 1740 in celebration of the Nativity; the composers include Alessandro and Dominico Scarlatti. A contemporary observer described how the marzipan *trionfi* looked in 1719:

The first ... represented a royal throne with two royal seats, on the first of which sat Christ crowned as King, with robes and royal cloak and with sceptre in his left hand; on the second [seat] was the Church dressed as Queen, who in the act of kneeling, received the ring from her spouse, Christ. At Christ's foot two angels knelt, each with a tray, in one of which were three imperial crowns, and in the other the sceptre; & next to the [female] spouse was a standing angel, who held the tablets of Moses in his left hand & in the right the book of Gospels: on the top of the said triumph one saw the Eternal Father with the Holy Spirit in the glory of the cherubs.[161]

The Nativity *cantata spirituali* was usually performed by five actor-singers, representing the shepherds, or the Magi, as dictated by the choice of main theme.

The musical Baroque made its way to England at the Restoration of Charles II in 1660. The Baroque anthem is characterised by the fact of its *musical imitation* of the meanings of the words of the psalm: in Henry Purcell's 'Jubilatio Deo', the bass makes the sea *sound like* the sea. Such musical mimesis or 'word-painting', playing upon the meanings of the words and expressing it, for example, in down-swings and up-swings, dramatises the sacred music, as the marzipan does the sacred figures. The styles invented by Gabrieli and Monteverdi trickled into England, bringing with them 'the new secular "anthem" with its dramatic vocal line and theatrical ritornelli and accompaniments'.[162] After the Glorious Revolution, William III 'restrict[ed] instrumental accompaniment in the Chapel Royal to the organ'. It was, once again, outside the church, and this time in the 'festival concert' that the religious and musical possibilities of the Baroque were developed.[163] One of Purcell's ventures in the musical-histrionic style,

160 Ibid., pp. 110–111.
161 Cited by Carolyn Gianturco, '"Cantati spirituali e morali", with a Description of the Papal Sacred Cantata Tradition for Christmas 1676–1740', *Music and Letters*, LXXIII (February 1992), 1–13 (7–8).
162 Franklin B. Zimmerman, *Henry Purcell: 1659–1695: His Life and Times* (Macmillan, London, 1967), p. 66.
163 Alexander Shapiro, '"Drama of an Infinitely Superior Nature": Handel's Early English Oratorios and the Religious Sublime', *Music and Letters*, LXXIV, May 1993, 215–245 (221).

his 'Te Deum', was performed at a festival concert, on the day after St Cecilia's day:

> For a Church service the 'Te Deum' and 'Jubilate' must have been a new kind of composition – new in its martial trumpet accompaniments, new in its unpolyphonic . . . settings of the old liturgical texts, and new, above all, in its theatrical expression.[164]

The music is 'theatrical' in that, first, it captures and expresses in sound the sense of the words, and, more generally, in that the musical *style* attempts to appropriate itself to the *sacred* theme. If music is to be 'about' God, then it must put on some of the divine majesty:

> The successive canonic entries at 'day by day we magnify Thee' suggest the dizzying passage of time, while the homophonic grandeur of 'the holy church throughout all the world doth acknowledge thee' signifies the unity of the Anglican faith. The use of trumpets . . . lends this sacred work an innovative grandeur. This dramatically descriptive use of the chorus . . . an adaptation to music of elements of the sublime poetic style – distinguished the ceremonial mode.[165]

Handelian oratorio came to England by two routes. Purcell and his lesser contemporaries created an 'indigenous English tradition' in which the composer was to anchor his own anthems, such as the 'Te Deum for the Utrecht Thanksgiving':[166] Handel's oratorio would be a 'magnification of the miniature sublime dramas' written by Purcell.[167] Secondly, Handel had witnessed the Italian tradition of oratorio in Rome. The Handelian oratorio is a progeny of Baroque culture, which was 'a drama, religious and secular. And its stage was the church, the street, the public place, the palace of wide rooms . . . and the formal fantastic garden. The peruke was the actor's wig . . . This baroque drama was polite . . . It was a comedy of manners'.[168]

After writing a few operas, Handel went to Rome in 1707. A papal ban on opera inspired him to direct his talents into oratorio, a musical form which he discovered at the court of Cardinal Pamphilj.[169] When the Lutheran composer was invited to alter his religious allegiance, he pronounced himself 'resolved to die a member of that communion, whether true or false, in which he was born and bred'. In 1709, he made a home in Anglican England. A British audience enjoyed its first oratorio in Handel's *Esther* (1732). The 'advertisements' sub-titled the unknown quantity a 'Sacred Drama', and 'warned that "There will be no Action on the Stage"'. Some critics found the performance lacking in the essentials of drama:

> The commentator . . . complained that 'I . . . found this Sacred *Drama* a mere Consort [concert], no Scenary, Dress or Action, so necessary to a *Drama*'. Preferring Handel's new operas, *Ezio* and *Sosarme*, he confesses: '(I am sorry I am so wicked) but I like one good Opera better than Twenty *Oratorio*'s: Were

164 Zimmerman, *Henry Purcell*, p. 249.
165 Shapiro, 'Drama of an Infinitely Superior Nature', 222–223.
166 Ibid., 216 and 224.
167 Ibid., 240.
168 E. I. Watkin, *Catholic Art and Culture* (Hollis & Carter, London, 1947), pp. 129–130.
169 Hamish Swanston, *Handel* (Geoffrey Chapman, London, 1990), pp. 7–10.

they indeed to make a regular *Drama* of a good Scripture Story, and perform'd it with proper Decorations, which may be done with as much Reverence in proper Habits, as in their own common Apparel . . . then should I change my Mind, then would the Stage appear in its full Lustre, and Musick Answer to its original Design.[170]

Thanks to the Bishop of London's insistence that the musical 'Sacred Drama' be put on without costumes or actions,[171] Handel's oratorios *look* less like plays than their Continental counterparts. They aim to *express* action and meaning musically. Handel taught his contemporaries that one can experience the Bible as drama without the visual props. Even if censorship had not ensured that his histrionics were not assisted by costumes and scenery, Handel would have wished to transpose the dramatic quality of the scriptural scenes into musical drama, conveying an aural and affective image. Some of his oratorios supplement the Author-ised Version or hale from stories which the Reformers had excluded from their canon. If, as it is fashionable to claim, *Judas Maccabeus* is a celebration of Protestant Britishness,[172] Handel drew on a text not found in King's James' Bible in order to offer this encomium to the United Kingdom. Handelian oratorio, with which British audiences have been enraptured for two and a half centuries, is perhaps more *European* than we realise; the Continental Counter-Reformer and the Welsh Methodist share a biblical affectivity.

The eighteenth-century Dissenters took against church music because it was Jewish: James Pierce, 'denounces instrumental music as a "Jewish ceremony"'.[173] The High Anglicans grounded their apology for church music in the Old Testament. The 'Three Choirs' sermon gave them an annual pulpit. Thomas Payne used it to remind his audience of these musical *figura*: 'When all the children of *Israel* sang the Song of *Moses*, upon the overthrow of *Pharaoh*, and his host, then *Miriam* the Prophetess, with her Choir of women, answer'd them, *with Timbrels in their hands*, sing ye to the Lord for he hath triumph'd gloriously.' That was the year before Handel's *Israel in Egypt* was put on:

> In the light of this passage, the Song of Moses which forms the concluding part of *Israel in Egypt* acquires a new *raison d'etre*, worth setting . . . as the . . . Ur-example of God's ratification of vocal and instrumental music in divine worship as practised in Anglican cathedrals (Payne . . . describes the Song as an exact harbinger of cathedral usage, performed by an accompanied, antiphonal double choir). Major characters of the librettos . . . are foreshadowed in this sermon tradition: Moses at the Red Sea (the last part of *Israel*), David the singer of psalms (portrayed as such while soothing the king in *Saul*) and Solomon the instigator of temple worship (the first part of *Solomon*).[174]

170 Ruth Smith, *Handel's Oratorios and Eighteenth Century Thought* (Cambridge University Press, Cambridge, 1995), p. 43.
171 Dean, *Handel's Dramatic Oratorios*, p. 33.
172 See, for example, Linda Colley's discussion of Handel in the chapter entitled 'Protestants' in her *Britons: Forging the Nation 1707–1837* (Random House, New York, 1992, Pimlico, London, 1994), pp. 31–32.
173 Smith, *Handel's Oratorios*, p. 228.
174 Ibid., p. 90.

Handel's contemporaries praised his music for its *sublimity*. Longinus' *On the Sublime* was repeatedly translated and reprinted in eighteenth-century England. The Song of Moses (Ex. 15) was found to meet Longinus' recipes for 'transport': the biblical paraphraser Aaron Hill claimed that 'the oldest and ... the most sublime poem in the world is of Hebrew origin ... God ... taught poetry first to the Hebrews'.[175] The 'librettist of Handel's *Deborah*, Samuel Humphreys' 'praised the Song of Deborah in his commentary on the Bible as far surpassing any classical attempts at sublime and affective poetry'. What they liked in the biblical verse was its potency viscerally to seize an audience: the way was 'prepared for Jennens' use of Isaiah in Messiah' by 'contemporary admiration for the energy and pathos of the very passages which he chose'.[176] Such 'pathos' is what I have labelled *audience attack*. What the eighteenth century admired as sublimity is a quality which carries the audience into the music. An eighteenth-century critic was hardly likely to praise Handel for his vulgarity. Handel's performers were allowed no mimetic gestures, but what cannot be done with the body can be done with the voice: 'The evidence suggests that in the heat of creation Handel saw Saul, Hercules and Belshazzar, strolling across the boards and that such a vision controlled the form and gestures of the music.'[177] The strong and obvious flavour of drama in his arias and choruses mark the oratorios with a certain commonness. The combination of audience attack and vulgar or immediate pleasingness will flower in the exuberant comedy of the *Messiah*. The *Messiah* is a musical *triumph*: 'Even the vitality that characterised the ancient world is not to be compared with the Renaissance and Baroque experience. Existence then was a celebration, and this uplifted mood found expression in the *trionfo*: indeed, in every great work a triumphal element was sought and celebrated.'[178]

Recent Christian Orthodoxy has responded to the liberalism of mid-twentieth century theology by making light of the Enlightenment. The novelist Henry Fielding caricatured the two sides in the religious skirmishing of eighteenth-century England in Tom Jones's two tutors, Mr Square and Parson Thwackum. The couple

> scarce ever met without a disputation; for their tenets were indeed diametrically opposite to each other. Square held human nature to be the perfection of all virtue, and that vice was a deviation from our nature in the same manner as deformity of body is. Thwackum, on the contrary, maintained that the human mind, since the Fall, was nothing but a sink of iniquity, till purified and redeemed by grace. In one point only they agreed, which was, in all their discourses on morality never to mention the word *goodness*. The favourite phrase of the former, was *the natural beauty of virtue*; that of the latter, was the *divine power of grace*. The former measured all actions by the unalterable rule of right, and the *eternal fitness of things*; the latter decided all matters by authority but, in doing this, he always used the Scriptures and their commentaries.[179]

175 Cited in ibid., p. 229.
176 Ibid., p. 118.
177 Dean, *Handel's Dramatic Oratorios*, p. 36.
178 Von Balthasar, *Glory V*, p. 382.
179 Henry Fielding, *The History of Tom Jones* (1749, Penguin, London, 1966, 1985), p. 98.

Thwackum's response to rationalistic naturalism was rather radically fideistic: his dictum was that 'The law of nature is a jargon of words, which means nothing'.[180] The argument between Square and Thwackum bypasses human nature and its innate affections and desires.

The Squares of eighteenth-century England were enemies of vulgarity and irrationality, and thus supernaturality in religion: when they lacked the temerity to profess atheism, they settled for Deism. Whilst his Anglican contemporaries set about to confute the Deists, between 1732 and 1755, Handel was composing his great oratorios.[181] The natural object of Tom Jones's desires is Sophia Western; her Papa was a Tory in his musical, as in his political, tastes:

> It was Mr Western's custom every afternoon, as soon as he was drunk, to hear his daughter play on the harpsichord, for he was a great lover of music, and perhaps, had he lived in town, might have passed for a connoisseur; for he always excepted against the finest compositions of Mr Handel. He never relished any music but what was light and airy; and indeed his most favourite tunes, were *Old Simon the King, St George he was for England, Bobbing Joan*, and some others. His daughter, tho' she was a perfect mistress of music, and would never willingly have played any but Handel's, was so devoted to her father's pleasure, that she learnt all those tunes to oblige him.[182]

If the largest novelty, in England, of Handel's work was 'to give the words and music narrative coherence',[183] his transposition of the biblical narrative into a musical language of drama was a response to Deism, which Thwackum would not have relished. While the Squares

> were . . . pointing to similarities between the stories preserved in the Bible and those of other cultures . . . those who established themselves as representatives of orthodoxy responded by dissociating Christianity from every form of story-telling.[184]

The a-theological Squares and the Thwackums held their contest about the historicity of the Scriptures on the ground prepared for them by Enlightenment philosophes. Voltaire's *Philosophy of History* teaches that it is a 'simple matter to distinguish between the true and the false in history' on the ground that the one is known by *reason*, the other merely by imagination.[185] Imagination distorts its object and is thus neither a means by which a contemporary historian can know historical truth, nor a trustworthy device in the hands of an ancient historian. Voltaire gave some pointers to the scientific historian in the article about 'Figurative Language' in his *Philosophical Dictionary*:

180 Ibid., p. 127.
181 Smith, *Handel's Oratorios*, p. 142.
182 Fielding, *Tom Jones*, p. 133.
183 Smith, *Handel's Oratorios*, p. 119.
184 Swanston, *Handel*, p. 25.
185 Hayden White, *Metahistory: The Historical Imagination in Nineteenth Century Europe* (Johns Hopkins University Press, Baltimore, 1973), p. 51.

Ardent imagination, passion, desire – frequently deceived – produce the figurative style. We do not admit it into history, for too many metaphors are hurtful, not only to perspicuity, but also to truth, by saying more or less than the thing itself.[186]

John Toland published his Deistic apologia, *Christianity not Mysterious*, in 1695. He considered Middle Eastern myths as mischievous as Babylonian ones. One response was to insist that Christianity can be as unimaginative as Voltaire-Square would wish. A critic writing in the *Spectator* under the name of Philalethes imagined a 'Mahommadan's' reaction to Handel's *Messiah* 'Will they not be apt to say that we ourselves believe it no better than a Fable?'.[187] Some of the more irregular features of Christian theology come to it through its liturgy. For Toland, the curvaceous images of 'Type, Symbol, Parable, Shadow, Figure, Sign, Mystery, signify all the same thing'.[188] If God intervenes, he must do so in one place and not another: the choice is difficult rationally to elucidate. Matthew Tindal's apologia for 'natural religion', *Christianity as Old as the Creation* (1730) was answered in kind by Joseph Butler, in his *Analogy of Religion: Natural and Revealed*. Having discerned that 'God governs the world by general fixed laws' and that this 'moral scheme of government' may be 'deduced from the eternal ... relations, the fitness and unfitness of actions', the Square *theologian* was able to infer that 'God's miraculous interpositions may have been all along ... by general laws of wisdom' which we have yet to grasp. If 'Christianity' is to be 'vindicated' by its 'analogy to the experienced constitution of Nature', that is because Nature and revelation obey the same 'general laws'.[189] Butler had, therefore, no need to venture into the liturgical reservoir which contains the precognitive conditions for the credibility of the belief that Isaiah's 'Suffering Servant' and Christ are typologically related. Whether the revelatory activities of Christ 'are or are not to be thought miraculous', Butler considered, 'is, perhaps, only a question about words'.[190]

The mediaeval typologies, set out in the Mystery Plays, display the episodes of the *narrative* parts of the Old Testament as prefigurations of Christ. The *Messiah* tackles the *prophets*, especially Isaiah, from whom nearly a third of its set pieces are taken. Handel's oratorio commences thus:

Comfort ye, comfort ye, my people,
   says your God.
Speak tenderly to Jerusalem,
   and cry to her
that her warfare is ended,
   that her iniquity is pardoned ... (Is. 40.1–2)

---

186 Cited in ibid., p. 53.
187 Cited in Swanston, *Handel*, p. 95: Philalethes is objecting to the mixture of the genres of drama and the sacred word: 'an Oratorio either is an act of religion or it is not', he says.
188 Ibid., p. 30.
189 Joseph Butler, *The Analogy of Religion: Natural and Revealed* (1736, Macmillan, London, 1900), pp. 50, 66–67, 181 and 258.
190 Ibid., p. 155.

The post-exilic prophets introduce such *emotions* as love and compassion into the biblical image of God.[191] Rather than drawing on the Gospels, Charles Jennens, Handel's librettist, turns to the Pauline Epistles, the most prophetically 'pathetic' and autobiographical texts of the New Testament.

For Joseph Butler,

> The law of Moses ... and the Gospel of Christ, are authoritative publications of the religion of Nature; they afford a proof of God's general providence, as moral Governor of the world, as well as of His particular dispensations of providence toward sinful creatures, revealed in the Law and the Gospel ... in the daily course of natural providence, God operates in the very same manner, as in the dispensation of Christianity.[192]

The Deist is convinced of the equivocity, or disjunctiveness, between nature and supernature: God is extrinsic to the natural machines he creates. Such literalism will find no meaning in biblical *analogies* or typologies. But nor does it help to make Nature and revelation (Butler always capitalises them thus) identical. Butler smoothly identifies the 'moral laws' of Nature, and her Governor, and the 'eminent Prophet' who 'confirmed the truth of this moral system of nature'.[193] Perhaps the path from nature to God, and thence to typological analogies between Isaiah's Servant and the Suffering Christ, is not as Natural as Butler indicates; perhaps Toland and Tindal were not best answered on paper. It does not follow that grace has no foundations in human sensibility, but must be brutally thwacked into us. Rather we must say that our perception of typological design is a supernaturally assisted feat of imagination. For the *spirituality* of eighteenth-century Anglicans and Catholics, the ground note is affective mysticism, which it articulated in the best of its oratorios. Mysticism is not cogent unless the mystic *herself* is believable. Fielding remarks, 'I am convinced I never make my reader laugh heartily, but where I have laughed before him':[194] the argument from *experience* is central to the *Messiah*. Handel said that, as he composed it, 'I did think I did see all Heaven before me, and the great God himself'.

In this oratorio, the two sopranos, tenor, alto, heroic bass and chorus *sing the story* of salvation history: they do not act out individual parts. For some, the *Messiah* is less dramatic than Bach's Passions, because the Gospel characters are not represented on stage. Peter Lang has it that

> the sequence of Promise, Incarnation, Passion and Resurrection provides an epic unity that dispenses with a dramatic plot ... the Oratorio does not present the life and passion of Jesus but the lyric-epic contemplation of the *idea* of Christian redemption. There is scarcely any narration or action in it, and most of the recitatives are undramatic.[195]

Philalethes' comments in the *Spectator* touch on the anxiety of the age: since a performance is either a sacred liturgy or a play for the secular stage,

191 Miles, *God: A Biography*, p. 234.
192 Butler, *Analogy of Religion*, pp. 141 and 184.
193 Ibid., p. 196.
194 Fielding, *Tom Jones*, p. 399.
195 Lang, *Handel*, p. 342.

where does Handel's oratorio fall? Perhaps it lies uneasily between the two. Roston finds the gap unbridgeable: oratorio was 'a magnificent substitute, but it was not drama in the true sense of the word'.[196] But perhaps Handel was compelled to create a 'miraculous' bridge, in the form of a pre-theoretical persuasion, an aural image which appeals to the 'reasons of the heart'. Though musical-mimesis, Handel tries to make us hear the truth of prophecy. A musical apology for Isaiah 40.1–3 may be expressed in this 'Air'

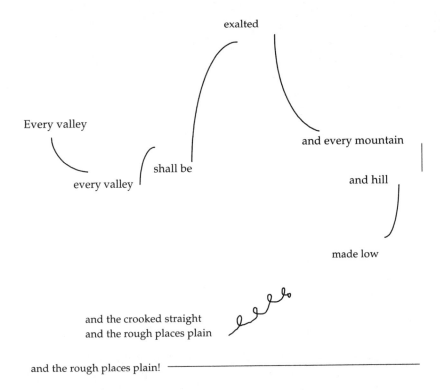

The vulgar feature of miracle is that it makes God visible. When the mimetic possibilities had been focused in music, one can still make the glory *shine*. One can take the three lines of Isaiah 40.5 and interweave them into choral 'rounds', so that one hears

> And the glory of the Lord shall be revealed
> and **all flesh** shall see it together
> [deeper] for the mouth of the Lord hath spoken it

almost simultaneously. The bass recitatives can bear the weight of the drama, as in 'Thus saith the Lord of Hosts' (Haggai 2.6, 7; Malachi 3.1). One can *bounce* through 'O thou that tellest good tidings in Jerusalem'

---

196 Roston, *Biblical Drama in England*, p. 189.

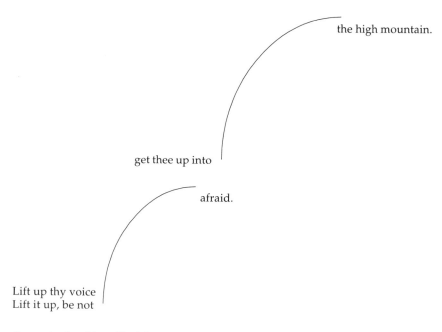

the high mountain.

get thee up into

afraid.

Lift up thy voice
Lift it up, be not

Say unto the cities of Judah:
Behold your God! Arise, shine [*bounce, bounce*], for thy light has come [*tum, tum, tum, tum*].
Arise shine for thy light has come

And the glory
of the Lord is risen upon *thee*! (Is. 40.9; 60.1)

The chorus can toe-tap through Isaiah 9.6. The recitative again bears the brunt of the drama: 'And Lo, the angel of the Lord came upon them.' And suddenly, with violins, the chorus can crash in with 'Glory to God in the highest!' A soprano must invoke the daughter of Zion to **SHOUT** (Zechariah 9.9–10). 'His yoke is easy and his burthen is light' (Matthew 11.30) is sung like good news. Thus far, thus relentlessly jolly. Part II begins in darkness: the chorus wails 'Behold the Lamb of God/that taketh away in the sin of the world' (John 1.29), and an alto mourns over the Suffering Servant (Is. 53.3; 50.6); 'he hid not his face from shame and spitting' is spat out with rapid and muscular vigour, not avoiding the horror, but vocally dramatising the evil play of the 'spitting'. The chorus begins on the same sad notes, if somewhat sweeter, with Isaiah 53.4–5. When it continues on an upper note with 'All we like sheep have gone astray/we have turned every one to his own way/every one to his own way/every one to his own way', it sounds as if the sheep are enjoying every minute of it; until we slide down into the reminder

And
   the Lord
      hath laid on Him
         the iniquity of
           us all (Is. 53.6).

The tenor recitative and chorus capture the satirical nastiness of the detractors ('let him deliver him'). We are taken to the underworld with the soprano's recitative on Isaiah 53.3. The last 'stricken' is immediately followed by the sounds of victory: 'Thou didst not leave his soul in hell!', followed by the great rhythmic 'Lift up your heads, O ye gates': the King of Glory triumphantly marches through the gates and into the citadel (Ps. 24.7–10). From here on, we know he has won the field, with the bass air challenging the nations (Ps. 2.1–2) and the chorus, like merry mice, threatening to 'break their bonds asunder' (Ps. 2.3). The Hallelujah chorus demands the mimetic response of vigorous bodily motion; it calls for the courtly gesture which George II accorded it. What biblical scholarship puts asunder, the soprano makes to belong together, in her 'air' on Job 19.25–26 and 1 Corinthians 15.20: *this* sweetness has known the pathos of death; she sings of resurrection with tears in her voice. We end in absolute confidence and the bassest sort of vulgarity: 'A Trumpet will sound' – and it does – and the dead shall be raised – and they are; and coming down to earth 'this mortal must put on immortality' (1 Cor. 15.52–53).

Joseph Addison, the founder and editor of the first *Spectator*, was interested in the relation between Greek drama and sacred mysteries. He believed that 'the first original of the drama was a religious worship, consisting of a chorus which was nothing else but a hymn to a Deity'. Such scholars urged the somewhat impractical plan of 'bringing the chorus back into drama' and 'stressed its original religious function, relating it to church music and arguing that it would add a rational and moral element to the theatre'.[197] If the scheme of recapturing the sacred for art by reincorporating the chorus was aesthetically unworkable with reference to *plays*, one could exercise more imagination when listening to music: Handel's 'Oratorio was not simply secular theatre music but a powerful fusion of ceremony and drama that had strong roots in an indigenous tradition of sublime religious art'.[198] The ensuing *Gestalt* brought a monarch to his feet: if audience participation is a mark of comedy from Aristophanes to Christmas pantomimes, the emotive Handelian overlapping of audience and players smacks more of the comic anabasis than of the awe-inspiring Aeschylean chorus. Handel's musical dramatisation of the miracle of typology is at its most biblical in the *Messiah*, and thus at its most genuinely and vulgarly comic: he has done what Fielding says a 'comic writer' must do, in his conclusion, that is 'make the principal characters as happy as he can'.[199] Players and audience move through the choral-sequence of the *Messiah* with the certainty of dancing through an exuberant ritual.

George Buchanan (1506–1582), humanist-scholar and one of the first moderators of the General Assembly of the Church of Scotland, was also

197 Smith, *Handel's Oratorios*, p. 242.
198 Ibid., p. 245.
199 Fielding, *Tom Jones*, p. 729.

the first to compose a tragic drama out of the tale of Jephthah. His Latin tragedy *Jephthes* takes its spiritual tone from the plays of Euripides, and its moral atmosphere from Seneca.[200] The play came down in the world after that. On their way to London, Tom Jones and Partridge stop to see a puppet-show at an inn,

> It was called the fine and serious part of the *Provoked Husband*; and it was indeed a very grave and serious entertainment, without any low wit or humour, or jests; or, to do it no more than justice, without anything which could provoke a laugh.[201]

The Puppet-Master has burdened himself with a Square aesthetic. His 'descanting on the good morals inculcated by his exhibitions' is interrupted by a 'violent uproar': the landlady has discovered her 'wench ... on the puppet-show stage in company with the Merry-Andrew, and in a situation not properly to be described'.[202] She notes her own biblical aesthetic as she expels the puppet players:

> I remember when puppet-shows were made of good Scripture stories, as Jephtha's Rash Vow and such good things, and when wicked people were carried away by the devil. There was some sense in those matters; but as the parson told us last Sunday, nobody believes in the devil now-a-days; and here you bring a parcel of puppets drest up like lords and ladies, only to turn the heads of poor country wenches.[203]

The puppet-play of 'Jephtha's Rash Vow' was first performed at Bartholemew Fair, in 1698; the text is preserved for us from the year 1733, when it was performed at 'Lee and Harper's Great Theatrical Book', in Southwark. It gives Jephtha's daughter a comic nurse and a lover, who commits suicide over the body of his bethrothed in a heart-rending dénouement.[204] We may inculpate, not the Calvinist Buchanan, but the Jesuits for the lover. Jakob Balde SJ was Professor of Rhetoric in the Jesuit college at Ingolstadt, and responsible for the school's annual performance of biblical plays. In his 1654 *Jephtias* Balde practically eliminated Mother and Daughter, and created a leading role for the lover, perhaps interpreting the Bible with the casting requirements of a boys' college in mind.[205]

Balde was also a 'pioneer' in drawing an analogical 'parallel between the story of the immolated virgin ... and the sacred human virgin, Jesus Christ'.[206] An inclusive affiliation for typology, both sacred and secular, is one of the features of the Baroque imagination, from Botticelli to Tiepolo, and from Carissimi to Handel. Handel mythologises *Jephtha*, in the direction of Hollywood sweetness. He gives the general a dove-like wife, whom he names Storge, as had Buchanan. Handel calls the daughter Iphis and creates a fiancé for her named Hamor. The love interest provides the

---

200 Wilbur Owen Sypherd, *Jephthah and His Daughter: A Study in Comparative Literature* (University of Delaware, Delaware, 1948), ch. 2.
201 Fielding, *Tom Jones*, p. 524.
202 Ibid., p. 526.
203 Ibid., p. 527.
204 Sypherd, *Jephthah and His Daughter*, ch. 3.
205 Ibid.
206 Ibid.

opportunity to let the pair of cupids sing to one another – 'Happy We!', for Hamor to volunteer to die for Iphis, which offer she rejects with the candidly melodic 'Whatever is, is right', and to end not only in a jubilant chorus of Hallelujah's, but in one another's arms.

The most untoward aspect of the biblical history is that its driving force is a God who does not remain external to the story, but appears from time to time to lift the plot threads in the right direction. As against the Deist objections to miracle, one may claim that not all divine interventions are sheer superimpositions, but tack into some element of the weave of nature. Handel's librettists are often marked down as rationalists for taking that biblical line: 'the librettists' of Handel's 'Israelite oratorios try to have it both ways, giving a rational explanation (or "second cause") while claiming divine intervention ... Jephtha has the skills of an outstanding general as well as the support of cherubim and seraphim'.[207] Jephtha's sprightly aria 'Virtue, virtue, goodness shall make me great', with its cha-cha-cha rhythm nods to the spiritual utilitarianism of the rationalists, and, but, at the same time, sends it up. Although he is on the verge of his 'rash vow' the sprightliness gets the better of the irony: this oratorio is set in a Rococo cherry orchard. When Iphis stands ready to die, Jephtha having invoked 'angels to waft her through the skies', and Iphis herself crooning that 'brighter skies I seek above/In the realms of peace and love', they are clearly envisaging von Balthasar's 'Pozzo and Tiepolo kind of heaven'. When the angel appears to annul the vow, we have dramatic comedy as the nineteenth century will understand it, with the suffering sugared over and the earthiness lightened to the point of disappearance, melodic drama and painless comedy.

Jephtha is indistinguishable from another superb Handelian oratorio, *Acis and Galataea*, and that is because the Baroque Enlightenment cannot quite find the relation of the profane to the sacred. Fielding has many great lessons about the 'natural goodness of heart'[208] neglected by Square the naturalist and Thwackum the theorist of supernatural grace. He can tell us about the 'analogy between the world and the stage':[209]

> Now we, who are admitted behind the scenes of this great theatre of nature (and no author ought to write anything besides dictionaries and spelling books who hath not this privilege) can censure the action, without conceiving any absolute detestation of the person, whom perhaps nature may not have designed to act an ill part in all her dramas: for in this instance, life most exactly resembles the stage, since it is often the same person who represents the villain and the heroe; and he who engages your admiration today, will probably attract your contempt tomorrow. As Garrick, whom I regard in tragedy to be the greatest genius the world hath ever produced, sometimes condescends to play the fool ...
>
> Those persons, indeed, who have passed any time behind the scenes of this great theatre, and are thoroughly acquainted not only with the several disguises which are there put on, but also with the fantastic and capricious behaviour of the passions, who are the managers and directors of this theatre (for as to Reason the Patentee, he is known to be a very idle fellow, and

207 Smith, *Handel's Oratorios*, pp. 146–147.
208 Fielding, *Tom Jones*, p. 101.
209 Ibid., p. 263.

seldom to exert himself) may most probably have learned ... to stare at nothing.

A single bad act no more constitutes a villain in life, than a single bad part on the stage. The passions, like the managers of a playhouse, often force men upon parts, without consulting their judgement, and sometimes without any regard to their talents. Thus the man, as well as the player, may condemn what he himself acts; nay, it is common to see vice sit as awkwardly on some men, as the character of Iago would on the honest face of Mr William Mills.[210]

Our search for the good, and our acting, is largely governed by pre-rational 'passions'. Here, also, is a common-sense adjustment to the Mystery Plays: we play neither the pure villain nor the perfect hero, but a bit of both, for practical observation indicates that human beings are 'inconsistent' or illogical, and do not automatically have all of the virtues if they have one.[211] The comic novelist's 'great theatre of nature' is true to *nature*, if it has little to say about the supernatural.

If we remove the horizon of the supernatural from our image of the human actor, he will be severely cut down to size, even when the mini-mising glance is merely that of Voltaire. If we treat the human subject as a causal mechanism our 'historiography' will be 'impelled toward a Satirical mode of representation', as will our fiction. Because it could not imagine human beings as great heroes

> This age produced no great Tragic historiography, and for the same reason that it produced no great Tragic theatre. The bases for believing in the heroic Tragic flaw, conceived as an excessive degree of virtue, were lacking in it. Since all effects had to be presumed to have both the necessary and sufficient causes required for their production, the notion of an existential paradox, a dialectical contradiction that was lived rather than merely thought, could hardly be conceived by the thinkers or artists of this age. This is why the Comedy produced by the age, even that of Molière, tends to correspond to that of the New, rather than the Old, Attic Comedy; it is in the line of the farce of Menander, rather than in that of the high-mimetic seriousness of Aristophanes, which is a Comedy based upon an acceptance of the *truths of tragedy*, rather than the flight from, or derogation of, those truths, as Menander's – and Molière's – tend to be ... Neither a Comic nor a Tragic vision of history was plausible to the [Enlightenment historians] and so they fell back upon Satirical and Ironic representations of the world they inhabited.[212]

The examples of Fielding's great novel, and of Handel's *Messiah*, in which Anglican comedies the biblical insights are alive, indicate that we need not write down the whole era as one of reductionist satire. The question of the right relation of nature to supernature remained, and unless we have an answer, we can seldom dramatise the biblical Good, which is both pre-sentable in the finite, and incommensurable with it. Unless we can juggle the torches of the presentability and the incommensurability of God, we shall not be able to express the analogy of goodness which runs through

210 Ibid., pp. 265–266.
211 Peter Geach, *The Virtues* (Cambridge University Press, Cambridge, 1977, 1979), pp. 161–168.
212 White, *Metahistory*, p. 66.

Scripture, the concordance and the discrepancy between God's intentions and their human fulfilments. One will then carry the torch *either* of the natural goodness of the generous if imprudent Tom Jones *or* that of Thwackum's transcendent grace. Our humane instincts incline us to the former, but the consequences of that choice are far from commonsensical.

Second Interlude: We Are Not Amused; or, Why to Avoid the Nineteenth Century

Joseph Butler was convinced that, if 'the soul be naturally immortal', and given a 'sufficient length of time' and a 'stage large and extensive enough', virtue must prevail in the universe.[213] We may then see 'the present world' as a 'theatre of action, for the manifestation of persons' characters, with respect to a future one: not to be sure to an all-knowing Being, but to His creation'.[214] That may tell us more about the fixed and moral laws of 'Nature' than about anthropidicy: human beings do not achieve their identities in action, in relation to the eyes of God. In 1809, John Larpent, the presiding Examiner of Plays 'expunged' the words 'Bring my grey hairs in sorrow to the grave'

> from a farce by Thomas Hook on the grounds that Biblical quotations were profaned by usage on the stage. His successor Colman (a profligate author of indecent plays) ... prohibit[ed] a stage lover from calling his mistress *angel* on the grounds that this constituted a slight on a scriptural figure ... William Donne, who supervised licensing from 1849 to 1874, stated categorically, 'I never allow any association with Scripture or theology to be introduced into a play.[215]

And yet, the spiritual utilitarianism of contemporary Christianity permitted the greatest philosophers of the nineteenth century to identify it with a prosaic and psychologising *Comedy*. The Idealists claim that the spirit of modern dramatic comedy is identical to that of Christianity, and this was not a compliment. If Schelling's mind lies behind the nineteenth century, it was not the fault of the pruriently censorious British Examiners of Plays that no dramatist was inspired to stage the biblical story.

Both Schelling and Hegel systematically deduce three genres of literature: lyric, epic and drama, which splits into tragedy and comedy. Drama is the higher synthesis of lyric and epic, uniting the necessity of epic with the freedom of lyric.[216] The first factor in drama is showing: 'in drama a specific attitude of mind passes over into an impulse, next into its willed actualization, and then into an action; it externalizes and objectifies itself'.[217] It is not merely that *something comes about*, but that the outward form of the presentation *expresses* the inward form of the characters:

213 Butler, *Analogy of Religion*, p. 60.
214 Ibid., p. 98.
215 Roston, *Biblical Drama in England*, p. 227. The single 'inexplicable exception' was Elizabeth Polack's *Esther, the Royal Jewess; or the Death of Haman* – performed in London in 1835.
216 Friedrich Wilhelm Joseph von Schelling, *The Philosophy of Art*, translated by Douglas Stott (University of Minnesota Press, Minneapolis and London, 1988), pp. 247–250.
217 G. W. F. Hegel, *Aesthetics: Lectures on Fine Art: Volume II*, translated by T. M. Knox (Clarendon Press, Oxford, 1975), p. 1161.

the chief thing in drama is not the objective action, but the exposition of the inner spirit of the action in respect of not only the general nature of the action and the conflict and fate involved, but also the dramatis personae and their passion, 'pathos', decision, mutual involvement and working on one another.[218]

If the act of *thinking* constructs an immobile duality of subject and object, the act of poeticising, especially that of the dramatic poet, produces an image of the two in the *act* of reconciliation: Hegel envisaged drama as 'the effort of poetic imagination to envisage *the movement* by which this tension is resolved and the unity of the subject with the object is achieved'.[219]

The second element in drama is *collision*. The Divine, so Hegel says, is at the 'bottom' of drama, and that in its 'essentially moral' nature.[220] The world of the Divine is intrinsically *one*. Realise it on the worldly stage, and the fragments of divine unity will fight it out, in a drama.[221] Each tragic hero represents, in the form of an objective 'pathos', only *one side* of the moral unity of the Divine. This is the cause of his guilt, and of the need for reconciliation.

The German Romantics find Greek mythology more imaginatively compelling than biblical typology. In search of the originary imagination, they found the Power which they sought in

the poetry of Antiquity ... What comes to light is: a previously imperceptible hiatus in Greek 'classicism', the traces of a savage prehistory and terrifying religion ... an ... art barely detached from ... 'orgiastic' ... fury. In sum, tragic Greece ... the Schlegels invent what becomes known ... as the opposition of the Apollonian and the Dionysian.[222]

Schelling and Hegel write enthusiastically of very real '*gods*'. Not just *gods*, taken as individuals, but the divine terrain which they together constitute is the object of the 'mythology of reason' which Schelling heralds in the 'System-Programme of German Idealism' (1796).[223] Schelling will claim that

The gods taken together necessarily constitute a totality, a world ... Since in each figure the absolute is posited with limitation, each figure therefore presupposes others; directly or indirectly each individual presupposes all others and all presuppose each individual ... they necessarily constitute a world in their own turn collectively, one in which everything together is mutually determined, an organic whole, a totality, a world ... *Only by collectively constituting a world in this way do the gods acquire independent existence for fantasy or an independent poetic existence.*[224]

218 Ibid., p. 1170.
219 White, *Metahistory*, p. 88.
220 Hegel, *Aesthetics II*, p. 1162.
221 Ibid., p. 1196.
222 Philippe Lacoue-Labarthe and Jean-Luc Nancy, *The Literary Absolute: The Theory of Literature in German Romanticism*, translated by Philip Barnard and Cheryl Lester (State University of New York Press, Albany, New York, 1988), p. 10.
223 David Farrell Krell, 'The Oldest Program towards a System in German Idealism', *The Owl of Minerva*, 17, 1, Fall 1985, 5–19 (9). Krell discusses the question of whether Hegel or Schelling composed the 'Program'.
224 Schelling, *Philosophy of Art*, p. 41.

With Hegel, 'the Divine', as a 'totality in itself', works its way out in the 'single individuals' through whose collision and reconciliation the drama is presented.[225]

Contemporary drama earns a negative assessment in the eyes of the two German aestheticians by contrast with the theatre of classical Greece. The Greek stage presents an idyllic metaphor of art and religion whilst the prosaic realism and sentimentality of the modern stage is damned. The two early nineteenth-century post-Kantian systematicians termed Christianity 'Romanticism', or 'Idealism'. Christianity falls short of the sturdy 'realism' of the mythology of the classical stage. Schelling states that, 'Realistic mythology reached its apex in Greek mythology. Idealistic mythology gradually came to dwell entirely in Christianity'.[226] The religious sense which lies behind the Greek theatre draws the infinite down into the finite:[227] this is what is *presented* or *expressed* on its stage. But Christianity dissolves the finite into the infinite: 'The principle of Christianity was the absolute predominance of the ideal over the real, of the spiritual over the corporeal.'[228] God cannot become incarnate and *suffer*, in the way in which Christ does, without 'nullifying' the finite, sacrificing it to the Infinite.[229] Hegel states that 'Greek art displays the inner life of spiritual individuality as entirely embodied in its corporeal shape, in actions and events, as expressed entirely in the outer',[230] whereas 'romantic', and that is, Christian art, deals with 'deep', and inward, 'feeling'. Thus, the outwardness essential to drama has no place in Christian or 'romantic' art. Hegel says that the Greek 'actor comes on the stage as a totally solid objective statue'.[231] Because 'the external shape' of the Incarnation 'does not rebuff' us 'with a classical rigorousness, but offers' to human vision what it has itself, or 'knows and loves in others around' itself, Christianity will do away with such firm and rebarbative externality.[232] Christianity offers direct, affective access to the divine heart. One can *sink into the Incarnate* Christ, because he is exactly like oneself. Because, as Hegel tells us, Christ incarnates the human spirit, he provides the faithful with a soft, watery, mirror-image of themselves. One may identify with him without banging one's head against the non-human otherness of the Greek gods. Romanticism-Christianity is submerged in subjective feeling: 'This being one with itself in the other', this finding one's reflection in Christ, 'is the really beautiful subject matter of romantic art, its Ideal which has ... for its form and appearance the inner life and subjectivity, mind and feeling'.[233] For Schelling, the suffering of Christ is unpresentable, the subsuming of the finite into the infinite; for Hegel, 'Christ scourged ... cannot be portrayed in the forms of Greek beauty', that is, outwardly, but only in 'the depth of

225 Hegel, *Aesthetics II*, pp. 1162–1163.
226 Schelling, *Philosophy of Art*, p. 57.
227 Ibid., p. 61.
228 Ibid., p. 77.
229 Ibid., pp. 63–64.
230 G. W. Hegel, *Aesthetics: Lectures on Fine Art: Volume I*, translated by T. M. Knox (Clarendon Press, Oxford, 1975), p. 531.
231 Hegel, *Aesthetics II*, p. 1186.
232 Hegel, *Aesthetics I*, p. 532.
233 Ibid., p. 533.

the inner life, the infinity of grief, present as an eternal moment in the Spirit'.[234] The biblical story is too complacently inward to require externalisation.

In tragedy, the necessity is objective and the freedom subjective; in comedy, conversely, freedom is objective, and necessity is subjectivised. A subjective fate holds no terrors, but is merely an indulged 'pretence'. The necessity in which comedy deals is that of *Character*.[235] 'Aristophanes conducts us', Hegel believes, to a 'world of private serenity. If you have not read him, you can scarcely realise how men can take things so easily.'[236] But the peace is *private* because it is subjective:

> The general ground for comedy is ... a world in which man as subject or person has made himself completely master of everything that counts to him otherwise as the essence of what he wills and accomplishes, a world whose aims are therefore self-destructive because they are insubstantial.[237]

If the subject has complete mastery, then the world in which it wins its battles is nothing.

The 'Ideas', as Schelling considered, are concretised as the gods of Greek myth:[238] as such they appear in the Greek tragedy. Greek theatre presents *universal* passions, because each of its characters manifests one aspect of the ethical *Gestalt* of an Olympian Good: each character in Greek tragedy represents an 'ethical power'.[239] By virtue of its reliance on mythology, Greek drama has access to an objective sacred world. Greek tragedy drama-tised a public body of mythology whereas Aristophanes and the comedians *invented* their mythology.[240] In so doing, comedy severs its link with the divine. Christianity completes the secularisation. For it has likewise *created* its mythology. Neither Schelling nor Hegel found the inventions as imaginatively entrancing as the *given* Greek myths.[241]

The triumph of Christian comedy must also be the dissolution of drama, the highest artistic genre, and thus of art itself. Schelling's *Philosophy of Art* concludes that

> Wherever public life disappears, instead of that real, external drama in which ... an entire people participates as a political or moral totality, only an *inward*, ideal drama can unite the people. This ideal drama is the worship service, the only kind of *truly* public action that has remained for the contemporary age, and even so only in an extremely diminished and reduced form.[242]

Hegel claims likewise that Western civilisation began with symbolic art, turned to the 'plastic art of Greece', and 'ended' two thousand pages later

---

234 Ibid., p. 538.
235 'Subjective absolutenesss ... expresses itself as character': Schelling, *Philosophy of Art*, p. 264.
236 Hegel, *Aesthetics II*, p. 1121.
237 Ibid., p. 1199.
238 Schelling, *Philosophy of Art*, p. 17.
239 Hegel, *Aesthetics II*, pp. 1195–1196.
240 Schelling, *Philosophy of Art*, p. 265.
241 Ibid., pp. 69–70; Hegel, *Aesthetics II*, pp. 1123–1224.
242 Schelling, *Philosophy of Art*, p. 280.

> with the romantic art of emotion and deep feeling where absolute subjective personality moves free in itself and in the spiritual world. Satisfied in itself, it no longer unites itself with anything objective and particularized and it brings the negative side of this dissolution into consciousness in the humour of comedy. Yet on this peak comedy leads ... to the dissolution of art.

If 'art aims at the identity', that is, the identical repetition of God 'in real appearance and shape to our contemplation', then Christian comedy destroys that perfect identity, by expressing it 'only on what is accidental and subjective', in the personality and historicity of Christ: but, in coming together with the contingent, the Christian Absolute 'cancel[s]' the world, subsuming all that is not itself into Divine Subjectivity.[243] Such a subjectivity floats in a void, having no external reality with which to coincide.

For Schelling, the reality of the aesthetic world of the imagination beggars that of historical contingency: '*The world of the gods is the object neither of mere understanding nor of reason, but rather can be comprehended only by fantasy.*'[244] The sacral terrain is apprehended by 'creative imagination', and rendered external by fantasy. It is thus the aesthetic sense which sees the divine:

> *The basic law of all portrayals of the gods is the law of beauty*, for beauty is the absolute intuited *in reality.* Now, since the gods are the *absolute itself* intuited actually (or synthesized with limitation) within the particular, their basic law of portrayal is that of beauty.[245]

The Greek Gods were truly beautiful; Schelling's Christ sacrifices beauty to Infinity; Hegel's Christ submerges beauty in inwardness. What do the German philosophers mean when they claim that the Classical gods, in their infinity, were *actually* and *really* made finite on the Athenian stage? Did Dionysius make himself present in the *Bacchae*; did the *Chordidaskalos* allow for an epiphany of Athena in the *Eumenides*? Or did the Greek dramatists have some notion of the analogical similarity and distance between actors and reality? For the Idealists, the best theatre is that in which this distance is abolished: they present a nostalgic dream of a drama of univocity, in which God or the gods are identical with their representations. The merely empirical fact of the historical appearance of a man in Palestine, who expresses the conjunction-in-difference of humanity and deity, throws a spanner into the works of the perfect machinations of Idealist theory. Which was real, and which a romantic opiate, Schelling's aesthetic gods or the crucifixion of Jesus of Nazareth under the Roman Governor Pontius Pilate in the 30s of the first century AD? The Idealists have reversed the prejudice that historical fact is more real than the products of the aesthetic imagination. They deem Christianity as 'subjectivism' because history is less real for them than concepts.

There is a twist in the tail of this deprecation of Christianity. For the Idealists ultimately identify comic and tragic drama.[246] One of Schelling's bizarre dicta is that 'Spiritually, Aristophanes is genuinely one with

---

243 Hegel, *Aesthetics II*, p. 1236.
244 Schelling, *Philosophy of Art*, p. 38.
245 Ibid., p. 40.
246 Von Balthasar, *Theo-Drama I*, pp. 439–442.

Sophocles, and *is* Sophocles himself'.[247] Hegel did not reserve drama for the stage, but defined human history as expression and collision: he 'not only historicized poetry and the drama' but 'poeticized and dramatized history itself'.[248] He considered that history is driven forward by tragic conflicts between individuals and their society: the historian who stands in the middle of events will perceive them as tragic.[249] As a culture rises to eminence, its historical figures come to the foreground. The death of a culture spells its resurrection in the idea: once Socrates had drunk the hemlock, the factual figure goes to his grave, and the Socratic Ideal can emerge. The historian knows the tragedy of Socrates; the philosopher knows something greater, and that is the concept of Socrates:

> The recognition that this 'death' is also the means to the transformation of human life and morality itself onto a level of self-consciousness greater than the 'life' which led up to it, was, for Hegel, the informing insight of the Comic vision and the highest comprehension of the historical process to which the finite mind can aspire.[250]

The flourishing real is known by the historian as tragedy; once it is past, its concept can be known by the philosopher as comedy. The rebirth of the real as the philosophical concept is the 'justification for belief in the ultimately Comic nature' of history.[251] The 'higher perspective of the Comic nature of the whole' of human history, in which we will perceive 'a theodicy which is not a justification not so much of the ways of God to man as of man's own ways to himself'[252] is not a given, even in Hegel's own philosophy. It is the unreachable goal which is set before us by the aesthetic imagination. And so, German romanticism 'involves a certain impossibility of exactly accommodating the vision of the Idea'.[253] Its belief that human and divine mind are *identical*, in the univocal concept, sets the human mind the impossible task of generating a revelation *to itself*. The Ideal, that perfect comic resolution, is ultimately unattainable, and so Romanticism is 'fascinated ... by the presentation of the absent and absolute Work'[254] which does not and cannot manifest itself.

3. *Jonah-Man Jazz*

Perhaps we can avoid this conclusion by starting again without the Enlightenment. Saul Bellow's Herzog asked, 'When exactly did the fall into the quotidian occur?' Hans Frei answers concisely, *c.* 1701. For, so he tells us, it was in the wake of the Enlightenment that the biblical narrative ceased to be the unitary meaning of the Christian's world. Now, instead of a unitary meaning, one is presented with *two* sets of meaning: the biblical text and the external world. Instead of being contained within the biblical

---

247 Schelling, *Philosophy of Art*, p. 265.
248 White, *Metahistory*, p. 88.
249 Ibid., p. 109.
250 Ibid., p. 120.
251 Ibid., p. 119.
252 Ibid., pp. 130 and 121.
253 Lacoue-Labarthe and Nancy, *Literary Absolute*, p. 122.
254 Ibid, p. 126.

text, the external world went its own way, taking *history* with it. Historical events gain their 'autonomy' from the text: one 'verifies' the text from the events, and not vice versa.[255] Secular history becomes an 'independent criterion' by means of which the biblical writings are judged. Historians and archaeologists *judge* the biblical narratives by 'independently establishable fact claims',[256] by non-biblical evidence. The Bible ceases to be the standard by which history is measured, and becomes the object of the higher judgement of biblical criticism.

In concentrating upon the narrative 'sense' of the Bible, Frei neglected its reference; the question of referential correspondence to truth has been tacitly elided, or, we might say more bluntly, tactically avoided. Frei believed that the *tradition* of the Church has usually directed it to the *literal* sense. But, Nicholas Wolterstorff says, he did not, and could not, ask why:

> Frei never addressed this question head on; the focus of his attention was always on how contemporary members of the Church should proceed, given that a sense has been established. But surely a large part of the answer is the Church wanted the content of its interpretation to be true, and chose from among its options in the light of that desire.[257]

Frei failed to link the beauty of narrative sense with the truth of history. The hope of returning to a 'unitary meaning' of the Bible orients us toward the apotheosis of aesthetic idealism, the philosopher who 'ended by deifying a purely aesthetic conception of history', that is, Friedrich Nietzsche.[258] Nietzsche takes up the original discovery of the Romantics, the Satyr chorus which, he considered, danced tragedy into existence. The musical-dance of the Satyr chorus does not resemble or re-present anything outside of itself. Its imagery is the purer for being non-verbal; this music is non-referential, and thus it creates 'a living wall against the assaults of reality'.[259] If Greek drama is the 'coupling' of Dionysus and Apollo, then it affirms both death and life; it is simultaneously tragic and comic. It represents that collision in a drama whose meaning is *itself*: 'The Tragicomic vision is identified with "the spirit of music" ... with nonrecitiative music which makes no statement *about* the world but simply exists alongside the world as pure form and movement.'[260] The impulse to history, to a mere description of things as they are and have been, made possible to human beings by their 'ability to name things, to confiscate things by linguistic means',[261] is a *descent* from this sheer dance of images. Nietzsche's historian turned tragic dramatist will be 'liberated from having to say anything *about* the past', for such scholars turned poets 'the past' will be 'only an occasion for

255 Hans Frei, *Eclipse of Biblical Narrative: A Study in Eighteenth and Nineteenth Century Hermeneutics* (Yale University Press, New Haven, 1974), p. 4.

256 Ibid., p. 77.

257 Nicholas Wolterstorff, *Divine Discourse: Philosophical Reflections on the Claim that God Speaks* (Cambridge University Press, Cambridge, 1995), pp. 235–236.

258 White, *Metahistory*, p. 373.

259 Friedrich Nietzsche, *The Birth of Tragedy and The Case of Wagner*, translated by Walter Kaufmann (Random House, New York, 1967), p. 61.

260 White, *Metahistory*, p. 345.

261 Ibid., p. 371.

his invention of ingenious "melodies". Historical representation becomes once more all *story*'.[262]

Nietzsche's dream of enabling the historical mind to regain 'its ability to "frolic in images"'[263] has been fulfilled by some of Frei's wayward disciples. Walter Brueggemann notes that

> in focussing on speech, we tend to bracket out all questions of historicity. We are not asking, 'What happened?' but 'What is said?' To inquire into the historicity of the text is a legitimate enterprise, but it does not ... belong to Old Testament theology. In like manner, we bracket out all questions of ontology, which ask about the 'really real'.[264]

Since he takes the words of the 'Biblical life world', which appear to speak about God, to have no referential meaning, Brueggemann *deifies* the biblical text. If

> Brevard Childs writes ... about 'the reality of God' behind the text itself ... one must ask ... What reality? Where behind? ... *the God of Old Testament theology ... lives in, with, and under the rhetorical enterprise of this text, and nowhere else, and in no other way.*[265]

The God of this theology is *in the possession* of anyone who understands the words of the biblical text. The driving force of this aesthetic philosophy is identity: the text's meaning is identical with itself, because it is identical with the self-expression of human imagination. Instead of dramatising a series of horizons, the biblical text closes the lid on itself: it is neatly contained within ourselves.

Is the villain the *spirit of tragedy*? We could trace an interpretative lineage which runs from the Calvinist transpositions of the Bible into Senecan tragedies, as in George Buchanan's *Jepthes*, to Kierkegaard's rendition of the Abraham and Isaac story. In the early twentieth century, Kallen hypothesised that Job is structurally modelled on the tragedies of Euripides; by the late David Robertson and James Williams make the Joban God an Imposter. Von Rad and von Balthasar, took Saul's story to be tragical; a Euripidean Jahweh does not merit Cheryl Exum's imaginative assent. Jack Miles's tragically oriented 'Biography' of God is akin to contemporary examples of the genre in finding the hero to have clay feet. Once one begins to 'frolic in the images' of a Bible which must not mean but be, one might say, Nietzsche's idea of tragedy will out-weigh the paradoxical faith of Kierkegaard.

Nietzsche left two things out of account. One is the historical individual, Thespis, who lived in the mid-sixth century BC, and whose combined thespian and entrepreneurial instincts led him to bring a 'rustic chorus' of dithyrambic actors to Athens, and to make their choral leader into the first tragic *actor*.[266] What did the 'padded dancers', or 'fat men', and satyrs, whose chorus Thespis directed to tragedy *do*? What did the 'fat men, satyrs,

---

262 Ibid., p. 372.
263 Ibid., p. 334.
264 Brueggemann, *Theology of the Old Testament*, p. 118.
265 Ibid., pp. 65–66.
266 The archaeological evidence, from the Parian Marble onwards, is overwhelming: Arthur Pickard-Cambridge, *Dithyramb, Tragedy and Comedy* (Clarendon Press, Oxford, 2nd edn rev. by T. B. L. Webster, 1962), pp. 69–88, 112 and 121.

birds, fish, knights, giants on stilts, ugly women, men in big cloaks', out of whose chorus comedy emerged, get up to on-stage?[267] It seems most likely that these protean actors were mimes. One of the stimuli to the invention of drama was the mimetic talents of the chorus: the fat men and satyrs did not just express themselves, but imitated their social and their religious world, which is why their stories were found tragic or comic.

One should credit a tragic, and dramatic, act of imagination to Calvin, to Bach, and to Kierkegaard; but not to anyone who cannot see in the literary life world of the Bible an analogical mimesis of historical facts, nor to anyone whose imagination does not stretch beyond a naturalistic conception of the good, or who denies to the biblical text its drama of signification, and who worships a text which has been swallowed by human understanding. If Brueggemann proposes as the method of biblical theology a 'fetishism of writing and ... narcissism of the reader', [268] we need not put it down to his tragic sense of life. If being trapped 'inside' is to be tragic, or comic, we must at least hope that there is an outside. Those who have sufficient imagination to perceive what it entails for us to be trapped can conceive tragically the predicament of a Jonah who, once swallowed, has never been regurgitated. The Romanian playwright Marin Sorescu deals out to his Jonah not one but three such swallowings. Inside his fish within a fish within a fish, Jonah sees

> Nothing but an endless row of bellies. Like windows placed next to each other.
> To be locked inside all those windows!
> I'm like a God who can't be resurrected. All his wonders have succeeded, his coming to earth, his life, even his death – but once here, in the grave, he cannot rise again. He beats his head against the walls, calls upon all the powers of mind and wonder, driving himself into Godliness like a circus lion through a halo of fire. But he falls amid the flames. He's jumped through that hoop so many times that he never once imagined he'd stumble, particularly at the resurrection!
> And everyone's expecting him above.[269]

The Christian Scriptures depict God as *facing* the world and yet other from it. The meaning of the comic drama of the Bible is in this proximity in otherness of God. Comedy perceives the difference of this face from every human face as an exuberant excess of being which freely creates, and makes way for, a finite 'heaven and earth' which is like and unlike itself. The story of Jonah expresses the difference-by-excess of the divine face in the outrunning and over-turning of Jonah's expectations, and the nearly-excessive similarity, by mere anthropomorphism. Ninevah's wickedness is so mythological as to lay itself open to comic-strip portrayal. As Michael Hurd transposes it, in his 'Musical Cantata', *Jonah-Man Jazz*,

---

267 Ibid., p. 173.
268 Hayden White, *Tropics of Discourse: Essays in Cultural Criticism* (Johns Hopkins University Press, Baltimore, 1987), pp. 259 and 265.
269 Marin Sorescu, 'Jonah: A Tragedy in Four Scenes', in *The Thirst of the Salt Mountain: A Trilogy of Plays*, translated by Andrea Deletant and Brenda Walker (Forest Books, London, 1985), pp. 24–25.

Ninevah city was a city of sin. The jazz-in and the jiv-in Made a terrible din,
Beat groups playin' A Rock an' roll; An' the Lord when he heard it said:
'Bless my soul!'[270]

The imaging of God as shocked by the wickedness of Ninevah, and his
selection of a man to prophesy destruction on it, is self-consciously literal:
we *think* that God is not a shockable old man, but that is how the story asks
how to picture him. The retributive justice of *this* God will not be
overwhelming:

Shout to the people, Shout from every steeple
Tell them the Judgement bell has chimed.
Tell them to stop their laughter, Or in the Great Hereafter
What's to come is all too sure. For I will smite 'em,
Ad infinitum, If they will not Turn to me once more.[271]

Moreover, this God appears to *need* the services of a prophet who has other
things in mind: or, he wants the prophecy to happen *this way* and no other.
God's omnipotence, his ability to command the necessities of the story's
logic brings about his dependence on the absurdly incompetent vehicle of
Jonah. D. S. Savage's 1956 radio play, *And also Much Cattle*, captures this:
Jonah

Preacher:	Thought he done give God de slip once dey gits afloat.
	Sits down in de scuppers wid a belly full o' booze.
	Pretty soon his head was down: Jonah's in a snooze.
	His fren's, you settin' in dis yere church,
	Has any of you lef' de Lawd God in de lurch?
The Lord:	Jonah. (*Pause*) Jonah. Don' yo' heah me no mo', Jonah?
	Ain't you gonta prophesy of' me, like I tol' you to?[272]

Jonah does not want this narrative logic. The storm-tossed sailors don't
want him in their story either:

Preacher:	Sure, dey got to die sometime, like evahone's gotta die –
	Geuss dey jest had a pre*fer*ence for doin' it dry.
	So dey pray fo' fo'giveness for doin' a sin,
	And dey grabs hol' of Jonah and dey tumbles him in.[273]

From Jonah's point of view, sinking into the waves is no laughing matter;
those who know that he is held in the grip of the divine plan *let him* sink, as
he offers a 'brisk' solo

When Jonah sank in-to the sea He
closed his eyes and prayed: Oh, Lord I'm very sorry that Your word I've
disobeyed. If you will only come and save me I will do as you command;
Instead of treading water Let me treat upon the land.[274]

270 Michael Hurd, *Jonah-Man Jazz: A Cantata Musical for Unison Voices and Piano, with
Guitar Chords* (Novello Publishing, London, 1966), pp. 1–2.
271 Ibid., pp. 5–7.
272 D. S. Savage, *And Also Much Cattle: Scenario for Four Voices* (Brentham Press, London,
1975), pp. 3–4.
273 Ibid., pp. 4–5.
274 Hurd, *Jonah-Man Jazz*, pp. 16–17.

We *know* that Jonah is on the end of the thread which is held by God: that turns the myth into a man bites dog story. Although Noah has some supernal fisherman's stories to tell, Jonah can out-brag him:

All I asks is this: Has one of ye been *'bait?*[275]

The consumption of the indigestible Jonah is perhaps not a laughing matter for the *whale*, the swelling of whose intestines are reflected in

Whale did,
whale did, whale did, Whale did have a pain just horrible!
Jonah,
Jonah, Jonah, Jonah was no airy bubble! trouble
trouble heaps o' trouble trouble heaps o'
Swallowin' him it was heaps o' trouble

Hm – Hm – Hm
Hm – Hm – Hm
Ah – Ah – Ah[276]

Savage draws on Tradition, or maybe just culture, to depict a worse fate for the whale:

Preacher: Ain't my part to speculate, an' I don' wanne be call' no liah,
              But dere is some as figure he was cold an' fixed hisself a
              fyah.[277]

He, or she, must have felt a good deal of relief upon vomiting Jonah on the shore. God's plans remain constant, as Savage returns to the word of Scripture:

Reader: And the word of the LORD came unto Jonah a second time,
            saying,
            Arise, go unto Ninevah, that great city, and preach unto it
            the preaching that I bid thee.

Ninevah is mythically unchangeable, ever the megalopolis of a Damon Runyon story. Jonah's preaching-word works like a magical incantation:

Jonah come to dis white-trash nation,
He prophesy dem hell an' he prophesy damnation.
Jehovah God his prophet done sent
To call on dis nation to repent.
No good brandy, no good rum,
[*Drums*]
No good bangin' on de ol' bass drum;
No good a-wailin' and a-makin' moan
[*Saxophone*]
No good a-rootlin on de saxophone;
[*Bassoon*]

275 Don Marquis, *Noah an' Jonah an' Cap'n John Smith: A Book of Humorous Verse* (Appleton & Company, New York, 1922), pp. 2 and 4.
276 Brian Hughes, arr., *Folk Songs for Male Voices*: Jonah. Spiritual for 4–part male chorus or quartet unaccompanied (Roberton Publications, Aylesbury, 1978), pp. 1–2.
277 Savage, *And Also Much Cattle*, p. 6.

No good blowin' on dat ole bassoon,
[*Drums*]
Destruction is a-comin' and a-comin mighty soon.[278]

Jonah did not expect his preaching to work with such omnipotentially powered logic; nor for God to change his mind about the Destruction. Its unforeseen conclusion will teach him to recognise the comedy of the likeness-in-unlikeness of God. The Face is close enough to bear human abuse:

Jonah: Reason I got on dat boat
                  gon' to Tarshish, caize I well knowed You woul'n't *do*
                  dat destruction You tol' me to prophesy on dis bum
                  town.

God accommodates to Jonah's heat: 'And the LORD GOD prepared a gourd, and made it to come up over Jonah, that it might be a shadow over his head, to deliver him from his grief. So Jonah was exceeding glad of the gourd'. The lengthening stem could be suggested by a saxophone, the gourd by a bassoon: Jonah is pleased by the 'pumpkin'[279] produced by the combined efforts of sound effects and miracle. 'But God prepared a worm when the morning rose the next day, and it smote the gourd that it withered'. When that is followed by an 'east wind', Jonah, like Job, wishes himself dead. The Lord God asks about the analogy between Jonah with his pumpkin, and God with his own city of Ninevah.

278 Ibid., p. 8.
279 Ibid., p. 11.

7

Images and Witnesses

1. How Do We Experience the Good?

As we made our way through the Bible we found human beings seeking the good. In the Pentateuch, the good informs the 'master image' of the promised land. The image of the good in the Pentateuch has two aspects. On the one hand, as Brueggemann emphasised, the good of Genesis, Exodus and Deuteronomy is no abstraction: it is tangible and tasteable; it is not the categorical imperative but vats running over with wine and barns bursting with corn. The promised land is constantly glimpsed but never quite grasped: 'The theme of the Pentateuch is the partial fulfilment – which implies also the partial non-fulfilment – of the promise to or blessing of the patriarchs.'[1] The Pentateuchal good is earthy and elusive, oscillating beyond possession. It is not only the object of a human quest but also, even before Abraham set out in search of it, the subject of a divine promise. In the Deuteronomistic history, the good is pictured in the person of the king. David is the promised and anointed king, God's beloved, God's gift to Israel, and the Old Testament's largest comic image of a giver of grace. He is no less a lusty, devious and once murderous human being. The image of the king oscillates between the ideal and the real. The satire in the Book of Job deconstructs an identification between the human and the divine good. But, if human and divine good must be cut apart, because cosmic order is not moral order, yet, as Job fleetingly sees, God's power extends into every crevice of human life. Job imaginatively travels into the heavens; his drama is the beginning of the transformation of the ancient image of death as Sheol into the apocalyptic image of death as Paradise. During the inter-testamental period the promised land is imaginatively relocated into heaven. The New Testament somersaults across this logic. The Good is supernatural, and also concrete and personal: it is the body of Christ.

Patrick defines biblical inspiration like this:

> the transcendent God has deigned to enter human consciousness as the *dramatis persona* of biblical literature . . . To use Jean Calvin's expression, God has 'accommodated' himself to human understanding by identifying with his *dramatis personae*.[2]

1 Clines, *Theme of the Pentateuch*, p. 29.
2 Patrick, *Rendering of God*, p. 135.

How far did he have to accommodate himself? Is the dramatic form which its authors gave the Bible foreign to human experience, or does something about us make us like to conceive of the good in the way that the Bible does? There are some ways in which the 'eye of faith' and the 'eye' overlap. Von Balthasar says: 'drama is human action, action as a way of imparting meaning to existence in its search for self-realisation'.[3] We act in search of meaning, and our desire for the good leads us to dramatise it. We know the truth, and we contemplate the beautiful, but 'the good is something done'.[4]

We sought four features in the Bible: freedom, eros or desire, alienation and integration. The biblical personae are free: there would be no drama if Abraham were a robot who *had* to obey God. The drama is driven by eros: these free beings are travelling toward their heart's desire. That marks the drama as comic. The biblical characters are jolted, and we call that alienation. Discrepancy has its place, but the last word is integration, that harmonious satisfaction of the desire for friendship in communion, expressed in the heavenly fish breakfast with which John's Gospel concludes.

We understand the meaning of one another's typical gestures by using common sense. A sophisticated common sense is the tool of the historian. She works toward understanding other times and places by training her own common sense to perceive what they would have found 'common-sensical'. Here, 'common sense' is akin to the aesthetic imagination. The common sense of distant cultures is present to the historian in the 'typical gestures' which are memorialised in its cultural artefacts. The gestures which have been captured in bricks, stone and writing are 'expressions': 'Families, peoples, states, religions may be said to express themselves. Accordingly, history may be conceived as the interpretation of such group expressions.'[5] For Lonergan, the dramatic is akin to the 'social expression of imagination'. The 'dramatic pattern of experience' is the operation of human meaning in social experience. Like it or not, human beings must interact with one another. They give an aesthetic meaning to their communal lives by stage directing their encounters with manners, and by determining their conversational script by allotting roles to themselves. These regulations are invented by imaginative play. The 'dramatic pattern of human action', the plumed hats and professorial titles with which we decorate ourselves, is a primary means by which we distinguish ourselves from our hatless, four-footed friends, an 'aesthetic liberation' from natural necessities. The display is put on for others, who tell us whether the product succeeds or fails. Lonergan says that

> Such artistry is . . . in the presence of others, and the others too are also actors in the primordial drama that the theatre only imitates. If aesthetic values . . . yield one the satisfaction of good performance, still it is well to have the objectivity of that satisfaction confirmed by others.[6]

---

3 Ibid., p. 413.
4 Von Balthasar, *Theo-Drama I*, p. 19.
5 Bernard J. F. Lonergan, *A Third Collection: Papers by Bernard J. F. Lonergan*, edited by Frederick E. Crowe (Geoffrey Chapman, London, 1985), p. 153.
6 Bernard J. F. Lonergan, *Insight: A Study of Human Understanding* (Longmans, Green & Co., London, 1957, 1958), p. 188.

Drama is a symbol by which we can understand human history. When we read the biblical narrative as theological drama, we are interpreting it along similar lines to every kind of history.

For von Balthasar, theological drama centres on the unique identity of each human person:

> It is not the sphinx's 'What is man?', but the question 'Who am I?' that the actor must answer, whether he wishes to or not, either before the play begins or as it unfolds.[7]

Human beings like the theatre because they find their own predicament reflected in it. That is, that they cannot act, freely and socially, without a 'role', which others have built for them, and yet no socially constructed role touches the rock-bottom of the self. We use our roles in order to be ourselves, but the social role does not use up everything there is in us: 'There is a point of loneliness and incommunicability in every role.'[8] For von Balthasar, 'drama' is an ethical conception, and one which can only make sense within the framework of a divine allotment of unique 'names' to individuals: 'I will give him a white stone, and in the stone a new name written, which no man knoweth saving he that receiveth it' (Revelation 2.17). This is the terrain of the 'eye of faith'.

Human identity is incarnate in history, and, that is, mediated through the moral and social roles which our civilisation gives us. If God gives us a unique name and mission, he gives it *through* our cultural self-understanding in a particular time and place. There is no perfect moment of disclosure of unique identity which does not require the mediation of cultural and *historical* identity. The drama of scriptural name-giving takes place within an analogous historical drama, of human role construction.

The good has to do with that which is done, and we may say this both of the human good and of the good which is God. Job demands that God show himself, and present himself in the court of Job's judgement: God assents to the first injunction, if he demurs as to the second. This terrifying God is not too transcendent to act: 'God's role is not spectatorship but involvement. He and man meet in the mysterious deed.'[9] We know from 'our faith in revelation [that] God is able truly to enter the world drama'.[10] The good as it is known by human beings and as it is known by God are in dramatic tension. They are analogous and not identical. If God is absolute light, then real human beings get going as fast as they can away from it. The fact of turning to face the Light is an 'act of epistrophe, of turning-around or conversion'.[11] The Light issues moral injunctions: Don't eat from the tree, Build a boat, Leave your home, or Follow me. Here again, a free decision is required:

> The fundamental element of all dramatic action on the world stage is man's
> . . . intelligent freedom that enables him to receive the 'instruction' that comes

---

7 Von Balthasar, *Theo-Drama I*, p. 129.
8 Ibid., p. 253.
9 Heschel, *Prophets*, p. 24.
10 Von Balthasar, *Theo-Drama II*, p. 529.
11 Hans Urs von Balthasar, *Theo-Drama: Theological Dramatic Theory: IV The Action*, translated by Graham Harrison (Ignatius Press, San Francisco, 1994), p. 111.

from the absolute light . . . together with the decision that this intelligent and responsible human being makes, embodying it in the form of history. This very act gives a shape to the continuing stream of events (which is . . . unforeseeable); it gives drama a beginning, a middle and an end, as Aristotle required.[12]

History is given its peripetiac shape by a series of free decisions.

The analogy between Job and his Creator is expressed in the form of a fierce combat between the two. The biblical stories, such as Moses' evasive manoeuvres around the divine Name, show that the historical encounter between God and human beings requires an act in which a human person turns around to see God. Conversion to the good happens to *someone*, whether we call that one the 'empirical self' or the 'unique I'. It does not make good sense either to speak of pure experience, on its way to faith, or of a 'life-world' of complete faith. We may draw it thus:

2. What Is Revelation?

I have taken it for granted that we are all capable of referring ourselves to fathers, daughters, Pharaohs, frogs, swords, swarms of bees, kings, concubines, potsherds, dungheaps, heavens, wells and fish; that the sentences including these particular words join up and project groups of objects in their inter-relation, and in which we find the master images: now that we have experienced the fact, I shall explain how we read 'the same' Bible. Taking a leaf from Master Schelling, we shall suggest that, if one begins with an epic or propositional notion of revelatory meaning and proceeds to a lyric or experiential one, one will arrive at the most encompassing and the best idea, that is, dramatic revelation. A trilogical theory of revelatory meaning includes the best elements of the propositional and the personal notions of revelation and fits the bill of our foregoing account.

a. An Objective Account of Communication

How could the author of the N-Town Cycle, Bilius Bale, Handel and the Jazz singers exercise their theatrical instincts upon the same script? The Polish phenomenologist Roman Ingarden (1893–1970) argues that it is by virtue of the 'ideal meanings' which are implicit in the book.[13] According to Ingarden, the literary work has four 'strata': **word sounds**, upon which are founded **meaning units**, out of which **schematised aspects** are built, by which **objectivities** are **represented**.

When we hear others speaking, we do not usually hear the rat-tat-tat of a hundred different noises. We hear combined sounds, sounds which

12 Ibid.
13 Roman Ingarden, *The Literary Work of Art: An Investigation on the Borderlines of Ontology, Logic, and Theory of Literature*, translated by George Grabowicz (Northwestern University Press, Evanston, 1973), p. 364.

express a 'phonic Gestalt', the conveyed impression, and the received expression, of a material form. A public speaker can do complicated things with sounds. Out of the 'mere sounds' there emerges an aural parade of sounds, marching together, slow, fast, syncopated, or melodic. If I tell a friend about an unfortunate encounter, and bark out abruptly what has happened, sinking to a gasping dénouement, the phonetic *Gestalt* tells my friend *what I feel* about the meeting. The *Gestalten* formed by a text's word sounds are its 'manifestation qualities'.[14] The 'sound' of a book makes it physically 'manifest'; it shows its meaning aurally. The literary work will not express quite the same feeling if its phonic level is altered. Especially, Ingarden says, in

> 'dramatic' works, the word sound material . . . play[s] the irreplaceable role of 'manifesting' the various psychic states of the represented personae. It is only on this path that the concrete physical life of these personae, which cannot be reduced to thoughts . . . arrives at its constitution. If the corresponding word sounds were to be eliminated, so that the meaning units were . . . naked . . . we would still know that the represented hero is thinking this or that . . . but the inexpressible, that aspect of psychic life which cannot be described conceptually would . . . remain indeterminate.[15]

Types of writing vary in their degree of translatability. Whilst lyric poetry barely survives the transmutation, scientific text-books can do so perfectly well: it depends upon how much the work depends upon its affective aura. The synagogue congregation who hears the Hebrew text in the original, and the Greek Orthodox audience who hear something close to the sound of the Gospel Greek, get the *affective* significance of biblical language. The Bible suffers in translation into other 'sound worlds' and would be thinned down into the expression of an idea if a structuralist transformed it into wordless sign–signifier patterns.[16] Nonetheless, although all word meanings require *a* phonic basis, only a few require a *specific* material basis. Although their sounds make us *feel* their object differently, 'Fish', 'poisson' and 'ichthus' all direct us to think about the same conceptual meaning.

Our *names* for things are names for their concepts.

> each word meaning . . . which in its formal content intends something . . . is an actualization of an ideal sense that is contained in the concept of the corresponding object . . . That aspect of the ideal sense of the concept that is actualized in each case creates the actual stock of the meaning.[17]

Thousands of different kinds of fish fall under the one concept. Any sentence which just mentions 'fish' is vague. It takes the interweaving of many concepts to pin down which ones this sentence is about. The sentence 'fish live in the sea' draws on a minuscule element of the meaning stock of the words, 'fish', 'live' and 'sea'; we draw out more from the *same* concepts if

14 Ibid, p. 55.
15 Ibid., pp. 60–61.
16 'The fact', Ingarden says, 'that the phonetic formations' have their 'own voice' in the 'polyphony' of the four strata of the literary work is demonstrated 'by the drastic change which the work undergoes when it is translated into a foreign language'. Ibid., p. 56.
17 Ibid., p. 87.

we say 'herring live in the North Sea, but dolphins live in the Mediterranean'. The word-concept is finite; it is the border on our appropriate interpretations of the word. Names are *intentional*: they direct us *to* some thing: the 'limits' of where we should point our thinking are enclosed in each name.

Names only do these things when we use them. Once contact with them has supplied us with a store of concepts relating to fish, we do not think about them *all* of the time. When we speak of kippers, part of that meaning-stock becomes activated in our usage. We just put into actual thinking some part of our knowledge of fish. The idea of 'actualising concepts' may bother us, if we think of concepts as floating in a Platonic heaven: but we need not think of concepts as existing apart from the cultural memory which we carry around with us, in our own intelligences.

Even a child draws on a medium which has been filtered through many acts of knowing when she talks. We need not insist that all concepts are constructed by scientific knowledge; some may be the dimmer and more obscure notes construed by common sense. If the term 'concept' sounds too, well, conceptual, or if we fear that most of our language use is not based on conceptualised knowledge, one could sometimes substitute the word 'region'. Husserl used that word to describe the different spheres of the world of common sense, the 'life world'. Perhaps most of our everyday use of words draws those words out of 'regions' of knowledge or experience. We have 'regions' of knowledge about oceans, and about world geography, and it is to such 'regions' which we apply when I say, 'A tidal wave hit Papua New Guinea', and you understand it, although neither of us may have a 'conceptual' understanding of 'tidal waves' or could readily locate that island on a map. Our common sense knowledge supplies us with *something by which to direct our thoughts at an object*, and it is part of our knowledge of these 'regions' which we 'pull out', 'draw on', or, why not say it, *actualise* when we exercise language.

1 Samuel is built of words like house, uncle, donkey, loaf, bread and ghost, whose meanings people have grasped. If no-one happens to be reading 1 Samuel, the meaning of the words lies dormant, or, in technical language, is in potentiality. In that potentiality lies the objectivity of the meaning of the work, because it contains a structure of meanings which lie in wait to be directed at their appropriate objects. To read or to perform 1 Samuel is to reconstitute its potential meaning. If we are not phenomenologists of religion, with a well-formed concept of a ghost in mind, then we have a workable 'regional' knowledge of what a ghost is; we know what we are looking at when we read about one. We do not actualise the meaning of every 'object' which could fall under the concept or region of 'ghost', but 'ghost' as the word is determined by its position in the sentence, and in the text as a whole: the 'actual stock' of the meaning which is expressed in any given sentence in any given literary work is a localised incarnation of the wider meaning the word can have. So some of its meaning is *left in abeyance, or potentiality*. Some of the possible meaning is selected out when the word is modified and qualified by the other words in the sentence, and in the other sentences by which it is surrounded. The Deuteronomist's Ghosts and those of Aeschylus are generically different, because they live in different 'worlds of words'; they are pinned down in

different shaped verbal nets. To attend to the difference is to say that some of the stock of the concept or region of 'ghost' is left in abeyance, when we understand the word in one particular 'world' or contextual 'net'. To attend to the similarity is to concede the existence of the concept or region, if our language use is immersed in experimental knowledge of things.

The term 'intention' is sometimes taken in an intransitive sense. Some physical and psychic processes do not relate us to anything outside of ourselves; digestion relates us only to a thing which we have already taken on board. One may have to perform an autopsy on an eater in order to find out what poisoned him. And one may likewise wish to recover the internal 'state' of a writer, in order to know what he 'intended'. Fielding commented thus on this notion of authorial 'intention': if ale

> is the liquor of modern historians, nay, perhaps their muse, if we may believe the opinion of Butler, who attributes inspiration to ale, it ought likewise to be the potation of their readers; since every book ought to be read with the same spirit, and in the same manner, as it is writ.[18]

It was such an intransitive 'intentionality' which we have been rightly advised to avoid under the term 'intentional fallacy'. Literary criticism is not an act of autopsy. Even if his biographer can exhume him to let us know what he had for breakfast, this surgeon cannot identify the causal connection between the fried eggs and the themes of the novels.

Other human processes, such as feeling, knowing, seeing, hearing, smelling, touching, intuiting, understanding, imagining, loving and perhaps even the invention of sentences are *of* or *about* other beings: they are relational or *transitive*. And some are more than relational/transitive: they are 'causal'. We transitively apprehend a camel; we say 'there is a camel', and the sentence *activates* that piece of information. Such an activating charge of apprehension never gets going without a mind: but once formed into a sentence *about* the facts, this *intentional* sentence carries the 'causality': it can make anyone who hears it or reads it *think* 'camel'. Talk of intentions which are intrinsic to sentences, or to texts, carries with it no murderous intentions towards authors. No sentence could make a reader or hearer refer to a camel, unless a writer or speaker had first seen them and mentioned it. It is not as if 'Language' wandered about, whether as a whole or in groups, 'intending' objects. That set of *causal* relations, whereby a thinker recognises a situation, describes it in a sentence, which makes other people intentionally refer to this situation, depends upon particular mental acts. A sentence is *intentional* because it is a way of relating to an object; the *intentional* judgement is an arrow in flight toward an object, not a plan to say something. The sentence is 'co-ordinated' with an event by its intentionality.[19] The intention carries us toward a reality, and not back to something 'in' the speaker. The sentence is 'bi-polar': the two poles are the intention and the object toward which the intention makes it fly. There can be no 'subjectless sentence meanings', but the same intentional meaning can be exercised by any number of speakers, with reference to the same ideal meaning.

18 Fielding, *Tom Jones*, p. 119.
19 Ingarden, *Literary Work*, p. 109.

Intentional sentences have subjects, objects and finite verbs. The 'object' to which a sentence-meaning directs us is a combination of a named thing ('camel') and a pure activity ('is there'): 'There is a camel!' The sentence points us to a 'state of affairs'. The sentence is *about* a state of affairs; a state of affairs just 'is'. The two can be aligned:

> the state of affairs that is developed and created by the sentence must be strictly distinguished from a state of affairs that 'objectively' exists and is rooted in an ontic sphere that is ontically independent with respect to the sentence. Thus, we shall call the first the 'purely intentional state of affairs' ... the two can be set 'in relation' to each other and ... in this way the sentence can attain coordination to an objectively existing state of affairs.[20]

A fictional sentence projects a purely intentional state of affairs and thereby constructs the third layer of the literary work, that is, the stratum of 'represented objectivities'. A non-fictional sentence refers to 'real objectivities'. It enables the speaker to consider 'that he has "found his mark"': the sentence now "claims to be true": "it becomes a 'judgement' in the logical sense, one that is subject to evaluation according to "true" and "false"'.[21]

If we describe someone caught up in a series of 'states of affairs', we run our object through its paces, and pin it down:

> If there are many sentences which, while connected, refer to one and the same object ... the state of affairs, figuratively speaking, merge into a 'net' in which the given object is 'ensnared'. One state of affairs is tied in this or that manner to another or is connected to it by a third, other states of affairs link up in various ways, and thus a field of connected states of affairs is developed. All of them exist within one and the same object and in their connection make up the delimited ontic range of the given object.[22]

Arising out of the many word concepts which the work uses, and tying all of them together, is a 'field'. Each sentence projects a 'state of affairs'; each state of affairs is connected with every other; out of these emerge the 'represented objectivities' of the work, the total picture which is being put together, and these objectivities 'sit' in a 'field'. Every sentence lights up its environs in a particular way, until we have a 'literary life-world'. Every literary world has a 'centre of orientation', out of which the world is constructed, which is the 'mind's eye' of the represented narrator:

> If, in our reading, we want to apprehend the world exactly as it is represented, we must ... fictitiously transpose ourselves into the represented centre of orientation and wander about in the represented world *in fictione* with the given person.[23]

The literary work is an *artistic object*. The artistic object is in a state of potentiality (to be read) until someone comes along and executes its verbal intentions: 'The playwright's work is *potentially* drama: it only becomes actual through the actor. He lends ... to the dramatic idea ... that reality

20 Ibid., p. 116.
21 Ibid., p. 110.
22 Ibid., p. 157.
23 Ibid., p. 231.

which *makes things present.'*[24] When we perform a script for others, or just make a novel or poem perceptible for ourselves, we co-create an *aesthetic* object. We *co-create* it because we bring the book to life by following through the sentence-meanings of the artistic object. Our aesthetic objects can vary enormously, across the *finite range* of its artistic meaning. If we are attuned to the 'phonic *Gestalt'*, execute the sentence-meanings by going *through* suitable concepts *to* their represented objectivities, and then see and enter a world, we shall be on the right path to knowing the unitary *artistic* work which the author left ready to be reconstituted in reading, or in performance.

The four strata of the artistic object gather together to display certain 'metaphysical qualities'.[25] Metaphysical qualities are such as: 'the sublime, the tragic, the dreadful, the shocking, the inexplicable, the demonic, the holy, the sorrowful, the indescribable brightness of good fortune, as well as the grotesque, the charming, the light, the peaceful':[26] we have encountered most of these in the Bible. They cannot be lumped on top of an artistic work: 'the polyphony of value qualities must not merely show a harmony that permits the appearance of a metaphysical quality; it must be harmoniously compatible with it, so that the given metaphysical quality is *required*' by it.[27] If a literary work has a single 'soul', a single driving 'idea', that is founded in

> the essential connection . . . between a determinate represented life situation . . . and a metaphysical quality that manifests itself in that life situation and draws its unique coloration from its content. In the revelation of such an essential connection, which cannot be determined purely conceptually, lies the poet's creative act.[28]

We need only read so far as Genesis 1 to find an 'organic polyphony': the *Gestalten* created by the Hebrew sounds, very hard to replace, as regards their affective quality; the 'meanings' intended by the words: the heaven and the earth, the light and the darkness, the waters and the dry land, the grass, the fruits with its seeds, the two great lights, the winged fowls, the great whales, the beasts of the earth, and 'man'; the words unite to form a teeming series of interconnected 'state of affairs', a field in which the 'represented objectivity' is the cosmos: the metaphysical quality which the narrator instructs us to find is *tōb*, 'good'. One could work one's way from Genesis to Revelation, and find a composite textual 'idea' which, barring the loss of 'phonic *Gestalt'*, through the translation of the Hebrew and Greek, speaks to every reader, in every and any place and time. Such an objective notion of textual language is suited to the epistemic or propositional theory of revelation.

b. Epistemic and Propositional Theories of Revelation

Some theologians treat revelation as a means of *knowing* God. I call their conceptions of revelation 'epistemic'. According to the epistemic theory,

24 Von Balthasar, *Theo-Drama I*, p. 281.
25 Ingarden, *Literary Work*, p. 294.
26 Ibid., p. 291.
27 Ibid., p. 298.
28 Ibid., p. 304.

the purpose of the divine revelation was to enable the biblical authors to recount *truths*. The principle is: 'Revelation occurs when ignorance is dispelled.' Not every exchange of information counts as revelation: 'Dispelling ignorance becomes *revelation* when it has . . . the character of unveiling the veiled, of uncovering the covered, of exposing the obscured to view.'[29] Christian theology would do well to take note of the epistemic theory of revelation because, if the broad outline of the Gospels do not give us knowledge about Jesus Christ, the whole caboodle goes up in smoke. 'Items of knowledge' are often conveyed in propositions, and so this notion is sometimes called a 'propositional' theory of revelation. But 'epistemic' seems better to get at what the theory is about: an act of knowing the truth towards which the biblical words fly.

If we look for a theory of knowledge in Thomas's writings, we cull his 'epistemology' from topics which are set to answer *metaphysical* questions. Situated towards the end of the First Part of a metaphysical epic, which begins with the revelation of 'Sacra Doctrina', moves to arguments for the existence of God, the nature of God, God's creation of the world, the angels, the seven days of creation, there is a 'Treatise on Man', and it is here that we find St Thomas's 'epistemology'.

Thomas's epistemology treats the human being as a creature which has been created by God, from whom being flows, and to which all creatures desire to return. Everything wants to be *united with* God: the 'aim' of all caused things is to return to the Cause. Intellectual creatures, such as human beings and angels, do so by way of their intellects. St Thomas's notion of revelation is largely concerned with knowing, and only peripherally with feelings, imaginings, or practical actions, because we achieve our aim, return to source, by knowing God. Theology is primarily a 'speculative science'[30] because the apparatus which God has given the human being to reach him with is her mind. The human animal is a *scientist*, as from *scio*, 'I know'. The *science* which sums up the purpose of human life is the knowledge of God. We push our way through things toward God. A person who lives through a body knows God through known things. The soul-form of the body is the single structuring and acting *agent* of the story which is the self. If we ask why we are all scientists in little and in greater ways, and why we are *made to think* our way into the *forms* of objects, St Thomas's answer is that there is a greater light, pulsing in and behind our thinking, and that is the Thinking of God. The overarching plot is the Odyssey of returning to God.

Here St Thomas gives a condensed definition of the action of the mind:

> the sense, moved by an external sensible object, places an impress upon the imagination, thus giving rise to an orderly process in all the powers down to the motive ones. Now, man's proper operation is understanding, and of this the primary principle is the agent intellect, which makes species intelligible, to which species the possible intellect in a certain manner is passive; and the possible intellect, having been actualized, moves the will.[31]

---

29 Wolterstorff, *Divine Discourse*, p. 23.
30 St Thomas Aquinas, *Summa Theologiae*, First Part of the First Part, Question 1, Article 4, *Whether Sacred Doctrine is a Practical Science*, Reply.
31 St Thomas Aquinas, *Summa contra Gentiles*, Bk II, 76, 19.

This can be elaborated by the description of one small episode within the mind's Odyssey: getting to know a fish. First we sense the object, and then we use our *imagination* to draw from it a 'phantasm'. One cannot define a fish without knowing what a fish 'looks like', the linear arrangement of their vertebrae, the underwater breathing apparatus hidden in their fins, and their gaping eyes. What the mind gets from the phantasm is a representation of the materiality of its object.[32] Now, while the imagination holds it up, the intellect probes the phantasm with its own 'microscopic light', trying to set up the material shape on the slide so that it can best see why the bones and flesh and flippers are put together like this: 'The object of understanding is supplied . . . materially by the imagination; formally . . . it is completed by intellectual light.'[33] The 'light' of the scientific intellect wants to see what the fish is, its *quod quid est*, its fishy *quid*dity.

First we *receive* the phantasms, drawing them out of their appropriate objects. The 'possible intellect' is the 'receptive intellect'. The receptive act of the intellect restructures the phantasm so as to make it intelligible. There is a further act of the same intellect which is active,[34] the 'agent' or the 'active' intellect. The active intellect uses the given intelligibility to relate itself back to the object: it *thinks* the fish, through the phantasm-shaped intelligible species.[35] Understanding is knowing things by means of their 'intelligible species'. We do not look at an internal likeness of the fish, but at the fish: the 'likeness' is between us and our object, a fishy intentionality directed upon a fish. We do not know 'in', but 'through' the phantasm and the intelligible species; they are intentionally related to the fish: of, or about, or toward it. The 'intelligible species', the form of the fish, is 'the thing by which one understands, and not . . . that which is understood'.[36]

Just as the concepts which stand behind words belong to our cultural memory bank, so our 'intelligible species' sleep in our 'possible intellect', which does not exist apart from individual human minds.[37] Just as, for Ingarden, the basis of linguistic meaning is the fact that the individual words fall under 'ideal meanings', so for St Thomas conventional speech is undergirded by 'intelligible species'. The act of understanding gives us an 'inner word'. 'Inner words' are 'pre-linguistic', if 'linguistic' means a human, historical language. A psychological explanation of this philosophical principle is the common experience of *knowing* something which we grope to put into words: we are struggling to express our 'silent' inner word in 'outer words', the medium of public discourse. Once we have defined our fish in inner words, convention supplies us with outer words,

---

32 St Thomas Aquinas, *Summa Theologiae*, First Part of the First Part, Question 75, Fourth Article, Reply.

33 Bernard J. F. Lonergan, *Verbum: Word and Idea in Aquinas*, edited by David B. Burrell (Darton, Longman & Todd, London, 1968), p. 81.

34 St Thomas Aquinas, *Summa contra Gentiles*, translated by James Anderson (University of Notre Dame Press, Notre Dame, 1975), Bk II, 77, 2: 'there is in th[e] soul an active power *vis-à-vis* the phantasms, making them actually intelligible; and this power is called the agent intellect; while there is also in the soul a power that is in potentiality to the determinate natures of sensible things; and this power is the possible intellect'.

35 St Thomas Aquinas, *Summa contra Gentiles*, Bk II, 73, 38.

36 Ibid., 75, 7.

37 Ibid., 73.

such as *ichthus*, fish, or *poisson*. The public exercise of outer words is rooted in our understanding of the things. When we speak, our knowledge of intelligible species wears the dress of a particular language. But no particular language, no social set of 'outer words', colours our knowledge: otherwise, Greeks, Englishmen and Frenchmen would know fish differently, and thus, by a long road, know God differently, and this does not fit the map of the human Odyssey which St Thomas draws.

St Thomas describes how God makes the prophet know supernatural *truth*. The prophets are minds blazing with knowledge from God: 'prophecy is first and principally a *knowledge*';[38] 'prophecy is a knowledge which divine revelation engraves in the mind of a prophet, in the form of teaching';[39] 'prophecy is brought about by a divine light'.[40] The light of prophetic revelation is 'supernatural': the intellectual light with which the prophet illuminates his objects is not his own, but comes from God. The prophet knows through the mind of God: 'prophecy calls for revelation as regards the actual perception of divine truths'.[41] We cannot know the divine essence, in this life,[42] so God does not show the prophet himself: 'the prophets see . . . in certain similitudes lighted up by a God-given light'.[43] We cannot look knowingly without looking through an intelligible species. God gives the prophet a 'similitude' to look through. These 'similitudes' can be pure 'intelligibility' ('an infusion of light only'), or a 'new species' illuminated by God (an image invented by God, such as the blazing bush), or 'species differently disposed'.[44] The *revelation* is the supernatural light which enables us to interpret the similitude correctly. Thomas provides a *largely* 'extra-textual theory' of revelation. He says little about the prophets' 'outer words', by which they spoke these truths to an audience. He evinces no concern for the practical question of how the Book of God was written, no interest in what Pierre Benoit calls 'Scriptural inspiration'.

The prophet Isaiah looked forward to the day when

> [T]he Lord will punish
> With His great, cruel, mighty sword
> Leviathan the Elusive Serpent –
> Leviathan the twisting Serpent;
> He will slay the Dragon [*tannin*] in the sea (Is. 27.1)

The representation of a fish which God supplied to Isaiah is not what the prophet is supposed to attend to: he must think his way past the image of a fish to the truth which it expresses. The phantasm-forming imagination is less *vital* in St Thomas's notion of prophetic knowing than in his common

---

38 St Thomas Aquinas, *Summa Theologica*, 2a2a, *Question 171, The Nature of Prophecy*, Article 1, Reply.
39 Ibid., Article 6, Reply.
40 Ibid., Article 3, Reply.
41 Ibid., Article 1, Reply objection 4.
42 With the apparent exceptions of Moses and St Paul: *Question 174, Divisions of Prophecy*, Article 4, 'Was Moses Greater than All the Prophets?': 'Moses excelled others in intellectual vision, seeing that he gazed upon God's very essence, as St Paul did in ecstasy, according to Augustine. Hence he beholds the form of the Lord. [*quod palam, non per aenigmata Deum vidit*]'.
43 *Question 173, The Manner of Prophetic Knowledge*, Article 1, Reply.
44 Ibid., Article 2, Reply.

epistemology, because Thomas is conceiving the human situation in relation to God differently. In the case of common-or-garden knowing, embodied 'Odysseus' has to use his phantasms as boats on his journey to Ithica. In the case of prophecy, God has lifted the voyager up, and is giving him an advance preview of the end of the journey: although the prophet does not leave his boated body behind, he is so close to the shore that he barely requires it. Since knowing is intentional, the prophet requires the maps of the intelligible species, to know what he is looking at: he looks *through* the 'maps' at 'Ithaca' made present to him in the act of supernatural revelation. But the phantasms cannot do much to help him now. When God makes him know supernaturally, he does not bypass the prophet's imagination: but nor does he linger there. For St Thomas, the prophetic *images* are an *almost extrinsic* means to an end: 'Whatever images are used to express the prophesied reality is a matter of indifference to prophecy.'[45] The same goes both for images taken from the prophet's life and for images supplied by God. Modern literary critics are concerned about the prophetic poetry. Not St Thomas: 'imaginative vision in prophetic knowledge is not required for its own sake, but for the manifestation of intellectual truth. So all the more effective is prophecy when it has less need of imaginative vision'.[46] St Thomas's absorption in the question of *how we know* supernatural truth, to the near exclusion of concern for the compositional process, entails that his theory of revelation describes an event of disclosure, not a field of imagery. St Thomas's unquenchable appetite to know included no taste for finding out how the Bible came to be written.[47]

The epistemic notion of revelation leaves something to be desired. A different portrait of Jesus emerges from each of the four Gospels and the Letters of Paul. Surely, if they are 'propositional revelation', each Gospel and Letter writer refers to the same truth. Given that the images are dispensable, it should be possible to distil these truths into an infallibly true *Life of Jesus: The Scientific Account*. This would consist of a chronologically arranged and systematic series of correct historical propositions about Jesus of Nazareth. Supposing that the books of the Old Testament are also propositionally inspired and thus historical, a *Life of David* can also be conceived, and perhaps even a *Life of Moses*. It is likely that such texts are no figment of my imagination but available for purchase in Fundamentalist bookstores; there are many Catholics who would find little odd about them, apart from the surreal absence of mystical elaboration.

Such worthy texts would have extricated the 'revelation' from the 'material shape' which the Bible gives it. Genesis' account of its numinous Heroes, the combat between Pharaoh and God, the wrestlings between the Pauline and the Christic ego, the four horsemen and the plagues of the Book of Revelation are unlike a set of supernaturally illuminated propositional truths, if *looks* are anything to go by. The Deuteronomist interleaves different accounts of David, each of which gives us an indispensable angle

---

45 *Question 172, The Cause of Prophecy*, Article 3, Reply Objection 1.
46 *Question 174, Divisions of Prophecy*, Article 1, Reply Objection 2.
47 Pierre Benoit comments that 'St Thomas never really studied the case of an author moved by God to write a book'. *Inspiration and the Bible*, translated by J. Murphy-O'Connor and M. Keverne (Sheed & Ward, London, 1965), p. 60.

on the man. The Christian canonists are editors of the same order. They compiled five portraits, Mark's Christ moving fast, John's treading a slow circle from above to below, and back, Matthew's pleromatic Moses-Christ, Luke's shrewd parable-speaker, and Paul's resurrected Christ, each with its own integrity. If we try to conceptualise a 'true' Christ without the composite images of the five portraits, we lose something essential. It takes too much re-arrangement and omission to read the Bible as a propositional 'epic'. The epistemic theory of revelation does not err by saying too much, although many, including the writer, will quail at the suggestion of the perfect truth of all the 'historical' books of the Bible. However true they are, the biblical books are *more than* a series of true judgements. Our study of the 'how' of the biblical narrative found an account of the interplay of persons, with an accent on their moral responsibility, their ability to play a part before God and humanity. If the material shape of Scripture is a part of its substance, the biblical revelation relates, not only to the True, but also to the Good.

c. Revelation as Personal Encounter

As we turn from St Thomas to Martin Buber, we find ourselves in the realm of what my philosophy teacher would call 'poetry'; we may lessen the sting of disparagement if we call it 'lyric poetry'. If we read *I and Thou* in our youth, we took away from it an ethical imperative. Most of our relationships fall into Buber's category of the 'I–It': we *ought* to try to have 'I–Thou' relations with other people, with animals, and with things, and, if we are average adolescents, we do not. But, Buber's 'I and Thou' is not something which we construct by our Anglo-Saxon and Pelagian efforts. 'In the beginning is the relation', he says: 'grasping form', that is, form grasping *us*, is there before we begin to think, and speak, and socially construct our worlds.[48] Reality is a 'Thou' which is calling us to be an 'I'. 'Thouness' is *the* objectivity of reality, drawing us into relation with itself:

> The world which appears to you . . . comes, and comes to bring *you* out; if it does not reach you, meet you, then it vanishes; but it comes back in another form . . . Between you and it there is mutual giving: you say Thou to it and give yourself to it, it says Thou to you and gives itself to you . . . Through the graciousness of its comings and the solemn sadness of its goings it leads you away to the Thou in which the parallel lines of relations meet.[49]

We are not born 'I's; the intentional relationship with the 'personal' Thou reforms us in its likeness: 'Through the Thou a man becomes I.'[50] Over against that is the dimension which we construct, space and time, the field in which things are a means to an end: the world of the I–It relations.

Our relations with things are below the level of language; our relations with other people take place in the form of speech, or dialogue: behind them, and giving rise to the possibility of language and dialogue, is the 'inner word', or rather, the 'inner dialogue', created by

48 Martin Buber, *I and Thou*, translated by Ronald Gregor Smith (T&T Clark, Edinburgh, 1937, 1958, 1987), p. 43.
49 Ibid., pp. 49–50.
50 Ibid., p. 44.

our life with spiritual beings. There the relation is clouded, yet it discloses itself; it does not use speech, yet begets it . . . In every sphere in its own way . . . we look out toward the fringe of the eternal Thou; in each Thou we address the eternal Thou.[51]

The young person is right, up to a point: Buber presents us with an ethics. But not *just an ethics*: the self-disclosure of the Eternal Thou is a *revealed* ethics. Buber tells us that a Person addresses us through being. But he shunts much of the realm of things in which the disclosure takes place into the realm of 'I–It'. That heightens the drama, and it is not as if the biblical writers are vivid landscape artists. The biblical characters have with them a sparse array of things, most of which, if we discount Balaam's ass, do not speak for themselves; there are just enough swords, plough-shares, flesh, onions and garlic to keep the action going. Buber's narrowing down to the 'I-and-Thou' is a *near* accurate account of what the Bible shows, and that is, very little, *in detail*, apart from the actors themselves. The stage does not require *that* many 'it's.

It may be because many of us who became Christian theologians began with Buber that we find that personalism makes some sense. The issue here is not the *knowledge* conveyed by divine revelation, but the person-to-person relationship which it creates. John Baillie states that: 'the revelation of which the Bible speaks is always such as has place within a personal relationship. It is not the revelation of an object to a subject, but a revelation from subject to subject, from mind to mind'.[52] It is as if, rather than objectively describing the life of Jesus of Nazareth, the Gospels put us face to face with him. There is no point in trying to describe God, for no exchange of 'abstract nouns' can 'exhaust the fullness of a living personality'.[53] A Catholic version of the personalist account of inspiration/revelation has been suggested by Edward Schillebeeckx:

> The quintessence of divine revelation in the Old Testament is expressed . . . thus: 'I will be your God and you will be my people' (cf. Ex. 6.7, Lev. 26.12, etc.). The significance of historical events derives from the people concerned (God and man). Revelation is not a thing, but an interpersonal event. To speak of revelation as historical events means events in the life of a human subject who grasps these events as relating him to God.[54]

In its Christianised versions, the experiential encounter of the 'I' and the Eternal Thou is an event with little empirical residue. It is true to say that the root of the biblical revelation is an I and Thou encounter. Personalism is scriptural in minimising the *things*, for the biblical actors take very few of those on stage, and the Gospels have minimal backdrops. But a *stage* there must be: that is, a *betweenness*. What is *between* can be Jacob's deception of Esau or the Angels bombing the earth with incense, something on stage, or something *between* the stage and the auditorium, between the 'Subject' of Christ, in the Gospels, and the hearers who encounter him through the text. The defect in Christian personalism is that it thinks of

51 Ibid., p. 19.
52 John Baillie, *Idea of Revelation in Recent Thought* (Oxford University Press, Oxford, 1956), p. 24.
53 Ibid., p. 26.
54 Cited in Gabriel Moran, *Theology of Inspiration* (Burns & Oates, London, 1967), p. 45.

experience as something *inward*, rather than *between*. Experience is not intransitive process, but transition: 'not a state but an event'.[55] The image of a journey expresses betweenness: 'the commandments of Sinai ... are precepts for an existence on the basis of hope';[56] Paul's experience is 'insight acquired by travelling to a place', which entails letting the action carry one: 'only he can have it who surrenders himself to the movement of the journey'.[57]

For the epistemicist, the issue is the truth which God makes the biblical writer see. This is indispensable. But we should avoid defining it as though it had been processed anonymously to be read by a machine; as if one could hand on the truth or the text without handing over oneself or engaging another. For the personalist, the key is intensive encounter, which is right, unless she sinks the extension of God's actions into herself.

d. A Trilogical Theory of Meaning

Ingarden's notion of 'ideal meanings' will do to explain how the same, 'artistic' text of *Hamlet* is reconstituted in different 'aesthetic' performances, or how we read the same Herodotean *History*. I would advise a literary critic or scientific historian to employ some such account. *However*, the Deuteronomist could have made most of his 'history' up, and some think he did. So could the Gospel authors, and ditto. The author of the Book of Revelation could have been stark raving mad, and one has encountered that opinion. These possibilities matter differently to the historian and to the theologian or believer. The historian can pick and choose what she finds to be probable; the believer requires a more certain and inclusive judgement. Christians take the Bible on trust. Christians believe these 'witnesses'; we can do so on the grounds that the witnesses are drawing upon their own experiences of the events. This forces us to give a third side of the 'triangle' of meaning.

Nicholas Wolterstorff argues that whenever we take a writer's meaning in a metaphorical sense, when it could otherwise have no rational meaning, we go beyond the 'essential' meaning of his words, and make a guess about the *author*: 'though we may profess to be engaged in textual sense interpretation, we all of us, surreptitiously or openly, engage in authorial-discourse interpretation.'[58] A glance at the author lets on whether to take a sentence metaphorically, or ironically. No matter how many well-formed intelligible species we have access to, sometimes we have to evaluate the speaker in order to know if her sentence is true or false. Following one another's sentences, from ideal meanings to objects, is not always like reading a science textbook. If we turn from an objective account of language to our confusing and contingent experience of the discovery of truth and falsity in personal communications, we may concede that we figure out whether a colleague's sentences *really* hit the mark by assessing their characters. Wolterstorff concludes that 'interpreters cannot operate without beliefs about the discourser: specifically, beliefs as to the relative prob-

55 Von Balthasar, *The Glory of the Lord: A Theological Aesthetics: Vol. I: Seeing the Form*, translated by Erasmo Leiva-Merikakis (T&T Clark Edinburgh, 1982), p. 222.
56 Von Balthasar, *Glory VI*, p. 179.
57 Von Balthasar, *Glory I*, p. 229.
58 Wolterstorff, *Divine Discourse*, p. 173.

ability of the discourser intending and not intending to say one thing and another'.[59] The objectivist theory of language explains how propositions can be true, by showing the conjunction of intention and object. This provides the *necessary* conditions of the stable meaning of the biblical account. But it does not give a *sufficient* explanation of how communication normally operates. In ordinary life, judgements about truth and moral judgements about persons are mixed up with each other; in practice, metaphysical epistemology and ethical discernment overlap. Ingarden and St Thomas are well aware that 'language' does not operate autonomously, like a separated intellect: they know that any thought or intention requires a mind, and any intentional sentence requires 'a' speaker. When we guess how far we can apply one another's intentional sentences, we look at this *particular* speaker, and decide whether he has the virtue of veracity. It may be that the historian *can* acquire sufficient evidential probability about the facts from either Herodotus' history of Greece or the Deuteronomic history of Israel, without reference to the moral status of the author. But a Christian or Jewish theologian or believer has to decide whether they can *trust* what the biblical authors say. If we decide that the 'Jahwist', writing in Babylonia in the fifth century BC, *invented* the exodus, or, conversely, that some of the events recorded in Exodus derive from Jewish historical experience, we are operating on the basis of a moral judgement: are we being manipulated or pointed at truth? The personalist invites us to study the *moral personality* who stands behind the text. That gives us three poles: a moral personality, a conjoined intention-object, and an audience which is invited to assent to the witness' experience. If we think that the Gospels and the Pauline Letters give us true portraits of Christ, that is because we combine our ability to operate the stable meanings of their sentences with a judgement that the writers are good, and that we must, as Rilke said, 'change our life' at their behest. The third pole, which requires us to 'assent' to the narrative is the personal and ethical injunction. Although we shall sink, with Stephen Moore, if we dispose of the elements of that picture which enable us to say that everyone reads the same Gospel of Mark, the language of the Bible is not only an epic language, sailing towards its Ithica whether or not anyone is on board. The boat is holed below the waterline if no experiences underlie the masterpiece, but the language of the Bible is not purely lyrical, built to adumbrate mystical contact between subjects. Rather, we should speak of a dramatic language, the trilogical language in which personal truth is conveyed.

A *true* portrait is not the same as a *perfect* portrait, where that means an itemisation of every fact that went into the event. To the criticism that no description of a person can be 'exhaustive', Helm rightly replies that no description of anything is exhaustive.[60] The true judgement gives a definition of an event or object: it *hits* the essence. Here, we may think, the analogy between a report on an event and a description of the life of Christ begins to falter. Did any one of the Apostles grasp his essence? Von Balthasar comments that

59 Ibid., p. 196.
60 Baillie, *Idea of Revelation*, p. 25; Paul Helm, *The Divine Revelation: The Basic Issues* (Morgan & Scott, London, 1982), p. 26.

Even in . . . a purely human life, no individual biography, however . . . con-
scientious, can give an exhaustive presentation of its total utterance. We can
only approach a multidimensional human life by taking a variety of
complementary perspectives. This applies even more, for three reasons, in
the case of the figure of Jesus. First, the latter does not make sense in purely
human terms but must be understood as the . . . portrayal of God. Second . . .
the figure of Jesus 'speaks' above and beyond the proportions of a finite life,
in the critical utterance of death on the Cross and Resurrection. Third . . . the
only possible response to it is the ecclesial faith it aims to elicit . . . No
portrayal of a personal, living reality can be exhaustive but can only point
the way, inviting us to see for ourselves . . . So there has to be a plurality of
New Testament theologies: only thus can they give an idea of the
transcendence of the one they proclaim.[61]

This statement supports the epistemic account: but it also stretches it out in
significant ways. Here the object which the statement intends, that is,
Christ, transcends the revealed descriptions, and a third factor, the readers
who are invited to 'see for ourselves', is added. This is a dramatic theory of
meaning. Many aspects of Scripture contradict one another: such contradictions, analogous to dramatic conflicts, create a constructive tension
amongst the parts of the Gospel:

> the plurality of perspectives in the New Testament Scriptures mirrors . . . the
> christological fact, which sums up the disparate Old Testament models . . . in
> a new synthesis. In the verbalized form, there will be a preponderance, now
> of one aspect of the synthesis, now of another – for example, the inner
> fulfilment of the 'law', or its being surpassed – but, in each case, the aspects
> are read from the transcending synthesis; they challenge each other, their
> apparent opposition expanding our vision so that we may contemplate this
> synthesis. Without this tension, the 'ever greater' quality of the word of God
> would lack essential contour.[62]

This draws out of the shadows elements which are implicitly present, in
St Thomas's position. If, as he says, we cannot know God's essence, then
we cannot abstract the 'truth of Christ' from the many and varied Gospel
portraits, in their combinations. Those combinations point above and
beyond themselves. Von Balthasar is drawing upon a theory of meaning
which is not a bi-polar objective essentialism, but an equally objective but
trilogical conception of verbal communication. In addition to the two
elements, the writer's 'essential definition' of his objects, and its objective
truth, its coming together with its object, we have a third party, which is
the writer's subjective 'taking responsibility' for his work, and its coming
together with the assent of the individual members of an audience.

A trilogical theory of revelatory meaning looks like this. God encounters the 'prophets', the experiencers of supernatural truth and goodness. The knowledge thus achieved as an 'inner word' passes into the
biblical language in the form of a description of a series of dramatic
encounters. The first pole begins in God and stretches across the narrative
descriptions: all are as if seen from the eye of God. That is the objective or
epical element of Scripture. A sequence of transitive experiences is caught

---

61 Von Balthasar, *Theo-Drama II*, pp. 143–145.
62 Ibid., p. 146.

in the net of the biblical life-world. What is thus manifested for judgement, by the audience, is the moral quality of the characters: can we trust what Buber's 'Moses' or Paul or John tell of themselves and of their experiences? What is held up to view is the Lyric or Subject-to-subject aspect of Scripture. The third party, who make the assessment, is the audience.

When we speak about the Bible theologically, we need something more than a stock of scientific concepts about physical objects; we need 'ideal meanings' which are able to point toward the supernatural. The biblical language appears to describe conversations between God and human beings. How do we phrase the human openness to conversation with the infinite? The widest, most open and inclusive notions have been traditionally called the 'transcendentals', such as being, truth, goodness and beauty. Such notions are turned out toward infinitude, without containing it: they are the medium between finite and infinite realities. Lonergan finds at the basis of the human person an 'unrestricted' intentionality. If the human mind is unrestrictedly desirous, it is always moving ahead of itself, asking questions before it knows the answers, and asking questions which are wider than any particular solution to a particular problem. It travels toward its promised land knowing what it looks like and not knowing, because its unrestricted desires discover an infinite horizon before it. The motor of this unrestrained questioning is the 'transcendental notions', notions which 'take us beyond' every experience, every intelligent grasp of truth, and every grasp of specific moral value.[63] Far from denying one another legroom, the transcendentals of being, truth, beauty and the good illustrate one another. The poetry of Job is the most beautiful in the Bible, and the book sums up the biblical drama of creation, or being, and the ensuing moral issue between a free God and free human beings. There is a bouncy reflection of an experience of *being* in the most *ethical* transpositions of the Gospel narrative, in the Mystery Plays, in Handel, and Gospel Jazz. Although we *know* whether someone's sentences are *true* by referring the meaning of their words to their objects, in the theatre of everyday life that usually works alongside a *moral* assessment of the speaker; the *truth* of the biblical narrative is bound up with the *veracity* of its speakers. Lonergan explains what the scholastics called the 'convertibility' of the transcendentals by reference to the unitary drive of human intentionality:

> the many levels of consciousness are just successive stages in the unfolding of a single thrust, the eros of the human spirit. To know the good, it must know the real; to know the true it must know the intelligible; to know the intelligible, it must attend to the data.[64]

Lonergan puts 'responsibility' at the summit of the four levels of intentionality, driving the empirical, the intellectual and the rational. If the rays of the transcendental notions are always ahead of us so that we cannot quite keep up with them, they are also behind our movement, just as is desire. If one is seeking the good, that transcendent object is at the same

---

63 Bernard J. F. Lonergan, *Method in Theology* (Darton, Longman & Todd, London, 1972), p. 11.
64 Ibid., p. 13.

time the medium of one's search. Or as Lonergan says: 'Besides particular acts of loving, there is the prior state of being in love, and that prior state is, as it were, the fount of all one's actions.'[65] When we read the Bible, looking through its world of words to the historical drama which it describes, the event takes place within a field: we, as readers or hearers, who 'think through' its meaning-intentions to their objects, are already immersed in, and constituted by, acts of being, knowing and loving. *This* field encapsulates that openness of created language to the language of God to which the transcendentals point. The analogy of being is actualised in the biblical field of revelation, as is the analogy of the good.

How then does a third party, that is, all readers of the Bible, know what its words mean? As an artistic object, the Bible holds its objective and conceptual meanings in readiness to be actualised by readers, who direct its sentences at their appropriate objects. Every reading of the Bible co-creates an 'aesthetic' object, that is, an object as perceived by someone. The potential stock of a word's meaning does not subsist in a Platonic heaven, but is part of our cultural memory. The biblical archaeologists add to the store of our cultural memory, refining the essential intentions of the words to their objects. Our aesthetic concretisations of the potential meaning of the biblical text also draw on a body of regional or commonsense knowledge: the word-conglomerations carried by tradition. Words rest and sleep, and get up and walk, in traditions, and people without much articulate access to many well-formed concepts use them as the tradition does. Practical experience may incline us to seize on particular imaginative aspects of a word's meaning. Tradition can dislodge the original meaning of a word; but pre-theoretical knowledge can sometimes get the intention right. Tradition has a feeling for the literal sense in those cases where it retains some living particle of the social life in which the word was originally employed. One has recourse to 'tradition', in understanding the Bible because it actualises the *moral* field in which its 'meanings' are constantly realised and actually live.

3. What Is Inspiration?

a. Inspiration Is Intentional

Homer leads us to think of inspiration as a sort of *menage-à-trois*. There is the poet, there is the goddess whom he asks to 'sing him' into his vision, and there is the Trojan War. We can reduce this three-party affair to a Christian marriage of two. We can place Homer's muse *inside* the Trojan War, making it perceptible to the poet. We have made her the genius of the object, which speaks to the poet. The 'by what' of inspiration is the object itself. The act of reduction enables us to see that inspiration is a way of knowing. Like any kind of knowing, inspiration entails relating to an object, and being guided by its form in what one says about that experience. Inspiration in the textual sense is the verbal embodiment of this relationality. The process of inspiration is intentional. It is *of* or *about* something outside of ourselves. The inspired writers perceived the form *of* some thing or event or person, and they communicated this 'ofness' to

---

65 Ibid., p. 33.

their text: a sentence retains its relationality even after it has been written down; the text-sentences of the *Iliad* are of or about the same imaginative and semi-real Troy of which Homer sang. When the process completes itself in a text we have the 'what' of inspiration. In this sense, we speak of the 'inspiration of Scripture'. Artistic inspiration comes about when an object, a tree, speaks to me as a Thou:

> This is the eternal source of art: a man is faced by a form which desires to be made through him into a work. This form is no offspring of his soul, but is *an appearance which steps into it* and demands of it an effective power. The man is concerned with an act of his being . . . if he speaks the primary word out of his being to the form which appears, then the effective power steams out, and the work arises.[66]

Inspiration differs from other acts of knowing in that its object further conspires in its self-disclosure.

b. Immanent, Angelic and Totally Supernatural
Rudyard Kipling recalled that

> My Daemon was with me in the Jungle Books, Kim and both Puck books, and good care I took to walk delicately, lest he should withdraw. I know that he did not, because when those books were finished they said so themselves with, almost, the water-hammer click of a tap turned off. One of the clauses in our contract was that I should never follow up a 'success', for by this sin fell Napoleon and a few others. Note here. When your Daemon is in charge, do not try to think consciously. Drift, wait, and obey.[67]

Kipling's Daemon and others of his kin have assisted the practitioners of the high and the low arts, from Homer to the horticulturist, and from Socrates to many a shambling Sheamus. The poets and composers ascribed their compositions to the inspiration of the company of daemons, muses, genii, goddesses and good faeries because their creations seemed to be *gifts*. Kipling's 'Drift, wait and obey' attests to the passivity which attends creativity. We may not say that artistic inspiration consists of the *self-expression* of a human being *whereas* religious inspiration is the expression of Another through a human instrument. Many artists feel themselves to be the unworthy recipients of a gift. Then how do we distinguish natural and supernatural inspiration?

At the height of the popularity of Shaeffer's *Amadaeus* it was remarked that the play-movie expressed the 'Lutheran' insight that a morally wretched human 'vessel' such as Mozart could receive divine inspiration whilst all the good works of Salieri could not gain divine favour. This is incorrect, unless the created powers who help us to make symphonies (gardens, Epic poems, Eggs Florentine . . .) are identical to the Uncreated power who lies behind the Scriptures. Being inspired by a Daemon and being inspired by God are different *if* Daemon and God are different sorts of chaps. Daemons are unlicensed and weird beasts; they carry no passports; we do not know whence they make their incursions into our

66 Buber, *I and Thou*, pp. 22–23.
67 Rudyard Kipling, *Something of Myself* (1936, Penguin, London, 1977, 1988), p. 143.

lives. Wherever that mysterious region is, it is within created reality. Isaiah's experiences were not unlike those of Mozart, and vice-versa, for they were both human beings, but Mozart was inspired by a mysterious natural power, Isaiah by a supernatural power.

The assumption of ontological identity between the created Muse of Music and God Almighty was an easy error to have made: the worthy monotheistic notion which leads to it is that the sacred is homogeneous. The opposite hypothesis is that the regions of being inhabited by the sacred are many; or that the sacred *is* many different kinds of thing. Von Balthasar comments that:

> The gods cannot be interpreted as the personifications of human or cosmic forces . . . As concrete forms, they are radiant, unique images and unveilings of Being, of human existence within experienced Being, of 'regions' of Being which cannot be divided by arbitrary borderlines.

That explains why they have no passports. Von Balthasar continues:

> A Michelangelo, a Goethe, a Keats must still have seen such gods with their inner eye; many of their figures presuppose such encounters. And we must ask ourselves whether the inability of the modern heart to encounter gods . . . is altogether to Christianity's advantage.[68]

'Experienced being' is reality as it is proportionate to the human mind; that is, created and finite being. Homer's gods, and that of process theology, inhabit this immanent realm. If an aspect of proportionate being forcibly presents itself to an artist, and says, 'This is what I look like', we have an 'inspiration from within immanence'. If that sounds rather pagan, and if Rilke, speaking for modern paganism, 'portrayed a God who "inherits" Christianity', a Christian valour with respect to the many regions of *being* can turn it around the other way: Friedrich Hölderlin and Gerard Manley Hopkins 'show us a Christ who "inherits" the gods of paganism: that is "inherits" the splendour of the theophanies'.[69] There are no border guards between the regions; the Christian must hold that they all belong to an Uncreated Austrian Reich, or to a British Empire, in which the rule of law prevails.

Dionysius the Areopagite favoured the latter opinion: his celestial hierarchy is set out in order to demonstrate the order ('taxis') between the Uncreated God and the lower orders of creation.[70] St Thomas spoke of inspiration on a level above that of immanent being but below that of God:

> it is a law of divine order, according to Dionysius, to govern lesser orders of being by intermediaries. But angels hold a middle position between God and men. They participate more perfectly than men in the perfection of divine goodness. And this is why divine enlightenment and revelations proceed from God by means of angels . . . the Holy Spirit distributes graces among men through the ministry and mediation of angels.[71]

---

68 Von Balthasar, *Glory I*, p. 500.
69 Ibid., p. 501.
70 Dionysius the Areopagite, *The Celestial Hierarchy*, chapters 3 and 4, pp. 153–158, in *Pseudo Dionysius: The Complete Works*, translated by Colm Luibheid (SPCK, London, 1987).
71 St Thomas Aquinas, *Summa Theologiae*, 2a2ae, Question 172, *The Cause of Prophecy*, Article 2 *Is prophetic revelation mediated by angels?* Reply and Reply Objection 2.

Angels are not merely walk-on actors in the Bible; often enough, they are the *dramatis personae* who appear to the Patriarchs, inspire the Judges with *ruaḥ* and give vision to prophets, from Genesis to the Apocalypse of St John. A biblical theology must mention inspiration by angels. Von Balthasar sets these 'forms' midway between the poetic-Daemonic and the angelic:

> What is the 'angel of Yahweh' in the Old Testament? What is the meaning of this radiant power, this passing face of the one without countenance, this flaming radiance of his might and presence, glorious and terrible as he wrestles with man near the River Jabbok (Gen. 32.25–33) or when he seeks to kill Moses . . . (Ex. 4.24ff.)? A primitive myth crying out for demythologisation? Or, rather, is it a tremendous experience of God in revealed forms which (as is usually the case in the 'religion of the fathers') cannot be interpreted completely as 'gods' nor completely as 'angels'?[72]

Such visions proceed out of the higher regions of *immanent* being. God stirs some form within immanent being to make itself present to a human being.

Heller shows that good novels can be made of the Old Testament stories; novels about the life of Christ are uniformly awful. Landy, Clines, Josipovici and Alter have no Christian competitors. It may be that the Old Testament is more susceptible to literary analysis than the New; and perhaps my own account of the New Testament has done something to convince the reader of this fact. The reason may lie in the greater concreteness of the Old Testament narrative. John Crowe Ransom defined aesthetic experience as the 'contemplation' of 'things as they are in their rich and contingent materiality':[73] the Old Testament has richer aesthetic roots than the New. Christ would be no comedy unless he carried the Hebrew Bible up with him, into incarnation, crucifixion and resurrection. If one takes them separately, the comic good of the Old Testament looks a little more immanent, that of the New a little more supernatural. Angelic mediators abound in the Old Testament and are thin on the ground in the New: the Book of Revelation is an exception in containing angels as revelatory agents. We may tend to think of angels as creatures more spiritual than ourselves: then we are following St Thomas, for whom angels function as disembodied intelligences.[74] That tradition will not help us here. Conversely, von Balthasar suggests that the angels 'represent heaven's whole approach and closeness to the material cosmos'.[75] Theology can account for the way that Old Testament attends to 'the thick *Dinglich* substance'[76] of finite facts, by referring the immediate inspiration of some of it to angels conceived as the superhuman characters which are nearest to 'the World's Body':

> The Old Testament experience of God has myth at its back and, ahead of it, the Incarnation of God . . . the experience has behind it the inner-worldly,

---

72 Von Balthasar, *Glory I*, p. 501.
73 John Crowe Ransom, 'Poetry: A Note on Ontology', in *The World's Body* (Charles Scribner's Sons, New York, 1938), p. 116.
74 St Thomas Aquinas, *Summa Theologiae*, First Part of the First Part, Question 50, Art. 1, *Whether an Angel is Altogether Incorporeal* [yes].
75 Von Balthasar, *Theo-Drama III*, p. 494.
76 Ransom, 'Poetry: A Note on Ontology', p. 142.

aesthetic relationship between 'ground' and 'form', and is moving towards the definitive form of theological aesthetics.[77]

As the inspiration – the region of reality which its object shows the author – of the Bible moves toward the supernatural, so the images become a bit less dense and poetic.

That does not mean that the whole of the Old Testament is inner-worldly, or mythological, but that there are more patches of 'immanence' in the Old, and greater attention to the self-presentation of the *supernatural* realm of the good in the New. The distinction between levels of inspiration in the Bible allows Christian theology to take all as inspired, but not all as historical (and that without allegorising the story into thin air). Von Balthasar draws out the implications:

> it is much less necessary than with the New Testament to determine what in the Old might be historical in individual details and what there might be of mythical material (derived from the general vision of the historical situation) ... This historical existence of Israel, half-way between paganism and Christianity, objectivises itself in images of unforgettable vividness and colour (regardless of how many of these images could individually be considered 'historical' in the modern sense).[78]

The same God inspires both the 'immanent' and the 'transcendent' aesthetics of Scripture, but sometimes more directly, and sometimes with more angelic mediation, which thickens the substance of the images. The dense images and the soufflés spiral around each other: the supernatural good of the New Testament is unimaginable without the natural goods of the Old. The 'great archetypal experiences' of God in the Old Testament cannot

> be classified as merely a lower stage which leads on up to Christian experience. Their very sensoriness and their celestial symbolism is something that cannot be surpassed by the New Testament; the seer of the Apocalypse was fully conscious of this.[79]

The Bible shows the whole range of the imagination: we have to keep the harmonium together.

c. Biblical Inspiration Concerns the Moral Imagination

Inspired knowledge sees what matters. If scriptural inspiration is the 'inspired description of the show', then the sacred writers have to know what counts and *make it count* for their audience. What we take away from Exodus or John's Gospel are certain master images: Moses approaching the burning bush, too fast, beating a retreat, taking his shoes off and returning to the divine fire. The scene which remains in the mind's eye is an image. To conjure up such images is to think and to feel imaginatively. The psycho-spiritual power driving the affections and the ratiocinations of the biblical authors is the imagination. Austin Farrer conceived of inspiration as a supernatural charge directed to the biblical authors' imaginations. He suggests that we

77 Von Balthasar, *Glory I*, pp. 337–338.
78 Ibid., pp. 625–626.
79 Ibid., p. 336.

suppose . . . the Apostle's . . . thought centred round a number of vital images, which lived with the life of images, not concepts. Then each image will have its own conceptual conventions, proper to the figure it embodies.[80]

When we say 'you cannot divorce inspiration from *language*', we sometimes mean that 'inspiration and its *imagery* are inseparable'. The language of Scripture is not external to its meaning. But, whilst the mediaeval dramatisations of the 'salvation history' retain as much biblical language as they can, they still re-arrange and invent. If they succeed in imparting the biblical story, it is because they retain its typical images: Noah and his wife sighting land, Abraham poised with the knife, the torture of Christ. It does not do to be over-rigidly textual or linguistic in our approach to Scripture. Rashi read between the lines of God's command to Abraham, and invented some additional dialogue and motivation of his own. Christian tradition has preserved some of the extra-canonical apocalypticists' *midrashim* on the Old Testament, such as the image of the Fall of the Angels. The image of Christ's descent into hell owes as much to the Apocryphal Gospel of Nicodemus as to the texts of the canonised ones. The great interpreters in the living tradition are sufficiently sensitive to the images to undertake a little inspired play with the language in which they are set. The objectivity of the exercise requires that the interpreter knows which of the images is central and which is dispensable: 'In the prophets, as in the apostles, we must distinguish between the master-images for which there are no equivalent, and the subordinate images by which the master-images are set forth or brought to bear.'[81] This accords with our experience of Scripture: we do not recall every word which Isaiah used; our memory of the prophetic text is overshadowed by the great images – the Suffering Servant standing at the centre of a circle of detractors, the people travelling along the high way. Both liturgical *tradition* and a culture's *spontaneous* re-creation of the tradition bring the indispensable images to the foreground. The substance of the Bible is neither its abstractable truths nor its discrete words. The words are the means by which the Bible captures the meaning of the inspired and representative gestures, its master-images and substance. Von Balthasar gets it about right:

> There will never be a theology that gives a fully valid translation into abstract concepts of the dimensions of poetry and image into Scripture; not because God's word is exclusively poetry and pictorial language, but above all because the verbal form of the Bible is the only proper form for all that is said by God's Son and Word concerning the Father.[82]

One cannot make sense of the Bible without *seeing the form* of the master-images, grasping their reality in their beauty, and thereby assenting to their claim to bind us into a network of moral obligations. There is more to seeing the form of the biblical story than cleverly grasping its master-images: we have to assent to them. Once we get here, 'we would have to speak,

---

80 Austen Farrer, *The Glass of Vision*, the Bampton Lectures (Dacre Press, Westminster, 1948, 1958), p. 45.
81 Ibid., p. 133.
82 Von Balthasar, *Glory VII*, 267–268

with Newman, of an ethically demanded perception of form, involving both the person's sense of responsibility and his freedom'.[83]

Farrer was clear that such inspired images are intentional: 'the inspired man . . . does not think about the images, but about what they signify'.[84] He was not as clear about whether the inspired images had their home in the *text* or in the *process* of composition. His discussion of inspiration slips back to the psychological 'who', as when he says that 'if we observe the perceptible process in the inspired mind, the psychological fact, then we may say that it is a process of images which lives as it were by their own life'.[85] He has therefore been taken to task for committing the intentional fallacy.[86]

Farrer's inclination to the intentional fallacy has this to recommend it: it serves as a reminder that empirical individuals wrote the biblical books. We are very often advised to the contrary. For example, Paul Achtemeier claims that

> the major significance of the Bible is not that it is a book, but . . . that it reflects the life of the community of Israel and the primitive church, as those communities sought to come to terms with the . . . reality that God was present with them . . . the Bible is the result of the experience of Israel and of the early church with the God who invaded their world and forced them to come to terms with that fact . . . our understanding of inspiration must reckon with the interrelation of community and Scripture, as well as the continuing process of reinterpretation imposed on Scriptural traditions . . . We must take seriously Paul's insight that the Spirit is given to the community . . . (1 Cor. 12).[87]

The theologians who have conceived the notion of inspiration as communal have taken their lead from the various source hypotheses concerning the Old and New Testaments. If biblical exegetes teach us to think of the Pentateuch as the compilation of 'J', 'E', 'P' and 'D', each emerging over hundreds of years and finally being edited after the exile, the systematic theologian is directed to cook up a theory of the inspiration of the long tradition of a religious community.

Source criticism has lately tended to reduce the sources of the Pentateuch, perhaps, as far as one plus an editor, if we follow John van Seters, or two ('P' and 'D'), if we take on board the hypotheses which have gained the widest acceptance. Once scholarly attention falls upon the final form of a text such as Job, the final editor looks more like 'an author' than a group of them. We no more have to think of the Book of Job as the product of a collective than we do the plays of Shakespeare, given that Shakespeare used Holingshed and other sources. Burridge's conception of the literary structure of the Gospels as ancient βιοι directs us to the same paradigm: if Mark's Gospel is like *Agricola*, then Mark is like Tacitus, that is, one man. Empirically, it makes sense to think in terms of one mind, lying behind each of the biblical books.

83 Von Balthasar, *Theo-Drama II*, p. 134.
84 Farrer, *Glass of Vision*, p. 57, cf. p. 113.
85 Ibid., p. 113.
86 Margarita Stocker, 'God in Theory: Milton, Literature and Theodicy', *Journal of Theology & Literature*, I, 1, March, 1987, 70–87.
87 Paul Achtemeier, *The Inspiration of Scripture: Problems and Proposals* (Westminster Press, Philadelphia, 1980), p. 92.

If one comes to the theology of inspiration from, say, von Rad's tremendous notion of salvation history, one may tend to imagine inspiration as a vast communal enterprise. But if one turns to the theology of inspiration from Gunn, Cheryl Exum, Alter and Heller, one is thinking of Abraham and Isaac, Pharaoh and Moses, Hannah, Samuel, Saul and David. And one may wish to ask the old-fashioned biblical scholars to put their finger on where this great wave of communal experience is recorded in the biblical text. The biblical narrative has its 'stock-characters' and comic 'types'. One of them is the 'children of Israel', whose cries went up to God in Egypt, which whinges its way through the wilderness of Leviticus, Numbers and Deuteronomy, and receives the abuse of the Prophets.

The literary imagination sometimes romanticises, or collectivises: that is, it tends to mythologise. We have collective *aesthetic* experiences, and the literary imagination sometimes obliges us with a collective object, or a myth. But the closer one brings the literary imagination and the literal historical imagination together, the more one has to depart from mythic hyperbole. Collective *moral* experiences are a problematic concept. Only an individual can take moral responsibility. The historically minded moralist cannot indict a *nation*. He or she can make particular assessments about particular persons in their given situations. Whatever their prejudices, or shortcomings, a nation does not give orders, or execute them, or give a little help. If the historian wishes to indict the whole nation, he or she will have to indict every single individual in it, for each of their omissions and commissions. No court of law can pass judgement on a group; if we find that all are equally guilty, that will be because, in deference to the requirements of justice, we have analysed each individual case. Likewise, one cannot canonise a troop. Praise and blame ultimately accrue only to individuals. Collective mythologies give us moral aspirations which only individuals can put into practice, or not, or sometimes. The aesthetic fiction is 'the Children of Israel' and John's 'the Jews': the moral and historical realities are David and Isaiah, Nicodemus and Caiaphas.

Meir Sternberg argued that the narrator of the Old Testament has an *omniscient* persona, as is shown in their telling things which a normal human being could not know.[88] Against this, Wolterstorff contends that this 'convention', of treating the author as a 'prophet-like' figure who has access to the divine mind, is not present in the Scriptures.[89] The biblical authors do not claim to know *everything*; they simply claim to know what they need to know in order to tell this story:

> to know by inspiration what Haman said in his heart, one doesn't have to be omniscient; one only has to know by inspiration what Haman said in his heart . . . As to why Sternberg should draw that extreme inference, I can only guess that he was letting the literary critical term of art, 'omniscient narrator', run away with him.[90]

Wolterstorff is overlooking the 'a priori' of the believing reader's approach to Scripture: if the narrator had added other or more things to his story, we

---

88 Sternberg, *Poetics of Biblical Narrative*, pp. 68–80.
89 Wolterstorff, *Divine Discourse*, p. 252.
90 Ibid., p. 249.

should believe these things too. In doing so, we take the narrator to be omniscient about whatever he may say. For the audience, the question of the author's role or persona comes down to that of *authority*: on what grounds do we believe him? The tradition takes the assertions of the biblical writers as 'a priori to be believed' because they cast each writer in the role of an authority, who knows the mind of God. We do not do justice to the biblical narrative unless we say that this is the authority of experience. It is no Schleiermacherian translation of the language of the Bible into secular categories to say that a series of individuals experience God; this is what the Bible describes.

St Thomas's paradigm of *prophetic* inspiration is criticised by proponents of collective inspiration on the ground that it leads us to conceive of *individual* authors behind individual books. I am afraid to say that this latter has been the burden of our empirical phenomenology of the origination of the sacred text. *Someone* experienced the 'I am that I am'; perhaps biblical tradition made matters too simple by calling him 'Moses'. Where the process begins with the collection of oral and written legends, as in the Deuteronomistic writings, one will have to speak of an editor who has sufficient experiential contact with the master images to create a good synthesis of the traditions. *Someone* reflected on the conflict between this worldly and other-worldly conceptions of God as the Good, and that judicious assessment gave rise to the Book of Job. *Someone* saw and assented to the set of master-images by which Christ, in the Fourth Gospel, identifies himself with the 'I am'. This prophetic or apostolic experience is our only authority for believing in the 'inspired' quality of the books which record them. The traditional word for the experiencers has been 'witnesses'.

It is not enough to say that God has directed his inspiration to the biblical writers' imaginations. There are different types of imagining. There is an aesthetic imagination and a historical imagination. There is also a moral imagination, which enables one to get out of tight spots with a good grace. It is that form of discernment which sees how to implement the good in particular situations. The author of the Song of Songs was an aesthete's aesthete: if the beautiful is that which pleases when seen, then biblical poetry contains that transcendental notion.[91] There are hints of a philosophical imagination in the Wisdom writings and in apocalyptic. There is little of the mathematical imagination, even in the case of the author of the Book of Revelation. There is much historical imagination, in the Deuteronomistic tradition, in the prophets, and in the Gospels. Wherever we find aesthetic, philosophical, or historical imagination in the Bible, they are put at the assistance of the intention to show us the good. That is why most of its matter takes the form of *actions,* and actions which impose a decision on the reader. The kind of imagination which predominates in the Old and New Testaments is the moral. The master-images of Scriptures display what St Thomas called the 'bonum honestas', the beauty of goodness.[92]

---

91 St Thomas Aquinas, *Summa Theologiae*, First Part of the First Part, Question 5, Article 4, *Whether Goodness has the Aspect of a Final Cause*, Reply Obj. 1.
92 Ibid., Second Part of the Second Part, Question 145, Third Article, *Whether the Honest Differs from the Useful and the Pleasant.*

The various individuals who composed the Bible took moral responsibility for the truth, the beauty and the historical factuality of their writing.
Sometimes theologians have been so concerned to safeguard the objectivity
of the biblical writers that they have downplayed this fact. The hardest
kind of objectivity which comes to their minds is the impersonal. That
might incline us to the notion of inspiration as divine dictation: a 'Strange
dictation which cost its literary fashioner so dearly. The fact of the matter
is that it is not dictation at all'.[93] We would not have the Bible unless some
one took responsibility for their work. The New Testament writers do not
only say 'believe *it*': they say, 'believe *me* that it happened; or see *it* through
my testimony'. Von Balthasar says,

> The Apostles are witnesses of the Resurrection and of the whole life of Jesus
> . . . the form of their objectivity coincides with the form of their witness. They
> are not uninvolved . . . reporters, but with their lives they vouch for the
> testimony they must give. Scripture, for its part, testifies to their giving of
> testimony. The two coincide entirely when Paul writes a letter and, in it,
> testifies with his whole life to the truth of revelation, putting God's action at
> the center but including himself . . . he shows how the drama comes from
> God, via Christ, to him, and how he hands it on to the community, which is
> already involved in the action and must bring it into reality.[94]

The inspired community has its place here. On the basis of the moral
witness of individuals such as Paul and John, they are drawn into the moral
conflict which these authors describe.

d. Inspiration Can Be Historical
Inspiration is a marriage of two, in which an object discloses itself. Some
objects may put on an especially suggestive posture. Inspiration does not
stay obediently behind the easel with the painter but begins on the side of
the 'sitter'. Holbein would have been a less memorable artist if the Tudor
aristocracy had worn less magnificent ruffs. The Elizabethan portrait
painter was one of the artists behind the Elizabethan portrait; but the man
who designed what Henry VIII or Elizabeth I are wearing is another; the
pose which the sitters put on also makes its contribution. One cannot paint
a good portrait of someone who cannot or will not project themselves; this
is why passport photographs look like policeman's mugshots. Docu-
mentary photographers and cinematographers often *capture* an expressive
face; but a wooden actress could not make a fashion-model: the sitter poses
the image. Thus, it is not just scriptwriters who require inspiration, but
also actors. This is not left to chance: the actors require the assistance of a
director. The director imagines how he wants the text to be re-constituted,
and prompts his performers to effect his imagined conception. Professional
actors do not act only with their mouths, by speaking their lines, but with
every movement and grimace.

We may think of inspiration as God showing the biblical writers *what to
write*. Scripture is *about* something. On the one hand, we have the historical
event, the life of Christ, and, on the other side of the easel, the interpreters,

---

93 Alonso Schökel, *The Inspired Word: Scripture in the Light of Language and Literature*,
    translated by Francis Martin (Herder & Herder, New York, 1965), p. 96.
94 Von Balthasar, *Theo-Drama II*, p. 57.

creating their inspired record. Not only its writers, but also many of the
actions which the Bible describes, are *inspired*, because inspiration overlaps
with history. We need not confine inspiration to the interpretation of the
actions; the exegesis may be suggested by the actions. In the case of the
inspired and imaginative re-creation of a script by directors and actors, the
script comes first, but, in the case of *historical inspiration*, the 'acting' comes
before the verbal description. If we look for this within the biblical narratives, we may think of the prophets' *representative* or *expressive gestures*. We
may think of Isaiah, dressed, or undressed, as a deportee; or of Ezekiel,
who 'gesticulates with his whole existence'.[95] Is that an example of *inspiration* or of *revelation*? Gesticulating is pointing, or making a sign of oneself:
the actor-prophets 'sign' a visual statement which is *about* the revelation of
God. These acted gestures may then be recorded in the inspired record of
the biblical text: this need be no more problematic than the fact that it takes
great actors *and* good cinematographers to make a decent movie. If one
sees no reason to think that, if he existed, he didn't dance, one can put the
question like this: Was David dancing before the Ark inspired, or was the
Deuteronomist who described him the sole recipient of supernatural
enthusiasm? Pierre Benoit attributes inspiration to both:

> For the composition of the Bible, we can speak of 'scriptural inspiration'. But
> it is more difficult to give a name to the role of the men chosen by God to act,
> and to live the biblical 'Deed' before it was recounted or written. 'Dramatic
> inspiration' would be suitable enough, were it possible to restore the
> adjective's etymological overtones.[96]

Benoit thus speaks of the 'dramatic inspiration' of the deeds which lie
behind the 'types' of the Old Testament; he speaks of the 'apostolic inspiration' of some of the historical words of the disciples, and of the scriptural
inspiration of the people who told their story. The principle is that the *first*
event of inspiration is not cognitional, but actual and salvific:

> Seen in this broad perspective, scriptural inspiration . . . takes its place in the
> centre of a current of the breath of God passing through the history of
> salvation from beginning to end, from the Spirit who stirred the primordial
> waters to the Spirit who will penetrate souls and bodies in the final mani-
> festation.[97]

Could an 'inspired actor' *be* God's self-disclosure? It would complicate
matters considerably. We should have to speak of many dimensions of
inspiration. In the first place, there would be the actor, and we should have
to place him in history. In the second place, his performance would have to
be captured by an inspired artist, or a series of them, positioned at different
angles to the stage. At a third remove, there would be the biblical text, the
inspired description of the show.

The clearest point of common ground belonging to inspiration and
history is the life of Jesus Christ. Von Balthasar speaks of Christ as the
'actor' who is enabled to 'carry out his mission' by 'the Holy Spirit's

95 Von Balthasar, *Glory VI*, p. 270.
96 Benoit, *Inspiration and the Bible*, pp. 103–104.
97 Ibid., p. 114.

"prompting"';[98] and of the 'transposition' of this inspired *historical* performance into the *living experience* of the apostles. He states that: 'Every transposition . . . has a theological a priori: the Holy Spirit, whose task is to universalise the drama of Christ'.[99] Thirdly, then, the performances are written down: 'the permanent meaning of pre-Easter discipleship had to be made available to those who came later; and this was the task of the Synoptics. John carried out a final transposition.'[100]

4. Inspiration and Revelation: Father, Son and Spirit

God the Father writes the play, God the Son acts it upon the stage of world history, and God the Holy Spirit directs the performances.[101] When we say that God the Father 'writes', the word is used in an analogous sense: we mean that the drama is gestated in him, and is brought about by his hand. The story would not be a drama if it were first and foremost a *book*. The Father writes in the language of actions. God's action in history is like the 'cinematographic' language used by Eisenstein: 'Though sound is important, a movie substantially consists of images' which tell a story; the great silent movies like the *Battleship Potemkin* show that 'action is a language – provided . . . that its "vocabulary" be carefully chosen and artistically handled'.[102] But those actions are overflowing with meaning, and meaning, for persons, naturally makes its way into words. The words with which the inspired writers recreate the actions seek to capture a massive meaning which is both built to flow into languages and exceeds them. The deed bubbles over into a surplus of symbols. Buber wrote that

> Prophets and psalmists praise the deeds of YHVH at the Red Sea with the same images of cosmic battles and victories in which the divine works of Creation are extolled and glorified. The defeated Egyptian 'dragon' grows into a symbol as vast as the world in the drama of rescue which serves as prelude to the revelation, but which in itself is also already revelation. For here the miracle is revelation through the deed, which precedes revelation through the word.[103]

If, as St Thomas said, 'The author of Holy Writ is God, in whose power it is to signify his meaning, not by words only (as man also can do), but also by things themselves',[104] one may think of the author of the 'thingly' quality of revelation as God the Father and Cause of things, and their being.

These actions also have a personal quality: The prophets, Samuel, David, Mary, John the Baptist and Jesus have not only to *be*, as things are, but to *do*: performance is the prerequisite of persons. And so we have stolen Benoit's notion of a 'dramatic inspiration', a doing inspiration: this we ascribe to the Holy Spirit. The Spirit enables the historical actors to commit actions whose

---

98 Von Balthasar, *Theo-Drama III*, p. 533.
99 Ibid., p. 96.
100 Ibid., p. 126.
101 Von Balthasar, *Theo-Drama I*, p. 319.
102 Schökel, *Inspired Word*, pp. 35–36.
103 Buber, *Moses*, p. 79.
104 St Thomas Aquinas, *Summa Theologica*, I, Question 1 *The Nature and Extent of Doctrine*, Article 10, Reply.

meaning others can interpret. It is by virtue of the 'stage-directing' of the Holy Spirit that the 'Father's will is encountered in history no less than in interior inspiration . . . the Baptist's appearance and fate served as a sign to Jesus that he should begin his public ministry'.[105] The Spirit prompts historical persons to transform their lives into 'legible patterns', and that works, as the Stanislavkian director would say, from inside out. Once 'out', on the stage of history, these practical gestures become cues to which the cast responds, and which the audience understands. 'Now its over to you, Cousin', says John, by inciting Herod to arrest him.

The Actor in the 'family' of the Trinity is God the Son: the Playwright Father's Word in historical flesh. We can translate the 'actor' into biblical categories. God has treated the figures of the salvation history like 'actors' at his disposal, by signifying their tasks in their names, making Abram become Abraham, Jacob Israel; the Jesus of the Gospels continues the series by making Simon Peter; Saul becomes Paul.[106] At the baptism, Jesus receives, historically, the mission: 'This is my beloved son' (Matthew 3.1). Everyone assumes social roles, but these parts do not quite fit our skin. The Christ who turns his eternal nature inside out into his historical mission *is* his role.[107] Christ's process through his historical life is the historical carrying forward of his eternal composition by the Father. The shape of Christ's life 'shows us the Father': that is what revelation is.

From the beginning of Genesis, we have seen two things. One was the onward moving dialogue between the two partners, One in heaven, and the others on earth. The second was the shifting apart, the increased 'distance' between the stage levels, after the Fall. The Deuteronomistic writings, the prophets, and then the Apocalypticists, imagine a growing disparity between the stage levels of heaven and earth. Christ's intimacy with the Father is something new, since 'Adam'. So that here, human and divine actors speak the same language. Divine revelation is not aimed at achieving a pompous monologue, but a dialogue, between heaven and earth. The two 'stage-levels' are both spacious things and events, ways of being. If Christ 'overcomes' the 'distance between heaven and earth' that is because, in his mission and nature, he performs the analogy between human and divine Good. The revelation of God is, and is made perceptible to us, because it is the construction of the analogy, the likeness between God and his world, heaven and earth. He is the 'similitude' by which we know God.

Christ's mission is to use his life to reveal the Father. He is a word, expressing the Writer's thought, an Actor putting the Playwright's idea into action, and thus an idea which shows us the whole mind of the Writer. Von Balthasar ascribes Christ's ability to perform this mission to 'grace': that is, to the directing of the Spirit. 'Grace' is the ability to be completely in line with the Father:

> at the point of distinction between the Father's purpose and the Son's obedience, we discern an essential poise, an essential communication between Father and Son, which can only be the operation of the Holy Spirit.[108]

105 Von Balthasar, *Theo-Drama III*, p. 178.
106 Ibid., p. 155.
107 Ibid., p. 201.
108 Ibid., p. 183.

The gift which enables us to discern value, or the good, comes to us from the Spirit: and this good is concretised in the way in which we direct our lives, the shape which our lives take. In his dramatic 'poise', his perfect showing of how it means to be related to God, Christ is dependent upon the Spirit. Here, in Palestine, in the first century of the Christian era, the Spirit does in time what the Spirit is in eternity: the linking of Father and Son. Jesus has to 'pray' for this stage direction.[109]

The Spirit shows the imperfect human cast, and the divine–human Actor how to make their lives interpretable. Once the Word is removed from the stage of world history, the Spirit presides over the translation of 'seeing' the form into knowing the form and putting it into language. The life of Christ is organically rooted in its historical, Jewish context: the 'task' of the 'Holy Spirit . . . is to universalize the drama of Christ'.[110] Now the deed is translated into language, and produces an even greater surplus of meaning than that of the 'deeds of YHVH at the Red Sea'. Translation from deed into word, the verbal inspiration of the Scriptures by the Holy Spirit, is an act of imagination.

From the perspective of the good, the book is a set of rules for a game which has barely begun, as the book is set in writing, and laid to gather dust on the presbytery shelf. Christ is both Actor and the stage on which the drama continues. How can an actor be a stage? Christ sets the scene; and he provides the model for new ways of directing a human destiny toward the 'acting area' which is 'a perduring event' and within which 'new players can continually act their parts, appearing on stage and leaving it';[111] my students tell me that it works like *What's My Line*. No matter how many ways we can imagine to instantiate the good, there are more. The Letter to the Ephesians says that we are 'Created for good works' (2.4–10): that 'means that . . . we are enabled . . . to engage in that "actio" to which the *bonum* shows itself to be . . . the *transcendentale*'.[112] If the Bible is about the good as *transcendental*, there is no closure on the human capacity to keep up with it; it directs its audience to keep going. The good of the Scriptures is incarnate in Christ. The infinitude of the transcendentally good specifies itself into a finite person. To be on the 'stage' which Christ creates, to be 'in Christ', through baptism, is to gain a unique name, which goes to the bottom of us. This name is a calling and mission. Since evil is still present, the mission will include biffing it.[113] The task requires stage directions from the Holy Spirit, lest our crusade run amok.

The audience of a play, a trial, and even a game, wait intensely to learn how the truth will be teased out. The drama is the question whether a reality which confronts the players can emerge; this reality imposes itself upon the players, but can only be made present at their instance: 'drama is an opening up or closing-off to the presence of some light that radiates from existence'.[114] The 'primordial drama which the theatre only imitates'

109 Ibid., pp. 510–511.
110 Von Balthasar, *Theo-Drama II*, p. 96.
111 Von Balthasar, *Theo-Drama III*, p. 54.
112 Ibid., p. 53.
113 Ibid., p. 231.
114 Von Balthasar, *Theo-Drama II*, p. 30.

is a matter of 'sacred presence and human response'.[115] In the biblical history, that light first takes the form of the 'Word'. God's 'word' is revealed to the people of Israel. That 'word' inches its way further and further into being, so that it becomes not only speech but also reality. The *Dabar* was always word and thing: now it takes human flesh, so that a human life is the revelation of the nature of God and 'becomes the visible presence of God's acting and speaking in the world'.[116] Now the drama is about the recognition of a person:

> When the Word who 'was God' 'becomes flesh', he steps forth among the figures that surround us and point us in various directions, and now comes the decision (and this is *the* drama, embracing all others): Will 'his own' recognize him and 'receive' him or not?[117]

Drama manifests a combat between good and evil, because it is a moral category.[118] Revelation includes God's assault upon human alienation.[119]

The fact that persons do battle symbolises the fact that they are *different* from one another: but if we shed the *clash* of personalities, the dialogue remains. We do not have to differ in order to be different, and to meet as one strange face to another: 'the core of the drama consists ... of that interplay, that wealth of dialogic possibilities, that is found in the permanent, reciprocal relationship between finite freedom ... and infinite Freedom'.[120] The New Jerusalem will be a place of eternal surprise:

> Human freedom, which lives and operates entirely within the inspiration pouring forth from the God, who is always eternally free, is not ... a puppet-play ... In inspiring us, God gives us freedom, launching us into far-expanded possibilities. Eternal bliss is not like the ceremonial of some oriental court; the scenery in Revelation 4 may seem reminiscent of the latter, but we should note the breathtaking abruptness with which the images of heaven in this book keep changing: we are even presented with battles fought in heaven itself, songs of victory, marriages, cities filled with life day and night, rivers and fruitful trees.[121]

Because human beings are free, they are unknowable; that is why 'we cannot know in advance what the stage will look like at the end of the play'.[122] This mystery at the heart of the *person* is retained, and perhaps even deepened, in the New Jerusalem. Such freedom will take the form of creative giving: we will be 'constantly being given new and unexpected gifts, through the creative freedom of others; and ... delight to invent other, new gifts and bestow them in return'.[123]

115 Thomas McPartland, 'History and Philosophy: The Existential Dimension', in Timothy P. Fallon and Philip Riley (eds), *Religion and Culture: Essays in Honor of Bernard Lonergan* (State University of New York Press, Albany, 1987), p. 110, citing, in the first phrase, Lonergan, *Insight*, p. 188.
116 Von Balthasar, *Glory VII*, p. 274.
117 Von Balthasar, *Theo-Drama II*, p. 26.
118 Von Balthasar, *Glory VI*, p. 16.
119 Von Balthasar, *Theo-Drama IV*, p. 193.
120 Ibid., pp. 200–201.
121 Von Balthasar, *Theo-Drama V*, p. 410.
122 Von Balthasar, *Theo-Drama II*, p. 186.
123 Von Balthasar, *Theo-Drama V*, p. 404.

God's revelation is addressed to *free* persons. It is addressed in such a way that it leaves the person free. There is a kind of biblical 'fact-value distinction'. In the biblical satires, it comes over as the difference between human inclinations and the reality of the good. In the 'testing', purgatorial arenas of the Bible, it is expressed in the partial success and the partial failure of the human combatants. We cannot quite see God as the Good in promised land or promised king, because the good hovers beyond complete manifestation. The paradisial comedy of the New Testament supplies, not a mechanical outcome of all that had gone before, but a good that over-reaches expectations. Now the good is incarnate, but too thick and rich to be automatically recognised. God does not

> create a freedom that is so confirmed in the good that it does not need to choose ... That is why ... we spoke of a necessary 'latency', according to which God initially keeps his free, inner self hidden: thus he gives the creature the opportunity to lay hold of its own freedom, a freedom that both is its own *and* comes from an external source.[124]

To will the good of another is to want them to be themselves, to permit them freely to move towards their own good. Human beings do not merely have an inbuilt 'orientation' towards the divine revelation; they have to be asked; only an 'invitation' respects their freedom.[125] If God's self-disclosure respects the freedom of its human recipient, so it also springs out of his own freedom: 'The drama portrayed by the Bible is God's initiative, and so between man's blue prints of existence there is not a continuous transition but a leap.'[126]

Human beings, alienated by sin, and free by creation, are directed by revelation towards integration: the surpassing return to the original stage-level, the intimacy with God from which Adam and Eve departed, with an angel waving a sword at them (Gen. 3.24). Adam and Eve were lent the *Nephesh*, the breath of life. The integration with which Revelation concludes is an eternal life which human beings desire, but which is beyond their means to create for themselves. The fact that they cannot climb up far enough to achieve the desire is symbolised by its 'coming down' from above.[127] For all of its transcendence of human self-extension, this is an *integration*, and not the imposition of a foreign reality. The conclusion will not abolish the drama of human history but intensify it:

> Mysteriously ... even what we call our 'drama' ... will be *present*, not *past* ... the One who sits upon the throne says, 'Behold, I make all things new'. Not: Behold, I make a totally new set of things, but: Behold, I refashion and renew all that is. And our faith tells us that this 'new' reality was already present in the 'old', in our drama, though in a hidden form ... So what will be manifested in glory is the depth and truth of our present life.[128]

The life-world of the drama of revelation is moved by the 'pull and counterpull' of Eros. Now the decision to 'pull' must come from God: 'for',

---

124 Von Balthasar, *Theo-Drama IV*, p. 150.
125 Ibid., pp. 165–166.
126 Von Balthasar, *Theo-Drama II*, p. 53.
127 Von Balthasar, *Theo-Drama IV*, pp. 43–44.
128 Ibid., p. 200.

St Thomas says, 'what exceeds the capacities of free-will, a man needs to be uplifted by a more powerful source of action'.[129] If the drama is driven by the 'appetites' of the human characters, its completion will never be 'ecstasy', or a stepping beyond themselves, because 'a man who desires some good is not in ecstasy but simply moving himself'.[130] But neither are the human agents dragged to their destiny by their hair: 'That a man should be so uplifted by God is not against nature but above the capacities of nature.'[131] The dramatist does not neglect the motivation of any of his characters: if we attend to *why* the human agents want this revelation: 'ecstasy can have its cause in the affective powers. In fact, should one's desire cleave very strongly to something, it can be that the great intensity of that love causes a man to become a stranger to all else'.[132] Thomas remarks that 'Goodness has the same relation to realities as truth has to knowledge':[133] that is, it causes them to *be*. The recipients of revelation are returning, like fish, to their source, the creative goodness of God. The desire to know God, seized upon, broken into, elevated beyond itself, and fulfilled in prophecy, is the desire to love God.

5. Revelation as Dramatic Comedy: Kenosis *Con Brio*

The Chalcedonian formula (451) speaks of the two natures of Christ, divine and human, co-existing in the one person of the Logos, 'without confusion, without change, without division, without separation'. The author of the Letter to the Philippians imagines that proposition like this: Christ,

> being in the form of God, thought it not robbery to be equal with God: but made himself of no reputation, and took upon him the form of a servant, and was made in the likeness of men: And being found in fashion as a man, he humbled himself, and became obedient unto death, even the death of the cross. Wherefore God also hath highly exalted him, and given him a name which is above every name: That at the name of Jesus every knee should bow, of things in heaven, and things in earth, and things under the earth. (Phil. 2.6–10)

Patristic, Russian Orthodox and Reformed theology have always made use of a distinction between the two *states* of Christ's person. These are the status *exaltationis*, the exalted state of the divine person in heaven, and the status *humiliationis*, the humiliated state of the divine person on earth. Kenotic Christology has consisted in seeing the divine Logos as moving between the *states* or *conditions* of exaltation and humiliation: his divine–human nature(s) remain divine and human, whilst moving through their various dramatic modes. The dramatic analogy helps to makes sense of it: Peisetaerus or Oedipus are always one person, *and* that identity is enacted under different conditions, as they proceed from complication to peripeteia/parabasis to dénouement. We cannot really ask: is Oedipus' 'nature' changed by the play (what becomes of dramatic causality if it does

129 St Thomas Aquinas, *Summa Theologica*, 2a2ae, *Question 175 Ecstasy*, Article 1, Reply.
130 Ibid., Article 2, Reply.
131 Ibid., Article 1, Reply Objection 2.
132 Ibid., Article 2, Reply.
133 *Question 172 The Cause of Prophecy*, Article 6, Reply.

not). The reason why the question is unanswerable is that there is no Oedipus outside of the particular set of interactions which is his play.

The *imaginative* note which the idea of kenosis adds to Chalcedon is that of drama. Kenotic Christology allows us to picture the life of Christ as activated by moral choice and decision. The framework is as much moral as it is metaphysical. Just as, P. T. Forsyth says, we restrict and 'mortgage' our selves by acts of 'freedom, love and duty', so did the Incarnate Christ.[134] Kenoticism enabled theologians to say things which make sense to a modern Christian: such as that Christ's 'personality' is 'constituted' by his relationship to the Father: 'his whole personality was absolute sonship'. That makes us think of movement and counter-movement: the elements of dialogue and drama. The notion of kenosis allows us to preserve the reality of Christ's human nature. The Incarnate life of Christ is, first, a 'retraction' and then a 'reintegration' of the fullness of the divine person.[135] But, if we begin our doctrine of incarnation from the eternal Father–Son relation, then we shall have to speak of an 'act of renunciation' which is 'outside the walls of the world'.[136] The 'will-warfare' in which the historical Jesus 're-deemed the world' is the 'exercise' and reflection of 'an eternal resolve'.[137] There is thus in the 'primal drama' of the Trinity, a 'Lamb slain from the foundation of the world'.

Von Balthasar says that the Christ of the Gospels is more transparently divine than the Christ of history. This is so because, after the event of the Resurrection, the interpretative spotlight of the Spirit picks out Christ's divinity and gives it a glow which was not apparent in the course of his historical life, and to his contemporaries. Look at him before Easter, and you will see in a glass darkly; look back from Easter Sunday, and his divinity is gloriously present throughout:

> The light shed by the Spirit was so bright that when its dazzling rays turned back on the hiddenness of Jesus, it bathed him proleptically in the light of Easter, and proleptically transfigured his kabod as pure momentum into doxa as brilliance, in some passages. As the Word become flesh, Jesus was more hidden than he is shown to be by the light of the Gospels, just as . . . God's deeds of salvation in the redeeming of Israel were more hidden and incon-spicuous than the transfiguring images in Exodus or Joshua portray them . . . the Gospels conceal by revealing: how else could it be otherwise, when God's humility, descending beneath all that may be uttered, can be fully grasped in no act of reverbalisation.[138]

This is a note which is in harmony with any Christian mind which has been chastened by two hundred years of biblical scholarship *and* which wishes to find in Christ an organic being, not a human nature which serves as a 'spacesuit' for the divinity. In the *status humiliationis* of Christ's human life, Christ's nature is divine, but his glory is concealed: his historical life carries the 'fundamental' sign of 'hiddenness'.[139] Von Balthasar asks

---

134 P. T Forsyth, *The Person and Place of Jesus Christ* (Independent Press, London 1909, 1961), pp. 296–297.
135 Ibid, pp. 288 and 308.
136 Ibid., p. 273.
137 Ibid., p. 270.
138 Von Balthasar, *Glory VII*, pp. 156–157.
139 Ibid., p. 218.

whether the Gospel writers 'look backwards from Easter and give a retro-
spective interpretation that pours too much paschal light over the life of
Jesus?' This does not mean that the miracles are fictions – 'at most, one can
speak of light, stylistic touches' – but that the miracles both reveal and
conceal.[140] In terms of his *being*, Christ is the manifestation of the divine
nature; from the perspective of our *knowing*, the *revelation* takes place after
the event: 'he leaves the *apokalupsis* of his enduring hiddenness to the Spirit
and the Church'.[141]

In some of our temperamental states, perhaps, we can lap up one sort of
apparently 'kenotic' picture of Christ all too readily: we should rather pity
Christ than be terrified by him. But what happens then to our notion of
Christ as a comic hero? If we follow out the imaginative logic of this image
of 'kenosis', we shall have to make him into a slightly depressing Bozo the
Clown figure, and I do not think that we want our conception of revelation
to step out into the world wearing odd shoes. A Christ without any oomph
can be the *object* of satire, but this deflated figure cannot hold earth *and*
heaven together. In other moods, we find the notion instinctively repellent:
one of my very good students once remarked that 'I want Christ to be
glorious and golden; I want to run to him and hug him, like Aslan'. There
is a lot of religious truth in that comment: but it is remarkable, that the
slaying of Aslan, in *The Lion, the Witch and the Wardrobe*, the only scene in
which the Lion suffers in the Narnia epic, has an undercurrent of sado-
masochism, almost as if, dare I say, the author secretly enjoyed writing it.
The miserabilistic desire for a purely pitiable Christ and the triumphalist
one, for a glorious and golden Christ, have a curious affinity. If we really
want to empty *ourselves* of our anger and guilt onto a sacrificial victim,
he must be strong enough to take it. A genuine idea of kenosis requires
that we recall, for the last time, that the *comical* victim of sadistic laughter
does not have the last word about *comedy*. The sublime tragic hero
suffers instead of the audience; a pagan means of cathartic sacrifice. The
lowly comic hero who is and remains at one with his audience can play
out a sacrifice for which there are no spectators, but only witnesses who
will lend a hand. We do not *expel* the gracious comic hero, we identify
with him. One can see a genuine comic hero in action in *Life is Beautiful*.
In that movie, Guido Orefice is taken with his wife and little son to a
concentration camp in 1944: he makes the boy imagine the hideous
world around him as a game. The expedient enables him to persuade
the boy to 'win points' by hiding, and thus helps him to survive: but it is
also his way of enabling the child to retain his innocence. The little play-
theatre which he builds between himself and the child is their way of
making the camp into a joke on the guards. Guido drinks the deception to
the dregs, winking and saluting to his concealed child as the guards
march him off to be shot. The kenotic Christ is a comic hero with that sort
of *brio*.

One of the paradoxes of theatre is that those enlarged egos which
perform their histrionics before an audience have to do so *as someone else*.
Actors disguise themselves in costumes so that they can strip themselves

140 Ibid., pp. 321, 322 and 335.
141 Ibid., p. 219.

down, and reveal the reality of a naked self, which has been dictated to them by the author, and imagined for them by the director. Far from making its practitioner into an object of helpless *pity*, kenosis is a way of putting on power. The more that Christ strips himself down into his humanity, the more scope is given to the power of the naked Sonship, as envisaged by the Father and prompted by the Spirit. The Son would not be the self-expression of the Father without the humiliation of self-hiddenness: it is by negating his *self* that the Son creates the 'emptied out space' in which the Father is seen.[142] Kenosis is not a static object, but an action. Christ's kenotic action is a way of mobilising his two natures, so that the Word and the flesh, the veiling and the unveiling, do not stand still, in motionless balance: rather, each makes a creative use of the other. The Logos does not express the Father only, but divine and the human in one single act: he disguises himself in flesh *so that* he can reach into his deity and perform the human. By veiling himself in flesh, he unveils his ability to be man.

We have said that drama is not just the smooth interplay of dialoguing selves, but also combat. An earlier age liked to imagine Christ as carrying the fight against Satan into hell: this militaristic and masculine figure carries less conviction in an age of atomic bombs. Von Balthasar pictures, rather, a Christ who defeats the powers of evil by being powerless:

> The complete disarming of the principalities and powers (Col. 2.14f.), the . . . breaking into the house of the strong man, in order to bind him in chains (Mk 3.24), the robbing of the 'gates of hell' of their power (Mt 16.18) – all this can take place only from within, in participation in the absolute passivity of being dead.[143]

That, and not the sword-wielding figure of the Mystery Plays, one may say, is what a dead man is like. But, if the triumph of the commanding Christ of the *Ludus Coventriae* is *satisfying*, the work of the kenotic hero, encountering the powers of evil in all of his mortality, is truly hilarious. That tiny and finite morality springs back from death in an act of complete assimilation. The more completely Christ enters into the reality of the kenotic 'deception', the more thoroughly hell is assimilated into his experience. And thus, by performing himself on every level of supernatural and natural reality, he holds all together, in the comedy of the *analogia entis*.

We find the features of comedy in the revelatory drama of biblical history: audience enjoyment, laughter, the resolution of conflict, a vital hero in a liberating space, and large, obvious symbols which unify the high and the low. The enjoyment of comedy is that of empathetic identification. If the 'identification' which we make in relation to the tragic character is like *knowing* how he must go on, comic sympathy is more like immersion. The lowly comic heroes and heroines lay themselves open to identification, inviting us to grab them. This immersion in a vital and lively character, which assuages our aloneness without taking away our identity, is so enjoyable that we would suffer to maintain it.

142 Ibid., pp. 379–380.
143 Ibid., p. 230.

Sophocles' Electra, Antigone and Oedipus, Euripides' Iphigeneia, and Shakespeare's Hamlet, are great and heroic *individuals*. We identify with them from the outside. This is not the kenosis envisaged by the biblical narrative. The liturgy and the secular dramatists show us the kenosis of inclusion, of the stock-hero of comedy. The large and obvious symbols which unify high and low are the great typological images, which run from Abel the sheep farmer to the Lamb of the New Jerusalem. We cannot keep the harmonium of Old and New Testament together unless we just as often Hebraise the New Testament as we 'Christify' the Old: this is the work of typology. The comic hero is *so* typically human that he includes *everyone*, and every thing ('and also much cattle'), but so much larger than life that he can give 'himself' away.

The ethical exercise of kenosis takes place within a *sacred* adventure: 'Christ's life is at the same time deed and cult';[144] his most significant achievement is to let himself be plundered and shared out in Passion and Eucharist.[145] The biblical history resolves conflict by means of paradox. If the paradox were static, it would be a mere conjunction of opposites. The dynamic paradoxes of the biblical history drive opposites into unification: the crucifixion *is* the glorification. In the Johannine 'bread discourses', Christ is represented as giving himself to be eaten. Before the 'cauldron of apotheosis' of crucifixion and death, this comic victor is so full of resurrected life, that he can describe himself as the meat and drink of resurrecting life: the status of exaltation surges out of the plunge down into finitude. In his offer of eternal life through the consumption of his flesh, he is the most liberating and fertile comic hero. His act of eucharistic kenosis is a surging river of *power*: the charge is ignited by paradox. The 'death' *is* the life and the life-giving power.

The meaning of biblical history is perceptible to the eye of faith; the sight which God enlightens is the moral imagination. Natural human experience of the good is open to this illumination. St Thomas does not establish the 'join' or the 'break' between nature and grace neatly. On the one hand, he says that the inclination to the supernatural is our inbuilt drive; on the other, that we have no inbuilt means of achieving it.[146] Thomas was content to leave us with a non-unified theory of natural and supernatural concourse with God, and this reflects the 'graced contingency' of the experience of the typical comic hero. In the life-world of comedy, helpers and sources of order may appear, at various intervals, but on their own terms, and from unforeseen directions. Odysseus has an inbuilt drive

---

144 Hans Urs von Balthasar, 'Nine Propositions on Christian Ethics', in Heinz Schurmann, Joseph Ratzinger and Hans Urs von Balthasar (eds), *Principles of Christian Morality*, translated by Graham Harrison (Ignatius Press, San Francisco, 1986), pp. 77–103 (80).
145 Ibid., p. 29.
146 St Thomas Aquinas, *Summa Theologiae*, Second Part of the Second Part, Question 175, Article 1, *Whether A Man's Soul is carried away to Divine Realities*, Reply Obj. 2: 'It belongs to the mode and worth of a man to be uplifted to the divine because man was created in the image of God. But as the divine goodness infinitely surpasses human capacities, man needs to be supernaturally helped to attain this good – and this takes place in any bestowal of grace. That a mind should be so uplifted by God is not against nature but above the capacities of nature.'

to get home, but, for all his many wiles, he would never have reached Ithaca without Athena. There is something *funny* about this waiting upon grace, which is why hitch-hikers experience undrugged ecstasies. Miracles are as at home in the terrain of comedy as dolphins in the Mediterranean. It is the *surprise* of the miraculous help, the unpredictable grace, which makes us laugh. A world in which 'nature' and 'grace' do not entirely overlap, but *can* overlap, we never know when or how, is laughter inspiring to inhabit.

6. Apologies for Our Shortcomings

I have taken advantage of a temporary disarray in the front of Biblical Studies to advance a philosophical interpretation of the Christian Scriptures. I have strengthened my arguments by pitting them against the best statements of the opposing case; if, as Chesterton said, the cap has sometimes come off the foil, I apologise. And if I have hurt anyone's feelings by my failure to write God several times in the same sentence ('God blows God's nostrils for Godself') in order to avoid saying he, himself or his, and have, instead, written 'God blew his nose', I apologise. I began rather a long time ago with the intention of *reading* the Bible. It would be twice as long ago if I had not turned Nelson's blind eye to the historical writings from 1 Kings onwards, the prophets, and the Pauline writings. I set out to read the Bible as *literature*. This tactic has led me to discover in the Bible a drama about the choice or the rejection of the good. The transcendentals, being, truth, goodness and beauty are convertible. And so I have mentioned the drama of *being*; I have attributed *truth* to the experiences of God which underlie the books of Exodus, of Job, and of John; the scriptural master-images are beautiful. The transcendentals show up different dimensions of an object. Because we have launched our forces against the dimension of the good in the Scriptures, the range of our forays into inspiration and revelation has been limited. Faith has many strategies, and we have enlisted that of the imagination. That choice was not intended to rule out other strategic plans, for those who know the terrain. If the good and being are, as St Thomas said, convertible, then we have done our part, for the present, to settle the Manichees.

Bibliography

ACHTEMEIER, PAUL, *The Inspiration of Scripture: Problems and Proposals* (Westminster Press, Philadelphia, 1980)

ACKROYD, PETER, *The People of the Old Testament* (Christophers, London, 1959)

ALTER, ROBERT, *The Art of Biblical Narrative* (George Allen & Unwin, London, 1981)

—— *The Art of Biblical Poetry* (T&T Clark, Edinburgh, 1985, 1990)

—— *Genesis: Translation and Commentary* (W. W. Norton & Co., New York, 1996)

—— *The World of Biblical Literature* (SPCK, London, 1992)

—— and FRANK KERMODE (eds), *The Literary Guide to the Bible* (Fontana, London, 1987)

ARISTOPHANES, *Birds*, edited with translation and notes by Alan H. Sommerstein (Aris & Philips, Wiltshire, 1987)

—— *Lysistrata*, edited with translation and notes by Alan H. Sommerstein (Aris & Philips, Wiltshire, 1990)

—— *Peace*, translated by B. B. Rogers (Loeb Classical Library, William Heinemann, London, 1924)

AQUINAS, THOMAS, *Summa contra Gentiles* II, translated by James Anderson (Notre Dame University Press, Notre Dame, 1975)

—— *Summa Theologica*, translated by the Fathers of the English Dominican Province (Sheed & Ward, London, 1911, 1920; Christian Classics, Maryland, 1981)

ARISTOTLE, *Poetics*, in the *Basic Works of Aristotle*, edited by Richard McKeon (Random House, New York, 1941)

AUERBACH, ERICH, *Mimesis: The Representation of Reality in Western Literature*, translated by Willard Trask (Princeton University Press, Princeton, 1946, 1974)

AUGUET, ROLAND, *Cruelty and Civilization: The Roman Games* (George Allen & Unwin, London, 1972)

BAILLIE, JOHN, *The Idea of Revelation in Recent Thought* (Oxford University Press, Oxford, 1956)

BALE, JOHN, *The Complete Plays of John Bale: Volume I*, edited By Peter Happé (D. S. Brewer, Cambridge, 1985)

—— *The Complete Plays Of John Bale: Volume II*, edited by Peter Happé (D. S. Brewer, Cambridge, 1986)

BALTHASAR, HANS URS VON, *The Glory of the Lord: A Theological Aesthetics: Volume I: Seeing the Form*, translated by Erasmo Leiva-Merikakis (T&T Clark, Edinburgh, 1982)

—— *The Glory of the Lord: A Theological Aesthetics: Volume III: Studies in Theological Style: Lay Styles*, translated by Andrew Louth, John Saward, Martin Simon and Rowan Williams (T&T Clark, Edinburgh, 1986)

—— *The Glory of the Lord: A Theological Aesthetics: Volume V: The Realm of Metaphysics in the Modern Age*, translated by Oliver Davies, Andrew Louth, Brian McNeil, John Saward and Rowan Williams (T&T Clark, Edinburgh, 1991)

—— *The Glory of the Lord: A Theological Aesthetics: Volume VI: The Old Covenant*, translated by Brian McNeil and Erasmo Leiva-Merikakis (T&T Clark, Edinburgh, 1991)

—— *The Glory of the Lord: A Theological Aesthetics: Volume VII: Theology. The New Covenant*, translated by Brian McNeil (T&T Clark, Edinburgh, 1989)

—— 'Nine Propositions on Christian Ethics', in Heinz Schurmann, Joseph Ratzinger and Hans Urs von Balthasar, *Principles of Christian Morality*, translated by Graham Harrison (Ignatius Press, San Francisco, 1986), pp. 77–103

—— *The Office of Peter and the Structure of the Church*, translated by Andrée Emery (Ignatius Press, San Francisco, 1987)

—— *Theo-Drama: Theological Dramatic Theory: I Prologomena*, translated by Graham Harrison (Ignatius Press, San Francisco, 1988)

—— *Theo-Drama: Theological Dramatic Theory: II The Dramatis Personae: Man in God*, translated by Graham Harrison (Ignatius Press, San Francisco, 1990)

—— *Theo-Drama: Theological Dramatic Theory: III Dramatis Personae: Persons in Christ*, translated by Graham Harrison (Ignatius Press, San Francisco, 1992)

—— *Theo-Drama: Theological Dramatic Theory: IV The Action*, translated by Graham Harrison (Ignatius Press, San Francisco, 1994)

—— *Theo-Drama: Theological Dramatic Theory: V The Last Act*, translated by Graham Harrison (Ignatius Press, San Francisco, 1998)

—— *The Theology of Karl Barth*, translated by John Drury (Holt, Rinehart & Winston, New York, 1971)

BARR, DAVID, 'The Apocalypse of John as Oral Enactment', *Interpretation*, 40, 1986, 243–256

BARTH, KARL, *Church Dogmatics I:1 The Doctrine of the Word of God*, translated by G. W. Bromiley (T&T Clark, Edinburgh, 1st edn, 1936, 2nd edn, 1975)

BAUCKHAM, RICHARD, *The Climax of Prophecy: Studies on the Book of Revelation* (T&T Clark, Edinburgh, 1993)

BAUCKHAM, RICHARD, *The Theology of the Book of Revelation* (Cambridge University Press, Cambridge, 1993)

BEAVIS, MARY ANN, *Mark's Audience: The Literary and Social Setting of Mark 4.11–12, Journal for the Study of the New Testament*, Supplement Series, 33 (JSOT Press, Sheffield, 1989)

BENOIT, PIERRE, O.P., *Inspiration and the Bible*, translated by J. Murphy-O'Connor and M. Keverne (Sheed & Ward, London, 1965)

BERGER, PETER, 'A Lutheran Looks at an Elephant', in *A Rumour of Angels: Modern Society and the Rediscovery of the Supernatural* (Doubleday, New York, 1969, rev. edn 1990), pp. 109–122

—— 'New York City 1976: A Signal of Transcendence', in *Facing Up to Modernity* (Penguin, London, 1979), pp. 258–268

—— *Redeeming Laughter: The Comic Dimension of Human Experience* (Walter de Gruyter, Berlin/London, 1997)

BERGSON, HENRI, *Le rire: Essai sur la signification du comique* (Presses Universitaires de France, Paris, 1947)

BEST, ERNST, *Mark: The Gospel as Story* (T&T Clark, Edinburgh, 1983)

BILEZIKIAN, GILBERT, *The Liberated Gospel: A Comparison of the Gospel of Mark and Greek Tragedy* (Baker Book House, Grand Rapids, 1977)

BLEVINS, JAMES, *The Genre of Revelation. Review and Expositor*, 77, 1980

BOLING, ROBERT G., *Judges: Introduction, Translation, and Commentary*, Anchor Bible Series, 6a (Doubleday & Company, New York, 1969)

BOMAN, THORLIEF, *Hebrew Thought Compared with Greek*, translated by Jules L. Moreau (SCM, London, 1960)

BOWIE, A. M., *Aristophanes: Myth, Ritual and Comedy* (Cambridge University Press, Cambridge, 1993)

BOWMAN, JOHN WICK, *The First Christian Drama: The Book of Revelation* (Westminster Press, Philadelphia, 1955)

BRAINE, DAVID, 'The Inner Jewishness of St. John's Gospel as the Clue to the Inner Jewishness of Jesus', *Studien zum Neuen Testament und seiner Umwelt* (SNTU), Serie A, Band 13, 1988, 101–157

BRENNER, ATHALYA, 'Job the Pious? The Characterization of Job in the Narrative Framework of the Book', in Clines, *Poetical Books*, pp. 298–313

BROWN, FRANCIS, S. R. DRIVER and CHARLES A. BRIGGS, *A Hebrew and English Lexicon of the Old Testament* (Clarendon Press, Oxford, 1951)

BROWN, JOHN RUSSELL, *The Complete Plays of the Wakefield Master in a New Version for Reading and Performance* (Heinemann, London, 1983)

BROWN, RAYMOND E., 'The Dead Sea Scrolls and the New Testament', in Charlesworth, *John and Qumran*, pp. 2–6

BRUEGGEMANN, WALTER, *David's Truth in Israel's Imagination and Memory* (Fortress Press, Philadelphia, 1985)

—— *Genesis*, Interpretation Series (John Knox Press, Atlanta, 1982)

BRUEGGEMANN, WALTER, *Theology of the Old Testament: Testimony, Dispute, Advocacy* (Fortress Press, Minneapolis, 1997)

—— 'Trajectories in Old Testament Literature and the Sociology of Ancient Israel', *Journal of Biblical Literature*, 98/2, 1979, 161–85

BUBER, MARTIN, *I and Thou*, translated by Ronald Gregor Smith (T&T Clark, Edinburgh, 1937, 1958, 1987)

—— *Kingship of God*, translated from the 3rd German edn by Richard Schiemann (George Allen & Unwin, London, 1967)

—— *Moses* (Phaidon Press, Oxford, 1966)

BULTMANN, RUDOLF, *Theology of the New Testament: Volume II* (SCM, London, 1955, 1979)

BURRIDGE, RICHARD A., *What Are The Gospels? A Comparison with Graeco-Roman Biography* (Cambridge University Press, Cambridge, 1992)

BUTLER, JOSEPH, *The Analogy of Religion: Natural and Revealed* (1736, Macmillan, London, 1900)

CASSUTO, UMBERTO, *A Commentary on the Book of Exodus*, translated by Israel Abrahams (The Magnes Press, Hebrew University, Jerusalem, 1951, 1961, 1st English edn, 1967)

CHARLESWORTH, JAMES, 'A Critical Comparison of the Dualism in 1QS 3.13–4.26 and the "Dualism" Contained in John's Gospel', in *John and Qumran*

—— (ed.), *John and Qumran* (Geoffrey Chapman, London, 1972)

CHILDS, BREVARD S., *Exodus: A Commentary* (SCM, London, 1974)

CLINES, DAVID J. A., *The Theme of the Pentateuch* (*Journal for the Study of Old Testament Literature*, Supplement 10, Sheffield, 1978)

—— (ed.), *The Poetical Books*, The Biblical Seminar, 41 (Sheffield Academic Press, Sheffield, 1997)

COLLEY, LINDA, 'Protestants', in *Britons: Forging the Nation 1707–1837* (Random House, New York, 1992, Pimlico, London, 1994)

COLLINS, JOHN J., *The Apocalyptic Imagination: An Introduction to Jewish Apocalyptic Literature* (William B. Eerdmans, Michigan, 1984, 1998)

COLLINSON, PATRICK, *The Birthpangs of Protestant England: Religious and Cultural Change in the Sixteenth and Seventeenth Centuries* (Macmillan Press, Basingstoke, 1988)

CORNFORD, FRANCIS MACDONALD, *The Origin of Attic Comedy* (1934, Peter Smith, Gloucester, Mass., 1968)

COWAN, LOUISE, 'The Comic Terrain', in Louise Cowan (ed.), *The Terrain of Comedy* (Dallas Institute, Dallas, 1984), pp. 1–18

CURTIUS, ERNST ROBERT, *European Literature and the Latin Middle Ages*, translated by Willard Trask (Routledge & Kegan Paul, London, 1953)

DANIÉLOU, JEAN, *The Bible and the Liturgy* (Servant Books, Michigan, 1979)

DAVIES, R. T. (ed.), *The Corpus Christi Play of the English Middle Ages* (Faber & Faber, London, 1972)

DEAN, WINTON, *Handel's Dramatic Oratorios and Masques* (Oxford University Press, Oxford, 1959, 1972)

DILLISTONE, F. W., *The Christian Understanding of Atonement* (SCM, London, 1968, 1984)

DIONYSIUS THE AREOPAGITE, *Pseudo Dionysius: The Complete Works*, translated by Colm Luibheid (SPCK, London, 1987)

DODD, C. H., *The Interpretation of the Fourth Gospel* (Cambridge University Press, Cambridge, 1965)

DOUGHERTY, JAMES, *The Five-Square City: The City in the Religious Imagination* (University of Notre Dame Press, Notre Dame, 1980)

DOUGLAS, MARY, *Purity and Danger: An Analysis of the Concepts of Pollution and Taboo* (Routledge & Kegan Paul, 1966, 1989)

DOZEMAN, THOMAS, *God at War: Power in the Exodus Tradition* (Oxford University Press, Oxford, 1996)

DRIVER, TOM F., *The Sense of History in Greek and Shakespearean Drama* (Columbia University Press, New York, 1960)

DRURY, JOHN, 'Mark', in Alter and Kermode, *Literary Guide to the Bible*, pp. 402–417

DUFFY, EAMON, *The Stripping of the Altars: Traditional Religion in England 1400–1580* (Yale University Press, New Haven and London, 1992)

DUKE, PAUL, *Irony in the Fourth Gospel* (John Knox Press, Atlanta, 1985)

DUPREE, ROBERT, 'The Copious Inventory of Comedy', in Cowan, *Terrain of Comedy*, pp. 163–194

EHRENBERG, VICTOR, *The People of Aristophanes: A Sociology of Old Attic Comedy* (Basil Blackwell, Oxford, 1943)

EICHRODT, WALTHER, *Theology of the Old Testament*, Vol. II, translated by J. A. Baker (SCM, London, 1967)

ELLIOTT, ROBERT, *The Power of Satire: Magic, Ritual, Art* (Princeton University Press, New Jersey, 1960)

ERASMUS, DESIDERIUS, *The Praise of Folly*, edited with an introduction and commentary by Clarence Miller (Yale University Press, New Haven, 1979)

EVANS, C. F., and P. R. ACKROYD (eds), *The Cambridge History of the Bible: Volume I: From the Beginnings to Jerome* (Cambridge Unviersity Press, Cambridge, 1970)

EXUM, CHERYL, *Tragedy and Biblical Narrative: Arrows of the Almighty* (Cambridge University Press, Cambridge, 1992)

—— and WILLIAM WHEDBEE, 'Isaac, Samson and Saul: Reflections on the Comic and Tragic Visions', in Radday and Brenner, *On Humour and the Comic in the Hebrew Bible* (Almond Press, Sheffield, 1990), pp. 117–159

FALLON, TIMOTHY, and PHILIP RILEY (eds), *Religion and Culture: Essays in Honor of Bernard Lonergan* (State University of New York Press, Albany, 1987)

FARRER, AUSTIN, *The Glass of Vision*, the Bampton Lectures (Dacre Press, Westminster, 1948, 1958)

—— *A Rebirth of Images: The Making of John's Apocalypse* (Dacre Press, Westminster, 1949)

FERGUSSON, FRANCIS, *The Idea of a Theatre: A Study of Ten Plays. The Art of Drama in Changing Perspective* (Princeton University Press, New Jersey, 1949)

FIELDING, HENRY, *The History of Tom Jones* (1749, Penguin, London, 1966, 1985)

FISCH, HAROLD, *Poetry with a Purpose: Biblical Poetics and Interpretation* (Indiana University Press, Bloomington and Indianapolis, 1990)

FOHRER, GEORG, *History of Israelite Religion*, translated by David Green (SPCK, London, 1972)

FOKKELMAN, J., *Narrative Art in Genesis* (Van Gorcum, Amsterdam, 1975)

FORSYTH, P. T., *The Person and Place of Jesus Christ* (Independent Press, London 1909, 1961)

FOX, EVERETT, *Now These Are the Names: A New English Translation of the Book of Exodus, Translated with Commentary and Notes* (Schocken Books, New York, 1986)

FRANKFORT, HENRI, *Ancient Egyptian Religion: An Interpretation* (Harper & Row, New York, 1948, 1961)

FREI, HANS, *The Eclipse of Biblical Narrative: A Study in Eighteenth and Nineteenth Century Hermeneutics* (Yale University Press, New Haven, 1974)

—— *The Identity of Jesus Christ: The Hermeneutical Bases of Dogmatic Theology* (Fortress Press, Philadelphia, 1974)

FRYE, NORTHROP, *The Anatomy of Criticism: Four Essays* (Princeton University Press, New Jersey, 1957)

—— *The Great Code* (Routledge & Kegan Paul, London, 1981)

GARRETT, GRAEME, '"My Brother Esau Is an Hairy Man": An Encounter between the Comedian and the Preacher', *Scottish Journal of Theology*, 33, 3, June 1980, 239–256

GEACH, PETER, *The Virtues* (Cambridge University Press, Cambridge, 1977, 1979)

GIANTURCO, CAROLYN, '"Cantati spirituali e morali", with a Description of the Papal Sacred Cantata Tradition for Christmas 1676–1740', *Music and Letters*, LXXIII, February 1992, 1–13

GIRARD, RENÉ, *The Scapegoat*, translated by Yvonne Freccero (Athlone Press, London, 1986)

GOLDHILL, SIMON, 'The Great Dionysia and Civic Ideology', in Winkler and Zeitlin, *Nothing to Do with Dionysius?*, pp. 97–129

GOOD, E. M., 'Apocalyptic as Comedy: The Book of Daniel', in *Semeia*, 32: *Tragedy and Comedy in the Bible*, edited by Cheryl Exum, 1985, 40–65

—— *Irony in the Old Testament* (SPCK, London, 1965)

GOMBRICH, RICHARD, *Precept and Practice: Traditional Buddhism in the Rural Highlands of Ceylon* (Clarendon Press, Oxford, 1971)

GORDIS, ROBERT, *The Book of God and Man: A Study of Job* (University of Chicago Press, Chicago, 1965)

GREGORY THE GREAT, *Morals on the Book of Job*, Volume I, translated by John Henry Parker (Oxford, 1844)

GRENSTED, L. W., *A Short History of the Doctrine of the Atonement* (Manchester University Press, Manchester, 1920, 1962)

GROUSSET, RENÉ, *Chinese Art and Culture*, translated by Haakon Chevalier (André Deutsch, London, 1959)

GUNN, DAVID M., *The Fate of King Saul: An Interpretation of a Biblical Story* (Journal for the Study of Biblical Literature, Sheffield, 1980)

—— '"The Hardening of Pharaoh's Heart": Plot, Character and Theology in Exodus 1–14', in David Clines, David Gunn and Alan Hauser (eds), *Art and Meaning: Rhetoric in Biblical Literature* (*Journal for the Study of the Old Testament*, Supplement Series, 19, Sheffield, 1982), pp. 72–96

—— 'Joshua and Judges', in Alter and Kermode, *Literary Guide to the Bible*, pp. 102–121

—— *The Story of King David: Genre and Interpretation* (JSOT Press, Sheffield, 1978)

GUTIÉRREZ, GUSTAVO, *On Job: God Talk and the Suffering of the Innocent*, translated by Matthew O'Connell (Orbis Books, New York, 1987)

HAFEMAN, S. J., 'Paul and His Interpreters', in Gerald F. Hawthorne, Daniel Reid and Ralph P. Martin (eds), *Dictionary of Paul and His Letters* (Intervarsity Press, Downer's Grove, Illinois, 1993)

HALLIWELL, F. S., 'The Uses of Laughter in Greek Culture', *Classical Quarterly*, ns., 41, 1991, pp. 279–296

HARDISON, O. B., JR., *Christian Rite and Christian Drama in the Middle Ages* (Johns Hopkins Press, Baltimore, 1965)

HARRIS, MAX, *Theatre and Incarnation* (Macmillan, Basingstoke and London, 1990)

HARVEY, A. E., *Jesus on Trial: A Study in the Fourth Gospel* (SPCK, London, 1976)

HEGEL, G. W., *Aesthetics: Lectures on Fine Art: Volume I*, translated by T. M. Knox (Clarendon Press, Oxford, 1975)

—— *Aesthetics: Lectures on Fine Art: Volume II*, translated by T. M. Knox (Clarendon Press, Oxford, 1975)

HEILMAN, ROBERT, *The Ways of the World: Comedy and Society* (University of Washington Press, Washington, 1978)

HELLER, JOSEPH, *God Knows* (Jonathan Cape, 1984; Black Swan, London, 1985)

HELM, PAUL, *The Divine Revelation: The Basic Issues* (Morgan & Scott, London, 1982)

HESCHEL, ABRAHAM, *The Prophets* (Harper & Row, New York, 1962)

HIMMELFARB, MARTHA, *Ascent to Heaven in Jewish and Christian Apocalypses* (Oxford University Press, Oxford, 1993)

HITCHCOCK, E. R. M., 'Is the Fourth Gospel a Drama?' in Stibbe, *Gospel of John as Literature*, pp. 15–25

HUGHES, BRIAN (arr.), *Folk Songs for Male Voices: Jonah. Spiritual for 4-Part Male Chorus or Quartet Unaccompanied* (Roberton Publications, Aylesbury, 1978)

HUMPHREYS, W. LEE, 'The Tragedy of King Saul: A Study of the Structure of 1 Samuel 9–31', *Journal for the Study of the Old Testament*, 6, 1978, 18–27

HUNTER, A. M., *According to John* (SCM, London, 1968)

HURD, MICHAEL, *Jonah-Man Jazz: A Cantata Musical for Unison Voices and Piano, with Guitar Chords* (Novello Publishing, London, 1966)

INGARDEN, ROMAN, *The Literary Work of Art: An Investigation on the Borderlines of Ontology, Logic, and Theory of Literature*, translated by George Grabowicz (Northwestern University Press, Evanston, 1973)

JACOBSON, HOWARD, *Seriously Funny: From the Ridiculous to the Sublime* (Viking, London, 1997)

JOBLING, DAVID, *The Sense of Biblical Narrative: Structural Analyses in the Hebrew Bible* (JSOT Press, Sheffield, 1986)

JOHNSTON, ALEXANDRA F., 'The Plays of the Religious Guilds of York: The Creed Play and the Pater Noster Play', *Speculum*, 50, 1975, 55–90

JOHNSTON, WILLIAM, *Exodus* (JSOT Press, Sheffield, 1990)

JOSIPOVICI, GABRIEL, *The Book of God: A Response to the Bible* (Yale University Press, New Haven, 1988, 1990)

KALLEN, HORACE M., *The Book of Job as a Greek Tragedy* (Moffatt, Yard & Co., 1918; Hill & Wang, New York, 1959)

KASS, LEON, 'What's Wrong with Babel', *American Scholar*, 58, 1, Winter 1989, 41–60 (49)

KERMODE, FRANK, 'Matthew', in Alter and Kermode (eds), *Literary Guide to the Bible*, pp. 387–401

KIERKEGAARD, SØREN, *Concluding Unscientific Postscript*, translated by David F. Swenson and Walter Lowrie (Oxford University Press, London, 1941)

—— *Fear and Trembling and the Sickness unto Death*, translated by Walter Lowrie (Princeton University Press, Princeton, NJ, 1941, 1974)

KINGHORN, A. M., *Mediaeval Drama* (Evans Brothers, London, 1968)

KIPLING, RUDYARD, *Something of Myself* (1936, Penguin, London, 1977, 1988)

KOLVE, V. A., *The Play Called Corpus Christi* (Edward Arnold, London, 1966)

KRELL, DAVID FARRELL, 'The Oldest Program towards a System in German Idealism', *The Owl of Minerva*, 17, 1, Fall 1985, 5–19

LACOUE-LABARTHE, PHILIPPE, and JEAN-LUC NANCY, *The Literary Absolute: The Theory of Literature in German Romanticism*, translated by Philip Barnard and Cheryl Lester (State University of New York Press, Albany, New York, 1988)

LANDY, FRANCIS, 'Humour as a Tool for Biblical Exegesis', in Radday and Brenner, *On Humour and the Comic in the Hebrew Bible*, pp. 99–115

LANG, PAUL HENRY, *George Frederic Handel* (Faber & Faber, London, 1964)

LANGER, SUZANNE, *Feeling and Form* (Routledge & Kegan Paul, London, 1953, 1979)

LASINE, STUART, 'Bird's Eye and Worm's Eye Views of Justice in the Book of Job', in Clines, *Poetical Books*, pp. 274–297

—— 'Guest and Host in Judges 19: Lot's Hospitality in an Inverted World', *Journal for the Study of the Old Testament*, 29, 1984, 37–59

LE GOFF, JACQUES, *The Birth of Purgatory*, translated by Arthur Goldhammer (Scholar Press, London, 1984)

LEEUW, GERARDUS VAN DER, *Religion in Essence and Manifestation: A Study in the Phenomenology of Religion*, translated by J. E. Turner (George Allen & Unwin, London, 1938)

—— *Sacred and Profane Beauty: The Holy in Art* (Holt, Rinehart & Winston, New York, 1963)

LEVENSON, JON D., *Creation and the Persistence of Evil: The Jewish Drama of Omnipotence* (Harper & Row, San Francisco, 1988)

LEVER, KATHERINE, *The Art of Greek Comedy* (Methuen, London, 1956)

LONERGAN, BERNARD J. F., *Insight: A Study of Human Understanding* (Longmans, Green & Co., London, 1957, 1958)

—— *Method in Theology* (Darton, Longman & Todd, London, 1972)

—— *A Third Collection: Papers by Bernard J. F. Lonergan*, edited by Frederick E. Crowe (Geoffrey Chapman, London, 1985)

—— *Verbum: Word and Idea in Aquinas*, edited by David B. Burrell (Darton, Longman & Todd, London, 1968)

LONGO, ODDONE, 'The Theater of the Polis', in Winkler and Zeitlin, *Nothing to Do with Dionysios?*, pp. 12–19

LYNCH, WILLIAM, *Christ and Apollo: The Dimensions of the Literary Imagination* (Sheed & Ward, London, 1960, University of Notre Dame Press, Notre Dame, 1975)

MALRAUX, ANDRÉ, *The Voices of Silence*, translated by Stuart Gilbert (Paladin, London, 1953, 1974)

MARQUIS, DON, *Noah an' Jonah an' Cap'n John Smith: A Book of Humorous Verse* (Appleton & Company, New York, 1922)

MARTIN-ACHARD, ROBERT, *From Death to Life: A Study of the Development of the Doctrine of the Resurrection in the Old Testament*, translated by John Penney Smith (Oliver & Boyd, Edinburgh and London, 1960)

McDOWELL, DOUGLAS, *Aristophanes and Athens: An Introduction to the Plays* (Oxford University Press, Oxford, 1995)

McLEISH, KENNETH, *The Theatre of Aristophanes* (Thames & Hudson, London, 1980)

MENDENHALL, GEORGE E., *The Tenth Generation: The Origins of the Biblical Tradition* (Johns Hopkins University Press, Baltimore, 1973)

MILES, JACK, *God: A Biography* (Simon & Schuster, London, 1995)

MILLS, DAVID, *The Chester Mystery Cycle: A New Edition with Modernised Spelling* (East Lansing Colleagues Press, 1992)

MOLTMANN, JÜRGEN, *The Coming of God: Christian Eschatology* (SCM, London, 1996)

MORAN, GABRIEL, *Theology of Inspiration* (Burns & Oates, London, 1967)

NIÇEV, ALEXANDRE, 'L'enigma des *Oiseaux* d'Aristophane', *Euphrosyne: Revista de Filologia Classica*, Nova Serie, 17, 1986, 10–30

NICOLL, ALLARDYCE, *The Theatre and Dramatic Theory* (George G. Harrap, London, 1962)

NIETZSCHE, FRIEDRICH, *The Birth of Tragedy and The Case of Wagner*, translated by Walter Kaufmann (Random House, New York, 1967)

OLSON, ELDER, *The Theory of Comedy* (Indiana University Press, Bloomington, 1968)

OTTO, RUDOLF, *The Idea of the Holy*, translated by John W. Harvey (Penguin, Harmondsworth, Middlesex, 1959)

PATRICK, DALE, *The Rendering of God in the Old Testament* (Fortress Press, Philadelphia, 1981)

PEARL, CHAIM, *Rashi* (Weidenfeld & Nicolson, London, 1988)

PICKARD-CAMBRIDGE, ARTHUR, *Dithyramb, Tragedy, Comedy* (Clarendon Press, Oxford, 2nd edn rev. by T. B. L. Webster, 1962)

POLZIN, ROBERT, *Samuel and the Deuteronomist: A Literary Study of the Deuteronomic History*, Part II, *1 Samuel* (Harper & Row, San Francisco, 1989)

PORTEOUS, NORMAN, *Daniel: A Commentary* (SCM, London, 1965, 1979)

PRICE, JAMES L., 'Light from Qumran on Some Aspects of Johannine Theology', in Charlesworth, *John and Qumran*

RAD, GERHARD VON, *Genesis: A Commentary*, translated by John Bowker from the 9th German edn (SCM, London, 1961, 1972)

—— *Old Testament Theology I, The Theology of Israel's Historical Traditions*, translated by D. M. G. Stalker (SCM, London, 1975)

—— *Old Testament Theology II, The Theology of Israel's Prophetic Traditions*, translated by D. M. G. Stalker (SCM, London, 1965)

—— 'Typological Interpretation of the Old Testament', in Claus Wester-mann (ed.), *Essays on Old Testament Hermeneutics*, English translation edited by James Luther Mays (John Knox Press, Richmond, Virginia, 2nd edn, 1964), pp. 17–39

RAD, GERHARD VON, *Wisdom in Israel*, translated by James D. Martin (SCM, London, 1972)

RADDAY, YEHUDA T., and ATHALYA BRENNER (eds), *On Humour and the Comic in the Hebrew Bible* (Almond Press, Sheffield, 1990)

RAHNER, HUGO, *Man at Play: Or Did You Ever Practice Eutrapelia?* translated by Brian Battershaw and Edward Quinn (Burns & Oates, London, 1965)

RANSOME, JOHN CROWE, 'Poetry: A Note on Ontology', in *The World's Body* (Charles Scribner's Sons, New York, 1938)

REDFIELD, JAMES, 'Drama and Community: Aristophanes and Some of His Rivals', in Winkler and Zeitlin, *Nothing to Do with Dionysios?*, pp. 314–335

RENSBERGER, DAVID, *Overcoming the World: Politics and Community in the Gospel of John* (SPCK, London, 1989)

RHOADS, DAVID M., and DONALD MICHIE, *Mark as Story: An Introduction to the Narrative of a Gospel* (Fortress Press, Philadelphia, 1982)

RICHES, JOHN, *Jesus and the Transformation of Judaism* (Darton, Longman & Todd, London, 1980)

—— *The World of Jesus: First Century Judaism in Crisis* (Cambridge University Press, Cambridge, 1990)

ROBINSON, BERNARD P., *Israel's Mysterious God: An Analysis of Some Old Testament Narratives* (Grevatt & Grevatt, Newcastle upon Tyne, 1986)

—— *The Priority of John*, edited by J. F. Coakley (SCM, London, 1985)

ROMILLY, JACQUELINE DE, *Time in Greek Tragedy* (Cornell University Press, Ithaca, New York, 1968)

ROSTON, MURRAY, *Biblical Drama in England: From the Middle Ages to the Present Day* (Faber & Faber, London, 1968)

ROWLAND, CHRISTOPHER, *The Open Heaven: A Study of Apocalyptic in Judaism and Early Christianity* (SPCK, London, 1982)

RUBIN, MIRI, *Corpus Christi: The Eucharist in Late Medieval Culture* (Cambridge University Press, Cambridge, 1991)

SACKS, JONATHAN, *One People? Tradition, Modernity and Jewish Unity* (Littman Library of Jewish Civilization, London, 1993)

SANDERS, E. P., *Jesus and Judaism* (SCM, London, 1985)

—— *Paul and Palestinian Judaism* (SCM, London, 1977, 1989)

—— and MARGARET DAVIES, *Studying the Synoptic Gospels* (SCM, London, 1989)

SACCHI, PAOLO, *Jewish Apocalyptic and Its History*, translated by William J. Short, *Journal for the Study of the Pseudepigrapha* Supplement Series, 20 (Sheffield Academic Press, Sheffield, 1998)

SAVAGE, D. S., *And Also Much Cattle: Scenario for Four Voices* (Brentham Press, London, 1975)

SCHELLING, FRIEDRICH WILHELM JOSEPH VON, *The Philosophy of Art*, translated by Douglas Stott (University of Minnesota Press, Minneapolis and London, 1988)

SCHLESS, HOWARD H., 'The Comic Element in the Wakefield Noah', in *Studies in Medieval Literature*, edited by MacEdward Leach (University of Pennsylvania Press, Pennsylvania, 1961)

SCHNEIDAU, HERBERT, *Sacred Discontent: The Bible and Western Tradition* (University of California Press, Berkeley, 1977)

SCHÖKEL, LUIS ALONSO, *The Inspired Word: Scripture in the Light of Language and Literature*, translated by Francis Martin (Herder & Herder, New York, 1965)

—— 'Toward a Dramatic Reading of Job', *Semeia*, 7, Studies in the Book of Job (eds) Robert Polzin and David Robertson (1977, Society of Biblical Literature), 45–59

SCREECH, M. A., *Laughter at the Foot of the Cross* (Allen Lane, London, 1997)

SEGOVIA, FERNANDO F., 'The Journey(s) of the Word of God: A Reading of the Plot of the Fourth Gospel', in *Semeia*, 53, edited by R. A. Culpeper and Fernando F. Segovia

SEITZ, CHRISTOPHER, *Word without End: The Old Testament as Abiding Theological Witness* (W. B. Eerdmans, Michigan and Cambridge, 1998)

SETERS, JOHN VAN, *The Life Of Moses: The Yahwist as Historian in Exodus– Numbers* (Kok Pharos Publishing House, Kampen, The Netherlands, 1994)

SHAPIRO, ALEXANDER, ' "Drama of an Infinitely Superior Nature": Handel's Early English Oratorios and the Religious Sublime', *Music and Letters*, LXXIV, May 1993, 215–245

SIMPSON, DAVID (ed.), *The Origins of Modern Critical Thought: German Aesthetic and Literary Criticism from Lessing to Hegel* (Cambridge University Press, Cambridge, 1988)

SMALLEY, BERYL, *The Study of the Bible in the Middle Ages* (Basil Blackwell, Oxford, 1952)

SMITH, RUTH, *Handel's Oratorios and Eighteenth Century Thought* (Cambridge University Press, Cambridge, 1995)

SORESCU, MARIN, 'Jonah: A Tragedy in Four Scenes', in *The Thirst of the Salt Mountain: A Trilogy of Plays*, translated by Andrea Deletant and Brenda Walker (Forest Books, London, 1985)

SPARKS, H. D. F. (ed.), *The Apocryphal Old Testament* (Clarendon Press, Oxford, 1984)

SPONSLER, CLAIRE, 'Festive Profit and Ideological Production: *Le Jeu de Saint Nicholas*', in Meg Twycross (ed.), *Festive Drama: Papers from the Sixth Colloquium of the International Society for the Study of Medieval Theatre, Lancaster, 1989* (D. S. Brewer, Cambridge, 1996), pp. 66–79

STACEY, W. D., *Prophetic Drama in the Old Testament* (Epworth, London, 1990)

STAIGER, EMILE, *Basic Concepts of Poetics*, translated by Janette C. Hudson and Luanne T. Frank (Pennsylvania State University Press, Pennsylvania, 1991)

STEINER, GEORGE, *Tolstoy or Dostoievsky: An Essay in Contrast* (Faber & Faber, London, 1959)

STENDAHL, KRISTER, *Paul among Jews and Gentiles and Other Essays* (SCM, London, 1977)

STERNBERG, MEIR, *The Poetics of Biblical Narrative: Ideological Literature and the Drama of Reading* (Indiana University Press, Bloomington, 1985)

STIBBE, MARK, 'The Elusive Christ: A New Reading of the Fourth Gospel', in Stibbe, *Gospel of John as Literature*, pp. 232–247

—— *John's Gospel* (Routledge & Kegan Paul, London, 1994)

—— (ed.), *The Gospel of John as Literature: An Anthology of Twentieth-Century Perspectives* (E. J. Brill, Leiden, 1993)

STOCKER, MARGARITA, 'God in Theory: Milton, Literature and Theodicy', *Journal of Theology & Literature*, I, 1, March 1987, 70–87

SWANSTON, HAMISH, *Handel* (Geoffrey Chapman, London, 1990)

SYPHER, WYLIE, 'The Meanings of Comedy', in Henri Bergson, *Comedy, an Essay on Comedy by George Meredith and Laughter* (Doubleday Anchor, New York, 1956; Johns Hopkins University Press, Baltimore, 1980, 1984)

SYPHERD, WILBUR OWEN, *Jephthah and His Daughter: A Study in Comparative Literature* (University of Delaware, Delaware, 1948)

TAPLIN, OLIVER, *Greek Tragedy in Action* (Methuen, London, 1978)

TAYLOR, JOHN V., *The Go-Between God: The Holy Spirit and the Christian Mission* (SCM, London, 1972)

TERRIEN, SAMUEL, 'The Yahweh Speeches and Job's Response', *Review and Expositor*, 68, 1971, 497–509

TURNER, H. E. W., *The Patristic Doctrine of Redemption* (A. R. Mowbray, London, 1952)

TWYCROSS, MEG, 'The Theatricality of Medieval English Plays', in Richard Beadle (ed.), *The Cambridge Companion to Medieval English Theatre* (Cambridge University Press, Cambridge, 1994), pp. 37–84

VANN, GERALD, *The Eagle's Word: A Presentation of the Gospel according to St John with an Introductory Essay* (Collins, London, 1971)

VAWTER, BRUCE, *Biblical Inspiration* (Hutchinson, London, 1972)

VERMES, GEZA (ed.), *The Dead Sea Scrolls in English* (Penguin, London, 1962, 4th edn, 1995)

VIA, DAN O., *Kerygma and Comedy in the New Testament* (Fortress Press, Philadelphia, 1975)

VOEGELIN, ERIC, *Order and History: Volume I: Israel and Revelation* (Louisana State University Press, 1956)

VOS, NELVIN, *The Drama of Comedy: Victim and Victor* (John Knox Press, Richmond, Virginia, 1966)

WAINRIGHT, GEOFFREY, *The Trinity in the New Testament* (SPCK, London, 1962)

WALEY, ARTHUR, *An Introduction to the Study of Chinese Painting* (Ernest Benn, London, 1958)

WATKIN, E. I., *Catholic Art and Culture* (Hollis & Carter, London, 1947)

WELLS, COLIN, *The Roman Empire* (Fontana, London, 1984, 1988)

WEVERS, JOHN WILLIAM, 'The First Book of Samuel', in Charles Laymon (ed.), *The Interpreter's One Volume Commentary on the Bible* (Collins, London, 1971)

WHARTON, JAMES A., 'The Secret of Yahweh: Story and Affirmation in Judges 13–16', *Interpretation*, 27, 1973, 48–65

WHEDBEE, WILLIAM, 'The Comedy of Job', in Radday and Brenner, *On Humour and the Comic in the Hebrew Bible*, 217–249

—— 'The Comedy of Job', *Semeia, 7: Studies in the Book of Job*, Edited By Robert Polzin And David Robertson, (1977, Society Of Biblical Literature), 1–39

WHITE, HAYDEN, *Metahistory: The Historical Imagination in Nineteenth Century Europe* (Johns Hopkins University Press, Baltimore, 1973)

—— *Tropics of Discourse: Essays in Cultural Criticism* (Johns Hopkins University Press, Baltimore, 1987)

WHITELY, D. E. H., *The Theology of Saint Paul* (Blackwell, Oxford, 1964, 1974)

WHYBRAY, NORMAN, *The Making of the Pentateuch: A Methodological Study* (Sheffield Academic Press, Sheffield, 1987)

—— *The Succession Narrative: A Study of II Samuel 9–20 and I Kings 1 and 2* (SCM, London, 1968)

WILLIAMS, JAMES G., 'The Comedy of Jacob: A Literary Study', *Journal of the American Academy of Religion*, 45/2, Supplement B, June 1978, 241–265

—— '"You Have Not Spoken Truth of Me": Mystery and Irony in Job', *Zeitschrift für die Alttestamentliche Wissenschaft*, 83, 1971, 231–255

WIMSATT, W. K., JR., with MONROE C. BEARDSLEY, *The Verbal Icon: Studies in the Meaning of Poetry* (University of Kentucky Press, 1954)

WINKLER, JOHN J., and FROMA I. ZEITLIN (eds), *Nothing to Do with Dionysios?* (Princeton University Press, New Jersey, 1990)

WOLTERSTORFF, NICHOLAS, *Divine Discourse: Philosophical Reflections on the Claim that God Speaks* (Cambridge University Press, Cambridge, 1995)

YOUNG, FRANCIS and FORD, DAVID, *Meaning and Truth in 2 Corinthians* (SPCK, London, 1987)

ZIMMERMAN, FRANKLIN B., *Henry Purcell: 1659–1695: His Life and Times* (Macmillan, London, 1967)

Index of Names